D1266871

THE BEST PLAYS OF 1926-27

# THE
# BEST PLAYS OF 1926-27

### AND THE

## YEAR BOOK OF THE DRAMA
## IN AMERICA

*Edited by*

## BURNS MANTLE

NEW YORK
## DODD, MEAD AND COMPANY
1960

# INTRODUCTION

TO add a dash of variety to the routine of selecting the ten plays that would most worthily represent the current theatre season in this book I called for suggestions.

To ten of the leading reviewers of plays in New York I sent a list of twenty-four dramas culled from a total of one hundred and sixty-three, from which I expected to make my own final selections, asking them to write in any of their favorites I had overlooked.

"If," I wrote, "if you were the editor of an American year book of the drama, boldly entitled 'The Best Plays of 1926-27,' which ten of these plays would you include therein?"

From the ten critics I received nine answers. The missing colleague was already lost in Europe. Each of the nine obligingly stipulated his preferences. Between them they named twenty-five plays.

When I had counted the votes I found that Philip Dunning and George Abbott's "Broadway" and Maxwell Anderson's "Saturday's Children" were the only two plays that had received unanimously the critics' endorsement.

Maurine Watkins' "Chicago" and W. Somerset Maugham's "The Constant Wife" were tied for second choice with eight votes each.

The Molnar-Wodehouse comedy, "The Play's the Thing," had seven votes, Robert Emmet Sherwood's "The Road to Rome" six. There were five each for Edouard Bourdet's "The Captive," S. N. Behrman's "The Second Man," and Sidney Howard's "The Silver Cord," and four each for Martinez Sierra's "The Cradle Song" and Paul Green's Pulitzer prize-winning play, "In Abraham's Bosom."

There were three votes each for Kenyon Nicholson's "The Barker," Richard Barry's "White Wings," and Sidney Howard's "Ned McCobb's Daughter," two each for George Kelly's "Daisy Mayme," the Goodrich-Palmer Browning adaptation, "Caponsacchi," the Copeau-Croué-Ivan "Brothers Karamazov" and Laetitia Macdonald's "Lady Alone," and one each for "The Constant Nymph," Pirandello's "Right You Are If You Think You

Are," Franz Werfel's "Juarez and Maximilian," the Brooks-Lister "Spread Eagle," the Lindsay-Robinson "Tommy," Frederick Lonsdale's "On Approval" and Vincent Lawrence's "Sour Grapes."

The ten best plays of last season, therefore, if you ask nine leading play critics, were:

| | |
|---|---|
| "Broadway" | "The Play's the Thing" |
| "Saturday's Children" | "The Captive" |
| "Chicago" | "The Silver Cord" |
| "The Constant Wife" | "The Second Man," and either |
| "The Road to Rome" | "The Cradle Song," or |
| | "In Abraham's Bosom." |

It is a good list and an intelligent list. Standing on the side lines, all dressed up in the pure white of an impartial referee, I can honestly felicitate my confreres on their selections. I had, before I wrote them, included eight of these eleven plays in my own list. These I have retained.

I have, however, substituted George Kelly's "Daisy Mayme" for "The Second Man." "Daisy Mayme," I think, is the more purposeful drama of the two, a more incisive study of native character and an equally well written play. Only the exceptional brilliance of its dialogue gives "The Second Man" its greater popular value.

Of the two plays that received four votes each, and were therefore tied for tenth place in the list, I had previously taken "The Cradle Song."

The only other play about which there was doubt in my mind was Bourdet's "The Captive." The doubt, however, was not inspired by the play, or by any question of its quality as written drama, but rather by the quite natural question as to its place in this particular year book.

Inasmuch as "The Captive" has been condemned, however unjustly, by law and voluntarily withdrawn, without benefit of trial, from our stage, it ceases actively to figure as a history-making contribution to the current drama.

Should it, or should it not, therefore, make way for another play of less historical significance theatrically but of equal material importance to the American theatre? Has "The Captive," on its record of success, a right to fill the space I otherwise would give to Paul Green's "In Abraham's Bosom," which was popularly classified as a failure?

I found Mr. Green's drama rather sketchy and somewhat dated; a promise, I would say, rather than a fulfillment of its author's undoubted genius, but it did win the Pulitzer prize as the American play of 1926 the writing of which brought the greatest credit upon a native playwright. And the judges who so proclaimed it, Walter Prichard Eaton, A. E. Thomas and Clayton Hamilton, I number among the most competent and sanely balanced of critics.

On the other hand "The Captive" was an outstanding dramatic success of the season of which this volume is a record. Before it was withdrawn it had been played for one hundred and eighty performances, attended by audiences that taxed the capacity of the theatre. These audiences could not have been drawn to the theatre or satisfied in the theatre by any salaciousness traceable to either the text or the action of the Bourdet drama. A play jury of twelve citizens voted seven for its continuance and five for its withdrawal. Admittedly written upon a theme that leers menacingly in the background, never coming quite into the picture, the auditor got from the play only so much knowledge of the evil he read into it as he brought to the theatre with him. Both Ibsen's "Ghosts" and Brieux's "Damaged Goods" would be barred by the application of the same moral standards. To leave "The Captive" out seemed only a little less cowardly than weakly to ignore the sensational adventure of which it was the center.

In this dilemma I took counsel. In fact I took generous counsel. I queried my fellow reviewers. Five out of nine voted for "The Captive." I took counsel with my friends. They either flushed embarrassedly or frankly confessed their unfitness to make a decision. I put the question to my percentage of the several million readers of those scattered newspapers for which I serve as dramatic correspondent, and the replies I received were strongly against "The Captive," and as strongly in favor of holding to the facts and the record.

I went into conference with my publishers and came out with the pleasant assurance that my judgment as editor would be respected.

I stood finally just outside Omar's door, having heard great argument to no definite purpose so far as I was personally concerned.

And then I decided that "The Captive," so far as this book and this editor and this year's record are concerned, shall remain where fate and circumstances have placed it.

The rest of the plays speak both for themselves and their patrons' choice of drama. Each of them has been popularly acclaimed. Few of the old-time artificial aids to play making are employed in any of them. They are forthright in expression, almost reportorial in subject and treatment and as timely in theme as last season's best selling novel. The imaginative drama of another day is represented only by the smilingly satirical "Road to Rome," the long popular sentimental drama only by the lovely "Cradle Song."

"Broadway" is a photographic account of thirty hours spent with the bootleggers and entertainers of a New York night club;

"Saturday's Children" is an observant and slightly cynical study of two young people who try to prove that two can live as cheaply and as contentedly as one on $40 a week and a fraying romance;

"Chicago" is a first-page story written by a free-handed and keenly alert reporter without fear of any copy editor's blue pencil and with something akin to joy in the thought that if the city editor doesn't care for it he is privileged to take as long a walk in the park as he feels may be necessary to restore him to normal;

"The Constant Wife" is a brilliant English dramatist's compliments to Everywoman's predetermined allegiance to the single moral standard and the logical philosophy of the goose and the gander;

"The Play's the Thing" is a freely expanded and slightly dubious anecdote admitted to parlor-story circles because of its wit and the turn-table twist given the story's point at the end;

"The Silver Cord" is a frank discussion of selfishly possessive mothers and the harm they are capable of doing in messing up the lives of their impressionable and often helpless progeny, and "Daisy Mayme" tears the fourth wall from the home of a more than usually typical circle of American kin, and reveals certain of us to ourselves with, I hope, beneficial results.

I should like to include in the bestowal of thanks to all those who have helped with the compilation of this eighth volume of "The Best Plays" series the names of the nine worthies who, after sitting with me through a majority of the hundred and sixty-three dramas and the hundred other exhibits we saw in the theatre, were still strong enough and friendly enough to give me the value of their advice in the selection of the ten plays to be honored. They were—naming them alphabetically, lest, like temperamental actresses, they accuse me of favoritism—

John Anderson of the New York *Evening Post*
J. Brooks Atkinson of the *Times*
Robert Benchley of *Life*
Gilbert Gabriel of the *Evening Sun*
Percy Hammond of the *Herald Tribune*
George Jean Nathan of the *American Mercury*
E. W. Osborne of the *Evening World*
Frank Vreeland of the *Evening Telegram* and
Alexander Woollcott of the *Morning World.*

My thanks also go to the playwrights and publishers of the dramas from which excerpts are quoted. They are of vast help in maintaining this current history of the American theatre, its achievements and its failures. And, most of all, thanks to the buyers who continue to encourage and make possible the annual issue of the year book.

B. M.

Forest Hills, Long Island,
June 15, 1927.

# CONTENTS

# THE BEST PLAYS OF 1926-27

## THE SEASON IN NEW YORK

ELUDING for the moment those statistical records drawn up in mass formation to the right and left of us, report is made that the New York theatre season of 1926-27 was one of comparatively few successes and several rather conspicuous failures. As, for example:

The failure of an elaborately organized play jury system to function,

The failure of John Citizen to win his case against the theatre ticket speculators,

The failure of certain producers of those bolder sex plays selected for test prosecution by the District Attorney to profit from the publicity gained, keep out of jail, and continue as before,

As well as the expected failure of 70 per cent. of the 260 odd plays newly produced or importantly revived to attract sufficient financial support to keep body and box office alive.

In the early summer complaint was made to the authorities that several plays and revues then running should be suppressed. District Attorney Banton thereupon assembled jury groups drawn from a panel of 300 citizens agreed upon the year before and sent them to see the plays.

The twelve playgoers who saw the most brazen of the then current revues, one called "Bunk of 1926," returned a majority verdict against it and the piece was ordered withdrawn. The management thereupon sued out the expected injunction, which served as an alibi for all concerned, and "Bunk" continued playing under court protection until it died a natural death a few weeks later.

There were sporadic agitations, mostly in the press, against what were called "the dirt shows" all through the early fall months of the new season. These began to crystallize in December, and the District Attorney's office frequently threatened action if something was not done. So did the governor of the state. Finally, catching the drift of the wind, Mayor Walker took a hand.  He called the theatre managers into conference and told them flatly that if they did not promptly order the "cleaning up" of their own theatres he would do it for them.

The managers, belatedly impressed with the seriousness of the situation, met and agreed again that something should be done. But what?  No one could, or did, offer an acceptable working plan.  So a committee was appointed to formulate one.

The committee was still formulating when Governor Smith hearkened again to church and other reform influences and the managers were frightened into a greater show of action.  They met and appointed a second committee of nine, representing actors, dramatists and producers, and promised to do their own censoring if given a chance.

By this time the list of allegedly objectionable plays included Bourdet's "The Captive," an admittedly powerful and, of itself, inoffensive drama written upon a theme previously barred from open discussion; "New York Exchange," a story of the night clubs and those handsome youths who accept support from the middle-aged women they fascinate; "Sex," a story of a prostitute's revenge upon a society mother who had sent her to jail, which was at this time playing its forty-first week in Daly's 63d St. theatre; Philip Kearney's dramatization of Theodore Dreiser's novel, "An American Tragedy"; Edward Sheldon and Charles MacArthur's "Lulu Belle," which was approaching its second successful year; "The Virgin Man," a story of an unkissed youth from Yale beset with temptation in New York, and the revived "Night Hawk," telling of a street woman's attempt to reëmbrace decency with the encouragement of an operation for rejuvenation.

In addition to these the producers of "Sex" were boldly threatening to bring in another and even bolder study of effeminate males called "The Drag."  This threat, being accepted as the very last of a wagonload of last straws, the District Attorney promptly ordered the raiding of three of the offensive dramas.

On these raiding excursions the police were accompanied by attorneys, newspaper reporters, photographers and interested citizens, and a pleasant time was had by all.

The actors in the casts of "The Captive," "The Virgin Man" and "Sex," together with their producers, were placed under arrest.  The next day "The Virgin Man" and the "Sex" companies were held for trial, but "The Captive" prisoners were dismissed when the management of that play announced its voluntary withdrawal from the stage.

This action threatened for a few days to precipitate serious complications in the offices of Charles Frohman, Inc., producers of "The Captive." The control of this company is held by the Famous Players-Lasky motion picture organization which, following the death of Charles Frohman, took over the active management of the Frohman interests with the intention of using the firm's output as a source of supply for the production of pictures.

For two years Gilbert Miller had been the producing director of Charles Frohman, Inc., and had been given a free hand in the selection of plays as well as in their casting and production. It was he who bought "The Captive," which had proved a sensation in the theatre capitals of Europe and was, at the time of its withdrawal, playing to weekly receipts of approximately $22,000 in New York.

Mr. Miller naturally resented the order to withdraw "The Captive," and was eager to fight through the courts the question of the play's alleged tendency to corrupt the morals of youth. Adolph Zukor, however, who had from the first been opposed to the production of the Bourdet drama, stood upon his ultimatum and Miller was whipped. He threatened withdrawal from the organization, submitted his resignation, but was held to the terms of a continuing contract which still had two years to run.

When the "Sex" and "Virgin Man" companies came to trial Miss West, as author and co-producer of "Sex," was fined $500 and sent to the workhouse for ten days. It was a jury verdict. "The Virgin Man," tried by three jurists in Special Sessions, drew jail sentences and fines of $250 for author and producer, and suspended sentences for members of the company.

The speculators' victory over those annoyed playgoers who insist they are wrongfully gouged by the brokers who control all the good theatre seats was won by the Tyson and Brother-United agency of New York. In March the Supreme Court of the United States, by a vote of 5 to 4, declared unconstitutional the New York state law denying speculators in theatre tickets a right to charge more than the 50-cent increase prescribed. Which altered nothing but the bookkeeping forms approved by speculators, so far as anybody hereabouts could see.

There were, this season, the usual revivals. The most interesting, and the most successful, adding the receipts of the road tour to those of the fifty-six performances given in New York, was that of Pinero's "Trelawney of the Wells," under the direction of George C. Tyler.

The cast was impressively starry, embracing the distinguished services of John Drew, Mrs. Thomas Whiffen, Henrietta Crosman, Effie Shannon, Wilton Lackaye, John Kellerd, Oliver Heggie, and Lawrence D'Orsay in the first line of veterans, with Pauline Lord, Helen Gahagan, Otto Kruger, Rollo Peters, Eric Dressler, Estelle Winwood, and J. M. Kerrigan to represent the present and future generations of popular players.

When the road tour was decided upon Miss Lord dropped out and Peggy Wood took over the rôle of the fluttery Miss Parrott. When Mr. Drew was stricken in the west Mr. Heggie played his part of the vice-chancellor.

Mr. Ames continued most successfully with his reëstablishment of a Gilbert and Sullivan repertoire. He followed "Iolanthe," his revival of the year before, with "The Pirates of Penzance," which was quite as joyously welcomed and ran through the season, "Iolanthe" being substituted at one, sometimes two, performances a week. Under other managements both "Ruddigore" and "Patience" were revived, but without success.

William A. Brady, hoping to duplicate the success he had with his revival of Barrie's "What Every Woman Knows" for Helen Hayes, brought back the same author's "Legend of Leonora" with Grace George in the name part, but the response was not encouraging.

The Actors' Theatre tried O'Neill's fine drama, "Beyond the Horizon," and it ran the better part of three months. Mr. Brady also brought back Bernstein's "The Thief," with his daughter Alice and Lionel Atwill in the principal rôles. It ran for ten weeks.

With "The Honor of the Family," Otis Skinner started another successful road tour by playing a four-week season on Broadway. A half success of the year before, "Night Hawk," was tried again in a small theatre at cut rates and played there the better part of the winter.

An interesting experiment was that of Murray Phillips who undertook to reëstablish the popular-priced theatre with revivals of certain former successes. He began with the Nugents in "Kempy," followed with Leo Carillo in "Lombardi, Ltd.," Margaret Anglin in "The Woman of Bronze," and Carroll McComas in "Madame X." His success was sufficiently encouraging to keep him going.

In the spring the Players' Club, continuing its annual practice of reviving at least one classic, staged eight performances of "Julius Cæsar," at the New Amsterdam Theatre. Tyrone Power was the Marcus Brutus, William Courtleigh the Cæsar, Basil Rathbone the Cassius and James Rennie the Marc Antony. In the cast were Pedro de Cordoba, Harry Davenport, James T. Powers, Frederick Warlock, David Glassford, Frazer Coulter, Joseph Kilgour, Kenneth Hunter, Marion Coakley, Mary Young and Mary Eaton.

Returning to the statistical department we note that when the season of 1925-26 passed out on June 15, 1926, there were still thirty-eight attractions being offered in Broadway theatres. This year there were no more than thirty-three still playing. Which may mean something, but probably no more than that there were five quicker failures one year than the other.

Taking up the record early in the evening of June 16, 1926, we discover that there were but two plays offered the last fifteen days of that June, "The Man from Toronto" (called "Perkins" when Henry Miller played it in 1918), and Florenz Ziegfeld's "No Foolin'."

This was the year, it may be recalled, that Mr. Ziegfeld again decided never to produce another "Follies." "Follies" were too expensive, read his statement; the best entertainers had adopted the arts of the highway robber in the matter of salary demands, and, after twenty years it just did not seem worth while to go on.

So he put the girls into "No Foolin'," certain portions of which were originally used in his "Palm Beach Girl" at Palm Beach, and went on as before. Everybody insisted on accepting "No Foolin'" as the annual "Follies," however, and after Mr. Ziegfeld had wearied of trying to explain the difference he agreed to go back to the old title for the road tour. Incidentally "No Foolin'" was the first Ziegfeld revue of many years which failed to register an immediate success on Broadway. After one hundred and eight performances it was withdrawn.

July was unexpectedly active, but only one of the six entertainments uncovered, a revue called "Americana," met successfully the test of weather and seasonal dullness.

The August productions lived up to expectations. There were fifteen of them, which is an average August record, and three or four promising hits. Among these were a new version of Earl Carroll's "Vanities," which ran the season out; Owen Davis's "The Donovan Affair," which had everything its own way for the better part of four months and then succumbed to the rapidly strengthening competition, and "The Little Spitfire," a moderate success that, with the help of the cut rates, lasted for two hundred performances.

There was a new "Potash and Perlmutter" comedy which could not overcome the absence of Barney Bernard and Alex Carr; a new Cohan comedy, "The Hometowners," which missed the old-time Cohan success; a light footed affair having to do with the gigolo boys and called "Loose Ankles" that went pretty well so long as it had a clear field, and an English mystery, "The Ghost Train," which failed to stand the strain of being Americanized.

The first outstanding hits of the season came a month later. The Philip Dunning-George Abbott melodramatic comedy, "Broadway," set the town buzzing on September 16, and Edouard Bourdet's "The Captive," the much discussed sensation of foreign capitals, came in the 29th.

"Broadway" piled up all sorts of box-office records and was still popular as this record was being compiled in June. "The Captive," as previously reported, ran for one hundred and eighty performances before it got into trouble with the authorities and was withdrawn by its producers.

Two musical plays from the West, "Castles in the Air," which was a favorite summer show in Chicago, and "Queen High," which had served Philadelphia with similar success, were popularly received. "Queen High" ran out the season, but "Castles" quit after one hundred and sixty performances.

Eddie Dowling, a local favorite, pleased the crowd and charmed the mayor, who is one of his buddies, with a music play called "Honeymoon Lane." He, too, ran through the season. The Shuberts brought in an operetta called "The Countess Maritza," which stayed all winter, and John Golden began his season with a homely little comedy about stenographers and rich men's sons called "Two Girls Wanted," which, without ever expecting to, continued until spring.

George Cohan's second production was a melodrama called "Yellow," boasting two as good acts as any melodrama needs and one that was no less effective but much less interesting. It lasted the better part of four months. David Belasco started his season with a failure, a comedy called "Fanny" which Willard Mack hoped would disguise the fact that Fannie Brice is a better singer of character songs than she is an actress. She went back to vaudeville after sixty performances.

Considerable excitement attended the approach of Anita Loos' "Gentlemen Prefer Blondes." It had been sensationally successful in Chicago and the Broadway crowd was so eager to see the play that even a doubled tariff for first night seats could not discourage it. The Loos comedy was far from a failure, playing six months to good receipts, but it was a disappointment to its promoters, who confidently expected it to play through one season at least and probably two. Two hundred performances was the best it could do.

Clark and McCullough carried "The Ramblers" through from September till spring, Alice Brady scored what many of us considered an undeserved failure with Vincent Lawrence's "Sour Grapes," and Joe Laurie, leaving vaudeville and musical comedy to star in "If I Was Rich," had the satisfaction of playing nearly a hundred performances before any one suggested his moving.

There was more to lament than there was to cheer over in October. Out of thirty-three productions in twenty-eight days I count less than a half dozen pieces of quality, and most of these failed.

It was in October that Arthur Hopkins put his heart and a fortune into the production of an operatic drama called "Deep River," Laurence Stallings having furnished the book and Frank Harling the score. It was, save for an overlong and rather monotonous second act, a lovely thing, a story of Creole days in Old N'Orleans, full of quaint customs and characters and exciting drama. But the opera-going public would not come down to it, nor could the theatre public rise to it, and so it failed, being withdrawn after thirty-two performances.

The Theatre Guild, grown now to an organization of sixteen or eighteen thousand subscribers (it had passed twenty-four thousand by the season's end), began its year October 12 with a production of Franz Werfel's "Juarez and Maximilian," a drama that had won Werfel a prize in Germany. This also was the introduction of the Guild's acting company which was to present a repertory of plays with the schedule of which long runs should not be permitted to interfere. "Juarez and Maximilian" was a fine drama, finely realized, but too episodic and broken in continuity of interest to be popular. It was the only Guild failure of the season, so far as the general public's support went.

Philip Kearney's dramatization of Theodore Dreiser's two-volume novel, "An American Tragedy," was a quick success this same week, and ran the better part of the season. Fred Stone, supported by Daughter Dorothy and Allene Crater Stone, came in with "Criss Cross" and was immensely popular, as usual, until early spring, when he moved on to Boston.

Philip Barry tried a satire called "White Wings," thus braving the paying theatre public's distrust of this subtle form of entertainment. His comedy, dealing with the pride of ancestry of a lowly street sweeper, despite a fine Winthrop Ames production, lasted but a fortnight. There was a dialect comedy, "We

Americans," that went better than most melting pot attempts, and the Actors' Theatre bravely started its season with a fantastic study of native character represented by the go-getters of the greeting-card industry called "God Loves Us," which was a disappointment.

Frederick Lonsdale's "On Approval," a brightly written society comedy, did fairly well; Willard Mack's melodrama, "The Noose," won a welcome by the sheer holding quality of its primitive drama and George Kelly, for whose new play both the "Show Off" and "Craig's Wife" publics were waiting, offered "Daisy Mayme." "Daisy" continued well past the holidays, but never equalled in popularity either of the other Kelly plays.

Eva LeGallienne, who had organized the Civic Repertory Theatre with the avowed intention of offering the best class of drama at a cost within the reach of its most appreciative public, which does not live in the more exclusive or more expensive sections of the town, began her season in October at a recently scrubbed Fourteenth Street Theatre. She offered first a production of the Spaniard, Jacinto Benevente's, "Saturday Night." Miss LeGallienne's ambition and intentions were heartily approved, but Mr. Benevente's play was not.

Walter Hampden, having tried "The Immortal Thief" without great success earlier in the month, turned to a Browning play he had for some time had in his road repertory. This was Arthur Goodrich and Rose Palmer's adaptation of "The Ring and the Book" called "Caponsacchi" after its priestly hero. The poetic drama pleased the Hampden crowd mightily, and ran the season out to fairly good returns.

It was in October, too, that a play based on the theosophical theory of the soul's progress through many reincarnations, called "The Ladder," was produced by Brock Pemberton and financed by a wealthy citizen named Edgar B. Davis. It was not a success, but so insistent was Mr. Davis that it should continue playing until the people in need of its message could be reached that he footed the weekly deficit all the rest of the winter, spending, it is estimated, something like half a million dollars. At this writing "The Ladder" is still playing, still losing money, and still, I hope, doing the good of which its courageous patron believes it capable.

Play producing having now reached its normal peak in New York, November followed October's thirty-three new plays with thirty-one of its own, though with little if any better luck. It was in November that Gilbert Miller, as producing director for

Charles Frohman, Inc., scored his second success of the year, which was the production of the Molnar comedy, "The Play's the Thing," freshly adapted by P. G. Wodehouse. With Holbrook Blinn playing the chief part this comedy ran merrily until early summer.

The Theatre Guild staged a revival of Bernard Shaw's "Pygmalion" at the Guild to alternate with "Maximilian" and also produced a Sidney Howard drama, "Ned McCobb's Daughter," at the new John Golden Theatre in 58th Street, on which it had taken a three-year lease. These plays were both popular hits.

Ethel Barrymore, having returned to the direction of Charles Frohman, Inc., helped Director Miller score a third success with Somerset Maugham's "The Constant Wife." David Belasco suffered his second failure of the season with an exciting but dated Western melodrama called "Lily Sue," which had been fashioned by Willard Mack primarily for the use of Beth Merrill, who had scored so notably as the heroine of "Ladies of the Evening" the year before. It was another "Salomey Jane," but not many seemed to care.

It having been announced that Sacha Guitry and his wife, Yvonne Printemps, were coming over to play in French M. Guitry's most successful comedy, "Mozart," of which Ray Goetz held the rights to the English translation, Mr. Goetz decided to present his version first with his wife, Irene Bordoni, in the name part. He did this handsomely, suffered four weeks' losses and retired.

Miss Le Gallienne revived two Ibsen dramas, "The Master Builder" and "John Gabriel Borkman," and two music play hits were those of "Oh, Kay," in which Gertrude Lawrence, the English comédienne of "The Charlot Revue," was popularly acclaimed, and "The Desert Song," which followed "The Vagabond King" at the Casino and remained all winter.

Two November entertainments that sold at popular prices, otherwise classified as cut rates, were "The Squall" and "Gertie." These, with proper nursing and many theatre parties, also remained with us until spring.

Several things happened through the holiday month of December. For one E. H. Sothern suffered his first failure as an independent star with a comedy called "What Never Dies." Haidee Wright, playing an octogenarian mater, took the play quite away from him. For another the Guild produced a second Sidney Howard play, "The Silver Cord," at the John Golden Theatre, scored a success with it and thereafter alternated two plays by the same author, "The Silver Cord" and "Ned McCobb's Daughter," at this theatre through the season.

It was in early December that Winthrop Ames resumed his Gilbert and Sullivan activities with a happily cast and nicely appointed revival of "The Pirates of Penzance." The same week George Tyler produced "The Constant Nymph," with an imported ingénue, Beatrix Thomson, playing the much-discussed rôle of Teresa Sanger. "The Pirates" ran the season out, and "The Nymph" stayed for one hundred and fifty performances.

Beatrice Lillie, another of the "Charlot Revue" stars, was taken over by Charles Dillingham and featured in an American music play, "Oh, Please," but with only moderate success. The Moscow Art Theatre Habima brought over a series of plays done in the original Hebrew, including "The Dybbuk." The Hebrew population liked them but did not support them.

The Guitrys arrived the 27th with "Mozart" and were enthusiastically welcomed, especially Mlle. Printemps. Otis Skinner revived "The Honor of the Family," preparatory to taking it on tour; Florenz Ziegfeld lost $150,000 for some one with a piece called "Betsy," in which Belle Baker hoped to star, and a music play called "Peggy-Ann," with Helen Ford featured, began a long run at the Vanderbilt.

Just before New Year's Maurine Watkin's "Chicago" startled the town into applause and laughter, scoring one of those immediate hits that frequently punctuates a theatre season and gives it color.

The same week there was obscurely produced in the Provincetown Theatre a folk drama of the southern negroes written by Paul Green of the University of North Carolina which was, to the surprise of many, destined to win the Pulitzer prize as the best play of the year. This was "In Abraham's Bosom," which ran for a few weeks in the Village, and was then transferred to the Garrick. After a few weeks here, without much attention being paid to it, the play closed. It was revived in May, after winning the prize, and again played at the Provincetown for six weeks to consistently good receipts.

In the theatre January is the starting point of the season's last half. The holidays are over, the early hits have become established, the early failures have been weeded out and it is time to take count of the near-failures that are barely holding on. Attractions were changed in thirty-one of the sixty odd playhouses along Broadway this January. And five of the newcomers were outstandingly popular.

These were "The Barker," Kenyon Nicholson's racy melo-drama of the street carnivals; Sierra's "The Cradle Song," the first popular success to give comfort to Eva La Gallienne and her Civic Repertory Theatre supporters in Fourteenth Street; "Saturday's Children," Maxwell Anderson's homely and truthful domestic drama, produced by the Actors' Theatre; "The Road to Rome," Robert Sherwood's expanded incident of history giving a possible explanation for Hannibal's retreat from Rome, and George Tyler's starry revival of "Trelawney of the Wells."

In January, too, the Guild replaced "Maximilian" with a Copeau-Croué compression of Dostoevsky's "The Brothers Karamazov." This brought the actors engaged much praise and proved sufficiently popular with the public, particularly the Russian-American public, to be listed with the Guild's suc-cesses.

Mrs. Fiske, who had been unsuccessful in finding a modern play to her liking, revived "Ghosts," playing such a Mrs. Alving as the Fiske folks approved and the more serious Ibsenites questioned.

George Tyler happily selected this month, which, as previously reported, saw the District Attorney flying to the support of decency in the theatre, for the production of Howard Lindsay and Bertrand Robinson's "Tommy." Save for the fact that its youthful hero becomes slightly woozy with liquor, "Tommy" is as clean as a kennel of hounds' teeth. It did not excite the play-goers unduly, but served beautifully as an alibi and some place to send apprehensive aunts and old-fashioned mothers.

It was in January, too, that Leon Errol achieved stardom in a music play called "Yours Truly," produced by that former Zieg-feld lieutenant, Gene Buck. It was a big and handsome produc-tion, but costly to maintain and its promoters were content to call it a season after one hundred and thirty performances.

February was a month of frustrated ambitions in the play-house. Such a month as tries the souls of professional play-goers. Only two out of twenty-five plays produced interested anybody for long, and there were many quick failures. I count ten plays that lived a fortnight or less, and three more that could not struggle past three weeks.

The two outstanding samples, however, were interesting. One was the Ziegfeld production of "Rio Rita," with which the new and gorgeous Ziegfeld Theatre was dedicated, and the other a frankly staged melodrama of gunmen, their "gats" and their "gals," called "Crime." These two finished out the season, "Rio

Rita" proving the biggest of all the Ziegfeld music play hits. It promises now to run through the summer and well into next season.

Other February items included an unfortunate venture on the part of Mrs. Patrick Campbell, who appeared in a comedy called "The Adventurous Age"; a series of matinée performances of an interesting Pirandello exhibit entitled "Right You Are If You Think You Are," and a drama of the bolder generation type written by Thompson Buchanan and called "Sinner," after the heroine. Her right name was Cynthia and her moral standards were adjustable.

March was another dull period, though two of its offerings jumped quickly into favor. These were "The Spider," one of those shiver-inciting mystery plays that spills over the footlights and is acted mostly up and down the aisles, and "The Cardboard Lover," a light-waisted but amusing French comedy in which Jeanne Eagels made her Broadway reëntry after four years of "Rain." "The Spider" success was sensational.

The Actors' Theatre, having gained new hope with the success of "Saturday's Children," tried an intelligent but somewhat depressing Clemence Dane drama called "Mariners," with Pauline Lord in its chief rôle. The reviews were favorable, but the attendance was not.

Grace George, emerging suddenly from an inactive season, played the name part in a revival of Barrie's "Legend of Leonora." Again the reviews were mostly encouraging but the public's support not even promising.

Three costly and, in the main, entertaining musical productions that proved expensive failures were "Lucky," with which Charles Dillingham hoped to duplicate the success of "Sunny," starring Mary Eaton instead of Marilyn Miller; "LeMaire's Affairs," named for the producer, and "Cherry Blossoms," an operetta the Shuberts had ordered made from the book of "The Willow Tree," which Fay Bainter played some years back. No one of these recovered anywhere near the cost of its production.

S. N. Behrman's "The Second Man," which the Guild offered in April as its last subscription production of the season, proved another interesting and popular comedy, giving the Guild the exceptional record of four hits out of five plays produced.

A second spring success that did not last, however, was Jed Harris's production of "Spread Eagle," a cynical drama tracing the origin of America's wars to Wall Street and the hysteria that follows to the dumbness of the citizenry.

The Guild revived "Mr. Pim Passes By" and, as reported, W. A. Brady restored Bernstein's "The Thief" to the stage, co-starring his daughter Alice in the chief feminine rôle with Lionel Atwill.

There was a production of "The Field God," written by the winner of the Pulitzer prize, Paul Green, which did not do well. "Hit the Deck," a musical comedy made from "Shore Leave," which Francis Starr once played, was the first of the summer shows to give promise of playing through the hot weather, if any arrived, and "The Circus Princess" opened promisingly at the Winter Garden. "Hit the Deck," incidentally, was the first musical piece ever to be played in the Belasco Theatre and one of the few attractions not owned by Sir David to be allowed to occupy its stage.

Spring had now come, or was lurking mischievously around the corner, and there was not much interest in the theatre. Still there were nineteen new plays and revivals introduced during May, twelve of which quickly passed out.

An interesting visit was that of the Spanish Art Theatre company, on its way home from a South American tour. Headed by a gifted young actress, Catalina Barcena, and directed by Martinez Sierra, the most modern of Spain's playwrights, the visitors gave five or six plays of their repertory. Many people liked them but comparatively few went to see them. Two weeks were enough to satisfy so many of our Latin Americans as were interested.

The fifth of the Little Theatre tournaments was held in May under the direction of Walter Hartwig and was the most successful of this annual series. There were entries from many parts of America and from England. The English players carried away the Belasco trophy, and thereby added to the international significance of the contest.

Two benefit performances of the "Electra" of Sophocles brought Margaret Anglin again to the attention of New York and crowded the Metropolitan Opera House, and another summer music show, "A Night in Spain," started well at the Forty-fourth Street Theatre. There was little of interest in any of the others.

The weather remained unseasonably cool and as a result five or six adventuresome showmen flirted with fate through the first two weeks of June, and Murray Phillips, who had done fairly well with a revival of the Nugents and "Kempy" at popular prices, continued his activities.

Roscoe ("Fatty") Arbuckle, still trying to beat his way back to popularity after an unfortunate experience with the courts in the West, made his reappearance on Broadway as a featured comedian in a revival of "Baby Mine." His reception was friendly, but the play could not sustain him, nor he the play. Two weeks and both were gone.

No two of the season's statisticians are agreed, each having his own system of classification, but a general average places the number of new and revived attractions at two hundred and sixty-four. Of the new shows, one hundred and sixty-three were dramatic, thirty-eight had musical trimmings of one kind and another and the rest were revivals and what not. Which is enough for any theatrical capital in any one year.

Incidentally it may be recorded that Alfred Lunt of the Theatre Guild company and Pauline Lord, at the moment unattached, were voted the winners of two gold plaques emblematic of the acting honors of the season. The *Morning Telegraph* sponsored the donation and provided the plaques and eighteen of the local play reviewers did the voting.

# THE SEASON IN CHICAGO

By Frederick Donaghey

Drama-Editor of *The Chicago Tribune*

HERE, as of June 15, is a report on and a record of the stage-year 1926-27 in Chicago: a stage-year that had its beginning in June of last year with "Lemaire's Affairs"; that was marked by the exhibition of more plays and shows of one kind and another than in any previous stage-year in the annals of the city; and that was from its gaudy beginning to its shabby ending a bedraggled, sad, mean, soiled, and prideless twelve-month. There was in it little or nothing important of Chicago origin or beginning: what was best in it, as to plays and acting, had been tested and proved in New York. And, as the stage-year neared June 4, the list of Chicago theatres devoted to drama was shortened by two, the Apollo, opened in 1921, and the La Salle, whose beginnings date back vaguely into what Thomas Beers has taught us to call the Mauve Decade. The Apollo is, as I write, being remodeled for the films; and the La Salle, the house of many a long and merry run, is already in use as what the trade calls a grind-movie, meaning a theatre wherein odds-and-ends of old film are made into a day's program and hawked from the sidewalk to passers-by who may be seeking a place wherein to loaf an hour or longer. Moreover, negotiations are on for the conversion of a third theatre, the Playhouse, into a film-place. This is one of the theatres in the Fine-Arts Building, which contains the Studebaker, also, and for a number of years contained the Little Theatre, operated by Mr. and Mrs. Maurice Browne, and, so far as I know, the first venture along the defined lines of little-theatre activities to bear that name: I don't count the Little Theatre of New York, built and for a time operated by Winthrop Ames; for that was merely a small theatre, and was used for professional performances.

That the number of theatres in the Loop district of Chicago should be decreasing against a mounting population is not a matter for surprise when the annual jumps in rates and taxes are taken into account. I offered more than a year ago to wager at

17

evens that by 1935 the Loop will not contain so much as one theatre devoted to the spoken drama. Where new theatres will be built to take the place of those being and to be converted to other uses I don't pretend to know: that is a matter which must await settlement of the question of local transportation. From time to time dispatches from New York to the Chicago newspapers explain that Mr. Ziegfeld, or Mr. Dillingham, or Mr. Woods is announcing to an unlistening universe that he has decided to build four or five theatres here either in Tribune Square, meaning opposite to or alongside the Tribune Tower, or in Wacker Drive. And the new office-boy for any firm of real estate men can figure it out for you in just four minutes that, in order for a theatre in either location to break even on the year, it would require to have not fewer than two thousand seats, and to sell each of those seats every night in the year, with Wednesday and Saturday matinées, at ten dollars apiece.

This bricks-and-mortar angle is exemplified, perhaps, by the fact that Mr. Woods is willing and eager to sell his one theatre here, the Adelphi; that anybody with the price can easily obtain the Cort from Mr. Frazee and Mr. Herrmann, although it is the theatre which annually turns in the largest profit on the investment; and that George M. Cohan, after virtually rebuilding the Grand Opera House at a cost of between five and six hundred thousand dollars, was glad within four months to dispose of a half-interest in his thirty-year lease to the Messrs. Shubert, that the house might be kept in something like continuous use. Two theatres seating fewer than nine hundred persons apiece are on ground so costly that the fixed expense of each is $104,000 per annum before an incandescent is switched on or the floor swept.

If you say, after reading thus far, that these matters have nothing to do with drama, I shall be orally in agreement with you, and of the unspoken belief that I've been wasting my time on you while telling you about them. They are most of the answer to the question of what's the matter with the drama in Chicago.

Now, as to the plays and shows of 1926-27, the best was, oddly enough, nothing else than the one for which the 1926 Pulitzer prize was awarded—"Craig's Wife"; and readers of the Year-book know all there is to know about that. Also, they know all there is to know about the plays which I regard as next-best: not necessarily in the order of such merit as they possessed, they were "The Butter-and-Egg Man," "Young Woodley," and "Ned McCobb's Daughter." Late in April "The Barker" was added to this loose list of seconds. The best of the four as drama was "Ned McCobb's Daughter"; the most interesting of the four, "Young Woodley"; the most amusing and (as parody) witty, "The Butter-and-Egg Man"; while "The Barker" brought a new theme into the theatre. The actors of "Craig's Wife," "Young Woodley," and "The Butter-and-Egg Man" were, as to the principal rôles, those who had been seen in the New York performances; but Sidney Howard's piece had John Cromwell, capital as the bootlegger; Miss Florence Johns, rather tenative in the title-part; and Spencer Tracey, bully as the younger of the Callahan blackguards; while Richard Bennett, as the Barker, and Miss Marjorie Wood, as the hula-dancer, gave to Kenyon Nicholson's play of love, lust, and license in the tent shows two fine performances.

Making a division of plays shown here that are as yet unknown in New York, the record runs thus:

"The Ragged Edge," George Abbott's arrangement of the piece known in Middle-Europe as "Periphery": put on here through the combined efforts of the Chicago Play-Producing Company, whose prospectus stressed uplift and betterment as the objectives, and Brady & Wiman. It was taken off after eleven nights; and the Chicago Play-Producing Company then quietly slipped out of business, leaving to others the task of staging Eugene O'Neill's "Lazarus Laughs."

"Sin of Sins," by William Hurlbut: this was a dirty and a cheap tribute to the box-office success of "The Captive" in New York, and the most offensive offering in the annals of the theatre in Chicago.

"Black Velvet," by Willard Robinson: something about black girls and white men, how the Old South feels about such things, and so on. Pretty bad as drama; but it prospered for weeks, owing, it is believed, to the popularity here of Frank Keenan, who appeared as an ex-officer of the Confederacy ninety-nine years old. The play calls on the old chap to die before he reaches one hundred. Arthur Byron may have the rôle in New York.

"Betsy Nobody," by David K. Higgins: in this, the put-upon drudge in a comic boarding-house found out, at 10:55 P.M. that her mother was legally married to her father, although secretly. Miss Flora Le Breton made her Chicago bow in this.

"Sisters," by John Willard: a stupid charade about how one

woman, married to a poor man, and another woman, kept by a rich one, arrived in a heated conflict as they sought to shape the future of their youngest sister, who had an offer of matrimony from a poor man, and an offer to be kept by a rich one.

"The Mender," by E. E. Rose: one of those attempts to rewrite "The Passing of the Third-Floor-Back" in order to blend it with "The Servant in the House."

"Different Women," by Eugene Walter: all about a stern old public prosecutor called upon to prove that his son killed a notorious woman right in her own night-club, although the truth was that the lad hadn't the nerve to do so.

"Tenth Avenue," by Jack McGowan and Lloyd C. Griscom: a tough piece in the key and tone of "The Deep Purple" and other things written by Wilson Mizner and the late Paul Armstrong.

"False-Faces": a guess-again piece whose authors, two Englishmen, didn't seem to know, as they wrote their text, that the sayings of Will Rogers, and the writings of Oscar Wilde, are known in this country. Nor, seemingly, had they ever heard of the piece, wherein the late Jerome Sykes was so funny, about Foxy Quiller, the detective who managed to trace the crime to himself.

"The Runaway Road," by Mrs. Gretchen Damrosch Finletter, and "Dice of God," by J. J. McGinnis: plays put on by Mrs. Insull in her first season as the actor-manager of the Studebaker, which she has leased for six years.

"Yes! Yes, Yvette!": the song-and-dance version of James Montgomery's 1916 farce, "Nothing But the Truth."

"The Madcap": a farce of French origin (first known in this country as "Green Fruit") fitted out with songs and dances as a conveyance for Mitzi. She is better in this than in anything else she had since "Sari," back in 1914. Her part calls for her, as a well-known film-player, to pretend to be a kid of twelve years in order to forward her mother's matrimonial designs.

"Listen, Dearie!": the song-and-dance version of Mrs. Gertrude Rankin Drew's 1909 farce, "Billy": the piece, you may recall, in which the hero lost his teeth.

"Sweet Lady," the song-and-dance version of the 1926 farce named "Papa Loves Mama."

"Trial-Divorce," by Joseph Sabath, for many years a judge in the Circuit Court of Cook County.

"The Open Door," by Walter Lawrence, and "The Comédienne," by J. Hartley Manners: patently designed as something

in the line of "Trelawney of the Wells," with the American
theatre of to-day as the immediate background. Laurette Taylor,
played the title-rôle.

These have been seen in New York: some of them were the
subject of mention in the Year-book of 1925-1926.

"The Last of Mrs. Cheney," wherein Ina Clair and her associates had a popular visit.

"The Jazz-Singer," with George Jessel and the cast much as it
was in New York.

"The Poor Nut," with Elliott Nugent: this had one of the
few long runs of the Chicago season.

"The Noose," fairly prosperous here: "Coal-Oil Jennie" (given
in New York later as "Money from Home"), "The Donovan
Affair," "Cradle-Snatchers," riotously successful until mid-Lent,
when the business dropped below the Plimsoll line; "Pay to
Bearer" (which was called something else in New York), "The
Shanghai Gesture," which has prosperity for what it was, "The
Ghost-Train," which wasn't wanted; "Twelve Miles Out," which
drew for five weeks and remained seven more; "The Little Spit-
fire," "One Man's Woman," "Honest Liars," "On Approval,"
"Not Herbert!," "A Woman Disputed," "That French Lady"
(which was called "The French Kiss" in New York), "The
Shelf" (wherein Miss Frances Starr drew fairly well), "Howdy,
King!," "Treat 'Em Rough!," "Love 'Em and Leave 'Em!,"
"First Love" (with Miss Fay Bainter), "Kongo," "New York
Exchange," "Our Country," "We Americans," "Alias the
Deacon," "She Couldn't Say No," "The Wild Westcotts," and
"The Great Gatsby," a good dramatization of Fitzgerald's best
tale.

In the way of revisits and revivals, there were Mrs. Fiske in
"Ghosts," Al Jolson in "Big Boy," Otis Skinner in "The Honor
of the Family," "No! No! Nanette!" "Abie's Irish Rose,"
Helen Hayes in "What Every Woman Knows," and Mr. Tyler's
cast of celebrities and somebodies in "Trelawney of the Wells,"
with Peggy Wood in place of Pauline Lord as Imogen Parrott.
I take a measure of delight in reporting that "Abie's Irish Rose"
failed to reënkindle the town. The Theatre Habima gave four
plays from its repertoire; Harry Lauder was back for a week;
and Ruth Draper came at length into her own, her own being
capacity audiences for six scheduled appearances.

Then as to the things with songs and dances in them, whether
in the general shape of operetta or just shapeless, there were
these:

"The Vagabond King," with Dennis King of the original New York cast, and otherwise performed by persons not regularly concerned in the run there. They gave what classified as a good show.

"Princess Flavia," the operetta based on "The Prisoner of Zenda," "The Nightingale," "Dearest Enemy," and "Katja," a fairish piece on the Vienna model.

Others were "Sunny," "Tip-Toes," "Kitty's Kisses," "Twinkle, Twinkle!" and "Oh, Please!" The last named, unsuccessful in New York, had by the time it was brought hither, been made into good entertainment by Beatrice Lillie and Charles Winninger, and prospered greatly through a real run. The others were just so many others,—although the clowning of Jack Donahue in "Sunny" was worth an evening of the time of any man with a nice disposition.

The best, by far, of the shapeless pieces was "The Cocoanuts," where Les Frères Marx again put up a sound argument in favor of their being the most amusing of the native buffoons. The Ziegfeld Follies (the show New York knew as the Ziegfeld Revue), a Passing Show (made up partly of the revue given in New York as "The Merry World"), an issue of Earl Carroll's Vanities, "A Night in Paris," "The Great Temptations," an emergency version of the Greenwich Village Follies, and "Gay Paree" complete that list.

It may be that the activities of the Goodman Memorial Theatre should have a division to themselves. To me, the trouble with the establishment is that it isn't "professional," although it insists that it is; that it isn't little-theatre, although that is its mental condition; and that it isn't *amateur* save in the American sense of the word. The end of the second season found the theatre about where it was in the beginning of the first season: that is, at work on the flagpole atop the tower before anything had been done in providing foundations. Where improvement had been displayed, it was due largely to the acquisition of two seasoned players from the professional stage in Alexandra Carlisle, in charge of the pupils-in-acting, and Whitford Kane. Miss Carlisle made two appearances in the season—in Maugham's "Penelope," acted in 1909 in New York by Miss Marie Tempest, and in "As You Like It"; and she was delightful in both comedies. She staged the revival of "Penelope" and that play was given with more ease and suavity than anything else put forward so far in the theatre.

The range of the plays attempted in 1926-27 is indicated by

the list of titles: Jesse Lunch Williams' "Why Not?," Romaine Rolland's "The Game of Love and Death," Mrs. Mowatt's "Fashion; or Life in New York," Sean O'Casey's "Juno and the Paycock," Molière's "Don Juan" and Galsworthy's "The Pigeon," with "Penelope," "Everyman," "As You Like It," and "A Mid-Summer Night's Dream." Something resembling popularity was evoked by "Juno and the Paycock." This theatre is conducted as a branch of the Art Institute, and is subvented.

# THE SEASON IN SAN FRANCISCO

## By George Warren
### Dramatic Critic *San Francisco Chronicle*

SAN FRANCISCO'S theatrical year, ending June 1, has on the whole been uneventful, the presentation of Morris Gest's "The Miracle" for three weeks being the high light. Gest was here, and Dr. Max Rheinhardt came from Berlin with Karl Vollmoeller, who wrote the book, to superintend the staging of the spectacle on the Pacific Coast. Receipts for the engagement for which extra matinées had to be given during the final week were reported to have run to nearly $300,000. The performances were given in the Civic Auditorium, which transformed easily into the Gothic cathedral needed for the pageant.

The enterprising Henry Duffy kept the public pretty well in touch with the type of domestic comedy and drama popular during the year on Broadway, producing at his two houses, the historic Alcazar, and the more recent President Theatre, plays that were still running in New York, so they were being presented simultaneously on both Coasts of the United States.

Among these plays were Harry Delf's "The Family Upstairs," "Love 'Em and Leave 'Em," which had a run of fifteen weeks; "Alias the Deacon," with Hugh Cameron as the Deacon, securing a run of eight weeks, Leroy Clemens being here to assist in staging the piece; "The Little Spitfire," on for ten weeks; William Anthony McGuire's "If I Was Rich"; "The Show-Off," for which Louis John Bartels came out from New York to play Aubrey Piper, carrying the comedy for ten weeks that might easily have been extended but for the reason Bartels was called East; Don Mullally's "Laff That Off," with eight weeks to its credit, and "The Patsy," by Barry Conners, which has run ten weeks and promises to go ten more, perhaps making a record here, for it is the most popular play Duffy has put on in his two and a half years of management in this city.

Other agencies, too, on the Pacific Coast have been keeping San Francisco in touch with the East. In fact, the growth of

Coast production is the outstanding feature of the year. A. G. Wilkes and C. O. Baumann made a handsome and well-acted production of Dreiser's "An American Tragedy," which Harry Mestayer directed and in which he played the District Attorney; Edward Smith presented Ruth Chatterton in "The Green Hat," and gave an elaborate staging to "Castles in the Air," which ran here for eight weeks; Belasco and Butler put on "The Dove" with Richard Bennett in the Holbrook Blinn rôle and Dorothy Mackaye as the "Dove"; Kolb and Dill made a brilliant presentation of "Queen High," and there was a well-meant attempt at putting on Edwin Justus Mayer's farce, "The Firebrand" with William Farnum, Ian Keith and Ethel Clayton in the principal rôles.

Louis Owen Macloon has made a number of productions, "Cradle Snatchers" and "Loose Ankles" among them, Lillian Albertson directing for him. His activities, however, have been confined to Los Angeles largely, for he has two or three theatres under lease there.

Few companies came across the continent during the year, but those that came with good casts and fresh productions prospered. Jeanne Eagels did a phenomenal six weeks in "Rain," and George Arliss, visiting the Coast for the first time in eleven years, played "Old English" to more than $80,000 in four weeks. Florence Reed drew very large audiences for a month in "The Shanghai Gesture," and "The Vagabond King" had six weeks of good business with a special company that included John Mealey, H. Cooper Cliffe and Mark Smith.

Blanche Bates and Margaret Anglin joined hands for a repertoire season in the summer of 1926, putting on in quick succession a double bill, "Peg the Actress," a condensation by George Creel of Tom Taylor and Charles Reade's old comedy, "Masks and Faces," and W. Somerset Maugham's "Caroline"; "Candida" with Miss Anglin playing the title rôle and Miss Bates as Prossy; "Footloose" and Zoe Akins' "The Texas Nightingale." The company toured the Coast and went to Honolulu, but returned quickly as business was bad in Hawaii.

While Miss Anglin was in California she gave a performance of Sophocles' "Electra" in the Greek Theatre at Berkeley, across the bay from San Francisco.

There were two other productions of Greek classics during the year. The girls at Mills College presented "Iphigenia in Taurus" by Euripides, and the University of California students, celebrating the twenty-fifth anniversary of the gift of the Greek Theatre to the institution, gave two performances of Euripides' "The Trojan Women."

Raquel Meller drew two very large audiences at $10 per seat, and other freak performances were Robert Mantell in a modern-dressed "Hamlet," and the same tragedy done in mufti at Stanford University with Lester Vail in the title rôle, Vail being a graduate of the Palo Alto institution.

Of new plays given original productions in San Francisco or its environs there were half a dozen of some importance and several others of minor significance. Richard Bennett put on "Creoles" by Samuel Shipman and Kenneth Perkins, a pornographic study of primitive passion, veiled under the conventions of life in the Old South just after the Civil War. The play did not do well, even with the reputation for "dirt" it had.

Edwin Carewe, the motion picture director, venturing into the realm of the regular theatre, made a production of "The Heaven Tappers," a melodrama by George Scarborough and his wife, Annette Westbay, done with an imposing cast. It failed here as it did later in Chicago.

"Oklahoma" Bob Albright, a baritone popular on the Pantages vaudeville circuit, made a production of a Western play with songs, called "Paint Pony." Thomas S. Van was the author and chief comedian, and Albright the star. The play lasted three nights.

The Playmakers, a group of men and women interested in the stage and the drama, gave four programs during the year at the Playhouse, Berkeley—seat of the University of California. Three of them were devoted to one-act plays, and the fourth evening to a full length drama, "The Pendulum," written by Minetta Ellen; story of a woman who took up a profession, that of acting, after she was 40 years old, and made a success of her work. The Playmakers write their own plays, direct them, stage them, physically, and act them. Many of the members are lecturers at the university.

Another original play, one that seemed to have the greatest promise of any of those acted here during the year, is "Deep River," by Ransom Rideout, who is connected with the University. It was done at the Berkeley Playhouse—an old church used as a theatre—by the Community Players.

It deals with the status of the negro in Europe, being particularly concerned with a New Orleans house servant who was left behind in France at the beginning of the Great War by the fleeing Americans to look after their luggage. Drafted, he served in the African regiment and after the armistice married a French woman, keeper of a little bar in a seaport town.

The discovery by the woman that he was a servant in America and her scorn of him give the story some psychological value.

A "Follies" by this same group of amateurs; a program of original plays done by the Pendragon Players of Palo Alto; original travesties by students of Stanford University and by students of the University of California were interesting, but ephemeral.

# THE SEASON IN SOUTHERN CALIFORNIA

By Margaret S. Carhart

University of California, Southern Branch

GOOD Year! say the playgoers of Southern California, good actors and up-to-date plays!

The outstanding dramatic event of the season was "The Miracle," which brought to Los Angeles both Max Rheinhardt and Morris Gest. With Lady Diana Manners, Elizabeth Shirmer, Elinor Patterson, Iris Tree, Rosamund Pinchot, and Olga Baklanova playing the rôles of the Madonna and the Nun in turn, and with Fritz Feld as the Piper Los Angeles had a chance to decide for itself as to the morality and the artistry of the spectacle. But Los Angeles has not yet decided just what it thinks. The only other foreign production of note was Mordkin and the Russian ballet, which was praised unreservedly by many critics.

Hollywood has come to the front this year as a legitimate theatre center. Two up-to-the-minute plays have succeeded there because of the plays, not because of great stars. "The American Tragedy" at the new Wilkes Vine Street Theatre began a two months' run on January 19th. On the second of May it was transferred to a down-town theatre for another month. In contrast to the New York production, the scenes were filled with all the color and life possible. The result was some startling color effects, about which the author and the audiences were enthusiastic. "The American Tragedy" was more generally talked about than any play in Los Angeles for several years.

Its closest competitor was "Chicago," which opened on March 25 at the new Music Box Theatre and in which Nancy Carroll played a kittenish Roxie Hart, far different from the tigerish interpretation of the New York production. Barry Townly played the rôle of the criminal lawyer in a thoroughly convincing manner. The production or perhaps the casting destroyed for the audience most of the humor of the satire and made one long to electrocute the entire tribe of reporters and lawyers. So a satirical comedy was turned into a melodramatic treatment of the travesty of justice in our present American system. Perhaps other audiences found more humor than the one to which the writer belonged, for "Chicago" continued for two months to teach Hollywood flappers how to handle the law.

The older plays of the season have really been more enjoyable than the newer ones. George Arliss in Galsworthy's "Old English" gave us our most artistic performance of the year. Ruth Chatterton starred in "The Green Hat" for a long run in the fall. She is a Los Angeles favorite in any rôle and was very successful in this Arlen comedy. Pauline Fredericks gave us a delightful renewal of "Madame X" and later of Maugham's "Lady Frederick." Otis Skinner in "The Honor of the Family," William Hodge in "The Judge's Husband," George Whitehead in "The Arabian," Lucile LaVerne in "Sun Up," and Ina Claire in "The Last of Mrs. Cheney" were all worth while. John Drew, who was on his way to Los Angeles with "Trelawney of the Wells" when he was taken ill, would have been a fitting close to this list of the season's offerings of good actors.

We have had some musical comedy, of course, such as the delightful "Vagabond King" and a revival of "Blossom Time." But our entertainment in lighter vein has been chiefly the Hollywood "Music Box Review," which starred Fannie Brice to our unlimited amusement and the perennially funny and pathetic "Topsy and Eva," which brought the Duncan sisters home for a long run.

Again this year Eugene O'Neill has furnished one of the most interesting plays of the season. "All God's Chillun Got Wings" had its initial presentation here this spring in a series of six special matinées under the direction of Dickson Morgan. Irving Pichel as Jim Crow and Violette Wilson as Ella were so successful that the drama has been put into regular performance at the Majestic Theatre. Acted with a restraint that disarms all race criticism, the play is proving as popular here as have O'Neill's more frequently acted dramas.

The catalog of the year's best plays would be incomplete without mention of the long run of "Cradle Snatchers," and of our joy in "The Tavern," which George M. Cohan finally allowed

Mr. Macloon to produce on the Coast. So many melodramas have come our way that it did us good to laugh over this burlesque, "an evening's entertainment all about nothing."

The little theatres, both professional and amateur, have had a thriving year. In Los Angeles the Potboilers have been reorganized into the Little Theatre of Los Angeles. This year the organization has given four interesting performances: "The Little Clay Cart" of Sudraka, one of the earliest dramas of India, "The Pleasure of Honesty" by Pirandello, which, by the way, was its first performance in America, "The Processional" by John Lawson, and "A Man's Man" by Patrick Kearney. These monthly performances are gaining rapidly in popularity with the thinking public.

Among the professional theatres I must not omit the truly remarkable Chinese Theatre in the heart of Chinatown. There a Chinese stock company has given this winter, in genuine Chinese fashion, dramas ranging from the classical tragedies of centuries ago to the most modern spicy interpretations of the American Review. Gorgeous costuming in stiff brocades, brilliant embroideries, and headdresses that almost over-shadow the wearers; acting which my Chinese friends tell me is as good as any seen in China and which puts over the main story without words; and Chinese music which taxes the endurance of every Occidental visitor, furnishing an entertainment never to be forgotten. The student of the drama feels himself back in Elizabethan England when the friendly audience was at one with the stage, and the novelty hunters find excitement enough and to spare from audience as well as actors.

The Pasadena Community Playhouse reports a season of unusual artistic growth, of marked innovation in program planning, and of sound financial advance. The policy of securing first Western rights to striking and unusual plays has been continued, and two interesting novelties have been offered: Luigi Chiarelli's "The Mask and the Face" and Eden Phillpotts' "The Farmer's Wife." The Italian "grotesque," with its peculiar self-mockery, and the English folk comedy, with its rural atmosphere and difficulties of dialect and diction, demanded the best ability of producers and actors. In addition to these, three Shaw plays have been outstanding successes: "Cæsar and Cleopatra," "The Doctor's Dilemma," and "Misalliance." Contrast in program has been secured by a range from Phillpotts' and Hastings' fantastic and nonsensical "The Angel in the House" and the exotic Italian-Chinese fantasy "Turandot" to a sequence of five historical

American plays. Beginning with Royal Tyler's "The Contrast," the series included "Uncle Tom's Cabin," "Aristocracy," "Her Own Way," and "The Show Off," and showed the styles in drama from the Revolution to the World War. The most successful plays of the year have been "The Angel in the House," "The Doctor's Dilemma," "Turandot," "The Farmer's Wife," and "Captain Applejack." Early in May the policy of the Playhouse was changed to repertory program. The first succession was of "Misalliance," "Two Gentlemen of Verona," and "Justice," to be followed at once by "The Duenna," "They Called Him Babbitt," and "Easy Virtue." At the annual membership meeting in June a delightful presentation of Witter Bynner's "Cake," with constructionist setting, was presented to members only. Another noteworthy production was a special performance of Browning's "The Return of the Druses," which, I understand, had never before been staged and which proved an amazing accomplishment. During the year thirty-two different plays have been produced in all, over five hundred people have been cast, and over forty-three hundred people have broken bread in the green room.

In connection with the Playhouse two other organizations have been functioning this winter, the Workshop and the Playbox. The Workshop offers a tryout for playwrights, directors, and actors who would prepare themselves for the bigger stage. For a first year the Workshop has had success, as several promising graduates are already at work in the Playhouse.

The Playbox has offered seven delightful plays again this year. "The Trackwalker's Child" was the first performance in English of a powerful and haunting drama by Alice Stein. "Anthony and Anna" by St. John Ervine was followed during Christmas week by the Chester Pageant of "Noah's Deluge." "Amelia" by Alice C. D. Ridley and Ibsen's "Rosmersholm" completed the series as it was originally announced. The demand for additional plays, however, was so general that Mr. Brown produced Ervine's "Ship" and Galsworthy's "Justice" as the concluding numbers of the series. During his stay in Los Angeles Max Reinhardt attended a performance of "Rosmersholm" and compared the work done at the Playbox with that at the Moscow Little Theatre. All of these plays lent themselves well to intimate production in a small studio without a stage. Those of us who were privileged to look through the window at "Rosmersholm" and to sit in the jurybox and declare Falder guilty would find it hard to forget the experience. The announcement by Director Brown of the plans for the formation of a permanent school of the theatre in connection with the Playhouse to be opened in September 1928, indicates the strides which this community theatre is making.

The Drama Branch of The Community Arts Association of Santa Barbara has also had a most successful year under the management of Irving Pichel, whom Southern California is glad to welcome as a permanent addition to its dramatic force. Sixteen plays have been produced this winter at the Santa Barbara theatre, plays covering the wide range from "Twelfth Night" to "Hay Fever." As a result of a ballot as to the best play of the year cast by several hundred patrons, the first choice was Shaw's "Cæsar and Cleopatra," followed closely by "Twelfth Night," "Loyalties," and "Peer Gynt." The unusual and beautiful impressionistic settings used for the Shaw and the Ibsen plays undoubtedly helped to deepen the impression made by good acting and directing. Next season the Lobero hopes to offer performances on two week ends of each month, thus increasing its contact with the community. For the end of June Mr. Pichel is loaned to Los Angeles for "All God's Chillun Got Wings," mentioned earlier in this account.

# BROADWAY

## A Comedy Drama in Three Acts

### By Philip Dunning and George Abbott

THERE had been rumors all through the summer of 1926 that the play called "Broadway" was a success. Or would be as soon as it reached town. And although many plays are similarly heralded as probable hits long before they appear on Broadway, in this particular instance the rumors were wise rumors, being largely circulated and vouched for by the wise folk of the theatre.

In Atlantic City in the early summer "Broadway" had been called "The Roaring Forties," and once before that Philip Dunning, its original author, had christened it "Bright Lights." "The Roaring Forties" title was discarded because many of the visitors in Atlantic City, missing the significance of the street reference, thought it referred to the California gold rush, and "Bright Lights" just naturally faded into "Broadway."

The night of the premier a representative Broadway crowd took the play immediately to its palpitating heart. There were cheers both for the players and the authors, but no speeches. Mr. Abbott was buried some place back stage and Mr. Dunning, then acting as stage manager of the Marilyn Miller production of "Sunny," at the New Amsterdam Theatre, had run over for a minute and was furtively dodging among standees at the back of the theatre, wondering a little whether the fuss the folks were making was really inspired by their liking for the play or was due to the fact that they had been away from the theatre for a long summer and were just happy to be back.

The play was, however, a very genuine success and for many months thereafter its popularity dominated the entire list of plays to be seen in New York. The reviewers were enthusiastic, accepting "Broadway" as the truest and most entertaining of those reportorial dramas whose authors recently had taken so heartily to reflecting native life in the rough.

"Of all the scores of plays that shuffled in endless procession along Broadway in the year of grace, 1926," writes Alexander

Woollcott in a preface to the published version, "the one which most perfectly caught the accent of the city's voice was this play named after the great Midway itself, this taut and telling and tingling cartoon which, produced with uncommon imagination and resource, was presented to New York at the Broadhurst Theatre on the night of September 16, 1926."

There is precious little waste in the action of "Broadway." Being cross-sectioned from the group life which it reflects the rising curtain catches its people in the midst of a definite daily activity. The scene is the private party room of the Paradise Night Club in New York and the time just before the first show, which would put it at about midnight.

"To the tinny obbligato made by 'Lil' Rice at the piano, five chorus girls are in line singing and dancing one of the numbers of the revue," report the authors. The rehearsal is under the direction of Nick, the proprietor of the Paradise, and Nick is "a middle-aged Greek, mercenary and hard." Lil, too, is a familiar night-club type, "a heavy, middle-aged woman with a certain amount of good looks, which, however, have long since lost their bloom. She rolls her own, and removes tight slippers from swollen feet whenever occasion permits."

The chorus girls are being paced in this rehearsal by the "hoofer" of the troupe, Roy Lane, "a typical song-and-dance man with his coat off, sleeves rolled up."

The girls are variously dressed, some in practice clothes, some with the skirts of their street clothes pinned up to give greater freedom to their legs. Everybody is irritable. Nick is raucously impatient because the girls are listless in the dance. The girls are sore because the rehearsal has really been called to help a newcomer in their group, Billie Moore, who has not even shown up. Roy Lane, being interested in Billie, is anxious because he fears Nick will fire her for being late. His effort is to cover Billie's tardiness and keep the Greek's mind on the rehearsal. He gets little encouragement, however, either from Nick or from Lil.

Roy—Listen, Mr. Verdis, Billie's only been in this game for a short while. (Joe *enters with a drink for* Nick.)

Nick—And she won't be in it a hell of a while longer. As soon as she comes in, she goes out. (Lil *plays "How Dry I Am."* Nick *pauses as he is about to drink and looks at her.*) Joe, get Lil a drink. (*He drinks. The girls lounge about the room, smoking, using nail files, etc.* Joe *exits to Hall.*)

Roy—Gee, Mr. Verdis, it's not like Billie to fall down on the

job. Why, that kid is one of the best lookers and neatest workers you got. You'll make one big mistake if you let her out—
she's a mighty nifty little trick.

Nick—Why all the talk? You don't work for her—you work
for me.

Roy—God knows I know that.

Nick—Whadda ya mean?

Roy—Well, not to pin any bouquets on myself, but where
could you get a guy to do what I'm doing for the coffee-and-cake
money you're paying me?

Ruby—He's off again.

Roy—You see it ain't only I can dance, but I got personality—

Mazie—Huh!

Roy—Personality plus—

Mazie (*to* Grace)—Ain't he a darb?

Grace—He hates himself.

Nick—Somethin' else ya got is a terrible swell head.

Roy—Who, me? Nothin' swell-headed about me, Boss—I
coulda been that way long ago, if I'd wanted to. (Katie, a
*cigarette girl, enters down hall.*)

Nick—Cut out the belly-achin' and quit any time you
want.

Roy—They must be some good reason why Billie ain't here.
Listen, Lil, don't put it into Nick's head to give her the air, will
you? 'Cause she needs the do-ray-me pretty bad—she's got a
mother and sister over in Trenton.

Lil—I never knew a jane in this business that didn't have.

Roy—On the level, I met 'em.

Mazie—I room with her and I happen to know she's a good
kid.

Roy—And believe me, it pays to be good.

Mazie—Sure, but not much.

Lil (*wisely—to* Roy)—So you met the family, eh?

Roy—Yeh, I went out there one Sunday. You see I take a
sort of brotherly interest in that kid.

Lil—Brotherly?—

Roy—You heard me. Anyhow I and her are fixing up a little
vaudeville act together.

Lil—Say, sweetheart, why don't you get hep to yourself?

Roy—What do you mean?

Lil—Ain't you wise that she's given you the bum's rush?
Why, that guy's got her so dizzy she don't know you're alive.

Roy—Who? Crandall? No, no, not at all. She'll get over

that. She ain't used to going to such swell places, that's all.
She's got more sense than to care a thing about Crandall himself, personally—it's just the buggy ride—I seen it happen lots
of times—young kids get taken out by a rich guy—everything
swell; music, lights—they get baffled, you know what I mean,
dazzled—and then suddenly they get wise to themselves that the
whole works is a lot of boloney and they realize where the
real guys in this world is at—

LIL—Hoofing in cabarets.

ROY—Yeah. That's no kid neither. Billie's ambitious to get
ahead in this game. I guess she'd want to stick with somebody
could learn her something, huh? . . . Her and me ain't long in
this joint anyhow. I'm going to make her something besides a
chorus girl.

LIL—What's coming off?

ROY—As soon as I get Billie ready we're all set for a lot of
nice booking on the big time.

LIL—Soon as you get Billie ready? Are you—all ready?

ROY—Who—me? Well, that's a funny question. You're
lookin' at me every night. You can see. I don't belong here.

Now Billie rushes in, breathlessly. "She is a beautiful little
creature, despite the obvious commonplaceness of her clothes."
And she is full of explanations. She has been out to dinner with
Steve Crandall, which, by Mazie's reckoning, will make everything all right with Nick. And Mr. Crandall promised to keep
track of the time. But it was so wonderful just to sit and listen
to the music they both forgot.

Roy is of the opinion that Billie should be warned about
"sugar daddies" like Crandall. They're only after one thing,
and they gotta be watched. . . .

Steve Crandall is "a tall man, handsome in a hard sophisticated way," and rather impressive in his dinner clothes. He is
also plainly master of the situation. Nick's tone toward Billie,
whom he is about to discharge, changes abruptly when Crandall
walks into the scene and nothing more is said about it.

Crandall is giving a party that evening after the show. He
wants to engage the supper room and he wants all the performers
to stay as his guests—his paid guests—and help him entertain.
He is not so very keen about Roy's staying, but he is willing to
pay the dancer for a little clowning. Roy agrees to oblige, knowing how parties need laughs, but he is still unsettled in his mind
about Crandall's obvious pursuit of Billie Moore and not above
admitting it.

"I been knocking around cabarets, dance clubs, vaudeville, everything, for a long time," he says to Steve, "and what I can't get through my head is this—why is it that all the guys like you are never satisfied with the hundreds of janes that will do anything you want—all the rummies and bums you can have, and by God—you'll quit 'em all to go after one girl that you know is good—why is that, huh?"

Steve might resent Roy's interference in his affairs if the dancer, to him, were not such a fool. As it is he passes it off with an implied warning that he is not in the habit of permitting any one to tell him what he should or should not do.

Two of Steve's men are in. Dolph, dark and wiry, brings a diamond bracelet he has picked up for his friend. Porky, placid and bald, has come to suggest that Steve sell Nick a load of liquor the boys had hi-jacked from a rival in the Bronx the night before. Steve's regular business, it soon appears, is that of bootlegging. A highly organized business as he runs it. And at the moment about to be expanded.

"Say, boys, this business of peddling booze is the second largest industry in the United States right now," is Steve's boast. "Give me a year more at it and we'll all retire." And again: "Listen, Nick, if my trade is going to grow I got to crush a little competition now and then—I'm taking Scar's booze when I can lay my hands on it, and I'm taking his territory. It's just business, that's all. Are you with me or not? You gotta declare yourself in or out."

Of course Nick is with him, and agrees to buy the liquor. But not without protest. He is opposed to hi-jacking because of the feud risk and he is convinced that Steve can easily run into a lot of trouble if he persists in defying "Scar" Edwards, who has long been in command of the Bronx territory above 125th Street. Steve is much too handy and too ready with a gun.

The matter of the liquor is settled, the final arrangements for the party are made and Dolph turns over the bracelet that Steve has ordered for Billie. It is a nice bracelet, "lifted off one of the classiest mammas in town," according to Dolph, and it cost "five yards." The fence had wanted a "grand," but Dolph beat him down.

For the moment things are pretty well settled at the Paradise. Then Scar Edwards appears! "He is a tense man, slightly over-dressed in the Broadway fashion," and he evidently is not there just to make a social call.

Scar has come to file a protest and to demand a show-down.

He is, he declares, unarmed and as friendly as the circumstances justify, but he isn't afraid of them or anybody else. They know damned well what he is there for, he ventures. They have been poaching on him and they know it, and they will quit it and keep below 125th Street, or they will get into a lot of trouble.

SCAR—We stocked that territory and we got a right to it. My mob worked for four years to get things the way we got 'em—and nobody—get that—nobody is goin' to cut in from down here and spoil a nickel's worth of it. You hi-jacked another truck-load last night (STEVE *rises*), yes, and you been spillin' more jack around for protection than we can afford—we ain't never come down here to horn in on your Broadway trade, but you're ruinin' our game up there and I'm here to tell you that you can't get away with it.

STEVE—If you knew me a little better, you'd know that yelling wouldn't get you much.

DOLPH—That's just what I was going to say.

SCAR—Peddle your papers, will you. (DOLPH *walks away squelched. In the cabaret the orchestra can be heard playing George Olsen's Battle Number.*) I'm talking to the boss now. I come here for a show-down with you guys, see.

STEVE—All right. I don't mind a little show-down myself once in a while. You're looking for trouble, is that it?

SCAR—No, I ain't lookin' for trouble. Nothin' like that. Not that my friends ain't capable of holding up their end, if it comes to that. But I say they's plenty of business for everybody and them that works up the trade should be the ones to get it.

STEVE—And supposing I say that I'll sell any damn place that I can get away with it?

SCAR—Then I'm warning you that it's dangerous for you to do business in Harlem cause from now on 125th Street is the dead line. Get me?

STEVE—Yeah?

SCAR—Yeah.

STEVE—Well, that's just dandy, Scar. Thanks for the tip-off. Now if you've spoke your piece you can take the air. I don't care about having a public fight with the likes of you because everybody in this place don't know my business yet, and I don't care to have you stand around and broadcast it.

SCAR—There's a lot of things I can broadcast, if I have to.

DOLPH (*comes to the other side of* SCAR)—You heard what the boss said, didn't you?

SCAR—You too—the both of you—since you're looking for tips, I'll give you another one.  I happen to be the guy who can clean up a few murder mysteries in this town.  I suppose you don't know who knocked O'Connell off!

DOLPH—What are you talking about?

SCAR—And who dumped his body up in Harlem so my mob would get blamed for it?

STEVE—What the hell are you driving at?

SCAR—This is what I'm driving at—

DOLPH—Wait a minute.

SCAR—I've waited long enough.  Now get this—you guys stay down here in your own territory and you leave my trucks alone.  See—cause I got the dope on you, Steve—you croaked O'Connell.

DOLPH (*grabbing his arm*)—Look here.

SCAR—Take your hands off me or I'll bust your goddam face.  You guys can't put me out of business.  (SCAR *is facing* DOLPH.  STEVE *quickly pulls out his gun, presses it against* SCAR's *back and fires.*  SCAR *pitches forward.*  DOLPH *catches him in his arms.*  SCAR's *hat falls off.*)

DOLPH—Jesus Christ, Steve, what have you done?

STEVE (*remaining cool*)—Get hold of him under the arms— quick—walk him out of here—

The orchestra in the cabaret is still playing the battle number, with its trumpet calls and drumming features.  Billie and Roy come down from their dressing rooms, look over the stair railing and see the three men walking toward the door.

"Who's the drunk?" calls Roy.

"Just one of the boys we're helping home," nonchalantly answers Steve, and the death march continues.

Roy and Billie are down early to do a little individual rehearsing to make up for what Billie has missed.  But they spend most of the time trying to square themselves with each other.  Billie is sorry about the rehearsal, but she refuses to be sorry about Mr. Crandall.  A girl should take advantage of all her wonderful opportunities.

A girl should also remember the chances she's got when a fellow wants to help her work up a great little dancing act that will put them both in the Palace, maybe, and at $300 a week, counters Roy.  Think of the thrill of that!  Think of the thrill of seeing their names spelled out in electric lights—"Roy Lane and Company!"  She can't afford to let anything get in the way of that honor.  Certainly she shouldn't be doing foolish things like staying to Steve Crandall's party. Steve's kind can get soused without her. Anyway, this is the night she is expected to go home to New Jersey to see her mother. What if the old lady should kick the bucket, or something?

Roy and Billie have gone to their dressing rooms when Steve and Dolph come back from getting rid of Scar Edwards. Dolph is plainly worried, but Steve is deliberately self-poised and calm. Nothing could have been prettier than the way everything has broken for them. With Edwards out of the way Steve plans to hook up the two gangs and organize the town right, with plenty of profits for everybody.

Plans for Steve's party go forward. Porky, making a choice early, thinks that with her permission he will stick close to Lil. She's more his style than the others. No skinny-legged, slat-sided baby pigeons for Porky. "Me?" says he; "I like a dame that can sit in a Morris chair and fill it."

There is, however, a note of apprehension injected into the proceedings. Dolph has just discovered Dan McCorn sitting out in the cabaret. Dan McCorn is a member of the homicide squad, a square dick and a good one. But Steve refuses to be startled even by that news.

Still he takes the precaution to tighten up his defenses. He sends for Billie Moore and gets her promise to forget that she has seen him helping a drunken man out of the Paradise earlier in the evening.

"You see, he's a big politician," Steve explains. "If it got out it might cause a lot of trouble. Just thought I'd warn you so that—you know—if you happened to talk you might get yourself in a bad jam."

He gives her the bracelet—for her birthday. She has already had one birthday, but Steve thinks she should be smart and have another. Billie is trying to protest convincingly that she cannot take the bracelet when the orchestra sounds the warning for the first number, and the girls and Roy Lane have lined up and danced into the cabaret.

Dan McCorn strolls in through the hall door. "He is a man about 30, matter of fact and rather well dressed." Dan is there, apparently, just to pass the time of day with Nick and the boys. He jollies Steve a bit on his ambition to "extend his trade," and questions the advisability of such a move. McCorn doesn't deny that Steve is going to peddle his goods wherever he pleases, but he has a feeling that breaking into "Scar" Edwards' territory is likely to cause trouble.

"That's a bad bunch up there," he warns; "some of 'em two-term men."

"Some of them gorillas of Steve's ain't such a sweet bunch, either," suggests Nick.

"That's what I say—that's why it looks like fireworks," agrees Dan.

NICK—Wouldn't you think with all the trouble it is to get it—they wouldn't fight over who sells it?

STEVE—Well, some people ain't never satisfied.

DAN—By the way, seen Scar Edwards lately?

STEVE (*with mild surprise—as though he hadn't quite caught the question*)—Speaking to me?—

DAN—Well, not exactly.   Have you?

STEVE—About two weeks ago I saw him—at the races.

DAN—Speaking to him?

STEVE—Why not?   I gave him a tip that paid 20 to 1.

DAN—Yeah?   You didn't see him, then, when he was here to-night?

NICK—Huh?

STEVE—Here?   Who?

DAN—You didn't, Steve?   Huh?

STEVE (*long pause*)—Your arm is swelling, Dan, what did you put in it?

DAN—Scar Edwards was here, wasn't he?

STEVE—Listen, Dan, Scar Edwards and me are personal friends, but we don't do business together.

DAN—Maybe that's why he came.

STEVE—Don't be silly.

DAN—I'm not.

NICK—He wouldn't come to my place.

DAN—Well, he was in this neighborhood anyway—that much I know, cause I saw him myself.

STEVE—You saw him?   Where?

DAN—Under a blanket in a Westcott Express truck, just a block and a half from here.

NICK—For God's sake!

STEVE—So they got him, eh?   That's too bad—Scar wasn't a bad sort when you knew him.

DAN—I hope to tell you.

STEVE—Well, that's a tough break—I'm sorry to hear it.

DAN—Now that I don't sound so silly—who pulled that off?

STEVE—How the hell should I know?

DAN—Funny part of it is, he didn't have a rod on him.

NICK—You find him?—

DAN—No, the Westcott driver found him, when he came out of the lunch room. I got there shortly after.

STEVE—Can you imagine that driver?

DAN—Yeh, lucky thing he found him so soon, still warm when I got there—

STEVE (*casually*)—What time was it?

DAN—Must have been—say—twenty minutes or half-past ten.

STEVE—Well, I've been here all evening, haven't I, Nick?

DAN—I didn't ask you for an alibi, but since you mention it—let's have it—who was with you?

STEVE (*revealing just a flash of chagrin at his slip, he controls himself and speaks calmly*)—Why, Porky Thompson, and Nick here part of the time; Billie Moore—one of the girls; most anybody could tell you, they all saw me. (PORKY *comes in from hall.*)

PORKY (*to* DAN, *surprised*)—Oh, you're here—I was looking at the show and—yeah—how are you?

DAN—Thompson, what time were you here with Steve and Nick to-night?

PORKY (*hesitatingly.* STEVE *signals with his hands*)—I came in—about—five minutes after nine—(STEVE *signals again.*) yes, sir—five minutes after ten. (STEVE *walks away with satisfied expression.*)

DAN—Why so positive?

STEVE (*cutting in*)—I happened to ask him for the correct time when he came in.

DAN—You didn't have a watch?

STEVE—Sure. But I wanted to see if I was right.

DAN—When he told you—then you knew you were right—is that it?

STEVE (*righteous indignation*)—Where the hell do you get off to sweat me?

PORKY—What's the matter—what's up?

NICK—Some one killed Scar Edwards.

PORKY (*smiles*)—Well, well— (*sees* STEVE's *look—changes mood*) Gee, that's too bad.

DAN—You guys ain't thinking of goin' in mourning, are you?

Roy and the girls prance in from the Paradise dancing floor, and prance back again to take their bows. Lil Rice prepares to follow as the next number. Dan McCorn decides there is nothing more for him to talk about and goes back into the cabaret, with Porky trailing him.

Now the girls have noticed Billie's bracelet and are properly impressed. Some ice! Roy Lane, however, is not pleased.

"You ain't gonna keep it?" he queries, anxiously.

"Certainly she is," Mazie, the friendliest of the gold diggers, answers for her.

Roy—Give it back to him.

Billie—Now, Roy—

Roy—Listen, Billie, for God's sake, don't be a fool! You know what everybody'll be saying about you.

Billie—Don't tell me what to do!

Roy—I tell you give it back to him.

Billie—Listen, General Pershing.

Roy—You do what I say!

Billie—Mind your own business.

Roy—Please, Billie, I'm telling you something straight from the heart—

Nick (*pushing* Billie *out of the way*)—Hey, hey, what you gonna do—have some heart talks instead of doing your number?

Roy—No, sir, Mr. Verdis. I'm right here waiting to do my stuff. Nobody can say I don't give the customers one hundred per cent. every performance. The night my old man died, I went out at the Regent Theatre in Danbury and give as good a performance as I ever done in my life. (*Turns and looks at* Billie.) And even if a jane I'd put my hope and trust in was going to hell, I could still go out and give them my best. Line up, kids. (Porky *enters from hall*.)

Porky—Dan McCorn is sittin' out there waitin'. What to hell's the matter?

Roy (*to girls*)—There's the cue. Give it to 'em! Cut 'em deep and let 'em bleed! Here we go! Here we go! Let's mop up! (*While the two men stand looking at each other inquiringly, the cabaret doors open, the music swells,* Roy *puts on a little hat with a feather in it, and dances out behind the girls*.)

The curtain falls.

## ACT II

It is a half hour later, and the Paradise show is on. From the cabaret come the muted strains of the jazz orchestra.

Steve Crandall and Porky, in for a moment after quieting
down the more riotous Chicago gorillas who are seeing the show,
are far from calm. Especially Porky.

Dan McCorn is still outside and giving no signs of leaving.
His presence strikes Porky as being ominous. Nor does Steve's
repeated statements that a gang shooting is not such a novelty
that any one need worry about it reassure him.

Dolph, too, is nervously anxious. He has just come in with
the early editions of the morning papers carrying lurid stories of
the Scar Edwards shooting and predicting a renewal of the old
gang feud as a consequence. The boys don't like the looks of
things, but Steve is cheered by the conclusions of the police reporters. "Here's the real dope," he tells them. "Listen—this
is good:

" 'It is learned from confidential sources that the police suspect
one of Edwards' own gang who is said to have nursed a grudge
against his leader. An arrest is expected within 24 hours.' "

"I'm worried just the same," repeats Porky. "What if the
Edwards outfit bumps me off?"

"Me, too," says Dolph.

"Well, what of it? You only have to die once. You got nothing to worry about—I'll bury you right—I may get a special professional rate from Campbell's if they get both of you. (*Laughs.*)
Say, quit worryin'. I wish they would start something. We'll
go up to Harlem in a couple of fast cars and let these Chicago
boys show off some of their machine-gun stuff."

Steve refuses to "blow the town" for a while, as they suggest.
He has other, and personal, interests at stake. He isn't going to
give up his pursuit of Billie just to ease their foolish fears. Besides, if he were to disappear now it would be the most damag-
ing evidence against him.

The "Hawaiian" number is finished and the girls dance in
wearing their shredded-grass costumes, dance back for their en-
cores and rush to their dressing rooms for their costume change.

Steve stops Billie. She is not wearing his bracelet and he
wants to know why.

Reluctantly she admits that she has taken it off because the
girls made dirty cracks about it. It's what they call a "slave
bracelet" and he knows what that means. "They said if a rich
man gives you one and you wear it, then that's a sign that you
belong to him."

STEVE (*urgently*)—You like me, don't you? I know you like me—I can tell—

BILLIE—Yes.

STEVE—And I sure like you—and—I want to be able to do things for you and—

BILLIE—It isn't fair to you—that—I mean I can't take this bracelet off you because it wouldn't be fair.

STEVE—Don't you think I'd treat you right?

BILLIE—I s'pose I shouldn't have let you take me out at all, Mr. Crandall, because I know it sounds silly, but I'm not that kind of a girl, that's all.

STEVE—Maybe that's why I like you.

BILLIE—I know there's nothing wonderful about being the way I am—I mean being virtuous, I s'pose you call it—I know lots of the best-hearted girls in the world that aren't, so it isn't that; but I mean it isn't fair for me to keep your bracelet because that's the way I am.

STEVE—Well, listen, baby, have I ever tried to pull any rough stuff?

BILLIE—No, you haven't, and that's what I always say—

STEVE—Then why haven't I got as much right to hang around you as some of these other yaps?

BILLIE—Well, you're married, of course and—

STEVE—No, I'm not.

BILLIE—They said you was.

STEVE—No, I'm divorced—I'm all right—I'm divorced twice. Just because you're here in the show, don't think I regard you in a light way—no, indeed—I'm no fly-by-night—I'm a very sincere sort of person, baby, and I want you to understand how I feel about you. I'm crazy about you. Honest, no foolin'. (*Draws her to him a little;* ROY *enters on stairs.*) Don't listen to nobody but me, kiddie—cause I'll treat you right—

ROY—Mazie wants to see you right away, Billie.

BILLIE—Oh, does she—all right—excuse me.

For this interruption Steve is of a mind to poke Roy right in the nose, but he recovers his poise and lets the matter drop with a warning.

Billie, too, is miffed at Roy's interference when she discovers that his sending her to Mazie was a trick. And Mazie backs her up. By what right has Roy constituted himself Billie's protector?

By the right of his interest in her, argues Roy. Billie isn't the kind of girl that can stand this night-club racket like some he knows. Furthermore, she isn't going to stay to Steve's party and she's going to give him back his bracelet.

She is, is she? That's a joke to Mazie. Billie could get five hundred on that bracelet in hock, and, besides, if she plays her points right there's a chance she may land Steve as a husband, marriage, hand-embroidered nightgowns and everything.

Is that so? Well, if there's any thought of that marriage stuff Roy has a thing or two to say for himself, and he'd like to say it privately to Billie, if Mazie will kindly chase herself, which she does.

Roy—I'm going to save you from getting into a lot of trouble.

Billie—I didn't ask you to.

Roy—I know you didn't. And take it from me I ain't achin' to play the hero in this picture myself, but there's nothing else to do. Now first, I'm going to put a plain proposition to you. (*He comes toward her half appealingly. She sits looking up at him.*) I guess you know pretty well that I'm very strong for you, but I ain't said nothing about matrimony on account of my old man has just recently died. But since this big four-flusher is talking about a wedding ring, I'll play my own ace. Listen, honey, how about getting hitched up?

Billie (*faintly*)—Roy, I don't know.

Roy—It would be better for the act, wouldn't it?

Billie—I never thought much about it.

Roy—I suppose I should of tipped you off how I felt before, but anyhow there it is in black and white.

Billie (*distressed*)—Gee, I don't know what to say.

Roy—Take your time. I know it's kind of sudden. But I sort of thought you was wise to how I felt anyhow.

Billie—Well, I did think you liked me—I mean I hoped you liked me.

Roy—Well, now that you know how much I like you, what do you think about the idea?

Billie (*rising*)—I don't know what to say.

Roy—I always thought way down in our insides we knew we was for each other. God knows I'm for you, Billie girl, so just say the word that you're for me and I won't let out no yells or nothing, but I sure would feel just like doing that little thing. (*She doesn't answer.*) What do you say?

Billie—Well, Roy, of course I'd have to think a thing like this over and—

Roy—Nothing doing. Just as easy to say it now as some other time.

Billie—How can I say it, when I don't know for sure whether I'm in love with you or not?

Roy—Well, we certainly get on well together.

Billie—Oh, I know we do, just wonderful.

Roy—Well, when you see me coming to say hello to you in the morning, don't your heart never beat no faster?

Billie—Yes, it does.

Roy—Well, that's it. That's what they call love at first sight, kid. It's wonderful. I'm the same way.

Billie—But I don't know if we ought to talk about marrying when we're so poor—

Roy (*he comprehends her reason for hesitating*)—Oh, you want a rich guy—

Billie—I didn't say that.

Roy (*contemptuously*)—A gold digger!

Billie—I'm not. I'm not. But I don't want to be fooling and say something that I'll be sorry for afterwards. All I say is that I ought to think about a thing like this.

Roy—Aw, you want to think.

Billie—Yes.

Roy—All right, my duty's plain—go on upstairs and think.

Billie—Well, don't talk to me that way or I never will marry you.

Roy (*dismissing her*)—Sure. Talk it over with you next week.

Billie gone, Roy puts in a long distance phone call for Trenton. He wants to talk to one of the Maloney brothers at the Capitol hotel. Getting his connection, he carries on an animated conversation with one of the Maloneys that cannot be heard above the racket the girls make coming back for their next number.

Dan McCorn is in again from the cabaret. He finds Pearl alone. She is trying to telephone to some one, but hangs up quickly at the sight of the detective. With some difficulty McCorn engages Pearl in conversation. Has she seen Scar Edwards lately? At first she denies knowing Edwards, only to confess in the end that she is Scar's girl, and is working in the Paradise club in his interest.

Pearl (*appealingly*)—He didn't want to put somebody down here he couldn't absolutely trust for fear they'd double cross him—a lot of dirty skunks, they wouldn't stop at nothing.

DAN—But Jim Edwards trusts you, eh?

PEARL—Sure! (*With a sudden burst of confidence.*) We're gonna be married as soon as he gets his final papers.

DAN (*walking away*)—That's too bad.

PEARL—What is? (*Pause.*) Has he done anything you want him for?

DAN—No, I haven't a thing on him, lady.

PEARL—Well, tell me straight—has something happened? You act so kind of funny.

DAN—You gotta finish this show to-night? Sing and everything?

PEARL—Sure, I go on again.

DAN—Well, I won't take up any more of your time then,—I just wanted to know if you'd seen Edwards to-night.

PEARL—No, I ain't seen him since breakfast, but— (*again decides to trust him*) I don't know why I shouldn't tell you—he told me he was coming down here to-night to have a show-down with Steve.

DAN—Oh, oh, he told you. . . . Well, I'll be going along about my business— Thanks, Mrs. Edwards.

PEARL (*pleased*)—In three weeks.

DAN—You just keep this under your hat, won't you?

PEARL—Will I? If I want to get out of here with all my neck, I will.

Billie has sent a telegram to her mother telling her about the party and that she won't be home. Roy, making a quick change of costume without going to his dressing room, is divesting himself of his trousers at the prop table. But he is too excited to be conscious of his bvd's under the circumstances. Billie's decision to stay to the party in opposition to his wishes irritates him.

BILLIE—You tried to boss me so much I just thought I'd find out if I had a mind of my own. So I just went and telegraphed that I wouldn't be home to-night cause I'm going to the party.

ROY—Well, I'm sorry you done that. (*Takes off trousers.*) Listen to me, kiddie, if it's just to spite me you're doing this, why, I'll eat mud.

BILLIE—It's not only that—it's because I have an obligation.

ROY (*throws trousers over arm and goes to her*)—Listen, partner, I've been your pal anyhow, and I got some right to talk to you. Who have you got the greatest obligation to in this world, huh—a big rounder like Steve Crandall, who's got no respect for pure womanhood, or your poor old gray-haired mother who's sitting at home alone waiting for you?

BILLIE—But she's not alone—my sister's with her.

ROY—Oh. (*In disgust he throws his trousers in corner and picks up others.*)

BILLIE—If you don't think I got enough character to be decent at a party, you better look for somebody you got confidence in. (PORKY *enters from hall.*)

PORKY—Your shirt-tail's hanging out. (*Exits to office.*)

ROY (*paying no attention to him*)—That ain't the life for you. (*Getting on trousers while he pleads earnestly.*) You don't want to be pegged with them bags, do you? They think they're wiser than Almighty God, the guy that wrote the book,—but when they're hittin' the home stretch for Potter's Field, they'll be wiser still. For God's sake, think of all the plans we made, Billie. Don't be a dumb-bell.

BILLIE—I'm not.

ROY—You're giving a good imitation of one.

BILLIE—I'd go if for nothing else just to show you good and proper that I don't belong to you.

ROY—If you did, I'd spank your bottom.

BILLIE—Oh, you would—would you?

ROY—You bet I would—and if I catch you inhaling any of that poison, I'll spank you before the whole mob.

BILLIE—Then I would be finished with you.

ROY—I don't care if you never spoke to me again. I gotta do my duty by my partner—first the artist, that's me—second, the human bein'. (*Buzzer.*) I done everything I could to appeal to your better instincts. I pulled every wire I knowed to keep you decent and we ain't heard from all the precincts yet. (*Tries out comedy hat.*) I told you just what my feelings for you is, nothing up the sleeve so far as I am concerned, so if you want to be sore, I guess that's how it'll have to be, that's all. (*Dances into cabaret.*)

Dan McCorn finds Porky alone during Roy's number and questions him rather pointedly about the events of the night. Porky is evasive but suspiciously anxious to establish his own alibi. Dan has always found it goes easier with a fellow if he comes clean when he knows anything about a murder. That's always been his belief, too, admits Porky. But he doesn't happen to know anything about Scar Edwards being there.

Neither does Dolph. Or Steve, when these two break into the conversation. And they are getting a little bit peevish about McCorn's nosey suspicions. All this snooping around is making a sort of coroner's inquest out of the place and interfering a lot with Steve's party.

McCorn tries to reassure them. "Trouble with you," he says, "is that you've had so much business with a lot of half-baked federal dicks you ain't used to talking to just a plain old New York cop any more."

"Well, maybe you're right."

"I ain't always—I've been wrong lots of times, but this case of Edwards interests me terribly. You see, whether a guy shoots square or not, according to the law, ain't always it—but no matter what he's done, to me, he should have a break; and somebody shot this guy in the back."

Bennie, one of the tough Chicago boys, is in from the cabaret. He doesn't like the nasty look of recognition Dan McCorn gives him in passing and demands of Steve to know what McCorn is doing there.

The girls are coming downstairs for the "Pirate" number and Pearl overhears Steve's reply:

"A local nuisance by the name of Scar Edwards got bumped off to-night, that's all."

Pearl gives a scream and falls fainting, trying to save herself by clutching the handrail. The other girls rush to her. Pearl revives quickly, however, and insists she is all right. The show goes on.

Before the girls go out Steve completes his arrangements for the party. Tearing six one hundred dollar bills in two, he gives each of them half of one. They are to get the other half when the fun is over if they are all good babies.

Now the Chicago bunch is in and eager to meet the lingerie. They are a rough crowd, a little less comfortable in their dinner coats than their New York friends. New York, to them, as Bennie says, is the place you got to go through to get to Chicago, but they are none the less impressed with the town's possibilities. Steve takes charge of the introductions and everybody is well acquainted in practically no time at all.

Soon the last cabaret number is finished and Steve's party has spread into the adjoining supper room to start the drinking. All but Steve and Billie. Some of the boys got a little rough with Billie and she runs to Steve for protection. He is awfully willing to give her that.

STEVE (*holding her*)—It's all right, Billie, don't be scared. Everything's all right.

BILLIE—Oh, Steve, what'll I do.

STEVE (*holding her*)—I won't let anybody bother you— (*He looks at her tenderly—is suddenly overcome by his passion.*) I love you—kid. (*Crushes her to him.*) God, I love you. I'd do murder for you. (*He kisses her passionately—she tries to break away.*)

BILLIE (*frees herself and goes to chair*)—Steve, please don't.

STEVE—All right—I'm sorry. (*Kneels beside her—contrite.*) Listen, Billie, just to show you that I appreciate what a real nice girl you are, you don't need to stay to the party. You can go home if you'd be happier about it.

BILLIE—No, I ought to stay because I owe that much to you, and anyhow— (*looking upstairs after* ROY) I said I'd stay and I'm going to.

STEVE—But you're such a little peach I want to make you happy—see? Listen, to-morrow night after the show let's get in the car—go for a ride and have a good talk. Will you? (*Nods.*) All right, that's a date. We'll stop at Ed's place and get a nice little supper and I've got something important to tell you. (*He starts to fondle her.*)

BILLIE—Make your hands behave, Steve.

STEVE (*drawing back*)—All right, I'm just as meek as a lamb, see! Whatever you say.

Suddenly the party threatens to get out of bounds. Mazie and Ruby are exchanging compliments and nasty looks. Mazie has a mind to make Ruby's shirt "roll up her back like a window-shade," and if she does that Ruby will certainly do something drastic in reprisal. Probably spit in her eye. Ruby, being no more than a "phoney blonde with store teeth," according to Mazie, is likely to be violently separated from life at almost any moment. Fortunately the men are able to quell the disturbance before definite damage is done.

Mazie is also a little disturbed at seeing Billie sticking so closely to the fringe of the party. She should get in and have some fun, seeing she's only going to live once.

"Don't be afraid," counsels Mazie. "Nothing'll happen to you. Listen, Billie, crack wise. It ain't so serious. Just kid 'em along that's all, kid 'em along. It ain't so bad as it looks. I wouldn't give you a bum steer, Kid, honest, I wouldn't—but you don't always want to pay too much attention to what people say. Take me, for instance, you think I'm a pretty tough character—sure I am, in a way,—but I seldom give up—very seldom—"

But Billie prefers to keep away from the rioting. A moment

later she is glad. A telegram is handed her. It is signed by her sister Mary and reads: "Mother very low. Come at once."

The next moment Billie is hysterical. To think of her staying to a party like this when her mother may be dying! It's terrible!

Both Roy and Mazie try to comfort her. Roy is sure everything will be all right and is ready to take her home. Good to her? Of course he's good to her. Ain't they pals through thick and thin? Sure they are!

Steve Crandall is also eager to be good to Billie. Of course she must go home right away. And his car is right out back waiting to take her. Steve will have her home in no time.

But before either Roy or Steve can do anything about it a sec‹ ond telegram arrives. This one is from Billie's mother herself.

"Your wire received," it reads, "stay to party and have good time. Mother."

"She musta got better," weakly suggests Roy. But he still insists so long as everything has been fixed they had better go on home.

"I wouldn't stay and entertain your gang of goofers if you kissed my foot in Macy's window at high noon." That's the way Roy feels about it. And he tells Steve so.

But Steve, equally angry, is certain her mother's telegram has cleared everything for Billie. Now they can all have a good time, and he's through with any further interference from any "waxed-floor bum."

It is Mazie who brings the incident to a climax. She scents a frame-up. Roy's talk with the Maloney brothers—that's when he did it. He asked them to send that first telegram.

Billie is reluctant to believe that Roy would do a dirty trick like that, making her think her mother was dying— When she reads the truth in his eyes, despite his denials, she declares she is through with him forever.

"Suppose I did do it," Roy shouts, his voice trembling, his eyes filling with tears. "I did it for you, didn't I? I know these kind of guys and you can't be right if you run with guys like Steve Crandall—he's just out to grab you—and he don't care what means he uses—I'm tellin' you he's just plain no good and I don't give a damn who knows it."

At a sign from Steve Porky clears the room by herding the men and the girls back into the supper alcove, leaving Roy and Steve alone. "Now, you lousy little bum, I got you where I want you!" shouts Steve, and with a swift blow he knocks Roy down.

Slowly the dancer rises to his feet, rubbing his chin. "Thanks," he sneers. "Ain't you a brave guy though—all right—look out for this one!" With that he rushes at Steve, who pulls his gun.

"And look out for this one," he warns as he is about to shoot.

Dolph bursts through the doors in time to see the gun and stop the shooting. Dan McCorn is coming, he warns. In the scuffle Steve's gun has fallen to the floor and Roy picks it up, defensively, without realizing what he is doing. The next minute Dan McCorn has taken it from him and demanded to know what the trouble is.

An argument, explains Steve, a little argument in which Roy has pulled a gun on him.

"Ever hear of the Sullivan Act?" McCorn demands of the protesting dancer.

"What time is it playing?" innocently inquires Roy.

"The Sullivan Act is a law—it gives you plenty of time for carrying one of these."

The gang drifts in, looking for trouble. They are convinced now that McCorn is stalling so far as Roy is concerned. He doesn't want the hoofer. He wants the gun.

Steve is excited by the suggestion and insists that McCorn give the gun back to Roy. "Listen, Mac, what the hell are you tryin' to do?" he demands of the detective. "You been gumshoeing around here all night. For what? Now you come buttin' in here around my party. Understand, mine!— You ain't got a warrant to go tearing around here as you like. This room is private. Now I'll thank you to run along and call it a day— give the kid back his cap pistol. I can settle my own arguments with him."

"I said I'd keep the gun," calmly answers McCorn.

But the boys, growing ugly, are not inclined to let him have his way, until he craftily convinces them that, for their own protection from the Edwards gang, he has stationed seven of his men outside the Paradise and left them there subject to call. Of course he is sorry if his asking questions and seeming to butt in, as Steve says, has interfered any, but asking questions is his business and he just has to do it. It doesn't mean, necessarily, that he suspects anybody in particular.

Roy Lane, however, has his suspicions, and is ready to voice them. He suspects Steve. Why? Because at 10 o'clock that night he had seen Steve and Dolph helping a fellow with a scar on his face out the back door.

STEVE (*starts for* ROY)—You're a liar.

DAN (*holds arm up—keeps* STEVE *from getting to* ROY)—
Wait! Wait a minute, Steve. Take it easy. (*Pause—to* ROY)
What time did you see Steve with Scar?

ROY—Before the show—about 10 o'clock.

STEVE—He's lying, Dan.

DOLPH—Sure he is.

DAN (*to* ROY)—Would you know this guy with the scar if
you saw him again?

ROY—Sure I would. I saw them and Billie Moore saw
them too. They were taking him out of that door. I asked,
"Who's the drunk?" and Steve said, "One of the boys we're
helping home." If you don't believe me, ask Billie—she'd never
tell nothing but the truth—ask her.

STEVE—Dan, this kid is sore at me—he's jealous—he made
up that rotten lie to get me in bad.

DOLPH—Sure. Dan can see through him.

DAN—Verdis, call in the Moore girl. (NICK *glances at* STEVE.
STEVE *makes sign, so* NICK *goes up, opens party door.*)

DOLPH (*during above, speaks to* DAN *confidentially*)—Don't
believe nothin' this hoofer says. I tell you, he's nuts.

DAN (*impressed*)—Yeah?

NICK—Billie—hey, Billie—come—want to see you a minute.

DOLPH—Sure—ask anybody—he's an awful liar. (BILLIE
*comes in. The other girls straggle after her, curious.*)

BILLIE—What do you want me for?

GRACE—What's the matter?

MAZIE—Why ain't you guys paying us attention—

RUBY—Shut up, look what's going on.

DAN—Miss Moore (*The room becomes quiet.*), Miss Moore,
about 10 o'clock to-night, before the show started, when you
came down to rehearse with the dancer here, did you see Steve
and this gentleman (*Points to* DOLPH.) helping a drunken man
out the back door?

BILLIE (*unable to grasp the situation*)—Why—

ROY—Tell the truth, Billie.

DAN—Did you? A man with a scar on his face? (STEVE
*turns and looks at her—she catches his eye—turns back to* DAN
*—pause.*)

BILLIE—No. (STEVE *shrugs, satisfied, as though to say, "I
told you."*)

DOLPH—I told you that kid was nuts.

DAN (*to girls*)—Did any of you see Scar here to-night?

GIRLS—No. (PEARL *steps forward, starts to speak, then walks toward stairs.*)

NICK—I'm here all the time. I didn't see him.

STEVE—Now are you satisfied?

DAN—Yes.

MAZIE—Say, copper, will you do me a favor? Take Personality with you before he tries to make any more trouble here.

STEVE—Is that all you want, Dan?

DAN—That's all for now. (*Pulls* ROY *by the arm.*) Come on, Lane. I'll tell you some more about the Sullivan Act.

ROY—You can't take me like this, officer— Who's going to look after Billie? She don't know what kind he is— (*The crowd starts back toward the party room.*)

DAN—Come on—

ROY (*desperately*)—No! Wait a minute— For God's sake give me a chance! She's only a kid! She don't know what she's up against! Mazie, tell him! This Crandall guy is out to grab her—

STEVE—Take him along.

ROY—I'll fix you. (*Breaks away. Makes a rush at* STEVE— *is stopped by* BENNIE.) I'll kill you if you touch her— I will, God damn you. (DAN *recaptures him; yanks him toward back door.*) Lil—somebody—why don't you say something! I don't care what you do to me— Oh, God, Billie. (*The music starts up.* DAN *is dragging* ROY *out.*)

The curtain falls.

## ACT III

It is just before show time the night following Steve's party. Everything is dead around the Paradise Club. Only a few of the girls have shown up. Roy Lane is still detained by the law. Lil isn't there. Nick, himself ragged from his adventures of the night before, is crazed with anxiety.

Nor does the arrival of Dolph to report that the truckload of liquor Nick has agreed to take will be delivered that night serve to lessen Nick's worries. Everything is being hurried a little it appears, because Steve Crandall is planning to take a short trip.

The reports concerning Lane, however, are somewhat exaggerated. He is not still in jail. He is out, and good and mad at having been put in. Also he is through with Nick and the Paradise for life. He has come now for his props.

Nick, however, reminds him that no great artist would act that way. An artist would always think of his public first. It is going to be a big disappointment to a lot of important people, some of them already gathered in front, if Lane doesn't appear in the Paradise show to-night. There is probably something in that, Roy agrees, and promises to work until the end of the week.

One by one the stragglers begin to appear. Billie is back from Trenton, contrite and eager to explain to Roy that she wouldn't have done anything or said anything she did if he hadn't tried to boss her. It isn't easy to get Roy to listen. He is terribly disappointed in Billie.

"When a fella's worked like I have to get together the best dancing act in the business, and gets all ready for bookings, he hates to see it go blooey just because a big stiff that's rancid with coin comes along and cops his partner," he explains.

BILLIE—What right have you got to say he's copped me?

ROY—Last night you lied to save him and against me.

BILLIE—Yes, but I didn't know—you got no right talking that way. All the girls around here are always saying I'm too good— and you're saying I'm too bad. I hate this damn place.

ROY—And another thing, last night you called me a sap in the presence of several witnesses.

BILLIE (*almost in tears*)—Oh, shut up. That's what you are. (NICK *enters from office.*)

NICK—All right—all right—get made up. (BILLIE *starts upstairs, so agitated that she scarcely notes* NICK'S *presence. She pauses and leans over the banister.*)

BILLIE—And I'll tell you something else, and it's most likely the last thing I'll ever tell you—the reason I went to my Mother's was to ask her, if a girl was terribly in love with a person, so much it was like regular love at first sight, was it all right to marry 'em even if they was poor,—that's what! Now, how'd you like to go to hell? (*Exit upstairs.*)

ROY (*gazes after her dumfounded; turns to* NICK)—They pick up that language quick around this honky-tonk.

NICK—She's right. Don't be interfering with her.

ROY—Well, they's a lot of personal things mixed up here you don't understand. I'll tip you off to one thing—my next partner is going to be a man.

Now Lil is back, but not exactly ready for work. She has Porky with her and they have continued the festivities inaugu rated by Steve by getting drunk and also married. It seems probable that they will both recover in time, but for the present it is doubtful if even many cups of black coffee can fix the queen of song so that she can go on with her part of the pro, gram that evening.

They are busy getting Porky stowed away in the office and Lil upstairs to her dressing room, when Steve Crandall puts in a sudden appearance. He is plainly apprehensive, anxious that no one should know he is around and ready to pay doormen and waiters liberally for protection. That he has cause to be nervous he indicates by a bullet hole straight through the top of his hat. He was coming through 49th Street when that happened—and not a suspicious soul in sight. Some one with a silencer on his gun had taken a shot at Steve and almost nicked him. It will be a lot better for him, he figures, if he leaves town for a few days, and he is making his plans accordingly.

Billie, dressed for the first number, is coming down the stairs when Steve sees her. He pauses on his way to the office to dig out the sleeping Porky when he sees her. "Hello, beautiful," he calls, gayly. "Well, you look as sweet as sugar. How's tricks?"

BILLIE—All right. (BILLIE *is ill at ease with him. She hurries up to the table with her props, trying to be casual, but betraying a new manner towards* STEVE, *that almost amounts to suspicion.*) I came in late and then I hurried so—that I'm about the first one ready.

STEVE—Found the folks all right, did you?

BILLIE—Oh, fine.

STEVE—That's good. That gives me a great deal of pleasure. Of course we missed not having you stay for the finish of the party last night.

BILLIE—Well, you were awfully nice about letting me go home, Mr. Crandall.

STEVE—Well, I'll tell you, Billie girl, any time I'm not nice to you, you remind me and I'll get nice, 'cause as far as you're concerned, that's the way I want to be, see?

BILLIE—Of course I don't understand about the detective and everything.

STEVE—Of course you don't, Girlie. But I'll explain it to you. It's just politics—that's all. I'll tell you all about it after the show to-night. It'll be very interesting. You're going for a ride with me to-night you know.

Billie—Well, I don't know. (*He has taken her hand, she draws it away, as though by accident, and steps back.*)

Steve—You haven't forgotten. That was a promise—you wouldn't try to go back on that.

Billie—Well—

Steve (*quite frantic*)—You did promise—don't forget that—

Billie—I wouldn't go back on my promise—

Nick has an inspiration. With Lil out of the show why not let Roy and Billie try out their big-time act? It will be a great chance for them to break it in.

Billie is willing, but Roy hesitates. So far as he knows, he hasn't any partner. But so far as Billie knows, he has. She's willing to go on if he is. Everything doesn't have to be the same as it was before—not everything.

"We might as well go on and try it," she argues, "now that we rehearsed it so much, even if you don't like me any more."

Roy (*hooking her dress*)—It isn't a question of liking you. But when I get a throw-down like last night, I get wise to myself.

Billie—Well, when I get a throw-down like I just got to-day, I'm wise to myself too. But lots of people don't like each other, still they work together. I mean, if you still think we'd make a good team, then it's just a business proposition. A couple can be in the same act without being crazy about each other.

Roy—Well, I used to think we'd make about the best combo I could imagine—but I'm the kind of a guy I don't want to butt in where I ain't wanted. (*Sniffs.*) You want to run over a few of them steps? (Billie *nods.*) Just remember your routine, that's all you got to do.

Billie—Let's try the finish—that's where we got mixed up at the last rehearsal.

Roy—All you gotta do is follow me. Watch me out the corner of your eye and you can't go wrong. (*Takes place to do steps. She puts arms around his neck, pulling their cheeks together. He takes her hand away and places it at waist.*) Down here.

Billie—The last time we did it this way.

Roy—Well, that was the last time. We'll do it now the old way. (*Stops acting and looks away from her.*) You see it's kinda spoiled it for me, thinkin' you might have had your arms around Steve that way.

Billie—I haven't. (*Pause.*) And when I lied last night about the drunken man, it was because I had promised Steve to say that, and I didn't know a thing about that you'd said the opposite. And I went home alone last night.

Roy (*looks at her—melts*)—We'll do the finish the new way—like this. (*Puts her arm around his neck.*) Billie, you know that, what you asked your mother when you went home to-day—about marryin' a poor fellow?

Billie—Yeah—

Roy—Well. (*Buzzer. They jump apart.*) Never mind. You can tell me later. We gotta think of our work now. On your toes, baby—don't get nervous. (*At door.*) Listen, Mr. Verdis is makin' an announcement—sensational newcomers—Roy Lane and Company— Oh, boy, don't that make you feel proud?

Billie (*overcome with sudden panic*)—Roy—I'm scared—

Roy—Don't be scared—remember I'm right beside you. It'll all be over before you know it.

Billie—Roy, I don't believe I can go on. Can't we wait till to-morrow till we have a chance to rehearse?

Roy—Pull yourself together. We can't have no stage fright gummin' our act. I'll give you a sock in a minute. There's our music. We'll finish in a blaze of glory. (*Pulls her to entrance—blesses himself.*) Lots of snap now. We'll show 'em. Let's go. (*They exit to cabaret, dancing gayly.*)

Dan McCorn is looking for Steve. He comes in the back way over the waiter Joe's protest and seems rather determined to stay for a while, despite the opposition. But Nick assures him he is wasting his time. Steve isn't there and hasn't been there. Anyway, Dan thinks he will wait awhile in the cabaret.

Now Steve knows his danger and takes Nick into his confidence in fixing his getaway. He doesn't like the looks of things. Even the girl Pearl, passing quietly through the room, startles him. And the report of Dolph, who is keeping watch outside, that there is a guy out there pacing up and down apparently waiting for some one does not lessen his anxiety. He sends Dolph back to watch. Nick is rather puzzled.

"I don't get this business, Steve," he says.

Steve—Listen, Nick, you and I been best kind of pals for a long time. I'd shoot the works for you and I hope you would for me.

Nick—Sure I would. What you want?

STEVE—I'm going to blow to-night. I don't want to have any slips. This damn bull McCorn is getting too curious. He thinks some of my mob got Edwards.

NICK—Did they?

STEVE—No, they didn't. Now listen, I want you to get Joe or some one you can trust to beat it over to Charlie's and tell him to bring his car, not mine, they know mine—and leave it at the back entrance for me.

NICK—You can phone him.

STEVE—No, these dicks might have the wires tapped. Sending Joe is safer. After the show, I'll take Billie and a couple of these broads and pile in the car. Looks like we're going for a joy ride, savvy? Then if they trail us, when I get 'em out on the Post Road, I can lose 'em, see, but they won't think I'm going to blow, so long as I got the girls with me. I can get rid of the ones I don't want later on.

NICK—You go to lots of trouble just 'cause a bull's asking questions. My Gawd, Steve, where's your guts?

STEVE—You think I'm yellow, huh? I don't want no man thinking that. Listen, Nick. (*Takes him roughly by wrist and comes close.*) I did that job myself. (NICK *motions quiet with both hands.*) Now, they can't get me for it—they got nothing on me but that gun—but it's getting on my nerves—I'm getting ragged and I want to get out of here. Now, have you got it?

NICK—Sure, I understand. But don't bump nobody else off in here.

STEVE—You won't get in trouble—I'll fix that. Now send for the car.

NICK—Sure, right away—you wait in the office, Steve. (*He hurries into cabaret.* STEVE *goes to big door under stairs, peeks out cautiously through peep hole—then crosses to cabaret doors, closes them. As he does so, the party door opens, and* PEARL *steps in with a pistol in her hand. It has a silencer affixed.*)

PEARL (*low*)—Turn around, Rat! (*He wheels about.*) I don't want to give it to you like you did him—in the back.

STEVE (*he can't move*)—For Christ's sake, don't!

PEARL—I'm giving you more chance than you gave him— I'm looking at you—and the last thing you see before you go straight to hell is Jim Edwards' woman, who swore to God she'd get you.

STEVE (*backing away*)—Don't—don't kill me—don't—

PEARL—Whine, you rat—I knew you would. (*She fires. There is just a pish as the gun goes off, a slight curl of smoke.* STEVE *lurches toward office and falls out of sight as he clutches at the door.* PEARL *stands paralyzed by the violence of her act. Then she thrusts the pistol into her handbag and scurries upstairs like a frightened rabbit.*)

Roy's big act is over. And what an act! The girls can hardly keep from laughing in Roy's face. But they are good sports. They wait until he isn't looking. Roy is too busy taking his bows to pay any attention.

Now Dan McCorn is back and more excited than before. Either Nick is going to help him find Steve Crandall or he is going to run the risk of being taken up for helping a guy that's wanted for murder. If he knows where Steve is he'd better say so, and say it quick.

Nick motions toward the office.

DAN—Tell him I want to see him. (NICK *goes reluctantly to office. He opens door and draws back with a gasp.*) What's the matter? (DAN *runs to door, sizes up situation, and steps past him into room.*) Come in. Shut the door. (*They go to office.* NICK *fearfully—the door is shut.* RUBY *enters, half dressed, followed by* MAZIE, *who catches her on stairs and chokes her—bending her over the banister.*)

MAZIE—Now you're going to eat mud.

RUBY—Quit.

MAZIE—Now what am I the son of?

RUBY—You're an angel.

MAZIE—Say uncle—

RUBY—Uncle.

MAZIE (*releases her*)—Now, get back; I'd drop you over if I wasn't feeling so good natured. (RUBY *exits.* MAZIE *dusts off her hands as* ROY *enters with a rush. He has supper card in his hand.*)

ROY—Look, Mazie—look at this— I got this from Mike Shea —he just caught our act.

MAZIE—Who's he?

ROY—He's one of the biggest booking agents in New York— he wrote me on this supper card—

MAZIE—Mike Shea? Never heard of him—

ROY (*at top of stairs*)—Listen, what he wrote. At last I got a break. "I can offer you and partner Chambersburgh and Pottsville next week—" Billie, Billie! (*Runs out to dressing room.*)

MAZIE (*laughs*)—That's one for the book! (*Follows him.*

NICK *comes out of office looking under great stress—*DAN *follows.*)

DAN—He's dead all right. (NICK *moans.*) Right through the old pump.

NICK (*turning back to him—suddenly alive*)—Lane! The hoofer! He's the one! He killed Steve! I'll betcha! He was out to get him!

DAN—The actor, you mean? (PEARL *enters on stairs—she starts down—hears the voices and halts.*)

NICK—Sure! He's been tryin' to get him. He's been lyin' about him.

DAN—No, it wasn't Lane—it was suicide.

NICK—Suicide?

DAN—Sure. (*Fascinated,* PEARL *comes slowly downstairs, her hands against the back wall.* DAN *talks to* NICK, *his eye on the girl.*) Here's Steve's own gun—with one chamber empty.

NICK—I thought you had that?

DAN—I gave it back to Steve to-day.

NICK—But Steve said—

DAN—I said I gave it back to him to-day. He knew I was going to pinch him, so he took the shortest way out. I'm calling up headquarters to report it suicide—so that's what it is.

NICK—All right—all right—whatever you say.

DAN—Give me the key to this door. (NICK *gives him key to the door;* DAN *locks it.* PEARL *sinks to the chair by piano.*) I want you to keep every one out of there till the Coroner gets here. I'll wait for him out back. (*He starts to back door; as he passes* PEARL *he speaks disinterestedly—out of the corner of his mouth.*) Pull yourself together, kid. (*Exits back door.* PEARL *lets her head fall forward, weak with relief, as* DAN *exits and the other girls and* ROY *enter on stairs, laughing and joking excitedly.*)

MAZIE—Pottsville and Chambersburgh! Gawd, Billie, you must love this guy.

BILLIE—I certainly do.

ROY—I been so busy gettin' the act framed, I ain't had time to show you how much I love you. But here goes. (ROY *and* BILLIE *embrace.*)

ANN—My Gawd, in front of everybody—

GRACE—When do you two play the matrimonial circuit—

MAZIE—Break! Time!

RUBY—Look at 'em. (*Girls laughing and pulling* BILLIE *and* ROY *apart.*)

NICK (*bursting out suddenly—his nerves unable to stand their hilarity*)—Cut out this noise—I—ah—we gotta cut it out, y' understand! (*They stand dumfounded by his violence. The buzzer sounds—and* ROY *snaps back to his job.*)

ROY—There goes the gong, girls. All ready! Come on, Pearl. Gee, I'm happy! Our names will be in bright lights soon. Roy Lane and Company! Remember you're all artists! Here we go —here we go— (*The girls form in line and dance into cabaret singing as* NICK *crosses himself and prays, leaning against the floor as though half fainting.*)

The curtain falls.

# SATURDAY'S CHILDREN

## Comedy in Three Acts

### By Maxwell Anderson

THE Actors' Theatre, having combined with the Greenwich Village Theatre group the previous spring, began the season with high hopes and the production of a fantastic drama called "God Loves Us," fashioned by J. P. McEvoy. This effort appeared to mystify rather than to enthuse the populace and was soon withdrawn. A revival of Eugene O'Neill's "Beyond the Horizon" fared somewhat better, but it was not until, following an internal reorganization resulting in the appointment of Guthrie McClintic as director in chief, that the Actors' Theatre took a definite step forward.

Under McClintic a new Maxwell Anderson comedy, "Saturday's Children," was produced and immediately accepted by those quoted arbiters of the drama's fate, press and public, as a success. It was, in many ways, the most important success of the year. It not only reëstablished the Actors' Theatre and justified its continuance as a subsidized institution, but it also brought a new confidence to Playwright Anderson at a time when he needed it most. He had earned critical praise with "The White Desert" but nothing more substantial. He had achieved a measure of fame and temporary financial independence as part author of "What Price Glory?" Thus encouraged he had given up his editorial jobs and gone in exclusively for writing for the theatre, only to be set back by the failure of "Outside Looking In." If "Saturday's Children" also had failed it might have been seriously discouraging to one of the most gifted of native dramatists.

"Saturday's Children," as noted, did not fail. From the date of its production (January 26, 1927) until late in the spring it played to the capacity of the Booth Theatre, and was still continuing prosperously in late June.

This comedy is another of those intimate studies of home life among the native middle class, an amusing exposure of human and familiar weaknesses touched with an individuality in characterization that sets it apart from the common run of plays of its type.

In June, 1926, we walk into the Halevy dining room in a typical city apartment. It is furnished with the usual dining-room accessories, including a "large 1910 model Grand Rapids buffet," and it lets into a hall at back on the other side of which the bathroom door can be seen.

At the moment the Sands, Willy and Florrie, Florrie being the elder Halevy daughter, are going over the *Morning World* want ads in search of a business opportunity that shall come within their means. These include stationery stores, cigar and pool rooms, garages situated in ideal locations, chances to buy in on flourishing collection agencies and such.

Mrs. Halevy is cleaning up the dinner things and from the adjoining living room the sounds of a radio concert, frequently interrupted by static, serves to locate Father.

The Sands are young married people and still playful. Florrie is addicted to occasional attacks of baby talk and Willy extracts much humor from his own veiled insinuations that his wife is in love with the iceman, even though the handsome dog is married and the father of seven children.

"It's Florrie's romance," Willy explains to the protesting Mrs. Halevy, who does not like to hear young folks joke about such things. "Everybody has to have his romance, and if your husband's a real estate agent you fall in love with the iceman, and if your husband's an iceman you probably run away with a real estate agent. I know how to handle her though. I stay so damn poor she never has enough pocket money to run away with anybody."

Whereupon Florrie launches a violent attack upon Willy, determined by pulling his hair to make him take back his outrageous statements, kiss her sweetly as he used to do when she was only his secretary, and, finally, agree to take her to the band concert in the park. At this point Mrs. Halevy succeeds in changing the subject to Florrie's sister Bobby.

Bobby is also a working girl, secretary to the president of the company by which Willy is employed. She is still unmarried at 23, and a cause of some anxiety to the family. Bobby's a good girl, but just the same Florrie, for one, would feel much better about her if she were married. It is quite easy for a girl to drift into an affair at Bobby's age.

WILLY—Maybe we could kill two birds with one stone—fix something up between Bobby and our iceman.

FLORRIE—You can read your paper, darling. You aren't so very funny.

WILLY—Yes'm.

FLORRIE (*more interested*)—Did she turn Fred down, really? I mean, was it final?

MRS. HALEVY (*speaking from viewpoint of the suitor's appeal to her, not to* BOBBY)—Oh, yes; but you couldn't blame her for that—he was—well, he was over thirty—and bald. (*This is the last word.*)

FLORRIE—I know. He wasn't a very romantic figure. But neither is old Helmcke, either, but he has got a lot of money. Is he ever here any more?

MRS. HALEVY—Yes, he's here, but he's deaf, and after all he's a widower. She's just sorry for him and doesn't want to hurt his feelings. You know he's so deaf (*disgusted at the very thought*) you have to write out what you want to say to him.

FLORRIE—But he's got a lot of money—and who else is there?

MRS. HALEVY (*a different tone*)—There's the O'Neil boy;—but he's going to South America—

FLORRIE—South America—! What for?

MRS. HALEVY (*startled, and quite unable to answer coherently*)—I don't know. Just some trip he got a chance to take. (*Drawing her chair closer to* FLORRIE.)—You know I did think it was getting serious, but he hasn't been here for a week or more and he's going day after to-morrow.

FLORRIE—Does Bobby mind?

MRS. HALEVY—I think she does. But her father doesn't—and she won't say a word.

FLORRIE (*disgusted*)—What a nuisance! To have him go away!

MRS. HALEVY (*dreaming*)—He is a nice boy.

FLORRIE—Does he make any money to speak of?

MRS. HALEVY—She told me he gets just as much as she does.

FLORRIE—Oh, well, they couldn't live on $40 a week. (*Thinking.*) I wonder if Bobby sees him at the office.

MRS. HALEVY (*proud of him*)—I guess she sees him, but he's so busy about his trip—

FLORRIE—Well, I suppose that ends that—

WILLY (*from the paper*)—Yep, looks like the boy's got away.

A moment later Rims O'Neil telephones. He is eager to see Bobby and evidently disappointed to learn she isn't there. It is, decides Florrie, who answers the phone, a good time to make things interesting for Rims. So in place of telling him that Bobby is expected home any minute and that she expects to stay home, as Mrs. Halevy reports, Florrie arranges a most exciting evening for her sister.

"Why, Mr. O'Neil," reports Florrie, "Bobby's going out tonight, but she'll have to be in shortly to dress, you know, and if you're near by—yes—yes. . . . It might be a party or a dance, because she couldn't get to the theatre now— Oh, I know she'd like to see you but I'm afraid she won't have much *time*. . . . Well, that is a shame. . . . Oh, you are? Oh, I see. I'm sure she didn't know . . . yes, I would tell her, of course . . . yes . . . good-by."

Continuing her investigations, Florrie sends Willy in to see whether or not it really is China that Mr. Halevy has got on the radio and learns from her mother that Bobby really is in love with this O'Neil boy, though she is too proud to admit it. Bobby has cried a great deal since Rims decided to go to South America and is terribly unhappy.

It is a case that demands treatment, Florrie is convinced of that. Bobby is such an egg, so unhatched, somehow, it would be just like her to wait and wait for Rims until the first thing they knew she would be an old maid and a public charge.

Further consideration of Bobby's affairs are interrupted by the arrival of the young woman herself. She is small and pretty, and quiet, given to short and definite answers and, in her present mood, resentful of any one's interfering interest in her.

She is hot and uncomfortable from her subway ride. She doesn't want any dinner because she has had dinner. At least she has a hazy recollection of having had dinner with her boss, Mr. Mengle.

"Since when does Mr. Mengle take you to dinner?" queries the interested Florrie.

"Ever since 6 o'clock," answers Bobby significantly, "and it's been a long time."

Probably Mr. Mengle was very talkative and very interesting, but unfortunately she had not heard a word he said. And she doesn't care. She will get him to say it over, and if he doesn't want to do that he can fire her. At the moment the only thing Bobby is interested in is a bath—until she hears Florrie saying that Rims O'Neil had telephoned.

BOBBY (*after pause, shielding herself with a casual tone*)—Rims? Rims telephoned?

FLORRIE—I think that's the name. Rims—Rims Murphy—

MRS. HALEVY (*reading*)—O'Neil, dear.

FLORRIE—Oh, yes, O'Neil.

BOBBY—What did he say?

FLORRIE—He wanted to know if you'd be in this evening.

BOBBY—Oh.

FLORRIE—I said you were going to a dance . . . or something, but if he came right over—

BOBBY (*turning to* FLORRIE)—Oh, I'm not going anywhere.

FLORRIE—Well, why tell him that? You don't want him to think you're sitting home weeping about him?

BOBBY—Why should he think I'm weeping? Did you know I wasn't going out?

MRS. HALEVY (*annoyed*)—I told her you weren't, Bobby—

BOBBY (*angry*)—Then I don't see what occasion there was for—

FLORRIE—Child, you'll never know; you'll never, never know. You're just that *innocent*.

BOBBY (*passing it off*)—Oh—well, he'll know I wasn't going anywhere—because I'll be here.

FLORRIE—Couldn't you change your mind? At any rate you can't tell him you weren't going out because I told him you were.

BOBBY—Couldn't you be mistaken, dear? I think you could. I even think you were.

FLORRIE—You would!

BOBBY—I think it's perfectly silly.

FLORRIE—You're quite hopeless, darling—I doubt if I can do anything for you, but I can tell you this.

BOBBY—Yes?

FLORRIE—If you want a man to be interested in you, let him see you going out the door with another man. And if you want a man to come running, just let him imagine you at a dance with some one else.

BOBBY—You're pretty tiresome to-night, Florrie. (*She turns and exits, through hall to bathroom.*) If I cared enough about anybody to want to keep him—I'd care too much to want to keep him that way.

FLORRIE—My God, can anybody be as young as that and live!

MRS. HALEVY—Well, Bobby is right, Florrie—Bobby is right!

FLORRIE—Mother, you never grew up a day after you were married.

MRS. HALEVY—Well—I'm glad I've stayed *young then*.

It is Florrie's idea that Bobby should put on her prettiest party dress—the pink one—and then after Rims comes and sees she is all ready for the party she should decide not to go.

It is a silly idea, according to Bobby. Any one would think that she is mad about this Rims and she isn't—not the least bit in the world. As for proposals—well, she has had two in a week—or three—from Mengle.

It was his proposal, Bobby suspects, that Mengle was talking about a good deal at dinner.

This news is a great shock to Mrs. Halevy. Mr. Mengle is a married man! What right had he—

But it wasn't a proposal of marriage, Bobby explains. It was just a proposal. Mother shouldn't be so indignant. It probably was Mr. Mengle's hopes of her that got Bobby a job with him, and it was always wise to keep hope springing eternal in an employer's breast. Mengle might be a beast, as Mrs. Halevy suggests, but he is "a rather friendly old beast, and very considerate, *really!*"

Finally Bobby agrees to put on the pink dress and has gone to take her bath. Florrie is delighted.

"Use just the right touch and you can get her to do anything," she boasts to her mother. "You see, mother, she's just a child. There's a psychologist writing for the *American* that says people don't really begin to think until they're nearly thirty. They walk around and talk and they seem human, but they're really practically unconscious."

"I do wish you wouldn't read the *American,* dear."

"Well, sometimes I think it's really true. That's one reason why it's easy for a girl to get married young, and not so easy afterward. The idea is to catch your man while he's still unconscious. If he begins to think about it there really isn't any reason why he should get married at all. And so the psychologist says the only hope for a girl is to start thinking young and that's why girls have to be cleverer than men."

There is a crash in the living room. A moment later Mr. Halevy, tensely and grimly satisfied, strides into the room humming a tune. He has finally and effectually silenced the infernal machine that has been wrecking the peace of their home.

"I have murdered the entire Philadelphia symphony orchestra," he gloats, "from Stokowski to the timpani player. I tried everything else on that goddam machine and it didn't do any good, so I tried smashing it. From now on if we want any music we'll go where it is."

"I don't know what's come over you, Merlin. You're so sudden."

"Yeah! Toward the end of his life the human male, having learned there is nothing to be gained by gentleness and compromise, begins to assert himself. You didn't want me to build a radio and I built it anyway. After I got it built I didn't like it so I smashed it. If you tell me to get another one I won't. If you tell me not to get another one I will."

With which ultimatum Mr. Halevy seats himself in the armchair with his paper and pipe.

The telephone bell rings again and Florrie jumps to answer it. It is Rims, and Bobby is out of the bathroom hurrying to adjust her robe the moment she hears his name. She is not quite in time to prevent Florrie assuring Rims that although Bobby seems awfully particular about her evening's engagement she is sure she will wait if—

When Bobby gets hold of the phone she promptly assures Rims that she hasn't any engagement, that she has not, and never has had, any intention of going out. It was just her infernal sister's little joke— She will be waiting for him and ever so glad to see him.

Furthermore, she warns Florrie, when Rims comes it is her intention to tell Rims exactly what has happened—and she isn't going to wear her pink dress either. She is also quite disgusted at Florrie's deliberate plan to maneuver everybody over to the band concert so the house will be free to her and Rims when he does come. Just for that she will ask her dad to stay home. Which she does. And Dad agrees, although he would like to hear a little music, now the radio is out of commission.

Later, when Florrie has explained to him why Bobby is acting the way she is, and that she really does want to be alone with Rims but doesn't want it to seem too deliberate, Mr. Halevy agrees to go with the others to the concert. Florrie is to stay and make her peace with Bobby and follow after them.

Now they are all gone except Florrie, and Bobby is in to have her dress—she has put on the pink after all—hooked. She is still angry with Florrie, however, and not inclined to make up with her.

She was only trying to help, Florrie explains. She knows Bobby loves Rims, and that Rims is in love with her. She could tell by his voice even over the phone. And if Bobby wants him she can have him. She needn't let him go to Buenos Ayres or any place else. And she shouldn't. They are in love with each other and they would be happier right there.

Bobby admits that she did expect Rims to ask her to marry him and that if he had stayed a little longer he would have.

"Then," predicts Florrie, confidently, "he'll ask you to-night."

BOBBY—No, he won't. He's made up his mind not to.

FLORRIE—Darling, he didn't tell you that?

BOBBY—No, but I know.

FLORRIE (*exasperated*)—Oh, if I could only be in your shoes half an hour—just half an hour—wouldn't I get it out of him!

BOBBY (*after pause—caught for a second*)—What would you do?

FLORRIE (*with a world of insinuation*)—I'd tease him—till he was wild.

BOBBY (*definitely*)—Well, I won't.

FLORRIE—I guess you're just too good to live.

BOBBY—No, it isn't that. I like him too much to cheat him into anything.

FLORRIE (*back to the game*)—Darling, if you knew just half a dozen sentences to say that would make him propose to you, would you say them?

BOBBY—No, I wouldn't.

FLORRIE—It's so easy— When he asks if you weren't really going out with somebody, tell him you were going out with Fred. Has he ever seen Fred?

BOBBY—No, but you're just wasting your time, Florrie.

FLORRIE (*getting pad and pencil*)—Look, dear, I'm writing it down—can you read my shorthand? (*Florrie sits and gets ready to write. She is facing* BOBBY.)

BOBBY—I could if I wanted to—

FLORRIE—You're going with Fred to a dance or a supper-club— you see?—and then Rims will come in and ask you to stay with him this evening—and you'll say (*writes*) yes, you'll call it off when Fred telephones—and then I'll telephone—isn't it easy?

BOBBY—It doesn't interest me.

FLORRIE—Then he'll ask you to go somewhere with him and (*writes*) you'll suddenly take out your hanky and begin to cry a little and say you don't want to go anywhere.

BOBBY—Me—cry—me?

FLORRIE—Yes, darling, you. You'll weep a little and he'll ask you what's the matter and try to comfort you, and—

BOBBY—I can't cry on order—

FLORRIE—Oh, yes, you can, dear.

BOBBY—Anyway, I never cry.

FLORRIE—Well, he'll ask you what's the matter, and then you'll say (*writes only what* BOBBY *says*)—"Oh, I'm so tired of—of everything, Rims—and I'm afraid I'm not good company"—and he'll say, "Oh, yes, you are," and he'll put his arm around you— or would he?

BOBBY (*sarcastic*)—How could he help it?

FLORRIE (*rapidly getting interested*)—Well, after that it gets easier all the time—you just say (*writes*), "Rims dear, sometimes you're the only person in the world I can talk to—sometimes I can't bear to be with anybody else—"

BOBBY—I simply couldn't—

FLORRIE—But that's exactly what you've got to say—and then you go right on and say (*writes*), "Rims, don't you ever get tired of poor me,—ever?"

BOBBY (*sarcastic*)—And then he'd say "Never" of course.

FLORRIE—Of course—and you say, "You're such a darling— and it's going to be awfully hard—"

BOBBY—What is?

FLORRIE—That's exactly what he'll say—"What is?" and you'll say (*writes*), "Marrying somebody else!" Then he'll draw back and say, "You getting married?" and you'll say (*writes*), "Oh, Rims, a girl has to get married sometime, you know, while she's got chances," and he'll say, "How many chances do you get in a week," or something like that, and you'll say (*writes*), "I've had two every other week for two weeks," or something, and he'll say, "Now, kid, you don't mean you've set to marry somebody?" and then you'll say—

BOBBY (*definite*)—Oh, no, I won't—

FLORRIE—Yes, you will, dear, you'll say (*writes*), "Fred wants me to marry him, and he's awfully in love with me and I don't want to go on working forever," and he'll say, "Well, if you're getting married this season, why not marry me?"—and there you are— (*She looks up pleased.*)

BOBBY (*after pause*)—No, because he wouldn't say it—

FLORRIE—Why not?

BOBBY (*she knows the answer*)—Because he isn't such a sap for one thing, and for another I don't think it's fair and I wouldn't do it.

FLORRIE (*she also knows the answer*)—My darling, how do you think people get married?

BOBBY (*looking away*)—I don't know.

FLORRIE—I'll say you don't—

BOBBY—Honestly, do you think a person of any sense would fall for a deliberate trap like that?

FLORRIE—Why, honeybunch, hundreds of thousands of them fall for it every *year*. (*The doorbell rings.*) There's one coming now. I'm running along, dear, and, look, I'm leaving those notes—see?—

Rims O'Neil is a good-looking boy in his late twenties—the peppy type of young business executive. He stands for a moment looking at Bobby and then admits that as a picture of Flaming Youth she is a dream in her pink gown. He just can't believe she made it herself. . . . Now she is trying to tell him that she really isn't going out; that she never had any thought of going out, but he won't believe her, so she lets it stand. Anyway, the fellow she was going with is going to telephone—and then she will see about "giving him the air," as Rims suggests.

Rims admits that he has not been particularly attentive of late. But it hasn't been his fault, really. He's been taking a little intensive instruction on the Argentine and he's learned more about South America in a week than he ever knew about New York.

And now he's ready to go, if they decide to send him. They'll do that, all right, Bobby agrees. As the boss's secretary, she has seen enough of the correspondence to know it is all fixed. Of course she can only tell him in strictest confidence, because she got it from Mengle the night he took her to dinner—

That dinner stuff doesn't go so well with Rims. Mengle's a pirate and Bobby ought to know it. Still, Rims is also free to admit that he himself has not been filling in any great number of dinner dates with Bobby recently and a girl must have some fun.

Anyway, theirs has been a great Spring while it lasted. Rims is going to carry away a memory of those rides on the old Fifth Avenue bus and those evenings along Riverside Drive that he will never forget. Not even if he were to fall in love again, which isn't at all likely. He could never forget those particular experiences.

Now the telephone is ringing. It probably is Fred. If it is, Rims reminds her, she is to tell him she's busy.

Bobby hesitates a little at the phone, but finally makes it plain to "Fred" that she can't go, and that he is not to come over. She will explain when she sees him again.

And now Rims, convinced anew that Bobby's really a brick, wants to do a little serious talking. What, for one thing, does she think about his going to South America? Does she think it's a good thing? Doesn't she think a young fellow really ought to see the world a little when he gets the chance? Just so he can kind of make up his mind what he wants to do? That's why he's going. It's a kind of adventure.

Surely it is, agrees Bobby, looking away from him. And surely he should go.

Rims is standing right close to her now and trying to tell her how grateful he is for the way she feels and everything.

RIMS—And, kid—

BOBBY—Yes?

RIMS (*placing a hand on her arm*)—You certainly have been wonderful to me.

BOBBY (*looking at him*)—We did have a good Spring together, didn't we?

RIMS (*he takes hold of both arms*)—You were certainly marvellous. (BOBBY *looks at him, and then turns away.*)

BOBBY—Well, it's Summer now.

RIMS (*following her*)—Yep. But that's no reason you shouldn't give me a *kiss*, is it?

BOBBY—I guess not. (*She turns suddenly to him and gives herself. They kiss. Then quite as suddenly she breaks away. She knows she is done for. She whispers.*) Maybe you'd better run along, Rims.

RIMS (*blind—he follows her*)—Why so, sweetie? (*He is behind her; he lays his cheek against her hair.*) The night's young.

BOBBY—Well— (*She looks down and her eye falls on* FLORRIE'S *note-book. She looks at it fascinated. There is a pause.*)

RIMS (*lightly*)—What you studyin', Bobby?

BOBBY—Nothing. Only— (*Still looking at book.*) Oh, I'm so tired of everything, *Rims,* and I'm afraid I'm not very good company.

RIMS—Oh, yes, you are.

BOBBY (*turns to him*)—Rims, dear—

RIMS—Yes.

BOBBY (*looks back at book*)—Rims, sometimes you're the only person in the world I can talk to. Sometimes I can't bear to be with anybody else.

RIMS—Gee, kid.

BOBBY (*looks at book*)—Rims, don't you ever get tired of poor me, ever?

Rims—Never! I should say not.

Bobby (*to Rims*)—You're such a darling.

Rims—Well, I wouldn't say that.

Bobby—But you are (*she turns and glances at the notebook*), and it's going to be awfully hard. (*A pause.*)

Rims—What is, sweetheart?

Bobby—Marrying somebody else.

Rims—You getting married? (*His hand drops from her shoulder.*)

Bobby—Oh, Rims, a girl's got to get married sometime you know, while she's got chances.

Rims—I suppose you get chances all right.

Bobby—Yes.

Rims—Do they come fast?

Bobby—I've had two, every other week, for two *weeks*. (*She looks at book.*)

Rims—Say, look here, you don't mean you're making up your mind to marry somebody in particular?

Bobby (*from book*)—Well, Fred wants me to marry him, and he's awfully in love with me, and I don't want to go on working forever.

Rims—I see. Yeah, I see. I didn't know you felt that way.

Bobby (*suddenly she can't go through with it. She breaks away*)—Well, I don't really. I was just—I was just joking. You'd better go, dear. (*She turns on him. It is her last stand.*) I wouldn't marry anybody. I wouldn't marry—anybody. Not even you.

Rims—You wouldn't?

Bobby—No, I wouldn't!

Rims (*going to her*)—Oh, yes, you will. I mean—

Bobby (*unable to believe, but wanting terribly to believe. She instinctively holds out her arms*)—Do you want me to?

Rims (*grabbing her in his arms*)—Sweetheart! (*They kiss.*)

Bobby (*breaking away and crying on his shoulder*)—But you're—you're going to South America—

Rims (*still holding her*)—South America can go to the devil—! Somebody *else* can go to South America!

The curtain falls.

## ACT II

It is five months later. Bobby and Rims are married and living in a two-room-and-kitchen house that Florrie and Willy had once looked at and would have taken if they could have slipped out of their apartment lease.

The scene is the O'Neil's kitchen-dining room. On one side is the stove and kitchen table, in the center an elongated cabinet which serves to divide the room, and on the other side of the cabinet a small dining-room table. "The whole thing is done in yellow and light blue, the furniture all of the Macy's arty-hours furnishing type. It is neat and clean. A chandelier hangs from the ceiling with large indirect lighters."

Bobby is cleaning up the supper dishes and Rims prowling about the adjoining living room in search of his pipe cleaners. Pretty angry, too, when he can't find them. And even angrier when, finding he is out of tobacco, he turns to his cigarettes and discovers those practically gone, too, though Bobby has left him one.

Reminded that he was to have brought Bobby cigarettes when he came home, Rims confesses that he has been a little short of change this particular week, and when he is taken to task for having exceeded his $5 budget he further confesses, with some show of defiance, that he had taken "a couple of passes at pinochle" and they ruined him.

If he is going to do that sort of thing, Bobby insists, they simply can't make ends meet. She has been going over the budget and it is awfully close figuring, which she insists upon proving by making him listen to her report.

Bobby—Well, we get $240 a month and when there's five weeks in a month we get $300.

Rims (*quickly*)—Sounds like too much money—how much is it in a year?

Bobby—Don't interrupt. Two hundred and forty a month and out of that we pay sixty for rent, about thirty-five for groceries, forty on the furniture, twenty for your allowance, ten insurance, about six for gas and light, and about three for ice. And it comes to a hundred and seventy-four.

Rims (quickly)—You must have left something out.

Bobby (*still intent*)—Please! A hundred and seventy-four from two hundred and forty leaves sixty-six dollars—

Rims—Then how do I happen to be broke all the time?

Bobby (*annoyed*)—Of course, if it doesn't interest you—

Rims—Sure it interests me, Bobby. (*Points at back, apparently very serious.*) You know, I've got a great idea, girlie. How about a little game of black jack for that sixty-six dollars?

Bobby (*she starts to get angry, but can't help laughing*)—

Rims, you idiot! If you don't take me seriously I'll never—never— (*She leans back and turns from him.*) You can take care of your own dirty old money! I can earn some for myself!

RIMS (*putting an arm on her shoulder, smiling*)—Ah, take it easy, Bobby. I was only fooling.

BOBBY (*turning and answering his smile*)—Will you really listen?

RIMS—Sure I will! Geez, I've been listening.

BOBBY (*trying to smile, but not succeeding. Her features merely stretch*)—Oh, it isn't any use. You don't think it matters . . . but I *know* it does.

RIMS (*mock-serious*)—Don't I know it matters? Why, kid, if you can figure out how we can save sixty-six a month—ha—ha—well—you're good.

BOBBY (*serious*)—I didn't say we could save that much. We have to use that for clothes and dentist and doctor bills and extras—

RIMS—No, say, there's certainly something wrong here—

BOBBY (*annoyed at interruption*)—But just a minute. I *know* we'll just throw it away and never know where it goes if we don't use some system, so I want you to write down everything you spend and I'll do the same and every evening we'll go over it—

RIMS—I see a long row of pleasant evenings ahead—

BOBBY—But I mean it, dear. I've been thinking about it all day.

RIMS (*definite*)—Well, that part's out.

BOBBY—What part?

RIMS (*he puts out his cigarette*)—About writing it all down. No, thanks. I knew a guy that did that.

BOBBY—I think it's very sensible.

RIMS (*flaring up*)—And make me accountable to you for every cent I spend?

BOBBY—Oh, is *that* the way you look at it?

RIMS—That's what it amounts to, isn't it?

BOBBY—Well, then, I guess we won't discuss the matter any further. (*She rises, puts out cigarette and goes to kitchen table.*) I'll finish the dishes.

It is Rims who discovers the error in Bobby's book-keeping. It happens that she is all wrong about that $240 a month stuff. He only gets $40 a week—that's $160. No wonder—

Bobby sees her mistake now. Mr. Mengle had spoken of a raise for Rims, and she had figured the budget on that before the raise was confirmed. That certainly does make a difference! They just can't live on $160, with their expenses $174, unless they cut everything away down.

It is a blow to Rims. Gee, he never used to have money troubles before he was married. He just ran along—

So did Bobby. She wishes she hadn't quit her job now. But, Rims insists, they couldn't both work in the same office after they were married. It wouldn't only be embarrassing, but it would make it look as though Rims couldn't support his wife.

"Wife! I won't be a *wife!*" flares Bobby. "It sounds so fat and stupid! I wish we hadn't got married! I wish you'd gone to South America!"

"Well," agrees Rims, "you haven't got anything on me!"

But the next minute they are apologizing for the thought, and agreeing that everything is all right.

"Honest, kid," swears Rims, holding Bobby very close to him, "nobody ever loved anybody the way I love you. I'm just silly about you. I think about you all day long. And then I come home at night and—we get into some goddam mess—and it just shoots the works—"

"I know. It's just the same way with me," answers Bobby, dreamily. "I think all day how marvellous it's going to be when you come home—and then you get here—and I don't know—it isn't marvellous at all— It's just a house and we're just married people—and—sometimes I hate it— (*She pauses. Then very quietly, but very definitely*) Everything's getting spoiled—"

"I guess it's mostly relatives and—money."

"And pipe cleaners and clothes and meals and—dishes—"

Now they are doing the dishes together, though Bobby insists she doesn't want Rims to help. She really wishes he never had to see her doing dishes. Sometimes she almost wishes that she had married some one else so Rims could be her lover. She'd be married to an old brute and Rims would hate him, and they would have to scheme and meet places, and Rims would always want to see her.

Rims is not altogether enamored of the idea of the old brute, but he assumes that Bobby means to be complimentary.

Now the subject turns to the problem of relatives—Bobby's relatives, mostly. They've been around a good deal lately. Especially Florrie and Willy. They seem to think they own the place just because they saw it first. Rims doesn't care much for Florrie. He can stand Bobby's father, but Florrie kinda gives him the pip.

Bobby thinks perhaps they had better move as soon as their lease is up. Which brings up the subject of the rent. It's due now, and with this week's salary they will have just enough to meet it. Rims, however, has other plans for a part of this week's salary. There is going to be a stag dinner for old Juan at the office and the boys were chipping in for a present.

Bobby sees no reason why old Juan should have either a present or a dinner, but she is interested in the date set for it. It is to be on Wednesday—which happens to be the very day—

BOBBY—Guess who called me up to-day?

RIMS—Fred?

BOBBY—No. . . . Mengle.

RIMS (*rising and facing her*)—The boss? What did he want?

BOBBY—Well, first he wanted to know if I'd come back and work for him—

RIMS (*belligerently*)—Oh, he did, did he? I'd like to see you—

BOBBY (*explaining it away*)—Well, I said "No," and he said, "Come down and see me sometime," and I said, "All right," and he said, "Why don't you come and have dinner sometime," and I said, "No, thanks" and he said, "How about Wednesday night?"

RIMS—What did you tell him?

BOBBY—I told him I'd call up and let him know.

RIMS (*furious*)—Why didn't you tell him to go to the devil?

BOBBY (*turning and following him*)—Well, I'd been going over these figures and I thought if our income was doubled—how easy it would be—and if I just took my job back—

RIMS (*turning on her. The possessive male*)—Get this from me right now, kid. I won't have you sitting in Mengle's private office taking dictation. It was bad enough before we were married.

BOBBY—Well, I guess I'll do as I please about that, my dear.

RIMS—You will not! You'll do as I tell you.

BOBBY (*icily*)—I might if you asked me nicely, but—

RIMS (*quickly*)—I'm not asking you! I'm telling you, and that's once for all! And you won't go to dinner with him, either!

BOBBY (*getting angry*)—I didn't intend to go to dinner with him, but if you say you won't let me, I certainly will.

RIMS—Oh, no, you won't!

BOBBY—Yes?

RIMS—Yeah, that'd put me in a nice position, wouldn't it? Me at the banquet and you dining alone with Mengle.

BOBBY—Well, I've had dinner with him before and it didn't seem to hurt your position much.

RIMS—That was before we were married!

BOBBY (*climaxing*)—Well, Good God, what's the difference?

RIMS—You know damn well what's the difference. (BOBBY *following him, touching his arm.*)

BOBBY (*gently*)—Oh, dear, we're quarreling again—over nothing.

RIMS (*turning halfway to her*)—You call that nothing! Anyway, what the hell do I care if we are? I come home here every evening just because you're here (*aggrieved*) and what thanks do I get for it? They had a game going over at Perry's and I certainly wish I'd gone.

BOBBY (*flaring up*)—I certainly wish you had. I suppose you come home every evening just to keep me company,—because you're afraid I'll be lonely—

RIMS (*over his shoulder*)—Sometimes I do.

BOBBY—Well, go to your game. I won't be lonely. Any time you don't come home I can amuse myself plenty.

RIMS—*All right!*

BOBBY—I had a bid myself to-night if you want to know.

RIMS (*turning to her*)—Who was it?

BOBBY (*flashing*)—Don't you wish you knew?

RIMS (*jumping up*)—Was it Mengle?

BOBBY—No, it was Fred. He said he was all alone at the club party to-night and he wished I was going to be there.

RIMS—Are you going?

BOBBY—Why, darling, I was staying home *to keep you company*. But I wouldn't mind seeing another man once in a while—now that's the *truth*. (*Door bell.*) (*Angry at interruptions.*) I wonder who that is?

RIMS (*disgusted*)—You know all right. It's that sister of yours and her Willy boy. That's who it always is.

Rims is right. Florrie and Willy are calling. And quarreling a little on their own account. But Florrie is used to that. She accepts it philosophically now.

Now Rims and Willy have gone out for some cigarettes and Florrie takes advantage of the quiet to warn Bobby that she should not take family tiffs too seriously. There's a man writing in the *American,* says Florrie, who says that there is always a period of adjustment before it is settled who's to boss the other one, and the period of adjustment is one long series of rows. She and Willy, Florrie declares with some pride, are nearing the end of their period of adjustment, though Willy still struggles a little.

This is discouraging news to Bobby. If that is what marriage is like she guesses she doesn't want to be married. But it can't be true that people always quarrel when they are married, even when they are madly in love! And if it is true, as Florrie insists, that the mad passion passes and a kind of disillusionment follows, Bobby will have none of it. She wants to be madly in love always. And with Rims. But—

"I know it can't go on the way it is," she confesses, on the point of tears. "He'll leave me, or I'll leave him—or something will happen. We want to be together and then as soon as we are together—it's no use. We always say the wrong things."

FLORRIE—Then do you know what I think?

BOBBY—No.

FLORRIE (*looking at her nails*)—I think it's time for you to begin having a baby.

BOBBY (*quickly*)—But if we don't get along together now—

FLORRIE—It makes everything different. It makes you so much more important, don't you see?

BOBBY—I don't want to be important.

FLORRIE (*with a meaning*)—You want to be important to Rims, don't you?

BOBBY (*pause*)—Yes.

FLORRIE—Well, if you are having his baby you instantly become the most important thing in the world to him. Men are funny that way. They take so much credit and they feel so responsible, it's pathetic. So long as you don't have a baby Rims is really free, you see—and he might get tired of you—but just you tie him down with two or three good fat ones—and he'll stay. (*Sighing.*) Willy used to get rebellious, but not any more. Not since the baby.

BOBBY (*meaning it*)—But that's terrible.

FLORRIE—What is?

BOBBY—To keep a man that way.

FLORRIE (*laughing*)—It's been going on a long time, my dear. I wasn't the first to think of it.

BOBBY—You mean that's why women have children?

FLORRIE—Why, surely.

BOBBY—But they want to have them.

FLORRIE (*as though it were too obvious to mention*)—Oh, yes. I suppose, partly they want to keep their husbands because they want to have children, and partly they want to have children because they want to keep their husbands. Anyway, it works.

BOBBY—It wouldn't—with us.

FLORRIE (*annoyed at her superiority*)—You're just like the rest of us. It's a scientific fact. It works. (*Leaning forward to make her point.*) Some morning you'll tell Rims it's going to happen, and all of a sudden everything will change. He'll bring you things and mother you, and smother you with kisses, and he'll be humble and happy and— (*Smiling and leaning back.*) Well, you see, there's no arguing about a thing like that—

Bobby is suspicious of Florrie's schemes. She still remembers the one by which she won Rims—with notes on the pad. And she will not trick him any more.

Maybe she won't, but it will be just as well if she gives the matter some thought, Florrie insists. If ever a crisis does arise it will be a good thing to remember.

Mr. Halevy drops in and Florrie decides not to wait for Willy. She is putting on her coat when she spies on the floor a bit of paper that Rims had dropped as he was leaving. It is an I O U, and Florrie hands it to Bobby. "You'd better look at that," she advises. "Somebody owes Rims some money. . . . Don't let the boy gamble, dear."

Bobby doesn't know exactly what an I O U is, and she is still mystified after her father explains that if Rims didn't have any money to lend he probably won the I O U.

If he had, why hadn't he told her? When they had been talking budget all evening!

Then there is that other matter that is worrying Bobby. She takes that up with her father. Does he think that she ought to have a baby?

Mr. Halevy is somewhat startled by the abruptness of the question, but he can see by Bobby's seriousness that it is not a subject to joke about. Yes, he supposes she is old enough to have a baby. But when he looks back on his own wasted youth he wonders why anybody should want to have a baby. Why anybody should even want to get married is more than Mr. Halevy can understand.

"From me, my dear," he admits, "I fear you will get nothing but ribald advice and evil counseling. I'd better go home."

BOBBY—No, don't go. This is serious!

MR. HALEVY—Bobby. I married young and brought up two

lovely children. I can't say I regret it, but there are moments, and those moments occur more frequently now that I'm a grandfather, when it appears to me that Don Juan and Casanova chose the better part. (*Pause.*)

BOBBY—Yes, I suppose that's true if you're a man, but I'm not.

MR. HALEVY (*a long pause*)—I used to wish you were.

BOBBY (*quickly*)—Why?

MR. HALEVY (*caught*)—Now, don't ask me to talk seriously on this topic, my dear. After all, I'm your father and I know my duty. If I said, "No, don't have any babies," you'd ask me if I was sorry we had you and Florrie, and I couldn't think of an adequate reply. Anyway, fathers shouldn't confide in their daughters. It isn't hundred per cent— No doubt it would be considered a kind of intellectual incest. (*Pause.*) But I can tell you lies by the yard—

BOBBY—Then you think having a baby—would be a mistake?

MR. HALEVY (*reaching out and patting her arm, not looking at her*)—I didn't even want you to get married.

BOBBY (*quickly*)—You didn't say anything—

MR. HALEVY—I came near it—the night you and Rims fixed it up. I was afraid it was going to happen.

BOBBY—Oh!

MR. HALEVY—Do you know how fathers feel about their daughters when they're growing up?

BOBBY—No.

MR. HALEVY (*turning half away*)—Well, they think—when they think about it—here I have two good-looking virtuous girls, and I'm putting in my whole life raising them up, feeding them, sending them to school—and for what? All for the service and delight of two unknown and probably disagreeable young men. So I used to wish I had sons, because they could have a good time at any rate. (*Pause.*) And then it occurred to me there was no reason why girls shouldn't have a good time.

BOBBY—How do you mean?

MR. HALEVY (*after a pause, looking at her*)—Fall in love—have your affair—and when it's over—get out!

BOBBY—Oh!

MR. HALEVY (*looking away, half-smiling*)—I told you I'd better go home.

BOBBY—But why not have a love affair—and get married?

MR. HALEVY—Marriage is no love affair. It's little old last year's love affair, my dear. It's a house and bills and dishpans and family quarrels. That's the way the system beats you

They bait the wedding with a romance and then they hang a three-hundred-pound landlord around your neck and drown you in grocery bills. If I'd talked to you that night I'd have said, "If you're in love with him, why, have your affair, sow a few oats." Why the devil should the boys have a monopoly on wild oats?

BOBBY—Yes, I see.

MR. HALEVY (*suddenly self-conscious. He becomes the commonplace father*)—No, I shouldn't say that. Marriage is fine, kiddie, it's grand. It's the corner stone of progress. It's the backbone of civilization. Don't you believe anything against it.

The philosophy of her radical parent is not of great help to Bobby. She might, she suggests, have gone on working. But if she went on being Rims' economic equal she might have lost him, too.

That danger was not as great then as it is now, insists Mr. Halevy. What was a love affair has become largely an affair of grocery bills. Still, Mr. Halevy admits that he and Bobby's mother passed successfully through their similar experience. Of course they had children! And didn't he want his children? Yes, he did want them—even when he discovered that what was started as an experiment turned out to be a life sentence.

"You don't understand me, Dad," concludes Bobby. "I'm young and foolish and Rims is everything in the world to me and I'm afraid I'll lose him. I can't help being young and foolish. . . . So I guess I'll make it—a life sentence."

Florrie is back. She met Willy and Willy was bringing a message to Bobby. Rims, says Willy, had a chance to get in a little game and sent word that Bobby was not to look for him until she saw him coming.

The hurt that Bobby feels is expressed in a stifled cry. They try to comfort her. Florrie advises her to give Rims lots of rope, and Mr. Halevy is torn between paternal solicitude and a desire to horsewhip his upstart cub of a son-in-law.

Before they have gone far Rims is back. He has come in search of his I O U. When Bobby hands it to him he turns on her angrily with the accusation that she has taken it from his coat pocket.

Awkwardly but discreetly the family withdraws, followed by sarcastic references to their character and quality by the still angry Rims. Now he turns on Bobby and boldly confesses how he came by the I O U. He got it playing blackjack. He has always played cards, and he expects to play a lot more. If she thinks she's got a mortgage on everything he gets she is mistaken. And he isn't going to write it down in any book so's she won't miss anything, either. If she's going to do as she pleases, says Rims, if she's going to have dinner with Mengle, and take back her job, by God he's going to do as *he* pleases. And anyway all the twenty-seven dollars wasn't his. He'd given his I O U for twenty-nine. He didn't tell her because he didn't want to. He isn't used to telling anybody everything.

Bobby understands. Let him run along and have a good time.

But he can't run along, or have a good time, with her feeling that way, and not saying good-by or kissing him or anything.

And now she is in his arms again, crying a little, and he is holding her close as he tries to explain that everything's the fault of the family. Especially Florrie. Bobby wishes she didn't have any family and Rims agrees that everybody ought to be born orphans.

Peace is reëstablished and harmony momentarily prevails, until Rims starts again to join the boys. For a moment Bobby holds him back while she suggests, a little hesitantly, that perhaps they would be happier if—if they had a baby!

The thought is more or less startling to Rims. Seems to him they have got trouble enough as it is. He hasn't any desire to join the chain gang. For the lova Mike!—she's not holding back any surprises on him, is she?

Bobby admits she was only thinking that perhaps they might be happier if there was a baby, and wondering how he would feel about it if that was the one thing she wanted more than anything else—

Gradually the idea appeals to Rims. Of course, if Bobby feels that way about it—

But Bobby cannot go through with her plan. It was just roping him in, that's all it was, just a scheme to keep him. And if she can't keep him on the level she will just have to lose him. She loves him too much for that.

Again Rims' anger flares. Bobby hadn't thought of this scheme by herself. It was that sister of hers who put the idea into her head, wasn't it?

BOBBY (*feverishly, fiercely*)—Well, what if it was? I'm being honest with you now anyway. I'm going to be so honest it hurts. It isn't the first time I tried to trick you. I tricked you into marrying me. (*This next dialogue as at fever heat.*)

RIMS—When?

BOBBY—When you asked me to marry you. Didn't you see it?

RIMS—No.

BOBBY—Well, it was obvious enough.

RIMS—Did she put you up to that too?

BOBBY—It doesn't matter. I did it.

RIMS (*slow and intense, but quiet*)—All right, I've got her number. And yours too. It's the last time you put anything over on me—

BOBBY (*desperate*)—I don't want to put anything over on you. If I'd wanted to, I could have, couldn't I?—and I didn't!

RIMS (*coming towards her menacingly*)—Listen, kid—I think we're going to have a show-down right here and now! A fellow gives up a lot when he gets married. As long as he's single, he owns the earth, but when he's married his money's not his own, his time's not his own, he's got to keep on working whether he wants to or not, and there's hell to pay if he spends an extra dime. (*He becomes louder and faster working to a climax.*) Whenever I tired of my job I used to quit—if I didn't like one town I tried another—and now I can't—

BOBBY (*quickly*)—Why not?

RIMS (*climaxing*)—Because I've got a wife—because I've got a family!

BOBBY (*screaming*)—Good God—am I a family? I won't be a wife—I won't be a family! I'm just me!

RIMS—All right, be yourself!

BOBBY (*very quickly*)—All right, I'll be myself—and if you think a man gives up a lot when he gets married, a girl gives up something when she gets married, and don't you forget it! I spend the whole day here taking care of this damned house for you and cooking your meals and washing your dishes and never going anywhere because we can't afford it—and every time I get a dime for myself I have to ask for it! It's *degrading!* (*She turns away.*)

RIMS—It's your own home.

BOBBY (*screaming*)—It's not mine. It's all yours. You earn the money so it's all yours! I tell you it's despicable! Asking!

RIMS—Throw it up to me I don't earn enough! That's right!

BOBBY (*still higher*)—Well, you don't!

RIMS—You knew how much I was earning when you married me. If you don't like it, why see what you can do about it!

BOBBY (*furious, incoherent, she turns on him*)—Gee! I know what I can do about it.

RIMS (*menacing*)—Well, you won't work for Mengle! If it's my house I'm going to have my way in it, and I won't have my wife working for Mengle! I give up a good deal to keep this damn place going and it's going to be the way I want it from now on—

BOBBY (*turning, going out in a rage*)—Oh, it will! Well, I still know my way to the front door! I guess I know when I've got enough!

RIMS (*calling after her*)—Where are you going? (BOBBY *stops in arch, turns and faces him.*)

BOBBY (*screaming*)—You can wash your own dishes! The hot water's in the right-hand tap! I'm running along! And I'm not coming *back!* (*She storms off, gets hat and coat.*)

RIMS (*calling*)—You mean you're leaving me?

BOBBY (*off*)—If you don't believe it, you watch me!

RIMS—All right! Suits me! Two can play at that game. I'm not stopping you. (*He grabs his coat and hat.*) Got any money?

BOBBY (*entering to get pocket book*)—I've got the rent money.

RIMS (*putting on coat*)—If you go to work for Mengle I *quit him.*

BOBBY—I don't care where you work. It's a free country. Good-by.

RIMS—Good-by.

Rims slams the kitchen door as he leaves. There is a pause and then the door slowly opens. Rims comes back. "Bobby!" he calls. There is no answer. He turns out the kitchen light and goes out again.

The front door is heard to open. Bobby rushes through the living room, calling excitedly: "Rims, dear!"

There is no answer. She switches off the living-room light as she passes through. The front door slams.

The curtain falls.


## ACT III

Three weeks later Bobby has a room in Mrs. Gorlick's boarding house in East 33d st. There is a window letting onto a fire escape, a bed extending into the room from the upper corner, the usual washstand and chest of drawers. The door into the hall is below the bed. "It is a gloomy room, fixed in bad late-Victorian manner. . . . It is altogether dark, save for the light outside the window. A breeze blows the curtains gently."

Mrs. Gorlick, on one of innumerable tours of inspection, slams down the window, muttering her opinion of fool girls that have no more sense than to leave windows open with robberies going on all about them. She finds further cause for irritation in the two pair of stockings hanging on the towel rack. Some things just ain't decent.

Mr. Halevy finds his way up the stairs, being directed by a voice from below and met by Mrs. Gorlick above. He will, he says, wait for Miss Halevy, if Mrs. Gorlick has no objections; wait either in her room or in the parlor. He is Miss Halevy's father.

Mrs. Gorlick, made suspicious by nature and experience, is not sure Mr. Halevy is Mr. Halevy, but if he is Miss Halevy's father it is a good thing he has come. It is Mrs. Gorlick's opinion that the young woman needs lookin' after. And she knows.

"When they come here looking for rooms late at night and when they have middle-aged gentlemen to call like she done last night—and when they smoke cigarettes—well—I can *tell*," declares Mrs. Gorlick.

From below the voice announces another gentleman to see Miss Halevy, and before Mrs. Gorlick can descend to stop him Rims is also in the room. He, however, has come to see Mrs. O'Neil and not Miss Halevy. He is a little surprised to see Mr. Halevy there. He really expected to find Mengle—

Rims has been having a pretty tough time of it for the last three weeks. His highly prized freedom has not meant as much to him as he thought it would. A chance to step out? Yeah—

RIMS—Listen, Mr. Halevy. I called her up. She said I can't see her. Then I tried having some fun, but it wasn't any good. I don't want to play cards. I don't want anything else in the world except her. And—she's gone. She doesn't need me. She's having a good time.

MR. HALEVY—You'll have to prove that to me.

RIMS (*turns to* MR. HALEVY)—Prove it! I hung around the office last night. I had to see her. And what happened? She comes out with Mengle—and they went to dinner together—Geez—

MR. HALEVY—Well—?

RIMS—Well— She didn't see me. So I followed them. And after dinner she let him bring her home. He brought her here in a private car—with a chauffeur. I guess that's what she wants. I don't earn enough. She's got to have a private car—with a chauffeur.

MR. HALEVY—Oh, no—no—no.

RIMS—Well, anyway, I waited outside. And pretty soon he went away. (*Starts to pace.*) God, I don't know what's the matter with me! I used to have a little sense. About girls, anyway. Now I act like a damn dummy. (*Turns to face* MR. HALEVY.) You don't know what it's like!

MR. HALEVY (*looking up at* RIMS, *emphatically*)—Don't I?

RIMS—Does everybody go crazy this way?

MR. HALEVY—Every last one of us.

RIMS—You know, when I came in and thought Mengle was here, I was going to beat him up.

MR. HALEVY—No, no—that wouldn't do any good, you know.

RIMS—No. But it'd be a lot of fun.

MR. HALEVY—You're lucky, Rims. You young fellows don't know how lucky you are. When a man's young he makes love—when he's middle-aged he makes money—or tries to—and when he's old he makes his soul. I never could make any money to speak of, so I suppose it's about time I began to make my soul. But I'd rather be young—and make love to a girl that was in love with me. There's nothing like it.

RIMS—She's not in love with me, Mr. Halevy. That's the hell of it. If she were, she wouldn't have gone away.

MR. HALEVY—Well, you went away, too, didn't you? And you were in love with her?

RIMS—Yeah. But—

MR. HALEVY—Maybe she left you because she was in love with you. Where are you going, Rims?

RIMS (*turns to face* MR. HALEVY)—I'm going to take a walk around the block.

At the door Rims runs into a chauffeur carrying a package which he has been instructed to deliver personally to Miss Halevy. The fact that he recognizes him as Mr. Mengle's chauffeur does not particularly please Rims. And as Miss Halevy isn't there, suggests Rims, he will have to come back.

Mrs. Gorlick, investigating voices, is up again to warn Bobby, if she is home, that the rule of the house respecting open doors when gentlemen are calling on ladies must be observed.

"If I was ever going into this business again I wouldn't take girls," explains Mrs. Gorlick, "only gentlemen. True, gentlemen do get drunk and smash things. But I will say this for them. They do know how to take care of themselves, and you don't have to watch them."

"Why do you have to watch the girls?" Mr. Halevy wants to know.

"Why, my dear Mr.— Well—if you knew the kind of goings on, and what was thought of girls that close their doors with gentlemen callers—well, you wouldn't want it said about your daughter."

"You mean they get drunk and break things?"

"I guess you know what I *mean*, all right."

Bobby is surprised and pleased to find her father waiting. And curious to know what he thinks of her room. He doesn't think much of it. He had lived in too many like it when he was a young fellow. There's nothing new about them except the girls and boys who live in them. Remembering how lonely the little house they used to have looked when he walked past it this afternoon, Mr. Halevy can't understand just what Bobby thinks she is doing there. There is her old room at home. She can always have that.

But Bobby doesn't want to go home. That would put her right back where she was, as though she were going around in a circle. No, she wanted to be alone and she has been alone. She has gone back to work and she is definitely on her own. As for Rims—

Rims is there to speak for himself. He stands in the doorway, calls pleasantly, if shortly, to Bobby, and refuses to be lifted out of his serious mood by the attempted pleasantries of the departing Mr. Halevy.

If Bobby would like to know how Rims found out where she lived, he followed her home after she had had dinner with Mengle the night before. And he had a bad time of it waiting for Mr. Mengle to leave. After all, Bobby is still his wife, and there are some things he can't stand.

Not being certain whether he has come to see her, or just to lecture her about Mengle, Bobby is not sure what she thinks of Rims' visit, but she asks him to sit down and stay awhile. He has a new job, she understands. And it pays just the same as the old one. Which is really marvellous—to start in a new business at the old salary.

It isn't jobs, however, that are of interest to Rims at the moment. He had come over to say something, and he finds it hard to say. Hasn't she really had enough of this sort of thing? And won't she come back? Back to the house?

No, Bobby doesn't think she will. Probably Florrie and Willy will take the house off their hands. She will go on living where she is.

The chauffeur is back with the package for Miss Halevy, which he delivers personally. It's flowers from Mengle, Rims assumes. Why doesn't she open the package and see. She doesn't want to. Anyway, she knows it isn't flowers.

RIMS—Then what is it?

BOBBY (*starting to open package, laughing*)—It's really something for Mrs. Gorlick.

RIMS (*looking at package. He takes out bolt*)—It's a bolt!—

BOBBY (*laughing*)—Yes—for the door!

RIMS (*taking out screw driver and hammer*)—And a hammer, and a screw to put it on with.

BOBBY (*laughing*)—Well—he said he was going to send me a bolt—but I thought he was joking. You see, when Mengle was here last night, the landlady seemed to think he was a shady character and kept opening the door all the time—

RIMS (*flashing*)—Hey! Wait a minute! (*Puts bolt and hammer and screw driver back into the box—and faces* BOBBY.) Let me get this straight!

BOBBY—I suppose he thought it would be funny. And I really did want a bolt.

RIMS (*belligerently*)—Yeah, go right ahead and explain. You're making it better all the time.

BOBBY—Rims—

RIMS—Yeah, explain some more! Did you ask for it?

BOBBY—I didn't tell him he couldn't send it.

RIMS (*grabbing hat from the bed post*)—Oh, you didn't! Well, all right—

BOBBY—You mean you think I haven't any right to let Mr. Mengle send me a bolt for my door?

RIMS—I mean it looks damned funny to me and it is damned funny!

BOBBY—Certainly it's funny! That's why he did it. Don't you see?

RIMS (*caustically*)—Do I see? I'll say I see! (*He starts to go.*)

BOBBY (*stepping in front of him*)—Rims, if you go now, it's the last you see of me as long as you live. (*Pause.*)

RIMS—Well, what I can't understand is why you'd let Mengle come to your room.

BOBBY—Well, why not, if I feel like it? It's my room. I can take care of myself.

RIMS (*turning on her, sarcastically*)—I doubt it.

BOBBY—Listen, Rims. I did want you to come. I've been waiting for you to come. But if you're going to begin to tell me what I can do and what I can't do—

RIMS (*breaking in on her, exasperated; tossing his hat on bed post*)—If you don't know enough to keep clear of Mengle, you shouldn't be at large.

BOBBY—That's just the point. I do know enough to keep clear of Mengle. Only I'm on my own now, and I'm going to use my own judgment.

RIMS (*caustically*)—Such as it is.

BOBBY—Exactly. Such as it is. You use yours such as it is, and you haven't any guardian.

RIMS (*he is completely at sea*)—What's the idea, anyway?

BOBBY—The idea is I'm a free agent. Just as free as you are.

RIMS (*he is really still very much in love*)—You don't care about me any more?

BOBBY—Yes, I do. (*Pause.*)

RIMS—Well, it's all right about Mengle. I can see how it was.

BOBBY (*nicely*)—It did look queer, I know.

RIMS (*turning to face her*)—Only any time you want a bolt on your door, I wish you'd ask me.

BOBBY—I will—if you're around.

RIMS—You know damn well I'd be around if I thought you wanted me.

BOBBY (*smiling*)—Well, I wasn't sure you would.

RIMS (*coming close to Bobby*)—Listen, dear—about that house! That isn't a bad little house—as houses go.

BOBBY—Any house is bad enough.

RIMS (*pleading*)—You won't try it again?

BOBBY (*dreaming*)—No. . . . You see— Oh, I wonder if I can tell you— What we wanted was a love affair, wasn't it? Just to be together and let the rest go hang—and what we got was a house and bills and general hell. Do you know what I think a love affair is, Rims? It's when the whole world is trying to keep two people apart—and they insist on being together. And when they get married the whole world pushes them together so they just naturally fly apart. I want my love affair back. I want hurried kisses and clandestine meetings, and a secret lover. I don't want a house. I don't want a husband. I want a lover.

RIMS (*weakly*)—So that lets me out.

BOBBY (*hoping he can see how it doesn't*)—Does it, dear?

Mrs. Gorlick's knock at the door is followed again by her insistence that it must remain open. "Of course, I understand the gentleman last night was your boss," observes the landlady, caustically; "and the old one was your father and I daresay this one's your husband."

"No. Oh, no," says Bobby.

"Then the door stays open."

But it happens also to be 10 o'clock and no gentlemen callers are allowed after 10. So it seems that Rims really has to go.

He does not accept his dismissal with very good grace. Bobby's idea that they are no longer married, just friends, and her hope that he will want to come and see her occasionally and maybe take her for a bus ride, or downtown to dinner, even to Childs, does not appeal to him. Rims is desperate— He would be willing to get a divorce, he admits, if Bobby will agree to marry him again. Which Bobby thinks is really darling of him.

BOBBY—But you never really wanted to get married, did you? Now tell the truth—

RIMS—I wanted you.

BOBBY—Of course you did, but you didn't want a house.   I wanted you but I didn't want a house.   And I don't now.

RIMS (*worried*)—How do I know you won't fall for somebody else sometime?   If I leave you here?

BOBBY—You don't.

RIMS (*beaten*)—Oh.

BOBBY (*she has her plan*)—How do I know you won't fall for somebody else?   I don't.   I don't want to.   You aren't to see me unless you just can't keep away.   You used to know me so well you didn't like me.   You used to know where I was and what I was doing all the time.   It was positively indecent, and we won't have any more of it.   It's like not wearing any clothes.

RIMS (*looking down*)—Well.   All right.

BOBBY (*backing away a step*)—So—now we're really free.

RIMS—I said all right.   I don't give a whoop about that.

BOBBY (*gently*)—What do you give a whoop about?

RIMS (*close to her*)—About you, you little fool!   Can't you see it?   Don't you see I can't get along without you?   I can't stand being away from you all the time.   I keep waking up in the night (*looks into her eyes*), wanting you.

BOBBY (*a whisper*)—So do I.

RIMS (*still closer*)—I want to see you to-night.

BOBBY—Well—?

RIMS—And the house is standing there waiting for us.

BOBBY (*turning away suddenly*)—It'll just have to wait, then. I got you into it in the first place—and you didn't like it—and I didn't like it. And now, thank God, we're out of it.

RIMS (*he is about through*)—I don't know what you want.

BOBBY (*turning to him, blurting*)—I don't either. I only know what I don't want.

RIMS (*he is furious now*)—All right! (*He puts on his hat and exits left, hurriedly.*)

BOBBY—Good-by!

Bobby stands still for a moment, then closes the door with a half completed gesture of despair. She is sitting on the edge of the bed, a picture of utter misery, when a knock at the door stirs her into excited action.

But it is only Mrs. Gorlick, come to make sure all the gentlemen have gone. And to make sure she comes boldly into the room and investigates all the possible hiding places. Mrs. Gorlick doesn't intend any one shall try any tricks on her! She tries at least to run a respectable house.

Now she has gone and Bobby languidly gets ready for bed. She has taken her nightgown and slippers from the closet and turned out the light. But by the time she has reached the side of the bed she is in tears. Now she has thrown herself flat upon the bed and is weeping convulsively.

The window alongside the fire escape is raised slowly and Rims climbs quietly in. He tiptoes across the room, carefully picks up the bolt, screws and hammer and is at the door starting to work when Bobby hears him.

"Oh, Rims!"

Bobby tries to smother her excitement.

"Bring me the screwdriver, will you, dear?" hoarsely whispers Rims, pointing to that silent but effective instrument.

And as she kneels beside him Bobby cautions Rims with a warning "Hush!"

He starts to fit the bolt against the door.

The curtain falls.

# CHICAGO

## A Satirical Comedy in Three Acts

### By Maurine Watkins

THE romance of the theatre enters excitedly into the writing, sale and production of the play "Chicago." Particularly as it concerns the experiences of its author, Maurine Watkins.

Miss Watkins had enjoyed but few contacts with the theatre when she decided she would like to write plays. But she had been greatly encouraged when Leo Ditrichstein thought enough of her promise not only to pay her $500 advance on a manuscript, but to ask her also to collaborate with him on a play for which he had an idea.

She worked with Mr. Ditrichstein in Chicago, and was ready to return to her home in Indianapolis when she decided suddenly that what she needed was more first-hand experience of people and the way they live. This, she believed, she could best get if she had a newspaper job. So she decided to go to work on the *Chicago Tribune*.

Many other young women have a similar urge, but few of them ever get past the doorman guarding the city editor's office. Miss Watkins, however, was blessed with sufficient force of personality to overcome the handicap. Given a chance at reporting, novice though she was, her freshness of viewpoint, her keen interest and her natural gift for writing attracted the attention of her editors. Her assignments included several court stories. One of them was an interview with a lady murderess. It was the written and unwritten facts gathered while she was pursuing this story that afterward appealed to her as being good play material.

She had learned, however, from her experience with Mr. Ditrichstein, that playwriting was not as simple as many amateurs believe it to be and she determined to learn more of the trade. She thereupon gave up her job on the *Tribune* and went back to school. She came East and made application to the drama writing class of Professor George Pierce Baker of Yale University. It was as a part of her class work that she wrote the first draft of "Chicago."

When it was finished, being a thorough feminist, Miss Watkins took her play to a woman play broker, Laura Wilck, who promptly bought it for herself and announced an intention of producing it. But before she got around to this the men interfered. She let a producing manager named Alfred Lewis read it. Mr. Lewis promptly ran with it to Sam Harris and Mr. Harris immediately opened negotiations with Miss Wilck for a production of the play with the interests of ownership satisfactorily adjusted. Successful during its preliminary tour, "Chicago" was an overnight hit in New York.

Miss Watkins is specific in noting the time and the locale of the opening scene of "Chicago." It is "6:58 P.M., Friday, April 3." The scene is the bedroom of Amos Hart, "a corner room, first floor, in a cheap modern flat on Chicago's south side, with flowered paper, gaudy rugs and shiny furniture. . . . Between the two windows at back with footboard to the front, is a large brass bed, with covers thrown back in confusion and pillows tossed together. At its head is a night table with telephone, a stoutish bottle and a couple of glasses, an ash tray and cigarettes. At the right is a large vanity dresser equipped with imitation ivory toilet articles, bottles with atomizers, perfumes, powder, rouge, eyebrow pencils and lipstick.

"A girl of twenty-two or so, in a flashy negligee of blue Georgette with imitation lace, sits on the edge of the bed and pours herself a drink. She is slender and beautiful, with short upper lip, pouting mouth, dark eyes, and bobbed hair the color of flame. A man in the thirties stands in the center of the room adjusting his tie, collar, etc."

These two are Roxie Hart and a man named Casely, and they are in the midst of a violent quarrel. The subject of the quarrel is evidently Mr. Casely's determination to withdraw from an acquaintanceship that has existed intimately for some months and Roxie Hart's vigorously voiced declaration that she will not be so treated. Mr. Casely is, she insists, "a double crosser, a dirty piker and a —— —— louse!" With which information she whips out a pearl-handled revolver from the dresser drawer and shoots him in the back. The curtain descends as Casely falls prostrate in the center of the room.

The lapse of time is sufficient to permit the gathering of the law's representatives and a newspaper reporter. At the curtain's second rise, the investigation has proceeded part way through the preliminary examination of Amos Hart, Roxie's husband, "an awkward creature of thirty-five with low forehead, snub nose and weak chin."

Amos wears "a noble, melancholy air and enjoys the procedure thoroughly." He is confessing to Sergeant Murdock of the force that *he* did the killing. He had come home late, his wife was peacefully sleeping and a man was crawling through the window. Mr. Hart had thereupon grabbed his gun and shot the intruder dead.

Sergeant Murdock is proud of that confession and the record time in which it is secured. Jake, the reporter, is mildly suspicious and the assistant state's attorney, Martin S. Harrison, who presently takes charge of the case, is frankly dubious. Harrison is looking for motives. Presently he learns more than he hoped for. Amos, in the next room while Roxie is getting dressed to go to jail, has proved an easy victim of Harrison's shrewdness. Faced with the fact that Roxie's men friends have been legion, as she has unwittingly admitted to her diary, Amos explodes in wrath and finally tells the truth. Amos is a "dirty little double-crosser," Roxie insists, with vehemence, but she admits her guilt.

ROXIE (*hysterically*)—Yes, it was me! I shot him and I'm damned glad I did! And I'd do it again—

JAKE—Once is enough, dearie!—I'm sure glad I met you to-night, sweetheart; to-morrow you'll sing another tune.

SERGEANT—Here's my confession—and the whole damn thing to do over again! (*Grabs* AMOS *by arm*.) Here, you, get your rags together! (*To* HARRISON.) We'll get her at the station (*shoves* AMOS *into room*) but let's finish him—now. (HARRISON *starts to follow, but* ROXIE *grasps his arm as he passes her*.)

ROXIE (*chattering*)—O God . . . God . . . Don't let 'em hang me—don't . . . Why, I'd . . . *die!* You promised—if I signed that— Can't—can't we—fix this up, you and me . . . fix it up . . . *you* know. . . .

HARRISON (*coldly*)—You don't frame anything with me! (*Shakes her off and goes into room*.)

JAKE—For crying out loud—what's the matter with *you!*

ROXIE—Matter? (*Half-shrieking*.) Matter? Are yuh crazy! (*Starts pacing up and down madly*.) O God, God, can't yuh do somethin'? Can't I get away, can't I?—

JAKE—Keep your clothes on, kid.

ROXIE (*weeping*)—They will hang me, I know they will. (*Throws herself on bed*.) I killed him and—

JAKE—What if yuh did? Ain't this Chicago? And gallant old Cook County never hung a woman yet! As a matter of fact—cold, hard statistics—it's 47 to 1 you go free.

ROXIE—*Free?* How?

JAKE—Sure, why, you're not even booked yet. But suppose they do, and the coroner's jury holds you, and you're sent to jail—

ROXIE (*shrieking, on bed*)—Jail! *Jail!* O God!

JAKE (*standing over her*)—Save those tears for the jury, sister: for jail's the best beauty treatment in town. You take the rest cure for a couple uh months at the County's expense; you lay off men and booze, and when you come to the trial you will look like Miss America, and that's when the big show starts with you for leading lady! It's a hundred to one they clear you—that's straight goods. But suppose an off-chance does happen—there's always a pardon—and you know our governor, God bless him! There you are: a thousand to one— Want uh bet?

ROXIE (*fearfully*)—And you'll . . . *help* me?

JAKE—Sure! I'll phone Billy Flynn in the morning.

ROXIE—Who's he?

JAKE—He's the best criminal lawyer in town—next to Halliday. Specializes in women: freed Minnie Kahlstedt, the hammer murderess, Marcelle Wayne, who fed her children arsenic—

ROXIE—Oh, yes, I read all about *them!*

JAKE—Oh, he's a wonder, and will make it a real fight. (*Coming towards her.*) For Harrison is an Ace on the Prosecutor's staff, and believe me, that boy won't leave a stone unturned to put you back of the bars. (*Smiles in satisfaction.*)

ROXIE—Well, you needn't be so *pleased*, if you really want me to go free.

JAKE—*Want* you to go free? How do you get that way? Oh, baby, your hanging would mean newspaper headlines six inches high. Say I'd give my last dollar—both of them—and every night when I kneel down by my little bed, I'll ask God to put a hemp rope around your nice white neck!

ROXIE—Aw, cut it out! (*Crying.*)

JAKE—Don't let my prayers worry you, for God's not on the jury. . . . And with a face like yours— Well, Justice ain't so blind in Chicago! (*Pointing to mirror.*)

ROXIE (*pleased*)—Oh, do you really think I'm—well—

JAKE—Sure! I'm callin' you "the most beautiful murderess"—

ROXIE—"Murderess!"

JAKE—Of course! What do you *think* I'd say? Prima donna?

ROXIE—But you needn't *say* it.

JAKE—Well, what the hell is going to put you on the front page? Why, a three-line want-ad would cost you two eighty-five, and you'll get line after line, column after column, for nothin'. Who knows you now? Nobody. But this time to-morrow your face will be known from coast to coast. Who cares to-day whether you live or die? But to-morrow they'll be crazy to know your breakfast food. They'll fight to see you, come by the hundred just for a glimpse of your house— Remember Wanda Stope? Well, we had twenty thousand at her funeral—

ROXIE—I'm not interested in any *funeral.*

JAKE (*grinning*)—Why, you may even end in wax works! Lord, girl, you're gettin' free publicity a movie queen would *die* for! Why, you'll be famous.

Jake and Harrison are pleased enough to enjoy a congratulatory drink which Harrison proceeds to pour from the law's flask. This case of Roxie Hart will probably mean promotion for Harrison, if he wants it, or sufficient reputation to set himself up independently. And it is a good front-page story for Jake.

Babe, the *Gazette's* photographer, is in with his camera and his flashlight assistant. There are snaps taken of the beautiful murderess, her captors, her probable prosecutor and her husband. Amos, in the picture, is shaking her hand and promising to stand by her.

Amos is, however, opposed to publicity until Jake explains its advantages to him. It will be a lot better for him to have the papers with him rather than against him, and, besides, he'll find himself in the news right along with President Coolidge and Harold McCormick.

As a last shot Babe calls for one of "the stiff." The dead Casely, however, has been moved into the other room, so Jake has to double for him. The reporter is prone on the floor, his coat collar turned high to complete the disguise and Roxie is bending over him, weeping a little and trying to smile at the camera at the same time, as the curtain falls.

## ACT II

It is Sunday afternoon, two days later, in the woman's ward of the Cook County jail. A row of cells are at the back of the room, and at its center, a long table surrounded by chairs. It is a sort of ante-room to the recreation and lounging rooms.

Roxie Hart and the matron have spent most of the day clipping out the pictures and stories telling of Roxie's crime. Now they have stopped for a minute while more newspaper photographers snap Roxie as she appeared "her first Sunday in jail."

Roxie is pleased with the attention and proud of her clippings. But she finds it hard to listen to the hymns of the Salvation Army and spending a dry Sunday in jail is far from her idea of perfect bliss. The lady bootlegger, it appears, calls Thursdays.

There are other things Roxie is advised to learn about being a murderess. She must not talk to any one until she has seen her lawyer. The Billy Flynn who is to defend her is one of the best in the business, the matron admits, even if he does cost $5,000. It doesn't pay, the matron has found, to economize either on trials or funerals.

Of course Velma, "the stylish divorcee," also awaiting trial as the slayer of her late mate, employs the same attorney who has secured all her divorces for her, but the criminal specialists are safer.

ROXIE (*taking up a clipping*)—"But the jazz slayer showed neither grief nor remorse; while the wife of the dead man sat with bowed head during the inquest. . . ." Say, they oughta run our pictures together and call it, "Why men leave home."

VELMA (*bitterly*)—You oughta cried and took on a lot.

MATRON—Well, it's only the papers, and the jury's all *you* care about.

VELMA—And thank God they're *men!* Tell her how they razzed *me*, Mrs. Morton.

MATRON—Terrible—the things they wrote.

VELMA—Made fun of my jewels, said my diamonds sparkled like real. And my pearls—my real Japanese pearls . . .

MATRON—And your coat—don't forget your coat, Velma.

VELMA—A real genuine mink, mind you, and they called it weasel! It was his—Mr. Clapp's—last gift to me before he—er—passed away.

ROXIE (*bewildered*)—Your husband?

VELMA—Yes. Wonderful to me—more like a friend than a husband. That very night, just before he went to his reward, he offered me two hundred a week alimony. I had just started my divorce, you know— Oh, my dear, didn't you see that?

All the papers had it with pictures of me and everything. . . .
And I said to him, "No, Clarence, you're too generous—I won't
take it. Hundred, yes, or maybe a hundred fifty; and not over
one seventy-five at the most." (*Triumphantly rises.*) Now in
the face of that, is it likely I'd shoot him. Would I trade an
offer like that for a measly ten thousand insurance? (*Goes to
the cell.*)

MATRON (*indignantly*)—Which the company won't pay.
Think of them holdin' out on her like that! Oh, what woman
suffers from men!

ROXIE—But she must have killed him, for the papers all
said—

MATRON (*severely*)—Now listen, dearie, if you're goin' to believe what the papers say, you'll be suspicious of ever'body here—
includin' yourself. You'll get along better if you just forget all
that and take each one as they come—that's my motto. . . .
And as for Velma, she's a pleasure to have around. No fightin',
no ugly language, refined and genteel—a real lady if I ever saw
one. And classy— (*With quick diplomacy.*) Well, of course
she ain't got *your* looks— Oh, my no! But she *is* a lady; uses
black narcissus perfume and never makes her bed.

In addition to Velma, Roxie's jail mates include "Crazy Liz,"
whose delusion is that she is a messenger of God and whose defense for having shot the man with whom she had been living
in sin for seven years, and who laughed when she asked him to
marry her, is, reasonably enough, insanity. Liz has her moments, however, when she is far from crazy.

Amos brings Roxie a box of clothes and lingers to inquire
solicitously after his wife's welfare and state of mind.

AMOS—How do they treat you here?

ROXIE—Terrible! Locked up all night in one of these sardine-
boxes! No make-up—not even a lipstick! And you have to
wash in cold water.

AMOS—My God.

ROXIE (*pacing up and down*)—And that damned Salvation
Army squawkin' out there and the radio tunin' in to health
talks, Y.M. meetin's, and sermons—this is a helluva joint!
Sunday here and not a drop of liquor in the house! (*To* AMOS
*who has started pacing in sympathy.*) What the hell are you
walking the floor about? *You* got it easy while *I'm* locked up
here with God's messenger! And food—it's terrible— I can't

eat this jail stuff— You'll have to send my meals in—from Weiser's around the corner—only twenty a week.

Amos—Twenty dollars!

Roxie—All right: I'll eat the damned stuff and *die!*

Amos—Oh, well—twenty a week—what's that! I got a raise —fifty-five now—

Roxie—My God.

Amos—And when I got back from the inquest, the whole office crowded around and shook hands with me and wished me luck—

Roxie—That's just because your my husband—you'd be nobody if it wasn't for me.

Amos (*indignantly; comes to her*)—It's because I'm stickin' by yuh! I guess there's not many guys would *do it.*

Roxie— Whatever it is you got a raise out of it, didn't you? I've got to have money for making the bed and cigarettes, and you know how penny a point counts up!

Amos—Say, listen here—

Roxie—Do you want me to look like a cheap skate before all these people? All right, there's plenty of money in the world, and you ain't got no corner on it. God, why did I ever marry you!

Amos—Will ten do? (*Holding out money to her.*)

Roxie—Yes, twenty! (*Grabbing both ten dollar bills out of his hand.*)

Amos (*in alarm*)—Yeah, but what about *me?*

Roxie (*turning away from him*)—My God, can't yuh think uh nothin' but yourself!

Amos is still there when Billy Flynn, the lawyer, calls. Flynn "is dressed with careful carelessness; tweed topcoat and fedora, pepper and salt sack suit, blue shirt with soft collar, striped necktie with golden horseshoe, and a red carnation."

Flynn is thoroughly a business man. At the moment his only interest is Amos Hart's success in raising the $5,000 retainer for Roxie's defense. Amos has so far been able to raise only $2,000 on his insurance (which he had no right to cash, according to Roxie, seeing that it was hers) $500 that he had already paid, $700 that he got out of the building and loan and $300 that he borrowed. He had tried Roxie's father, but so had Flynn, and the old man had been cold. Roxie, her father said, had gone to hell five years ago and could stay there so far as he was concerned.  That leaves $3,000 still to raise and it has got to be raised.  And not by installments either.

"I wouldn't be bothered with your chickenfeed," announces the attorney, positively.  "I play square, Hart, dead square.  When you came to me yesterday I didn't say, 'Is she innocent, is she guilty, will it be an easy case or a hard one'—nothing like that, now *did* I!  No.  I said: 'Have you got five thousand dollars?' and you said, 'Yes.'  (*Eyes him in contempt.*)  You dirty liar! . . . And I took your case—and I'll *keep* it.  But she'll rot in jail before it comes to trial!"

Amos promises to do his best and is summarily dismissed. Roxie, worried about the possible delay of her case, suggests a compromise.  Maybe she and Flynn might reach an agreement, if he was agreeable.

"Why can't we be friends?" inquires Roxie, coyly.

"Good!" replies Flynn, with vigor.  "You've got that out of your system.  Now, listen: I'm not interested in your looks, your age, your sex—nothing *except* as it affects the case.  You mean just one thing to me: five thousand dollars.  Get that."

Roxie "takes the slap philosophically," and Flynn outlines the preliminaries of his campaign.

FLYNN—Now, the sob sister from the *Evening Star*—

ROXIE—Mary Sunshine?

FLYNN—Yes.  And the woman from *The Ledger* are coming.

ROXIE—I don't want to see her.  She said I was knock-kneed.

FLYNN—You've talked so much, damn it, you can't stop now.

ROXIE—But not *her*—  I'll be damned if I do!

FLYNN—You'll be hanged if you don't.  And pipe down on that swearing.  What we have to do now is to shout for public sympathy.  Heart stuff.  The story of your life starts to-morrow in the *Star*.

ROXIE—What?

FLYNN—"From Convent to Jail."  I'll have my secretary write it to-night—signed with your name, of course.  Now here's where you've got to learn to act like hell. . . . Here's the idea— Beautiful southern home—every luxury and refinement—edu- cated at the Sacred Heart—parents dead—fortune swept away. Runaway marriage—  You're a lovely innocent child, bewildered by what has happened.  Young, full of life, lonely, you were caught up by the sad whirl of life in a great city—  I'll have a red hot picture of cabaret life—jazz stuff is always good. . . . You were drawn inevitably like a moth to the flame!  And now

the mad whirl has ceased; a butterfly crushed on the wheel. . . .
And you sob remorse for the life you took—

ROXIE—Oh, God!

FLYNN—Cut out God. Stay where you're better acquainted.
And don't overdo it. Go as far as you like with Mary Sunshine— She'll swallow hook, line and sinker, for it's what *she*
wants, but easy with the *Ledger* girl— The important thing is
*Regret*.

ROXIE—Regret?

FLYNN—You're *sorry—sorry*— You'd give your life gladly to
bring him back.

ROXIE (*drops pose*)—Say, why did I do it? What's my defense? Drunk? Crazy?

FLYNN (*shakes head*)—Nobody cares about a lunatic unless
they got money. Whenever they ask "Why,"—all you remember
is a fearful quarrel— He threatened to kill you— You can see
him coming toward you with awful look in his eyes—that *wild*
look— And—get this now— You *both* grabbed for the gun.
Whatever else we weave in afterwards, that's there from the
start. You spent a sleepless night tossing about—

ROXIE—And walking the floor— (*Buzzer.*)

FLYNN—Here comes Sunshine now, and that dress—

ROXIE—What's the matter with it?

FLYNN—You ought to have something simple—plain—dark—
And slick down your hair—

ROXIE—How will this do?

FLYNN—All right, get into that,—and don't forget—Regret—
Remorse—

ROXIE—I got you— (*Turns to* FLYNN.) And we both
grabbed for the gun.

Mary Sunshine, of the *Star*, is a sweet child and fearfully sympathetic. The Roxie Hart case is just thrilling to her. Her
story has aroused every one's sympathy. Ever so many lovely
letters have come in as a result of the *Star's* offer to pay $10 a
day for the best letter received, and there have been flowers
from groups of college boys.

Jake, who is still on the story for the *Gazette*, is also in for
new material. It is Jake who suggests a way to raise the remaining $3,000 which worries Flynn so desperately. Let them
organize a sale, an auction, of Roxie's junk—her furniture,
clothes, anything. The public is sure to fall for that. "They'll
go wild at the chance to own a tea cup drank out of by a real

live murderess," Jake insists, "and of course *if she dies* by due process of the law the value is enhanced. And we could use a carload of underwear."

There is one small stumbling block in the way, admits Roxie, when she is called into the conference. Her stuff isn't paid for! But Jake is still excited by the possibilities of the scheme. "The mirror of Marie Antoinette, Carrie Nation's Hatchet, the bed of Roxie Hart—why, kid, they're museum pieces!"

The auction is finally agreed upon, the first $500 to go for another outfit of clothes for Roxie, and the beautiful murderess is turned over to Mary Sunshine.

SUNSHINE—Now, my dear—let's finish our little talk. You were saying you had given your all.

ROXIE (*having seated herself in chair*)—I have given all. All that a woman can give.

SUNSHINE—Yes—yes!

ROXIE—And now the mad whirl is over—crushed on the wheel of life—butterfly—a butterfly—the moth and the flame—

SUNSHINE (*scribbling*)—And what caused you to—

ROXIE (*sadly*)—But dancing feet find sorrow—

SUNSHINE—Dancing—jazz? The Charleston? Shall we say the Charleston, Mrs. Hart? And er—drink—you *had* been drinking?

ROXIE—Oh, yes, I was drunk, my dear, dead drunk!

SUNSHINE—Oh, lovely, lovely—my paper's dry, you know. . . . So you would advise girls to avoid jazz and drink—what else, Mrs. Hart? How did you happen to . . . just *why* did you . . . shoot . . .

ROXIE (*grows dramatic*)—I was insane! Crazy!

SUNSHINE—Oh, dear!

ROXIE (*hastily*)—Not enough for the asylum, you know—over with right away.

SUNSHINE (*nods*)—Temporary insanity.

ROXIE—For I really have the tenderest heart in the world—wouldn't hurt a worm . . . not even (*with* VELMA'S *tremolo*) a worm. . . .

SUNSHINE (*sympathetically*)—And what brought it on?

ROXIE—He—he threatened my life—

SUNSHINE—What a terrible man!

ROXIE (*bows head in hands*)—Oh, he *was! Very terrible!*

Two dinners arrive for Roxie—one from Weiser's around the corner, another, a chicken dinner, from an Unknown Admirer with a card reading "My heart and hand are at your feet, with you my life would be complete."

A moment later Roxie is busy with her meal, although she is sure that every mouthful will choke her.

ROXIE (*forces herself to a more languid pace*)—The first bite I've tasted since he went to his reward. . . . (*Presses handkerchief to her eyes.*)

SUNSHINE—*Dear* Mrs. Hart!

ROXIE—Oh, if I could only bring him back! How gladly . . . how gladly I'd give my own life! (*Chokes with emotion, takes a few healthy bites.*) And sleep—I can't sleep either. . . . *All* night I walked about—tossing the floor.

SUNSHINE—Oh, my *dear*.

ROXIE (*in hollow tone*)—Always his face coming toward me (*her emotion raises as she lives through it all*) with that terrible look—that *wild* look in his eyes—(*dramatic pause as she reaches forth her hand*)—and we both grabbed for the gun!— And I shot—to save my honor— (*Listening to the singing.*) Isn't that lovely—The Salvation Army—I love to hear it! I'm so awful refined— I was born in a convent!

The curtain falls.

A month elapses. It is an early afternoon in May. Roxie is resting in her bunk and Velma is being groomed for her trial, the matron helping her fit one of her newer gowns. "Velma looks ten years younger. Her shingle bob glistens, and there's a tangerine rouge (from the huge makeup box on the table) on her cheeks and lips." Velma is not happy, however. The gown she has counted on most has not arrived. She could just kill Marshall Field!

Liz, scrubbing the floors and sane for the moment, is inclined to make sneering remarks about Velma and her success as a decorative plaintiff. Roxie, too, is bitter because of the attention that is being paid this bunch of four-flushers who think they're so important. Roxie's jealous, according to Liz. She's out of the limelight now, and miserable.

"Says she's got a headache, but it ain't," Liz reports to Jake, when the *Gazette* happens in. "No, sireee. A broken nose— that's what it is—out of joint because Velma's *IT* now instead uv her. No more presents or letters—except from that durned fool admirer."

Jake's attitude bears out Liz. He frankly confesses to Roxie that she is no longer in the news, though she tries desperately to convince him that she is.

Roxie (*wearily*)—I can't sleep—my head hurts so!  I've had a terrible night!  Tossed and wept, sobbed remorse—

Jake—Oh, my God, don't start that again!  Nobody gives a damn how you're sleeping.

Roxie (*shrilly*)—They do too!  Don't you remember—(*Follows him.*)

Jake—Sure, *once*—when the story was new, but it's dead now. You'll have to pull a better line than that.

Roxie (*with sudden inspiration*)—*I*'ve got it: a scoop for you—a front-page story!

Jake (*skeptically*)—Yeah?

Roxie—It's a dress—you can raffle it off—sell chances on it—(*takes from box and goes on, inspired, as he shakes his head in rejection—impressively*)—the dress I wore the first time I ever went *wrong!*

Jake—Oh, my God!

Roxie—It's a museum piece.

Jake—Then put it back in the case.

Roxie—I'll give it to another paper.

Jake—Try it—  Roxie, you sure are a publicity hound! You've got it bad, kid.  Now listen: You'll have another fling at the front page when your trial starts, but until then there's not a chance in the world!  For they've caught Kitty Baxter!

Roxie—Oh, my God, *another* one!

Jake—And she's got you faded, Roxie.  She's a Tiger Cat and you're just a little white kitten.  But I will do this for you: use you in a picture with her: "The Jazz Slayer meets the Bandit Queen."

Roxie—Nothing doing.

Jake—Whole cheese or none, huh?

Roxie—Yep.

Jake—Suit yourself.  But if you can't play ball, you'd better curl up (*nods toward cell*) and go to sleep for the next four months.

Roxie (*genuinely startled*)—Four months!  It ain't goin' to be *that* long!

Jake—Sure!  The September calendar—maybe October.  Billy goes abroad for July and August.

Roxie—*What*!  Hoofs it to Europe on *my money*—the clothes

I sold off my back to pay him? And I stay cooped up here!
(*Eyes flash.*) Do you think I'm goin' to stand for that?

JAKE (*calmly*)—Sure. What can you do about it?

ROXIE (*determinedly*)—I don't know, but . . . (*Taps foot,
thinking.*) God damn it, and I got my clothes all planned for a
summer trial!

Roxie is increasingly depressed as she sees herself slipping farther and farther from the center of interest and begins to worry
about the outcome of her case. She hears the story of Moonshine Maggie, the ignorant Hunyak convicted for the death of a
man to whom she sold liquor. What is it that juries think
about? They don't think, Jake tells her. What counts most
with them is bein' a woman.

"But look at Maggie," prompts Roxie.

"That wasn't the jury's fault," insists Jake. "She had a bum
lawyer. . . . D'yuh remember the Harlan case? She fed lysol
to her two step-children and the baby died; and the last day of
the trial they had the other one run down the aisle cryin'
"Mamma! Mamma!" and the jury sent her home to her husband and the dear little one who needed her! . . . And now this
Hunyak. God, what a waste—a decent lawyer with a sob like
that would have had a jury wiping its eyes and giving her a
medal. Gee! Kinda gets me, wastin' a kid like that!"

Now Velma is off to her trial, amid the shouts of her mates.
And the police have brought in "Go-to-hell Kitty," "a wiry young
tough with insolent eyes set deep in a thin white face, square
hard jaw and straight scarlet mouth." Kitty is defiant and proud
of her crime. She stuck up a guy and they got her, and that's
that! Jake is interested in Kitty's story. Mary Sunshine tries
to interview her and is cursed for her pains. Roxie even tries
to get into the new story by giving her opinion of the newcomer,
and offering to fight her, only to be pulled away and set back
for her pains.

Suddenly the light of inspiration flashes in Roxie's eyes. She
shrieks and falls in a fake faint. Now the excitement swirls
around her again. The matron rushes for water. Jake offers to
call the doctor. Mary Sunshine is all sympathy and attention.
Gradually Roxie recovers from the attack. Her eyes open
slowly, she moans and cries.

"Oh, dear—oh, dear—I can't stand it?"

"Stand what, darling?" sympathetically inquires Mary Sunshine. "Tell me."

"Go 'way, let me alone," wails Roxie. "Here in jail—oh, dear! My—my baby!" And then she adds, wanly—"When my child is born!"

She has the attention now—all of it. Jake is sure a doctor is needed. Sunshine is filled with womanly anxiety. Even Flynn, rushing in, feels the excitement and exults at the news.

FLYNN—What's this, young lady? Why didn't you let me know?

ROXIE (*sweetly*)—I did try to but you wouldn't come.

FLYNN—Umm, yes. . . . I was busy. Well, well, it's all right now.

ROXIE (*with sweet bitterness*)—"All right?"

SUNSHINE (*to* ROXIE)—Isn't it gorgeous? Aren't you *glad?*

ROXIE—"Glad?" Oh! (*Gives a moan.*) To have your baby born *here?*

SUNSHINE—Wonderful! I'll phone all the women's clubs, the Parent-Teachers, the Civic League! We'll ask for letters: "Shall an Innocent Child Bear the Stigma of Jail?"

JAKE—They'll eat it alive!

FLYNN (*to* SUNSHINE)—Good! And then a petition—

SUNSHINE—Oh, yes, miles and miles of names!

FLYNN—Asking that she be granted bail so that an innocent babe can be born in God's great outdoors! (*Arm sweeps the Western hemisphere.*)

JAKE—But you won't wait for *that,* will you? When—?

SUNSHINE—When is it to be?

ROXIE—Oh! (*Closes her eyes a minute.*) Not till fall— September.

FLYNN—Then I'll rush it to the jury in June.

SUNSHINE—What jury would condemn a mother-to-be!

JAKE (*to* FLYNN)—*Could* a jury condemn her to death, or would it be passing judgment on two lives instead of one? And if they did, could the sentence be executed, or—

FLYNN—See the State's Attorney on that. (*Chuckles.*) It's a solar plexus for them, all right!

ROXIE (*sits up dramatically*)—My *own* life doesn't matter, but that of my child . . . (*Sinks back.*)

FLYNN—Don't worry, my dear: The American public will fight to death for your innocent unborn babe!

JAKE—Say, this will make the editorial page as well as the news—somethin' to scrap about.

FLYNN—A challenge to every red-blooded man!

SUNSHINE—And every true woman! Why, motherhood itself is at stake, *isn't* it, Mr. Flynn? Oh, wouldn't it be *wonderful* if the trial could come just before Mother's Day! (*Buzzer—* MATRON *exits.*)

ROXIE (*soulfully*)—You've been so kind to me. . . . If it's a girl, I'm goin' to name it after you!

SUNSHINE (*pats her head*)—You darling . . . that's just too *sweet.* . . .

ROXIE—And if it's a boy, after *you*, Jake.

JAKE—*Hell,* no! (*Quickly.*) Name it for Billy here.

FLYNN (*also in alarm as she looks up at him*)—Oh, no—no.

Then the question arises as to the paternity of Roxie's child. Who is the father? Amos Hart happens to call at the moment, and he too is interested—until he hears the baby is to be born in September. Being a bookkeeper he can figure quickly and as quickly he withdraws from the situation. Nobody is going to put anything over on Amos.

FLYNN—My client needs your support, Mr. Hart.

AMOS (*bitterly*)—Yeah—"Meal Ticket"—that's all I've ever been!—Say, you can't make a fool out of *me!*

JAKE—What are you going to do—divorce her?

AMOS (*loftily*)—I ain't sayin' *what* I'll do! (*Starts off but hangs on the edge as* BABE *is admitted with camera.*)

MATRON—All right, Babe, go right in.

JAKE—Oh, Babe, a couple uh flashes here! (BABE *has started towards stairs. Turns back and looks at* ROXIE.)

BABE—Not that lens-louse—I'm after the Tiger Girl!

JAKE—It's a scoop, kid, come on! (*With a grand gesture toward* ROXIE.) Waitin' the works. A baby—

BABE (*sets up camera; to* AMOS, *who has gradually edged closer*)—Well, Court-plaster, you in on this?

FLYNN (*doesn't give him a chance to answer*)—No! He's cast her off, forsaken her. . . .

AMOS—Wait till I see my lawyer. September—hell! (*Exits.*)

JAKE—Here you are, Roxie. (*Places chair for her.* ROXIE *sits and stretches out her arms to where* AMOS *has gone—when she's sure he has gone.*)

ROXIE—Amos! My husband! He deserted me in my hour of need!

BABE—Look at the camera, sweetheart!

ROXIE—Wait a minute. (*To* SUNSHINE.) My sewing.

(SUNSHINE *hands her the baby dress left by Hunyak in rocking chair.*)  I made every stitch myself.  (*Holds up baby dress.*)

FLYNN—Deserted wife and mother.

JAKE—Hot stuff!

BABE—Hold it!  (*Flash!*)

The curtain falls.

## ACT III

Seven weeks later, a morning in June, Roxie Hart and Billy Flynn are rehearsing the closing scenes planned for the trial. They are in the prisoner's room adjoining the courtroom.  A bailiff is sitting by the door asleep in a tilted chair.  Roxie is sitting in a chair turned relatively as it will be later in the witness stand.  "She wears a dress with meaning, heavy white crêpe with surplice collar and bishop sleeves, white shoes and hose of perplexing nudity.  Her feet are crossed carelessly and one lily hand dangles a cigarette.  Her eyes, wide and innocent, stare soulfully at the blank wall that represents the jury.  Flynn paces up and down, coaching from the sidelines."

Roxie has got as far as "My innocent unborn babe—"

"Throw your head back—nobly," prompts Flynn.  "That's right.  Wait—don't look at the jury on that—you forget them— seek the eyes of your husband."

The rehearsal proceeds.  Roxie knows her story now—knows it so well she could repeat it in her sleep.  Now she is instructed as to her attitude toward Prosecutor Harrison.  "Remember, no matter what he *says*, or how mad he gets—you shrink—and cower—and cry—till the jury are ready to knock him down. They always lose when they bulldoze a woman."

There is the matter of the confessions, and the force, the brutal force, used to extract them from her.  "And when you answer him—'I don't know!' 'I don't remember!' (*he acts the part for her*) weak, faint, frightened—always to the jury—with a little flutter—especially that 20-minute egg in the corner."

"Say, you don't have to tell me how to handle *them* babies. I ain't watched them three days for nothin'.  I've done everything but give them my telephone number."

"That'll come later.  Beautiful work!"

Mary Sunshine is in with a big bouquet of flowers from the Parent-Teachers Society.  She also reports the arrival of another baby carriage, which makes five in all.  There have also been more proposals of marriage. One from a New York millionaire who wants to adopt Roxie. Outside the courtroom is jammed with the biggest crowd since the Loeb-Leopold trial.

With the room to themselves again Flynn goes on with his plea. He and Harrison have agreed on three hours each for the summing up. "To the jury by 8, and a verdict by 10—that'll catch the home editions," is Flynn's plan.

Roxie is a little worried about her clothes. If she goes free to-night how can she walk out without a coat? "I don't give a damn if you wear gunny sack after the verdict," coldly admits Flynn. But Roxie is awfully afraid she won't be able to remember her part unless she has a new coat. And Flynn reluctantly advances the money.

FLYNN—He'll ask you why you didn't tell the police this story in the first place. . . .

ROXIE—Yeah, I've been worried about that, too.

FLYNN—You droop your head. . . . "Gentlemen" . . . "Let us think." . . . (*She puts her head up. He motions her to put her head down.*) "When and to whom did she finally reveal the dearest secret of a woman's heart?" (ROXIE *crosses her legs.*) Uncross your legs. . . . "Only after long gray days in jail when her soul cried out for sympathy. . . ." Then I'll point to Mary Sunshine. . . . (ROXIE *watching* FLYNN.) "To a woman. And the State's Attorney wonders why she didn't confide in him!" And you look modest.

ROXIE—Still droopin'?

FLYNN (*nods*)—"They threatened and tortured and were successful in tearing from her the confessions of her weakness—"

ROXIE (*looks up*)—What do I do?

FLYNN (*waves for silence;* ROXIE *looks down*)—"The frailty that is woman in loving too well, but she kept locked within the sanctuary of her heart (ROXIE *with her own initiative, tries to follow with effective pantomime*) the sacred secret of her coming motherhood." (*Looks up and catches her in ludicrous pose.*) What the hell—

ROXIE (*with dignity*)—I'm only trying to do what you *say*.

FLYNN (*grimly*)—We're not playing charades. Droop— (*she droops*) that's all you do: *droop*. . . . Then I turn toward you: "I'm thankful! I'm glad! I'm *proud* that you did, Roxie Hart!"

ROXIE (*lifts her head expectantly*)—Then what do *I* do?

FLYNN (*glares at her*)—What do you *want* to do—turn a cart-wheel?

ROXIE (*rebelliously*)—Looks kinda dumb just to *sit* there.

FLYNN—I'll take care of that. You *droop* and that's all, for *you*.

Roxie isn't as well pleased as she might be with Flynn's attitude. She feels that this is her show and she is paying for it. And she doesn't propose that any damned old crook is going to take it away from her.

Flynn answers her as vigorously as she attacks him and they are on the point of a serious quarrel when the reconvening of court is announced.

"Come on, Cinderella, the stage is set," shouts Jake.

"Flynn hands Roxie a bunch of lilies of the valley, Roxie adjusts her expression to one of wistful innocence and walks slowly toward the door.

"A brave little woman," agrees Flynn, for the benefit of the listeners. He gathers up his briefs and papers and the procession to the courtroom starts as the curtain falls.

The scene changes to the courtroom, with the trial in session. Judge Canton, "a closely shaven gentleman in the forties, is on the bench, and the jury, largely the middle-aged fatherly type, are in the box."

A half dozen reporters occupy the press seats. Amos Hart is on the stand and Harrison is trying to get him to acknowledge his familiarity with Roxie's confession. He gets little from Amos but evasions and disgustedly turns him over to Flynn.

Flynn worms from Amos his doubt of the paternity of Roxie's child, his admission that it was because he did not intend to have anything put over on him that he had divorced his wife in May, and that it was largely on the statements of the district attorney's office that he had decided on that action. If he were convinced that he was the father of Roxie's child, Amos hesitatingly admits, he would be willing to take her back, and is quickly excused.

The state rests and Roxie is called. Immediately the courtroom is in turmoil. The moving picture men are summoned, the Judge adjusts his tie and moves over by Roxie, to be sure he is in line with the cameras, the photographers set their machines and call for the Kleig lights. As the witness is being sworn the cameras whir and click and the action is of the scene officially recorded. Then the lights and cameras are taken out and the trial is resumed.

Modestly and in subdued tones Roxie retells the story of her meeting with Casely; of how she and a girl friend were seeking shelter from a sudden rain and Casely appeared, offering his umbrella; of how he escorted the girls home; of how he met them again the next day, and the next, and finally of the time he took her to the Policemen's Benefit ball. Gradually their friendship deepened into a more intimate relation, largely because Roxie had quarreled with her husband. She had wanted a home, a real home, and kiddies. She never, never knew that Casely was a married man and she was most unhappy when she realized what she was doing.

She admits her confession, but *not* the confession the state has produced. She doesn't remember that at all. She was much too hysterical at the time.

Arrived at the night of the killing she tells of Casely's visit, of his plying her with liquor, and of his ungovernable rage when he learned of her delicate condition. Because of that he swore to kill her.

FLYNN—Now, Roxie, tell the jury *just* what happened next.

ROXIE—The pillows were thrown back, and my—Mr. Hart's revolver was layin' there. He grabbed—I knocked it from his hand. It fell to the floor and he whirled me aside—back by the dresser now—and we both grabbed for the gun. I reached it first, then he started toward me. . . . I can see him now with that awful look in his eyes—

FLYNN (*slightly behind and to left of* ROXIE *through the speeches, coaching her and egging her on*)—What kind of look? Describe it to the jury.

ROXIE—I can't describe it; but a terrible look—angry— wild—

FLYNN (*purrs*)—Were you afraid? Did you think he meant to kill you?

ROXIE (*shudders*)—Oh, yes, sir! I knew if he once reached the gun . . .

FLYNN (*purrs more deeply*)—It was his life then or yours?

ROXIE—Yes, sir. (*Faintly as she lifts her eyes.*) And not . . . *just* mine . . . (*Pause, then continues dramatic narrative.*) Coming right toward me, with that awful look—that wild look . . . I closed my eyes . . . and . . . (*Barely whispers.*) shot. . . .

FLYNN—In defense of your life?

ROXIE (*lifts her head nobly*)—To save my husband's innocent unborn child!

FLYNN (*with wave of hand to* HARRISON)—Take the witness.

The dropping of the curtain covers a lapse of several hours. When it rises it is late afternoon and Flynn is making his closing plea. "He stands before the jury—this is the hour he earns the five thousand. And Billy Sunday himself never worked harder, with muscle as well as brain, minus coat and collar, with perspiration standing in great beads on his forehead. He's fighting, gentlemen, fighting, with every drop of his blood, for the life of that brave little woman. The jury half asleep, enthralled, hang on each word and follow every gesture. The press watch benignly; they know his whole bag of tricks, but Billy's always worth watching. Even the Judge listens, but in sleepy pose— All are reclining in seats or against walls. And Roxie? This scene is really the close of an hour's duel between Roxie and Flynn. When the curtain goes up, honors are even and she is faithfully registering the emotions outlined for her in rehearsal. Gradually, however, she extends her field; deeper emotion, gesture, writhing. She works for her audience—the jury; and they, fascinated, are torn between her contortions and the fervid orator. Flynn, who feels them slipping, turns—when his speech permits— and tries to stop her with furtive gesture. Of course she is oblivious, and he is forced to redouble his own efforts—louder tone—wilder manner—to drown her out. Until toward the end you have them both playing in grand crescendo."

FLYNN—Do *you* believe, gentlemen, that's a word-for-word confession? Of *course* not! No human being could have made such a deliberate, coherent statement—certainly not this delicate, frightened girl. . . . No, there was careful selection; a bit here— (*lifts out morsels from the air*)—a bit here—an addition, deletions—*any*thing to build up his case! (*He is hoarsely confidential.*) He's *got* to bring home a conviction or LOSE HIS JOB! (*All eyes are turned in scorn toward* HARRISON, *who slinks down with eyes downcast.*) And then when he read it to you: malicious twists of meaning . . . (*reads as* HARRISON *read in former scene*) "but he didn't get that far . . ." "Question: Why not?" "Answer: Because, by God, I shot him." (ROXIE *bangs table.*) That's the way he read it to you, isn't it? (*Jury look aggrieved—it's true; he flings the paper on the table.*)

He would have you believe, gentlemen, that child sitting there—
(ROXIE *lifts her head—the picture of girlish innocence.*) *swore*—
(*He gestures toward* ROXIE—*then back to the jury—then back
to* ROXIE *again—calling attention to her innocence.*) Those were
her words, yes, but—ah! what a different meaning! This beast,
this drunken brute, who had forced his way into her home—and
remember, gentlemen, if she had shot him down then, the law
would have upheld her!—was coming toward her, threatening her
life . . . (*Breaks off and resumes in melancholy tone.*) What
was the future to her? Crushed, betrayed, broken-hearted . . .
Nothing—*less* than nothing. But the little life that fluttered
beneath her heart (*taps his fountain-pen pocket*) ah! mother-
love stirred within her . . . and those words were a tribute to
her Omnipotent Maker who stood by in her hour of need: (*He
brings it out with ministerial reverence*—ROXIE'S *gaze is directed
heavenward and her hands clasped to her heart in prayer.*) "By
God I shot him." (*Jury looks relieved—effective pause while
little Eva does her stuff.* FLYNN *goes on quickly.*)

I'm sorry she loved as she did. I'm sorry this monster preyed
upon her innocence—I wish he had never entered that happy little
home. (*Crosses down stage—looks at* ROXIE—ROXIE'S *legs
crossed—she immediately straightens up.* FLYNN *turns his back
on her.*)

If sorrow could avail (*he warms up*) Fred Casely would be
here now, for she'd give her life and gladly to bring the dead
man back! (*Looks at* ROXIE *who nods her head in ecstatic con-
firmation and begins enthusiastic pantomime.*)

But we can't do that, gentlemen. (*Melancholy.*)

You may take her life as the State asks, but it won't bring
Casely back. (*Looking fixedly at her.* ROXIE *starts to cry.*
FLYNN *turns back with satisfaction to jury.*)

And for what purpose? (*Voice rings out.*)

Do *you* hear that weeping girl? (ROXIE *has her head in her
hand—gives a big cry.* FLYNN'S *finger darts to the tailor.*)

Do *you?* (ROXIE *lifts her head.*) (ROXIE *puts her head down
again at each "do you."*) (*To the hard-boiled egg in the corner.*)

Do *you?* (*They don't—he continues.*) For her reformation?
She learned her lesson, gentlemen, in that dark hour alone. For
punishment? My *God*, she's punished enough! No—none of
these! But to satisfy the greedy ambition of the prosecution!
*Pro*secution?—No, *Per*secution.

(ROXIE *rises—crying—to her feet. She is crying so loud now
she is almost drowning his voice.* FLYNN *is trying to stop her.*)

You ask for her life, gentlemen—by one who would climb to fame on dead bodies! (*Pause, filled with* ROXIE's *sobs, almost wails.*) We can't give her happiness— (*Looks at* ROXIE. *The Jury are with her.*) No, it is too late for that. (*Crosses quickly to her.* ROXIE *has stretched her arms out towards jury.* FLYNN *tries to block her from jury by turning his back on her— As he moves towards jury* ROXIE *follows.*)

ROXIE—Mine baby—mine baby!!! (*Holding out her arms toward jury.*)

FLYNN (*moving towards jury*)—Betrayed, crushed, we can only let her pick up the broken fragments of life, the tangled threads— (*During this scene* ROXIE *tries to appeal to the jury, and* FLYNN *tries to keep in front of her as she shifts up and down to right and left of him, she finally lands below him.*) We can give her another chance! (*She totters and flops into his arms, in a faint, jury rise and bend forward. Everybody bends forward.*) We rest, your Honor; you may give the case to the jury.

The curtain is down again briefly. At its rise it is ten o'clock that night. The courtroom is gloomy and dull. Only Flynn, the reporters and photographers await the final scene. A poker game has just been finished at the clerk's desk. Jake, at the door of the jury room, is listening for some evidence of activity inside. He hears enough to know that the jury has finished discussing the Klan and Prohibition and should be ready to report before long. It stands, he believes, 10 to 2.

"Lights!" shouts Babe, the photographer, loudly, and slyly adds, "If that don't bring 'em, it's Gabriel's cue."

Immediately there is a stir. The judge enters with his robe on his arm. Roxie dashes in from the next room, her face alight.

"Pitchers?" she inquires, eagerly.

Now the lights are turned up and the court attachés take their places. "Flynn leads Roxie from the prisoner's room as in a bridal procession. Roxie has a handsome new coat over her dress." They face the judge. The jury foreman hands up the verdict.

"We, the jury, find the defendant not guilty!"

"Roxie rushes with a wild shriek—to judge. Everybody cheering. Roxie kisses Judge. Then she embraces Stenographer—and anybody else within reach. Rushes down to table—the chairs being pulled out for her to mount it. Jury crowd out towards her filling stage."

Roxie (*on table*)—Dear friends, kind friends, who have stood by me in the dark hours of the past—His Honor—Mr. Flynn— Mr. Callahan—Mary Sunshine—and all you guys on the jury: You've been so kind to me—so—so *encouragin'*—that I'm goin' to do somethin' for you— (*Bang, bang, bang—outside. Three shots.*) (*Woman's shriek—Sergt. of Police yells out—general murmur.*)

Jake—What the hell!

Sunshine—Another murder! (*Police whistle off Left. All break and rush off.*)

Roxie—Hey, you! Come back here! Wait a minute— I want to *tell* you something! (*Rocks arms.*) Mine baby, mine baby! (*Bursts into rage.*) You God-damn bums, walkin' out on me when I want to make a speech! (*Climbs down and starts after them.*) It's important—it's *news*—

Flynn—Forget it; you're all washed up.

Roxie—I am not washed up! I'm goin' in vaudeville—I'm famous!

Amos (*who has entered after the walkout*)—What!

Roxie—Sure! Booked solid for ten weeks.

Amos—But the wedding—

Roxie—No wedding—it will ruin my career—

Amos—But the ring—

Roxie (*grabs it*)—I'll keep it to remember you by!

Amos—But the baby, Roxie, the baby—

Roxie—What baby? My God, do I look like an amachure!

Flynn—Oh, my God! (Babe *rushes in—across to* Roxie.)

Babe—Another case for you, Billy. It won't take a minute, Sergeant, a pitcher uh the two with you here between 'em.

(*Sergeant enters dragging on* Machine-Gun-Rosie. *Woman reporter backing on in front of her—*Sunshine *following her.*)

Jake—Another jane out for trigger practice—bumped off the boy friend! Gee, ain't God good to the papers! Come on, Carrots,—a picture of you with Machine-Gun-Rosie!—The Jazz-Slayer meets the Cicero-Kid! Shake hands!

Rosie—No! (*Jerks away and throws arm up to cover face.*) I don't want to be in the papers!

Roxie (*who has crossed to her—jerks her arm down*)—Come on, sister, yuh gotta play ball; this is Chicago! Pitchers!

Babe—Right in the camera now! sweethearts—smile, more, just a little more—big—

The curtain falls.

# THE CONSTANT WIFE

## A Comedy in Three Acts

### By W. Somerset Maugham

AFTER the death of Charles Frohman Ethel Barrymore, among other stars directed by him, continued briefly with the succeeding management and then ventured into other fields. For a number of seasons she was with Arthur Hopkins, and once she tried a Shakespearean repertoire with Walter Hampden.

This season, however, she came back to the Frohman Company at the suggestion of Gilbert Miller, general director of Charles Frohman, Inc., to play a part eminently suited to her style in W. S. Maugham's comedy, "The Constant Wife." It proved a happy move. Miss Barrymore's successes have been rather widely spaced the last several years, and she has been far from satisfied. This one quickly reëstablished her with a public that had temporarily suffered a strain upon its loyalty.

The Maugham comedy, produced at the Maxine Elliott Theatre in late November, was popularly acclaimed and had not the slightest difficulty running through the season. It was the nearest thing to a high comedy success the winter boasted.

The Barrymore part is that of Constance, wife of John Middleton, an eminent London surgeon. At the moment of the play's beginning Constance is avoiding with not a little effort the gossip she feels her friends and well wishers are determined to relate to her—gossip concerning her husband and one of her best friends.

Constance's sister Martha, for one, is positive that Constance should be told about John and she has come to the Middleton home in Harley Street this morning to be the bearer of the interesting but unhappy tale. She is temporarily deterred, however, by her mother, Mrs. Culver, who is elderly, pleasant and wise. They meet in Constance's drawing-room.

It is Martha's argument that the truth, being the truth, should be told. She is sure that her sister is a very unhappy woman and doubtless greatly in need of confidants.

Their mother, on the other hand, is equally convinced that

Constance is as happy as any woman in her set and likely to remain so if she can be protected from her friends. "She eats well, sleeps well, dresses well and she's losing weight," reports the mother. "No woman can be unhappy in those circumstances."

Furthermore Mrs. Culver has been brought up to believe that men are naturally wicked. "Constance and John have been married for fifteen years," she reminds Martha and Barbara Fawcett, who has joined them. "John is a very agreeable man. I've sometimes wondered whether he was any more faithful to his wife than most husbands, but as it was no concern of mine I didn't let my mind dwell on it."

Marie-Louise Durham, it now appears, is the object of John Middleton's philanderings. Marie-Louise is, according to the women, a pretty thing but a little silly, and Constance's best friend. The younger women are righteously indignant that Constance should be so publicly humiliated. Still, Mrs. Culver repeats, many worse situations might be as easily imagined.

MRS. CULVER—It may be that with advancing years my arteries have hardened. I am unable to attach any great importance to the philanderings of men. I think it's their nature. John is a very hard-working surgeon. If he likes to lunch and dine with a pretty woman now and then I don't think he's much to blame. It must be very tiresome to have three meals a day with the same woman for seven days a week. I'm a little bored myself sometimes at seeing Martha opposite me at the dinner table. And men can't stand boredom as well as women.

MARTHA—I'm sure I'm very much obliged to you, mother.

BARBARA (*significantly*)—But they're not only lunching and dining together.

MRS. CULVER—You fear the worst, my dear?

BARBARA (*with solemnity*)—I know the worst.

MRS. CULVER—I always think that's such a comfort. With closed doors and no one listening to us, so long as a man is kind and civil to his wife, do you blame him very much if he strays occasionally from the narrow path of virtue.

MARTHA—Do you mean to say that you attach no importance to husbands and wives keeping their marriage vows?

MRS. CULVER—I think wives should.

BARBARA—But that's grossly unfair! Why should *they* any more than men?

MRS. CULVER—Because on the whole they like it. We ascribe

a great deal of merit to ourselves because we're faithful to our husbands. I don't believe we deserve it for a minute. We're naturally faithful creatures and we're faithful because we have no particular inclination to be anything else.

BARBARA—I wonder.

MRS. CULVER—My dear, you are a widow and perfectly free. Have you really had any great desire to do anything which the world might say you shouldn't?

BARBARA—I have my business. When you work hard eight hours a day you don't much want to be bothered with love. In the evening the tired business woman wants to go to a musical comedy or play cards. She doesn't want to be worried with adoring males.

MARTHA—By the way, how is your business?

BARBARA—Growing by leaps and bounds. As a matter of fact I came here to-day to ask Constance if she would like to come in with me.

MRS. CULVER—Why should she. John earns plenty of money.

BARBARA—Well, I thought that if things came to a crisis she might like to know that her independence was assured.

MRS. CULVER—Oh, you want them to come to a crisis too.

BARBARA—No, of course I don't. But, you know, they can't go on like this. It's a miracle that Constance hasn't heard yet. She's bound to find out soon.

MRS. CULVER—I suppose it's inevitable.

MARTHA—I hope she'll find out as quickly as possible. I still think it's mother's duty to tell her.

MRS. CULVER—Which I have no intention of doing.

MARTHA—And if mother won't I think I ought.

MRS. CULVER—Which I have no intention of permitting.

The talk has turned to what will happen when Constance does find out, as she inevitably must do, when Constance herself appears. "She is a handsome woman of six and thirty," and she is all apologies for not being there when her callers arrived. She has been shopping with Marie-Louise.

A moment later Marie-Louise pops in. "She is a very pretty little thing, beautifully dressed; of the clinging, large-eyed type."

In the exchange of intimacies Marie-Louise admits that it was because she had been lunching with a beau that she could not go to lunch with Constance. But she refuses, on the advice of Constance, to tell who her beau was. Casually, and with no suspicion of her questioners' implied doubts, Marie-Louise admits that her husband is quite devoted to her and is such a sweet thing that even if he were to see her with a beau it would require more than the evidence of his eyes to persuade him that she was doing anything she shouldn't.

John Middleton is heard arriving below and is brought up. "He is a tall, spare man of about 40," and in a mood of such amiability that he is even ready to pay pretty compliments to his mother-in-law.

His greeting of Marie-Louise is quite formally correct, and he inquires politely as to the whereabouts of her husband. Marie-Louise as formally reports that gentleman as being as incorrigible as usual. She has just been talking with him over the phone and he has told her that he will have to go down to Birmingham for the night. It's such a bore.

Constance promptly invites Marie-Louise to dine with her and John, but Marie-Louise doesn't think she will. She's so tired out. Neither can John be home to dinner. He remembers he has an acute appendix to do.

"You've got a wonderful profession, John," observes the suspicious Martha. "If you ever want to do anything or go anywhere you've only got to say that you've got an operation and no one can prove it's a lie."

"Oh, my dear, you mustn't put suspicions in my innocent head," quickly interposes Constance. "It never would occur to John to be so deceitful. Would it, John?"

"I think I'd have to go an awful long way before I managed to deceive you, darling."

"I sometimes think you might," agrees Constance, with the suggestion of a smile.

Now Martha and Marie-Louise are going, but Marie-Louise must stay a minute while John looks at her knee, if he will. It has been paining her a lot of late. She and John retire to the consulting room for the examination, which again arouses the resentment of Martha.

"What's the matter with her knee?" she demands.

"It slips," calmly reports Constance.

"What happens then?"

"She slips, too."

But Constance refuses to see any reason why she should be jealous of the women her husband sees alone in his consulting room. If they are the kind who want to be made love to with a lively odour of antiseptics about they probably are also the kind that wear horrid undies, and are not at all dangerous.

"They're like little boys—men," muses Constance. "Sometimes, of course, they're rather naughty and you have to pretend to be angry with them. But they're such lambs. They're so irresponsible. They attach so much importance to such entirely unimportant things that it's really touching. And they're so helpless. Have you never nursed a man when he's ill? It wrings your heart. It's just like a dog or a horse. They haven't got the sense to come out of the rain, poor darlings. They have all the charming qualities that accompany general incompetence. They're sweet and good and silly, and tiresome and selfish. You can't help liking them, they're so ingenuous, and so simple. They have no complexity or finesse. I think they're sweet, but it's absurd to take them seriously."

Now Martha and Marie-Louise, with her knee fixed, have gone, and Barbara has made her business proposition. Why won't Constance come in with her and make a name for herself as an interior decorator? Success beckons, and a woman who is economically independent can look at the future with confidence.

But Constance is not interested. John would not be likely to approve, and so long as they are happy she does not care to risk vexing him. She is flattered that Barbara wants her so much she is willing to hold the offer open indefinitely, but for the present she is content.

When they are alone, after Barbara goes, Mrs. Culver tries, discreetly, to win her daughter's confidence.

MRS. CULVER—If at any time anything went wrong with you, you would tell your mother, wouldn't you?

CONSTANCE—Of course.

MRS. CULVER—I hate the thought that you might be unhappy and let a foolish pride prevent you from letting me console and advise you.

CONSTANCE—It wouldn't, mother dear.

MRS. CULVER—I had rather an odd experience the other day. A little friend of mine came to see me and told me that her husband was neglecting her. I asked her why she told me and not her own mother. She said that her mother had never wanted her to marry and it would mortify her now to have to say that she had made a mistake.

CONSTANCE—Oh, well, John never neglects me, mother.

MRS. CULVER—Of course I gave her a good talking to. She didn't get much sympathy from me.

CONSTANCE—That was very unkind, wasn't it?

MRS. CULVER—I have my own ideas about marriage. If a man neglects his wife it's entirely her own fault, and if he's systematically unfaithful to her in nine cases out of ten she only has herself to blame.

CONSTANCE (*ringing the bell*)—Systematically is a grim word.

MRS. CULVER—No sensible woman attaches importance to an occasional slip. Time and chances are responsible for that.

CONSTANCE—And shall we say, masculine vanity?

MRS. CULVER—I told my little friend that if her husband was unfaithful to her it was because he found other women more attractive. Why should she be angry with him for that? Her business was to be more attractive than they.

CONSTANCE—You are not what they call a feminist, are you?

MRS. CULVER—After all, what is fidelity?

CONSTANCE—Mother, do you mind if I open the window?

MRS. CULVER—They are open.

CONSTANCE—In that case do you mind if I shut them? I feel that when a woman of your age asks such a question I should make some sort of symbolic gesture.

MRS. CULVER—Don't be ridiculous. Of course, I believe in fidelity for women. I suppose no one has ever questioned the desirability of that. But men are different. Women should remember that they have their homes and their name and their position and their family and they should learn to close their eyes when it's possible or they may see something they are not meant to.

There is one confidence Constance is willing to share with her mother. She is expecting a caller. His name is Bernard Kersal and she has not seen him for the fifteen years that she has been married.

Surely, Mrs. Culver must remember Bernard Kersal? He was the young man who proposed to Constance most frequently; a tall young man with brown hair and brown eyes who danced divinely. So far as Mrs. Culver can recall, all Constance's young men were tall and brown-eyed and danced divinely.

But Bernard was, Constance insists, a special suitor, and one she very nearly married. Would have married him, she thinks, if he had not been the kind that was much too inclined to lie down on the floor and let her walk over him.

"I was quite certain that he loved me, and I was never absolutely sure that John did," Constance explains.

Now Bernard Kersal, back from Japan, where he has been

located for all the fifteen years he has been away, is in England again and has asked if he might call. Bernard must be nearing 45 now, Constance admits; and certainly he cannot still be in love with her, which Mrs. Culver suggests as at least a possibility.

MRS. CULVER—Have you been corresponding with him?

CONSTANCE—No. One can't write letters to any one one never sees for fifteen years. He always sends me flowers on my birthday.

MRS. CULVER—That's rather sweet of him.

CONSTANCE—And the other day I had a letter from him saying he was in England and would like to see me. So I asked him to come to-day.

MRS. CULVER—I wondered why you were so smart.

CONSTANCE—Of course he may be terribly changed. Men go off so dreadfully, don't they. He may be bald and fat now.

MRS. CULVER—He may be married.

CONSTANCE—Oh, if he were I don't think he'd want to come and see me, would he?

MRS. CULVER—I see you're under the impression that he's still in love with you.

CONSTANCE—Oh, I'm not.

MRS. CULVER—Then why are you so nervous?

CONSTANCE—It's only natural that I shouldn't want him to think me old and haggard. He adored me, mother. I suppose he still thinks of me as I was then. It wouldn't be very nice if his face fell about a yard and a half when he came into the room.

MRS. CULVER—I think I'd much better leave you to face the ordeal alone.

CONSTANCE—Oh, no, mother, you must stay. I particularly want you. You see, he may be awful and I may wish I'd never seen him again. It'll be so much easier if you're here. I may not want to be alone with him at all.

MRS. CULVER—Oh.

CONSTANCE—On the other hand I may.

MRS. CULVER—It seems to me you're getting me in a slightly embarrassing situation.

CONSTANCE—Now listen. If I think he's awful we'll just talk about the weather and the crops for a few minutes and then we'll have an ominous pause and stare at him. That always makes a man feel a perfect fool and the moment a man feels a fool he gets up and goes.

MRS. CULVER—Sometimes they don't know how to, poor dears, and the earth will never open and swallow them up.

CONSTANCE—On the other hand if I think he looks rather nice I shall just take out my handkerchief and carelessly place it on the piano.

MRS. CULVER—Why?

CONSTANCE—Darling, in order that you may rise to your aged feet and say, well, you really must be running along.

MRS. CULVER—Yes, I know that, but why should you carelessly place your handkerchief on the piano?

CONSTANCE—Because I am a creature of impulse. I shall have an impulse to place my handkerchief on the piano.

MRS. CULVER—Oh, very well. But I always mistrust impulses.

The signals do not always work as expected. When Kersal arrives—"a tall, good-looking man, sunburned and of healthy appearance, who carries his 45 years well"—Constance is convinced at sight of him that his call should not be too quickly interrupted. She promptly takes a small handkerchief out of her bag and places it on the piano. But Mrs. Culver does not see it.

The formal greetings over, Constance, who has been giving her mother significant glances without result, produces a second handkerchief and places it beside the first. Still Mrs. Culver finds many things to ask Mr. Kersal about. It is not until a third handkerchief is found and placed in line with the others that mother suddenly remembers what she is to do and, somewhat flustered, recalls a forgotten engagement. She could not think, she hoarsely whispers to Constance in the doorway, whether the handkerchiefs meant that she was to go or to stay.

"You had only to use your eyes," protests Constance. "You can see at a glance that he is the kind of man one would naturally want to have a heart-to-heart talk with after fifteen years." And she hustles Mrs. Culver out of the door.

The Bernard-Constance reunion is entirely happy. She thinks he has changed very little and he thinks her even more lovely than she was as a girl. Ten times more lovely, as a matter of fact. And each confesses some little feeling of trepidation when the meeting was thought of.

Constance is just a little surprised that Bernard has never married, and Bernard is frank to confess that the reason is perfectly simple to him.

"I never wanted to marry any one but you," he says, quite simply.

"Oh, come," she laughs, "you're not going to tell me that you've never been in love since you were in love with me."

"No, I've been in love a half dozen times. But when it came to the point I found I still loved you best."

"I like you for saying that."

She would not have believed him if he had said he had never loved anybody else, and she would have been vexed with him for thinking she would have believed it.

Bernard remembers John Middleton, and is sure Constance was very wise to have married him. Is she happy with him?

She is very happy, Constance reports. Naturally there have been times,—but in the main her marriage has been both happy and successful.

Does John love her? Yes, she is convinced that he does, and that she loves him—very much.

BERNARD—May I make you a short speech?

CONSTANCE—If I may interrupt at suitable moments.

BERNARD—I hope you're going to let me see a great deal of you during this year I've got at home.

CONSTANCE—I want to see a great deal of you.

BERNARD—There's just one thing I want to get off my chest and then I needn't refer to it again. I am just as madly in love with you as I was when I asked you to marry me fifteen years ago. I think I shall remain in love with you all my life. I'm too old a dog to learn new tricks. But I want you to know that you needn't have the smallest fear that I shall make a nuisance of myself. I should think it an awfully caddish thing to try and come between you and John. I suppose we all want to be happy, but I don't believe the best way of being that is to try and upset other people's happiness.

CONSTANCE—That's not such a very long speech after all. At a public dinner they would hardly even call it a few remarks.

BERNARD—All I ask for is your friendship and if in return I care to give you my love I don't see that it's anybody's business but my own.

CONSTANCE—I don't think it is. I think I can be a very good friend, Bernard. (*The door opens and* JOHN *comes in.*)

JOHN—Oh, I'm sorry. I didn't know you were engaged.

CONSTANCE—I'm not. Come in. This is Bernard Kersal.

JOHN—How do you do?

BERNARD—I'm afraid you don't remember me.

JOHN—If you ask me point blank I think it's safer to confess I don't.

CONSTANCE—Don't be so silly, John. He used to come home to mother's.

JOHN—Before we were married, d'you mean?

CONSTANCE—Yes. You spent several week-ends with us together.

JOHN—My dear, that was fifteen years ago. (*To* BERNARD.) I'm awfully sorry not to remember, but I'm delighted to see you now.

CONSTANCE—He's just come back from Japan.

JOHN—Oh, well, I hope we shall see you again. I'm just going along to the club to have a rubber before dinner, darling. (*To* BERNARD.) Why don't you dine here with Constance? I've got an acute appendix and she'll be all alone, poor darling.

BERNARD—Oh, that's awfully kind of you.

CONSTANCE—It would be a friendly act. Are you free?

BERNARD—Always to do a friendly act.

CONSTANCE—Very well. I shall expect you at eight-fifteen. The curtain falls.

## ACT II

A fortnight later Bernard Kersal, who has come to take Constance to the polo games, and Martha Culver meet in Constance's drawing room. Bernard is flourishingly happy and Martha inclined to tease him a little regarding what she assumes to be the obvious cause. That he is desperately in love with Constance is as plain as anything can be, says Martha. And that she is a prying and rude young woman for suggesting any such thing is Bernard's equally fixed conviction.

Constance, he is sure, is in love with John and he with her. Their marriage was a wise marriage. And it is something less than kind for any one to suggest anything to the contrary.

Bernard, Martha retorts, is a good deal of a donkey if he can't see more clearly than that. Practically every one knows that John Middleton has been notoriously unfaithful to Constance for ages.

Bernard both doubts and resents this statement. But Martha is pitiless. Not only is it true, but Marie-Louise is the lady involved, even if she is Constance's best friend. And, so far as Martha is concerned, Marie-Louise's brazen attitude is, in the circumstances, positively maddening. She still wants to tell Con stance what is happening, but her mother won't permit her to.

Martha slips out when she hears Constance coming, leaving Bernard with the shock of her disclosures plainly indicated in his depressed expression. Constance demands to know what is troubling him, but he makes light of the suggestion that anything at all is wrong.

Bernard's anxiety is plain, however, in his eagerness to assure Constance of his hope that she will let him fly to her aid if she were ever to need his counsel or his help. He has been very happy for the fortnight that he has been in London, and even though he has taken great pains to talk to her of quite casual things he does not want her to think it is because he loves her less devotedly than he has confessed. He knows now that he loves her at least ten times more than he ever had before and he is eager that she should know it.

Constance admits that she is pleased and flattered, but a little insistent, too, that he shall hold to his agreement not to make love to her.

BERNARD—I've been very good during the last fortnight, haven't I?

CONSTANCE—Yes. I kept on saying to myself: I wonder if a pat of butter really would melt in his mouth.

BERNARD—Well, just for a minute I'm going to let myself go.

CONSTANCE—I wouldn't if I were you.

BERNARD—Yes, but you're not. I want to tell you just once that I worship the ground you tread on. There's never been any one in the world for me but you.

CONSTANCE—Oh, nonsense. There have been half a dozen We are seven.

BERNARD—Shadows. I love you with all my heart. I admire you more than any woman I've ever met. I respect you. I'm an awful fool when it comes to the point. I don't know how to say all I've got in my heart without feeling like a perfect ass. I love you. I want you to know that if ever you're in trouble I should look upon it as the greatest possible happiness to be allowed to help you.

CONSTANCE—That's very kind of you. I don't see why I should be in any very great trouble.

BERNARD—Always and in all circumstances you can count on me absolutely. I will do anything in the world for you. If ever you want me you have only to give me a sign. I would be proud and happy to give my life for you.

CONSTANCE—It's sweet of you to say so.

BERNARD—Don't you believe it?

CONSTANCE (*with a charming smile*)—Yes.

BERNARD—I should like to think that it meant—oh, not very much, but just a little to you.

CONSTANCE (*almost shaken*)—It means a great deal. I thank you.

BERNARD—Now we won't say anything more about it.

CONSTANCE (*recovering her accustomed coolness*)—But why did you think it necessary to say all this just now?

BERNARD—I wanted to get it off my chest.

CONSTANCE—Oh, really.

BERNARD—You're not angry with me?

CONSTANCE—Oh, Bernard, I'm not that kind of fool at all . . . it's a pity that Martha doesn't marry.

BERNARD—Don't think that I'm going to marry her.

CONSTANCE—I don't. I merely thought that a husband would be a pleasant and useful occupation for her. She's quite a nice girl, you know. A liar, of course, but otherwise all right.

BERNARD—Oh?

CONSTANCE—Yes, a terrible liar even for a woman. . . . Shall we start now? It's no good getting there when the polo is over.

BERNARD—All right. Let's start.

It is while Constance is changing her hat for the ride down to Ranelagh that Marie-Louise arrives. She is plainly flustered, and visibly relieved when Bernard offers to wait for Constance in an adjoining room so Marie-Louise can see John a minute alone. It is quite important, as she knows how John hates being called away from his patients.

What Marie-Louise has to report to John is that she fears that Mortimer, her husband, at last suspects something. Last night Mortimer had appeared for a moment and sat on the edge of her bed while he asked what she had been doing while he was away. She had dined with the Middletons, she told him. Suddenly, and without reason, he had stood up and left the room. Next morning he had not come in to bid Marie-Louise good-by, which was his custom. It all looks very suspicious to Marie-Louise.

John is convinced that she is making a mountain out of a mole hill. Suppose Mortimer were suspicious. There is a devil of a distance between suspicion and proof. She is just over-excited.

Still, Marie-Louise is not greatly cheered. She could probably twist Mortimer around her finger if she had to. Mortimer is fearfully in love with her, and that does give a woman an advantage. But she would simply die of shame if Constance were to know.

John is as sure of Constance. Constance, he says, is a peach, and if he really thought there was anything in Marie-Louise's suspicions he would be in favor of going directly to Constance and making a clean breast of everything. She would kick up a row, probably—any woman would—but she would do anything in the world to help them out.

"A lot you know about women," Marie-Louise answers him. "She'd help you out, I daresay, but she'd stamp on me with both feet. That's only human nature."

"Not Constance's."

"Upon my word, it's lucky I'm fairly sure of you, John, or the way you talk of Constance would really make me jealous."

She smiles as she says it, and he is glad to see she is getting her courage back. Their restored confidence, however, is not for long. Martha and Bernard have come in, Constance is back and ready to start for the polo games and John is about to go back to his patients when the butler brings in the card of Mortimer Durham.

There is something ominous in the fact that Mortimer should suddenly adopt the formality of sending up a card, and Constance is puzzled. She has the foresight to get Marie-Louise on the couch beside her before Mortimer comes in, and covers the wait by being as casual as possible with the others.

"What are you doing here, John?" she demands of her husband. "Haven't you got any patients to-day?"

"Yes, there are two or three waiting," John admits. "I'm just going down. As a matter of fact I thought I deserved a cigarette."

But when John reaches in his pocket for his cigarette case he cannot find it. It has been missing all morning. He is still worried about it when Mortimer enters the room. Mortimer "is a stoutish, biggish man of about 40, with a red face and an irascible manner. At the moment he is prey to violent emotion."

At sight of her husband Marie-Louise starts forward, but Constance quickly seizes her wrist and holds her to her place. "Sit still, you fool!" she whispers. And then, to Mortimer—

"Hello, Mortimer. What are you doing in these parts at this hour? Why on earth did you send up a card?"

Mortimer pauses, looks a little wildly around the room and then faces Constance.

"I thought you might like to know that your husband is my wife's lover!" he says.

CONSTANCE (*keeping a firm hand on* MARIE-LOUISE *and very coolly to Mortimer*)—Oh? What makes you think that?

MORTIMER (*taking a gold cigarette case out of his pocket*)—Do you recognize this? I found it under my wife's pillow last night.

CONSTANCE—Oh, I am relieved. I couldn't make out where I'd left it. (*Taking it from him.*) Thank you so much.

MORTIMER (*angrily*)—It's not yours?

CONSTANCE—Indeed it is. I was sitting on Marie-Louise's bed and I must have slipped it under the pillow without thinking.

MORTIMER—It has John's initials on it.

CONSTANCE—I know. It was presented to him by a grateful patient and I thought it much too nice for him. So I just took it.

MORTIMER—What sort of a fool do you take me for, Constance?

CONSTANCE—My dear Morty, why should I say it was my cigarette case, if it wasn't?

MORTIMER—They had dinner together.

CONSTANCE—My poor Morty, I know that. You were going into a City banquet or something, and Marie-Louise rang up and asked if she might come and take pot-luck with us.

MORTIMER—Do you mean to say she dined here?

CONSTANCE—Isn't that what she told you?

MORTIMER—Yes.

CONSTANCE—It's quite easy to prove. If you won't take my word for it we can ring for the butler and you can ask him yourself. . . . Ring the bell, John, will you?

MORTIMER—No, don't do that. If you give me your word of course I must take it.

CONSTANCE—That's very kind of you. I'm grateful to you for not exposing me to the humiliation of making my butler corroborate my statement.

MORTIMER—If Marie-Louise was dining here, why were you sitting on her bed?

CONSTANCE—John had to go out and do an operation and Marie-Louise wanted to show me the things she'd got from Paris so I walked round to your house. It was a lovely night. You remember that, don't you?

MORTIMER—Damn it, I've got more important things to do than to look at the night.

CONSTANCE—We tried them all on and then we were rather tired, so Marie-Louise got into bed and I sat down and we talked.

MORTIMER—If you were tired, why didn't you go home and go to bed?

CONSTANCE—John had promised to come round and fetch me.

MORTIMER—And did he? At what time did he come?

JOHN—I couldn't manage it. The operation took much longer than I expected. It was one of those cases where when you once start cutting you really don't know where to stop. You know the sort of thing, don't you, Mortimer?

MORTIMER—No, I don't. How the devil should I?

CONSTANCE—All that is neither here nor there. This is a terrible accusation you've made against John and Marie-Louise and I'm very much upset, but I will remain perfectly calm till I've heard everything. Now let me have your proofs.

MORTIMER—My proofs? What d'you mean? The cigarette case. When I found the cigarette case I naturally put two and two together.

CONSTANCE (*with her eyes flashing*)—I quite understand, but why did you make it five?

MORTIMER (*emphatically in order not to show that he is wavering*)—It isn't possible that I should have made a mistake.

CONSTANCE—Even the richest of us may err. I remember when Mr. Pierpont Morgan died he was found to own seven million dollars' worth of worthless securities.

MORTIMER (*uneasily*)—You don't know what a shock it was, Constance. I had the most implicit confidence in Marie-Louise. I was knocked endways. I've been brooding over it ever since till I was afraid I should go mad.

CONSTANCE (*bearding him*)—And do you mean to say that you've come here and made a fearful scene just because you found my cigarette case in Marie-Louise's room? I can't believe it. You're a man of the world and a business man. You're extremely intelligent. Surely you have something to go upon. You must be holding something back. Don't be afraid of hurting my feelings. You've said so much now that I must insist on your saying everything. I want the truth and the whole truth. (*There is a pause.* MORTIMER *looks from* MARIE-LOUISE, *who is quietly weeping, to* CONSTANCE *with the utmost bewilderment.*)

MORTIMER—I'm afraid I've made a damned fool of myself.

CONSTANCE—I'm afraid you have.

Mortimer's humiliation is complete. He apologizes humbly to Constance and to Marie-Louise, but neither is inclined to forgive him out of hand. He had no right to jump to such damnable conclusions. The idea of his thinking Marie-Louise, Constance's best friend, could be guilty of such a violation of that friendship.

"You might have accused me of having an affair with any one else—but not John," protests Marie-Louise.

"Not her greatest friend's husband," echoes Constance. "The milkman or the dustman, if you like, but not her greatest friend's husband!"

"I've been a perfect swine," insists Mortimer.

It will probably be just as well if he leaves Marie-Louise there for a little while, Constance suggests. She is such a sensitive little thing. And, by pantomime, she makes him understand that perhaps if he were to come home with a string of pearls it would greatly help the situation.

There is a notable change in the tenseness of the atmosphere as soon as Mortimer withdraws. John and Marie-Louise are consumed with gratitude for what Constance has done for them, John a little conscious and Marie-Louise tearfully indebted to her friend. Constance accepts their explanations calmly. After all the exposure is not as complete a surprise to her as they think.

"Do you mean to say that you've known all along?" demands Marie-Louise, aghast at the thought.

CONSTANCE—All along, darling. I've been spending the last six months in a desperate effort to prevent my friends and relations from telling me your ghastly secret. It's been very difficult sometimes. Often mother's profound understanding of life, Martha's passion for truth at any price, and Barbara Fawcett's silent sympathy, have almost worn me down. But until to-day the t's were not definitely crossed nor the i's distinctly dotted, and I was able to ignore the facts that were staring at me— rather rudely I must say—in the face.

MARIE-LOUISE—But why, why? It's not human. Why didn't you do anything?

CONSTANCE—That, darling, is my affair.

MARIE-LOUISE (*thinking she understands*)—Oh, I see.

CONSTANCE (*rather tartly*)—No, you don't. I have always been absolutely faithful to John. I have not winked at your intrigue in order to cover my own.

MARIE-LOUISE (*beginning to be a little put out*)—I almost think you've been laughing at me up your sleeve all the time.

CONSTANCE (*good-humoredly*)—Oh, my dear, you mustn't be offended just because I've been taken away from you the satisfaction of thinking that you had been deceiving me all these months. I should hate you to think me capable of an intentional meanness.

MARIE-LOUISE—My head's going round and round.

CONSTANCE—Such a pretty head, too. Why don't you go and lie down? You want to look your best if you're dining with the Vancouvers.

MARIE-LOUISE—I wonder where Mortimer is.

CONSTANCE—You know that pearl necklace you showed me the other day and you said that Mortimer thought it cost a lot of money. Well, he's gone to Cartier's to buy it for you.

MARIE-LOUISE (*excitedly*)—Oh, Constance, do you think he has?

CONSTANCE—I think all men are born with the knowledge that when they have wounded a woman's soul—and our souls are easily wounded—the only cure is a trifling but expensive jewel.

MARIE-LOUISE—Do you think he'll have the sense to bring it home with him so that I can wear it to-night?

CONSTANCE—Oh, my dear, don't be such a fool as to accept it with alacrity. Remember that Mortimer has grievously insulted you, he's made the most shocking accusation that a man can make against his wife, he's trampled on your love and now he's destroyed your trust in him.

MARIE-LOUISE—Oh, how right you are, Constance.

CONSTANCE—Surely I need not tell you what to do. Refuse to speak to him, but never let him get a word of defense in edgeways. Cry enough to make him feel what a brute he is but not enough to make your eyes swell. Say you'll leave him and run sobbing to the door, but take care to let him stop you before you open it. Repeat yourself. Say the same thing over and over again—it wears them down—and if he answers you take no notice, but just say it again. And at last when you've reduced him to desperation, when his head is aching as though it would split, when he's sweating at every pore, when he's harassed and miserable and haggard and broken—then consent as an unmerited favor, as a sign of your forgiving temper and the sweetness of your nature, to accept, no, don't consent, *deign* to accept the pearl necklace for which the wretch has just paid ten thousand pounds.

MARIE-LOUISE (*with peculiar satisfaction*)—Twelve, darling.

CONSTANCE—And don't thank him, that wouldn't be playing the game, let him thank *you* for the favor you do him in allowing him to make you a paltry gift. Have you got your car here?

The tension is not greatly relieved, even with the withdrawal of Marie-Louise. Bernard takes that crestfallen lady to her taxi. This leaves Martha, with many things she would like to say, and Mrs. Culver, whose only advice to Constance is that she do nothing hastily.

As for John, he is quite properly humiliated and ready, as he assures Constance, to take whatever is coming to him.

"I'm expecting you to make a scene, Constance," he says, humbly. "It's your right and your privilege. I'm willing to bear it. Give me hell! I deserve it! Drag me up and down the room by the hair of the head. Kick me in the face. Stamp on me. I'll grovel. I'll eat the dust. My name is mud. Mud!"

But Constance sees no excuse for a scene. Of course her mother and her sister may think what they like. That John's conduct has been outrageous; that he has humiliated her before all her friends, and that the least she can do is to divorce him. Certainly, they insist, he is no fit person to be the father of his daughter. All of which John ruefully admits.

But John has been an excellent father, Constance insists, and for some reason she does not feel the least bit bitter toward him.

"When I look into my heart," she says, "I can't find a trace of resentment, except perhaps for John's being so stupid as to let himself be found out."

What puzzles Mrs. Culver is that Constance had not taken some action the minute she discovered that her husband was having an affair. Again Constance repeats that she had no such impulse. What John did actually seems to her to be none of her business. In fact she considers that she and John have enjoyed that rare experience, an ideal marriage.

"For five years we adored each other," she explains. "That's much longer than most people do. Our honeymoon lasted five years and then we had a most extraordinary stroke of luck. We ceased to be in love with each other simultaneously."

John would deny this, and yet finds himself unable to make the denial sound reasonable. Constance has been a perfect wife to him, he asserts, and there is no other woman whose society he enjoys as much as he does hers.

True, as she insists, his heart does not leap into his mouth when he hears his wife's footsteps on the stairs, and when she comes into the room he has no impulse to catch her in his manly arms. Naturally, he doesn't want to make a fool of himself.

And that, Constance concludes, is a complete answer to her question. He is no more in love with her than she is with him.

John is still worried and puzzled at his wife's attitude. When did she come upon this discovery that he no longer loved her?

CONSTANCE—I'll tell you. One night as we were dancing together all at once I noticed that we weren't keeping such good step as we generally did. It was because my mind was wandering. I was thinking how it would suit me to do my hair like a woman who was dancing alongside of us. Then I looked at you and I saw you were thinking what pretty legs she'd got. I suddenly realized that you weren't in love with me any more and at the same moment I realized that it was a relief because I wasn't in love with you.

JOHN—I must say, it never occurred to me for a moment.

CONSTANCE—I know, a man thinks it quite natural that he should fall out of love with a woman, but it never strikes him that a woman can do anything so unnatural as to fall out of love with him. Don't be upset at that, darling, that is one of the charming limitations of your sex.

MARTHA—Do you mean mother and me to understand that since then John has been having one affair after another and you haven't turned a hair?

CONSTANCE—Since this is the first time he's been found out, let us give him the benefit of the doubt and hope that till now he has never strayed from the strict and narrow path. You're not angry with me, John?

JOHN—No, darling, not angry. But I *am* a little taken aback. I think you've been making rather a damned fool of me. It never struck me that your feelings for me had changed so much. You can't expect me to like it.

CONSTANCE—Oh, come now, you must be reasonable. You surely wouldn't wish me to have languished for all these years in a hopeless passion for you when you had nothing to give me in return but friendship and affection. Think what a bore it is to have some one in love with you whom you're not in love with.

JOHN—I can't conceive of your ever being a bore, Constance.

CONSTANCE (*kissing her hand to him*)—Don't you realize that we must thank our lucky stars? We are the favored of the gods. I shall never forget those five years of exquisite happiness you gave me when I loved you, and I shall never cease to be grateful to you, not because you loved me, but because you inspired love in me. Our love never degenerated into weariness. Because we ceased loving one another at the very same moment we never had to put up with quarrels and reproaches, recriminations and all the other paraphernalia of a passion which has ceased on one side and is still alive and eager on the other. Our love was like a cross-word puzzle in which we both hit upon the last word at the same instant. That is why our lives since then have been so happy, that is why ours is a perfect marriage.

MARTHA—Do you mean to say that it meant nothing to you when you found out that John was carrying on with Marie-Louise?

CONSTANCE—Human nature is very imperfect. I'm afraid I must admit that at the first moment I was vexed. But only at the first moment. Then I reflected that it was most unreasonable to be angry with John for giving to another something that I had no use for. That would be too much like a dog in the manger. And then I was fond enough of John to be willing that he should be happy in his own way. And if he was going to indulge in an intrigue . . . isn't that the proper phrase, John?

JOHN—I have not yet made up my mind whether it really is an indulgence.

CONSTANCE—Then it was much better that the object of his affections should be so intimate a friend of mine that I could keep a maternal eye on him.

JOHN—Really, Constance.

CONSTANCE—Marie-Louise is very pretty so that my self-esteem was not offended and so rich that it was certain John would have no reason to squander money on her to the inconvenience of myself. She's not clever enough to acquire any ascendancy over him, and so long as I kept his heart I was quite willing that she should have his senses. If you wanted to deceive me, John, I couldn't have chosen any one with whom I would more willingly be deceived than Marie-Louise.

JOHN—I don't gather that you have been very grossly deceived, darling. You have such penetration that when you look at me I feel as though I were shivering without a stitch of clothing on.

They are all quite mystified by Constance's attitude. Her mother still feels that she should do some of the things deceived wives always have done. Her sister Martha finds it almost past belief that she is not even going to divorce John. And John himself, humble, contrite, hopeful of forgiveness and willing to make all the expected promises as to his future conduct, can't understand what really is expected of him. What more can he do? He is willing to give his wife his word of honor— But even that makes but light appeal to Constance.

"That," she interrupts him, "is the only gift you can make me for which I can find no use. You see, so long as I was able to pretend a blissful ignorance of your goings on we could all be perfectly happy. You were enjoying yourself and I received a lot of sympathy as the outraged wife. But now I do see that the position is very difficult. You have put me in a position which is neither elegant nor dignified."

At one decision, however, Constance has definitely arrived. She will accept Barbara's business offer. Nor will she listen to John's protest that she is welcome to all he has, or her mother's insistence that she is silly.

She is tired of being a modern wife and she wants to stand on her own. That she is up to some deviltry; that she at least is thinking many more things than she is saying, Mrs. Culver is positive, but it does no good to question her.

Now Bernard Kersal is back, after having taken Marie-Louise home, and Mrs. Culver and Martha happily recall that they have other things to do.

Alone with Constance Bernard has an opportunity of relieving his overweighted chest of many conclusions. He has been terribly distressed by all he has seen and heard, but it has greatly increased his admiration for Constance, if that were possible. Now, at least, there is some reason for his repeating the statement of his adoration and his eagerness to do anything and everything he can do to make up to her for the unhappiness she has gone through. If things were different he would not think of breaking his agreement, but under the circumstances he feels free to urge her to come to him and cease wasting her life with a man she does not love and who does not love her. Won't she marry him?

Constance is grateful, but still of no mind at the moment to make a change. Furthermore she is not entirely convinced that John has treated her so very badly.

"My dear Bernard," she says, "have you ever considered what marriage is among well-to-do people? In the working classes a woman cooks her husband's dinner, washes for him and darns his socks. She looks after the children and makes their clothes. She gives good value for the money she costs. But what is a wife in our class? Her house is managed by servants, nurses look after her children, if she has resigned herself to having any, and as soon as they are old enough she packs them off to school. Let us face it: she is no more than the mistress of a man of whose desire she has taken advantage to insist on a legal ceremony which will prevent him from discarding her when his desire has ceased."

"She's also his companion and his helpmate," protests Bernard.

"My dear, any sensible man would sooner play bridge at his club than with his wife, and he'd always rather play golf with a man than with a woman. A paid secretary is a better helpmate than a loving spouse. When all is said and done the modern wife is nothing but a parasite."

Bernard insists that Constance is wrong, but she will not admit it. He is in love, she says, and his judgment is confused. John has really done pretty well by her. He has given her board and lodging, clothes and amusement, as well as a position in the world, merely because fifteen years before he fell under the spell of his desire for her. He paid a pretty high price then for something that he couldn't get cheaper. It doesn't seem altogether fair that he should go on paying, now that he is no longer conscious of that desire.

BERNARD—That might be all right if a man had only to think of himself. What about the woman?

CONSTANCE—I don't think you need waste too much sypmathy on her. Like ninety girls out of a hundred when I married I looked upon it as the only easy, honorable and lucrative calling open to me. When the average woman who has been married for fifteen years discovers her husband's infidelity it is not her heart that is wounded but her vanity. If she had any sense, she would regard it merely as one of the necessary inconveniences of an otherwise pleasant profession.

BERNARD—Then the long and short of it is that you don't love me.

CONSTANCE—You think that my principles are all moonshine?

BERNARD—I don't think they would have much influence if you were as crazy about me as I am about you. Do you still love John?

CONSTANCE—I'm very fond of him, he makes me laugh, and we get on together like a house on fire, but I'm not in love with him.

BERNARD—And is that enough for you? Isn't the future sometimes a trifle desolate? Don't you want love? (*A pause. She gives him a long reflective look.*)

CONSTANCE (*charmingly*)—If I did I should come to you for it, Bernard.

BERNARD—Constance, what do you mean? Is it possible that you could ever care for me? Oh, my darling, I worship the ground you tread on. (*He seizes her in his arms and kisses her passionately.*)

CONSTANCE (*releasing herself*)—Oh, my dear, don't be so sudden. I should despise myself if I were unfaithful to John so long as I am entirely dependent on him.

BERNARD—But if you love me?

CONSTANCE—I never said I did. But even if I did so long as John provides me with all the necessities of existence I wouldn't be unfaithful. It all comes down to the economic situation. He has bought my fidelity and I should be worse than a harlot if I took the price he paid and did not deliver the goods.

BERNARD—Do you mean to say there's no hope for me at all?

CONSTANCE—The only hope before you at the moment is to arrive at Ranelagh before the game is over if we start this very minute.

BERNARD—Do you still want to go?

CONSTANCE—Yes.

BERNARD—Very well. I love you.

CONSTANCE—Then go down and start up the car, put a spot of oil in the radiator or something, and I'll join you in a minute. I want to telephone.

BERNARD—Very well. (*He goes out.* CONSTANCE *takes up the telephone.*)

CONSTANCE—Mayfair, 2646. . . . Barbara. It's Constance. That offer you made me a fortnight ago—is it still open? Well, I want to accept it. . . . No, no, nothing has happened. John is very well. He's always sweet, you know. It's only that I want to earn my own living. When can I start? The sooner the better.

The curtain falls.

## ACT III

It is a year later, and the day on which Constance is planning to start on a holiday. Barbara Fawcett and Martha are in to say good-by to her, much interested in her plans and a little curious about them.

It has been a happy year for Constance. She has made a great success of her business venture with Barbara and now, something accomplished, something done, she is eager for her six weeks of freedom. She refuses point blank to do any shopping for Barbara, or for the business, or to give so much as a thought to houses and furnishings all the time she is away.

Martha is impressed with the great good spirits of her sister, and has some little hesitancy about suppressing them—but Martha has just met Marie-Louise Durham in Bond Street, and she thinks Constance should know about it. Marie-Louise has been away for a year, traveling with her husband.

Constance is not at all surprised. As a matter of fact she has just been talking with Marie-Louise over the phone and is waiting now for her call. It will be their only chance of seeing each other before Constance leaves.

It may be all right with Constance, but Martha counts it as at least unfortunate that she should be starting a six weeks' holiday, with John staying home, just as Marie-Louise is back from her trip. She also considers it rather a pity that John can't get away to go with Constance.

But Martha must do her worrying alone, because Constance is quite satisfied with such arrangements as she has made. She is confident they will all work out beautifully. She wants to go to Italy because she likes Italy, and John doesn't.

And yet John, who appears shortly, intimates that he would have been perfectly willing to go anywhere Constance cared to go if she had given him any encouragement.

Constance doesn't believe much in husbands and wives taking their holidays together. The only good of a holiday is to get rest, change and recreation.

"I know nothing more depressing," she insists, "than the sight of all those couples in a hotel dining room, one little couple to one little table, sitting opposite to one another without a word to say. Sometimes the woman, with her greater social sense, after racking her brains for five minutes, utters a remark, and the man says yes or no and then they fall again into a dreary silence."

John also has heard of Marie-Louise's return and he wants Constance to feel perfectly satisfied that that affair is not going to be resumed. He never could do a thing like that. Of course he realizes that Marie-Louise is madly in love with him, and he doesn't want to be unkind, but he is determined that the old relations shall not be resumed, both on Constance's account and because—well, if the truth must be told, John is a little fed up with Marie-Louise. He would like awfully to have it definitely understood between them that their more intimate friendship is a thing of the past. And he is anxious that Constance should take on the job of telling Marie-Louise so. It isn't the sort of thing a man can tell a woman.

"Women are funny," John has discovered. "When they're tired of you they tell you so without a moment's hesitation and if you don't like it you can lump it. But if you're tired of them you're a brute and a beast and boiling oil's too good for you."

Constance agrees to tell Marie-Louise the worst. John is greatly relieved. Certainly no man ever had a better wife than Constance. She is, he agrees, a ripper.

Curiously, Marie-Louise, bustling in full of news and charged with affection for Constance, is in much the same frame of mind as John. No sooner has that embarrassed and unhappy man left than she confesses the completeness of her change of heart toward him. She has, among other things, come to assure Constance that she need have no further fear so far as her husband is concerned. Marie-Louise has had a wonderful trip, Mortimer has been an angel and bought her some of the most wonderful things, and now she is ready to make all possible amends for her former misdeeds. She owes so much to Constance she is ever and ever so grateful. Of course she realizes John is madly in love with her, and for that reason she thinks it best that he be told at once what to expect and what not to expect.

CONSTANCE—This is very sudden. I'm afraid it'll be an awful shock to John.

MARIE-LOUISE—I've quite made up my mind.

CONSTANCE—There isn't much time for a very long and moving scene, but I'll see if John is in still. Could you manage it in ten minutes?

MARIE-LOUISE—Oh, but *I* can't see him. I want you to tell him.

CONSTANCE—Me!

MARIE-LOUISE—You know him so well, you know just the sort of things to say to him. It's not very nice telling a man who adores you that you don't care for him in that way any more. It's so much easier for a third party.

CONSTANCE—Do you really think so?

MARIE-LOUISE—I'm positive of it. You see, you can say that for your sake I've made up my mind that from now on we can be nothing but friends. You've been so wonderful to both of us, it would be dreadful if we didn't play the game now. Say that I shall always think of him tenderly and that he's the only man I've really loved but that we must part.

CONSTANCE—But if he insists on seeing you?

MARIE-LOUISE—It's no good, Constance, I can't see him. I shall only cry and get my eyes all bunged up. You will do it for me, darling. Please.

CONSTANCE—I will. . . . Now tell me the real reason why you're so determined to get rid of John without a moment's delay. (MARIE-LOUISE *looks at her and gives a little roguish smile.*)

MARIE-LOUISE—Swear you won't tell.

CONSTANCE—On my honor.

MARIE-LOUISE—Well, my dear, we met a perfectly divine young man in India. He was A.D.C. to one of the governors and he came home on the same boat with us. He simply adores me.

CONSTANCE—And of course you adore him.

MARIE-LOUISE—My dear, I'm absolutely mad about him. I don't know what's going to happen.

CONSTANCE—I think we can both give a pretty shrewd guess.

MARIE-LOUISE—It's simply awful to have a temperament like mine. Of course you can't understand, you're cold.

CONSTANCE (*very calmly*)—You're an immoral little beast, Marie-Louise.

MARIE-LOUISE—Oh, I'm not. I have affairs—but, I'm not promiscuous.

CONSTANCE—I should respect you more if you were an honest prostitute. She at least does what she does to earn her bread ana butter. You take everything from your husband and give him nothing that he pays for. You are no better than a vulgar cheat.

MARIE-LOUISE (*surprised and really hurt*)—Constance, how can you say such things to me? I think it's terribly unkind of you! I thought you liked me.

CONSTANCE—I do. I think you are a liar, a humbug and a parasite, but I like you.

MARIE-LOUISE—You can't if you think such dreadful things about me.

CONSTANCE—I do. You're good-tempered and generous and sometimes amusing. I even have a certain affection for you.

MARIE-LOUISE (*smiling*)—I don't believe you mean a word you say. You know how devoted I am to you.

CONSTANCE—I take people as they are and I daresay that in another twenty years you'll be the pink of propriety.

MARIE-LOUISE—Darling, I knew you didn't mean it, but you will have your little joke.

CONSTANCE—Now run along, darling, and I'll break the news to John.

MARIE-LOUISE—Well, good-by and be gentle with him. There is no reason why we shouldn't spare him as much as possible. (*Turns to go and at door stops.*) Of course I've often wondered why with your looks you don't have more success than you do. I know now.

CONSTANCE—Tell me.

MARIE-LOUISE—You see—you're a humorist and that always puts men off.

John is greatly relieved when Constance tells him that Marie-Louise has accepted the situation as it stands. He is a bit surprised that she did not make more of a fuss, and he agrees with Constance that later, probably, when she realizes the full extent of her loss Marie-Louise is likely to cry like anything. However, that's over and John is happy to think that now Constance can set off on her holiday with a perfectly easy mind. Which reminds him that he has not yet given her a check.

Constance does not need money. She has plenty of her own. Her year's work with Barbara has netted her fourteen hundred pounds. Two hundred she is taking with her, and two hundred she has spent on clothes and the preparations for her trip. The remaining thousand she has paid into John's account at the bank, and she wishes him to accept it in payment for her board and lodging during the last twelve months.

That, to John, is all nonsense. He is perfectly able to support her in her proper station, and for her to offer to pay him is almost insulting. Doesn't she love him any more?

Constance feels that it is an insult that he probably can bring himself to swallow. And what has love to do with it? Does he think a woman can only love a man if he keeps her? No, she feels that she is no longer of much value to him as wife or housekeeper. He has not been less comfortable since she has been in business than he was before, proving that his home is quite competently run by the servants. Blink the matter as they may, the fact remains that she had become in his house little more than a parasite.

"You are the mother of my child," he reminds her.

"Let us not exaggerate the importance of that," she calmly answers him. "I performed a natural and healthy function of my sex. And all the tiresome part of looking after the child when she was once born I placed in the hands of much more competent persons. Let us face it, I was merely a parasite in your house. You had entered into legal obligations which prevented you from turning me adrift, but I owe you a debt of gratitude for never letting me see by word or gesture that I was no more than a costly and at times inconvenient ornament."

JOHN—I never looked upon you as an inconvenient ornament. And I don't know what you mean by being a parasite. Have I ever in any way suggested that I grudged a penny that I spent on you?

CONSTANCE (*with mock amazement*)—Do you mean to say that I ascribed to your beautiful manners what was only due to your stupidity? Are you as great a fool as the average man who falls for the average woman's stupendous bluff that just because he's married her he must provide for her wants and her luxuries, sacrifice his pleasure and comfort and convenience, and that he must look upon it as a privilege that she allows him to be her slave and bondman? Come, come, John, pull yourself together. You're a hundred years behind the times. Now that women have broken down the walls of the harem they must take the rough and tumble of the street.

JOHN—You forget all sorts of things. Don't you think a man may have gratitude to a woman for the love he has had for her in the past?

CONSTANCE—I think gratitude is often very strong in men so long as it demands from them no particular sacrifice.

JOHN—Well, it's a curious way of looking at things, but obviously I have reason to be thankful for it. But after all you knew what was going on long before it all came out. What happened then that made you make up your mind to go into business?

CONSTANCE—I am naturally a lazy woman. So long as appearances were saved I was prepared to take all I could get and give nothing in return. I was a parasite, but I knew it. But when we reached a situation where only your politeness or your lack of intelligence prevented you from throwing the fact in my teeth I changed my mind. I thought that I should very much like to be in a position where, if I felt inclined to, I could tell you, with calm courtesy, but with determination,—to go to hell.

JOHN—And are you in that position now?

CONSTANCE—Precisely. I owe you nothing. I am able to keep myself. For the last year I have paid my way. There is only one freedom that is really important and that is economic freedom, for in the long run, the man who pays the piper calls the tune. Well, I have that freedom and upon my soul it's the most enjoyable sensation I can remember since I ate my first strawberry ice.

JOHN—You know, I would sooner you had made me scenes for a month on end like any ordinary woman and nagged my life out than that you should harbour this cold rancour against me.

CONSTANCE—My poor darling, what are you talking about? Have you known me for fifteen years and do you think me capable of the *commonness* of insincerity? I harbour no rancour. Why, my dear, I'm devoted to you.

JOHN—Do you mean to tell me that you've done all this without any intention of making me feel a perfect swine?

CONSTANCE—On my honour. If I look in my heart I can only find in it affection for you and the most kindly and charitable feelings. Don't you believe me? (*He looks at her for a moment and then makes a little gesture of bewilderment.*)

JOHN—Yes, oddly enough, I do. You are a remarkable woman, Constance.

CONSTANCE—I know, but keep it to yourself. You don't want to give a dog a bad name.

And then, to John's further amazement, he discovers the details of Constance's plan for a holiday. She is not, as he has feared, to be subjected to the inconveniences of travelling alone. Bernard Kersal is going with her! Bernard and no one else!

Of course they have taken the ordinary precautions to lessen as much as possible the spread of gossip. They have told no one and they plan to visit only the less frequented places. Otherwise they will have to take their chances of being seen.

And, of course, they will travel as man and wife!

JOHN—Don't be a fool, Constance. You don't know what you're talking about. That's not funny at all.

CONSTANCE—But, my poor John, whom do you take us for? Am I so unattractive that what I'm telling you is incredible?

Why else should I go with Bernard? If I merely wanted a companion I'd go with a woman. We could have headaches together and have our hair washed at the same place and copy one another's night-dresses. A woman's a much better travelling companion than a man.

JOHN—I may be very stupid, but I don't seem able to understand what you're saying. Do you really mean me to believe that Bernard Kersal is your lover?

CONSTANCE—Certainly not.

JOHN—Then what *are* you talking about?

CONSTANCE—My dear, I can't put it any plainer. I'm going away for six weeks' holiday and Bernard has very kindly offered to come with me.

JOHN—And where do I come in?

CONSTANCE—You don't come in. You stay at home and look after your patients.

JOHN (*trying his very best to control himself*)—I flatter myself I'm a sensible man. I'm not going to fly into a passion. Many men would stamp and rave or break the furniture; I have no intention of being melodramatic, but you must allow me to say that what you've just told me is very surprising.

CONSTANCE—Just for a moment, perhaps, but I'm sure that you have only to familiarize yourself with the notion in order to become reconciled to it.

JOHN—I'm doubtful whether I shall have time to do that, for I feel uncommonly as though I were about to have an apoplectic stroke.

CONSTANCE—Undo your collar then. Now I come to look at you I confess that you are more than usually red in the face.

JOHN—What makes you think that I'm going to allow you to go?

CONSTANCE (*good-humouredly*)—Chiefly the fact that you can't possibly prevent me.

JOHN—I can't bring myself to believe that you mean what you say. I don't know whatever put such an idea into your head.

CONSTANCE (*casually*)—I thought a change might do me good.

JOHN—Nonsense.

CONSTANCE—Why? You did. Don't you remember? You were getting rather flat and stale. Then you had an affair with Marie-Louise and you were quite another man. Gay and amusing, full of life, and much more agreeable to live with. The moral effect on you was quite remarkable.

JOHN—It's different for a man than for a woman.

Constance—Are you thinking of the possible consequences? We have long passed the Victorian Era when asterisks were followed after a certain interval by a baby.

John—That never occurred to me. What I meant was that if a man's unfaithful to his wife she's an object of sympathy, whereas if a woman's unfaithful to her husband he's merely an object of ridicule.

Constance—That is one of those unconventional prejudices which sensible people must strive to ignore.

John—Do you expect me to sit still and let this man take my wife away from me under my very nose? I wonder you don't ask me to shake hands with him and wish him good luck.

Constance—That's just what I am going to do. He's coming here in a few minutes to say good-by to you.

John—I shall knock him down.

Constance—I wouldn't take any risks in your place. He's pretty hefty and I'm under the impression that he's very nippy with his left.

John—I shall have great pleasure in telling him exactly what I think of him.

Constance—Why? Have you forgotten that I was charming to Marie-Louise? We were the best of friends. She never bought a hat without asking me to go and help her choose it.

John—I have red blood in my veins.

Constance—I'm concerned at the moment with the gray matter in your brain.

Mrs. Culver arriving just after John, in impotent rage, has smashed a blue and white vase, is equally excited, and similarly helpless in dealing with Constance. For one thing she cannot admit that because John had an affair with Marie-Louise it gives Constance any excuse for indulging herself in a similar adventure with Bernard Kersal.

"The circumstances," she points out, "are entirely different. It was very naughty of John to deceive you, but he's sorry for what he did and he's been punished for it. It was all very dreadful and caused us a great deal of pain. But a man's a man and you expect that kind of thing from him. There are excuses for him. There are none for a woman. Men are naturally polygamous and sensible women have always made allowances for their occasional lapse from a condition which modern civilization has forced on them. Women are monogamous. They do not naturally desire more than one man and that is why the common sense of the world has heaped obloquy upon them when they have overstepped the natural limitations of their sex."

"It seems rather hard that what is sauce for the gander shouldn't also be sauce for the goose."

"We all know that unchastity has no moral effect on men," answers Mrs. Culver. "They can be perfectly promiscuous and remain upright, industrious, and reliable. It's quite different with women. It ruins their character. They become untruthful and dissipated, lazy, shifty and dishonest. That is why the experience of ten thousand years has demanded chastity in women. It has learnt that this virtue is the key to all the others."

"They were dishonest," ventures Constance, "because they were giving away something which wasn't theirs to give. They had sold themselves for board, lodging and protection. They were chattels. They were dependent on their husbands and when they were unfaithful to them they were liars and thieves. I'm not dependent on John. I am economically independent and therefore I claim my sexual independence. I have this afternoon paid into John's account one thousand pounds for my year's keep."

"I refuse to take it," speaks up John.

"Well, you'll damned well have to."

Constance does not pretend to be in love with Bernard. She doesn't exactly know whether she is or not. She is mightily grateful to him and rather touched by his fifteen years' devotion to her, and she hopes in some small way to repay him for that devotion. In six weeks Bernard is going back to Japan.

"I came to the conclusion," she confesses to them quite frankly, "that it must be now or never, and so I asked him if he'd like me to spend these last six weeks with him in Italy. When I wave my handkerchief to him as the ship that takes him sails out of the harbour at Naples I hope that he will feel that all those years of unselfish love have been well worth the while."

"Six weeks? Do you intend to leave him at the end of six weeks?" demands John.

"Oh, yes, of course," replies Constance, sweetly. "It's because I'm putting a limit to our love that I think it may achieve the perfection of something which is beautiful and transitory."

Now Bernard is announced and Mrs. Culver is taking her departure, a saddened mother, but wisely philosophical. "I don't approve of you, Constance," she says in farewell to her daughter, "and I can't pretend that I do. No good will come of it. Men were meant by nature to be wicked and delightful and de-

ceive their wives, and women were meant to be virtuous and
forgiving and to suffer verbosely. That was ordained from all
eternity and none of your new-fangled notions can alter the de-
crees of Providence."

Bernard's greeting is impressively formal and his chatter
discreetly chosen to deceive the most trusting husband. He is,
apparently, in complete ignorance of Constance's plans and eager
in inquiry concerning them. His disappointment that he will not
be able to see her again is almost intense. He might drop in
frequently on John while she is away, suggests Constance, the
shadow of a threatening grin playing about the corners of her
mouth. John is likely to be a little lonesome.

But Bernard cannot do that, unfortunately. He also has been
ordered away by his doctor. He must, he finds, devote the rest
of his stay in Europe to a cure. And so he will have to say
good-by.

By the time Bernard has left Constance is hysterical with
laughter and John again apoplectic with rage. Bernard, insists
John, is little if any better than a drivelling idiot. Not particularly good looking, not any too well tailored, certainly no more
amusing than he is himself. All of which Constance admits as
true. Then, John demands, in heaven's name, why does she
want to go away with him?

"Shall I tell you?" she asks. And answers: "Once more before it is too late I want to feel about me the arms of a man
who adores the ground I walk on. I want to see his face light
up when I enter the room. I want to feel the pressure of his
hand when we look at the moon together and the pleasantly
tickling sensation when his arm tremulously steals round my
waist. I want to let my head fall on his shoulder and feel his
lips softly touch my hair. I want to walk along country lanes
holding hands and I want to be called by absurd pet names. I
want to talk baby talk by the hour together."

Eagerly John makes his last bid. Let her give up Bernard as
he had given up Marie-Louise; let them go away on a second
honeymoon of their own; let him prove to her again that he
can be a lover as well as a husband. But Constance is not impressed.

JOHN—You know what you're doing. I was determined in
future to be a model husband and you're driving me right into
the arms of Marie-Louise. I give you my word of honour that

the moment you leave this house I shall drive straight to her door.

CONSTANCE—I should hate you to have a fruitless journey. I'm afraid you won't find her at home. She has a new young man and she says he's too divine.

JOHN—What!

CONSTANCE—He's the A.D.C. of a Colonial governor. She came here to-day to ask me to break the news to you that henceforth everything was over between you.

JOHN—I hope you told her first that I was firmly resolved to terminate a connection which could only cause you pain.

CONSTANCE—I couldn't. She was in such a blooming hurry to give me her message.

JOHN—Really, Constance, for your own pride I should have thought you wouldn't like her to make a perfect fool of me. Any other woman would have said: "What a strange coincidence, why, it's only an hour since John told me he had made up his mind never to see you again." But of course you don't care two straws for me any more, that's quite evident.

CONSTANCE—Oh, don't be unjust, darling. I shall always care for you. I may be unfaithful, but I am constant. I always think that's my most endearing quality. (*The butler opens the door.*)

JOHN (*irritably*)—What is it?

BENTLEY—I thought madam had forgotten that the taxi was at the door.

JOHN—Go to hell.

BENTLEY—Very good, sir. (*He goes out.*)

CONSTANCE—I don't see why you should be rude to him. Bernard will pay the taxi! Anyhow I must go now or he'll begin to think I'm not coming. Good-by, darling. I hope you'll get on all right in my absence. Just give the cook her head and you'll have no trouble. Won't you say good-by to me?

JOHN—Go to the devil!

CONSTANCE—All right. I shall be back in six weeks.

JOHN—Back? Where?

CONSTANCE—Here.

JOHN—Here? Here? Do you think I'm going to take you back?

CONSTANCE—I don't see why not. When you've had time to reflect you'll realize that you have no reason to blame me. After all, I'm taking from you nothing that you want.

JOHN—Are you aware that I can divorce you for this?

CONSTANCE—Quite. But I married very prudently. I took the precaution to marry a gentleman and I know that you could never bring yourself to divorce me for doing no more than you did yourself.

JOHN—I wouldn't divorce you. I wouldn't expose my worst enemy to the risk of marrying a woman who's capable of treating her husband as you're treating me.

CONSTANCE (*at the door*)—Well, then, shall I come back? (*He hesitates a moment.*)

JOHN—You are the most maddening, wilful, capricious, wrong-headed, delightful and enchanting woman man was ever cursed with having for a wife. Yes, damn you, come back! (CONSTANCE *lightly kisses her hand to him and slips out slamming the door behind her.*)

The curtain falls.

# THE ROAD TO ROME

## Comedy in Three Acts

### By Robert Emmet Sherwood

THE theatre season had covered half its length before "The Road to Rome" came to Broadway. The Sherwood comedy, lightly touched with satire, had been tried in both Washington and Newark, and though the reports from these minor centers were promising they were accompanied by certain reservations and a wise shaking of certain heads. It was a bold comedy, reported the out-of-town conservatives, and defiant of many of the theatre's conventions. Its best chance of success lay in the fact that Jane Cowl was playing the heroine.

As it turned out "The Road to Rome," produced January 31, 1927, at The Playhouse, proved to be exactly the type of entertainment for which Broadway is most willing to make the speculator sacrifice and pay double fees. It is sufficiently plain in speech and implication to excite the slyly expectant play follower, and sufficiently intelligent to flatter his choice. Like that other happy compromise of this pro-censorship season, "The Play's the Thing," Mr. Sherwood's quasi-historical romance could be depended upon to both startle and amuse visitors from the West. With their support added to that of the intellectually adult residents of Manhattan it ran far into the summer.

Following the course charted twenty years ago by Bernard Shaw with his "Cæsar and Cleopatra" and successfully adapted to the novel form recently adopted by Professor Erskine with "The Private Life of Helen of Troy" and "Galahad," Mr. Sherwood has skillfully woven an imaginative romance into a semi-historical background.

History records that Hannibal turned back from the very gates of Rome after he had marched 3,000 miles through fire and flood to lay the city low. Why? Mr. Sherwood's guess is that he had a reason particularly his own, and this guess serves as the motivating inspiration of his comedy.

The opening scene is the courtyard of Fabius Maximus in

Rome. The time is just before sunset on a June evening in 216 B.C.

"The house, which surrounds the courtyard on all three sides, is one story in height," records the author. "It is simple and unostentatious in design, being representative of Rome in the period of the Republic, when the sterner virtues of economy and almost Spartan frugality were practised."

There is a gaily painted awning stretched over the fore part of the garden, and looking between the columns at the rear an expansive view of the blue Italian sky is visible above the rear wall of the house.

Varius and Meta, slaves to Maximus, are laying the table for the evening meal. "He is a fair young man, obviously not a Latin, with the air of one who has known better circumstances than these," and she is "a slim, lovely young girl."

Varius and Meta are frankly in love with each other and Varius is of a mind to attempt an escape, though Meta discourages him. The chances against the success of such an attempt are much too great, she protests, and failure means death. It is impossible now for them to think of escaping from Rome. Rome is everywhere. Rome is about to corner the last of her active enemies, Hannibal and his army of Carthaginians, and once they are out of the way Rome will be the whole world.

Besides, Meta could not think of deserting her mistress, who is also bored to death in Rome and still cannot herself escape. The slave girl is trying dutifully to make Varius content with his lot and to reassure him of her own love and loyalty when Fabia comes suddenly upon them, embraced.

"Fabia is the mother of Fabius—a cross, narrow-minded old lady whose world is her home. For all her 73 years she is brisk and vigorous and rules the establishment with an iron hand."

Fabia is much shocked to find the young people thus occupied. Their behavior is at least shocking, and they should know that love-making among the slaves is strictly forbidden.

Now Fabius Maximus, the head of the house, is home from the senate. "Fabius is a typical senator—pompous, unctuous, consciously important and 100 per cent. Roman. His most casual utterance is delivered, as it were, from the eminence of the rostrum. He is not, however, just an old windbag—inflated, for purposes of this play, merely to be punctured. On the contrary, he should convey a definite sense of authority, distinction and real power. He is, at the moment, at the head of the Roman state; he must 'fit the picture-frame.'"

Fabius is tired and troubled. His mother is maternally solicitous. The people, Fabius reports, are worried about Hannibal, who continues most irritatingly to win victories and to continue his advance on Rome. But the Senate has at last taken intelligent, constructive measures to combat this advance. The Senate has this day elected Fabius Maximus Dictator of Rome with full power to conduct the state and the armies as he sees fit!

· Fabia is duly impressed by the honor that has come to her son, and conscious of what it means to them all. Even the best families are bound to take note of the Dictator's mother. And of his wife, Amytis.

Amytis is not there to hear the good news. She is, Meta reports, at the market place, in conference with a merchant recently arrived from Antioch. Which distresses Fabius slightly. Not only because he had hurried home from the senate to tell Amytis the good news, but because he is strongly opposed to merchants from Antioch. They might easily be spies. Anyway, it doesn't look well for the wife of Fabius to be patronizing a dirty foreign peddler.

Fabius and his mother have started their supper when Amytis arrives, followed by a slave carrying numerous garments and materials of brilliant colors.

"Amytis is young, beautiful, gracious and obviously civilized. She has an air of culture, sophistication and refinement that is not evident in any of the Romans. Her mother was an Athenian Greek—her father a Roman officer—and within her are combined the worthiest characteristics of these two widely contrasted races: superficially, she is frivolous, frothy, apparently oblivious of the more serious problems with which her distinguished husband is continually wrestling; but behind this surface artificiality are profound depths of sympathy and understanding. Her external fluffiness and levity are masks for an essential thoughtfulness. She gives the impression, to Fabius and his friends, that she is weak and inconsequential; actually, she is strong, and brave and wise."

Amytis is sorry if she is late, but she has had a most wonderful time making selections from the goods brought by the merchant from Antioch. So full is she of her purchases that she cannot pause in her description of them to listen to what they have to tell her of the honor that has been done her husband.

Amytis has brought with her a most gorgeous Phœnician nightgown, said to be from the court of Antiochus the Great and to have belonged to the Emperor's favorite concubine. She has materials, ravishing, gorgeous materials that the looms of Rome could never have woven. And a peacock-green dress from Damascus, made of silk, real silk, that was carried on the backs of camels across the desert. And—

But finally they manage to tell her that now she is the wife of the Dictator of Rome.

"Yes, my dear," beams Fabius, "they have placed me at the head of the Roman state."

"Isn't that nice," agrees Amytis. "Tanus, put those things in my room. Go on with dinner. I'll be right back." And she is gone.

"She took it calmly," admits Fabius.

"She doesn't understand what it means," ventures Fabia. "After all, she's only a Greek."

Still, Fabius is convinced they should not be too hard on Amytis. She has many queer Athenian ideas imbred in her. Yes, and look at Athens to-day! Completely gone to seed. "No state can succeed unless it is founded on good, sound military strength and a policy of progressive conquest," declares Fabius. And now that the Romans have Hannibal on the run—

Amytis is back and ready to go on with the meal. But again she is unfortunate in her choice of subjects. They have been talking about Hannibal, they explain, and Amytis doesn't even know who Hannibal is!

"My dear Amytis," ejaculates the astounded Fabius, "you're not serious?"

AMYTIS—Why not? How should I know who Hannibal is? I'm not a member of the Senate.

FABIUS—Amytis! Hannibal is the arch-enemy of Rome, the invader of Italy. He has threatened the very sanctity of our homes.

AMYTIS—Where does he come from?

FABIUS—From Carthage.

AMYTIS—Really. I've heard that Carthage is a very beautiful city.

FABIUS—Quite possibly. But Carthage happens to be at war with Rome, and Hannibal is in command. . . .

AMYTIS—Now, please don't ask me to keep track of our wars, or just who our enemies happen to be at the moment. With one war after another—and sometimes two or three wars at a time— I can't follow them. The mental effort is too great.

FABIUS—Perhaps you'd take a more lively interest if Hannibal marched into Rome, with his army of Africans and Spaniards and Gauls. How would you like to see this house burned down about you, and your loved ones slaughtered before your eyes? Would that amuse you?

AMYTIS—It might serve to break the monotony of life in Rome.

FABIA—I have lived in Rome for seventy-three years. I have not found it monotonous.

AMYTIS—But, my dear mother, you must remember that you've never been anywhere else. I had the misfortune to be born in Athens, where gaiety is not listed among the unpardonable sins.

FABIA—It was bad luck for you that your mother married a Roman officer.

FABIUS—Sometimes I wish that you had inherited more of your father's traits.

AMYTIS—Perhaps I did. Perhaps my Athenian frivolousness is purely artificial. Perhaps, in the depths of my soul, I am a stern, relentless, world-beating Roman!

FABIUS—I'm afraid I know nothing about the depths of your soul, Amytis.

AMYTIS—I'm afraid you don't.

FABIUS—You'll never believe that I am in sympathy with you.

AMYTIS—The trouble with me is—I'm bored. And I don't like it. Being bored is so—so snobbish.

FABIA—It is your own fault if you are bored. There are many subjects of interest in Rome.

FABIUS—My mother is right, Amytis. Rome to-day is the liveliest, most progressive city in the world. Why, just consider the population figures. Ten years ago . . .

AMYTIS—That's just it. Rome is too busily engaged in the great work of expanding to think about such trivial matters as happiness or even contentment. If we could only stop being successful for a change—if we could only *lose* a war, now and then, just for the sake of variety . . .

FABIUS—Our community life is well organized. Why don't you associate with the wives of my friends?

AMYTIS—Now, really, Fabius, you know that Senators themselves are dull; you ought to know that, having to listen to them make speeches all day. But even Senators are marvels of intellectual brilliance compared to their wives.

FABIA (*with obvious scorn*)—I've noticed that you don't care to associate with ladies of the better class. You seem to prefer the companionship of *slaves*.

FABIUS—Please, mother. We needn't mention that.

Now Amytis is eager to know the plans for the evening. Couldn't they go out somewhere? To a play, perhaps? There is a company of players in Rome. They come from Athens. They are playing "Œdipus Rex," and Amytis loves it. She simply adores a good, exciting tragedy. She loves to go to the theatre and just sob. And she resents Fabius's description of "Œdipus Rex" as a questionable drama, when he hasn't even seen it.

Fabius does not feel that he can go out again. He is all worn out. Nor could he think of letting Amytis go by herself. No, they had better stay home. And just sit around? Oh, no. Fabius will go to bed presently.

"That will be fun," agrees Amytis.

The meal is finished, and without a sweet. This, Fabius is the one to remember, is sweetless Saturday. And now Fabia has retired and Fabius and Amytis are alone. There are things Fabius feels should be mentioned.

FABIUS—It is always difficult for me to talk to you, Amytis. Sometimes I feel that you and I don't speak the same language.

AMYTIS—Are you angry with me because I spent so much money in the market-place?

FABIUS—No—it isn't that—although, I must say, that Phœnician nightgown seems a little—perhaps—

AMYTIS—Indecent? What of it? None of the Senators will see me in that, will they? I bought that in the hope that it might be just the least bit stimulating to you.

FABIUS—And then that green dress—the one that the camels carried—do you intend to wear that in the streets of Rome?

AMYTIS—Of course. It will make all the women in Rome envious, and cause them to complain to their husbands that the wife of Fabius Maximus is not quite respectable.

FABIUS—But that's what we must avoid. We can't afford to have that sort of talk going on. Don't forget that you are now the first citizeness of Rome.

AMYTIS—And therefore the arbiter of fashion, the leader of thought, the ultimate authority in all matters relating to feminine deportment.

FABIUS—Of course, of course. You are the Dictator's wife—

and for that very reason, you are expected to set a good example in all the more desirable virtues.

AMYTIS—Such as?

FABIUS—Well—ah—respectability, modesty, economy, devotion to duty, reverence, chastity, and—and—

AMYTIS—Mediocrity! I see.

FABIUS—It is in the best interests of the state as a whole. Do you understand?

AMYTIS—I understand perfectly, and I shall do my best to be a model of all that is most virtuous and most thoroughly uninteresting.

FABIUS—And there is one other thing, Amytis.

AMYTIS—I suppose I am to be more regular in my attendance at the temple.

FABIUS—That goes without saying. What I wished particularly was to influence you to take a more lively interest in public affairs. For instance, I was shocked to learn that you know nothing of Hannibal.

AMYTIS—Why should I know anything about Hannibal? Remember, you confessed to me the other day that you had never heard of Aristotle.

FABIUS—That's quite true, my dear. But, after all, you must admit that Aristotle never did anything to make himself famous.

AMYTIS—What has Hannibal done? Has he contributed anything to the advancement of science or philosophy or art?

FABIUS—I'm afraid not. But he has led an army of footsoldiers, cavalry, and elephants from Africa to Spain, from Spain to Gaul, across the Alps and into Italy—a distance of over three thousand miles. Hannibal is cruel, he is treacherous, he is a menace to our Roman civilization, but he is a great soldier. We must be generous with him and concede him that much.

AMYTIS—You say he is cruel. Is there any soldier who is otherwise?

FABIUS—Hannibal has spread destruction wherever he has gone. His army has burned homes, destroyed crops, butchered men, and despoiled women.

AMYTIS—That is the immemorial privilege of the conqueror. . . .

FABIUS—Hannibal has taken undue advantage of that privilege. Last winter, when his army was quartered in Cis-Alpine Gaul, there was a veritable epidemic of pregnancy.

AMYTIS—Good for Hannibal! He sounds like a thoroughly commendable person.

FABIUS—Amytis! Please don't say such things, even in fun.

AMYTIS—Why not? Is it wrong for me to admire good, old-fashioned virility in men? I certainly haven't seen any too much of it in my own life.

FABIUS (*falteringly*)—What do you mean?

AMYTIS—You know perfectly well what I mean, Fabius. . . . Has there been any epidemic of pregnancy around here?

FABIUS—I wish you wouldn't harp on that subject, Amytis. You know that I've been working hard lately. I've had so many worries. It's the state that demands all my time—all my energy. . . .

AMYTIS—Of course—the state! What else is there in life but the state, and the state's business, and the state's public brawls. . . .

FABIUS—We can have no other thought until Rome rules the world.

AMYTIS—When that happens, I suppose the orgies will start.

FABIUS—The splendid morale of the Roman people will never weaken.

AMYTIS—Morale—there's no such thing in Rome. There's nothing here but a narrow-minded, hypocritical morality. You Romans call it godliness; it's nothing but worldliness, of the most selfish, material kind.

FABIUS—Amytis! I can't bear to hear you talk that way. It—it's cruel.

AMYTIS—Oh—I'm sorry, Fabius. I don't mean to hurt you. Don't pay any attention to the things I say. My ideas don't fit in Rome, anyway. . . . (*She strokes his hair. He is easily mollified.*) Now! Go ahead and tell me all about your success in the Senate, and whatever it was they made you to-day.

FABIUS (*expanding*)—Dictator. They proclaimed me Dictator of All Rome. I control everything.

AMYTIS—Everything except Hannibal.

FABIUS—I'll have him under control before long. His head will be mounted on a spear in the center of the market-place, as a warning to all those who lack faith in the glorious destiny of Rome.

With the least encouragement Fabius would grow oratorical in his descriptions of what he plans to do to, and with, the arch enemy of Rome, but Amytis has a way of suppressing his flights of eloquence by gently pushing him into a seat whenever he would rise in senatorial majesty to emphasize a point. He manages to make her listen to enough, however, to let her know that Hannibal and his disorganized army are about to be caught in a trap not two hundred miles from Rome. The Carthaginians are on the defensive, reports Fabius, and the Roman army, outnumbering that of the invader by two to one, is about to advance.

"Poor Hannibal!" sympathizes Amytis. "After traveling three thousand miles he has to die ingloriously and be exhibited in the market-place as a horrible lesson to little children."

It is difficult for Amytis to understand Hannibal. Surely he cannot hate Rome so much that he should want to obliterate it, as Fabius insists, merely because of a fear that Rome may ultimately destroy Carthage. Sounds so silly.

And when she is told that Hannibal is young—no more than 30 years old—the situation seems more tragic to her than ever. She can't help thinking how wasteful it is to sacrifice a young man who has the genius to lead a troop of elephants across the Alps.

"Just think," she muses, "if he were allowed to live some day he might do something useful."

"If he were allowed to live, Amytis," answers Fabius, "he might some day cause the downfall of Rome."

Still Amytis cannot get the Carthaginian conqueror out of her mind. What would happen if the Roman legions, and Fabius, should fail to conquer Hannibal? What would it be like to be despoiled? It may not be a proper subject for a lady's thoughts, she admits, but it can't be unusual. Are there, she wonders, any women in Rome who have been so unfortunate as to encounter Hannibal's army? If so she would like to have some of them up to dinner. Their comments should be interesting.

The faint sound of a bugle is heard, as from a distance; a shrill, barbaric sound. It interests Amytis, but Fabius dismisses it as probably the pipe of a shepherd bringing his flocks in from the field. Anyway it is nothing to keep a tired man from his bed, and Fabius is soon on his way, with the best wishes of both wife and mother for his sweet repose.

Amytis thinks she will sit up awhile. She has just given Varius and Meta permission to go for a walk and is sympathizing with them because the laws of Rome prohibit their marrying, and because there is so little hope of their escaping, even if she could help them, when there is a vigorous knocking at the outer door.

The caller is Cato, an excited youth, come to report the sudden appearance of hundreds of campfires off to the east. It must be the army returning, Varius thinks, probably after having conquered Hannibal.

Soon the knocking is repeated and Cato admits Scipio, "a handsome young man wearing the helmet, breastplate, etc., of a Roman officer. His cloak is torn, dirty and spotted with blood. His left arm is bandaged. He is a fine, upstanding type of soldier—earnest, sincere, intense—one of the men who aided materially in Rome's conquest of the world."

Scipio has come to arouse Fabius and to report to the surprised dictator that the Roman army has suffered a terrible defeat. At Cannæ the Romans were routed and disgraced and Hannibal is even now at the gates of Rome!

"The Roman army has been wiped out! Our strength and our prestige are gone! Hannibal rules the world!" There is desperation in Scipio's voice.

"What shall we do? What shall we do?" mutters the stunned Fabius.

"You are the Dictator, Fabius. It is for you to decide."

Fabius decides that all he can do at the moment is to summon Sertorious, Tibullus and Drusus for a conference.

Now Amytis, hearing the clatter, returns excitedly. The news, however, does not stun her. She is apparently delighted with the way everything is going.

"So Hannibal got here after all," she murmurs.

FABIUS—Yes—and it means death to us all!—the end of everything for Rome.

AMYTIS—Think of it . . . Hannibal!

FABIUS—Rome has been betrayed by the gods.

AMYTIS—Why don't you sit down, Scipio? You must be fearfully tired.

SCIPIO (*ungraciously*)—I'm perfectly able to stand, thank you. (*It is obvious that he bears no love for* AMYTIS, *an attitude that is not uncommon among the friends of* FABIUS.)

FABIUS—Is there a remnant of the army left, Scipio?

SCIPIO—None, Fabius. We were annihilated at Cannæ. A few of us cut our way back to Rome, but even then we travelled no faster than Hannibal with his entire army. He is a superman—a god—against whom mortal strength is of no avail.

AMYTIS—A god!

FABIUS—But I can't understand it, Scipio. Superman or no superman—we outnumbered his army two to one. I thought we had him caught in a trap.

Scipio—Hannibal let us think so. He forced us to attack the center of his line, where his weakest troops were massed. He allowed us to drive through—and then surrounded us, with his infantry and Numidian cavalry.

Fabius—More of his damnable deception.

Amytis—We would never have resorted to such foul tactics—would we, Fabius?

Fabius—Never!

Amytis (*sits*)—No—we wouldn't have thought of them. (Fabius *paces up and down in a turmoil of baffled rage, nervous apprehension and utter bewilderment.*)

Scipio—I saw Hasdrubal, the Numidian cavalry leader, cut down dozens of our men with his own sword. He fought like a fiend sent down by the gods to punish us.

Amytis—And did you see Hannibal?

Scipio—I saw him in the distance.

Amytis—What was he doing?

Scipio—He was standing on a little hill . . .

Fabius—Laughing, I suppose?

Scipio—No—he was not laughing. He was watching the battle as though it were a play that he had written, being performed by actors in a theatre.

Amytis—Is Hannibal good-looking?

Scipio—Hannibal's personal appearance did not interest me at the moment.

Fabius—This is a serious matter, Amytis. I must ask you not to bother us with irrelevant questions now. . . .

Amytis—But this isn't irrelevant. It is very important for Hannibal to be handsome. Think of the statues.

Fabius—What else happened, Scipio?

Scipio—They closed in on us and butchered us . . . and all through the battle their terrible African war drums kept on beating—louder—louder . . .

Amytis (*without enthusiasm*)—It must have been thrilling!

Scipio—Our army was a confused mass of struggling, writhing men—battling against an enemy that attacked from every side. The slaughter was unspeakably awful. . . . When it was over, at last, seventy thousand Romans lay dead on the field of Cannæ.

Amytis (*slowly*)—Seventy thousand! Why did they die?

Scipio (*bitterly*)—Ask Hannibal why they died.

Fabius—Seventy thousand! What horror! What is this terrible thing the gods have done to us, Scipio—to us who have made our sacrifices regularly in the temple and have spared no

effort to show our gratitude for past favors. I can't understand
it.

AMYTIS—Perhaps Hannibal was nice to the gods, too.

FABIUS (*vehemently*)—Hannibal's gods are false gods!

AMYTIS—Oh—I see.

Action must be taken at once, Scipio insists, but Fabius is
completely crushed. Nothing, he fears, can save Rome now.
There are no more than 5,000 men to defend the walls, and they
would be as nothing against the army of Hannibal!

They must think first of the women. Both Amytis and Fabia
must escape. They at least must be spared from the bestiality
of Hannibal's men. Still Amytis is not excited. Can it be that
all Carthaginians are such extremely warm-blooded men? If
they are it should be quite an experience for the women of Rome!

As for Fabius, being a man, he is prepared to die. "And I,
too, am prepared to die," echoes Fabia, proudly. "I am a Roman. Here I was born. Here I have lived and borne children,
here I shall die!"

"Well, I am *not* prepared to die!" announces Amytis, emphatically. "I am not a Roman. I was not born here—and I
have certainly borne no children, here or anywhere else. I shall
go to Ostia and join my mother."

"Spoken like a true Greek," sneers Scipio.

Amytis can't help that. She loves life, even monotonous life,
and she cannot bear to part with it. She is a coward, she confesses, and Fabius probably hates her because she is less brave
than his mother.

No, Fabius doesn't hate Amytis, but he does think it would
be beautiful if they could die together. Which is not Amytis'
idea of beauty at all.

It is Fabia who is consumed with hatred of Amytis and glad
of an excuse for expressing it. She hates Amytis because she has
flippantly thrown aside the love of a good man and put on the
airs of a goddess! And she is glad that the clean streets of
Rome are not to be soiled with the vile blood of so heartless
and soulless a traitor.

"I may be a traitor to Rome," admits Amytis, calmly, "but I
am not a traitor to my own convictions. I didn't start this war.
I've never given it my support or encouragement. I have no axe
to grind with Hannibal. Why should I sacrifice my life merely
because the Roman army has failed to subdue a weaker enemy?"

"If you feel that way about it, you'd better go," wearily admits Fabius.

Amytis agrees. He certainly would not want her to stay and be subjected to whatever she might be subjected to, and Rome would gain nothing by her bravery if she were to stay and offer up her beautiful body to the conquerors.

By the time the senators have gathered and are hysterically trying to think of something to do, Amytis has got together a bundle of her belongings and is ready to go as soon as Varius brings around the horses.

She is cheerfully contemplating a visit to her mother on the seacoast and her attitude strikes Fabius as being at least callous. Why should she be blamed for being cheerful in the face of danger, Amytis demands. "You might try it yourself. If Hannibal should march into Rome and find you all laughing, he might forget what he came for and join in the merriment."

VARIUS—The horses are ready, my lady.

AMYTIS—Then we must start.

FABIUS (*tremulously*)—Good-by, Amytis. I'm afraid I shall never see you again.

AMYTIS—Don't say that, Fabius. Hannibal hasn't conquered Rome yet. There is still hope.

FABIUS—Hope is a poor defense against the Numidian cavalry.

AMYTIS—It's the only defense you have, isn't it?

FABIUS—Yes, I suppose so. We're doomed.

AMYTIS—Had you ever thought of treating with Hannibal?

DRUSUS—What do you mean?

AMYTIS—I mean—why don't you go out, under a flag of truce, meet Hannibal and talk the thing over in a civilized manner. He sounds to me like the type of man who might listen to reason.

FABIUS—I wonder if he would?

SCIPIO (*indignantly*)—Nonsense! Hannibal talks only on the field of battle, with words of steel. The Roman does not live who can argue with him successfully there.

DRUSUS—Scipio is right. We'll have to fight it out.

SERTORIUS—We can at least show him that Romans know how to die. (*From a distance, the faint sound of many drums is heard, beating rhythmically, ominously.*)

FABIUS (*starting*)—What's that?

SCIPIO—It's the drums—the African war drums.

TIBULLUS (*hysterically*)—O gods of Rome—save us. Save us!

Fabius—The gods can't hear you, Tibullus.

Amytis—In that case, I had better hurry. I don't even know how to die gracefully. . . . (Fabia *enters from the right.*) Good-by, my husband. Don't eat too much starchy food while I'm away. Good-by, mother. Good-by, gentlemen. Good-by, good-by. . . . . (*She goes out with the two slaves at the left. Fabia is still standing at the right, gazing after the departed Amytis.*)

Fabius—Now let's get down to business. (*He sits down, surrounded by the others. The sound of the drums becomes slightly louder, more emphatic.*) We must concentrate our infantry outside the city walls, prepared to withstand the first shock of assault . . .

Fabia—Fabius . . .

Fabius (*paying no attention*)—Our cavalry, such as it is, can be held within the city, prepared to make a sortie through the east gate when the situation becomes desperate . . .

Fabia—Fabius . . .

Fabius (*still not listening*)—You, Drusus, will take command of the infantry on the left . . .

Fabia (*louder*)—Fabius!

Fabius—And you, Scipio . . . What is it, mother?

Fabia—Did you notice anything about Amytis when she left?

Fabius—She seemed to be in a hurry.

Fabia—Did you notice anything strange in her appearance?

Fabius (*impatiently*)—No, I did not.

Fabia—She was wearing that new green silk dress!

Fabius (*not interested*)—She was, was she? . . . Now, if Hannibal attacks us on the right, you, Scipio, will move forward to meet him in pitched battle. If he concentrates on the left . . . The—the green dress, eh! Isn't that a rather strange costume for traveling. . . . (*In the distance, the war drums continue to beat their weird tattoo as the curtain falls.*)

## ACT II

Hannibal's headquarters are in a temple about a mile east of Rome. "The temple, normally open, has been converted into a sort of tent by means of rich, crimson draperies." Through parted curtains at the rear the Italian landscape may be dimly seen. A door at the left gives entrance to Hannibal's sleeping quarters.

"Although the scene is a Roman temple," notes the author,

"and although it is probable that Hannibal did not carry many household effects with him on his long march, strict realism and logic may be sacrificed for purposes of dramatic effectiveness in this scene. The barbaric splendor of Carthage itself must be reflected in all the trappings in this distant camp; the audience must feel that the action of the play has shifted from the virtuous but unimaginative simplicity of Rome to the Oriental opulence of its enemies."

The headquarters guard, consisting of a corporal and five stalwart Carthaginians, is being inspected by a sergeant. "The Sergeant is a rough, husky, brutal veteran whose counterpart is to be found on every drill ground from Quantico to Aldershot. The guardsmen are fine, upstanding soldiers—young, vigorous, confident and cheerful. . . . In their speech they are tough and hardboiled, exactly in the manner of the corporals in "What Price Glory," it being not unreasonable to assume that professional soldiers 2,100 years ago did not differ materially from the professional soldiers of to-day."

The Sergeant's inspection is ruthless and thorough. He bawls out this one for having a rusty sword, that one because his helmet is on crooked. He is keen to have them shined up for a meeting of the general staff that impends.

Free to speak their minds when the Sergeant is gone, the guardsmen have their own opinions about this particular man's army and its methods. There's the matter of being disciplined by being given a turn with the elephants, for instance. They're Hannibal's pets, the elephants are, and they sure need a lot of attention. That's why Hannibal put his own brother, Mago, in charge of them; that and because he wanted to give Mago the rottenest job in the army just to show how impartial he was.

Mago has had two years wet-nursing those elephants now, and even the guardsmen are a little sorry for him. He is a well-meaning kid. Once he tried to get Hannibal to stop the war because he suspected one of his charges was unfit for travel.

" 'Hannibal,' he says, 'we can't move yet. One of my elephants is about to become a mother,' " reports a guardsman. "And Hannibal says, 'That's interesting, but what are we going to do about it? Do you think we ought to hold up the army till the child is born?' And young Mago says, 'Yes, brother, I think we should, because that elephant ought not to be moved, not in her condition.' Well, sir, Hannibal tried not to laugh, and he finally told the kid, 'Mago,' he says, 'we've got a very important war on our hands, and however much we may sympathize with this poor, wayward elephant, I'm afraid we can't afford to wait for her. . . .'"

Seeing that an accouchement takes seven years out of an elephant's life, the guardsmen figure that they would have still been parked with the elephants had it not been that their chief was a farseeing and practical man. As it is here they are at what looks to be the end of the war—Rome a mile away just waiting to be cleaned up. Yet Rome's a bust to at least one of them.

"Don't talk to me about Rome," says he. "It's the biggest disappointment of my life. Why, I expected to see a real city, with big palaces, all made out of marble and gold and jewelry. I thought I'd take home enough souvenirs to keep me and the missus in luxury for the rest of our lives . . . and just look at the little dump! We'll be lucky to pick up a square meal in the whole town."

"It's your own fault, soldier. You *would* see the world."

Hasdrubal is the first of the generals to arrive. He is the second in command of the Carthaginian army—"a dark, ominous, explosive, fire-eating cavalry officer"—and he immediately clears the tent of the headquarters guard and spreads his maps ready for the conference.

Hasdrubal is followed by Carthalo, "a rough, bluff old warrior," and Maharbal, "a gaunt, hard, cynical strategist." Soon Mago comes. "He is Hannibal's younger brother—a personable youth, well set up and handsome. At the start of the campaign, he had been terribly enthusiastic and overwhelmed by the craving for adventure, but most of the thrill has worn off by now. Nevertheless, he is still fresh and jaunty, with an irrepressible self-assurance."

Mago is weary. He has been superintending the toilet of his elephants, and he's all in. The generals try to cheer him. His reward will come when he marches the elephants into Rome. The army will be going in next day.

Maharbal is not so sure. Hannibal may decide to let Rome rest for the present. There has been a call for help from Capua, where the Carthaginian allies are being besieged by a Roman army, and it may be Hannibal will want to go there first. The very thought of such a decision exasperates Hasdrubal.

"Hannibal," roars the fire-eater, "Hannibal is insane if he turns away from Rome now. The city is ours. They have only two legions to defend it. We could walk in this minute . . . and if we fail to destroy Rome now, you know what'll happen in Carthage, don't you? They'll turn against Hannibal. He'll be discredited—stripped of his power. . . . Oh, he can't make a mistake like this."

The sergeant's rough " 'Tshun!" outside announces the arrival of Hannibal. The four officers salute him stiffly as he enters.

"Hannibal is tall, thin, dark—quiet and surprisingly unemphatic in his speech—rather diffident in his manner. He is obviously terribly tired, but he has trained himself to such a point that he can readily ignore fatigue. He is the sort of man who is apparently none too powerful physically, but manages to exist on an inexhaustible supply of reserve strength. He provides not only the brains which direct his army, but the vitality which animates it? He is regarded with absolutely unqualified respect by his officers and men alike; his mildest whisper is instantly obeyed."

He returns his generals' salute, hands his helmet and sword to Bala, his huge Nubian attendant, and sits down at the table, relaxing easily in his chair.

HANNIBAL—Have you been looking at Rome?

MAGO—Yes, sir. It's not very impressive.

HANNIBAL—You'll have a closer view to-morrow.

HASDRUBAL (*excitedly*)—Are we going in?

HANNIBAL—We attack the city on the morrow.

HASDRUBAL—Thank the gods! We're going in at last! (*The four officers are obviously delighted at the prospect.*)

MAHARBAL—I was afraid you might decide to turn off and raise the siege of Capua.

HANNIBAL—Capua can wait. The men need a little rest and recreation after all they've been through. The destruction of Rome will be in the nature of harmless diversion.

CARTHALO—Are we going to burn Rome to the ground?

HANNIBAL—I suppose so. That's what we came for, isn't it?

HASDRUBAL—Of course it is! We'll show those damned Roman upstarts that they can't dispute the supremacy of Carthage. When we get through with Rome, there'll be nothing left of it but a memory.

HANNIBAL (*thinking of something else*)—Nothing left but a memory.

MAGO—I suppose the elephant brigade, as usual, will miss all the fun.

HANNIBAL—On the contrary, Mago, the elephants will lead the procession into the city. I want you to put on your finest uniform, comb your hair, and shave carefully, because we expect you to look your best. We must convince these Roman upstarts, as Hasdrubal calls them, of our importance.

MAGO—I'll have those elephants painted every color of the rainbow.

HANNIBAL—I wouldn't exactly overdo it. We want the Roman citizens to think that we're an army. We mustn't look too much like a circus parade.

HASDRUBAL—They know we're an army, all right. They found that out at Lake Trasimenus and Cannæ.

HANNIBAL—Don't boast about your victories, Hasdrubal. You can save them for your wife when you get home.

HASDRUBAL—Damn it all, sir, you don't seem to get any satisfaction out of anything. You ought to feel proud that our army has beaten the Romans whenever we've met them. You ought to be like the rest of us and celebrate a victory now and then. Sometimes, by the gods, I actually think you don't care whether we win or lose.

(HANNIBAL *stands up, and walks slowly across the stage during the following speech.*)

HANNIBAL—It's not quite as bad as all that, Hasdrubal. I *do* care whether we win or lose. I suppose it's the only thing I have to care about in the whole world. . . . But—if we win a victory, that's that. We have to go on to the next battle, then the next, and the next, until we've finished this war. Then we go home to Carthage and start looking for another.

MAHARBAL—You ought to take a rest, sir.

HANNIBAL—That's just the trouble with victory, Maharbal. You can't rest. You're only allowed to quit when you're losing. . . . Look at those seventy thousand Roman soldiers we butchered at Cannæ. They don't care now whether Rome is destroyed or not. Their work is done. They're at liberty to take a rest— a long rest.

HASDRUBAL—They can have their rest. I'd rather go on fighting.

HANNIBAL—Of course, Hasdrubal. You're a soldier, and a damned good one. You live on cavalry charges, flank movements and counter-attacks; it's your whole existence.

HASDRUBAL—How about yourself, sir? I haven't noticed *you* signing any peace treaties.

HANNIBAL—I know it. But then, I have my oath to think of— undying hatred of Rome. I have had that with me ever since I was nine years old, and I can't very well get rid of it until there's no more Rome left for me to hate.

CARTHALO—That's the proper spirit, sir. It's much easier to kill a man if you hate him.

HANNIBAL—Very true, Carthalo, very true. I never thought of you before as a philosopher.

MAHARBAL—Have you any orders for to-morrow, sir?

HANNIBAL—Never mind them now, Maharbal. They're very simple, and we can talk them over in the morning. We all need some rest to-night.

The generals are worried about Hannibal. He is not taking the care of himself that he should and the army can't afford to have him wreck his health. They couldn't go on without him, Carthalo insists.

Mago stays on, with Hannibal's permission, after the generals go. He gets lonesome with nobody to talk to except the elephants, and he is curious about news from home. Hannibal has had a letter from their mother, but there's not much in it, aside from the news that Uncle Hamilcar fell and broke his hip again.

Hannibal is cleaning up for supper and Mago is alone when the sergeant reports the capture of a spy—a woman spy—and would like to know what to do with her. Hearing the prisoner seems to be a lady and is not bad looking, Mago decides to have a look at her.

The soldiers bring in Amytis, Varius and Meta. They were picked up, the sergeant reports, just outside the camp. They said they were refugees from Rome who had lost their way.

"We were trying to escape from the city and took the wrong road," explains Amytis. Which Mago concludes is a highly improbable story. He promptly sentences all three to death.

Despite Amytis' protest that his action is entirely unfair, that he has no right to condemn them unheard nor to refuse to let her see Hannibal, the sergeant is about to lead them away when it occurs to Mago that perhaps they should be searched for incriminating documents before they are killed. The guard begins the search of Varius and Meta and the sergeant starts to search Amytis, but again she protests. Does she have to be pawed by a sergeant?

On second thought Mago decides to search Amytis himself, but his success is little better than the sergeant's. Amytis giggles hysterically and insists she is being tickled. Her levity in the face of an order of execution interests Mago and he decides, as he holds her at arm's length, that she is rather beautiful. He tells her so.

"I always try to look my best when going to an execution," she admits.

The more he thinks of it the more he is convinced that it would not be quite the thing to execute Amytis. Certainly not before she has seen the elephants. But, unfortunately for Mago's changed plans, Hannibal returns to the room before he can conclude them. For a moment the chief stands where Mago cannot see him and is listening to his brother's proposition. Not until Amytis has poked him repeatedly in the ribs does Mago turn and discover that he is being observed. He comes promptly to a salute and explains, a little lamely:

"We caught a spy, sir—a Roman spy."

HANNIBAL—I was wondering . . .

AMYTIS—You're Hannibal, aren't you! (*A statement rather than a question.*)

HANNIBAL—I am. (HANNIBAL *walks past her and crosses to the table. Presently* AMYTIS *follows him.*)

AMYTIS (*surveying him*)—So you're Hannibal. . . . You're not the way I pictured you, at all.

HANNIBAL (*politely*)—I hope I'm not a disappointment.

MAGO—We caught this woman red-handed, sir. She and these others were trying to sneak through our line.

HANNIBAL—That was highly injudicious of you, madam—I mean, to be caught.

AMYTIS—I realize that now.

MAGO—I cross-examined her.

AMYTIS—He did not. He tickled me.

MAGO—It was my duty, sir, to search her person for any documents that might be of value. She chose to interpret my actions as a personal advance.

AMYTIS—He told me he was going to take me down and show me the elephants. (HANNIBAL *laughs.*) Scipio told me you never laugh.

HANNIBAL—Scipio has happened to encounter me only in my less mirthful moments. (*He sits down at the table.*) I must apologize for my brother, madam. He's very young, and has much to learn about the gentle art of soldiering.

AMYTIS—Oh, that's all right. I understand perfectly. (*To* MAGO.) You're forgiven.

HANNIBAL—In this delightful conversation that went on between you two, was any mention made of the possible penalty for espionage?

MAGO—Of course there was. I sentenced all three of them to death.

HANNIBAL—Is there any particular reason why this ceremony should be delayed?

MAGO (*looking at* AMYTIS)—There certainly isn't.

HANNIBAL—In that case, Sergeant, you may proceed in the usual manner.

SERGEANT—Come on, you! (*He starts to lead her out. AMYTIS breaks away from him, goes to the table at which HANNIBAL is sitting, and speaks directly to him.*)

AMYTIS—I'm not asking for mercy, Hannibal. I know that there is no such thing in war.

SERGEANT (*starting for her*)—I told you to come with me.

HANNIBAL—Stand back, Sergeant. Let her talk.

AMYTIS—I'm ready to die—for the glory of Rome, or whatever it is we're fighting for now. I'm not afraid—no, I mean that. I'm really not afraid. That's not heroism, either. It's just the attitude of stoicism that comes to every one, I suppose. You soldiers who have been in battle must know what I mean.

MAGO—Must we listen to all this?

HANNIBAL—Go on.

AMYTIS—In Athens, when men were condemned to death, they were granted one last request—provided, of course, that it was within reason. If they wanted a sumptuous repast, they could have it. Or they might crave a last hour with their loved ones. They could have that, too. . . . Some of these men were murderers, some traitors, but all were accorded the same final favor. It didn't amount to much—it cost the state nothing. But it did help to send those poor creatures out with a somewhat less anguished conscience. . . . That's what I ask of you, Hannibal— one final favor.

MAGO—Don't listen to her, Hannibal. She's a bad woman.

HANNIBAL—What is it that you want?

AMYTIS (*hesitantly*)—I can't tell you before all these people.

MAGO—I thought not. I tell you, Hannibal, she's dangerous. I wouldn't listen to a word she says.

HANNIBAL—Dismissed, Sergeant. Take these prisoners with you.

SERGEANT—Yes, sir. Hup! (*VARIUS and META are led out by the Corporal and Guardsmen.*)

AMYTIS—Nothing will happen to them . . . ?

HANNIBAL—Sergeant, you will be responsible for the safety of the prisoners.

Sergeant—Yes, sir. . . . (*He salutes and goes out.*)

Mago—Well, what is it?

Amytis (*to* Hannibal)—Does *he* have to stay?

Hannibal (*smiling*)—You can go, Mago.

Mago (*ominously*)—I wouldn't do this, Hannibal.

Hannibal—Don't worry, Mago. I think I can take care of myself. She doesn't seem to be armed.

Mago—She doesn't have to be.

"For an instant Hannibal regards Amytis in silence. Then he motions her gracefully to a chair across the table from his."

After she is seated there is another awkward pause. Then Hannibal politely, and with due apology, suggests that he is quite busy and would she mind coming to the point with the least possible delay. Further, he would like to assure her that the indignity to which she is being submitted is not in any way intended as a personal affront. They have nothing whatever against her as an individual, but as a representative of Rome, seeing there happens to be a war on at the moment, she should understand that there is an ancient law that prescribes instant death for all those caught in the act of espionage.

"If we violated that law," Hannibal concludes, "we should ourselves be guilty of delinquency, and Carthage would undoubtedly be expelled from the Mediterranean League."

Amytis, for her part, understands the difficulties of Hannibal's position. It is natural, too, that he should assume that she has been sent, probably by her husband. But what he doesn't know is that her husband is Quintus Fabius Maximus, Dictator of Rome. Furthermore her husband not only did not send her, but he does not even known she is there. She is on her way to join her mother in Ostia.

As to the situation in Rome, which she is ready to report, Hannibal is already well informed. One of his best officers happens now to be inside the city posing as a merchant from Antioch. The very man, as Amytis admits with enthusiasm, who sold her the green dress she is wearing. Does he like the dress? Hannibal thinks it charming. Which naturally leads to further confidences.

Amytis—I don't want you to think that I'm disloyal to Rome. I'm not really a Roman at all. I was born in Athens, and for some reason I've never been able to understand the Roman ideals of civic virtue. They think I'm an awful coward. . . . This evening they asked me to stay and die like a true Roman. . . .

HANNIBAL—To stay and die? Is the situation as hopeless as all that?

AMYTIS—We may as well be frank with each other, Hannibal. You know that the defenses of Rome haven't a chance against your army, and the Romans know it even better than you do. They've been desperately afraid of you ever since you crossed the Alps.

HANNIBAL—I suppose I should feel flattered.

AMYTIS—You should. To-day young Scipio described you as a superman, a god, against whom mortal strength is of no avail. I heard him say it—and that's why I'm here.

HANNIBAL (*puzzled*)—That's why you're here?

AMYTIS—I wanted, for once in my life, to see a superman. . . . When I left Rome in disgrace, I had no intention of going to visit my mother. That was just an excuse—I led my slaves along the wrong road, deliberately. When your sentries captured me, they wanted to put me to death at once. I told them I had a message for Hannibal. (BALA *comes in, bearing a huge tray laden with food for* HANNIBAL *and* MAGO. *He sees* AMYTIS, *looks at her curiously, and then sets the tray down on the table.*)

HANNIBAL—I haven't yet heard what that message is.

AMYTIS—Oh, food! How nice! I'm simply famished! It was very thoughtful of you to have supper for me, Hannibal. (BALA *serves the meal, and then takes up his position by the column, upstage.*)

HANNIBAL (*elaborately polite*)—I must apologize for the simplicity of the meal. We're living on army rations, you know.

AMYTIS—Army rations! Why, it's de*lici*ous! We never have anything as good as this in Rome. We have to deny ourselves all luxuries on account of the war. . . . What marvellous wine!

HANNIBAL—Yes, the wine is rather good. It's a Spanish wine that we brought with us. There's very little of it left, but we hope to replenish our supply to-morrow.

AMYTIS—In Rome? (HANNIBAL *nods,* AMYTIS *laughs.*) You won't find much of that in Rome . . . or anything else, for that matter.

She is not, she admits, particularly patriotic. Her husband, who is a true, 100-per-cent. patriot, has often told her so. Poor Fabius, he is so easily annoyed with her. She can, happily, talk him out of his irritations. Probably because Fabius is fond of her. But theirs has never been much of a love match. Her father had left her as Fabius' ward and their marriage followed inevitably.

No, Amytis has never fallen in love with any one else. And she must say that Fabius has been a good, kind, considerate husband. It probably is her own fault that she has not been able to find much to interest her.

Greatly as he dislikes to interrupt, Hannibal suggests that it is just possible the sergeant is growing a trifle impatient.

Of course! Amytis had practically forgotten the sergeant! And Varius and Meta, too! They must be famished. Would he mind seeing that her slaves were given supper?

Again Hannibal rises magnificently to the emergency. Let Varius and Meta be served. But now, if Amytis doesn't mind, wouldn't she please return to the statement she wished to make? The last favor she wished to ask?

Amytis is perfectly willing to oblige. But before she asks her last favor she would like to ask Hannibal a question—"not as a Carthaginian conqueror speaking to a Roman victim—but as one civilized human to another. . . . Why have you done it?"

HANNIBAL—Why have I done it? Why have I done what?

AMYTIS—Oh, everything that you've done—fighting wars, winning battles . . . why?

HANNIBAL (*after a moment's pause*)—That's a strange question.

AMYTIS—You must know the answer. You must have had some definite motive to inspire you.

HANNIBAL—But who cares about my motives? It's only my actual accomplishments that count.

AMYTIS—I care about your motives.

HANNIBAL—Why?

AMYTIS—I just happen to be curious, that's all.

HANNIBAL—I should think that my reasons would be fairly obvious. I came here to destroy Rome. Isn't that reason enough?

AMYTIS—Is it enough to satisfy you?

HANNIBAL—I can't see that that makes any difference.

AMYTIS—Oh—but it does. It makes an enormous difference. You know, some day you'll have to reason this thing out with yourself. Some day, you'll say to yourself, "Here I've marched three thousand miles, and crossed mountains and things, and spilt a lot of blood—and what good has it done?" It would be most embarrassing if you suddenly realized that you'd been wasting your time.

HANNIBAL—I'm not supposed to think about such things. I'm a soldier. I have to content myself with a soldier's rewards.

AMYTIS—As, for instance?

HANNIBAL—Well—when I get back to Carthage, I shall receive medals, and testimonial documents, and I shall be the guest of honor at state banquets, and . . .

AMYTIS—Yes, and they'll give you the key to the city. I know all about that. My husband once was given the key to the city. We have it at home, somewhere. Take my word for it, it doesn't do you any good.

HANNIBAL—I suppose not. But it's a nice sentiment.

AMYTIS—So that's what you've been striving for—fighting for —all these years. A nice sentiment!

HANNIBAL—If you choose to put it that way—yes.

AMYTIS—No. I don't believe it. You'll have to offer a better reason than that.

HANNIBAL—I'm beginning to sympathize with your husband. . . . By the way, what is your name?

AMYTIS—Amytis. But why do you sympathize with my husband?

HANNIBAL—I shouldn't care to live with a woman who asked so many questions.

AMYTIS—If you'd only give me an intelligent answer, I'd stop.

HANNIBAL (rising)—Perhaps I can't explain my actions.

AMYTIS—Perhaps you don't even know yourself?

HANNIBAL—That question of yours disturbed me a little. . . . I've asked myself that same thing so many times.

AMYTIS—I rather imagined that you had.

HANNIBAL—One morning we were camped on the banks of the Rhone River. It was swollen with the spring floods. I had to get my army across—eighty thousand infantry, cavalry, elephants—with all their supplies. We had no boats of our own; there were no bridges. Across the river, a howling mob of Gauls was waiting to slaughter us as we landed. From the south, a large Roman army was advancing to attack us. . . . I sent a small body of men upstream to get across as best they could and to attack the Gauls on their right flank. I was waiting for the signal from that detachment, and wondering whether I should ever set foot on the opposite bank. . . . As I stood there, I asked myself, "Why do I do this? Even if a miracle occurs, and we

do cross the river, what then?  What will we have gained?"  I
didn't know.

AMYTIS—But you did cross the river, didn't you, Hannibal?

HANNIBAL—Yes—we routed the Gauls, and tricked the Romans, and marched on to the Alps. . . . Have you ever tried to
lead an elephant over a snow peak?

AMYTIS—No—that's one of the many adventures I've missed.

HANNIBAL—Our men, who were accustomed to the fierce heat
of Africa, had to plod through the Alpine snows, many of them
in their bare feet.  They had to drag the elephants and all the
machinery of war with them, while the natives pushed avalanches
down on our heads. . . . When we came to the last line of mountains, and saw Italy spread out at our feet, I asked myself that
same question. . . . I've never been able to find an answer.  I've
watched our men slaughter the Romans in one terrible battle after
another.  Through all these years, I've seen nothing but death—
death—and I've never been able to find an answer.  (*He crosses
over to the right and stands gazing off toward Rome.*)

AMYTIS—Not even in the key to the city?

HANNIBAL—For ten years I've followed the road that leads to
Rome—and it's a hard road to travel, Amytis.  It's littered with
the bones of dead men.  Perhaps they know why they died.  I
don't.  (AMYTIS *rises and stands behind him.*)

AMYTIS—And now you've come to the end of that road, Hannibal.  There's your goal—before you.  You can see the lights
of Rome clearly, can't you?  Even the lights seem to tremble
with fear of Hannibal. . . . They know that to-morrow they'll ·
be snuffed out forever. . . . Poor little Rome. . . .

Hannibal is not particularly pleased when Amytis accuses him
of being proud because people think of him as a cruel, merciless,
terrifying brute.  True, he is not averse to having his enemies
afraid of him.  In fact it would not displease him if Amytis were
herself at least a little more respectful.

Again he admits that he has no idea why she is there, unless
it is as a spy.  In which case her methods are inexcusably crude.
Nor can he credit her statement that hers is merely a pleasure
trip—not with swift, violent death staring her in the face.

Still she persists such is the fact.  She had seen the smoke
from Hannibal's camp and she wanted to see the fire.  That she
might get burned she knew—but that only made the adventure
all the more exciting.

Nor is she afraid of what he is pleased to call the divine vengeance of the gods. She is not afraid, though she is not ready to die.

AMYTIS—I don't want to die until I have lived. That's perfectly reasonable, isn't it?

HANNIBAL—I can give you death—but I can't give you life.

AMYTIS—How do you know you can't?

HANNIBAL—I don't know what it is. I don't want to know.

AMYTIS—I do want to know. I came here because I was determined to find out.

HANNIBAL—Mago was right. Amytis—you're dangerous.

AMYTIS—That's what they said of me in Rome. But it isn't so. I'm not dangerous. I'm only real.

HANNIBAL—You might be dangerous to me.

AMYTIS—Because you're afraid I might make *you* real.

HANNIBAL—You can't do it. No one can. When I was a child, my father laid me on the altar of Ba-al and consecrated me to the destruction of Rome. Since that moment, I've never been an individual—I've been a force, divinely inspired to crush the enemies of Carthage.

AMYTIS—You're using the gods again—as an excuse for your own murders.

HANNIBAL—Those who kill for the glory of the gods are not murderers.

AMYTIS—Who told you that? One of the high priests, I suppose.

HANNIBAL—Ba-al himself has spoken to me. Throughout my life I have been driven forward by his voice, saying, "Go on, Hannibal, go on, with sword and flame, until you have destroyed the glory of Rome."

AMYTIS—That wasn't the voice of Ba-al, Hannibal. That was the voice of the shopkeepers in Carthage, who are afraid that Rome will interfere with their trade. . . . Hatred, greed, envy, and the passionate desire for revenge—those are the high ideals that inspire you soldiers, Roman and Carthaginian alike . . . and when you realize the shameful futility of your great conquests, you turn around and attribute it all to the gods. . . . The gods are always convenient in an emergency. . . .

HANNIBAL (*slightly nettled*)—What, may I ask, is the object of all this conversation? Do you think you can talk me away from Rome?

Amytis—I don't care *what* happens to Rome. I'm trying to find something in you, something great, something noble, something exciting.

Hannibal—And you expect to accomplish this by insulting me, by calling me a rotten murderer, blaspheming my gods.

Amytis—Good! You're getting angry at last. That's an encouraging sign!

Hannibal—I'm beginning to entertain an extreme dislike for you. If you'll forgive me for saying so, you're becoming something of a pest.

Amytis—I've tried to be interesting.

Hannibal—You've succeeded in being exceptionally irritating. I don't want to hear any more. You'll have to die.

Amytis—Right this minute?

Hannibal—Yes. I'll be glad to get it over with. (*In the subsequent speeches,* Amytis *betrays signs of tremulousness. Much of her amazing assurance is gone.*)

Amytis—But isn't this very unusual?

Hannibal—The execution of an enemy? No, I'm sorry to say that it is entirely according to regulations.

Amytis—Oh, I know that. But you ought not to kill me at once, without—without—

Hannibal—Without what? I've given you a meal, I've answered your damned questions—what more can I do?

Amytis—There's a certain—a certain ceremony to be gone through with, isn't there?

Hannibal—What sort of a ceremony?

Amytis—But it—it's so embarrassing to put it into words.

Hannibal—I'll count five. If you can't find words in that time, I'm afraid the subject—whatever it is—will have to remain   closed   forever. . . . One. . . . Two. . . . Three. . . . You'd better hurry. . . . Four. . . .

Amytis—I can't say it, Hannibal. You'd better call the Sergeant. (*There is a long pause, while* Hannibal *studies her expression of mute but eloquent desperation.*)

Hannibal—Oh! (*He backs away from her.*) Is *that* the ceremony you had in mind?

Amytis—But no soldier ever kills a woman until he . . . and es*pec*ially if she happens to be attractive.

Hannibal—You rather fancy yourself, don't you?

Amytis—Naturally, I shouldn't have come here at all if I had been lacking in a certain amount of self-confidence.

Hannibal—I'm sorry to disappoint you. I should have been

delighted to justify your confidence if the circumstances had been more favorable for a—an event of this kind.

AMYTIS—More favorable! How could any circumstances be more favorable. Here you are—alone, in the night—with your triumphant army behind you, with Rome cringing at your feet. Here you are, Hannibal—and here am I! (*He makes a step forward, toward her, and for a moment there is the suggestion that he has weakened. But he braces himself, and again steps back.*)

HANNIBAL—I'll have to decline your kind offer and put you to death . . . and this time you won't be allowed to talk your way out of it.

A piercing shriek is followed by the appearance of Meta, sobbing hysterically. A second later she is followed by Varius, and from them and the report of the sergeant it is learned that a guardsman had attacked Meta and been promptly knocked down by Varius. Amytis is furious and accusing. Hannibal had given his word that Meta and Varius would be protected!

And so they shall be. The offending soldier shall be put to death. There has been too much of that sort of misconduct in his army, Hannibal admits, and a stop shall be put to it.

But now they must return to Amytis and the disposal of her case. Mago is waiting to take her out and turns to Hannibal for the order.

HANNIBAL—Yes, you can take her out.

AMYTIS—Is it all over, Hannibal? Am I going to die?

HANNIBAL—You're going to die.

MAGO—Come on. (*He takes her toward the steps.*)

AMYTIS (*turning*)—You'll be sorry, Hannibal. (*She turns and is about to go down the steps.*)

HANNIBAL—Wait a minute, Mago.

MAGO—We mustn't delay any longer.

HANNIBAL—Bring her here.

MAGO—You haven't changed your mind?

HANNIBAL—Give me your sword. (MAGO *draws his sword, a long dagger, and hands it to* HANNIBAL.) I'm going to kill her myself. I'll send for you when it's over. (*There is a shrill bugle call. Outside, the Corporal is seen changing guard. When this is over, the Corporal stands by the curtains at the back, prepared to lower them.*)

MAGO (*crestfallen*)—Can't I stay and watch?

HANNIBAL—Go on, Mago.

MAGO (*to* AMYTIS)—It's an honor to die by the hand of Hannibal. Perhaps you deserve it. (*There is a note of admiration in his voice. He goes out. The Corporal lowers the curtains, and as he does so the lights are dimmed.* HANNIBAL *and* AMYTIS *face each other.*)

HANNIBAL—You've called me a murderer. You say that I glory in my reputation for cruelty. Now I'm going to justify that reputation. I shall give you the final satisfaction of knowing that Hannibal, the merciless conqueror of Rome, is not a myth. . . . Come here. . . . (*She advances to him, slowly but without hesitation. He clutches her throat with his left hand. His right hand holds the dagger.*)

AMYTIS—Why do you choose to have me die this way?

HANNIBAL—I couldn't trust Mago to do this. You might have told him some of the things you have told me. He might have weakened.

AMYTIS—Yes—Mago is a man. You, of course, are a god. . . . Perhaps some day you'll discover that you're a man, too, Hannibal—and not ashamed to weaken. . . . Perhaps, some day, you'll realize that there's a thing called the human equation. It's so much more beautiful than war.

HANNIBAL—The human equation does not interest me.

AMYTIS—Because you don't know what it is. If you could ever find it, you'd know that all your conquests—all your glory—are only whispers in the infinite stillness of time—that Rome is no more than a tiny speck on the face of eternity—that the gods are the false images of the unimaginative—and then you'll wish that all that you've done could be undone.

HANNIBAL—Where can I go to find this human equation?

AMYTIS—It is here—on earth—not on the heights of Olympus.

HANNIBAL—Perhaps I'll find it—but never with you. You must die. (*He is very close to her.*)

AMYTIS—War is death, Hannibal. Rome is dying, Carthage is dying—but we're alive. . . . You can conquer men, Hannibal. You can conquer armies. But you can't conquer life.

HANNIBAL—You must die.

AMYTIS—Go out and destroy the wind, Hannibal. Destroy the stars, and the night itself—if you can. Then come back and kill me. (*A bugle is heard, blowing the Carthaginian version of "taps"—softly, slowly.* HANNIBAL, *using all his strength, tries to thrust her away from him and lifts the dagger higher, preparing to plunge it in her heart. She clings desperately to his arms.*)

HANNIBAL (*his voice now tremulous*)—You're going to die!

AMYTIS—Yes—I'm going to die . . . but not until to-morrow.
. . . (*Her face is close to his—too close. He kisses her. Presently,* AMYTIS *draws away from him and gazes, unsmilingly, into his eyes.* HANNIBAL *raises the sword, thinks better of it, and throws the sword away, vehemently. Again he seizes her in his arms and kisses her.*)
The curtain falls.


## ACT III

Early the next morning the generals, Maharbal, Catharlo and Hasdrubal, are gathered in Hannibal's tent awaiting their instructions as to the assault upon Rome.  So eager to fight are they that they are ready to fight with each other.

The cavalry, says Hasdrubal, will go in first.  Not, insists Maharbal, until after the infantry, which has earned that privilege, inaugurates the assault.  The Numidian cavalry, repeats Hasdrubal menacingly, will go in first.  They will not!  The infantry—

Bloodshed, thinks Hannibal, who now appears, can be averted if the honors of entrance are divided.  Let Hasdrubal attack from the west, Carthalo from the south and Maharbal from the north.  Mago will take the elephants through the east gate, and as all the Romans will concentrate there to see the show the others will have no trouble.

"You can all start at the same time," he tells them, "and the first one to reach the Forum will win a prize."

The generals have gone to fall their men in.  The sergeant has been given his orders to pack up the tent equipment and Bala to get his kitchen ready.  Hannibal is taking a hasty breakfast, principally of bread and wine, while he stands by the table.

"The change in his manner is apparent; he is now gay, buoyant, carefree and reluctant to concentrate on the serious business at hand.  He has the air of one who doesn't much care whether school keeps or not."

Hannibal sends for Varius and Meta, who come in with their hands tightly clasped, "as though they were clinging to each other in the face of a common danger."  They are wanted, he tells them, in the sleeping room.

Outside the camp is bestirring itself actively.  The orders to pack and be prepared to move have been issued.

Mago, wearing a shiny new uniform, wanders in.  Mago is

a little miffed, not to say angry. For hours the night before he had waited to be sent for and when finally he gave up and looked in the tent it was empty and even his supper had been eaten.

"She ate it," confesses Hannibal, with a sly glance in the direction of the inner room.

"Of all the damned outrages!" explodes Mago.

The army is to move in half an hour. Mago might eat his breakfast there to make up for the supper he missed, suggests Hannibal, but the pleasantry is wasted on Mago. "I can't understand it, Hannibal," he confesses, a little dolefully; "it's the first serious mistake you've ever made."

"I've made many mistakes, Mago," Hannibal admits, "but this isn't one of them."

Hannibal has left the tent and Mago is eating breakfast when Amytis appears. "She is wearing the Phœnician nightgown and a brilliant blue cloak. She passes behind the column, going to the right to gaze out after Hannibal. . . . Amytis is also a changed person. There are no evidences of her cheerful flippancy. She is languorous, meditative, reserved."

She accepts Mago's invitation to breakfast and listens interestedly to his description of the things that are about to happen to Rome. By nightfall there will be nothing left of the city.

"First we'll slaughter the men," explains Mago. "When we've got them out of the way we'll start plundering and see what we can pick up in the way of loot. After that we'll set fire to the houses. . . . And then . . ."

Amytis can guess what will come next. And that Mago will prove irresistible to the women of Rome she can have little doubt. For his part, Mago would much rather feel that his conquests are fairly won than that he is accepted as one of the inevitable consequences of war. With that thought in mind he has been saving the new uniform for the Rome Campaign.

"To-day the women of Rome will feast their eyes on a real Carthaginian soldier," says he.

"I'm sure that the women of Rome will be duly appreciative," encourages Amytis.

The thought that Hannibal may join in the general merriment when the army runs wild in Rome is not, however, a particularly pleasant one to Amytis.

A delegation of Romans is announced. They have come under a flag of truce. They would like to talk with the commander-in-chief and they are headed by one who gives the name of Fabius

Maximus. At the mention of which name Amytis hurriedly leaves the tent.

"You'd better not try to communicate with your husband," Mago calls after her.

"Don't worry. I won't," says she, with conviction.

Hannibal is summoned and the Romans are brought in. They are Fabius, Scipio and Drusus. "Fabius is obviously nervous, moving as one who expects to be stabbed in the back at any moment. He looks apprehensively toward Mago, Maharbal and Carthalo. Scipio also regards them, but there is a belligerent flash in his eye. He had objected strenuously to this attempt at compromise, and during the parley he shows his impatience and dissatisfaction with the whole proceeding."

As Hannibal confronts his enemies he is very serious. "Which of you is Fabius Maximus?" he demands.

"I am," proudly answers Fabius.

For a second Hannibal gazes intently at Fabius. "So you're Fabius Maximus," he continues, finally. And adds, as partly to himself: "That explains a great deal."

Fabius has come, he explains, to talk things over in a civilized manner. Here, he points out, is Hannibal at the gates of Rome with a mighty army. Even they, his enemies, are willing to admit that. For years Carthage and Rome have been at each other's throats, with terrible losses of men on both sides. And now the conflict appears to have reached a crisis.

Hannibal is willing to admit that Fabius is not overstating that fact.

So, continues Fabius, with Hannibal at the gates of Rome, which is protected by at least twenty legions of men (they have two legions at the outside, and they are all great-grandfathers, Hasdrubal interrupts) what is to be gained by a siege? Many gallant young soldiers will be sacrificed, in addition to the innocent victims, the women and children. Why should that be?

And what, asks Hannibal, would Fabius suggest be done about it.

Fabius suggests that Hannibal abandon the idea of capturing Rome, move his army to some spot not *quite* so near the city and that the Roman soldiers come there in due time to meet them in honorable battle.

In due time, Hasdrubal sneers, will probably be after Fabius can get his armies back from Capua and Spain.

Hannibal is not impressed by Fabius' plan. "If you think you can beg us off with a few hollow words you're damned well mistaken," he answers the Roman. "Our army is mobilized at this minute—forty thousand men, waiting for the order to move. Within an hour we'll have surrounded Rome—and then we'll see what sort of defense your twenty legions can put up."

Scipio can stand no more. He, for one, is ready to fight. He has fought Hannibal before and he is ready to fight him again. He knew the idea of talking the thing over was all wrong from the first. Only a damned woman would have suggested it in the first place. Fabius had no business listening to his wife.

Hannibal is not surprised at this revelation, but at the moment he cannot consider domestic affairs of vital importance. He sends the Romans back under escort, but he refuses to order the attack of his own army, much to Hasdrubal's disgust. He wants time to think it over, and nothing will move him from that stand, even though Hasdrubal warns him that to delay the destruction of Rome another day means mutiny among the troops.

The generals are gone and Hannibal is alone when Amytis comes to ask still another favor. She wants Varius and Meta to be set free and sent back to Sicily. Hannibal agrees to that. He will see that they are sent home, and Amytis is grateful.

HANNIBAL—You too can be saved, Amytis—if you choose.

AMYTIS—If I choose?

HANNIBAL—Did you hear my conversation with your husband?

AMYTIS—Yes—I heard it all.

HANNIBAL—I delayed my decision—because I wanted to give you your choice. Last night, I should have put you to death. I shouldn't have listened to a word of protest or persuasion. But I did listen—and you didn't die. . . . This morning, it is different. . . . I can't destroy Rome until I know what your choice is to be. . . . I will spare your husband's life. You can go back to him, and I'll see that you both are allowed to escape—to go wherever you please . . . that's one part of your choice, Amytis.

AMYTIS—And the other part?

HANNIBAL—To go with me. To forget Rome—to forget Carthage—to be with me, forever. . . .

AMYTIS—And if I agree to that part of it, will Rome be spared?

HANNIBAL (*emphatically*)—No! Whatever your choice, Rome must be destroyed!

AMYTIS—Then I choose to go back to my husband. . . . Go ahead with your great work, Hannibal. Burn Rome to the ground; obliterate it. Keep your army here forever, to make sure Rome stays destroyed. Instruct your men to crush any blade of grass, any flower that dares to thrust its head above the ashes of the dead city. Prolong your victory. Glory in it till your dying day. . . . But don't ever look to me, or to my memory, for sympathy or applause.

HANNIBAL (*angrily*)—I think I understand you at last. You came here to save Rome. If you fail in that, you're prepared to die. For all your talk, you care nothing for me.

AMYTIS—You mustn't believe that, Hannibal. (*There is a shrill bugle call.*)

HANNIBAL—You thought you could save Rome from the destiny that is ready to overwhelm it! You have tried to build walls of words as a defense against my army.

AMYTIS—I'm not trying to save Rome, Hannibal. I'm trying to save you.

HANNIBAL—Why do you imagine that I'm worth saving?

AMYTIS—Because I want to have you—always—as my possession. Let Rome and Carthage remember you as a great general. I want to remember you as a conqueror who could realize the glory of submission.

HANNIBAL (*challengingly*)—And does Rome realize the glory of submission?

AMYTIS—No, and for that very reason Rome will destroy itself. Success is like a strong wine, Hannibal; give a man enough of it, and he'll drink himself to death. Rome will do that, too, if you leave it alone.

HANNIBAL—So I'm to leave Rome—and to leave you. Is that your choice?

AMYTIS—Yes, Hannibal—to leave me with something beautiful—something that is worth remembering. I don't want you to spoil that.

HANNIBAL—And what shall I have to remember? That I marched three thousand miles—and failed.

AMYTIS—Ah, but that's just the point, Hannibal. You haven't failed.

HANNIBAL—I came to conquer Rome. Anything short of that is failure.

AMYTIS—Are you sure of that? Are you sure that you didn't come all this way to find your own soul?

HANNIBAL—My own soul doesn't matter, Amytis. I myself amount to nothing. All of us amount to nothing. . . . We stand aside and watch ourselves parade by! We're proud of the brave manner in which we step forward, and of the nobility of our bearing, and the sparkle of divine fire that is in our eyes—and actually we have no more idea of where we're going, no more choice in the matter, than so many drops of water in a flowing river.

AMYTIS—Yes, and at the end of that river is an endless sea of things that are passed. It is called history. When you reach that sea, other drops of water may murmur respectfully, "Here comes Hannibal, the conqueror of Rome." But you won't care. You'll only be thankful for the interludes that you have known— the moments when you drifted from the main current and found peace and contentment in the deep, quiet pools. (*They are standing close together, facing each other. With sudden, fierce strength,* HANNIBAL *takes her in his arms.*)

HANNIBAL—I'll turn away from Rome now, Amytis, if you'll come with me. . . . Rome can live, Amytis. You can save it. . . .

AMYTIS—I don't want it to be that way. . . .

HANNIBAL—I'll bury my sword before the gates of Rome. I'll hand over my command to Hasdrubal. I'll do the one thing I thought was impossible: I'll quit when I'm winning. But I can't do this alone. . . . I can't. . . .

AMYTIS—No, Hannibal. I don't want it to be that way. I don't want Rome to be saved because I made this choice. . . . I want you to do it—to make the decision—to prove that you are stronger than your own victorious army. . . .

HANNIBAL—If I recognize your truths, I'll have to believe that all my life has been wasted—that all those men who have fallen along the road to Rome have died for nothing. Do you want me to believe that?

AMYTIS—I do! I do! I want you to believe that every sacrifice made in the name of war is wasted. When you believe that, you'll be a great man. (*Gently she strokes his hair.*) I want you to be a great man. (*He kisses her desperately.*)

They are still embraced when Mago enters to warn Hannibal that the Romans are awaiting his decision. Slowly he relinquishes his grip on Amytis and steps back.

"You were right, Mago," he sighs. "I should have let you put her to death without further delay."

"I'm glad you realize that at last," replies Mago. "You see I've had a lot more experience in these matters than you've had. I understand the risks."

Now Hannibal has ordered that the Romans be brought in

again, and when Amytis, eager to avoid her husband, starts hurriedly to leave Hannibal calls the guard and places her under arrest.

A moment later Fabius, back from a visit to the elephant camp, is startled to come face to face with Amytis. She starts weakly to explain when Hannibal interrupts her.

"Our sentries arrested this woman," he declares, harshly. "She represented herself as your wife."

"She is my wife! Amytis, why did you come here?"

"She told me that she was concerned for your safety," continues Hannibal. "She came to find you."

"Amytis! My true, my loyal wife! Do you hear that, Scipio? She came to find me."

Amytis tries to interrupt. "I can't let you believe . . ." she begins.

"She evidently told us the truth," declares Hannibal, quickly. "There is no reason why we should suspect the wife of Fabius Maximus. You may release her!"

Now the Carthaginian generals are in and eager for the word to attack. But Hannibal has changed his mind. The Carthaginian army will proceed at once to Capua.

But Hasdrubal will not stand for this! What in the name of all the gods is the matter with Hannibal? Let him take his damned army to Capua if he will—the cavalry will attack Rome!

Back of him now stand Maharbal and Carthalo. "The trouble with you, sir," ventures Maharbal, respectfully, "is that you know how to gain victories, but not how to use them."

But Hannibal is not to be moved. Even though they threaten to take over the army and force him to go with them, a prisoner, he is not impressed. They have been soldiers too long not to take orders. They'll do as he says and they know it.

Now they turn to pleading. And to demanding a reason for his decision. He at least owes them that.

HANNIBAL (*vaguely*)—Every one seems to be so damned curious about my motives.

HASDRUBAL—You owe that much to me—to every man in this sweating army. Tell us why—why? (HANNIBAL, *suddenly collected, steps forward toward* HASDRUBAL.)

HANNIBAL—I'll tell you why, Hasdrubal. . . . I've had a portent. (*He says this mysteriously.*)

HASDRUBAL (*awed*)—A portent?

CARTHALO (*even more awed*)—From the gods?

Hannibal—Yes—a portent from the gods.

Maharbal—From Ba-al?

Hannibal—No—from Tanit, the daughter of Ba-al. (*This last with a furtive glance toward* Amytis.)

Hasdrubal—Then there is no hope. If Ba-al has sent his daughter to rule our destiny, then we are lost forever.

Hannibal (*speaking now directly at* Amytis, *as though they again were alone.*) She told me to look for the human equation. . . . "When you have found that," she said, "you will know that all your conquests, all your glory, are but whispers in the infinite stillness of time—that Rome is only a speck on the face of eternity."

Carthalo—The gods speak strangely.

Hannibal—She told me that I must realize the glory of submission. . . . I could only obey.

Hasdrubal—The gods are cruel.

Hannibal—Cruel—but convenient, in an emergency. . . . (Amytis *smiles tenderly.*) We're going to Capua—to rest. We need rest, more than we need Rome. . . . Get to your posts! (Hasdrubal *steps forward and confronts* Fabius *menacingly.*)

Hasdrubal—The Carthaginian army retreats, for the first time. But don't try to take credit for that, you Romans! Don't ever forget that it was only the gods themselves who saved Rome from the strength of our swords. (*He turns, salutes* Hannibal, *and strides out, followed by* Maharbal *and* Carthalo. Mago *ambles in a leisurely manner across the stage and faces* Amytis.)

Mago—So Hannibal had a portent, did he? (*He turns to* Hannibal.) That's a new name for it. (*He salutes and goes out.*)

Hannibal—Fall in the guard, Sergeant.

Sergeant—Yes, sir. Hup! (*The Sergeant, Corporal, and Guardsmen march out.*)

Hannibal (*to* Thothmes)—Give me your records, Thothmes. (Thothmes *hands him the records.*) You may go. (Thothmes *goes out. Three bugles are heard.* Hannibal *looks through the sheets of papyrus, and then turns to the Romans.*) I have here a complete record of our march from Carthage to the gates of Rome. I need hardly explain to you that this is a document of great historical importance. That being the case . . . (*he tears the sheets into small pieces*) it is now no longer a document of any importance whatever. The exploits of Hannibal's magnificent army will live only as long as our own memory survives. That's the end of the story, gentlemen.

FABIUS—Hannibal—you've destroyed a chapter of History.

HANNIBAL—What difference does it make? In the end, there'll be more than enough history to go 'round.

SCIPIO—I have seen you before, Hannibal—in battle. Gods or no gods—it is not like you to do this—to retreat.

HANNIBAL—I'm leaving Rome to an enemy that is crueller even than I am. . . . I shall allow Rome to destroy itself.

SCIPIO—Perhaps we'll have the chance to fight it out some day.

HANNIBAL (*bowing*)—I'm afraid so. (*He walks slowly to the back, then turns.*)

HANNIBAL—Fabius, I wish happiness and prosperity to you, your wife, and your sons.

FABIUS—Thank you—but I have no sons.

HANNIBAL—You may have . . . and if you do, I hope that your first-born will inherit the qualities of greatness that were so evident in his father—that he will duplicate his father's signal triumphs and that he, too, will ultimately discover the human equation. . . . (*He turns to* AMYTIS.) It is so much more beautiful than war.

AMYTIS (*in a whisper*)—Hannibal! You're a great man. (*He takes an indecisive step toward her as she stands before the column; the impulse, however, is only momentary. He steps back.*)

HANNIBAL—Good-by, gentlemen. I wish you luck with your conquest of the world. (*He goes out.* BALA *comes in from the left, picks up* HANNIBAL'S *shield, and follows his master out. There is a shrill bugle call.*)

FABIUS—What was all that he said about "the human equation"? (DRUSUS *goes down the steps at the right, standing at the back—still visible—and gazing out after* HANNIBAL.)

SCIPIO—Hasdrubal was right. Hannibal has gone mad. (*He goes to the back to join* DRUSUS.)

FABIUS—Let this be a lesson to doubters. Hannibal, with all his elephants and all his men, could not subdue the high moral purpose of Rome.

AMYTIS—Virtue is rewarded—isn't it, Fabius? (*The African war drums start beating. The bugles come in, with a suggestion of wild, barbaric marching music.*)

FABIUS—Virtue, my dear, is the one perfect defense against all the evil forces on this earth.

SCIPIO—Look, Fabius—the army has started to move! (FABIUS *goes to the back and looks off toward the left.* AMYTIS *remains alone before the column.*)

FABIUS—What a glorious sight!

SCIPIO—There's Hannibal—riding away. . . . (*The terrifying sound of the drums and bugles swells in volume, the bugles seeming to shriek a final message of savage defiance to Rome. . . . AMYTIS goes to the top of the steps at the back, so that she is behind* FABIUS *and the others. She smiles sadly, and waves her hand to the departing Carthaginians.*)

The curtain falls.

# THE PLAY'S THE THING

## A Comedy in Three Acts by Ferenc Molnar

### Adapted by P. G. WODEHOUSE

FOR several seasons last passed Gilbert Miller has served as managing director of Charles Frohman, Inc. This, as most of the world knows, is the firm that assumed the play-producing obligations of the late Charles Frohman. A majority of its stock, if not all of it, is owned by the Famous Players-Lasky Motion Picture Corporation, and to some extent its policies have been shaped to serve the interests of the cinema. That, at least, was the intention when the picture magnates secured control.

Mr. Miller, however, being an independent sort and convinced in his own mind that a theatre is a theatre while a picture is something else entirely, insisted upon and managed to maintain a reasonable independence of action in his selection of plays.

His first production this year, for instance, was "The Captive" (September 29), which immediately achieved a sensational popularity but never, never could be considered a picture possibility. His second production was that of a boldly amusing comedy written by Ferenc Molnar, called "The Play's the Thing" (November 3), and adapted from the Hungarian for Mr. Miller by the English writer, P. G. Wodehouse. There are picture possibilities in the Molnar script, but it is seriously to be questioned whether they can be so utilized that the censors will approve their being capitalized upon the screen.

Thus Mr. Miller found himself early in the season with two big Broadway successes to his credit, which brought him nothing better than suspicious glances and limp handshakes from his business associates.

"The Play's the Thing" had been tentatively tried in a Great Neck, Long Island, theatre in late October. Two weeks later it was brought to the Henry Miller Theatre in New York, opening November 3. The reviews were mostly enthusiastic, with only a dissenting Puritan here and there questioning the good-natured boldnesses Mr. Wodehouse had carried over from the

Hungarian original. The approval of the first audience was a little uncertain, but promising, and within the month a popular success was assured.

The scene is a room in a castle on the Italian Riviera. It is two o'clock in the morning, but a distant orchestra is still playing Leoncavallo's "Mattinata" and the feeling is that a favored part of the world is still awake and enjoying itself.

The castle room is in darkness. "The only light comes through two large French windows at the back. Through them we see the moonlit Mediterranean far below, the vague outlines of the precipitous coast, twinkling lights along quays and esplanades and here and there the faint glow from some lighted window."

There are, it is soon discovered, three darker shadows moving about in the room. "The lighted ends of their three cigarettes prick the blackness. There is a long pause. It is almost embarrassingly long. Just before one wonders if anything is ever going to happen a man's voice breaks the silence."

Then one of the three finds an electric switch, the lights are turned on and a room beautifully furnished in Italian Renaissance is revealed.

The three shadows are likewise discovered to be two playwrights and a composer. The playwrights are Sandor Turai and a chap named Mansky, his collaborator. The composer is their youthful protégé, Albert Adam, who, if their confidence in him is not misplaced and nothing happens to halt or interfere with his career, is destined to achieve a sensational success.

These three, it is further revealed, largely by their "shop talk," which is aptly concerned with the most practical way in which a playwright may introduce his characters in a play,— these three have come to the castle to surprise their prima donna, Ilona Szabo, with whom young Adam is in love, and, second, to celebrate the completion of the play in which Ilona is to appear.

Incidentally the visit may be classified as one having its "good business" aspects. "When a composer is happy he writes song hits," asserts Turai. "When a prima donna is happy she stops singing off the key. And the librettists gather royalties from the resulting triumph."

Till now everything has worked out beautifully. Turai has been able to secure the suite adjoining that occupied by Ilona and although he is a little disappointed to find that the prima donna is not in the castle, but away on a picnic, he feels sure the success of their surprise will be all the greater.

It is his plan that they shall wait until Ilona comes in and is all comfortably tucked in her little bed and then, with Adam softly playing the waltz from the forthcoming opera on the piano, and Turai singing, they will waken their divinity and bring her forth to greet them. Particularly to greet Adam.

Mansky, however, is for going to bed. There is no telling when the picnic party will return. Adam frankly confesses an intention of taking a hot bath. But Turai is wide awake and full of thoughts. Sentimental thoughts, many of them. Thoughts of Adam's grandmother, who had brought the boy up after his parents died. Of Adam's mother, a gentle and beautiful woman. And of Adam himself, who, if Turai can bring it about, is going to escape most of the struggles and heartaches and wasted energy genius is so often heir to. "You've got a very clever man behind you pushing you on," he laughingly assures Adam. "So run away and have your bath and sleep and dream and love and enjoy this beautiful world and all that there is in it. Happiness will make your music all the sweeter."

Mansky grumbles something about it being a shame to encourage Adam to be a dreamer when he ought to be "learning that life isn't all music and roses and happiness." But Turai is satisfied and so is Adam.

ADAM—I think I'm going to like this place. Well, gentlemen, before I go, one last word. I am very fond of both of you. I am finding life very beautiful. And I am very happy. (ADAM *goes out. Once again the distant orchestra is heard, this time playing the Brise Argentine.*)

TURAI—Which startling utterance seems to call for a glass of very old brandy. (*He crosses to the bell rope on left wall and pulls it.*)

MANSKY—Make it two.

TURAI—It's nice to see the boy so happy. Now I'm on the shady side of fifty, I find myself full of parental affection and nobody to lavish it on. (*Reflectively.*) Yes—his mother was a gentle, beautiful woman. (*He goes up to window, and looks down the cliff.*) They're still dancing down there on the hotel terrace. With spotlights on the dancers. With that dark blue sky in the background and the colored lights on the water, that wouldn't make a bad setting for a first act finale. (MANSKY, *who has just taken a cigarette from his case, snaps it shut with irritation.*) Yes, I'm coming to think the boy's right and life is beautiful.

MANSKY—Sandor.

TURAI—Yes?

MANSKY—I didn't like to tell you before, though it really belongs to Friday, too.

TURAI—Tell me what?

MANSKY (*sits on bench with the unconscious relish of the confirmed pessimist*)—Something rather unpleasant. A little piece of news. Rather unpleasant. (*The music has stopped.* TURAI, *who has been at the window, turns toward* MANSKY.)

TURAI—You're a queer chap. Just when a man's feeling happy for five minutes you have to come along and take the joy out of life.

MANSKY—It concerns you, too. It's rather unpleasant.

TURAI (*going to* MANSKY—*speaks ironically*)—Well, come on, old friend. Ruin my evening. What is it?

MANSKY—I was looking in the visitors' book downstairs, and I saw a certain name. (*Puffs cigarette.*) Yes, it's rather unpleasant.

TURAI—Don't sit there making my flesh creep. What name did you see in the visitors' book?

MANSKY—Almady.

TURAI—The actor?

MANSKY—Yes.

TURAI—He's here?

MANSKY—He is.

TURAI—H'm. This *is*, as you say, rather unpleasant.

MANSKY—You realize what this means?

TURAI—It means that you're thoroughly happy.

MANSKY—Not at all. I may be a pessimist, but unfortunately I'm a tender-hearted pessimist. When I am proved right, I do not enjoy the fact. The fact is that Mr. Almady is here.

TURAI—But how? Why? He hasn't been invited here for ten years. I always understood he spent his summers with his wife and children at Lake Balaton.

MANSKY—I suppose he fished for an invitation. He probably had his reasons.

TURAI—Does our young friend know anything about that business?

MANSKY—He hasn't an inkling of the part Mr. Almady has played in his fiancée's life.

TURAI—Well, hang it all, it wasn't so much of a part. What does it amount to? When she was starting on the stage he gave her lessons in voice production. And then—well, it was just the usual business—the romantic leading actor and the little pupil.

The sort of thing that lasts a couple of months at the outside. And, besides, it was all over and done with long ago.

MANSKY—Apparently it is *not* over and done with.

TURAI—Rot!   Because by *pure* chance he happens to be in the same house?

MANSKY—It isn't pure chance.   It's impure intention.   Use your intelligence, man.   Ilona was Almady's discovery—he taught her all she knows.

TURAI—That's a thing of the past.   Ilona's intelligent.   She's in love and she's engaged to be married.   And you know how wholeheartedly, how passionately, an actress can be engaged when she *is* engaged to be married.   I'm bound to say I'm not remarkably enthusiastic about this match, but if it makes the boy happy that's the main thing.   My dear chap, you're crazy. She wouldn't be such a fool . . . with a worn-out elderly actor— a father of a family—with four children.   She's got too much sense.

MANSKY—I never said a word about that.   I merely said I had seen his name in the visitors' book.   That means he is stay-ing here.   Is that pleasant?   No.   It is unpleasant.   That was all I said.   I now say something more.   We *ought* to have *wired* Ilona that we were coming to-night.

TURAI—I admit it.   You're right again.   So be happy.   Never surprise a woman.   Always wire her in plenty of time.   On several occasions in a longish life I have prepared a joyful sur-prise for a woman, and every time I was the one surprised.   The telegraph was invented for no other purpose than that women should not get surprises.

The footman's name is Johann Dwornitschek.   He is a loqua-cious and a solicitous servant, eager to serve, eager to talk, sorry he is unable to tell Turai more than that the fair Ilona is popu-lar at all the hotel picnics, that she is, as the playwright suspects, frequently in the company of Almady the actor and that, in view of the fact that the picnickers have taken a considerable supply of liquor and a gypsy band with them, it is extremely unlikely that they will return early.

In this surmise, however, he is wrong.   A slamming door plainly suggests that Ilona is already back in her room.   Soon there can be no mistake, because Ilona is singing joyously an aria from a popular operetta.   Turai, made happy by the turn of events, orders champagne from Dwornitschek and goes to call his companions.

Now the voice of Almady is heard through the wall. It rises above Ilona's singing, and is a voice of protest. How can she sing when he is tortured—tortured by the very dear nearness of her and by her coldly repeated suggestions that inasmuch as she did not invite him to come home with her, and certainly not to walk thus boldly into her bedroom at such an hour in the morning, the least he can do is to get out and stay out.

"Everything's over and ended," Ilona's voice is heard saying. "I've put you out of my life forever. I'm engaged to be married and I intend to be a good little wife. You've no right to behave like this."

"No right? I, who made you? I, with whom you have lived so many hours of madness—wonderful—unforgettable—"

"Not unforgettable at all. Watch how quickly *I'm* going to forget them. Do go away and leave me alone. Don't touch me. (*Pause.*) Stop, I won't let you kiss me. Can't you understand my fiancé will be arriving any day now?"

"I'll kill him!" threatens Almady.

Soon it appears from Ilona's protests that Almady is actually crying, acting like a great baby in fact, and she is sufficiently sorry for him to let him kiss her. After which she again insists that he must go. Go into the ante-room, if he likes, and help himself to the liquor, but go. She is tired, she wants to get into her nightie, and she doesn't want him either coming back or peeking.

Now the three organizers of the surprise visit return and, under Turai's direction, arrange themselves close to Ilona's wall. They are all ready with their welcoming song, Turai's hand is uplifted to give them the beat, when they, too, hear voices.

ALMADY'S VOICE—I worship you—I adore you! (*The three are riveted where they stand, transfixed with amazement.*)

ILONA'S VOICE—Are you starting all over again?

ALMADY'S VOICE—Yes, I am. All over again. I love you as the church steeple loves the cloud that settles above it and floats away with the first passing breeze. I can't go on living without you. Not a week, not a day, not an hour. (*The three men turn simultaneously.*)

ILONA'S VOICE (*contemptuously*)—Just words.

ALMADY'S VOICE—It's the truth. I'm crazy about you. And you—you've used me up and squeezed me like a lemon, and now you want to throw me away.

ILONA'S VOICE—I don't want to throw you away, silly.

Where's the sense in raving like this? Oh, come on, then. Come here and let me kiss your beautiful classic brow.

ADAM—She said—did you hear what she said?

ALMADY'S VOICE—That's not a kiss—that's a tip— Nothing but a paltry tip.

MANSKY (*sinks into chair*).

ILONA'S VOICE—Don't shout like that.

ALMADY'S VOICE—I will shout. I'm a squeezd lemon. That's what I am— (*Sobs.*) A lemon! The whole world shall know that I'm a lemon.

ILONA'S VOICE—Get off your knees. And, oh, please, do stop crying. I can't bear it. You know how fond I am of you. (TURAI *and* MANSKY *clap their hands to their heads.* ADAM *collapses on the piano stool.*)

ALMADY'S VOICE—Those nights of love—those flaming wonderful nights! Have you forgotten them so completely?

ADAM (*looking up*)—That's Almady.

MANSKY—You can't be sure.

TURAI (*turns to* MANSKY)—Don't be an ass. Don't try to deceive a musician about a voice. There's no use talking—the thing's a tragedy and we've got to face it.

MANSKY—Friday!

ILONA'S VOICE—Stop! Control yourself.

ALMADY'S VOICE—You ask me to control myself—when I look at *that*—at that perfect shape. The rose flush of that skin.

ILONA'S VOICE—Hands off!

ALMADY'S VOICE—My God! How round it is! How smooth, how velvety—and how fragrant. (*A pause.*)

ILONA'S VOICE—Don't bite!

ALMADY'S VOICE—I must. I am *so hungry*. . . .

TURAI (*to* ADAM *and patting him on the shoulder*)—I think you had better go, old man. Go and turn in in our room.

ADAM (*bitterly*)—And I thought she was a Madonna. Holding her in his arms—stroking— (*Rising in sudden fury and rushing to the door.*) God, I could kill him!

TURAI (*restraining him*)—Steady, old man, steady. (ADAM *covers his ears with his hands.*)

ALMADY'S VOICE—Ah, well! I see I am nothing to you any more.

ILONA'S VOICE—Oh, for goodness sake. I swear that no man has ever meant so much to me as you. From the top of your head to the soles of your feet you are a *man!* Who should know that better than I?

TURAI—Come, come, my boy—let's get out of this.

MANSKY (*goes to* ADAM)—Come on, old chap. You're going to sleep in our room. (TURAI *and* MANSKY *lead him to stairway.*)

ADAM—Sleep! (*He goes out at right.* TURAI *and* MANSKY *are on the landing.*)

ILONA'S VOICE—Oh! Don't look so pathetic. . . . Well, come here—kiss me.

MANSKY—I was right— We ought to have sent a telegram. (*He goes out at right.* TURAI *comes down to table, lights a cigarette and sits on edge of table.*)

ALMADY'S VOICE—I want you to remember that kiss forever.

ILONA'S VOICE—It was your old kiss. Sweet and burning— like hot punch. But do be a dear and go away now. It was mad of you to come here. If my fiancé ever hears of this I'll kill myself. Oh, damn my idiotic sentimentality for getting me into this mess. You must leave here to-morrow on the first train. He'll be here any day now. (TURAI *shifts uneasily.*) Every day I've been expecting a telegram. (TURAI *groans.*) Get out, I tell you, get out!

ALMADY'S VOICE—If you insist, dear heart, so be it! Your word is law. I am going to bed now. Farewell, dear heart. But grant me one last kiss.

TURAI (*to himself*)—Damn all fools who don't know when they've had enough.

ILONA'S VOICE—Go *now*—

ALMADY'S VOICE—So be it. Good night, dear heart.

ILONA'S VOICE—Good night, you baby. (*Silence. A door is heard closing.*)

TURAI (*to himself*)—*At last!* Good night, dear heart! (*After a moment he sits down in armchair. Pause.* MANSKY *reënters.*)

MANSKY (*with a gesture of inquiry toward* ILONA'S *room*) This silence—what does it mean?

TURAI—This silence is a highly moral silence. The baritone hero has departed. And the fair heroine has deposited herself in bed.

MANSKY—After depositing *us* in the worst mess in my whole experience. Wasn't it awful?

TURAI—Awful!

It is Adam's future that most concerns Turai. Careers have been ruined by no greater shocks than that the boy will suffer thinking of Ilona's duplicity. Something must be done about that.

Suddenly, despite the interruptions of the chattering Mansky, an idea forms in Turai's mind—that he prefers to work out alone. He needs no collaborator. Mansky doesn't relish that kind of talk, but he can do nothing more than make the best of it. He is, however, not without ideas of his own.

MANSKY—My own humble suggestion would be to wake her up now and have a little chat.

TURAI—What about?

MANSKY (*starting across*)—I'll rout her out.

TURAI (*excitedly*)—For heaven's sake, no! The only thing a woman can do is deny everything. What could she deny? Could she unsay those words of hers? Gloss over that mad sensual outburst? Explain her half-hearted resistance? Of course, she might point out that it was nice of her to forbid the man to bite. No, I can't quite see where denials come in.

MANSKY—Women have lots of other tricks. Falling on their knees—fainting—bursting into tears—laughing hysterically—or just going *rigid* all over.

TURAI—That might be good enough for you or me. When you're a middle-aged dramatist, you welcome a chance to do the noble, forgiving business. It's good theatre. But that boy in there is twenty-five and he isn't a dramatist. So think again.

MANSKY (*collapsing hopelessly in armchair*)—Then there's no solution to the problem.

TURAI—There's a solution to everything—one has only to find it.

MANSKY—By Jove! Rather a good line, that.

TURAI—Not bad. Jot it down. (MANSKY *does so, on his cuff*.) And now the most important thing is—be very tactful and understanding with the boy. Sit by his bed till he falls asleep.

MANSKY—He won't sleep to-night.

TURAI—Give him something to make him . . . he must have sleep. To-morrow's going to be a big day. One false move and he will be the center of a record scandal. It would break his heart. And on his peace of mind depends . . .

MANSKY—Our success. Capacity business. A year's run.

TURAI—Beastly words.

MANSKY—And yet only yesterday—how beautiful they sounded!

TURAI—Go away. I'll take on this job. (*Rises.*) Leave everything to me, and base your confidence on past experience. Which shows the moment *you* stop trying to help me, I can solve anything.

MANSKY (*bows stiffly and turns toward stairs*)—Thank you, my dear fellow.

TURAI—Not at all.

MANSKY—Good night.

TURAI—Good night. See you to-morrow. Till then, don't leave him for an instant. That's official. I've enjoyed our little talk so much. Good night.

MANSKY—Good night. (*Goes out at right.* TURAI *goes to table, sits and jots down some more notes. There is a knock at door left to hall.*)

TURAI—Come in. (DWORNITSCHEK *enters with cooler and champagne, four glasses on a tray.*)

DWORNITSCHEK—The champagne, sir. Mumm's Cordon Rouge—just as you ordered.

TURAI (*motioning it away*)—'M yes. But that was a long time ago. A very long time ago. Since then the world has changed quite a good deal. However, the motto of the Turais is "Never refuse champagne," so put it down. (DWORNITSCHEK *places tray on the table and the cooler on the floor.*)

DWORNITSCHEK—Will four glasses be sufficient, sir?

TURAI—Three more than sufficient.

Armed, then, with the champagne, writing materials, and a promise of complete quiet until he is called for breakfast at 6, Turai goes to the library to work out his idea.

The curtain falls.

## ACT II

Next morning as the clock is striking six Dwornitschek opens the door of the playwright's sitting room to find Sandor Turai up and dressed, enjoying the golden sunshine that streams over the very blue Mediterranean and into the room. Turai is reading over the loose pages of a manuscript and he is ready for the breakfast that Dwornitschek and his lackeys bring him.

With the lackeys gone, the breakfast partly disposed of and Dwornitschek finally convinced that there is nothing more he can do to make his favorite guest comfortable, Turai picks up a phone and calls the number of Ilona Szabo's room.

Ilona, heard again through the thin partition, sleepily answers and is finally made conscious of her friends' nearness and the advisability of her immediate attendance upon them. A moment later Ilona appears. "She is an extraordinarily beautiful blonde young woman. Having just got out of bed and slipped a flimsy, alluring negligee over her nightie, she is somewhat disheveled."

Ilona is also considerably perturbed by Turai's account of the previous night's revelations. Quite hysterical in fact, and eager to do anything she can do to help them all out of the mess they seem to be in. Otherwise she can think of nothing to do but kill herself.

"You know I worship Albert," she insists, weepily; "if anybody knows that you do. I've been a different woman since I met him. He looks on me as a saint. (TURAI *gives her a quick ironic glance.*) And he's right. I *have* turned into a saint since I began to love him. It was the only thing I wanted to do in life—to keep straight for his sake. I was so happy. (*She sinks into armchair crying.*) I love him so."

"And yet you can't be true to him."

"You've no right to say that. It was nothing but my damned sentimentality. You know very well that affair with that beast Almady didn't last a couple of months. First he gave me breathing lessons and taught me how to throw my voice—"

"Yes, he taught you that all right," admits Turai, with a significant glance at the bedroom wall.

Ilona swears she is through with Almady, and thoroughly ashamed of herself for having even let him linger over his farewells. Now she is eager to know and to help with Turai's plan.

Almady is also summoned by telephone, roused from his bed and informed that his attendance upon the conference is a matter of life and death, particularly death. The summons hurries the actor, and a moment later he all but bursts into the room in a high state of nervous apprehension. "He is attired in elaborate, not to say loud, house pajamas. A tall and but recently handsome man, now well into middle age, Almady is first, last and always the actor. He dramatizes every moment of his existence. He does not walk, he struts; he does not talk, he declaims."

Almady is, in his turn, also greatly excited by Turai's recital of the situation. Being the father of a family, he sees even more plainly than Turai had hoped he would the necessity of doing what he can to keep his recent activities from becoming public. Failing in that, he, too, is willing to die. He would like to die with Ilona, but she won't let him. She prefers to die alone.

They will neither of them do anything so silly, Turai insists. They will do nothing more than to follow his orders, and follow them scrupulously. Then he outlines his plan.

TURAI—In that room next door—last night—something occurred.

ILONA (*ashamed*)—Yes, yes, *please*. We know what occurred.

TURAI—That is just what you don't know. You are now going to hear. What occurred was the rehearsal of a play. Do you grasp my meaning?

ILONA—In the middle of the night?

TURAI—In the middle of the night.

ALMADY—How do you mean—the rehearsal of a play?

TURAI—Your very loud remarks, so loud that they actually penetrated the wall—were dialogue from a play. Now, do you understand?

ILONA—I do. (*To* ALMADY.) Don't you—idiot? (*Rises.*) It's the most marvelous, wonderful idea, you old darling. . . . (*She is just about to embrace* TURAI, *when she stops in consternation.*)

TURAI—What's the matter?

ILONA—It's no good. He'd never believe it.

TURAI—Why wouldn't he believe it?

ILONA—Where on earth is there a play with lines in it like those?

TURAI—Where? (*Picking up pile of papers from the table.*) Here!

ILONA—What do you mean?

TURAI (*pointing*)—Here you are. Here's the play. This is it.

ILONA—Who wrote it?

TURAI—I did. Don't stare at me, my dear child, with those starry eyes of blue. (*Sits on bench.*) Rather ask when I wrote it.

ILONA—When could you have written it?

TURAI—This morning—between four and six. After all, one is either a playwright or one isn't. Half of it I heard through the wall; the other half I wrote to fit. In this life, every one has to fight with his own weapons. My weapon is the pen! And on this occasion I hope it will prove considerably mightier than the sword. I am feeling this morning like an acrobat who for once has the chance to use his skill to save a life. I don't suppose any play has ever yet been written with such purely altru-

istic motives. Well, there you are. There's the play. Read it—
learn it and play it. (*He gives her the manuscript.*)

ILONA—*Play* it?

TURAI—Naturally you must play it. How else can you make
him believe without a shadow of doubt that what you were saying last night was just dialogue? Off you go. Dress rehearsal
early this evening. Opening to-night.

ALMADY—To-night? But where?

TURAI—At the concert, of course. After dinner in the ballroom. (*To* ILONA.) You're down on the program already for
something or other.

ILONA—A couple of songs. (*Contemptuously.*) He's to recite
some poems.

TURAI—Then there'll be a slight change in the program. He'll
act with you instead—a one-act play.

ILONA (*looking at script*)—But how on earth can I learn all
this by to-night?

TURAI—Well, really! Last night you knew it well enough.
(ALMADY *sighs deeply.*) What's the matter with you?

ALMADY—Mr. Turai, that was a sigh of relief. Do you *know*
my wife?

TURAI—I do. Didn't I tell you that it was a matter of death?

ALMADY—How can I ever thank you? (*He holds out his hand.*
TURAI *ignores it.*)

TURAI—Don't bother to try. If you think I'm doing this for
your sake, my good man, you're greatly mistaken. Unfortunately, my life-saving apparatus is so constructed that you auto-
matically have to be rescued too.

ILONA—Oh, but listen. . . .

TURAI—Now what is it?

ILONA—What earthly reason could we have had for rehearsing
at three in the morning?

TURAI—That's what I ask myself, but I answer myself—quite
simple. You had to play the thing to-night. You'd lost a lot
of time on a picnic. Every moment was precious. You were so
conscientious that when you came home you insisted on rehearsing even though it was three o'clock in the morning.

Ilona phones to Mr. Mell, the director of the concert, to warn
him of the change that will have to be made in the program. She
and Mr. Almady have decided to do a sketch—a little thing
from the French by—by Geraldy. Mr. Mell is delighted. He
knows every line of Geraldy. In that case, Turai whispers

hoarsely, the sketch is by Sardou. Mr. Mell is not so well acquainted with Sardou. Only knows his "Hedda Gabbler." Which clears that situation nicely.

But now Ilona, glancing through the script, takes exception to the first of the inaccuracies she discovers.

"You make me say: 'Your kiss is revolting to me.' What I really said was—"

" 'That was your old kiss. Sweet and burning, like hot punch,' " quotes Turai. "I know. My memory is excellent. But fortunately we got the boy out of the room before you got that far."

Almady, too, objects to this reflection upon his osculatory gifts, but gets little satisfaction from Turai. Whether they like his play or do not like it, they will have to play it and play it as it is written. And they will do well to study with particular care those parts of it which are quoted verbatim from their slushy conversation of the night before.

ILONA (*reads*)—Odd—I hardly remember—

TURAI—I do. Nor is your fiancé likely to have forgotten.

ILONA (*reading*)—"I worship you. I adore you. I love you as the church steeple loves the cloud that settles on its summit." (ALMADY *turns away, embarrassed.*) Just words!

ALMADY (*takes script*)—"You have used me up and squeezed me like a lemon."

ILONA (*takes script*)—Yes, now I remember—

ALMADY—It's all down, word for word. (TURAI *takes script.*)

TURAI—Yes, the passage is underlined in red ink. Three pages—here—from page sixteen. It goes on "Come here and let me kiss that beautiful classic brow"—and then—this is the worst bit, here—this mad outburst of sensuality— (*Reads rapidly.*) "When I look at *that*—at the perfect shape. The rose flush of that skin— Just to stroke it . . .

ILONA—Yes, but I . . .

TURAI—I know, I know. (*Reads.*) "Hands off!" you said. But he couldn't have obeyed you for he goes on "My God! How round it is! How smooth! How velvety!" And then I'm afraid he must have got very close indeed for he adds, "And how fragrant." That's right, isn't it?

ALMADY—Quite right. It *was* fragrant.

ILONA—But I . . .

TURAI—No, my dear, you did *not*. There was a complete silence until you exclaimed, "You mustn't bite . . ." (*Both turn away.*) Yes, I should think you *would* be ashamed of yourselves. (*He gives* ILONA *the script.*) All right, then; copy it out and learn it. If you ever studied parts in your lives, study these. We'll have the dress rehearsal at seven-thirty sharp, here in this room. I'll give you a run through. And after dinner, first performance. And now—?

ILONA—Out we go, eh?

TURAI—You took the words out of my mouth. And don't forget, we've not seen each other for three months.

ILONA—All right—three months.

ALMADY (*going out*)—A colossal brain! (*They bow.*)

TURAI—I thank you.

Ilona and Almady are in Ilona's room studying, and Turai has resumed his interrupted breakfast when Mansky puts in an appearance. He is a doleful and dejected collaborateur this morning. Hasn't slept. Can't eat. Adam, he reports, lay awake all night staring at the ceiling. He is now dressing, and the worst can be expected.

Still, Turai refuses to be downcast. He has decided, he tells Mansky, to do everything he can to cause Adam to break with Ilona, because that is the surest way to bring them together.

"If he casts her off forever—in two weeks he'll be rushing after her and falling at her feet. The lady—after a little coaxing—will allow herself to melt. He will coax a little more. She will melt a little more. Finally she will melt altogether—and the curtain will fall on the lovers' slow embrace."

Adam has put on his white flannels, but he also is very solemn and miserable when he meets his friends this morning. He has decided that he wants to get away. There is a great crack in his heart and he is very unhappy. Once away he will tear up all the music he has ever written for Ilona, tear it up and burn it. After that he is not certain what will happen. Turai tries to help him.

TURAI—Now listen to me, my boy. Sit down. (ADAM *sits.*) What has happened, has happened. It's over, done with, a thing of the past. And I'm going to say something to you now which no young person will ever believe. You're twenty-five and you're gifted. The world's at your feet. And that world, let me remind you, contains a great many million women.

ADAM—What good are they to me? I only wanted this one. (*Rises.*) Can't we get away now—at once. I won't see her!

TURAI—Oh, yes, you will. No scandals, if you please. You arrived here late at night; everybody knows she is your fianceé; you can't run away this morning. Now, I'm not going to urge—in fact, I—er—positively forbid you to become reconciled to her,—but you must do the sensible thing. In the course of the morning we will go to her and pay our respects, and stay on here another day or two, and we will not breathe a word of what happened last night. You will behave towards her quite nicely and naturally. I know it will hurt. It's a bitter pill to swallow. But to-day you are a man.

ADAM—Yes. You're right.

TURAI—Up with the head and out with the chin and damn everybody! That's the stuff. The day after to-morrow, when we leave, you shall write her a letter, and let yourself go as much as you like. And, no matter how it may hurt, you have finished with that woman forever.

ADAM (*with an effort*)—Very well. And if—it should hurt *too* much, don't be afraid that I'll go back to her. I'll always have pluck enough to put a bullet through my head.

MANSKY—There! See where you have got us to with your psychology.

TURAI (*to* ADAM)—You ought to be ashamed of yourself.

ADAM (*smilingly*)—It's all right. It was silly of me to talk nonsense like that. I won't let you down. You shall be satisfied with me.

MANSKY (*to* ADAM)—Good. Then you won't—er—tear anything up?

ADAM—No.

TURAI—You'll behave towards Ilona as if nothing had happened?

ADAM—Yes. Honor bright. (*He holds out his hand.*)

TURAI (*rises*)—I am satisfied.

Mansky is sufficiently relieved to eat a second breakfast. He tries earnestly to get Adam to join him, but the boy has little interest in food. At the moment he is more concerned for Turai than he is for himself. The playwright has suddenly fallen into a state of deep thought and it is not easy to rouse him.

Turai, it appears, taking up again the subject of the technique of playwriting, is now faced by a new problem. Last night he was asking them the best and most interesting way to begin a play. Now he would like to know the best way to end a second act.

"Oh, come and end your breakfast," growls Mansky.

"No, it's worrying me," insists Turai. "Take this situation of ours, for instance—just as we did yesterday— We have had a curious experience. We arrived perfectly happy and immediately got a terrible shock—a ghastly disillusionment. We've managed to survive it, and we've got ourselves in hand again. But, suppose these things had happened not in real life but on the stage—suppose this were not a real room but a painted set—suppose we three were characters in a play who had just passed through the experiences we have passed through—"

"Well?"

"Well, how would you end the act?"

It is Mansky's belief that the act is ended already, but Turai disagrees. There is still something that might happen, something that should happen. A new note of suspense is needed, and a punch if possible. Something to snap up the interest of the audience and give it a jolt.

Mansky has an idea. He prefers a quiet, effective, French type curtain—the "sophisticated, lightly sentimental, smile-behind-the-tear" sort of thing. They sit down to breakfast (audiences always like to see actors eat according to Mansky), they fill their glasses and, following a couple of smart lines, like "Always remember that in affairs of the heart it is not the first victory that makes us men, but the first defeat," they drink to the toast, "To woman's treachery, which has made our child a man!"

"Rotten!" grunts Turai. "Tame! Feeble! Nothing in the nature of a high spot. I'm not saying it isn't pretty and graceful. Charming, even—but it lacks suspense."

They ask Adam how he would end the act. Adam answers with considerable intensity that he would take it up to the point of Mansky's toast "To woman's treachery," then he'd say: "No, I won't drink any toast," and smash the glass against the wall, which he does, somewhat to their consternation. Mansky admits such a scene might be effective.

"That woman was not just an incident in my life," continues Adam, rapidly losing control of himself and becoming somewhat hysterical. "She was my first great passion. I promised to act as if nothing had happened. I meant to keep that promise. But when I remember that I gave her my life and that she whispers words of love to another man—and—and kisses another man, that's such unbearable, burning torture that the only right solution—"

Suddenly Adam stops, grabs the small game carving knife from the table and would have stabbed himself if Turai had not leaped forward and caught his arm.

"What the devil do you think you're doing?" demands Turai.

"Just—finishing the act," bitterly replies Adam.

But that, too, would be a quite impossible curtain, insists Turai. "Death's all right for the end of a play, but absolutely no good for a second act. Besides, the scene was too crude. I don't say the gallery might not like it, but think what the critics would say. They would despise melodrama. Suspense is what you want—suspense and then a quick curtain."

Then Turai undertakes to show how the act should be finished. He goes to the telephone and calls Ilona Szabo's room. Casually Ilona answers, and her answers can be heard through the wall. She is quite surprised, she gurgles, and ever so delighted to hear her old friend's voice and fairly ecstatic at the knowledge that Albert has come, too. A moment later Ilona is with them, assuming a joy and excitement that are altogether deceiving.

ILONA—Well, this is wonderful of you all. (*She kisses* TURAI *lightly and crosses quickly to* ADAM *who kisses her hands.*) What a surprise. Albert, darling! This *is* a surprise. (*She hangs onto* ADAM'S *arm.*) Sandor! To think that it's—

TURAI—Three whole months—

ILONA—Three whole months since I've seen you. How brown you're looking. And younger than ever. Let me look at you. Wonderful! (*She crosses to* MANSKY *and kisses him on each cheek.*) And Mansky—how are *you,* Mansky dear? I think this is too sweet of you all. You don't know how I've been longing to see you. When did you get here? (*She returns to* ADAM.)

TURAI (*very gravely*)--Just a minute, Ilona. (*He looks through door into her room.*) Why, Mr. Almady! Of all people! Won't you come in? (*Enter* ALMADY.)

ALMADY (*nervously*)—Good morning.

TURAI—Fancy finding *you* after all these years.

ALMADY (*pompously*)—Passing through. Just passing through. I only wanted to say how-d'you-do to the Count, but they wouldn't let me go. The—er—the shooting-party you know, and the concert. They insisted on my staying.

ILONA—I was *so* surprised to see him.

TURAI—Pardon me for disturbing you and possibly casting a slight gloom on what must have been a joyful reunion, but I have something rather important to say. (ILONA *drops* ADAM'S *arm*.)

ILONA (*crosses to* TURAI)—What do you mean? Nothing— nothing unpleasant, I hope?

TURAI—Yes—extremely unpleasant. (ILONA *sits down, terrified. To* ALMADY.) Please. (*He motions them to sit down.*) Well, then. We arrived here last night— (*Long pause.*) And just now we were sitting having breakfast—we three— (*To* MANSKY.) Weren't we?

ADAM (*puzzled*)—Yes.

MANSKY—Well?

TURAI—Keep quite calm, please. We were sitting here, having breakfast—all three of us. (*He lowers his voice and speaks very earnestly.*) I must entreat you all to hear what I am about to say quite calmly— Don't lose your heads—

ILONA—For God's sake—

ALMADY (*uneasily*)—Well? What is it?

TURAI (*holds up his hand*)—Please! (*Dead silence.*) What I am about to say—and I shall not detain you long now—must almost inevitably have a shattering effect on the lives—both the private and the professional lives—of all us five people. I have asked myself—is it wise to speak? And I have answered myself—wise or not, it is unavoidable. Ilona—(ILONA *rises, gasping*) I have a question to ask you— (*Breaks off. Dead silence. Then very simply to* MANSKY.) How's that for suspense?

MANSKY—Yes. Yes. Well? What now?

TURAI—Nothing. That's all. (*Smiles.*) Curtain! (*Curtain comes down quickly and rises immediately. He offers* ILONA *his arm, as the rest of the group breathe again and relax their tension.*) We've just been having an argument about the proper way to end a second act. (*Leads* ILONA *slowly to the door, left to hall, the others following.*) I couldn't resist the temptation to show these colleagues of mine how, by the most simple methods, you can make an act end on a note of suspense. You see— (*He goes out, talking, followed first by* ALMADY, *then by* ADAM *and* MANSKY.)

MANSKY (*going out; to* ADAM)—Crazy! Absolutely crazy. Thinks of nothing in the world but the theatre—

The curtain falls.

## ACT III

It is 7:30 the same evening. The room is set for a rehearsal of Turai's play. "A large and elaborately painted screen in silver and green has been placed in front of the window. It is painted to suggest an orchard."

Mr. Mell, the director, assisted more or less vicariously by Dwornitschek, is putting the final touches to the setting, getting the properties in place.

The first to arrive is Almady. He is in a beastly temper. Because he has had to devote the day to studying the perfectly terrible part Turai has written for him, in addition to copying the entire play, he has missed a shooting party.

They call Ilona. She is resplendent in evening dress and eager to begin the rehearsal.

Adam wanders in. He, too, is in far from a contented frame of mind. His attitude toward Ilona is distant and, despite his effort to make it otherwise, plainly distant. But Turai has asked him to stay and help out with the rehearsal and he is prepared to make the sacrifice. He is even willing to relieve the flustered Mr. Mell, who admits frequently that he is quite all of atwitter, of the task of holding the book.

The rehearsal starts. Ilona, as the Countess, is on alone. She hears hoofbeats. Mr. Mell obliges with the hoofbeats. Can this be her husband, the Countess is eager to know. It is.

Almady as the husband follows the hoofbeats. He is rather distrait. He suspects the Countess of being a traitress. Thinking him a simple fellow, she has been philandering with another man.

Now Turai and Mansky have arrived. The rehearsal goes on, but not to Turai's satisfaction. He takes the book away from Adam, who is plainly unhappy.

The Count makes his accusation. He repeats that the Countess has been making mock of him. He is angered and excited. He stumbles uncertainly through his speeches.

ALMADY—Silence, woman! The proofs are in my pocket. Mon Dieu, is there no gratitude in this world? When I married you, who were you? A nobody! Your father, Brigadier-General Pierre Jean Bourmond de la Seconde-Chaumière-Rambouillet, fell in battle at Grande-Lagruyère Sur Marne, and you eked out a scanty living as a seamstress at your mother's home in the village of Saint Genevieve, in the Department of Seine et Oise. So, madame! And then what happened? *I* came! I gave you name, rank, and wealth such as you had never dreamed of. You became Madame La Countess du Veyrier de la Grande Contumace Saint Emilion. I bestowed upon you not only my estates in Pardubien-Grand-Amanoir, but also my two castles in the Challenges-

Debicourt de la Romanée and at Rivalieux-Quandamouzières Sur Vantera-aux Alpes Maritimes. (*He stops exhausted.*)

TURAI—Don't stop. What's wrong? (ALMADY *takes off his hat and gloves, puts the whip down on the table, and, stepping out of character, comes down to* TURAI.)

ALMADY—It's these damned *French names;* they're perfectly frightful.

TURAI—I don't see what we can do about it.

ALMADY—You surely don't need them all?

TURAI—They're in the script.

ALMADY—But I'll go mad trying to memorize them. Titles with six hyphens in them and names of places with a dozen "aux" and "de la's" and "sur's." And, damn it, they're all in *my* part. (*Choking with fury.*) It's deadly. At least, let's leave out that second castle.

TURAI (*coldly*)—My dear fellow, have you no sense of dramatic construction? If he had given her only one castle, the audience would think her perfectly justified in deceiving him. If he had given her three, they would look on him as a purse-proud fool who didn't deserve a faithful wife. No, two is exactly the right number. You can't beat Sardou when it comes to technique. Go on please. (ALMADY *goes up hopelessly and replaces his hat and gloves and takes up the whip.*)

ALMADY—I made you a countess and a wealthy woman. And what return do I get? You betray me—yes, madame, betray me—with my best friend and nearest neighbor, the Marquis Jean François Gilette de la Tour d'Argent, lord of Perigord des Champignons and Saint Sulpice de la Grand Parmentière. (*He breaks off, and removes hat and gloves as before.*) My God, it's enough to give a fellow apoplexy.

TURAI (*surprised*)—I beg your pardon? That doesn't seem to be in the script.

ALMADY (*down to* TURAI *as before*)—I'm sorry. I can't help it. It's these names.

TURAI—Well, I'm always open to suggestion. What would *you* like to call the gentleman?

ALMADY—Foche or Briand—or something short like that.

TURAI (*sarcastically*)—Perhaps—Vichy! Get on, please. (ALMADY *goes upstage more hopeless than before.*)

ILONA (*nervously*)—Oh, do let's get on. Count, you have said enough.

TURAI—So *he* seems to think.

ILONA—I will not endure these shameful accusations. You are insulting the woman who bears your name.

ALMADY (*again taking off hat and gloves and putting down whip*)—It's a damned shame.

TURAI—What is?

ALMADY—I always have to say the whole infernal thing from beginning to end, and she just says "Your name."

TURAI—(*coldly*)—We're wasting time.

ALMADY—Another word, madame, and I produce the proof.

ILONA (*laughing*)—The proof? One is amused. One smiles.

ALMADY (*takes stage and turns*)—A smile which I will make to die upon your lips. Behold! The proof! (*He fuddles in his coat-tail pocket from which he belatedly takes the peach with a sinister flourish.*)

ILONA (*with insincere terror*)—Ah, gracious heaven! The peach! (*Sits.*)

The rehearsal goes on. The peach, it appears, is the first that has ripened on the pet peach tree in all the Count's garden, "days ahead of any other peach in the whole of France." And what happens to it? The Count goes for a ride, meets the Countess's maid, questions her and finally worms a confession from her that she is taking the peach, the prize peach, the last word in peaches in fact, to his hated rival with a note. The note reads: "My beloved, this is the first peach that has ripened in France this year. I send it to *you*. Eat it reverently."

The Countess denies the accusation. The hated rival is not her lover. But the Count laughs, laughs derisively, although a little artificially. (Almady's heart is plainly not in his part.) The Count continues. He is insistent. Not only has the Countess betrayed him with the peach, but she also has been guilty of giving her lover the first white-heart cherries that ripened in the garden, cherries that he, her husband, had sent to her. There is another letter to prove that, a letter in which she refers to him as a "doddering old idiot." "Drop in this evening, darling, and we'll eat the old fool's cherries." That, too, is in the letter.

Now the Countess is defiant. If her husband wishes to distrust her, let him! But the truth of the matter is that she had really told her maid to stay behind when she (the Countess) had been called to her mother and give him both the letter and the peach. It was her little joke. She laughs merrily.

Now it is the Count who is beaten. He had been wrong. He

is wildly apologetic. He loves her distractedly. She will, she must, forgive him. He is at her feet, begging her forgiveness.

ILONA—The idea! A count, and an *elderly* count—groveling like that. (ALMADY *gets up and turns away.*) All the same, you have touched me. So I will forgive you. But you are not to get off without punishment. Firstly, I forbid you to eat this peach.

ALMADY—My God! Not that!

ILONA (*firmly*)—Yes.

ALMADY—So be it.

ILONA—Secondly, you will permit me to go to Paris alone—

ALMADY (*despairingly*)—Yvonne!

ILONA—Not a word. Either you trust me or you do not! If you *do,* I will return. If *not, not.*

ALMADY—Oh, heavens! And how long do you expect to stay in Paris?

ILONA—A week. (*Short pause.*)

ALMADY (*suddenly bursting out*)—No! I can't live without you. I worship you. I adore you. I love you as the church steeple loves the cloud that settles on its summit, only to be wafted away by the first passing breeze. I can't live without you. Not a week. Not a day. Not an hour.

ILONA—Just words. (*At the word "church steeple"* MANSKY *and* ADAM *have exchanged a glance of utter astonishment.*)

MANSKY (*rises*)—But . . . but . . . but . . . Just one moment. . . . *What* was that you said?

ILONA—I beg your pardon?

TURAI—Now, listen, *please.* We can't have these interruptions. Don't pull them up the moment they've got nicely into the swing of it.

MELL—I can't wait to see how it all ends. (*To* ADAM.) Will she leave him? Or will the memory of their past love prove too strong?

MANSKY (*goes to* ADAM—*aside to* ADAM)—This is devilish queer.

TURAI—Quiet, quiet, please. (*To* ALMADY.) All right. Go on. Better go back to "Not a week! Not a day! Not an hour!"

ALMADY—*Not a week! Not a day! Not an hour!*

ILONA—Just words.

ALMADY—It's the truth. I'm crazy about you. And you—you have used me up and squeezed me like a lemon, and now you want to throw me away. (*At the word "lemon"* MANSKY *and*

Adam *again exchange glances.* Mansky *gets up, deeply agitated.*)

Mansky—Sandor . . .

Turai—What is it?

Mansky (*to* Ilona *and* Almady)—You'll excuse me?    I have something very urgent to say to Mr. Turai. (*He crosses to* Turai *and drags him over to the corner below the fireplace.*)    Do you hear what they're saying?

Turai (*feigning non-comprehension*)—How do you mean, do I hear what they're saying?

Mansky—I mean . . . didn't those last lines sound familiar to you?

Turai—That's right. Now you mention it. I did notice something, only I thought it was my fancy.

Mansky (*to* Adam)—Come here. (Mell *tries to become a part of the whispered conference, but* Adam *waves him away, and he withdraws upstage, disconsolate.*) (*To* Turai.)    I give you my word, Sandor—those lines were syllable for syllable the ones we heard last night through the wall.

Turai (*looking at script*)—By Jove, you're right. . . . This is uncanny.

Mansky—Go on with the rehearsal, or they will be suspecting something. I want to hear some more. (Mansky *takes hold of* Adam's *arm.* Adam *is very excited.    Both listen intently.*)

The rehearsal proceeds, with sundry interruptions, through the fateful lines:

Ilona—Please, please. Don't cry. I can't bear it. You know how fond I am of you. (*She goes to table where peach is.*)

Almady—Those nights of love—those flaming, wonderful nights!    Have you forgotten them so completely? (*He stands up, and starts to touch the peach.*)

Ilona—Stop! Control yourself.

Almady (*gazing at peach*)—You ask me to control myself— when I look at *that?*    At that perfect shape!    The rose flush of that skin! (*Starts to touch peach.*) Just to stroke it . . .

Ilona—Hands off.

Almady (*snatching up the peach, holds it in one hand and with the other strokes it voluptuously*)—My God!    How round it is!    How smooth—how velvety—and how fragrant! (*Raises it to his mouth.*)

Ilona—You mustn't bite it. (*She snatches his hand.*)

(MANSKY *gives a shriek and goes into fits of laughter.* ADAM *stretches his arms out to* MANSKY *and roars.* ADAM *slaps* MANSKY *on the back,* MANSKY *laughing uninterruptedly.* AL-MADY *turns away furiously.* ILONA *turns away, ashamed.*)

MANSKY (*putting his arm around* ADAM'S *shoulder, still laughing.*)—Heavens! What fools we've been!

ADAM—Haven't we?

MELL (*eagerly*)—Won't you tell me the joke?

ADAM—You wouldn't understand.

ILONA—What are you two so amused about?

TURAI (*curtly*)—Come, come. We're wasting time. Let's get on.

MANSKY—Yes, get on. I want to hear this. "Round, smooth, velvety and fragrant."

ADAM—"And you mustn't bite."

ILONA—You mustn't bite it.

ALMADY—I must—I am so hungry. (ADAM *and* MANSKY *go on laughing.* MELL *laughs too, but with a puzzled look, as much as to say, "I'm joining in, but I really don't understand."*)

ALMADY (*sits*)—Ah well! I see I am nothing to you any more.

ILONA—Oh, for goodness' sake! I swear that no man— (*Breaks off, unable to go on.*)

TURAI (*prompting*)—No man who has ever come into my life . . .

ILONA— . . . has meant so much to me as you. From the top of your head to the soles of your feet you are a *man*.

It is Turai's idea that perhaps that last line should be cut. It is, after all, a wee bit coarse, and there will probably be many young girls in the audience. The audience must be considered. It is quite plain to Mansky, too, that the author of the sketch must have loathed the character of the Count.

Turai suggests a substitution. Let Almady admit that he is 'a ridiculous old petticoat-chaser." That would be true, and strong. And let him bear down on that line, giving it emphasis and point.

Almady is of a mind to rebel, but is overruled. He speaks the line and the sketch ends with the Countess's forgiveness. "Then, Maurice," she says, "I will be generous. I will not go to Paris and you may eat the peach."

Almady is far from mollified, and in his distraction he eats the property peach! Now Mr. Mell will have to rush about and find another for the regular performance.

But Adam is happy. Shakespeare at his best never wrote anything more than half so good as this little sketch that Ilona is to play. He is sure of that.

Now Turai, on pretext of wanting to talk her part over with Ilona, has gotten rid of the others, Almady still grumbling but grateful, Mansky plainly delighted with the outcome and Adam happily relieved of all his suspicions. The moment they are alone Ilona throws her arms about Turai. She, too, is very happy.

ILONA (*going to* TURAI *and embracing him*)—Sandor, you're an angel. Was it awfully difficult, writing that play?

TURAI—Oh, no. That damned peach stumped me for a while. "Smooth, round, velvety and fragrant, and you mustn't bite." It wasn't easy to get round that. Believe me, there are very few things in this world that are round, smooth, velvety—and respectable.

ILONA (*turns head away*)—Oh—he was talking about my shoulder.

TURAI (*with delicate irony and gazing at her shoulder, then kissing it*)—Really? I thought it was your forehead.

ILONA—You're an old devil—that's what you are.

TURAI—Just what I expected. Now that it's all over, everybody else is a gentleman and I'm an old devil. But somehow I don't think I am. My little Ilona, I have saved a young man a bad heartache. It's a negative kindness, but is there a positive one that's better? Yes, on the whole, I think I'm fairly well satisfied with myself. And there's a little old woman looking at me from somewhere—probably from hell—and her eyes seem to be twinkling, as if she was satisfied, too. It's unfortunate that you won't have me always on hand to . . . (*Reënter* MANSKY *and* ADAM.)

MANSKY (*on the landing, to* ADAM)—Poor old Turai's feeling awfully sore about all this. He had a wonderful scheme for bringing you two together, based on what he calls psychology. And now he's furious because that won't be needed. (*Enter* DWORNITSCHEK *from hall.*)

ADAM—Sh! Ilona will hear you. Let's drop the subject.

DWORNITSCHEK (*standing at center*)—Dinner is served. (ADAM *meets* ILONA *at center. They embrace and kiss lovingly and go out to the hall arm in arm.*)

MANSKY (*with self-satisfaction to* TURAI)—So, my friend, it comes down to this. There are many clever writers, but the most successful of them all is still Old Man Life himself.

TURAI—That's because he doesn't have to collaborate with you. (*He takes* MANSKY's *arm. As he passes* DWORNITSCHEK *he stops and looks at him.*)

DWORNITSCHEK (*smiling*)—Dwornitschek, sir.

TURAI—Still Dwornitschek—thank you.

DWORNITSCHEK—Thank *you*, sir.

TURAI—No, no, my dear Dwornitschek, thank YOU. (TURAI *and* MANSKY *go out.*)

The curtain falls.

# THE SILVER CORD

## A Drama in Three Acts

### By Sidney Howard

THE THEATRE GUILD, as has been noted in previous volumes of this series, has achieved the leadership of the theatre in America by bringing into the theatre an intelligence in the selection and direction of its offerings that previous to its advent had not generally existed. This year the Guild enjoyed a particularly successful season. With its first five productions the score stood at least 80 per cent. in its favor in respect to popular endorsement.

Of these five plays Sidney Howard, who in 1925 won the Pulitzer prize with "They Knew What They Wanted," wrote two, "Ned McCobb's Daughter" and "The Silver Cord."

I could, I feel, justify the inclusion of either or both plays in this book. Taking one, I feel "The Silver Cord" is entitled to the preference. It is a weightier and more significant study of American character, strikes closer to the problems of the home, is more incisively direct in its human analyses and tells, to me, the more absorbing story of the two.

Herein we find the harmful extremes to which a selfish mother love may extend as ruthlessly and as convincingly exposed as were the similar characteristics of the selfish wife in George Kelly's "Craig's Wife."

The chief feminine rôle in "The Silver Cord" is that of Mrs. Phelps, the idolizing parent of two grown sons, David and Robert, whom she has hoped and confidently expected to keep always, if not tied to her apron strings, at least never more than arm's length away from her for long at a time.

We meet her first the day of David's return from two years of study abroad. Dave is an architect. During his stay in Europe he has met and married Christina, to the none too tactfully suppressed disappointment of his mother. Christina is a young student specializing in biology.

The opening of the play reveals the living room of the Phelps home, "situated in one of the more mature residential developments of an eastern American city—a living room built and decorated in the best manner of 1905, and cluttered with the souvenirs of maternal love, European travel and an orthodox enthusiasm for the arts. There is a vast quantity of Braun Clement and Arundel Society reproductions of the Renaissance Italian masters. The piano features Grieg, Sibelius and MacDowell."

Hester, a house guest, is deep in the rotogravure sections of the Sunday press. "She is a lovely, frail phantom of a girl with a look of recent illness about her. She wears the simplest and most charming of house frocks."

A commotion in the hall heralds the arrival of David Phelps. "He is a personable young man, well enough dressed and a gentleman. He belongs to the somewhat stolid or unimaginative type which is generally characterized in this country as 'steady.' . . . His principal quality is a rare and most charming amiability, but he is clearly lacking in many of the more sophisticated perceptions and he is clearly of a conventional bent in his attitude toward life."

David is followed by Christina. "She, as David's wife, presents something of a contrast to her husband. She is tall, slender, grave, honest, shy, intelligent, most trusting, and, when need be, courageous. . . . One suspects that, where David is stubborn, she is open-minded, where he is blind she is amazingly clear-sighted. . . . David is incapable of subtlety; Christina will not bother with it. The result is congeniality."

The greetings as between David and Hester are effusive. Hester has grown up in the two years David has been away. Now she is a young lady and engaged to marry his brother Robert.

At the moment Robert and Mrs. Phelps are away, not having expected David and Christina until later. But Robert is soon back from a skating expedition and joyfully surprised at his brother's arrival. It will be a great surprise for their mother,— their really marvelous mother,—he assures Christina, with David's endorsement.

"Mother's immense," echoes David. "I'm glad for Chris's sake that things worked out this way. First Chris sees the old house. Then she meets Hester. Then Rob comes breezing in, full of health. And, last of all, Mother."

Mother is not far behind Robert. They hear her coming down the hall, excitedly discovering their hand luggage. "She is pretty, distinguished, soft, disarming and, in short, has everything one could possibly ask including a real gift for looking years younger than her age, which is well past fifty. She boasts a reasonable amount of conventional culture, no great amount of intellect, a superabundant vitality, perfect health and a prattling spirit. At the moment she is still wearing her hat and furs and she looks wildly about her."

MRS. PHELPS—Dave! Dave, boy! Where are you, Dave? Where are you? It's Mother, Dave! (*She does not see him in the room and she is already turning back to the hall without a word or a look for anybody else.*) Where are you, Dave? Come here this minute! Don't you hear me, Dave? It's Mother! (*Then Dave appears in the hall.*) Oh, Dave!

DAVID (*a little abashed by the vigor of this welcome*)—Hello, Mother.

MRS. PHELPS—Dave, is it really you?

DAVID—Guess it must be, Mother!

MRS. PHELPS—Dave, dear! (*She envelops as much of him as she can possibly reach.*)

DAVID (*prying loose*)—Well! Glad to see us, Mother?

MRS. PHELPS—Glad!

DAVID—You certainly seem to be glad . . . But you haven't spoken to . . . (CHRISTINA, *at his look, steps forward.*)

MRS. PHELPS (*still not seeing her*)—To think I wasn't here!

DAVID—We're ahead of time, you know. Christina . . .

MRS. PHELPS—I must have known somehow. Something just made me put down my cup and rush home. But you're not looking badly. You *are* well, aren't you? I do believe you've put on weight. You must be careful, though, not to take cold this weather. Was the crossing awfully rough? Were you seasick? You haven't been working too hard, have you, Dave, boy?

CHRISTINA (*unable to stand on one foot any longer*)—He hasn't been working at all. Not for weeks!

MRS. PHELPS (*she turns at the sound of a strange voice*)— Eh? Oh!

DAVID—I've been trying to make you take notice of Christina, Mother.

MRS. PHELPS (*with the utmost warmth*)—Oh, my dear Christina, I *am* sorry! (*She kisses* CHRISTINA *on both cheeks.*) Seeing this big boy again quite took me off my feet. Let me look at *you*, now. Why, Dave, she's splendid. Perfectly splendid! I always knew Dave would choose only the best. Didn't I always say so, Dave, boy? (*Which takes her back to* DAVID.) Dave, you *have* been working too hard. I don't like those circles under your eyes.

DAVID—Nonsense, Mother!

CHRISTINA—I think he looks pretty well.

MRS. PHELPS—But only pretty well. I can't help worrying about these big boys of mine. (*Her emotion stops her. She turns gallantly to Robert.*) Did you skate, Bob?

ROBERT—As a matter of fact, I couldn't. They've been cutting ice on the pond and it's full of holes.

MRS. PHELPS—I must have signs put up to-morrow. Remember that, everybody. If any of you do go out in this freezing cold, don't take the short cut across the pond. . . . Dave, boy, this is too good to be true. After two whole years away and five, nearly six, months married. (*The maid brings tea.*)

DAVID—Here's tea.

MRS. PHELPS—Sit down here beside me, dear, dear Christina. And, Dave, boy, sit over there where I can see you. Just take my furs, Delia, so I can do my duty in comfort. My boy, my boy, you don't know—you don't know how happy I am to have you home again! Just hand me my salts, will you, Robin? This excitement has laid me out. Christina, my dear, how do you take your tea?

There is the usual neighborhood and personal gossip during tea. Most of it is directed by Mrs. Phelps, and mostly it is spoken in reminiscent eulogy of David and all his works, both great and small, and a mother's guiding hand in bringing him from building blocks to architecture.

No one ventures any opposition. David is slightly embarrassed and Robert convinced that everybody must expect to take a back seat when his older brother is home.

Hester protests politely at this mother's almost too complete devotion to her sons. "What I say about children is this," ventures Hester. "Have 'em! Love 'em! And leave 'em be!" With which Christina agrees. But the Phelpses stick together.

Even when Mrs. Phelps, in sending the boys upstairs with the bags, puts Christina in a front room and David in his old room at the back of the house the protests are no more than politely feeble. The arrangement, Mrs. Phelps explains, is necessary so that Hester, who is really there for a rest, will not have to give up the guest room.

Now Mrs. Phelps has her new daughter-in-law to herself and

the probing begins. Dave's mother is ever so glad to know Christina, but she still is a little afraid of her. She never has seen a lady scientist before and she is free to confess that when David reported that he was marrying a talented and charming "geologist" she was a little startled. She finally gets the geologists separated from the biologists and seeks to be sympathetically interested in all that has happened to Christina and David on their tour. She is so glad they saw Sicily. She so hopes they read "Glorious Apollo" before they went to Venice. She is so hopeful that Christina likes to read, and does read. Books mean so much to Mrs. Phelps. And have always meant so much to David.

Christina reads, of course, but she naturally is more or less confined to scientific works. Which Mrs. Phelps plainly regards as a great pity.

Soon they have reached the question of future plans. She and David, explains Christina, are to live in New York, where she has an appointment at the Rockefeller Institute and where David can most advantageously continue his career as an architect.

The news is rather startling to Mrs. Phelps, though she makes an effort to accept it graciously. If Christina's "geology" is taking David to New York, so be it. She will make the best of it. But the thought is disturbing. So is the thought of Christina's being a professional woman. And being called "doctor." And being determined to continue with her work, just as though she hadn't married! They are all disturbing thoughts. There is, however, some little satisfaction in Christina's admission that she has no intention of practicing, especially on David.

How did Christina come to select her career? Naturally enough. "My father was a doctor," Christina explains. "I grew up in his hospital. Everything followed quite naturally." Now Christina's father is dead, a victim of his devotion to his profession and his experiments on infantile paralysis. Her mother, however, is still living in Omaha. Which in itself is something of a blow to Mrs. Phelps.

MRS. PHELPS—And you'll go on with your father's experiments?

CHRISTINA—Oh, no! That's not at all in my line.

MRS. PHELPS—What *is* your line?

CHRISTINA—It's hard to say. I did some rather hard work this last year at Heidelberg on the embryos of chickens. In the egg, you know.

MRS. PHELPS—For heaven's sake, what for?

CHRISTINA—Trying to find out something about what makes growth stop.

MRS. PHELPS—Why . . . ?

CHRISTINA—Curiosity, I guess. Now I'm admitting what low people we scientists are. I think that curiosity's all we have. And a little training.

MRS. PHELPS—Does David follow your work?

CHRISTINA—No. And I don't expect him to.

MRS. PHELPS—Quite right. David wouldn't be appealed to by rotten eggs. . . . Not that he couldn't understand them if they did appeal to him.

CHRISTINA—Of course.

MRS. PHELPS—Isn't the Rockefeller Institute one of those places where they practice vivisection?

CHRISTINA—One of many. Yes. . . .

MRS. PHELPS—Have you . . .

CHRISTINA—What?

MRS. PHELPS—Experimented on animals?

CHRISTINA—Isn't it a part of my job? Dave understands that. You must try to understand it.

MRS. PHELPS—Very well, I shall try, my dear. Now you must listen to me and try to understand me. . . . Look at me. What do you see? Simply—David's mother. I can't say of you that you're simply David's wife, because, clearly, you're many things beside that. But I am simply his mother. . . . I think, as I talk to you, that I belong to a dead age. I wonder if you think that. In my day, we considered a girl immensely courageous and independent who taught school or gave music lessons. Nowadays, girls sell real estate and become scientists and think nothing of it. Give us our due, Christina. We weren't entirely bustles and smelling salts, we girls who did not go into the world. We made a great profession which I fear may be in some danger of vanishing from the face of the earth. We made a profession of motherhood. That may sound old-fashioned to you. Believe me, it had its value. I was trained to be a wife that I might become a mother. (CHRISTINA *is about to protest.* MRS. PHELPS *stops her.*) Your father died of his investigations of a dangerous disease. You called that splendid of him, didn't you? Would you say less of us who gave our lives to being mothers? Mothers of sons, particularly. Listen to me, Christina. David was five, Rob only a little baby, when my husband died. I'd been married six years, not so very happily. I was pretty, as a girl, too. Very pretty. (*This thought holds her for a second.*) For twenty-four years, since my husband died, I've given all my life, all my strength, to Dave and Rob. They've been my life and my job. They've taken the place of husband and friends both, for me. Where do I stand now? Rob is marrying. Dave is married already. This is the end of my life and my job. . . . Oh, I'm not asking for credit or praise. I'm asking for something more substantial. I'm asking you, my dear, dear Christina, not to take all my boy's heart. Leave me, I beg you, a little, little part of it. I've earned that much. I'm not sure I couldn't say that you owe me that much—as David's mother. I believe I've deserved it. Don't you think I have?

CHRISTINA (*deeply moved*)—My dear, dear Mrs. Phelps!

MRS. PHELPS—It's agreed then, isn't it, that I'm not to be shut out?

CHRISTINA—Of course you're not!

MRS. PHELPS—Not by you, Christina. Nor by your work?

CHRISTINA—No! No!

MRS. PHELPS—Nor by anything?

CHRISTINA—You must know that I should never come between a mother and her son. You must know that I appreciate what you've done for Dave and all you've always been and meant to him. You *must* know that!

MRS. PHELPS—Christina, my dear, you're a very disarming person. You are indeed. I've known you ten minutes and unloaded my whole heart to you.

CHRISTINA—I'm proud that you trust me.

MRS. PHELPS (*patting her hand*)—Thank you, my dear. And now . . . now that you know how I feel . . . now you won't go to New York, will you? You won't take Dave to New York?

CHRISTINA (*drawing back in alarm*)—But, Mrs. Phelps!

MRS. PHELPS—Because that *would* be coming between mother and son as you just now said. That could mean only one thing—crowding me out, setting me aside, robbing me . . .

CHRISTINA (*completely baffled*)—You're quite mistaken, Mrs. Phelps! You've no reason to think any such thing!

MRS. PHELPS—Well, it's nice of you to reassure me, and we don't have to worry about it for some time yet. You'll have plenty of time to see how carefully I've worked everything out for David—and for you, too, my dear. You've a nice, long visit ahead and . . .

CHRISTINA—I only wish we *had* a nice long visit, Mrs. Phelps.

MRS. PHELPS—What do you mean?

CHRISTINA—I start work at the Institute a week from to-morrow.

Mrs. Phelps is fairly staggered by this information, though with an effort she controls her feelings. She will not submit without a contest, however. To have David for only a week after he has been away for two years! When he practically has been her sole companion for twenty-five years! And now to see his career, everything, sacrificed; to see him taken off to New York to live in a stuffy tenement, or apartment—they're much the same thing —without proper heat or sunshine or food? It is all very disappointing.

Mrs. Phelps had planned everything so differently. She owns a large tract of land to the north of the Country Club and she expected David to join her in its development and exploitation. Phelps Manor it was to be called, and David was to design all the houses and gates and lay out the streets. Surely Christina can see the advantages to accrue from such an opportunity. And as for herself and her career—why not fit herself up a laboratory in the local hospital?

But Christina is still firm in her belief that David should stand on his own feet and not depend upon his mother's being back of him. She had rather see him "a mere polliwog" in New York than a big frog in a small town puddle. David has a chance in New York, a place with one of the big firms. Christina has not given a thought as to whether he will succeed or not, that depends upon his own talent. But she is convinced that it is best that he should work it out for himself, that they should work together, and she is sure that it will come straight in the end. "Life takes care of such things," calmly insists Christina. "All we have to do is to keep out of life's way and make the best of things as *healthily* as possible."

Now Christina has gone to her room to dress for dinner and Mrs. Phelps seeks the sympathetic support of Robert. Of course, she admits to him, she should have been prepared to lose her two great, splendid sons, but now she finds she is too great a coward to face the issue.

That, Robert agrees, is because she is what she is, a wonderful ideal of womanhood. And if Dave can't appreciate her the loss is sure to be his.

"It's a funny business, isn't it?" suggests Robert. "After a woman like you has suffered the tortures of the damned bringing us into the world, and worked like a slave to help us grow up in it, we can't wait to cut loose and give up the one thing we can be sure of! And for what? To run every known risk of disillusionment and disappointment."

Robert is rather blue about his own affairs. He may be right in marrying Hester and drawing away from home, but it is difficult for him to feel sure about it. His mother immediately detects the note of apprehension in his voice. Here is a new and more promising problem to be settled. She draws Robert to a stool at her feet, by the fire where they can have a real old-time talk. Soon he is confessing his doubts and his fears concerned with his immediate future.

Hester is a sweet girl, Mrs. Phelps admits, but it *is* strange that she does not take more interest in her own wedding. She has come to no decision about her honeymoon except that she wants to spend it abroad. She hasn't even picked out her flat silver, nor given the least thought to the furnishing of her home.

"She says I know more about such things than she does," Robert reports.

"How little she understands my poor Robin, who ought never to be bothered," sympathizes mother.

MRS. PHELPS--Do you happen to know if Hester *has* many friends? I mean many *men* friends? Did she have lots of suitors beside you?

ROBERT—I daresay she had loads.

MRS. PHELPS—Do you know that she had?

ROBERT—She never told me so. Why?

MRS. PHELPS—I was wondering. She's been out two years. One does wonder how much a girl has been sought after. But, then, why should she have bothered with others when she thought she could land you? You are rather a catch, you know.

ROBERT—I, Mother?

MRS. PHELPS—Any girl would set her cap for you.

ROBERT—I don't believe Hester did that.

MRS. PHELPS—My dear, I wasn't saying that she did! But why shouldn't she? Only . . .

ROBERT—Only what?

MRS. PHELPS—I can't help wondering if Hester's feeling for you *is* as strong as you think it is. (ROBERT *wonders, too.*) I've been wondering for some time, Robin. I've hesitated to speak to you about it. But after what you've just told me . . .

ROBERT—Well, it's too late to worry now.

MRS. PHELPS—I can't help worrying, though. Marriage is

such an important step and you're such a sensitive, shrinking character. It would be too terrible if you had to go through what you were just speaking of—the disillusionment and disappointment. . . . I'm only trying to find out what it is that's come between you two young people.

ROBERT—Nothing has, Mother. Hester isn't you, that's all!

MRS. PHELPS—Nonsense, Robin! . . . It isn't that awful woman I was so worried about when you were at Harvard?

ROBERT—I'm not raising a second crop of wild oats.

MRS. PHELPS—Then it *must* be that risk you were speaking of! Oh, why do boys run that risk! Why will they break away!

ROBERT—I wish I knew!

MRS. PHELPS—Perhaps your trouble is that—(*a pause. Then, very low.*)—that you don't love Hester.

ROBERT—Oh, love! I must love her or I wouldn't have asked her to marry me. I guess she loves me in her way. Is her way enough? I'll find that out in time. A man ought to marry.

MRS. PHELPS (*a little more positively*)—You *don't* love Hester, and it isn't fair to her!

ROBERT—Yes, I do love her! Only I wonder if I'm the marrying kind—failing the possibility of marrying you. I mean your double.

MRS. PHELPS (*always increasing*)—You don't love Hester.

ROBERT—I do, I tell you! Who could help loving her? I mean . . . Good God, what do I mean?

MRS. PHELPS—Either you don't love Hester or Hester doesn't love you.

ROBERT—She does love me.

MRS. PHELPS—She may say she does, but I haven't seen her showing it.

ROBERT—Mother!

MRS. PHELPS—You don't love Hester and Hester doesn't love you. It's as simple as that, Robin, and you're making a very grave mistake to go on with this. These things may be painful, but they're better faced before than after. Children come after, Robin, and then it's too late! Think, Robin! Think before it's too late! And remember the happiness of three people is at stake!

ROBERT—Hester's and mine and . . .

MRS. PHELPS—And mine! And mine! . . . Only, I was wrong to say that! You must put my fate out of your mind just as Dave has done. Let Dave find out for himself what he's done. She won't be able to hold him. She won't have time for a home and children.  She won't take any more interest in him than Hester takes in you.  But you, Robin, *you* can still be saved!  I want to save you from throwing yourself away as Dave has.  You will face the facts, won't you?

ROBERT—You mean . . . I'm to . . . to break with Hester?

MRS. PHELPS—You will be a man?

ROBERT (*pause, then*)—Well . . . I'll . . . I'll try, Mother.

In a flutter of excitement over this triumph Mrs. Phelps promises to make the opportunity that Robert will need to tell Hester of his decision.

"Thank God I've saved my boy one more tumble!" she says fervently.  "You'll see I've still plenty to give you and to do for you."

"My blessed, blessed mother," echoes Robert.

They are locked in each other's arms when David comes down, dressed for dinner.  David, too, is happy.  Happy to be home.  Happy that his mother likes Christina.  Happy that he is married to Christina, who is so much more wonderful than his mother guesses that she will have to wait to find out how really wonderful she is.  And he is happy because Christina and Hester have hit it off so well.

"You're not going to let your happiness crowd me out entirely, are you, Dave, boy?" pleads Mrs. Phelps.

"Oh, Mother, lay off!" answers David, amiably irritated.

Now Robert has made the cocktails and passed them and the three of them are about to proceed with the dinner preliminaries.

"Shan't we call Chris and Hester?" asks David.

"No!" quickly answers Mrs. Phelps.  "Just we three!"

ROBERT—It'll never be we three any more.  I heard them coming as I crossed the hall.  (*He pours the cocktail into the glasses and goes about passing them.*)

MRS. PHELPS—My two boys!  My big one and my little one!

DAVID (*calls out*)—Hurry up, Chris!

MRS. PHELPS—If I can keep the little corner Christina doesn't need, Dave . . . that's all I ask . . .

DAVID—Don't you worry, Mother.  (CHRISTINA *and* HESTER *enter.  They are both dressed appropriately for the evening.* CHRISTINA *is particularly lovely.*)  Here we are!

CHRISTINA—Thank you, Robert.  (*They sip their cocktails.*)

DAVID—Chris!

CHRISTINA—Yes?

DAVID—Let's tell Mother.

CHRISTINA—Now? In front of everybody?

DAVID—It won't hurt 'em to hear.

CHRISTINA—I don't mind, if they don't.

ROBERT—Mind what?

DAVID—It'll make Mother so happy.

MRS. PHELPS—What will?

DAVID—A surprise Chris and I have got to spring on you!

MRS. PHELPS—How nice! What is it?

CHRISTINA (*a smiling pause—then*)—In about four months I'm going to have a baby.

HESTER—Oh, Christina, how wonderful!

ROBERT—Are you really!

DAVID—Isn't that a grand surprise, Mother?

MRS. PHELPS (*recovering as from a body blow*)—Of course . . . David. I'm very glad, my dear. Very glad. . . . Have you a napkin there, Robin? I've spilled my cocktail all over my dress.

The curtain falls.

## ACT II

That evening, after dinner, Mrs. Phelps got out a great Indian basket filled with family photographs. Pictures of David when he danced the hornpipe at Miss Brigg's dancing school; pictures of David at ten months, sitting in a seashell—"David on the halfshell," as Christina sees it.

"I didn't always sit in shells," protests David. "Mother's got one of me on a white fur rug."

"It hangs over my bed to this day," proudly admits Mother.

"In the nude?" queries Christina.

"No. In an undershirt," answers David. And Hester giggles.

"Fashions change," calmly declares Mrs. Phelps, plainly displeased by their levity.

"I suppose they must," admits Christina. "David wouldn't think of being photographed in his undershirt now. Let me see the picture again, Mrs. Phelps."

"I think that's enough for this evening," icily replies Mrs. Phelps, and the photographs are promptly put away.

Nor does the atmosphere of family harmony improve as the evening wears on. Her pride hurt in the matter of the photographs, Mrs. Phelps is fairly insulting to Christina, and with seeming deliberateness.

"I'm afraid of boring Christina," she admits. "Christina has other interests, of course. Higher interests than her husband. Higher even than children, I suspect."

Nor is she quite satisfied with that. She takes occasion a moment later to criticise her daughter-in-law's clothes and, by implication, her figure. And again, after Christina has related a particularly moving experience in which an aged German professor had figured Mrs. Phelps suggests that it is possible Christina's studies at Heidelberg have made her just the least little bit pro-German.

But Christina and David have gone for a walk by this time, and it remains for Hester to rise to her prospective sister-in-law's defense. This she does with spirit. And again when Mrs. Phelps is alarmed lest David catch cold, being dragged out as he has been by Christina to spoon in the road "like a couple of mill hands—"

"In the first place it was David who dragged *her* out," declares Hester, a little hotly. "In the second, they *are* in love and *do* want to be alone. In the third, I don't see any reason for worrying over the health of any man who looks as husky as David does. And in the fourth, if there *is* any worrying to be done, let me remind you that it's Christina and *not* David who is going to have a baby. (MRS. PHELPS *at the piano breaks off her playing in the middle of a phrase.*) I'm sorry if I've shocked you, but the truth is, you've both shocked me."

They have shocked her particularly, Hester continues, by not being a great deal more thrilled over Christina's baby, and she sees no sense at all in their prudish sensitiveness in avoiding the subject. As for herself, Hester is frankly interested in babies and intends when she is married to have as many as possible.

"Is that why you are marrying Bob, Hester?"

"What better reason could I have?" demands Hester, and Mrs. Phelps, plainly angered and with significant glances at Robert, leaves the room.

So long as Robert is angry at Hester's attitude toward his mother he finds it possible to show some spirit of disappointment and resentment. But after Hester has explained and apologized and asked to be understood and forgiven he finds it a little difficult to approach the subject of their engagement.

He tries to recall all of his mother's objections. Did Hester have many suitors? Hester can't remember. She did not take count. None ever came to the point of proposing, she admits, but she attributes that to the fact that she usually laughed at them.  She wonders a little that she did not laugh at Robert.  He was funny enough.

Robert brings up the question of his career, at least the career he expects to have, and the possibility that children will interfere with it.  That doesn't worry Hester, either.

"You just leave things to me.  If we're poor, I'll cook and scrub floors.  I'll bring up our children.  I'll take care of you whether we live in New York or Kamchatka.  This business is up to me, Rob.  Don't let it worry you."

Nor is Hester concerned about the honeymoon.  Or where they are to live.  She believes marriages are things of feeling.  They shouldn't be talked about too much.

Suddenly a tone in Robert's voice frightens her and she faces him seriously.

HESTER (*suddenly frightened*)—What's the matter, Rob?  I'll talk as seriously as you please.  Do I love you?  Yes.  Am I going to make you a good wife?  I hope so, though I *am* only twenty and may make mistakes.  Are you going to be happy with me?  I hope that, too, but you'll have to answer it for yourself.

ROBERT—I can't answer it.

HESTER—Why can't you?

ROBERT—Because I'm not sure of it.

HESTER—Aren't you, Rob?

ROBERT—These things are better faced before than after.

HESTER—What is it you're trying to say?

ROBERT—If only we could be sure!

HESTER (*stunned*)—So that's it!

ROBERT—Are you sure you want to marry me?

HESTER—How can I be—now?

ROBERT—Marriage is such a serious thing.  You don't realize how serious.

HESTER—Don't I?

ROBERT—No. . . . I hope you won't think harshly of me. . . . And, mind you, I haven't said I wanted to break things off . . . I only want . . .

HESTER—Please, Rob!

ROBERT—No.  You've got to hear me out.

HESTER—I've heard enough, thank you!

ROBERT—I'm only trying to look at this thing . . .

HESTER—Seriously. . . . I know . . .

ROBERT—Because, after all, the happiness of three people is affected by it.

HESTER—Three?

ROBERT—As Mother said, before dinner.

HESTER—So you talked this over with your mother?

ROBERT—Isn't that natural?

HESTER—Is your mother the third?

ROBERT—Wouldn't she be?

HESTER—Yes, I suppose she would. . . . I think you might tell me what else she had to say.

ROBERT—It was all wise and kind. You may be as hard as you like on me, but you wouldn't be hard on poor, splendid, lonely Mother.

HESTER (*savage—under her breath*)— So she's lonely, too!

ROBERT—You *will* twist my meaning!

HESTER—You *said* "lonely."

ROBERT—Perhaps I did. But Mother didn't. You know, she never talks about herself.

HESTER—I see. What else did she say about me?

ROBERT—Well, you haven't been very interested in planning our future. She notices such things.

HESTER—What else?

ROBERT—She sees through people, you know.

HESTER—Through me?

ROBERT—She thought, as I must say I do, that we didn't love each other quite enough to . . . At least, she thought we ought to think very carefully before we . . .

HESTER (*gripping his two arms with all her strength, she stops him*)—If you really want to be free . . . if you really want that, Rob, it's all right. It's perfectly all right . . . I'll set you free. . . . Don't worry. . . . Only you've got to say so. You've got to. . . . Answer me, Rob. Do you want to be rid of me? (*There is a pause.* ROBERT *cannot hold her gaze and his eyes fall. She takes the blow.*) I guess that's answer enough. (*She draws a little back from him and pulls the engagement ring from her finger.*) Here's your ring.

Before Robert can take his ring and get out of the door Hester is sobbing hysterically. "She drops into a chair and sits, staring straight before her, shaken by her sobs of outraged fury and wretchedness."

Christina and David are back, and Mrs. Phelps. They all try to help Hester control herself, but without great success. She is trying to stop, she wails between sobs, but she cannot so long as "those awful people" are in the room. She must get away. Some one must take her away.

Gradually, after she has drunk aromatic spirits of ammonia, Hester becomes calmer. She is able to tell them then what has happened—that Rob has jilted her—and to demand of Mrs. Phelps a reason for her having induced Rob to do such a thing. What reason had she for doing it? What reason?

Mrs. Phelps would dissemble, if she could, and deny that she had anything to do with Robert's change of heart. But angered by the lashing accusation of Hester and faced with some of her own words of advice to her son, she confesses defiantly that she did advise the break. She did it, first, because of Hester's seeming indifference as reported by Robert; of the doubt that Hester really loved him, and of his own doubt that he ever loved her. Such a marriage would be appalling and should be broken off.

Hester denies Mrs. Phelps' statements. She denies that Robert ever said the things, or thought the things, his mother attributes to him. And Christina supports her in this belief, to Mrs. Phelps' further irritation. Mrs. Phelps is finally forced to admit that perhaps she has misquoted her son slightly, but as to his meaning and his intentions she stands firm.

Hester demands that she be permitted to leave the house at once. Whatever people may think, or say, she refuses to remain another night under the Phelps roof. If there are no more trains, and Mrs. Phelps will not permit her to take the car, she will go to the hotel in town. This is a decision that concerns Mrs. Phelps very seriously.

MRS. PHELPS—You've got to think of appearances!

HESTER—Appearances are your concern. Yours and Rob's. I'm going to the hotel. I don't care what people say! I don't care about anything. I won't stay here!

MRS. PHELPS—Can't you talk to her, Christina? Surely you see . . . for all our sakes!

HESTER—If you won't let me have the car, I'll call a taxi . . . (*She plunges towards the telephone.*)

MRS. PHELPS—I forbid you!

HESTER (*seizing the instrument*)—I want a taxi . . . a taxi. . . . What *is* the number? . . . Well, give it to me . . . Locust 4000? Give me Locust 4000! (MRS. PHELPS *hesitates an instant, then, with terrible coolness, steps forward and jerks the telephone cord from the wall. Except for a startled expression, very low, from* CHRISTINA, *there is not a sound.* HESTER *hangs up the receiver and sets down the dead instrument.*)

MRS. PHELPS (*after an interminable silence*)—You are the only person in the world who has ever forced me to do an undignified thing. I shall not forget it. (*She goes nobly.*)

HESTER (*weakly, turning to* CHRISTINA)—Christina, it isn't true what she said. . . . He did . . . he did want to marry me! Really, he did! He did!

CHRISTINA—Of course he did, darling!

HESTER—I won't stay! I won't stay under that woman's roof!

CHRISTINA—Hester, darling!

HESTER—I'll walk to town!

CHRISTINA—Don't, Hester!

HESTER—That wasn't true, what she said!

CHRISTINA—Of course not!

HESTER—I still love him. . . . Let me go, Christina, I'll walk . . .

CHRISTINA—You can't, at this time of night! It wouldn't be safe!

HESTER—I don't care! I won't stay!

CHRISTINA—There! There! You'll come to bed now, won't you?

HESTER—No! No! I can't! I'd rather die! I'll walk to town.

CHRISTINA—You'll force me to come with you, Hester. I can't let you go alone.

HESTER—I won't stay another minute!

CHRISTINA—Do you want to make me walk with you? Think, Hester! Think what I told you before dinner! Do you want to make me walk all that way in the cold?

HESTER (*awed by this*)—Oh, your baby! I didn't mean to forget your baby! Oh, Christina, you mustn't stay, either. This is a dreadful house! You've got to get your baby away from this house, Christina! Awful things happen here!

CHRISTINA—Hester, darling! Won't you please be sensible and come up to bed?

HESTER (*speaking at the same time as her nerves begin to go again*)—Awful things, Christina. . . . You'll see if you don't come away! You'll see! . . . She'll do the same thing to you that she's done to me. You'll see! You'll see!

The curtain is down briefly. It rises again "upon David's little bedroom, untouched since the day when David went away to

Harvard and scorned to take his prep school trophies and souvenirs with him." The room has been freshly done up by Mrs. Phelps "in a spirit of maternal archæology."

David, in pajamas and socks, is ready to retire. The room is more or less untidily strewn with his clothes. With tooth brush and paste he slips into the bathroom. "After he has gone a few seconds a tiny scratching sound is heard on the other side of the other door and that is opened from without. We see the scratcher at work conveying the impression that a wee mousie wants to come in. The wee mousie is none other than Mrs. Phelps, all smiles in her best negligee, the most effective garment she wears during the entire play. She is carrying the largest eiderdown comfort ever seen on any stage."

Mrs. Phelps is a little disappointed at finding the room empty, but its untidiness catches her eye and she spends the next few minutes putting it to rights, loving her work and putting her whole heart into it. "One or two of the garments receive devout maternal kisses and hugs." Then she spreads the eiderdown, smooths the pillow and kisses that, and sits down to wait.

David is not nearly as enthused by his mother's surprise visit as she evidently had hoped he might be. Her beaming smile "arouses his usual distaste for filial sentimentality."

David tries politely to suggest that he is ready to turn in, but Mrs. Phelps is there to have a talk, just as she used to come in the old comrade days. David is doubtfully grateful but plainly uneasy. He can't, for one thing, get the scene downstairs out of his mind. He is awfully glad to be home, delighted to see his mother, and sure that a boy's mother is always his best friend, both in song and story and out of them. But still—

There is a knock at the door which Mrs. Phelps concludes must be that of Christina and she quietly slips out. But it is only Robert come to extract, if possible, a little moral support from his present trouble.

He gets little. David frankly admits that he doesn't think much of Robert's treatment of Hester. And less of his childish charge that he, David, is trying to turn their mother against him. Robert admits he has always been jealous of his mother's greater interest in David, and now—

"I know from experience what to expect when you and Mother get together," charges Robert. "I used to listen at that door, night after night, while you and Mother sat in here and talked me over. Then I'd watch for the change in her next morning at breakfast when I hadn't slept a wink all night."

They are at the point of a quarrel when the "wee mousie" scratches at the door again. She is afraid that her two beaus are quarreling and she can't have that.

David is for letting the matter drop, but Mrs. Phelps is not. She must know what is in her boys' minds. And she resents David's implied championship of Hester. It is wicked of Robert to so far forget his loyalty to his brother and to her.

David stands firm. He agrees with Chris that a lot of trouble can be caused by too much "mythologizing." "You mythologize Rob into a little tin god," he asserts. "Along comes Hester and falls in love with the real Rob. She never heard of your little tin god Rob. She doesn't deliver the incense and tom-toms. That makes you and Rob sore and the whole works goes to hell. That's mythologizing. Believe me, it can make plenty of trouble."

Mrs. Phelps is relieved that the criticism is so general, but she still is strong in Robert's defense. If he has seen fit to break with Hester because she, as he says, does not reach his ideal of womankind, the ideal that his mother has inspired, it is a sentiment to be admired. David has hurt her more than she ever has been hurt before by not standing by them. He has shown her, she says, that what she has most dreaded has come to pass— he has permitted the bond between them to be loosened.

"Act upon your treachery if you will," sighs Mrs. Phelps, "but don't, please, don't say another thing. Remember, 'The brave man does it with a sword, the coward with a word.'" With this she sweeps out of the room, slamming the door behind her.

She is not gone long, however. With his room to himself at last David has no more than kicked off his slippers and flounced into bed than his mother is back again. She has come now to apologize, to hold his hand as she used to do, and to ask him to forget that she has permitted herself to be hurt. Now she wants to talk about Christina and to be reassured that, although she herself is not at all modern and not a bit clever, "just a timid old lady of the old school," that Christina will like her. She is sure that Christina is all that David thinks her, and she is sure that if Christina does not quite live up to all David expects of her, or if she should feel a little out of it in their family, seeing that she and David and Robert have always been so much to each other, that David will be reasonable and understanding.

MRS. PHELPS—At first I thought Christina was going to be hard and cold. I didn't expect her to have our sense of humor and I don't believe she has much of that. But we've more than we need already. If only she will learn to care for me as I care for her, we can be so happy, all four of us together, can't we?

DAVID—You bet we can!

MRS. PHELPS (*dreamily*)—Building our houses in Phelps Manor. . . . Deciding to put an Italian Villa here and a little bungalow there. . . . (*As* DAVID *grows restive.*) But the important thing for you, Dave, boy, is a sense of proportion about your marriage. I'm going to lecture you, now, for your own good. If, at first, Christina does seem a little exacting or unreasonable, particularly about us, remember that she has to adjust herself to a whole new world here, a very different world from her friends in Omaha. And you must never be impatient with her. Because, if you are, I shall take her side against you.

DAVID—You *are* a great woman, Mother!

MRS. PHELPS—You're the great one! How many boys of your age let their wives undermine all their old associations and loosen all their old ties!

DAVID—Chris wouldn't try that!

MRS. PHELPS—She might not want to. But jealous girls think things that aren't so and say things that aren't true. Morbid things.

DAVID—Morbid things? Chris?

MRS. PHELPS—Only you won't pay too much attention or take her too seriously. I know that, because you would no more let any one strike at me than I would let any one strike at you.

DAVID—But Chris wouldn't. . . .

MRS. PHELPS—As I said to Christina this afternoon: "Christina," I said, "I cannot allow you to sacrifice David!"

DAVID—Chris sacrifice me! How?

MRS. PHELPS—Why, by taking you away from your magnificent opportunity here.

DAVID—Oh!

MRS. PHELPS—Be master in your own house. Meet her selfishness with firmness, her jealousy with fairness and her . . . her exaggeration with a grain of salt. . . .

DAVID—What exaggeration?

MRS. PHELPS—Well, you know . . . a girl . . . a young wife, like Christina . . . *might* possibly make the mistake of . . . well, of taking sides . . . in what happened downstairs, for instance . . . and without fully understanding. . . . You can see how fatal *that* would be. . . . But, if you face the facts always,

Dave, boy, and nothing *but* the facts, your marriage will be a happy one. And, when you want advice, come to your mother always.

DAVID—Thanks.

MRS. PHELPS—Now, isn't your mother your best friend?

DAVID—You bet you are, Mummy!

MRS. PHELPS—How long it is since you've called me that! Bless you, my dear, dear boy!

She is bending over, "to seal her triumph with a kiss," when there is a slight knock at the door and Christina appears. "She has changed her dress for a very simple negligee. Her mood is dangerous."

Mrs. Phelps is sweetly apologetic. She doesn't want Christina to feel that she is intruding. Christina is one of the family now and must feel free to come and go as she likes in the house. Then Mother quietly finds David's dressing gown for him, that he may observe the proprieties, and sweetly assures him that they will not look while he is getting into it.

Then she leaves them, with a final maternal warning that Christina should not keep David up too late.

Christina is a little lonesome, and a little apprehensive. She wants to be held in her husband's arms, and kissed and told that he loves her and that he wants to be in love with her. "Because just loving isn't enough," she insists. "It's being in love that really matters."

David is tender and reassuring, but there is a certain reserve in his manner that worries Christina. She doesn't like it. She doesn't like being so far away from him. Of course his mother wanted him to be near *her*, but—

Christina has come to talk with David because there are some things she must know. "Do you look upon me as apart from all other women?" she demands, seriously. "I mean do you think of all the women in the world and then think of me quite, quite differently? Do you, Dave? . . . Because that's how I feel about you and all the other men in the world. Because that's what being in love must mean and being properly and happily married. Two people, a man and a woman, together by themselves miles and miles from everybody, from *everybody* else, glancing around now and then at all the rest of mankind, at *all* the rest, Dave, and saying: 'Are you still there? And getting along all right? Sure there's nothing we can do to help?'"

That is a little deep for David, but he can't see that it is as serious as she seems to think. Sure, Christina's right. He feels that way. And he agrees that any person who breaks in on that feeling between a man and a woman is the blackest sort of sinner. It may be, as she says, that Robert didn't feel that way about Hester, but Rob always was a queer egg. And he hopes Chris will be careful to keep out of the mess Rob and Hester have got into. It's none of their business. But as to that Christina is not so sure.

"You see what comes of taking things so hard?" David points out. "I'm just as distressed over what's happened as you are. Maybe more. But I certainly don't want to run away. It wouldn't be right. Mother'd never understand. I'd feel like a bum going off and leaving her in the lurch after this. Think what Rob's put her through to-day and what she'll have to go through with Hester's family and all her friends and everybody else before she's done!"

David feels that perhaps it would be unfair now for them to think only of themselves and their own plans. It might be better for him to move slowly, and to look around. Take the matter of the houses his mother wants him to build in Phelps Manor. He can't be throwing away opportunities, now, with the baby coming.

Of course he can't, Christina agrees. But there is also the question of *her* opportunities. What about her appointment? She is not at all intrigued by Mrs. Phelps' generous offer to "scare up" a laboratory where she can "putter around."

David is convinced that he and mother can "dope out something for her." "And I must say, Chris," he goes on, "that I don't think you're quite playing ball to judge my home and my family entirely on what you've seen to-night. Besides the whole purpose of this visit was to bring you and Mother together and to show Mother that a lady scientist mayn't be as bad as she sounds. Because you and Mother have just got to hit it off, you know."

He doesn't want Chris to be impatient, and he is afraid she is a little intolerant. She'll see. Things will straighten out. Mother gets on his nerves, too, sometimes, but she's had a hard life. His father, Chris must remember, didn't amount to much. True, he left them rich when he died, but that isn't everything. Then there's the matter of Mother's health. She's never been robust. And she has been a great mother, nursing them through their illnesses, working for them day and night, taking an interest in all they did, in school and afterward.

Christina is sure that Mrs. Phelps has been most devoted to her boys. Of course he must admit she never was particularly sweet to his girl friends, especially those he seemed in danger of caring for. She had broken off several unpromising affairs both for him and for Robert, as he admits. And now there is Hester!

It all adds up perfectly to Christina. And she has come to one or two definite conclusions. First, they have got to get out of there immediately, and, second, they've got to "take sides" with Hester. Even if he thinks it is none of their business they owe it to themselves to *make* it their business. In a word it has come to this: "Who comes first with you? Your Mother or me?"

DAVID—Now what's the good of putting things that way?

CHRISTINA—That's what things come to! If your mother and I ever quarreled about anything, if it ever came up to you to choose between sticking by me and sticking by her, which would you stick by?

DAVID—I'd . . . I'd try to do the right thing. . . .

CHRISTINA—That isn't an answer. That's another evasion.

DAVID—But why ask such a question?

CHRISTINA—Because I love you. Because I've got to find out if you love me. And I'm afraid . . . I'm afraid. . . .

David—Why?

CHRISTINA—Because you won't see the facts behind all this. I'm trying to tell you what they are and you won't listen. You can't even hear me.

DAVID—I *can* hear you. And a worse line of hooey I've never listened to in my life.

CHRISTINA (*gravely, but with steadily increasing fervor*)— Have you ever thought what it would be like to be trapped in a submarine in an accident? I've learned to-night what that kind of panic would be like. I'm in that kind of panic now, this minute. I've been through the most awful experience of my life to-night. And I've been through it alone. I'm still going through it alone. It's pretty awful to have to face such things alone. . . . No, don't interrupt me. I've got to get this off my chest. Ever since we've been married I've been coming across queer rifts in your feeling for me, like arid places in your heart. Such vast ones, too! I mean, you'll be my perfect lover one day and the next I'll find myself floundering in sand, and alone, and you no-where to be seen. We've never been really married, Dave. Only now and then, for a little while at a time, between your retirements into your arid places. . . . I used to wonder what you did there. At first, I thought you did your work there. But you don't. Your work's in my part of your heart, what there is of my part. Then I decided the other was just No-Man's Land. And I thought: little by little, I'll encroach upon it and pour my love upon it, like water on the western desert, and make it flower here and bear fruit there. I thought: then he'll be all alive, all free and all himself; not part dead and tied and blind; not partly some one else—or nothing. You see, our marriage and your architecture were suffering from the same thing. They only worked a little of the time. I meant you to work all the time and to win your way, *all* your way, Dave, to complete manhood. And that's a good deal father than you've got so far. . . . Then we came here and this happened with Hester and your brother and you just stepped aside and did nothing about it! You went to bed. You did worse than that. You retired into your private wastes and sat tight. . . . I've shown you what you should do and you won't see it. I've called to you to come out to me, and you won't come. So now I've discovered what keeps you. Your mother keeps you. It isn't No-Man's Land at all. It's your mother's land. Arid, sterile, and your mother's! You won't let me get in there. Worse than that, you won't let life get in there! Or she won't. . . . That's what I'm afraid of, Dave: your mother's hold on you. And that's what kept me from getting anywhere with you, all these months. I've seen what she can do with Robert. And what she's done to Hester. I can't help wondering what she may not do with you and to me and to the baby. That's why I'm asking you to take a stand on this business of Hester's, Dave. You'll never find the right any clearer than it is here. It's a kind of test case for me. Don't you see? What you decide about this is what you may, eventually, be expected to decide about . . . about your marriage.

DAVID (*a pause, then, with sullen violence*)—No! I'm damned if I see!

CHRISTINA (*breaking*)—Then I can't hope for much, can I? . . . I feel awfully like a lost soul right now. . . . Oh, my God, what am I going to do! What am I going to do!

DAVID—I hope you're going to behave. You ought to be ashamed. Just as I was bringing Mother around to you and . . .

CHRISTINA (*violently*)—You'd better think a little about bringing me around to your mother!

David—Chris!

CHRISTINA—Why should your mother and I get on?

DAVID—Because you should, that's why. Because she's an older woman and my mother. And you know, just as well as I do . . .

CHRISTINA—I know a great deal better than you that your mother dislikes me full as much as I dislike her. You're wasting your time trying to bring your mother and me together, because we won't be brought. You say you believe in facing the facts. Well, let's see you face that one!

David never heard anything more outrageous than that. Christina knows what his mother means to him, and a man's mother is his mother.

"And what's his wife, may I ask?" demands Christina. "Or doesn't she count?"

It is all morbid rot, insists David, and he doesn't intend to stand for any more.

Christina is desperate now. "Hester's escaped," she cries, "but I'm caught. I can't go back and be the old Christina again. She's done for. And Christina, your wife, doesn't even exist! That's the fact I've got to face! I'm going to have a baby by a man who belongs to another woman."

The door opens and Mrs. Phelps, "white, but steady," stands before them. She has heard every word, she admits, and now the three of them know where they stand. She is not resentful. She is sarcastic, but she would be noble and sacrificing. She is on Christina's side, just as she warned David she would be.

"I accept my fate," she says to David, after Christina has left them. "You have your own life to live with the woman you have chosen. No boy could have given me back the love I gave you. Go to Christina! Make your life with her! No bond binds you to me any longer."

DAVID—That isn't true!

MRS. PHELPS—I'm not complaining. I'm only sorry for one thing. I'm only sorry to see you throw away your chance here, your great chance!

DAVID—But I haven't thrown it away. I'll stay here and work for you if you want me to.

MRS. PHELPS—Christina won't let you. You know that!

DAVID—She's my wife, isn't she?

MRS. PHELPS—Think what that means, Dave! Think what that means!

DAVID—And you're my mother. I'm thinking what that means, too!

MRS. PHELPS—Then it *isn't* good-by? Then I've still got my big boy, after all?

DAVID—You bet you've got him!

MRS. PHELPS (*triumph*)—Oh, Dave! Dave! Dave!

DAVID—Now, Mummy! (*But a sound downstairs distracts him.*) Hello! What's that? (*She listens, too.*)

MRS. PHELPS—Heavens, it isn't a fire, is it?

DAVID—Wait. . . . I'll see. . . . (*He opens the door into the hall and stands listening.*)

CHRISTINA (*from below*)—I went into her room and she wasn't there and then I looked for her and I found the dining-room window open.

ROBERT (*from below*)—What do you think has happened?

CHRISTINA (*from below*)—I don't like to imagine things, but . . .

ROBERT (*from below*)—Hester, where are you?

CHRISTINA (*from below*)—She's got away! I tell you, she's got away! I shouldn't have left her . . .

DAVID (*speaking during the above*)—What?

MRS. PHELPS—It's Christina and Robert.

DAVID—Something's happened to Hester.

MRS. PHELPS—No!

DAVID—Chris, what's going on?

ROBERT (*below*)—Hester! Where are you, Hester?

CHRISTINA (*appearing in the hall*)—Hester's got away, Dave. Out by the dining-room window. You'll have to get dressed and find her. She can't get to town to-night in this cold.

DAVID—All right. We'll have a look.

MRS. PHELPS—The little fool! Let her go, Dave!

CHRISTINA—But, Mrs. Phelps, she isn't properly dressed. She didn't even take her coat. . . .

ROBERT (*still calling from below*)—Hester! Where are you, Hester! Hester! . . . Oh, my God! (CHRISTINA *has walked to the window to look out. She utters an inarticulate scream.*)

DAVID—What is it, Chris?

MRS. PHELPS—Good heavens!

CHRISTINA (*strangled with horror*)—It's the pond! The holes in the pond! Quick, Dave, for heaven's sake!

DAVID—What? . . . Oh! . . . (*He runs out as* CHRISTINA *opens the window.*)

MRS. PHELPS—Dave! . . . (*To* CHRISTINA.)  What is it you say?

ROBERT (*from below*)—Dave!  For God's sake!  Hold on, Hester!  Don't struggle!  (DAVID'S *shouts join his.*)

CHRISTINA (*as she collapses on the bed*)—The pond. . . . I can't look. . . .

MRS. PHELPS—Oh, I've no patience with people who have hysterics.

CHRISTINA—Mrs. Phelps, the girl's drowning!

MRS. PHELPS—Oh, no! . . . Not that!  (*She, too, goes to the window, but recoils in horror from what she sees.*)  They'll save her, won't they?  They must . . . they must save her. . . . If only . . . (*Then a new fear overwhelms her.*)  If only those two boys don't catch pneumonia!  (*And she leaps to the window to call after her sons as they race, shouting, across the snow.*)  Robin, you're not dressed!  Dave, get your coat!  Are you crazy?  Do you want to catch pneumonia?

The curtain falls.

## ACT III

The next morning Mrs. Phelps is busily fixing a great many flowers about the living room.  The doctor who has been attending Hester has gone, Robert reports, and has left word that Hester will be able to travel immediately.  She will be much better off traveling than she would be staying there in his opinion.

Between Christina and Hester, Robert says, they managed to tell the doctor the whole story and the medic's sympathies were all too plainly with them.  He did not even ask to see Mrs. Phelps.

"He said there's nothing the matter with your heart, and never has been anything the matter with it," repeats Robert, with cruel frankness.  "He said it would take a stick of dynamite to kill you."

"Damned homeopath!"

"And that isn't the worst.  He said that I'd always been a rotter, and that I couldn't be anything else with such a mother."

There is venom in Robert's last remark and Mrs. Phelps' lips stiffen under the sting of it.  "I think you might have spared me that, Robin," she protests.  "There are things one doesn't repeat to sensitive people."

Robert insists he had no intention of being nasty, but it is quite evident that his feelings are far from friendly and sympathetic this morning. He still is trying to escape from the memory of Hester's experience, shuddering at the thought that she really tried to drown herself and of his own and his mother's responsibility. Nor do Mrs. Phelps' attempted alibis in any way comfort him. He feels that they are a good deal like Macbeth and Lady Macbeth. They've got into a mess they can't ever get out of.

There is more spirit in Mrs. Phelps' defiance of circumstances. It is ridiculous, she thinks, for Robert to feel as he does. Neither can she understand his regrets over the loss of Hester or his feeling that he will all the rest of his life regret that loss. For these regrets Robert holds his mother to blame. It was she who put the idea into his head. It was she who persuaded him and made him promise. If she didn't come between him and Hester, who did?

Mrs. Phelps is deeply hurt at this preposterous suggestion and quite sure that he will live to regret it—even more than he will regret the loss of Hester—when it's too late.

"I daresay I've got a life full of regrets ahead of me," solemnly agrees Robert. Of one thing he is certain. They will have to do something, he and his mother. They will have to go somewhere. He can't stay there and face people.

"This story'll be all over this damned town," he predicts. "And Hester's people aren't going to keep quiet in New York. Her brothers go everywhere I go. My friends will begin cutting me in the street."

Mrs. Phelps has been thinking, too. It might be wise for them to go away for a while, so Robin can study interior decorating abroad. They could, by hurrying the passports, sail on the *Paris* Saturday. She already has taken the precaution to wire for passage.

"I see. . . . Then we're to sneak away like two guilty fugitives!"

"Sh! Don't say such things!"

David, who has been putting up danger signs around the pond, is back and glad to hear that Hester is better. He also thinks that, everything considered, it probably would be as well if he and Chris were to go, say, in a couple of days. Time is bound to make things a lot easier for everybody. Mrs. Phelps agrees—but she also has another plan.

She does not know just what to do with Robin, she confesses to David. She feels that she must get him away, send him abroad perhaps. But he can't go alone. She could go with him, but her own health is nothing to be relied upon, and if Robin should collapse with a nervous breakdown on the other side—

Perhaps, she suggests, if Christina could spare him for a little while David might go with them. Just long enough to see them settled. Of course, she would like to have Christina go along, too. But that would be asking too much—making Christina put off her work when she is so set upon it!

It is really all on Robin's account that Mrs. Phelps has thought of asking David—and Christina—to make this additional sacrifice. Unless they do something Robin is sure to "slip back again to drinking and fast women." She is quite hysterical at the thought of that, and becomes suddenly so faint that David is frightened.

She is much improved the next few minutes, however. And her plan is still uppermost in her mind. So long as David is going to build the houses at Phelps Manor it might be an excellent thing for him to have a month or two drawing plans and getting ideas abroad.

David is the least bit persuaded that she may be right, and Mrs. Phelps grows ecstatic at the thought of what may easily happen. Robert abroad studying interior decorating! David building his houses!

"My two boys in partnership," she croons. "Oh, that's always been my dream! Oh, how simply things come straight when people are willing to coöperate and make little sacrifices! If there's one thing I pride myself on it's my willingness to make little sacrifices. Here we are, we three, a moment ago all at odds with life and with each other, now united and of a single mind."

And then in walks Christina, just in time to hear Dave say that before any real decisions are arrived at he must talk them over with his wife. Christina "is dressed as she was when she first came to the house. She wears her hat and her fur coat and carries her bag in her hand."

Christina is going away with Hester, she announces. She has come to see whether or not David is coming, too.

David is staggered by the suddenness of this decision, and the firmness of its statement. Both Mrs. Phelps and Robert, sensing a gathering storm, would withdraw.

"Don't go, Mrs. Phelps," Christina calls. "And won't you stay, too, Robert? I think it's best that we should thrash this question out together, here and now, for good and all.'

"What question, Christina?"

"The David question, Mrs. Phelps. Whether David is going on from this point as your son or as my husband."

The family is greatly disturbed. David, half pleadingly, begs Christina not to stir it all up again, just as he is getting everything straightened out. But Christina is firm. She must be firm, she feels, if there is ever to be any chance of happiness for any of them. As they stand they are all perfectly miserable and they know it.

"Thank you for being sorry for us," sneers Robert.

"You give me such good reason, Robert," calmly answers Christina. "Such awfully good reason! Because you're not really bad people, you know. You're just wrong, all wrong, terribly, pitifully, all of you, and you're trapped. . . .

MRS. PHELPS—What we say in anger we sometimes regret, Christina. . . .

CHRISTINA—Oh, I'm not angry. I was, but I've got over it. I rather fancy myself, now, as a sort of scientific Nemesis. I mean to strip this house and to show it up for what it really is. I mean to show you up, Mrs. Phelps. Then Dave can use his own judgment.

MRS. PHELPS (*blank terror at this attack*)—Oh! Dave, I . . .

DAVID—Now, Mother! Chris! Haven't you any consideration for our feelings? Are they nothing to you?

CHRISTINA—I'm trying to save my love, my home, my husband and my baby's father. Are they nothing to you?

DAVID—But surely I can be both a good son and a good husband!

CHRISTINA—Not if your mother knows it, you can't!

MRS. PHELPS (*a last desperate snatch at dignity*)—If you'll excuse me, I'd rather not stay to be insulted again. (*She is going.*)

CHRISTINA—You'll probably lose him if you don't stay, Mrs. Phelps! (MRS. PHELPS *stays*. CHRISTINA *turns to* DAVID.) No, Dave. There's no good in any more pretending. Your mother won't allow you to divide your affections and I refuse to go on living with you on any basis she will allow.

MRS. PHELPS—I cannot see that this is necessary.

CHRISTINA—It's a question a great many young wives leave unsettled, Mrs. Phelps. I'm not going to make that mistake. (*Back to* DAVE *again.*) You see, Dave, I'm not beating about the bush. I'm not persuading you or wasting any time on tact.

Do you want your chance or don't you?   Because, if you don't,
I'll have to get over being in love with you as best I can and . . .

DAVID—I wish you wouldn't talk this way, Chris!

CHRISTINA—Are you coming with me?   On the understanding
that, for the present, until your affections are definitely settled
on your wife and child, you avoid your mother's society entirely?
Well?   What do you say?

DAVID—I don't know what to say.

CHRISTINA—You never do, Dave darling.

DAVID—I'm too shocked.   I've never been so shocked in my
life.

CHRISTINA (*a glance at her wrist watch*)—Just take your time
and think before you speak.

DAVID—I don't mean that I don't know what to say about
taking my chance, as you call it.   I can answer that by reminding you of your duty to me.   I can answer that by calling all
this what I called it last night.   Morbid rot!   But I *am* shocked
at your talking this way about my mother and to her face, too!

CHRISTINA—Is that your answer?

DAVID—No, it isn't!   But a man's mother *is* his mother.

CHRISTINA—So you said last night.   I'm not impressed.   An
embryological accident is no grounds for honor.   Neither is a
painful confinement, for I understand, Mrs. Phelps, that you're
very proud of the way you bore your children.   I know all about
the legend of yourself as a great woman that you've built up
these thirty years for your sons to worship.   It hasn't taken me
long to see that you're not fit to be any one's mother.

DAVID—Chris!

ROBERT (*speaking at the same time*)—See here, now!

MRS. PHELPS—Let her go on!   Let her go on!   She will explain that or retract it!

CHRISTINA—I'm only too glad to explain.   It's just what I've
been leading up to.   And I'll begin by saying that if my baby
ever feels about me as your sons feel about you, I hope that
somebody will take a little enameled pistol and shoot me, because
I'll deserve it.


Mrs. Phelps objects to the insult, but Christina insists that no
insults are or have been intended.   She is trying desperately to
be as scientific and impersonal as possible.

If, however, insults are to be considered, how does Mrs. Phelps
explain her appalling rudeness to a guest in her home?   Why
does she openly resent the fact that Christina is going to have

a baby?  Because she is afraid the baby will give her another and a stronger hold on David?  Why did she bend every effort to separate Robert and Hester, even to the point of lying deliberately and brutally to Hester about Robert and his unwillingness to marry her?

Mrs. Phelps may deny that she did these things, but Christina heard her.  Furthermore she heard her call her boys back from saving Hester from drowning for fear they might catch cold. Mrs. Phelps, Christina charges, is deliberately trying to keep her sons dependent upon her, she instinctively opposes every move either of them makes toward independence and she is outraged by their natural impulses toward other women.

"I deny all of it," furiously declares Mrs. Phelps.

CHRISTINA—You may deny it until you're black in the face; every accusation I make is true!  You belong to a type that's very common in this country, Mrs. Phelps—a type of self-centered, self-pitying, son-devouring tigress, with unmentionable proclivities suppressed on the side.

DAVID—Chris!

CHRISTINA—I'm not at all sure it wouldn't be a good idea, just as an example to the rest of the tribe, to hang one of your kind every now and then!

ROBERT—Really!

CHRISTINA—Oh, there are normal mothers around; mothers who want their children to be men and women and take care of themselves; mothers who are people, too, and don't have to be afraid of loneliness after they've outlived their motherhood; mothers who can look on their children as people and not be forever holding on to them and pawing them and fussing about their health and singing them lullabies and tucking them up as though they were everlasting babies.  But you're *not* one of the normal ones, Mrs. Phelps!  Look at your sons, if you don't believe me.  You've destroyed Robert.  You've swallowed him up until there's nothing left of him but an effete make-believe.  Now he's gone melancholy mad and disgraced himself.  And Dave! Poor Dave!  The best he can do is dodge the more desperate kinds of unhappiness by pretending!  How he survived at all is beyond me.  If you're choking a bit on David, now, that's my fault because you'd have swallowed him up, too, if I hadn't come along to save him!  Talk about cannibals!  You and your kind beat any cannibals I ever heard of!  And what makes you doubly deadly and dangerous is that people admire you and your kind. They actually admire you! You professional mothers! . . . You see, I'm taking this differently from that poor child upstairs. She's luckier than I am, too. She isn't married to one of your sons. Do you remember what she said about children yesterday? "Have 'em. Love 'em. And leave 'em be."

MRS. PHELPS—You are entitled to your opinion, Christina, just as I am to mine and David is to his. I only hope that he sees the kind of woman he's married. I hope he sees the sordidness, the hardness, the nastiness she offers him for his life.

CHRISTINA (*an involuntary cry of pain*)—I'm not nasty! I'm not!

MRS. PHELPS—What have you to offer David?

CHRISTINA—A hard time. A chance to work on his own. A chance to *be* on his own. Very little money on which to share with me the burden of raising his child. The pleasure of my society. The solace of my love. The enjoyment of my body, to which I have reason to believe he is not indifferent.

MRS. PHELPS (*revolted*)—Ugh!

CHRISTINA—Can you offer so much?

MRS. PHELPS—I offer a mother's love. Or perhaps you scoff at that?

CHRISTINA—Not if it's kept within bounds. I hope my baby loves me. I'm practically certain I'm going to love my baby, but within bounds.

MRS. PHELPS—And what do you mean by within bounds?

CHRISTINA—To love my baby with as much and as deep respect as I hope my baby will feel for me if I deserve its respect. To love my baby unpossessively, above all, unromantically.

MRS. PHELPS—I suppose that's biology! You don't know the difference between good and evil!

CHRISTINA—As a biologist, though, I do know the difference between life and death. And I know sterility when I see it. I doubt if evil is any more than a fancy name for sterility. And sterility, of course, is what you offer Dave. Sterility for his mind as well as for his body. That's your professional mother's stock in trade. Only we've been over that, haven't we? Well, Dave! How about it?

For the moment David apparently can think of nothing that may be done about it, and Robert is of the opinion that the discussion has gone far enough. But Mrs. Phelps still has a defense to make.

Christina has married at 29. When she married, says Mrs.

Phelps, she was 20, Hester's age. Her husband was fifteen years older than she, a widower and an invalid. Within a week all her illusions were shattered, her marriage miserable and empty. She sought happiness and romance where she could find it, and she found it in motherhood. She found it in devoting her life to her two boys, in doing for them all the things nurses and governesses are hired to do to-day. The night her husband died, Mrs. Phelps relates, Robin had the croup—and she remained with Robin. If she made a mistake then, if she has made mistakes since, she can point to her two sons and insist that at least they were not serious mistakes. At 25 Mrs. Phelps was a widow, rich and attractive. There were other chances to marry, and marry well, but she preferred to place her sons first in her life, always.

"I shall not stoop to answer any of the foulnesses you have charged me with," she cries to Christina. "They are beneath my dignity as a woman and my contempt as a mother. No, there is one I cannot leave unanswered. That word 'sterility.' Sterility is what I offer David, you say. I wonder, is sterility David's word for all he has had of me these thirty years? Let him answer that for himself. All my life I have saved to launch my two boys on their careers. I offer David a clear field ahead and a complete love to sustain him, a mother's love, until a real marriage, a suitable marriage, may be possible for him. And I do *not* deny that I would cut off my right hand and burn the sight out of my eyes to rid my son of you! . . . That is how I answer your impersonal science, Christina."

Christina's answer is quick and sharp before either of the boys can speak.

"Well," she says, "it's a very plausible and effective answer. And I'm sure you mean it and I believe it's sincere. But it *is* the answer of a woman whose husband let her down pretty hard and who turned for satisfaction to her sons. . . . I'm almost sorry I can't say more for it, but I can't. . . . (*She turns from* MRS. PHELPS *to the two sons.*) It's a pity she didn't marry again. Things would have been so much better for both of you if she had. (*Then, with an increasing force, to* DAVID.) But the fact remains, Dave, that she did separate you and me last night and that she separated us because she couldn't bear the thought of our sleeping together. (*They flinch at this, but she downs them.*) And she couldn't bear that because she refuses to believe that you're a grown man and capable of desiring a woman. And that's because, grown man that you are, down,

down in the depths of her, she still wants to suckle you at her breast!"

The Phelpses stand aghast at this charge, but their excitement has little effect on Christina. She is not surprised that they find the thought revolting, because it is just that. And she is sorry that David feels as he says, that she hasn't any sense of decency left in her. Still—

"Is that your answer?" she demands of him.

"I want to do the right thing, but—"

"Remember me, won't you, on Mother's Day!" she says, preparing to leave. "Are you ready, Hester?"

Hester is dressed for the journey when she comes down stairs and Christina's arm goes protectingly around her shoulders as she stands waiting. Hester is on the verge of tears again, but she gathers herself together at Christina's command and stands ready. Robert, at sight of her, cries out impulsively:

"Hester! Hester! Couldn't we try again? Couldn't you? . . ."

"I don't know," she answers. Then a tiny smile spreads over her face. "Yes, I do, too, know. I'm going to marry an orphan!"

Christina's voice is choked and she finds it hard to say good-by finally to Dave. "I'm sorry it has come to this," she says. "It might easily have been so . . ."

She can say no more. She picks up her bag and goes quickly out, followed by Hester.

"David stands rigid, Mrs. Phelps watching him. Robert covers his face with his hands. Then the front door slams and David comes suddenly to life."

DAVID (*a frantic cry*)—Chris! (*He turns excitedly to his mother.*) I'm sorry, Mother, but I guess I'll have to go.

MRS. PHELPS (*reeling*)—No, Dave! No! No!

DAVID—I guess she's right.

MRS. PHELPS—Oh, no! You mustn't say that! You mustn't say that!

DAVID (*holding her off from him*)—I can't help it. She said we were trapped. We *are* trapped. I'm trapped.

MRS. PHELPS (*absolutely beyond herself*)—No! No! She isn't right! She can't be right! I won't believe it!

DAVID (*breaking from her*)—I can't help that!

MRS. PHELPS (*speaking at the same time*)—For God's sake, Dave, don't go with her! Not with that awful woman, Dave! That wicked woman! For God's sake don't leave me for her,

Dave! (*She turns wildly to* ROBERT.) You know it isn't true, Robin! You know it was vile, what she said! Tell him! Tell him! (*But he is gone.*) Dave! My boy! My boy! My boy! Oh, my God! Dave! She isn't right! She isn't, Dave! Dave! Dave! (*The front door slams a second time. An awful pause, then:*) He's gone!

ROBERT (*uncovering his face*)—Who? Dave?

MRS. PHELPS—Can you see them from the window?

ROBERT (*looking out*)—Yes. . . . They're talking. . . . Now he's kissed her and taken the suitcase. . . . Now he's helping Hester . . . Hester into the car. . . . Now he's getting in. . . . Now they're starting.

MRS. PHELPS—I loved him too much. I've been too happy. Troubles had to come. I must be brave. I must bear my troubles bravely.

ROBERT (*turning to her*)—Poor Mother!

MRS. PHELPS—I must remember that I still have one of my great sons. I must keep my mind on that.

ROBERT (*a step or two toward her*)—That's right, Mother.

MRS. PHELPS—And we'll go abroad, my great Robin and I, and stay as long as ever we please.

ROBERT (*as he kneels beside her*)—Yes, Mother.

MRS. PHELPS (*her voice growing stronger as that deeply religious point of view of hers comes to her rescue*)—And you must remember that David, in his blindness, has forgotten. That mother love suffereth long and is kind; envieth not, is not puffed up, is not easily provoked; beareth all things; believeth all things; hopeth all things; endureth all things. . . . At least, I think *my* love does?

ROBERT (*engulfed forever*)—Yes, Mother.

The curtain falls.

# THE CRADLE SONG

## Comedy in Two Acts

### By Gregorio and Maria Martinez Sierra

EVA LE GALLIENNE'S season of repertory, some account of which will be found in the chapter devoted to the season in New York, had preceded half its scheduled distance before, on January 24, she produced "The Cradle Song."

It was not a new play and, in many respects, seemed to be the frailest, dramatically, of all her repertory. But it developed, as it had done fifteen years before in Spain, a holding quality in sentiment that soon made it the favorite of the season.

This Martinez Sierra drama, in the writing of which his wife, Maria, is an accredited *collaborateur,* dates back to 1911, when it was first produced at the Teatro Lara in Madrid. It established Sierra, who had started as a poet and took up the drama after a season's association with Benevente, the idol of the Spanish drama lovers and the organizer at that time of the Art Theatre in Madrid.

Ten years later "The Cradle Song" was given at several matinée performances in English by Augustin Duncan, but gathered unto its promoters nothing more substantial than kind words and best wishes. Quite naturally no great store was set by it in the Le Gallienne camp.

It is the simplest of stories molded in the simplest of dramatic forms. There are but two acts, and only two major dramatic situations. The play violates,—if not all of the rules, at least most of the conventions of the theatre, and yet is one of the most moving of entertainments. Or proved so with the Le Gallienne following.

The scene of the opening act is "A room opening upon the cloister of a Convent of Enclosed Dominican Nuns in Spain. The walls are tinted soberly; the floor is tiled. In the right wall a large door with a wicket in it, leading to a passage communicating with the exterior. A grilled peephole for looking out. Beside the door an opening containing a revolving box, or wheel, on which objects may be placed and passed in from the outside without the recipient's being seen or a view of the interior disclosed."

It is broad daylight and the curtain rises upon a scene of cheerfulness and animation. The Prioress, flanked by the Mistress of Novices and the Vicaress, is surrounded by a group of Nuns and before them stand four novices, Sister Marcella, Sister Joanna of the Cross, Sister Maria Jesus and Sister Sagrario.

The gathering, it soon transpires, is a sort of impromptu celebration of the reverend mother's birth anniversary, her saint's day. Sister Joanna of the Cross has written verses in commemoration of the event and begs, with some trepidation, permission to read them.

They are simple verses, beginning "Most reverend Mother, on this happy day your daughters unite for your welfare to pray," and ending "And may the years vie in good with each other, in holiness and joy our dearly loved Mother." The Nuns are quite delighted with them, though Sister Inez suggests that they might have been copied from a book. But the Prioress is pleased, and that is sufficient reward for Sister Joanna of the Cross and her sister novices.

Only the Vicaress seems touched with misgiving. There has been of late a seeming laxity of attention on the part of the Novices, she suggests, and the success of this plan of theirs to keep as a secret and a surprise the gift for the Prioress on her birthday is not unlikely to lead them to pride themselves upon their accomplishments. "Evil combats us where we least expect it," solemnly warns the Vicaress, "and ostentation is not becoming in a heart which has vowed itself to poverty and humility." That the Prioress is much too lenient with the young women is plainly the thought of the Vicaress, but none of the others is inclined to support her in that thought. Especially not on a beautiful day like this.

Another gift comes by way of the revolving wheel. It is a canary and cage, sent by the mayor's wife. She would have brought it herself had it not been that she is detained at home interestingly but none the less definitely.

The Prioress is much pleased with the canary, and the Nuns as well. The novices are quite excited and vastly interested in the ways of caged canaries. As they go to their cells they ask another great favor of their holy mother. Could they be allowed to talk a little while they are waiting for the beginning of the fiesta? The Vicaress is opposed to this dispensation, but the

Prioress sees no harm in it, if her charges will refrain from whispering and offending the Lord with foolish talk.

Now the bell at the entrance gate has rung twice, which is the signal that the Doctor is outside. But before he may be allowed to enter the Nuns must cover their faces and file silently out through the cloister. Only those who are ailing may remain behind—Sister Sagrario, who is bothered with a felon, and Sister Maria Jesus, whose complaint is more mysterious.

The Doctor is a small man of about 60 years, active and interested in his charges, but none too sympathetic with many of the rules and observances of their order. A heretic, the Prioress playfully calls him, and is quite scandalized when he insists he knew there were novices about. As soon as he came in he distinctly smelled fresh meat.

DOCTOR—But I say no more. Come! To work! To work! What is the trouble with these white lambs?

SISTER SAGRARIO—Your handmaid has a felon, Doctor.

DOCTOR—Eh? On the hand? And such a lovely hand! Well, we shall have to lance it, Sister.

SISTER SAGRARIO (*alarmed*)—What? Not now?

DOCTOR—No, to-morrow, Sister. To-morrow, unless it yields first to a poultice and five *paternosters.* Remember, not one less!

SISTER SAGRARIO (*in perfect earnest*)—No, Doctor.

DOCTOR—And this other one, eh?

PRIORESS—Ah, Doctor! She has been giving me a great deal of worry. She falls asleep in the choir; she sighs continually without being able to assign any reason; she cries over nothing whatever; she has no appetite for anything but salads. . . .

DOCTOR—How old are you?

SISTER MARIA JESUS—Eighteen.

DOCTOR—How long have you been in this holy house?

SISTER MARIA JESUS—Two and a half years.

DOCTOR—And how many more do you remain before you come to profession?

SISTER MARIA JESUS—Two and a half more, if the Lord should be pleased to grant this unworthy novice grace to become his bride.

DOCTOR—Let me see the face.

PRIORESS—Lift your veil. (SISTER MARIA JESUS *lifts her veil.*)

DOCTOR—Hm! The Lord has not bad taste. A little pale, but well rounded, well rounded.

SISTER TORNERA—Don José! But who ever heard of such a doctor?

DOCTOR—So, we have melancholy then, a constant disposition to sigh, combined with loss of appetite—well, there is nothing else for it, Sister: a cold bath every morning and afterwards a few minutes' exercise in the garden.

SISTER TORNERA (*somewhat scandalized*)—Exercise? Don José!

DOCTOR—Unless we write at once home to her mother to hurry and fetch her and find us a good husband for her.

SISTER MARIA JESUS—Oh, Don José! But this Sister has taken her vows to the Church!

DOCTOR—Well, in that case cold water. There is nothing else for it. For melancholy at eighteen, matrimony or cold water.

SISTER SAGRARIO (*summoning her courage*)—You always talk so much about it, Doctor, why don't you get married yourself?

DOCTOR—Because I am sixty, daughter; and it is fifteen years since I have felt melancholy. Besides, whom do you expect me to marry when all the pretty girls go into convents?

PRIORESS—Doctor, doctor! This conversation will become displeasing to me.

DOCTOR—Is this all the walking infirmary?

SISTER TORNERA—Yes, Doctor.

DOCTOR—And the invalid? How is she?

SISTER TORNERA—She is the same to-day, Doctor. Poor Sister Maria of Consolation hasn't closed her eyes all night! Don't you remember? Yesterday she said she felt as if she had a viper gnawing at her vitals? Well, to-day she has a frog in her throat.

DOCTOR—Goodness gracious! Come, let me see, let me see. What a continual war the devil does wage against these poor sisters!—Long life, Mother, and happy days!

The Prioress has retired to the choir and the Novices left to guard the door while the Doctor is making his rounds. It is a gay time with the young women because of the permission to talk, and the hope of the Novices is that Sister Marcella, who is the latest from the world outside, will tell them a story. Sister Marcella is doubtful. They probably hope to be shocked and then, likely as not, one of them will tell the Mother Mistress on her. It wouldn't be the first time, either.

But they are diverted from the story to the canary, which has been left behind. Why not open the cage and let him fly away? suggests Sister Marcella. Surely he can't be happy left in a nest of silly women! And it is she who opens the door of the cage. But the bird refuses to fly. "He'd rather stay shut up all his life like us nuns," concludes Sister Maria Jesus.

"Then you're a great fool, birdie," says Sister Marcella, as she closes the cage. "God made the air for wings and He made wings to fly with. While he might be soaring away above the clouds, he is satisfied to stay here all day shut up in his cage, hopping between two sticks and a leaf of lettuce! What sense is there in a bird? *Ay,* Mother! And what wouldn't I give to be a bird!"

They are talking of dreams now. Sister Sagrario often dreams of flying in the night time, or of just floating in the air without wings. And Sister Marcella that she is running downstairs, ever so fast, and never touching her feet to the stairs or to the ground. Many, many times she has dreamt that dream and she suspects it is because one is likely to dream of the things one wants to do most, and can't.

Now they are telling where they would fly if flying were possible. Sister Marcella would fly straight to the end of the world. And Sister Maria Jesus to the Holy Land, to Mount Calvary. And Sister Joanna of the Cross to Bethlehem and the garden of Nazareth, where the Virgin lived with the child.

SISTER SAGRARIO—How do you know that there is a garden at Nazareth?

SISTER JOANNA OF THE CROSS—Of course there's a garden there, with a brook running by it. The song says so:

> "The Virgin washed his garments
> And hung them on the rose.
> The little angels sing
> And the water onward flows" . . .

(*Simply.*) There was a garden, too, by our house in the village, with a big rosebush on the border of a brook that ran by it; and I used to kneel beside the brook, and sing that song while I washed my baby brother's clothes, for there were seven of us children, and I was the oldest. (*Feelingly.*) And that's what I miss most! (*Drying her eyes with her hands.*) *Ay,* Mother! And I always cry when I think of that baby boy! But it isn't right, I know. . . . He loved me more than he did mother, and the day that they took me away to the Convent, and I left home, he cried—he cried so that he nearly broke his little baby heart!

SISTER MARCELLA—I have a brother and a sister, but they are

both older than I am. My sister married two years ago, and now she has a baby. (*With an air of importance.*) She brought him here once to show me.

SISTER JOANNA OF THE CROSS (*interrupting her, greatly interested*)—I remember. He stuck his little hand in through the grille and you, Sister, kissed it. Did you ever think how soft babies' hands are? Whenever I take communion I try to think I am receiving our Lord as a little child, and I take and press him like this to my heart, and then it seems to me that he is so little and so helpless that he can't refuse me anything. And then I think that he is crying, and I pray to the Virgin to come and help me quiet him. And if I wasn't ashamed, because I know you would all laugh at me, I'd croon to him then, and rock him to sleep, and sing him baby songs.

Again there is a ring at the door, and the novices are startled. The more startled when, after Sister Marcella has found courage to ask who's there, no one answers.

"Ave Maria purissima!" she calls a second time, and Sister Sagrario joins her with something almost like a shout. Still no answering "Conceived without sin!" is heard. It is very strange. Still, it may be only the prank of a mischievous boy.

Sister Marcella peeps through the wicket and sees no one. But it looks very much as though something had been left on the wheel. Yes, there is something there!

Sister Joanna of the Cross turns the wheel around to see, and, sure enough, there is a second basket, carefully covered with a white cloth like that in which the canary arrived.

There is a card attached to it. "For the Mother Prioress," it reads. The gift is probably a surprise from some of her friends. It is a much heavier present than the canary. They discover this when they carry it across the room, and their curiosity is greatly excited.

Sister Marcella simply must have a peek. She lifts a corner of the cloth, looks inside and immediately starts back with a blanched face and a sharp cry.

Sister Joanna also looks and is as excited. Soon the others are in a similar state of commotion and now the Prioress, the Vicaress and the Nuns come flocking back to learn whatever can have happened at the gate.

For a moment none of the novices can speak, but finally they manage, in disjointed sentences, to tell of the finding of the basket and the reverend Mother, lifting off the cloth, discovers the cause of their excitement. There is a baby in the basket!

Now the excitement spreads, with nuns and novices alike hovering over the infant and wondering, all in excited sentences, how it came there, whence and why? Nobody knows until they find the paper with the address on it and discover a letter inside. From the letter the Prioress reads:

"REVEREND MOTHER:

"Forgive the liberty which a poor woman takes, trusting in your Grace's charity, of leaving at the grille this newborn babe. I, my lady, am one of those they call women of the street, and I assure you I am sorry for it; but this is the world, and you can't turn your back on it, and it costs as much to go down as it does to go up, and that is what I am writing to tell you, my lady. The truth is this little girl hasn't any father, that is. to say it is the same as if she didn't have any, and I—who am her mother—leave her here, although it costs me something to leave her; for although one is what one is, one isn't all bad, and I love her as much as any mother loves her baby, though she is the best lady in the land. But all the same, though she came into this world without being wanted by any one, she doesn't deserve to be the daughter of the woman she is, above all, my lady, of her father, and I don't want her to have to blush for having been born the way she was, nor for having the mother she has, and to tell it to me to my face, and I pray you by everything you hold dear, my lady, that you will protect her and keep her with you in this holy house, and you won't send her to some orphanage or asylum, for I was brought up there myself, and I know what happens in them, although the sisters are kind—yes, they are—and have pity. And some day, when she grows up and she asks for her mother, you must tell her that the devil has carried her away, and I ask your pardon, for I must never show myself to her, nor see her again, nor give you any care nor trouble, so you can do this good work in peace, if you will do it, for I implore you again, my lady, that you will do it for the memory of your own dear mother, and God will reward you, and she will live in peace, and grow up as God wills, for what the eyes have not seen the heart cannot understand, my lady."

VICARESS—Bless us! *Ave Maria!*
MISTRESS OF NOVICES—Poor woman!

SISTER JOANNA OF THE CROSS—Baby dear! Darling baby!

VICARESS—What pretty mothers the Lord selects for his children!

PRIORESS—God moves in his own ways, Sister. God moves in his own ways.

SISTER INEZ—Is that all the letter says?

PRIORESS—What more could it say? (*The* DOCTOR *and* SISTER TORNERA *have reëntered during the reading.*)

DOCTOR—Exactly. What more could it say?

PRIORESS—What do you think, Don José?

DOCTOR—I think that somebody has made you a very handsome present.

PRIORESS—But what are we going to do with it? Because I . . . this poor woman . . . she has put this poor creature into our hands, and I would protect her willingly, as she asks, and keep her here with us. . . .

NOVICES—Yes, yes, Mother! Do! Do!

MISTRESS OF NOVICES—Silence!

PRIORESS—But I don't know if we can . . . that is, if it is right, if it is according to law . . . for, when we enter this holy rule, we renounce all our rights . . . and to adopt a child legally . . . I don't know whether it can be done. How does it seem to you?

DOCTOR—I agree with you. Legally, you have no right to maternity.

VICARESS—And even if we had, would it be proper for our children to be the offspring of ignominy and sin?

PRIORESS—I would not raise that question, reverend Mother, for the child is not responsible for the sin in which she was born, and her mother, in renouncing her motherhood, has bitterly paid the penalty.

VICARESS—Yes, it didn't cost her much to renounce it.

PRIORESS—Do we know, Mother? Do we know?

VICARESS—We can guess. It is easy enough to go scattering children about the world if all you have to do is leave them to be picked up afterwards by the first person who happens along.

DOCTOR—How easy it is might be a matter for discussion. There are aspects of it which are not so easy.

SISTER SAGRARIO—Oh! She's opened her mouth!

SISTER JOANNA OF THE CROSS—The little angel is hungry.

SISTER MARIA JESUS—She's sucking her thumb!

SISTER JOANNA OF THE CROSS—Make her take her thumb out

of her mouth. She'll swallow too much and then she'll have a pain.

SISTER SAGRARIO—Don't suck your fingers, baby.

SISTER JOANNA OF THE CROSS—Isn't she good, though? You stop her playing and she doesn't cry.

PRIORESS—There is another thing we must consider. What are we to do for a nurse?

SISTER JOANNA OF THE CROSS—The gardener's wife has a little boy she is nursing now.

PRIORESS—In that case I hardly think she would care to be responsible for two.

SISTER JOANNA OF THE CROSS—But it won't be any trouble— she's so tiny! Besides, we can help her out with cow's milk and a little pap. The milk will keep on the ice and we can clear it with a dash of tea.

DOCTOR—It is easy to see Sister Joanna of the Cross has had experience with children.

SISTER JOANNA OF THE CROSS—Your handmaid has six little brothers and sisters. Ah, reverend Mother! Give her to me to take care of and then you will see how strong she'll grow up.

VICARESS—Nothing else was needed to complete the demoralization of the Novices. You can see for yourselves how naturally they take to this dissipation.

PRIORESS—I want you to tell me frankly what you think—all of you. (*All speak at once.*)

MISTRESS OF NOVICES—Your Sister thinks, reverend Mother . . .

SISTER TORNERA—Your handmaid . . .

SISTER INEZ—It seems to me . . .

PRIORESS (*smiling*)—But one at a time.

SISTER TORNERA—It is an angel which the Lord has sent us, and your Sister thinks that we ought to receive her like an angel, with open arms.

MISTRESS OF NOVICES—Of course we ought. Suppose, your Reverences, it hadn't been a little girl, but . . . I don't know— some poor animal, a dog, a cat, or a dove, like the one which flew in here two years ago and fell wounded in the garden trying to get away from those butchers at the pigeon-traps. Wouldn't we have taken it in? Wouldn't we have cared for it? And wouldn't it have lived happy forever afterward in its cage? And how can we do less for a creature with a soul than for a bird?

SISTER TORNERA—We must have charity.

VICARESS—I am glad the Mother Mistress of Novices has brought up the incident of that bird, for it will absolve me from bringing it up, as it might seem, with some malice. It was against my advice that that creature was received into this house, and afterward we had good reason to regret it, with this one saying, "Yes, I caught him!" and that one, "No, I took care of him!" and another, "He opens his beak whenever I pass by!" and another, "See him flap his wings! He does it at me!" —vanities, sophistries, deceits, all of them, snares of the devil continually! And if all this fuss was about a bird, what will happen to us with a child in the house? This one will have to dress it, that one will have to wash it, another will be boasting, "It is looking at me!" and another that it's at her that it googles most. . . . There is Sister Joanna of the Cross making faces at it already!

SISTER JOANNA OF THE CROSS—What did your Reverence say?

VICARESS—Dissipation and more dissipation! Your Reverences should remember that when we passed behind these bars, we renounced forever all personal, all selfish, affection.

MISTRESS OF NOVICES—Is it selfish to give a poor foundling a little love?

VICARESS—It is for us. Our God is a jealous God. The Scriptures tell us so.

MISTRESS OF NOVICES—Bless us! Mercy me!

VICARESS—And this quite apart from other infractions of our order which such indulgence must involve. For example, your Reverences—and I among the first—take no account of the fact that at this very moment we are transgressing our rule. We are conversing with our faces unveiled in the presence of a man.

PRIORESS—That is true.

DOCTOR—Ladies, as far as I am concerned—take no account of me.

True, they are all unveiled, and the Prioress had not noticed. Let them veil their faces, or not, as their consciences dictate. The harm has been done. The Vicaress is the only one who lowers her veil. The others remain uncovered.

Again the discussion as to what to do with the foundling waxes warm. The Prioress frankly confesses that her heart prompts her to keep the child. And the others mostly are agreed that it is God's will that they should have her. Sister Joanna of the Cross is particularly anxious that the baby be not sent to an asylum.

Only the Vicaress represents the opposition. It is all utter foolishness to her. "Christian Heroism!" indeed! "Compassion on those who have fallen and are down!" Faugh! "Mush and sentiment!" that's what it is.

Finally the Prioress must intervene. Let them all be silent. Whatever they decide to do there are certain legal technicalities to be considered. The birth will have to be reported to the Register, and then if nobody wants the child it will be taken away.

But, if they can make up their minds to keep her the Doctor has a solution that will be perfectly legal.

"Thanks be to God, I am a single man," he explains. "But, although I am not a saint, yet I cannot take to myself the credit of having augmented the population of this country by so much as a single soul. I have not a penny, that is true, but like everybody else, I have a couple of family names. They are at the service of this little stranger, if they will be of use to her. She will have no father and no mother—I cannot help that—but she will have an honorable name."

"Do you mean to say—"

"That I am willing to adopt her; exactly—and to entrust her to your care, because my own house . . . The fact is the hands of Dona Cecilia are a little rough for handling these tiny Dresden dolls, and perhaps I might prove a bit testy myself. The neighbors all say that the air grows blue if my coat rubs against me as I walk down the street. . . . Is it agreed?"

"God reward you for it!" answers the Prioress. "Yes, in spite of everything. We shall notify the Superior immediately. It is not necessary that the child should live in the cloister. She can remain with the gardener's wife until she has grown older, and enter here later when she has the discretion to do so. She has been entrusted to our hands, and it is our duty to take care of her—a duty of conscience."

A moment later the gardener's wife has been sent for and the Doctor has departed for the Register to become a legalized parent.

And now they have all been called to devotions and have left Sister Joanna of the Cross with the infant babe. She is on her knees beside the basket bending over it tenderly and alternating with her responses to the prayers being intoned inside the cloister.

But soon she can hear the voices no longer. Only the child interests her. She is embracing it passionately, oblivious of all else.

"Little one! Little one! Whom do you love?" she croons as the curtain falls.

## ACT II

Between the acts there is an "Interlude" spoken before the curtain by a poet. It is at once a greeting and a promise, an explanation and a tribute, recalling in verse what has passed, predicting by inference what is to come. Thus the author combines his tribute to woman with the theme of his play.

> Ah, love of woman, by whose power we live,
> Offend so often—but to see forgive!
> Whence do you draw your grace but from above?
> Whence simply?  Simply from maternal love!
> Yes, we are children, woman, in your arms;
> Your heart is bread, you soothe our wild alarms,
> Like children give us the honey of your breast,
> In a cradle always your lover sinks to rest
> Although he prostitutes our groveling flesh.
> Mother if lover, mother if sister too,
> Mother by pure essence, day long and night through,
> Mother if you laugh, or if with us you cry,
> In the core of being, in fiber and in mesh,
> Every woman carries, so God has willed on high,
> A baby in her bosom, sleeping eternally!

Eighteen years have passed when the curtain rises on the parlor of the convent. It is a somber room. "At the rear a grille with a double row of bars. A curtain of dark woolen cloth hangs over the grille and intercepts the view of the outer parlor, to which visitors are admitted. . . . A number of oil paintings of saints hang upon the walls—all of them very old and showing black stains."

In the parlor a dozen of the Nuns are sewing, and Sister Maria Jesus is reading to them. "A bride's trousseau is spread out upon the table and chairs. It is embroidered elaborately, trimmed with lace and tied with blue silk ribbons. A new trunk stands against the wall, the trays being distributed about the benches and upon the floor."

The novices of the first act have long since professed their faith and changed their white veils for black. They are intent upon their work, but interested, too, in Sister Maria Jesus' reading from "The Treasury of Patience, the Meditations of an Afflicted Soul in the Presence of Its God."

At least they would be interested if from the garden a young girl could not be heard singing joyfully of flowers and spring. The Prioress tries to affect a severity she does not feel.  But not

the others.   They smile happily, even proudly, as they listen.
"She sings like a lark," sighs Sister Joanna, sympathetically.

Again Sister Maria Jesus continues with her reading.   ". . .
Every moment I am buffeted and borne down.   I am sucked into
the uttermost depths, and there is no health in me!"

And from outside again the girl Teresa's voice interrupts joyously.   Sister Sagrario must go and warn Teresa.

"There is no health in me," continues Sister Maria Jesus.   "I
cannot support myself; I cannot resist the shock of the horrible,
onrushing waves."   And again Teresa's voice is heard:

> "You, too, were happy, Mary,
>     Happy in His love,
>   Flowers of love and springtime
>     That bloom above!"

Now the singing stops suddenly and there is a peal of light
laughter following.   "It cannot be helped," admits the Prioress,
and smiles as she says it.   "The child was born happy and will
die so."

There is little more of the reading.   Sister Marcella's temptation to melancholy distracts the attention of the reverend mother.
Sister Marcella is given much to sighing of late.   Nor is she alone
in suffering the temptation.   It seems to be almost an epidemic,
and the Prioress is disturbed.

The Vicaress, who has been making her rounds of inspection
of the cells, is also disturbed, but not melancholy.   She has just
found under the mattress of Sister Marcella's bed "an object
which should never be found in the hands of a religious, an object
which, to say nothing of the sin against the rule of holy poverty
which the private possession and concealment of any property
whatever must presuppose, is by its very nature a root of perdi-
tion and an origin and source of evil—in short, a piece of looking
glass."   And with this offending glass, it is the opinion of the
Vicaress, Sister Marcella has been in the habit of "amusing herself with the sight of her beauty, thus offending her maker with
pride and vainglory and the exhibition of her taste."

But it is for no such purpose that she has used the glass,
Sister Marcella protests to the reverend mother.   She had used it
only to combat those very temptations to melancholy which she
has confessed.   When these temptations seized upon her too
strongly, putting it into her head to climb trees, run along the
tops of walls, and jump over the fences, it was Sister Marcella's
custom to catch a sunbeam in the mirror and make it dance

among the leaves and across the ceiling of her cell as a sort of spiritual proxy, imagining the beam to be a bird or a butterfly free to go where it pleaseth.

That is not a grave fault, the Prioress admits, but still it is well that Sister Marcella be assigned a penance. Let her repeat the psalm, "Quam dilecta," four times in her cell before she retires.

Now Teresa comes, out of breath and a little hurried. "She is 18, very pretty, very sunny and very gay, with nothing about her to suggest the mystic or the religious. She is dressed simply in gray and wears a white apron. She has a flower in her hair, which is arranged modestly, and without an excess of curls or ornament." When she speaks it is "always with the greatest simplicity, without affectation or pretense of any sort."

Teresa has been dressing the altar of the Virgin, and she is out of breath because she has been climbing acacia trees to get the white blossoms she needed. Climbing trees is not exactly the thing the good nuns can approve a day like this, but even the Prioress is forgiving. The thought that it is the last day Teresa will ever dress the altar is a sad one and they are distressed, even though she tries to cheer them.

TERESA—Ah, Mothers! You mustn't talk like this. Don't be sad.

VICARESS—No, we had better behave like you do, though it doesn't seem possible when you consider the day that it is, and you laughing and carrying on like one possessed!

PRIORESS—The Mother is right. A little more feeling to-day, daughter, a manner more subdued, would not have been out of place.

TERESA—You are right, reverend Mothers—you always are, in the holiness which like a halo surrounds your reverend heads; but when a girl wants to laugh she wants to laugh, although, as Mother Anna St. Francis says, it may be the solemnest day of her life.

MISTRESS OF NOVICES—It is a solemn day, a very solemn day. You are leaving this house in which you have passed eighteen years, without scarcely so much as taking thought how it was you came to be here. To-morrow you will be your own mistress, and you will have upon your conscience the responsibilities of a wife.

VICARESS—Which, believe me, are not light. Men are selfish, fickle . . .

TERESA (*timidly*)—Antonio is very good.

VICARESS—However good he may be, he is a man, and men are accustomed to command. They have been from the beginning of the world, and it has affected their character. And since you are very independent yourself, and like to have your own way . . .

TERESA—Yes, I have been spoiled I know; but you will see now how good I will be. It will come out all right.

SISTER JOANNA OF THE CROSS—Do you want to spoil the day for her?

TERESA—No, Mother—no; you won't spoil it, for I am very, very happy. You have all been so good to me!

VICARESS—Nonsense! No such thing.

TERESA—But it isn't nonsense. I know this is God's house, but you might have closed the doors to me, and you have flung them wide open, freely. I have lived here eighteen years and in all this time, to the very moment that I am leaving it, you have never once reminded me that I have lived here on your charity.

SISTER JOANNA OF THE CROSS—Don't say such things!

TERESA—Yes, I must say them. On your charity, on your alms—like a poor beggar and an outcast. I don't mind saying it nor thinking it, for I have been so happy here—yes, I am happy now—happier than the daughter of a king: for I love you all so much that I want to kiss even the walls and hug the trees, for even the walls and the trees have been kind to me. This has been the Convent of my Heart!

SISTER MARCELLA—It has been your home. If you had only been content always to remain in it!

PRIORESS—We must not talk like this. God moves in His own ways.

MISTRESS OF NOVICES—And in all of them His children may do His service.

VICARESS—The child was not born to be religious. The things of the world appeal to her too strongly.

TERESA—It is true. The world appeals to me—poor me! It seems to me sometimes as if everybody loved me, as if everything was calling to me everywhere to come. I have been so happy in this house, and yet, all the time, I have been thinking how great the world was, how wonderful! Whenever I have gone out into the street, how my heart leaped! I felt as if I were going to fly, it was so light! My brain was in a whirl. Then I was so glad to come back again into this house, it felt so good, as if you were all taking me up once more into your arms, as if I had fallen to sleep in them again and was warm, folded beneath the shelter of the everlasting wings.

VICARESS—The wings of your good angel, who stood waiting at the door—stood waiting till you came.

PRIORESS—Why should he have to wait? Her good angel always has gone with her, and surely there never has been a time when he has had to turn away his face. Am I right, daughter?

TERESA—You are, Mother. (*Sincerely.*)

SISTER JOANNA OF THE CROSS—They needn't have asked her that!

The trousseau is ready to be packed in the trunk. It is all beautifully sewed, and in the fashion, too, according to the patterns, even though the Vicaress does not approve of fashions. There are fashions in hell, she's certain of that.

"But you don't want the child to be married, do you, in the dress of the year of the ark?" demands Sister Maria Jesus.

"A pure heart and an upright spirit are what she should be married in," answers the Vicaress, "and if that is the case no one is going to notice whether she has one bow more or less."

"They say men pay a great deal of attention to such things, Mother Crucifixion," ventures Sister Marcella.

"And we must render unto Cæsar the things which are Cæsar's, and unto God the things which are God's," prompts Sister Maria Jesus.

Now the trunk is packed, and locked and the key tied to a ribbon ready to be hung around Teresa's neck, with her rosary. And Teresa is happy, though conscious, too, of all that has been done for her. She can't feel that she deserves so much kindness.

"Yes, you do. You deserve it," admits the Vicaress, testily. "And you might as well tell the truth as a falsehood. You have a good heart; you are a sensible girl. When you said what you did, you were thinking of your clothes; but you need have no scruples. Everything that you take away with you from this house, and more too, you have earned by your labor. That is the truth and you know it. Maybe we have taught you here how to sew and embroider, but you have worked for us in the convent, and outside of it. You owe us nothing. Besides, you had two hundred and fifty pesetas from the doctor to buy the material. Here . . . (*producing a paper from under her scapular*) is the account of the way they have been spent, so you can see for yourself and answer for it, since delicacy will not permit that we should be asked how it was used."

"What do you mean?" Teresa demands, embarrassed and confused. "Why, Mother Crucifixion!"

"That is all there is to it," tartly answers the Vicaress; "you will find the account is correct."

Teresa is to go at 5, but before she goes she hopes the Prioress will permit Antonio to see them all and thank them. He has asked if he could and the Prioress will be glad to have him come.

They have all gone now, except Teresa and Sister Joanna of the Cross. Together they are straightening up the room. For a moment they are silent, but suddenly Teresa throws herself on her knees before the nun.

TERESA—Sister Joanna of the Cross!

SISTER JOANNA OF THE CROSS—What do you want, my child?

TERESA—Now that we are alone, bless me while there is no one here to see—no, not one—for you are my mother, more than all the rest!

SISTER JOANNA OF THE CROSS—Get up. (TERESA *gets up*.) Don't talk like that! We are all equal in God's house.

TERESA—But in my heart you are the first. You mustn't be angry at what I say. How can I help it? Is it my fault, though I have struggled against it all my life, that I have come to love you so?

SISTER JOANNA OF THE CROSS—Yes, you have struggled. You have been wilful . . . (*Then seeking at once to excuse her*.) But it was because you were strong and well. When a child is silent and keeps to herself in a corner, it is a sign that she is sick or thinking of some evil. But you . . .

TERESA—*Ay*, Mother! Where do you suppose that I came from?

SISTER JOANNA OF THE CROSS—From Heaven, my daughter, as all of us have come.

TERESA—Do you really think that we have all come from Heaven?

SISTER JOANNA OF THE CROSS—At least you have come from Heaven to me. You say that I am your mother more than the rest; I don't know—it may be. But I know that for years you have been all my happiness and joy.

TERESA—Mother!

SISTER JOANNA OF THE CROSS—I was so glad to hear you laugh and see you run about the cloisters! It was absurd, but I always felt—not now, for you are grown-up now—but for years I always felt as if you must be I, myself, scampering and playing.

For I was just your age now, a little more or less, when you came
into the Convent. And it seemed to me as if I was a child again
and had just begun to live. You were so little, so busy—yes,
you were—but I was busy too, if you only knew, before I entered
here, at home in our house in the village. I was always singing
and dancing, although we were very poor. My mother went out
every day to wash in the river or to do housework—she had so
many children!—and I was always carrying one about in my
arms. And when I entered here, as I could do thanks to some
good ladies who collected the money for my dowry—God reward
them for it—although I had a real vocation, I was sorrowful and
homesick thinking of my little brothers and sisters! How I used
to cry in the dark corners, and I never dared to say a word!
Then the Mother told me that if my melancholy didn't leave me
she would be obliged to send me home. And then you came and I
forgot everything! That is why I say you came to me from
Heaven. And I don't want you to think I am angry, or ashamed
—or that it has ever given me a moment's pain to have loved
you.

Teresa—Is that the reason that you scold me so?

Sister Joanna of the Cross—When have I ever scolded
you?

Teresa—Oh, so many times! But no matter. I always tell
Antonio, Sister Joanna of the Cross is my mother. She is my
mother, my real mother! So now he always calls you mother
whenever he speaks of you.

Teresa is quite sure she will be ever so happy with Antonio,
because he is good and because he is happy, too, though his
mother was sad. Perhaps sad mothers have the happiest children.
If that be true Teresa is fearful lest her first son will be the most
solemn of men. She has plans for many sons. The first will be
an architect, like his father. The second may be a missionary
and go to China to convert the heathen. And if he were to become a saint that would give Teresa influence in heaven. When
she was little, Teresa confesses, she had often wished she was a
boy. Then she could have grown up to be almost anything she
wanted to be—a captain general or an archbishop or even a pope,
perhaps. But now she is satisfied. She loves Antonio so very
much it makes her humble. It is sweet to be in love.

And Antonio loves her, Teresa is convinced. But how much
she doesn't know. Nor care, greatly. It is loving him that
makes her happy. Some days there has been the fear that An-

tonio might stop loving her, and the thought made her sad. But better that she should die than that she should ever stop loving Antonio, for then what would be the good of life?

So much does Teresa love Antonio that she feels she would be willing to sit at his feet all the rest of her life, just listening to him talk. "I don't know how to explain it," she admits, "but it is his voice—a voice that seems as if it had been talking to you ever since the day you were born! . . . Ah, mother! The first day that he said to me 'Teresa'—you see what a simple thing it was, my name, Teresa—why, it seemed to me as if nobody ever had called me by my name before, as if I never had heard it, and when he went away, I ran up and down the street saying to my-self, 'Teresa, Teresa, Teresa!' under my breath, without know-ing what I was doing, as if I walked on air!"

It is a little frightening to Sister Joanna to hear Teresa talk so of an earthly love. For, after all, that is all such love can be—"a little brightness that God grants us to help us pass through life, for we are weak and frail"—but which must surely pass away.

Now Antonio has arrived in the outer parlor and Teresa pulls the curtain cord which shows that part of the room brightly lighted. Where Sister Joanna of the Cross and Teresa stand the room is still in darkness, but they can see the boy perfectly. "He is 25 years of age, well built, manly and sensitive of feature."

In whispers they discuss Antonio as he paces nervously up and down. He is tall, that is plain, and his hair, Teresa reports, is dark brown and his eyes between violet and blue and they sparkle when he talks.

Now Teresa calls Antonio by name, and though he can hear her voice he is not sure where it comes from, so little accustomed is he to calling on nuns. But soon he places them and stands be-fore the grille eager to be nearer.

With enthusiasm Teresa tells him she is with her mother, and is greatly pleased when he guesses it must be Sister Joanna.

Teresa (*to the nun, delighted because he has guessed it*)— There! Do you see? (*To* Antonio.) Sister Joanna of the Cross—exactly. We have been watching you through the grille, and she says that she thinks you are a very handsome young man.

Sister Joanna of the Cross—Goodness gracious! You mustn't pay any attention to what she says.

TERESA—Don't be angry, Mother. I think so myself.

ANTONIO—You never told me that before.

TERESA—That is because in here, where you can't see me, I'm not so embarrassed to tell you. Listen! We have to send in word now that you are here; but I want you to tell my mother something first, for if you stand there like a blockhead without opening your mouth, I am going to be very much ashamed, after all the time I have spent in singing your praise.

ANTONIO—What do you want me to tell her?

TERESA—What you have in your heart.

ANTONIO—But I don't know whether it is proper to tell it to a religious, although it is in my heart, for I love her dearly.

TERESA—Ah! I tell her that a million times a day.

ANTONIO—Then let us tell her together two million; because I must say to you, Madam, that it is impossible to know Teresa and not to love you.

TERESA—What a treasure is this mother of mine!

SISTER JOANNA OF THE CROSS—For shame, my child! (*Blushing, to* ANTONIO.) I also have a great affection for you, sir, for this child has been teaching me to love you. She is a little blind perhaps, and trusting, for that is natural. She knows nothing of the world, and we—how were we to teach her? And now you are going to take her far away; but don't take her heart away from us, sir, and break ours, when we let her hand go.

ANTONIO—Madam, I swear to you now that I shall always kneel in reverence before the tenderness and virtue which you have planted in her soul.

TERESA—I told you that he was very good, Mother.

SISTER JOANNA OF THE CROSS—May God make you both very happy. And may God remain with you, for his handmaid must go now and seek the Mother.

ANTONIO—But you are coming back?

SISTER JOANNA OF THE CROSS—With the sisters. . . . Yes, I think so. Good-by. I have been so happy to know you.

Silently, and under stress of a great emotion, Sister Joanna leaves the room. Antonio, too, has been much affected by the meeting, and is eloquently hopeful that all the convent has meant to Teresa, its peace and its calm, she will carry away with her.

"I the mistress of calm!" laughs Teresa. "Mother Crucifixion says that since I was passed in on the wheel there hasn't been one moment in this house of what the rules call 'profound calm.' "

But Teresa will try her best, and so wonderful is Antonio's love for her—his love that is really a religion and has remade him quite—that all is sure to be well with them.

Soon the nuns file in, quietly, the youngest first, the Prioress last, and take their places before the grille. Sister Joanna of the Cross comes close to Teresa that she may hold her hand. There is a moment of expectant silence, and then the Prioress speaks. "Good afternoon, young man."

"Good afternoon, madam—or madams—for behind the mystery of this screen it is impossible for me to see whether I am speaking with one or with many," answers Antonio.

Then the curtains are run back and the interview continues. Antonio is in the light, but the nuns are still in the shadow that his eyes cannot penetrate.

The impression he makes is good. The sisters smile and nod to each other as they are pleased with what he says. Their agitation is noticeably in the young man's favor, though he, too, is plainly ill at ease. He meets their queries openly, however, and speaks his compliments with compelling sincerity, while begging their pardon for his nervousness and fear.

MISTRESS OF NOVICES—You are not afraid of us?

ANTONIO—I am, Madam, very—because of the respect and admiration in which I hold you all. I came here more disturbed than I ever have been before in my whole life. I do not know whether I should thank you, or whether I should beg your pardon.

PRIORESS—Beg our pardon?

ANTONIO—Yes, because I fear that I am not worthy of the treasure which you are entrusting to me.

PRIORESS—We know already through the doctor that you are an honorable young man.

MISTRESS OF NOVICES—And the love which our daughter bears you is our guarantee. Surely the Lord would not permit His child, brought up in His fear, to throw herself away upon an evil man.

ANTONIO—I am not evil, no; but I am a man, and you, ladies, with all the great piety of your souls, have been nurturing a flower for the skies. When I first knew her, my heart whispered to me that I had met a saint. She was a miracle. When I first dared to speak to her, there came over me a fear and a trembling that were out of the course of nature; and when I told her that I loved her, my heart stopped, and bade me to fall on my knees, and now that I have come here to beg my happiness of you, I don't know what I can promise you in token of my gratitude, nor how I can give you thanks enough for the great honor which you do me.

VICARESS—It may be you are speaking more truly than you think, Señor Don Antonio.

MISTRESS OF NOVICES—Why, Mother.

VICARESS—No, let me speak. For he has said well. The girl is not one of those worldly creatures who take to their husbands a great store of physical beauty. That is certain. You cannot call her ugly, but it is the most that can be said. Nor does she bring with her any dower. She is poorer than the poor. But she carries in her heart a treasure, the only one which we have been able to give her, which is more priceless than silver or gold, and that is the fear of God. For this, sir, you must be answerable to us, and we ask you your word now, that you will always respect it in her and in her children, if you should have any, if it should be God's holy will.

ANTONIO—Teresa shall always be the absolute mistress of her conscience and of my house, and my children shall ever be that which she desires. I pledge my word.

Antonio tells them that he is taking Teresa across the sea—to America, where he is to become the resident director of a firm of architects. They are much worried lest she be seasick on the voyage. Each of them would advise him what to do in such emergency, but Teresa gently insists that she will be able to take care of herself, even though she may be self-willed and none too good at taking medicine.

Antonio promises that he will telegraph them of their arrival at the ship and will later send them word from the middle of the ocean, which is strange news indeed to some of the sisters. That words can be sent through the air sounds somewhat like the works of the devil. It is Sister Inez's idea that it will be safer to sprinkle any telegram that comes with holy water.

As the final good-bys are about to follow the final words of cheer and advice Antonio craves an indulgence.

"Although, as it seems, you have run back a curtain," he says, "yet the mystery of this screen still remains a mystery to me, a poor sinner, inscrutable as before; and I should be sorry to go away without having seen you face to face. Is it too much to ask?"

"For us this is a day of giving," graciously answers the Prioress. "Draw back the curtains, Teresa."

In the light that pours in from side windows the nuns stand revealed, facing him. Before them he bows low in salute.

"Well," demands the Vicaress, "how does the vision appear to you?"

"I shall never forget it as long as I live," he says.

"Then may God go with you, and may you live a thousand years," answers the Prioress, taking Teresa's hand and placing it in his. "Here is her hand. See, we give her to you with a great love, and may you make her happy."

"I answer for her happiness with my life," solemnly answers Antonio.

Now the curtains are drawn again and Antonio has gone. Outside a tinkling bell tells of the arrival of the Doctor, and soon he comes, on the arm of Sister Tornera. The Doctor is very old now, but neither decrepit nor cast down. He recognizes the ceremony of parting and is glad they have seen Antonio and liked him. The boy is waiting outside and it is time for them to be going.

Two of the nuns carry Teresa's trunk out the door and the Doctor valiantly tries to lift the mournful atmosphere that threatens to settle down upon them all. It is not an easy task. The nuns are in no mood for levity this day.

Now Teresa and Sister Joanna have joined the group, their eyes red with weeping, and the reverend mother has embraced and blessed Teresa with evident effort at self-control.

"Remember all the blessings God has showered upon you from the cradle," she admonishes; "remember that your whole life has been as a miracle, that you have lived here as few have ever lived, that you have been brought up as few have ever been brought up, like the Holy Virgin herself, in the very temple of the Lord. . . . Remember that you are the rose of His garden and the grain of incense upon His altar."

TERESA—Yes! Mother, yes! I will! . . . I will remember all . . . all . . . all . . .

MISTRESS OF NOVICES—And do not forget each day to make an examination of your soul.

TERESA—No, Mother.

SISTER JOANNA OF THE CROSS—And write often.

TERESA—Yes, Mother.

DOCTOR—It is time to go, Teresa.

TERESA (*throwing herself suddenly into his arms*)—Oh, father! Promise me never to leave them! Never abandon them!

DOCTOR—Child of my heart! Ah, may they never abandon me!—for this is my house. For more than forty years I have been coming here day by day, hour by hour, and now there is nobody within these walls who is older than I. I have no children. I have had my loves—yes, a moment's flame—but it was so long ago! I have forgotten them. And these Sisters, who have been mothers to you, have been daughters to me; and now, when I come, they no longer even cover their faces before me. Why should they? It seems to me as if I had seen them born. And in this house (*greatly moved*) I should like to die, so that they might close my eyes, and say a prayer for me when life itself has closed!

MISTRESS OF NOVICES—Who is thinking of dying, Doctor?

PRIORESS—It is time to go.

TERESA (*looking from one to the other*)—Aren't you going to embrace me? (*The nuns, after hesitating and glancing a moment doubtfully at the* MOTHER PRIORESS, *embrace* TERESA *in turn, in perfect silence. Only* SISTER JOANNA OF THE CROSS, *taking her into her arms, says*)—

SISTER JOANNA OF THE CROSS—My child!

PRIORESS—May you find what you seek in the world, daughter, for so we hope and so we pray to God. But if it should not be so, remember, this is your Convent.

TERESA—Thanks . . . thanks . . . (*Sobbing.*)

DOCTOR—Come, daughter, come. . . . (*The* DOCTOR *and* TERESA *go to the door, but* TERESA *turns when she reaches the threshold and embraces* SISTER JOANNA OF THE CROSS, *passionately. Then she disappears.* SISTER JOANNA OF THE CROSS *rests her head against the grille, her back to the others, and weeps silently. A pause. The bells of the coach are heard outside as it drives away.*)

MISTRESS OF NOVICES—They are going now. (*The chapel bell rings summoning the nuns to choir.*)

PRIORESS—The summons to the choir.

MISTRESS OF NOVICES—Come, Sisters! Let us go there. (*All make ready to go out sadly. The* VICARESS, *sensing the situation, to her mind demoralizing, feels it to be her duty to provide a remedy. She, too, is greatly moved but, making a supreme effort to control herself, says in a voice which she in vain endeavors to make appear calm, but which is choked in utterance by tears:*)

VICARESS—One moment. I have observed of late . . . that some . . . in the prayer . . . have not been marking sufficiently the pauses in the middle of the lines while. on the other hand, they drag out the last words interminably. Be careful of this, for your Reverences know that the beauty of the office lies in rightly marking the pauses, and in avoiding undue emphasis on the end of the phrase. Let us go there. (*The nuns file out slowly.* SISTER JOANNA OF THE CROSS, *unnoticed, remains alone. With a cry, she falls upon her knees beside an empty chair.*)

The curtain falls.

# DAISY MAYME

## Comedy in Three Acts

### By George Kelly

WITH the production of "Daisy Mayme" George Kelly faced a public in which expectancy had created a super-critical attitude. He had the year before won the Pulitzer prize with "Craig's Wife," and two years before that he had scored the comedy hit of the year with "The Show-off." He would have had to be something a little better than a mere genius to have fully met the expectations of that public.

"Daisy Mayme" was favorably received by the reviewers, though with reservations. It was not, they were in the main agreed, as good as they had hoped it would be, but it was much better than the general average to which they were accustomed. They unanimously continued Mr. Kelly in his earned position among the first of American dramatists, and repeated their belief in him as a technician of superior gifts and a writer whose observation of middle-class American life was admirably exact. The rest they left to the public's decision.

"Daisy Mayme" started splendidly October 25 at The Playhouse, was played for fourteen weeks, and was then sent on tour. Officially it was classified as one of the moderate successes of the season. The road tour proved none too encouraging and the stock companies, an increasingly vital factor in prolonging the lives of the best plays of any season, fell heir to the comedy.

The locale of "Daisy Mayme" is a small town indefinitely located as being approximately a three-hour motor trip from Atlantic City. The family upon which Mr. Kelly turns his penetrating binoculars is that of Cliff Mettinger and his married kin.

Cliff is a bachelor in his early forties who has always been the mainstay of his family. For years he took care of his widowed mother and kept up the home. When his mother died a widowed sister, Mrs. Phillips, had moved in with her young daughter May and taken over the responsibilities of housekeeper. Following the death of Mrs. Phillips a month before the play opens, Cliff had taken May, now 17, to Atlantic City to help her recover from the shock of her mother's loss.

This is the morning of the day on which Cliff and May are expected home. A second married sister, Mrs. Laura Fenner, and her daughter Ruth have got the key from the woman next door and are straightening up the house and getting a dinner on.

"Mrs. Laura Fenner, the eldest of the Mettinger girls, is a tall, genteel-looking woman of about fifty years of age, with a furtive eye and a bitter smile. Ruth, an attractive brunette of 25, with a lithe body and good style, is a smart girl, and holds a very responsible position, most of the profits of which are spent upon clothes for herself.

"The parlor of the Mettinger home, in which the entire action of the play takes place, has been a parlor for fifty-seven years, so that it gives the impression of being thoroughly accustomed to its own dignity: and fully aware of it, in a decorous sort of way. It has a mood, so to speak, of rather somber tranquillity, which seems to rebuke the fevered tempo of the times."

Ruth, who is dusting the furniture of the parlor while her mother is at work in the kitchen, has just reached the keys of the baby grand piano, and been warned to be careful of the noise she makes lest any one passing in the street should think she is playing the piano too soon after the funeral, when through the window she sees her Aunt Olly Kipax getting off the trolley car at the corner.

The Fenners are a bit irritated by this belated arrival of Olly. First, because it is belated and all the work is done. And also because, as they can see through the window, Olly is decked out in another new mourning outfit, including a new hat. If she thinks thus to excite their envy, however, Olly is about to be surprised. The Fenner women are agreed that they will not even let her see that they notice the new things.

"Olly is the second Mettinger girl, two years older than Cliff. She is one of those fussy fatties that never has a well day,—to hear her tell it: so a great deal of her time is spent in going to the doctor—and bridge parties. For Ollie has social aspirations." She is trying now not to be too conscious of her new clothes and refuses to be unduly excited by her sister's criticism of her lack of interest in the homecoming of their brother and niece. She is also prepared to give as good as she gets in the exchange of subtle sarcasm.

If, as Mrs. Fenner intimates, she has not given any too convincing an exhibition of industry or desire to do her part, Olly insists she has done quite as much as others who talk more about it. And, furthermore, she has no intention of trying to take credit for anything she has not done.

"That's what's the matter with you, Laura," she charges. "I know all your tricks. You wanted Cliff to come in here and find you overpowered with work, so that he'd realize what a good sister he had; and you're furious that he should find me here, too. . . . If you were so very anxious to have me here you could have called me up."

"A lot of good that would have done me; you've never been in once yet to my knowledge when I *have* called."

"Well, if I haven't been in I've been out. I knew the minute ever you'd see this new suit and hat on me you'd start *something*. (MRS. FENNER *laughs lightly with pained amusement*.) You can laugh all you like, but that's what's the matter with you—I saw it in your face the minute I came into the room."

Ruth and her Aunt Olly also indulge in a few veiled pleasantries. Aunt Olly is sure Ruth is thinner than she was, and Ruth can't believe it, seeing she actually weighed 122 pounds last time she was on the scales.

Aunt Olly can hardly credit that. It's three pounds more than she weighs, or did weigh, the last time she was at Dr. McShanty's office. Which, Mrs. Fenner is convinced, was not only a long time ago but was probably the time Ollie forgot to put both feet on the scales.

Whatever she weighs or doesn't weigh, Olly snaps back, she is far from well. She is still going to the doctor, and though he insists she is better than she was, the chances are she will have to keep on going to him for another six months at least.

"He says I'm very much better," admits Olly, "but I still have those shooting pains. And he says it's a wonder I'm here at all, the way my eyes are. The first day I went in to him, the minute he looked at me, he said, 'My, my, my, what *have* you been doing to your eyes, Mrs. Kipax!' 'Why,' I said, 'nothing, particularly, Doctor, that I know of; why?' 'Oh,' he said, 'you've been doing something, Mrs. Kipax,' he said, 'I don't think I have ever looked into such tired eyes.' So he sent me right over to Doctor Entwistle to have my glasses changed. And I think it's helped my neuralgia a lot. I was telling him about May to-day, too; he said he'd like to see her some time when she gets back."

MRS. FENNER—I imagine she must be better, or we'd have heard something.

Olly—What do you think Cliff'll do here, Laura—about this house, I mean?

Mrs. Fenner—I don't know any more about what he'll do than you do, Olly.

Olly—I think he should break up.

Mrs. Fenner—Cliff'll never do that, Olly.

Olly—He might have to do it.

Mrs. Fenner—He's too fond of his own home.

Olly—Well, he can't very well have a home, Laura, if there isn't some woman here to run it.

Mrs. Fenner—He'll find some one.

Olly—I wish him luck; I've been trying for nearly a year to find some one, but you might just as well look for gold dollars.

Mrs. Fenner (*becoming very positive*)—You know, if May were any good *she'd* turn in here and keep house for Cliff.

Olly—May couldn't keep house, Laura.

Mrs. Fenner—She could learn; she's not a child.  If she were married she'd have to do it.

Olly—Cliff wouldn't want her to do it.

Mrs. Fenner—That's the whole trouble; he's spoiled her. And every one of them has spoiled her from her grandmother down.  They've made her think she was too good to do anything but sit in the parlor here and play the piano.  And I've never heard her play anything yet that I knew what she was playing.

Olly—Lydy didn't want her to do housework.

Mrs. Fenner—I know she didn't; I've heard her say so.

Olly—She wouldn't let her wet her finger.

Mrs. Fenner—Well, it might be better for her now if she'd *let* her do something once in a while.  But, Cliff has spoiled her as much as her mother ever did.  And I guess now that she's through that school she's been going to, the next we know he'll be sending her to college.

Olly—He'll send her if she wants to go, I guess.

Mrs. Fenner—And you may be sure she'll want to go, too.  She has no more idea what things cost than her mother had.

Olly—Well, if he wants to spend his money that way, Laura, we can't stop him.

Mrs. Fenner—Well, I don't think it's fair, Olly.  (Olly *makes a gesture of conditional surrender.*)  I know I'd hate like fury to ask him to send *my* daughter to college; and she's his niece as well as May.

Olly (*powdering her nose*)—Well, it isn't exactly the same thing, Laura.

Mrs. Fenner—Why isn't it?

Olly—Why, May, has no father, dear, and Ruth has.

Mrs. Fenner—It'd be all the same if she did have.

Olly—Well, somebody's had to look out for her, Laura.

Mrs. Fenner—I'm not talking about him looking out for her; he's always done that. But I certainly don't think it's right for him to be squandering his money on her the way he does. It isn't fair to himself.

Olly (*rising*)—Well, maybe he might as well be squandering it on her, Laura, as saving it for somebody else.

Mrs. Fenner—He might need some of what he's squandering later on.

Olly has gone upstairs in search of slippers or something to change to so she may rest her tired feet, and Mrs. Fenner is surreptitiously trying on Olly's new coat when Cliff arrives.

"Cliff is a tall, bony man, with a good head and a good laugh. But, in repose there is something essentially wistful about him,— that unexpressed or unfulfilled something—that usually gets into the personality of a faithful son. His family had a profitable hardware business for many years, but after the death of his parents he sold it out and began to dabble in real estate. And he has been successful. And kind of a good thing for everybody belonging to him."

He has come on ahead to open the house and bring in the suitcases. The others stopped at the corner to get some things for dinner. It never occurred to him that any one might be there. Nor to May, either. But it was Miss Plunkett who suggested that probably they had better stop and get something.

"Who is Miss Plunkett, Cliff?"

"She's a woman that May got acquainted with at the hotel down there. A good-natured kind of a woman. She certainly cheered May up a lot. We brought her with us."

"Does she live around here?"

"No, she lives in Harrisburg; but nothin' 'ud do May but she'd stop here for a few days on her way home. Two of these suitcases belong to her. I'll have to wait until they get here to see where May wants to put her."

Hearty laughter at the gate heralds the arrival of May, who is pretty and blonde, and Miss Plunkett.

"Daisy Mayme Plunkett is one of those women that is usually described by men as 'a card.' A quick little body, with a bright

face and good teeth and an enormous amount of energy. She
is perfectly at home dragging down boxes of notions from the
shelves of her dry goods store in Harrisburg, and she can wrap
up a package while you'd wink. And she's held her own too long
with the lingerie salesmen not to be smart. Naturally, her familiarity with the fashion magazines has developed in her a certain
amount of style; and as her business has grown, she has been
able to afford some of the creations, at wholesale."

Daisy and May come in laden with bundles, making a joke of
their shopping, only to learn that their preparations were all un-
necessary. Aunt Laura and Aunt Olly and Cousin Ruth are all
there and dinner is nearly ready.

At the moment the aunts are scattered powdering their noses
to receive the company. Which gives May a chance to show
Miss Plunkett about downstairs and to adjust herself to the shock
of coming home for the first time without finding her mother
there.

The diplomatically forced gayety of Miss Plunkett helps May
over this emotional crisis. She loves old homes, such as this of
the Mettingers, Miss Plunkett enthuses. Loves the yard and the
trees, too. And she is going to have a fine visit helping May get
started with her housekeeping.

MISS PLUNKETT—Well, just watch me, dear, for the next week
or so; I love to keep house. We'll have a grand time. (*She
laughs and* MAY *tries to reflect it.*) Say, listen, dear—is this
the Aunt Laura that you were telling me about,—that you don't
like?

MAY—Yes. She doesn't like me, either. She only came over
here to-day for fear she'd miss something.

MISS PLUNKETT—Ruth's her daughter, isn't she?

MAY—Yes, and she's as stingy as she can be.

MISS PLUNKETT—Well, the one *I* want to see is your Aunt
Olly. (*They both laugh, and* MISS PLUNKETT *turns and goes
towards the windows at the back.*)

MAY (*following her, with a glance toward the right door and
the stairs*)—You'll see her.

MISS PLUNKETT—I'm dying to get a peek at Olly.

MAY—Don't get her telling you about her ailments—

MISS PLUNKETT (*raising the shades in the right alcove window*)—Not a chance, darling, not to me.

MAY—She has everything that was ever heard of.

Miss Plunkett—She won't tell it to me; I have to listen to enough of that in Harrisburg.

May—And I don't think there's a thing the matter with her.

Miss Plunkett (*coming briskly out of the right alcove and into the left one to raise the shades*)—Of course there isn't.

May—For she's everlastingly on the go.

Miss Plunkett—Hasn't she any children?

May—No.

Miss Plunkett—Don't you think we ought to put these shades up, dear?

May—Yes, put them up.

Miss Plunkett—Let in some of that grand sunlight.

Ruth (*entering from the right*)—Hello, May.

May (*giving her her hand*)—Oh, hello, Ruth.

Ruth—Glad to see you back again.

May—Thanks.

Ruth—Are you feeling better?

May—Yes, I feel ever so much better, thank you.

Ruth—Mama'll be right in; we were getting the dinner out there.

May—Isn't that nice of you? Miss Plunkett and I were all ready to get our own. (*They laugh.*) This is Miss Plunkett, Ruth.

Ruth—How do you do?

Miss Plunkett (*shaking hands*)—Hello, darling.

May—My cousin, Miss Fenner.

Ruth—Did you have a nice ride up?

Miss Plunkett—Too long for me.

May—Miss Plunkett doesn't like automobiles.

Ruth—You don't?

Miss Plunkett—I can't see sitting still for three hours at a stretch.

Ruth—Oh, I could spend the rest of my life in an automobile.

Miss Plunkett—I'd rather be walking.

May—Did it take us three hours, Daisy?

Miss Plunkett—Just about; we left there around three.

Cliff (*entering*)—How do you think the patient looks, Ruth?

Ruth—Why, I think she looks wonderful.

Cliff—You'd think so if you'd seen her when I left her down there. (Olly *appears on the stairs, with her hat on.*)

May—Hello, Aunt Olly.

Olly (*on the bottom step*)—Have the dead arisen?

Cliff—What do you think of her now?

OLLY—Come here till I see you, dear.

CLIFF—I think we can thank you for a lot of this, Miss Plunkett.

MISS PLUNKETT—We had a lot of fun. (*She whispers something to* CLIFF *and they both laugh convulsively.*)

OLLY—Why, my dear, you're transformed—I'd hardly know you.

MAY—I feel fine.

OLLY—But, you know, I think you're a wretch, and I think your Uncle Cliff is a brute— (CLIFF *stops laughing abruptly.*)

CLIFF—What!

OLLY—For we haven't had even a card from either of you.

CLIFF—She's been having too good a time I guess.

MAY (*turning towards* MISS PLUNKETT)—This is my friend, Aunt Olly.

OLLY—Oh, I'm so delighted to meet you, Miss Plunkett.

MISS PLUNKETT—How do you do?

CLIFF—Miss Plunkett's the lady that's been looking after May down there.

OLLY—Well, I'm sure you must have some miraculous power, Miss Plunkett, for I'd hardly know her.

MISS PLUNKETT—I think it was the air down there.

OLLY—Oh, it must have been something more than that; for I've been to Atlantic City any number of times for poor health; (MAY *glances at* RUTH) and it's never done me a bit of good.

CLIFF (*to* MRS. FENNER, *who has just entered without her apron*)—This is Miss Plunkett, Laura.

MRS. FENNER (*bowing coldly*)—How do you do?

MISS PLUNKETT—How do you do?

CLIFF—The lady that May's been going around with at the shore.

MRS. FENNER—I suppose I'm a sight, Miss Plunkett, but we've been going like the Gold Dust Twins here all day.

CLIFF—We thought we'd all have to pitch in and get our own dinner.

MRS. FENNER—No, Ruth and I tended to that.

CLIFF—Well, that's fine. How soon will dinner be ready, Laura?

MRS. FENNER—In about ten minutes; I just have to wait for a couple of things.

Having found out that Miss Plunkett is to have the front room, Cliff and May and their guest load themselves with suit cases and start up the stairs, laughing and making sport of their loads and of each other. Miss Plunkett and Cliff are particularly hilarious, what with her giving him a push or two to help him along with his burdens.

At a deft signal from Mrs. Fenner Ruth hurries after them. Now Mrs. Fenner can hardly wait to express to Olly her opinion of the situation and of Miss Plunkett's intrusion.

She resents particularly the bursts of laughter that have followed her appearance in the house—laughter, with every window open and probably neighbors passing to hear it—laughter, in a house where there'd been a funeral only a month ago!

"Miss Plunkett certainly must be a great joker to make you all laugh so," ventures Mrs. Fenner; "especially Cliff. I don't think I've ever heard him laugh that way before in my life."

"Well, she seems a very good-natured kind of person, Laura."

"I know all about what kind of person she is, Olly—you don't have to tell me one solitary thing about her; all I had to do was look at her. (*There is a general laugh from upstairs.*) She's got them going again. (*Closer to* OLLY.) And she's going to stay here for a while; you know that, don't you?"

OLLY—How do you know she is?

MRS. FENNER—Cliff told me so. You saw him take her suit cases upstairs, didn't you?

OLLY—But I thought maybe she was just staying over night here, on her way home.

MRS. FENNER—That one has no more home, Olly, than a tomcat. Couldn't you tell that by looking at her?

OLLY—Well, they must have invited her here, Laura.

MRS. FENNER—May invited her; and that's enough for Cliff. And she probably fixed it so that they couldn't get out of inviting her. But even if they did, that's no excuse for her accepting it; women that have homes are not taking people up on every invitation that's made them. And what's she doing at Atlantic City at this time of year in the first place; it isn't vacation time; and she's certainly not sick.

OLLY—How long is she going to stay here?

MRS. FENNER—From now on, if she can manage it; remember what I'm telling you. (OLLY *looks at her blankly.*) You heard her call him Cliff, didn't you?—and she's known him about four days, for he only left here last Tuesday. That's the kind she is—doesn't lose any time. You know, the woods are full of women like her, Olly,—that hang around fashionable hotels, with their ear to the ground. And May has very likely been talking her head off to her down there about the way things are around here, and she's wise enough to see the way the land lays. She figures that there's a nice home on the verge of being broken up here, and she's decided to step in and stop it.

OLLY—I don't think Cliff'll ever marry anybody now, Laura.

MRS. FENNER—He wouldn't have to marry her at all,—she could marry him.

OLLY—But I don't think he has any such idea in his head, Laura.

MRS. FENNER—Well, we've got to keep *her* from putting it there.

OLLY—Well, I don't know how you're going to do it, dear.

MRS. FENNER—Well, it'll certainly never be done by standing around laughing at everything she says.

OLLY—I mean if Cliff wants to marry some time, Laura, we certainly can't stop him.

MRS. FENNER—We can stop *her*.

OLLY—But, why should we, Laura?

MRS. FENNER—Because I don't think he should marry.

OLLY—Not if he wants to?

MRS. FENNER—Not at his age.

OLLY—Why, Cliff isn't old!

MRS. FENNER—He's old enough to have married long ago, if he intended to marry.

OLLY—But, how could he, Laura?

MRS. FENNER—Others have done it, haven't they?

OLLY—But a lot of them have walked away and left their mothers and widowed sisters to shift for themselves, too, Laura; don't forget that; and Cliff didn't. He stayed right here till the day Mother died; and then he had Lydy and May on his hands. And he's been very good to us, in the bargain. I know he has to me,—and I guess he's been just as good to you. (MRS. FENNER *gives her a look*.) So that I think that now that he's in a position to marry, if he wants to,—of course he probably hasn't any such idea in his head at all, but if he should have,—I think we're the last two in the world that should attempt to interfere with it.

MRS. FENNER—I wouldn't attempt to interfere with it, but I certainly wouldn't want it to be somebody from Harrisburg. Let it be somebody that people know something about. (*She lowers the shades in the right alcove window.*)

OLLY—Is that where she's from, Harrisburg?

MRS. FENNER (*after a glance toward the stairs*)—That's what she told them. But I guess she's from wherever the last place was that she was invited.

OLLY—I wonder what she does for a living.

MRS. FENNER—Just what she's doing now; you can take my word for it. For if she had any occupation she couldn't be galli- vanting all over the country at this time of the year. (*There is a general laugh from upstairs. She turns and looks darkly in the direction of the stairway.*) I love this house; I've always loved it; and it would just about break my heart to see some strange woman come into it; especially one that wasn't worthy of it. (*Turning sharply to* OLLY.) That's the reason I let both those housekeepers that have been here see that I was up to their tricks. I'm just as positive as I am that I'm standing here that both of those women had made up their minds that they were going to marry Cliff; particularly that Polish one, with the good color. And this one upstairs has made up her mind to do the same thing.

OLLY—Now, you may be entirely mistaken, Laura.

MRS. FENNER—Oh, don't be so soft, Olly. (*There is a gen- eral laugh from upstairs.*) You ought to know the way women figure as well as I do. Why do you suppose she came here at all, —when she knew there wasn't even a woman here to make her a cup of tea?—for they stopped at the corner to buy some food on the way up. But she made up her mind she'd make her own tea; and his, too.

OLLY—Such an idea may never have entered the woman's head, Laura.

MRS. FENNER—Well, we must see to it that it doesn't enter it.

OLLY—Well, we'd better not see too hard, Laura, for it might have just the opposite effect,—(LAURA *looks at her*)—and put the idea into her head.

MRS. FENNER—We don't have to *do* anything at all: only don't let her think we're dying about having her here; and if she's as sharp as I think she is, she'll take the hint and go.

Another thing that distresses Mrs. Fenner is the dress May is wearing. Evidently she bought herself a light dress in Atlantic City and she certainly should be wearing black, like Ruth and the rest of them, even if she is only 17. No doubt Miss Plunkett is responsible for the light dress, too. And she'll be responsible for a lot more if one of them does not stay around and keep an eye on her. It is Mrs. Fenner's idea that Olly should stay at Cliff's over the week-end, seeing her husband is away playing in a golf tournament. That will give Mrs. Fenner time to arrange things at home so she can come over and stay the rest of the time.

Miss Plunkett will certainly have to be watched by one or the other of them. Look at the way she pushed Cliff when he had the suit-cases in his hands. Like as not she will be throwing her arms around him the next thing. And probably Cliff would think that was funny, too. Men are all alike.

Charlie Snyder drops in to see if Ruth is there. Charlie is Ruth's young man, but his chief excuse for calling at the moment is to say hello to Cliff and May.

When Miss Plunkett comes she insists on adding somewhat to Charlie's embarrassment by accusing him of being May's beau, which May quickly denies. May hasn't any beau. Never has had. She may have her eye on one or two, but none of them is her beau.

"I didn't know there was a fellow in the world until I was 25," laughingly admits Miss Plunkett, "and after that they didn't know I was in the world."

She's glad Charlie is somebody's beau, with all that grand curly hair of his, which she would run her fingers through if Charlie hadn't ducked away from her. Miss Plunkett is putting up the shades Mrs. Fenner has carefully put down so she can get a better look at Charlie when through the window she notices old Mr. Filoon sprinkling the lawn next door.

Being a community character and the "funniest old dodo" she has ever set eyes on, Filoon amuses Miss Plunkett greatly. She simply can't resist the impulse to go out on the porch and get a better look at him. Although they warn her that old Filoon is just as apt to turn the hose on her as not, she is soon in gay conversation with him from the porch, her voice, raised to overcome his deafness, carrying plainly through the windows.

Such actions, Olly and Laura are agreed, indicate that Miss Plunkett must be a little crazy. Just making a show of herself, that's what she's doing. And dinner's waiting.

Finally Miss Plunkett comes running back from the porch, still greatly amused by her conversation with the amusing neighbor. He's not only a funny, but a nice old dodo as well.

CLIFF—I think you made a hit with him, Daisy.

MISS PLUNKETT—Oh, I think he's grand; I'm crazy about him. Did you see his hat, Olly?

OLLY—Yes, I've seen it many times, Miss Plunkett.

Miss Plunkett—It looks exactly like a rowboat turned upside down on his head.

Olly—I've seen it. (Miss Plunkett *looks out again and laughs.*)

Cliff—He's had that hat since I was a kid.

Olly—You'd better not let him hear you laughing at him, Miss Plunkett; he's a very wicked old man.

Miss Plunkett (*turning to* Olly)—Oh, I think he's grand.

Olly—I was talking to him out there one evening and he deliberately turned the hose on me. (*They all laugh.*) Well, you needn't laugh, for he did.

Cliff—I don't think he can see very well, Olly.

Olly—Oh, he can see—a great deal more than he pretends.

Miss Plunkett—Maybe he was flirting with you, Olly.

Olly—Well, if he was, he was wasting his time; for I don't like old men. And I told him so at the time, too.

Mrs. Fenner (*in the right door*)—This dinner'll be cold unless some of you come in here and eat it.

Cliff—Come right along, Laura.

Mrs. Fenner—Come on here, Ruth—what are you waiting for?

Cliff (*offering* Miss Plunkett *his arm*)—Are you ready, Miss Plunkett, and May?

Miss Plunkett—Lead me right in, Cliff; I'm nearly starved.

Ruth (*to* Snyder)—Come on, Charlie.

Cliff—You've got to go some to beat me. (Mrs. Fenner *lowers the shade on the lower left window.*)

Miss Plunkett—We look like a wedding, going in this way.

Mrs. Fenner (*in a suppressed rage*)—Put down those shades, Olly. (*But* Olly *is frozen to the spot.*)

Cliff (*indicating* Ruth *and* Snyder)—There go the bridesmaid and the best man ahead of us there.

Miss Plunkett (*turning back*)—Come on here, May, you've got to be the flower girl.

May (*following the procession*)—I haven't got any flowers.

Miss Plunkett—You won't need them at my wedding, dear; it'll be one of those "Please omit flowers" affairs. (May *laughs.*) Come on here, Laura and Olly; you two can be the matrons of honor. (*The curtain commences to descend slowly.* Miss Plunkett *turns, laughing, back to* Cliff *and they go out together.*) Got to do this thing right you know; it's the nearest to it I'll ever come, I guess. (May *reaches the door, and, with a glance back at her two aunts, who are still glaring narrowly after* Miss

PLUNKETT, *goes out.* MISS PLUNKETT'S *voice dies away in a laugh.* OLLY *looks at* MRS. FENNER, *their eyes meet, and* OLLY *breaks down, burying her face in her hands.*)

MRS. FENNER (*with a quick, impatient gesture*)—Now, don't start that, in front of Cliff— Come out here and get your dinner. (OLLY *hobbles after her, touching her eyes.*)

The curtain falls.


## ACT II

It is an hour later. Dinner is over. Evidently it has not been an altogether happy meal. May, flouncing out of the dining-room, glares back resentfully and hurries up the stairs as though she had had about all she could stand of that party.

Ruth and Charlie Snyder are next to leave the table, seeking some measure of privacy. It is the first chance they have had to discuss their own affairs. Ruth and Charlie are engaged to be married, it now appears, and they are hopeful that when they pass that news on to Uncle Cliff that he will do something about one of a group of houses he is building for speculation purposes.

Ruth thinks Charlie should speak to Uncle Cliff to-night. There is only one single house left and that is the one they would like very much to have if they can get it. It may be just a hint or two will be all that Uncle Cliff will need.

Charlie is not very good at hinting. And Uncle Cliff is not particularly apt at taking a hint. As a result there is a great deal of fencing with no tangible results between them when Cliff comes in. Charlie admires the houses and Uncle Cliff is pleased that he does. Charlie notices that most of them have been sold and Uncle Cliff is glad to report that his observation is correct. Charlie thinks perhaps he would be interested in getting hold of the single house, seeing Ruth and he are to be married and Ruth seems to have her heart set on that particular location. And Uncle Cliff is ready to entertain any proposition Charlie may like to make—

At which crisis Daisy Plunkett breaks in upon the conversation. She has been trying to edge her way into the dish-washing and drying sections in the kitchen, she reports, but the women won't let her do a thing. Cliff thinks that perhaps she would like to take a ride through the park with the rest of them, but Miss Plunkett has had enough riding for the present. So has Cliff. Let Charlie Snyder take them. They can drop Olly at her home. As for Cliff, he will stay home and keep Miss Plunkett company, though she assures him she will not get lonesome. If she does she can talk to herself, a practice he smilingly warns her against.

"You know what people say about people who talk to themselves, don't you, Daisy?" queries Cliff.

"I guess they say it about me, anyway," answers Daisy; "so I might as well enjoy the privileges of my reputation. (*They all laugh.* Miss Plunkett *strikes a couple of chords on the piano,* Cliff *sits down and* Snyder *goes out. Then* Miss Plunkett *rests her elbow on the keyboard and turns to* Cliff.) You know it's a funny thing, though, Cliff,—people think you're crazy any more if you laugh. (*He is amused.*) That's a positive fact. I catch people looking at me all the time as though I didn't have a grain of sense. I know your sister Laura here thinks I'm completely gone. (Cliff *laughs.*) And Olly thinks I never *was* here. (Cliff *laughs again.*) But, I should worry. (*She strikes a rather ambitious chord on the piano.*) Anytime I can't laugh, I want to call it a day. (*Turning to* Cliff.) What else is there to it, Cliff, if you don't get a laugh?"

"Not much, I guess, Daisy."

"There's nothing at all that I can see. Going around with one of those faces that looks as though it got caught in a wringer. (*He laughs hard and low.*) Not me. Give me liberty or give me laughs. And you can have the liberty."

A moment later, however, Miss Plunkett grows serious despite her philosophy of laughter. Seeing Cliff sitting there, quietly smoking, suggests to her that he never has played very much at anything. Life has been pretty much of a slavish business to him. And why? What is he slaving for? To leave what he may accumulate to a lot of relatives when the fight is over?

Miss Plunkett—You know I can't quite picture you as a boy, Cliff.

Cliff—How is that, Daisy?

Miss Plunkett—I don't know; somehow or another, you look to me like a man that's never had very much fun.

Cliff—Oh, I've had some pretty good times, Daisy.

Miss Plunkett—Not many, I'll bet.

Cliff—No, not so many; but I expect to have a few before I finish up.

Miss Plunkett—Well, you'd better start in, Cliff, while you're young enough to appreciate it.

Cliff—I'm not any spring chicken now, Daisy.

MISS PLUNKETT—You've got a few good years ahead of you. And I hope you'll use them, Cliff. (*She looks out and away off.*) It seems to me we're young such a short time and old so long.

CLIFF—It isn't always so easy to do just what you want to do in this world, Daisy.

MISS PLUNKETT—No, but I think a lot of us could do it oftener than we do.

CLIFF—It seems to me that it's always been necessary for somebody to stand by around here. Somebody had to look after my mother after the girls went. And I knew that the dread of my mother's life was that I'd bring a daughter-in-law in to her. And by the time she went, there were May and her mother here.

MISS PLUNKETT—Well, things happen that way sometimes for people, Cliff. But I think it's a terrible thing to let yourself be cheated out of life. Of course, it's all right to do the right thing by people, but be sure you do the right thing by yourself while you're at it. Because half the time they don't appreciate it. And then where do you get off? Just a funny old bird that never married. Good picking for them, if you happen to have a few dollars. I've been through it all, Cliff; nobody can tell me anything about it. It was a great joke at home whenever a fellow looked at me. They used to laugh me out of it. One of those eldest daughter things. I wasn't supposed to marry; I was needed at home, to wait on the rest of them. But the minute they took a notion to go,—try and stop them. The last of them went about four years ago and left me nice and flat, out in the alley—at thirty-five years of age—without a home or a job. A couple of them offered me a home, but because I wouldn't let their kids kick me in the shins and say nothing, I was just a cranky old maid. And their mothers thought it was funny. So I dropped them all cold after a bit and started a little store. Dry goods and notions—mostly notions. I didn't know how to do anything else—but housework. But it turned out all right, thank God! I have a nice little business now; and my own dollar. And that's the way I'm going to stay, too. And they've all been eating out of my hand ever since. And believe me, they don't eat anything out of my hand unless they earn it, either. So much for so much. Any time any of them want anything out of me, they come right down to my store and work for it. And it's been the making of a couple of them. (*She folds her arms and rocks back and forth, narrowing her eyes shrewdly. Evidently the chair annoys her, for she glances at the side of it disapprovingly and then gets up.*) This chair is too much of a lady for me; I think I'll play the piano some more. (*She moves up the middle of the room towards the piano, fluttering the fingers of her right hand towards* CLIFF, *as though running a scale. He leans forward on his knees, looking critically at the tip of the cigar.*)

CLIFF—Are you sorry you didn't marry, Daisy?

MISS PLUNKETT—Sometimes. . . . Although if I had I wouldn't know as much as I know now. Of course I might have been happier, but I think it's better to be wise than happy: because if you're wise you've always got something; and if you're just happy,—you haven't. (*She sits down at the piano.*) Besides, I think if you're going to marry, you should do it when you're young;—go through the hard days together; then there'll be something to keep you together when the good ones come. (*She touches the keys moodily. There is a pause, and then* MRS. FENNER *comes in from the right, drying a glass pitcher. She stops just inside the door and shifts her eyes from one to the other.*)

CLIFF—Want to go for a ride, Laura?

MRS. FENNER—No, thanks, there's too much to be done out here.

MISS PLUNKETT—I'll do the dishes for you, Laura, if you want to go.

MRS. FENNER—No, you won't, now, Miss Plunkett; I told you I would not allow that.

MISS PLUNKETT—Well, you see they're all leaving you flat, so it's your own fault if you have to do them all yourself.

MRS. FENNER—Well, I'm used to being left flat, as you say, Miss Plunkett.

MISS PLUNKETT (*moving to the middle of the room*)—So am I, Laura; you've got nothing on me. I've been left flat so many times that I'm all flattened out. (*She laughs to* CLIFF, *and he reflects it.*) Don't have to diet or exercise or anything. (*She laughs again and turns to* MRS. FENNER.) But not any more; you can put that down in the book—not if I see it coming. Oh, no. Anybody shows any signs of leaving me flat, I beat them to it. Ain't that right, Cliff?

CLIFF—That's the right idea, Daisy, if you can do it.

MISS PLUNKETT—You can do it; but you've got to get over all your illusions first—especially your illusions about your own people. (*She looks at* CLIFF, *and then shifts her eyes to* MRS. FENNER.) That's what I had to do. (*Standing at* CLIFF's *right shoulder.*) And I've been a happy woman ever since. Ever since I woke up to the fact that they'll let the willing horse pull the load.

Mrs. Fenner suggests that Miss Plunkett join the others for the ride, but Daisy is firm in her refusal. She is going to stay at home and vamp Cliff. She never has tried to vamp anybody before and she is eager to see how good she is at it. He may be as innocent as he looks, but the chances are strong that he is one of those wise old birds who knows all the tricks. Probably ten years ago Cliff used to be a regular Atlantic City sheik. Look at all the nice hair he used to have!

Now Cliff and Mrs. Fenner are outside seeing the party off. "Miss Plunkett moves up to the windows at the back and looks out keenly. Then she turns away, with a bitter little sound of amusement to herself, and moves to the piano. Upon reaching the piano she laughs hard and strikes the keyboard three times with both hands as though giving vent to some devilish amusement in herself. Then she straightens up and laughs heartily, sinking against the piano finally. When she has finished her laughter, she starts picking notes on the keyboard. Mrs. Fenner comes in, closes the door, picks up the pitcher and towel, and, with a narrow look toward Miss Plunkett, goes towards the right door."

Mrs. Fenner—I thought you'd gone upstairs, Miss Plunkett.

Miss Plunkett—No, I'm taking a music lesson here.

Mrs. Fenner—I'm sorry to tell you, Miss Plunkett, but the piano is supposed to be closed. You know we had a death in this house only a month ago.

Miss Plunkett (*quietly*)—How long are you going to close it for?

Mrs. Fenner—Why, it's customary to close it for a year.

Miss Plunkett—That's a thing I could never see any sense to,—closing up a piano for a whole year.

Mrs. Fenner (*going up to close the piano*)—Well, I don't think it would sound very nice to hear music coming from a house where there'd been a funeral within a month.

Miss Plunkett—There's nothing the matter with music, Laura, if it's the right kind. They have music at funerals.

Mrs. Fenner—Well, of course, one has to consider other people occasionally in this world, Miss Plunkett.

Miss Plunkett—I know all about considering other people, Laura;—that's the reason I think it's silly.

MRS. FENNER (*settling the piano scarf*)—The neighbors would certainly have a very fine impression of this family, I *must* say.

MISS PLUNKETT—That shouldn't worry *you* a lot, Laura;—they're not your neighbors.

MRS. FENNER—It was my sister that died, Miss Plunkett.

MISS PLUNKETT—That shouldn't worry you much either—

MRS. FENNER (*stonily*)—Well, I happen to be one of the kind that it does worry.

MISS PLUNKETT—May told me at Atlantic City that you didn't speak to your sister for nearly four years before she died—(*Turning slowly and looking directly at* MRS. FENNER.) Why should *you* go into such heavy mourning?

MRS. FENNER (*starting for the door*)—Well, the piano is to be closed, whether it meets with your approval or not.

MISS PLUNKETT—Close it up, Laura—

MRS. FENNER (*going out*)—And I wish you'd remember it.

MISS PLUNKETT—I can't play on it, anyway. (*There is a slight pause, and then* MRS. FENNER *comes in again.*)

MRS. FENNER—And I also wish you'd remember, Miss Plunkett, that *my* name is Mrs. Fenner. (MISS PLUNKETT *turns quietly and looks at her, steadily.*) I'm not in the habit myself of calling people I've known only a couple of hours by their first names, and I don't expect them to call me by mine.

MISS PLUNKETT—Now, do you think it's necessary, Laura, for you to tell me what *your* name is.

MRS. FENNER—Well, evidently you don't know it.

MISS PLUNKETT—I know it better than I know my own.

MRS. FENNER—Well, then, I wish you'd use it, if you do.

MISS PLUNKETT—I might do more than that for you, Laura, if you're dumb enough to drive me to it. I'll spell your name out for you here sometime—backwards;—and right in front of your brother too. (*There is a slight pause.*)

MRS. FENNER—Have you come here to make trouble in this family, Miss Plunkett?

MISS PLUNKETT—No, I'll leave that to you; you're good at that. But I'll see to it that you don't make any trouble for *me*, while you're about it. This is not your house, and I've been invited here for a week. And my name is Daisy Mayme Plunkett; and I'm going to *plunk* right here till my week is up (*she moves to the stairs, holding* MRS. FENNER's *eye*) unless your brother lets me see that he doesn't want me here.

Cliff has been to the corner to get the evening paper, but he has little chance to read it. Mrs. Fenner is too insistent upon carrying to him her campaign against certain intruders in the home. She is surprised, she frankly admits, that Miss Plunkett decided to come home with Cliff and May if she understood as thoroughly as he insists she did that there would be the housework to do. And she refuses to believe, as Cliff believes, that Daisy not only expected to pitch in and help, but that she really wants to. Not only to give May a hand, but to help cheer her up through her first weeks at home.

If that is the case, Mrs. Fenner submits, May should have discouraged in place of encouraging Miss Plunkett. She should have known that Cliff's sisters would never allow a perfect stranger on a visit to do housework. Of course, as she was saying to Olly before dinner, they would have to make some arrangement so one of them could take over the management of the house until Cliff can get some one.

Furthermore, notwithstanding Cliff's fixed belief that Miss Plunkett would not have come if she had not wanted to, and that she and May can get along fine with the work without any help from either Olly or Laura, Mrs. Fenner is convinced that he should say *something* to Miss Plunkett that will show her he does not want her to inconvenience herself out of consideration for May. Of course he can suit himself, but—

May has no confidence in her Aunt Laura's sudden interest in her and in the house, she tells her Uncle Cliff at the first opportunity. And she certainly hopes neither of her aunts is going to stay with them all week. What fun could she and Daisy have knowing their every move was being watched? That's what Olly and Laura had been doing—that and giving Daisy dirty looks in the hope she will get her feelings hurt and leave. May was embarrassed to death at the dinner table. Cliff insists he didn't see his sisters do anything. What were they doing?

"Why, the looks they were giving each other every time Daisy said anything to you," explains May. "That's the reason Daisy was laughing so much. And the way Aunt Laura was talking that time about it being necessary for one of them to be over here all the time to take care of *you*. I simply couldn't eat my dinner,—that was the reason I went upstairs."

When Miss Plunkett comes down stairs she laughingly confirms the report of the dirty looks. She has never seen so many kinds in her life. They range all the way from black to pale blue. But she doesn't mind. Still Cliff can't believe they are right.

CLIFF—Why, your Aunt Laura was saying to me here just before you came down that I ought to say something to Daisy about not inconveniencing herself—(MAY *looks at* DAISY.) She said she thought you were just staying here out of consideration for May.

MISS PLUNKETT—That's the best thing I've heard yet.

CLIFF—No, I mean she was afraid that perhaps May had played on your sympathies by telling you that there was nobody here to do anything; (DAISY *turns and looks at him, steadily*) and she said she thought I ought to tell you not to let that influence you, if you had a house or a business of your own to attend to.—*You* see what I mean, don't you, Daisy?

MISS PLUNKETT—Sure, *I* see what you mean.

MAY—Daisy was going to stay down at Atlantic City another week, anyway, weren't you, Daisy?

MISS PLUNKETT—Yes, I don't have to go home at any certain time.

CLIFF—Well, that's what she meant, Daisy. (MAY *gives him a pitying look.*) And I guess the looks that May imagines she saw were simply Laura's and Olly's embarrassment that you might think that they expected you to do any housework around here. (MISS PLUNKETT *laughs lightly.*)

MISS PLUNKETT—Oh, that's all right, Cliff, I don't mind. I didn't come here to visit them anyway; I came to visit May.

CLIFF—Well, I want you to feel that you're more than welcome, Daisy.

MISS PLUNKETT—I know I am, Cliff.

CLIFF—And if you've gotten any other kind of an impression, I want to assure you it isn't the right one. Anybody that's here to visit May is here to visit me; and if Laura and Olly don't want to put themselves out a bit to wait on us—they don't have to; we can get along very nicely without them. May says that you two can get along yourselves till I get somebody.

MAY—That's what we wanted to do, isn't it, Daisy?

MISS PLUNKETT—Sure; I wouldn't have come at all if I'd thought anybody was going to have to wait on me.

CLIFF—Well, I don't think your Aunt Laura understands that right, May; so if she says anything about it to you, you just tell her that that's the way you'd like it to be. No use in dragging them back and forth over here when you'd rather do things for yourself.

MAY—Do you want to go round and see those big trees at the back of the house, Daisy?

Miss Plunkett—Grand! I'd love to, darling.

May—Do you want to go, Uncle Cliff?

Cliff—Where are you going?

May—Daisy wants to see the trees at the back of the house.

Cliff—Sure, I'll go with you.

Miss Plunkett—But before we go, May, I'll tell you what I wish you'd do for me.

May—What?

Miss Plunkett—Play me something on the piano.

May (*moving to the piano*)—Certainly, dear.

Miss Plunkett—Do you mind?

May—I'd love it, Daisy.

Cliff—May'll play for you any time, Daisy; she likes to play.

Miss Plunkett (*with her eye on the right door*)—I'd love to hear her play right now.

Cliff—She often plays for us here in the evening.

Miss Plunkett—I think I'll enjoy the trees better after I've heard her play.

Cliff—Play her something nice now, May.

May—What do you want me to play, Daisy?

Miss Plunkett—I don't care; just so it's kind of nippy. (*They laugh a little.*) Play me that piece you used to play for me at Atlantic.

May—Berceuse?

Miss Plunkett—Berceuse! The one with all the little doodas in it. (May *laughs.*)

Cliff (*lifting the shade in the alcove above* May)—Have you got light enough there, May?

May—I think so. (*She starts to play,* Cliff *standing above her, watching her; and* Miss Plunkett *moves forward looking out through the right door, waiting for* Mrs. Fenner. *After several bars of the music,* Mrs. Fenner *enters hurriedly from the right and stands aghast, just inside the door, looking from one to the other.*)

Miss Plunkett (*casually*)—You're just in time for the concert, Laura.

Mrs. Fenner—Is that *you* playing the piano, May? (May *just raises her eyes and looks at her.*)

Miss Plunkett—I asked her to play something for *me; I* was feeling kind of romantic.

Mrs. Fenner—Isn't the piano going to be closed, Cliff? (May *stops playing, and looks at* Cliff.)

CLIFF—Why, I hadn't thought about it at all, Laura, to tell you the truth.

MRS. FENNER—Well, I certainly think it ought to be closed for a while.

MAY—It's *been* closed for a month.

MRS. FENNER—But it's customary to close a piano for a year, May, after a death in the family.

MAY—Well, it can't be closed for a year, Aunt Laura, for I have to practice, and Mama wouldn't want me to stop that.

MRS. FENNER—The neighbors'll certainly have a good opinion of us, Cliff.

CLIFF (*thoughtfully*)—Well, I'm afraid we'll have to leave that to May, Laura. (MAY *looks straight at her aunt and resumes playing; and* MRS. FENNER *shifts her eyes to* MISS PLUNKETT *and looks at her with a smoldering bitterness.* MISS PLUNKETT, *however, disregards it utterly, simply touching her necklace and looking away off, rather meekly. There is a terrific banging at the street door.* MAY *stops playing abruptly and* MISS PLUNKETT *whirls nervously and looks toward the door.*) Holy Smoke!

MISS PLUNKETT—I thought somebody was taking a shot at me.

Chauncy Filoon, the nonagenarian neighbor, is calling. He has come to see "that young woman from Harrisburg," seeing he has a few minutes before his bedtime. He goes to bed every night at 8, summer and winter, three hundred and sixty-five days in the year.

Mr. Filoon has come over to talk with Miss Plunkett about Harrisburg. Hasn't been there since 1882, when he went on the Lancaster County Letter Carriers' excursion. "Use to raise a lot o' hell in those days," admits Chauncy, to the discomfiture of Olly and the amusement of the others. Nor is Olly's interest in the visitor increased by his absent-minded habit of referring to her as "Mrs. Pickax" and "Mrs. Skipjack" when he should very well know that her name is really Kipax.

But it doesn't matter much to Mr. Filoon what any of them thinks. He has come to talk to Miss Plunkett about Harrisburg. Never lived there. Lived in the city of Lancaster.

"That's where I was first married," he recalls. "In the year 1867. Two years after the War of the Rebellion. Fifty-nine years ago. I was turned thirty-two years of age. And if I live till the twenty-eighth day of this coming August, I'll be ninety-one."

"That's a very good age, Mr. Filoon."

"That's right, so it is. A cat at that age won't play with a whisk broom."

Yet Mr. Filoon enjoys reasonably good health. All but his legs. "Won't carry me nowhere," he admits. "All shot to hell."

Outside of that he is as fit as a fiddle.

He does not warm much to Laura Fenner when she comes in from the kitchen. Hasn't seen her in many a day; remembers her when she used to swing on the gate; she must be getting along in years. He remembers Mrs. Phillips best of all, and liked her best. Likes May, too; thinks she ought to have a beau; thinks Cliff ought to be lookin' around for a wife too, and not spend too much time lookin'. Here's Miss Plunkett, for instance; nice young woman, all ready to step right in—

There is much nervous laughter at the suggestion. "You mustn't wish anything like that on him, Mr. Filoon," warns Miss Plunkett.

"Mustn't waste time," the old man rumbles on, as he gets up to go. "One woman's good as another once you get used to her. I've had three of them and I'd have another if my legs'd carry me far enough to find her."

"Most people don't think that way about marriage, Mr. Filoon," ventures Cliff.

"Shouldn't think too much about marriage at all; just go and do it. Chances of it turnin' out all right are just as good that way as if you thought of it from now till Kingdom Come."

CLIFF (*opening the door*)—Yes, I guess that's so, Mr. Filoon.

FILOON—Just as good, just as good. Well, good-by, young woman. (*He touches his hat.*)

MISS PLUNKETT—Good-by, Mr. Filoon.

FILOON—I've got to get along; it's gettin' on to my bedtime.

MISS PLUNKETT—Come over again some time before I go. (MRS. FENNER *is distressed.*)

FILOON (*touching his hat again*)—Thank you kindly, I will. (*He beckons her closer to him.*) And set your cap for this man here, young woman; (*they all laugh*) good steady man.

CLIFF—Now, you mustn't be putting her up to any tricks, Mr. Filoon.

FILOON (*turning on him*)—You'll need a woman around here now to look after things. No use wastin' time. (*He raises his finger with a touch of solemnity.*) If you don't *put* somebody in, somebody'll *come* in. That's the way it goes. It's a wife's place, and she might as well be in it. Good night to you all. (*He goes out, followed by* CLIFF.)

MAY, MISS PLUNKETT, AND CLIFF (*together*)—Good night.

He's gone now, but Mrs. Fenner ventures to predict that it is not for long. They will probably have "that dreadful old man" as a steady thing, so long as Miss Plunkett is there.

The idea does not distress May in the least. She is used to Mr. Filoon. He often used to visit them while her mother was alive; if her Aunt Laura never saw him it was because she was herself an infrequent visitor. And, for that matter, she doesn't have to worry about seeing him again because there is no real reason why she should be there. May and her Uncle Cliff can get along quite nicely without any one's help. Aunt Laura is no more needed now than she was at any time in the four years she did not set foot in the house while May's mother was alive. As to that Mrs. Fenner insists that she had very good reasons for staying away.

MAY—You make up reasons for things, Aunt Laura.

MRS. FENNER—Oh, I suppose you know all about it.

MAY—I know what Mama told me. And she said you were mad because she and I were living in a better house than the one you and Ruth were living in. (MRS. FENNER *gives a little deprecatory laugh.*) When I asked Daisy up here I told her that we were going to wait on ourselves; and that's the reason she came. And if I had known that you and Aunt Olly were going to be here, I wouldn't have asked her.

MRS. FENNER (*turning to her furiously*)—Well, it's too bad you *didn't* know we were going to be here.

MAY (*taking* MRS. FENNER'S *tone*)—Well, I *didn't* know it; and she's here. And Uncle Cliff said that if you and Aunt Olly can't wait on her without giving her a lot of funny looks that we can get along very nicely without you.

MRS. FENNER (*slightly dismayed*)—I don't believe your Uncle Cliff said anything of the kind.

MAY—Well, *ask* him, when he comes in, if he didn't.

MRS. FENNER—And what did you *say* to your Uncle Cliff that *made* him say such a thing?

MAY—I told him about the way you and Aunt Olly were treating Daisy.

MRS. FENNER—And what have we been *doing* to Daisy?

MAY—You've been doing everything you *could* to insult her.

Mrs. Fenner—What?

May—Giving her a lot of funny looks; and the way you were looking at each other every time she spoke.

Mrs. Fenner—Because we were embarrassed at the way she was carrying on.

May—She was only carrying on that way because of the way you two were acting. And you were acting that way before she started carrying on at all. You've been looking at each other ever since she came in that door; and Uncle Cliff says it's got to be stopped. And he says that if Daisy and I want to wait on ourselves, that that's the way it's got to be.

Miss Plunkett (*from outside*)—Are you coming, May?

May (*at door*)—Yes, I'm coming, Daisy.

She slams the door as she leaves the room. Mrs. Fenner is looking out the window after her when Olly comes down the stairs, quite evidently annoyed. She is back early from the ride through the park she had started on with Ruth and Charlie Snyder, she explains, because there had been no ride. They had left her at her home and understood very well they were to wait for her while she got her things. When she came out they were gone. They had, a neighbor told her, driven off the minute she was out of sight. Olly had had to come back on the trolley, and she is pretty mad.

Mrs. Fenner is quite sure the children did not understand that they were to wait for Olly. Anyway, they have more important things to consider now. May has said that Cliff has said that if they could not be a bit more civil to Miss Plunkett they could go home and stay there. Mrs. Fenner does not believe he really said it, nor does Olly. May probably made it up. But Mrs. Fenner is going to find out.

If he did say it, Olly snaps, she would not stay there a minute. Which, as her sister sees it, would be extremely foolish—to walk out and leave a clear field to Daisy Plunkett?

But, Olly insists, after all it isn't their house, and if Cliff wants Miss Plunkett there they certainly can't put her out. No, but they can at least stay around and see what's going on, counters Laura.

Olly (*becoming extremely nettled*)—I don't know why Cliff should say a thing like that about me; *I* haven't been doing anything to the woman.

Mrs. Fenner—Well, you've been doing as much as *I've* been doing, and he said it about me, too.

Olly—No, I have *not* been doing as much as you've been doing, Laura; (Mrs. Fenner *turns upon her*) now, *don't* tell a lie.

Mrs. Fenner—You haven't been looking at her funny?

Olly—I didn't look at her funny till you looked at her funny.

Mrs. Fenner (*sitting down*)—You looked at her just as funny as I did.

Olly—I wasn't even in the room when the woman came in.

Mrs. Fenner—Well, you looked at her when you *came* in.

Olly—Well, it was you that started to talk about her first, Laura; you must admit that.

Mrs. Fenner—I know I did.

Olly—And I defended her.

Mrs. Fenner—Well, why did you run over home for your things, then?

Olly—Because you told me to. (Mrs. Fenner *makes a sound of contemptuous amusement, and* Olly *starts to cry.*) You got me all upset, saying that she'd come here to marry Cliff.

Mrs. Fenner—And don't you think that that's what she *did* come here for?

Olly—I don't know whether she did or not. (Mrs. Fenner *makes an impatient movement.*) And you don't either. And I said that when you first mentioned it. (Mrs. Fenner *attempts to interrupt her but* Olly *stops her.*) I remember distinctly saying that the woman may not have any such idea in her head.

Mrs. Fenner—Ho!

Olly—Well, even if she has, Laura, that is Cliff's business and not ours. And if he doesn't want us here, I think we're very, very foolish to stay.

Mrs. Fenner—Well, I'm going to stay, whether I'm foolish or not.

Olly—Well, I'm not.

Mrs. Fenner—Well, nobody's holding you.

Olly (*touching her hair at the mirror*)—I'm not in the habit of staying where I'm not wanted. And I think you're very short-sighted, Laura, if you have any trouble with Cliff. I don't think you can afford it any more than I can.

Mrs. Fenner (*indignantly*)—You talk as though Cliff were keeping me.

OLLY (*with great conviction*)—He's *helped* to keep you, Laura, many a time; you know that as well as I do.

MRS. FENNER—You don't know anything *about what* Cliff has done for me.

OLLY—I know what he's done for *me;* and I know that you're not the kind that would stand by and see it without getting the same for yourself. (*She starts away, then thinks of something else to say and comes back.*) You live in a rented house; and you have a delicate husband; and your son is on his own, and your daughter is going to be married.

MRS. FENNER—How do you know that my daughter is going to be married?

OLLY—Never mind how I know it; she is, just the same.

MRS. FENNER (*feigning amusement*)—I don't know how you could know a thing that she doesn't know herself.

OLLY—But she does know it herself, and so do you.

MRS. FENNER—Do I?

OLLY—Yes, and I know it too, Laura.

MRS. FENNER—Well, I'd like to hear when it's going to be.

OLLY (*in a very level tone*)—Just as soon as Cliff's houses are finished, Laura, that's when it's going to be; for that's what you've all been waiting for: in the hope that Cliff'll give them one as a wedding present. (MRS. FENNER *turns away, laughing deprecatingly.*) And between you and me, Laura, I think somebody'll need to give her something; for, from what I hear, this young man hasn't even got a job. But Ruth'll marry him, whether *you* like it or not; that's the reason, if I were you, I'd be wiser than to have any trouble with Cliff—for Ruth's sake, as well as your own.

Now Ruth, back with Charlie Snyder, tells her mother that she is quite indifferent to her Aunt Olly's charge that they had deliberately left her. They hadn't. Olly must be going out of her mind if she thinks they did. As a matter of fact Olly hadn't enjoyed riding in the car at all. She kept pestering Charlie to put the top down. "She thinks," declares Ruth, "that she looks good in that black veil and she wants people to see it." And Ruth doesn't care *that* whether Olly hears her or not.

Still, Mrs. Fenner advises caution. Olly apparently knows a lot more than they have given her credit for knowing. She knows, for instance, about Ruth's engagement and she knows that she plans to get married as soon as her Uncle Cliff's houses are finished. Furthermore she has heard May say that her Uncle

Cliff had intimated that he was not at all pleased with the way Miss Plunkett was being treated.

Ruth doesn't believe Uncle Cliff has said anything at all, but she feels that it would be unwise for them to say anything to him about it, now that she and Charlie have spoken to him. There's no use of their spoiling everything.

Mrs. Fenner and Ruth have left the living room when Olly comes down from upstairs. She has packed her satchel and wears her new veil, which, seeing no one is watching, she takes some pains in readjusting before the mirror. She is starting toward the street door when Daisy Plunkett breezes in.

Miss Plunkett—I've got to get something for my shoulders; it's too chilly for me out there.

Olly—Yes, it is a bit chilly this evening.

Miss Plunkett—Are you leaving town, Olly?

Olly—No, dear; I'm going home.

Miss Plunkett (*stopping at the foot of the stairs*)—Do you want me to tell May and Cliff that you're going when I go out?

Olly—No, it isn't necessary, dear, thanks; I'll be over again in a day or two.

Miss Plunkett—Be sure you come over before I go, Olly.

Olly (*softening*)—Yes, I'll be over.

Miss Plunkett—I mustn't get away without seeing you again.

Olly (*melting completely*)—No, I'll be over again. (*She laughs faintly, comes to a decision, crosses directly to the foot of the stairs and calls up.*)—Oh, Miss Plunkett—

Miss Plunkett (*from upstairs*)—Yes?

Olly—Miss Plunkett, if you and May should want to go any place while you're here—(Mrs. Fenner *appears in the right door and stands regarding her stonily*)—I'll be only too delighted to come over and look after things for you, if you'll just give me a call.

Miss Plunkett—Thanks, Olly; that'll be grand.

Olly—I haven't so very much to do these days. (*She laughs a little and sidles forward, then becomes conscious of* Mrs. Fenner's *icy gaze. Her laughter freezes.* Snyder *bursts in.*)

Snyder (*holding the door open*)—Oh, did you just get here, Mrs. Kipax? (*She sails across to the door, looking at him from a great height, and goes out.*) We might have stopped for you on the way over if we'd thought you'd be— (*His voice dies away.*)

MRS. FENNER—Ruth says if you got the ice cream, Charlie, to bring it out to her.

SNYDER (*tossing his hat onto the table*)—I got a quart and a pint: I thought that'd be enough.

MRS. FENNER—Oh, plenty. She'll put it on the ice out there till Cliff and the rest of them come in. (*She watches* OLLY *down the street, then turns and looks straight out, thinking.* MISS PLUNKETT *can be heard coming down the stairs; so she turns suddenly to the windows again and pretends to be looking out.*)

MISS PLUNKETT—I had to come in for something to put around my shoulders.

MRS. FENNER—Yes, I've been thinking about you being out there with nothing around you.

MISS PLUNKETT—It's awfully chilly out there along the water.

MRS. FENNER (*with a touch of meekness*)—I was going to bring you out something. (*The curtain commences to descend slowly.* MISS PLUNKETT *glances over her right shoulder at* MRS. FENNER *and continues to the door. She opens the door quietly, and, looking suspiciously at* MRS. FENNER, *glides out, drawing the door slowly to after her.* MRS. FENNER *rocks back and forth, meekly.*)

The curtain is down.

## ACT III

Two weeks later Mrs. Fenner comes over to Cliff's house to call. She is much interested in finding out how everything is going, and a little curious as to how long Miss Plunkett is going to stay. She was going back to Harrisburg, Mrs. Fenner had been given to understand, a week ago. But she had not gone.

Mrs. Fenner finds Olly Kipax at Cliff's. She comes from the kitchen now, her arms full of clothes. She has been helping Miss Plunkett with her packing, pressing some lingerie for her. Mrs. Fenner is plainly disappointed in Olly. The idea of her being there at all after being told she wasn't wanted! And working!

Olly doesn't care. She is helping because she wants to, and as for being there, she doesn't intend to be kept out of her brother's house by anybody—not even by Laura. Nobody has asked her to work. Miss Plunkett has cooked every meal that has been cooked in the house the last two weeks. She's a wonderful cook, Cliff says. And she did try to go home when her week's visit was up. She only stayed on because May begged so. And Cliff asked her. Anyway it's Cliff's house and who stays in it is up to Cliff.

Mrs. Fenner is quite disgusted. It is all so obvious to her. And Miss Plunkett will make a fine stepmother for May, won't she? Making May as common as herself. Common? Certainly she's common. Nobody could laugh the way Miss Plunkett does and not be common. Just free with people? She's more than that. She's free and easy, too. Look at the way she calls people by their first names the minute she meets them! A nice one she'd be to have to introduce to anybody!

"Well, now, you may not *have* to introduce her to anybody, Laura," ventures Olly. "They're not married yet."

"They *will* be, if she can manage it. I felt it the minute ever I heard she was coming here. And when I heard her laugh I was sure of it. People are not called *Daisy* for nothing."

Speaking of marriage, it is Ruth's marriage to Charlie Snyder that has brought Mrs. Fenner over to see Cliff. She wants to talk to him about it. The plan, at present, is for a very simple, inexpensive wedding and the young people will probably live with the Fenners for awhile, until they decide just what to do.

Mrs. Fenner and Olly are in the kitchen having a cup of tea when Miss Plunkett and May come downstairs. Cliff is in from the garage after putting the car away. The girls are just back from looking at the new houses and May is delighted because Daisy has liked them a lot, though not as much as she likes the Mettinger house.

"There's something set and sensible looking to me about an old-fashioned house," agrees Daisy. "It looks as though it's been in the business of living a long time. . . . This room's my idea of a good time. I think if I were dying and they let me sit in this room for fifteen minutes I'd come to again."

May is in a teasing mood. She won't let Miss Plunkett alone, or let her uncle read his paper in peace. Now she wants to know if Cliff doesn't think Daisy is good looking.

Miss Plunkett—Don't pay any attention to her, Cliff.

May—I say, don't you think Daisy's nice looking? (*He looks at* Miss Plunkett *and laughs.*) She says she isn't.

Cliff—What am I supposed to say to that, Daisy?

Miss Plunkett—Well, don't say anything too sudden, Cliff, for I'm sitting in an antique here, and if I go over backwards, it's all off. (Cliff *laughs.*)

May—*Don't* you, Uncle Cliff?

Cliff—Why, yes,—I think Daisy's very nice looking.

Miss Plunkett—Now, don't kid me, Cliff, because I'm from Harrisburg.

Cliff—Sure I do.

May—Now, see.

Miss Plunkett—Let the man read his paper. And go and play me something on the piano, like a nice child.

May (*going to the piano*)—What do you want me to play?

Miss Plunkett—I don't care, anything at all. (May *settles herself at the piano, and* Cliff *turns the page of the newspaper.* Miss Plunkett *glances over at him.*) That must be a good cigar you're smoking, Cliff.

Cliff—It's a Corona.

Miss Plunkett—I love the smell of a good cigar.

Cliff—I always smoke these. (*He resumes his reading, and* May *goes very softly into "Chanson Triste."* Miss Plunkett *sits looking away off, listening to the music. Gradually her eyes wander to* Cliff, *then she turns herself all the way around and looks at* May. *She sits very still for a pause, then feels in the pocket of her dress for a handkerchief. She turns back again, and, touching her handkerchief to her eyes, sits rocking herself back and forth, quietly weeping. Presently* May *happens to glance at her, and it dawns on her that* Miss Plunkett *is weeping. She stops playing quietly, gets up, and, with a glance at* Cliff, *comes forward softly at* Miss Plunkett's *left.*)

May (*in a lowered tone*)—Are *you* crying, Daisy?

Miss Plunkett (*hastily using handkerchief*)—No, of course I'm not crying,—what would I be crying about?

May—Oh, you are so, Daisy.

Miss Plunkett—I always cry when I hear music, May.

May—I wouldn't have played if I thought it would make you cry.

Miss Plunkett (*getting up*)—I love to cry, darling,—I'm having a grand time. (*She laughs weakly.*)

May—Don't cry, Daisy,—I don't like to see you cry.

Miss Plunkett—Well, I'm not crying now, dear, I'm laughing. (*She laughs strangely, holds* May *close to her, then breaks away suddenly.*) I must go upstairs and pack, dear.

May (*following her towards the stairs*)—Oh, I can't bear to think of you going, Daisy.

Miss Plunkett (*coming back to the chair for her pocket-book*)—I've got to go some time, Kid; I can't stay here forever. I've been here now a week longer than I said I would. (*She hurries back to the foot of the stairs.*)

MAY—You could stay here, Daisy, if you lived here.

MISS PLUNKETT—But I don't live here, child; I live in Harrisburg.

MAY—But you said you didn't *like* Harrisburg.

MISS PLUNKETT—Well, nobody likes Harrisburg, dear, but if a person's business is there he's got to stay there.

MAY (*turning away and starting to cry*)—Well, I think it's terrible for you to go.

MISS PLUNKETT (*stepping to* MAY's *side*)—Now, you said you wouldn't do that, May, if I stayed the last time you asked me.

MAY—Well, I can't help it, Daisy.

MISS PLUNKETT (*starting abruptly for the stairs*)—Come upstairs and help me pack.

MAY—No, I won't help you pack. (MISS PLUNKETT *goes up the stairs, and* MAY *sits down in the lady's chair and cries. After a second* CLIFF *looks sharply over at her.*)

CLIFF—What's the matter, May? (MAY *cries harder.*) What's the matter, Kiddie? What is it?

MAY—Daisy's going away to-morrow.

CLIFF—Is she going to-morrow?

MAY—That's what she said; she's gone upstairs to pack.

CLIFF—Well, now, you know she has to go some time, May.

MAY—I don't see why she should.

CLIFF—Why, she's got a business to tend to, May; she can't neglect that.

MAY—It'll be terribly lonesome in this house when she goes. We won't have any fun any more.

CLIFF—Well, she can't stay here forever, May; you know that as well as I do.

MAY—I don't see why she couldn't; we've got lots of room.

CLIFF—But Daisy lives in Harrisburg, May.

MAY—But she doesn't *like* Harrisburg, Uncle Cliff, for she says so. She says *nobody* could like it.

CLIFF—Well, it's her home, May, whether she likes it or not.

MAY—She *hasn't* any home, Uncle Cliff; she says she lives in two rooms, all by herself. And she loves this house. She says when she hears the rain on those trees outside her window upstairs, she says she wants to pass right out of the picture.

CLIFF (*amused*)—Well, I don't know how we're going to keep her here for you, May.

MAY—I think she'd stay if *you'd* ask her; (*he turns and looks at her*) she stayed the last time you asked her.

CLIFF—But it isn't fair to ask her again, May; she's stayed a week longer already than she intended to.

MAY—I mean to ask her to stay here all the time.

CLIFF—Now, I can't do that, May; Daisy has a business to look after.

MAY—Well, other people have businesses too, and they go to live in other places.

CLIFF—They don't unless they're going to get married or something.

MAY—Well, why couldn't Daisy get married; *you* could marry her. (CLIFF *laughs.*) Why couldn't you?

CLIFF—Well, there's no reason why I couldn't; but I thought you didn't *want* me to get married; you always said so.

MAY—I wouldn't mind if it was Daisy. Old Mr. Filoon says you ought to marry Daisy, and he ought to know; he's over ninety years old.

CLIFF—But Daisy doesn't *want* to get married, May.

MAY—How do you know?

CLIFF—She said so,—the night she came here. She said she was a free woman and that was the way she was going to stay.

MAY—I don't think she knew then that she'd like it so well here. Will *I* ask her?

CLIFF—Ask her what, May?

MAY—If she'd stay if *you'd* marry her?

CLIFF (*startled*)—No, of course you won't, May; you mustn't ask Daisy anything like that.

MAY—Why not?

CLIFF—Because you mustn't. If Daisy's going to be asked anything like that, *I'm* the one that must ask her.

MAY—Well, will you?

CLIFF—I don't know whether I will or not, May; you can't just go and *ask* a person a thing like that—you've got to think about it.

MAY—Old Mr. Filoon says you *shouldn't* think about it; he says you ought to just go and do it. And *he's* been married *three times.*

CLIFF—Well, maybe he wouldn't have done it so often if he'd thought a little more about it.

MAY—Well, he says he'd do it again, only for his legs. (CLIFF *laughs and turns away.*) So it couldn't have been so terrible.

There is a suggestion of method in May's wild dash up the stairs as her Aunt Laura comes from the kitchen, which causes

Mrs. Fenner to gaze a little apprehensively after her. Nor is she entirely satisfied with Cliff's explanation that May is all broken up at the thought of Miss Plunkett's leaving.

Mrs. Fenner has come over to talk with Cliff about Ruth and Charlie Snyder getting married. She finds Cliff rather doubtful as to the wisdom of that move. And not at all confident of young Snyder's ability to take care of Ruth. So far as known Snyder has no job at present and has never held any that he has had very long.

Charlie's so terribly ambitious, Mrs. Fenner explains, that he can't stay in a job when he thinks the chances of advancement are slight. It is Cliff's opinion that Charlie had better hold on to one of his jobs if he's thinking about getting married and buying a house. Nor does Cliff approve of Ruth's plan to keep on working after she is married until Charlie is settled. She'd much better let Charlie get settled before she marries him.

Ruth and Charlie take up the argument when they arrive, but they have no better success interesting Uncle Cliff than Mrs. Fenner had. He still thinks they are very foolish to even think of marrying without giving serious thought to just what they are doing. It isn't good business.

SNYDER—Do you think it's wise to be too businesslike about marriage, Mr. Mettinger?

CLIFF—That depends on the circumstances. But I think it's only fair to give a thought to the business end of it, for if you don't, somebody else's got to.

RUTH—Well, why don't you think this is good business, Uncle Cliff?

CLIFF—Because, from what I understand, the young man there hasn't even got a job.

SNYDER—I'm taking a job Monday.

CLIFF—And how long are you going to keep it?

SNYDER—That depends on the job, I suppose.

CLIFF—I understand that you've taken quite a *few* jobs since you've been here.

SNYDER—Well, there wasn't any particular future in any of them that *I* could see.

CLIFF—I don't think there's any particular future in any job unless you stay long enough at it to make one. If the two of you are so set on getting married, I can't see why you don't go in and live with Ruth's mother for a while, 'til things get going for you. That's a pretty big house, and there'd only be the four of you.

MRS. FENNER—Well, Ruth doesn't seem to want to do that.

RUTH—Well, you said you didn't want it either, Mama.

MRS. FENNER—Because I think it's a mistake for young couples to go in to live with other people. Besides, you've always said you hated that house.

RUTH—I know I did; I *never* liked it.

CLIFF—Well, it doesn't seem to me, Ruth, that it's a question of what you like or dislike, it's what you've got to *do*. Those houses of mine are selling at twelve thousand apiece, and I'd like to know how you're going to make payments on a debt like that, and keep it going in the meantime, when you haven't even got a job.

RUTH—But I have got a job, Uncle Cliff.

CLIFF—And what are you going to do, stick at it after you're married?

RUTH—Well, I thought of staying at it for a while, till Charlie gets started. (CLIFF *makes a little sound of amusement.*) Why, I know lots of girls, Uncle Cliff, that have stayed at their positions after they married.

CLIFF—I'm surprised at you, Ruth. I thought you had better sense. Taking a burden like that on your shoulders and not a chance in the world of meeting it.

RUTH—I think if people absolutely know they've *got* to meet a thing, they manage to do it some way.

CLIFF (*impatiently, and raising his voice*)—How are you going to *do* it, Ruth, when *he* hasn't even got a job!

RUTH—But he *has* got a job, Uncle Cliff; he starts at it on Monday.

CLIFF—What job has he got?

RUTH—Tell him about it, Charlie.

SNYDER—It's a proposition that the Stoddard Transportation Company is putting on the market.

CLIFF—What kind of a proposition?

SNYDER—It's a collapsible barrel.

CLIFF—A collapsible what?

RUTH—Barrel.

SNYDER—A collapsible barrel; for the transportation of fluid commodities to shipping centers.

CLIFF—And, what do they want it to collapse for?

SNYDER (*getting mad*)—They don't want it to collapse at all, till it's emptied.

RUTH—Now, don't get mad, Charlie.

SNYDER—No, but he's treating the thing as though it was a joke.

CLIFF—I don't know anything about what it is; that's why I'm asking you.

SNYDER—Well, I'm trying to tell you, if you'll cut out the kidding.

CLIFF—What happens after the barrel collapses?

SNYDER (*looking at him suspiciously*)—They can remit it to the shippers, without taking up any space.

CLIFF—What is it, a patent of some kind?

SNYDER—Yes. A fellow in Brooklyn had the idea; and the Stoddard Transportation Company bought it from him.

CLIFF—And what are you going to do, go out and try to sell it?

SNYDER—I'm going to try to sell stock in it. (CLIFF's *interest relaxes.*) I know a couple of fellows who are cleaning up on it, on a straight commission salary.

CLIFF (*turning to him sharply*)—And what if you find there's no future in that for you?—what about the payments on the house then?

SNYDER—Well, I'm not talking about buying any houses, Mr. Mettinger; it's Ruth that's talking about that.

CLIFF—You'd *live* in the house, though, wouldn't you?

SNYDER—I'd expect to live with my wife, naturally.

CLIFF—And I'd be expected to keep a roof over you till you'd find a job—

CLIFF AND SNYDER (*speaking together*)—

CLIFF—And Ruth would have to keep you.

SNYDER—Oh, no, you wouldn't be expected to do anything of the kind.

CLIFF (*swinging down the middle of the room*)—That's a hell of an arrangement.

SNYDER—Nobody has to keep me.

MRS. FENNER—Keep quiet, Charlie.

SNYDER—Don't get wrong on that.

CLIFF—What else would it amount to?

SNYDER—I haven't spent any nights in the Park so far.

RUTH—Listen, Uncle Cliff; Charlie's perfectly right in saying I'm the one that talked about the house.

CLIFF AND SNYDER (*speaking together*)—

CLIFF—Listen, Ruth—there's no use saying anything more about it.

SNYDER (*snatching his hat from the sofa as he goes*)—Ha! That's the best laugh I've had since I left Syracuse.

RUTH (*rushing towards* SNYDER)—Where are you going, Charlie?

CLIFF—The whole thing is too silly to talk about.

SNYDER—I'm going to get out of here.

RUTH—Now, don't be silly, dear; listen to *me*.

MRS. FENNER—Listen, Charlie.

SNYDER—What do you expect me to do, stand here and let him bawl me out? (OLLY *appears in the right door and looks wonderingly at the scene.*)

RUTH—Uncle Cliff didn't mean anything by that.

SNYDER—You might think *I* had to sit out in the alley till *he* gave me a house.

RUTH—Well, he didn't understand, dear, that I'm the one that's been talking about the house.

SNYDER—Well, I wouldn't let you live in one of his houses, now, if he gave it to you. (CLIFF *laughs.*) No, I wouldn't. I had a house to live in before I ever saw this burg.

CLIFF (*sternly*)—Well, I think you'd better write home for it, boy, if you intend to settle around here.

SNYDER (*coming forward*)—Well, I may not *settle* around here, Mr. Mettinger, what do you think of that? (*He starts for the door again.*)

CLIFF—Fine! I think it'd be a good idea.

SNYDER (*opening the door*)—Come on here, Ruth.

RUTH—Where are you going, Charlie?

SNYDER—That's *my* business.

Snyder dashes out of the house, Ruth after him, and Mrs. Fenner does what she can to clear up matters with her brother. She makes little headway, however. Cliff is convinced he knows Snyder and the Snyder type of boy.

"He's one of those drifter boys that's going to get it easy at somebody else's expense," according to Cliff. "I've met him three times in town during the past two weeks, and every time he's been coming from a pool match. And you know what kind of material those pool rooms turn out. Ruth'll pick up the paper some morning and discover that she's married to a first-class bandit. And then my house'd be used as a storage room for a lot of stolen goods."

Charlie Snyder is largely Ruth's idea, Mrs. Fenner admits, but she still is eager to defend both him and Ruth. To do Charlie justice, it was Ruth's idea that her Uncle Cliff might give them a chance to get a house, seeing that he would be giving them a wedding present anyway. And they would get it paid for eventually.

But Cliff had no idea of giving his niece a wedding present that cost twelve thousand dollars and he is less inclined now to give her any kind of present than he has ever been before. As a matter of fact he hasn't even seen Ruth more than a half dozen times in the last five years, and she certainly has made no effort to keep May company. And if she hasn't any more sense than to figure the way she's figuring, he doesn't want to talk with her any more about anything.

Mrs. Fenner is ready to change the subject. She would like to talk now about her own affairs. Of course, after Ruth goes, it will be rather foolish for just two of them to stay on in their big house, and she thinks it might be a solution of both their living problems if she and Mr. Fenner were to move in with Cliff and let her do the housekeeping. He'll need somebody, after Miss Plunkett goes—

"You'll have to have somebody," she says, as he turns his head slowly and "pins her with a look," "and I don't think you have any realization of what a job it is to find a good housekeeper. Of course, Dan and I would pay our way here, just as we do now,—but I thought it would save you the bother of everlastingly looking for housekeepers, and at the same time split the living expenses for both of us."

Olly bustles in from the right with more lingerie before Cliff has a chance to reply to his sister's proposition. His expression is set and a little troubled as he leaves them and goes up the stairs.

Olly is eager to know what all the loud talking was about, and not at all surprised when she learns that it was started by Cliff's refusal to help Charlie and Ruth with their wedding plans. She, too, has heard a thing or two about young Snyder; heard it from the woman who works both for Charlie's landlady and comes to Olly on Fridays. Snyder, according to this woman, is both mysterious and shiftless, and there is at least some doubt as to where he hails from. Sometimes he has a lot of money, and then for days he will have none at all.

Mrs. Fenner is waiting for Olly to get her things on so they may go home together when Miss Plunkett comes upon her.

Mrs. Fenner—I hear you're going home to-morrow, Miss Plunkett.

Miss Plunkett—Yes, I'm going, Laura; so you'll have the field all to yourself again—till Cliff gets another housekeeper—then I suppose you'll start in on *her* the way you started in on me.

Mrs. Fenner—Why, what did I do to you, Miss Plunkett?

Miss Plunkett—Now, don't try to be meek, Laura; I like you better when you're yourself. You were running around here in a panic two weeks ago when I got here for fear I was going to steal your brother. (Mrs. Fenner *makes a sound of amused deprecation.*) And you fixed it with Olly so that one of you would be here all the time to watch me.

Mrs. Fenner—I don't know that *I've watched* you very much during the past two weeks.

Miss Plunkett—Because you were afraid of having trouble with your brother; and you knew that wouldn't pay you: so you packed up your things and went home, and took a chance on my doing the same thing. (*With a shift of tone.*) As though your brother wasn't safer from me than he was from you. (Mrs. Fenner *darts a hard look at her, and* Miss Plunkett *holds it.*) I *work* for *my* living; I'm not one of those women that has to hang on some *man* all her days.

Mrs. Fenner—I went home because I was given to understand that you wanted to wait on yourself.

Miss Plunkett—So we did. But that wasn't the reason *you* went home. And to wait on us wasn't the reason you came over here, either. May told me you haven't been inside this *house* in the last four years.

Mrs. Fenner (*turning away*)—Well, there were *reasons* for that, Miss Plunkett, that you know nothing about.

Miss Plunkett—I know the principal reason, though, Laura; there was nothing to *get.* (Mrs. Fenner *pierces her with a sudden look.*) But now that your sister's gone, you're very much in evidence,—because you want to come in here yourself; (Mrs. Fenner *turns away*) and you're frightened to death that Cliff'll take a wife and beat you to it. (Mrs. Fenner *continues to be amused.*) That's your game, Laura, I knew it before I was in here five minutes.

Mrs. Fenner (*in quiet fury*)—Why should *I* want to come in here? I have a home of my own.

Miss Plunkett (*maintaining her level tone*)—And you have a delicate husband; and two children that wouldn't lose a five-cent *piece* by you; and *you* know it. For that's the kind of children that women like you raise, Laura; that's the reason you

want to saddle yourself on your brother, now that he's free to
marry.

Mrs. Fenner (*turning away again*)—Well, he hasn't married
*you,* anyway.

Miss Plunkett—And you're going to see that he *doesn't*—
by insulting me—(Mrs. Fenner *glares at her*)—and every other
woman that he's civil to.

Mrs. Fenner—Why, who has insulted you around here?

Miss Plunkett—Do you think I'm blind? That I didn't get
a few of those looks you shot at me the night I came here.
And trying to get Cliff to blunder into telling me to go home, for
fear I'd be inconvenienced. As though *you* cared whether I was
inconvenienced or not. That was when you made your mistake,
Laura; for I'd have been on my way a week ago only for that
move. I didn't mind the looks; they were just a laugh for me;
and I expected them anyway, from what May had told me at
Atlantic City. But when you started that other thing, I decided
to stay here just for devilment. And I'd stay here longer only
for my business.

Mrs. Fenner—I thought May had given you quite a report
on me.

Miss Plunkett—Oh, she didn't have to give me much,
Laura,—just one or two things, and I could add all the rest.
I have a sister that's so much like *you* that you could be her
twin. One of those women that goes with her *man;* and after
that all is fish that comes to your net—even if it's from your own
people. I had no more idea when I came into this house about
marrying your brother than you had. But you *put* it into my
mind; and that's a dangerous thing to do sometimes, Laura, for
some people's minds have a way of putting ideas into practice.
And I think it'd be a good thing if somebody *did* put that idea
into practice; let Cliff have a bit of life of his own for a change.

Now Olly and Mrs. Fenner are gone, Olly after pleasant good-
bys and many conventional good wishes and Mrs. Fenner after
giving Daisy no more than a deadly look.

And now May has come rushing down the stairs, all excitement
and ready to dance around Miss Plunkett while she imparts the
gladsome tidings that she has spoken to Uncle Cliff and that he
has agreed to ask Daisy to stay on all the time. He had intended
to ask her anyway, May reports, and Cliff, following her down
the stairs, is ready to confirm the report.

Miss Plunkett is slightly overwhelmed by what she assumes to be May's news, and eager to get it straight. It is plain that she has been saying something to her Uncle Cliff.

Miss Plunkett—What's this nut kid been saying to you up-stairs there, Cliff? (Cliff *laughs. He has put on a rather fancy tie, and combed his hair a bit more carefully.*)

May—I didn't say anything, did I, Uncle Cliff?

Miss Plunkett—She's been giving me a line of talk here that's got me all non compos McGinnis.

Cliff (*laughing as he lights a cigar*)—She doesn't like the idea of your going home, Daisy.

Miss Plunkett—Well, I'm not so crazy about it myself, to tell you the truth, Cliff, after bumming for a whole month. But what can a poor girl do? I'm a business woman.

Cliff—I don't think you've done much bumming this past two weeks, Daisy.

Miss Plunkett—Oh, that was fun for me, Cliff; I've had a grand time. And I don't mind housework, anyway—I'm used to it; especially in a house like this, where there's lots of light and air: and where it looks like something when you've finished.

May—Do you want me to take those things upstairs for you, Daisy?

Miss Plunkett (*turning to her and giving her the lingerie*)—Yes, I wish you would, May. Just put them with the others, and I'll pack them when I come up. (May *runs up the stairs, and* Cliff *turns away and looks thoughtfully out the window.* Miss Plunkett *steps forward to the mirror and touches her hair.*) I don't think you ever realize how much junk you've got till you start to pack it up to go away somewhere. You know, that little nut thinks all I've got to do is fool around here with *her* from now on. My business will take care of itself, you know.

Cliff (*rather solemnly*)—Well, I'll tell you what I was thinking, Daisy. The three of us seem to get along so well together here, and you seem to like this place so well, that I was wondering if you'd care to *change* your business.

Miss Plunkett (*casually*)—How do you mean, Cliff?

Cliff—I'd like you to come in here as my wife,—if you'd care to. (Miss Plunkett *regards him for a second with amused suspicion.*)

Miss Plunkett—Now, listen, Cliff,—you don't want to marry *me?*

Cliff—Why not?

Miss Plunkett—Because you don't. You're only asking me because *May* wants me here.

Cliff—No, I'm not, Daisy; I've been thinking about asking you for over a week.

Miss Plunkett—But it's twenty years since I was twenty, Cliff; and you're a good-looking man.

Cliff—Well, it's twenty-*three* years since I was twenty; and I think you're a good-looking woman.

Miss Plunkett—Now, I *know* you're kidding me.

Cliff—No, I'm not at all, Daisy.

Miss Plunkett—But, listen, Cliff—can you see *me* with the veil and the orange blossoms? Ho! My God, there'd be a riot in Harrisburg. (*She laughs.*)

Cliff (*laughing with her*)—Well, I'd like you to think it over, Daisy. I haven't exactly been in a position to marry up till this time; but I think it's the thing for me to do right now. You and May seem to get along so well together; and you heard Old Filoon say that if I didn't *bring* somebody in, somebody would *come* in. (*He laughs.*)

Miss Plunkett (*laughing faintly*)—Well, I think myself, Cliff, from what I've seen around here, that it'd be the wise thing for you to do.

Cliff—I think so myself. And the more I've thought of it, the more I've realized that it might be a very difficult matter to find somebody that'ud just— (*He becomes inarticulate.*) I don't know just how to say it to you, Daisy. Of course, the proposition may not appeal to you at all. I remember you said the first night you were here that you were a free woman and that that was the way you were going to stay.

Miss Plunkett (*leaning on the back of the chair, and with a touch of weariness*)—Oh, I guess we all say a lot of things in a lifetime, Cliff, that we don't really mean. We say them because we think there's nothing else *for* us, I guess,—and try to kid ourselves into believing we mean them.

Cliff—I think you'd be happy here, Daisy.

Miss Plunkett—Yes, I'd be happy, Cliff.

Cliff—We'd do our best to make you so, anyway. *May* is fond of you; and, personally, I'd like to feel that there was some woman to have an eye to her. And as far as you are concerned, I think we're both sensible enough to make a go of it. (*She looks at him and laughs, a bit ironically; and he laughs too.*)

Miss Plunkett—I will, Cliff; I guess I'd be foolish if I didn't. For I've always thought I'd *like* to be married—to some steady man—that smoked good cigars—(*she gives a faint little laugh, which he reflects*)—and live in an old-fashioned house—with trees around it—and just sit there in the evening and listen to some doll of a daughter play the piano—while I made dresses for her. (*She laughs a little again.*)

CLIFF—Well, I'm sure May'd be only too glad to play the piano for you if you'd make dresses for her. (*He laughs.*)

MISS PLUNKETT (*still looking wistfully out and away*)—Yes, I guess this is it. And I guess it's coming to me. (MAY *comes running down the stairs.*)

CLIFF—How about that, May?

MAY—What? (*She stops in the middle of the room, between* CLIFF *and* MISS PLUNKETT.)

CLIFF—Daisy says she'll marry me and stay here if you'll play the piano for her.

MAY (*turning to* MISS PLUNKETT *eagerly*)—Did you, Daisy?

CLIFF—And she says she'll make dresses for you while you play.

MAY—Oh, Daisy—you'll be a June bride. (CLIFF laughs, but MISS PLUNKETT *merely smiles, strangely, and lays her hand on* MAY's *arm.*)

MISS PLUNKETT—There's not going to be anything like that, dear. Just in and out, and get it over with.

MAY—Do you want me to play something now for you, Daisy?

MISS PLUNKETT (*still abstractedly*)—Yes, play me something, Kid. (MAY *rushes to the piano.*)

CLIFF—And I'll blow cigar smoke at you, Daisy. (*She looks at him and smiles faintly.*)

MISS PLUNKETT—That'll be grand. (*She moves forward,* CLIFF *watching her.*) And I'll sit here in the lady's chair. I've always wanted to *be* a lady. (*She sits down in the lady's chair and rocks quietly back and forth.* MAY *starts to play the piano, Grieg's "To Spring." After several bars,* MISS PLUNKETT *slowly shifts her eyes and they meet* CLIFF's. *He smiles, and blows a long line of smoke towards her. Then he laughs faintly. But she only smiles and lets her gaze wander away off again. She is listening to the music of "To Spring."*)

The curtain descends very slowly.

# IN ABRAHAM'S BOSOM

## Drama in Seven Scenes

### By Paul Green

THE East and the North began to hear of Paul Green two or three years ago when he wrote a one-act play called "The No 'Count Boy." It was published in the Theatre Arts magazine and later, being peculiarly fitted to the personality and talent of an amateur actor in Dallas, Texas, Ben Smith by name, was brought to New York and entered in the Little Theatre tournament of that year, 1925, by the Little Theatre of Dallas.

The judges of the tournament not only awarded the play a cash prize, but also gave the Dallas players the Belasco trophy, for which the amateurs strive annually. "The No 'Count Boy" was afterward played successfully in vaudeville.

Later Robert M. McBride & Co. published Prof. Green's short plays, and Barrett Clark wrote an appreciation and a prophecy respecting the young man who, as he now disclosed, had joined the faculty of his alma mater and was teaching English in the University of North Carolina at Chapel Hill; teaching English and writing plays to help along the Little Theatre movement of the South, which was much beholden at this time to the enthusiastic support of Prof. Koch, a fellow worker with Prof. Green.

Last season "In Abraham's Bosom," the first long play written by Prof. Green, a study of negro life in the eastern section of North Carolina, was produced in New York by the Provincetown Players, in their Greenwich Village Theatre. The date was Dec. 30, 1926, which is the particular time in the theatre year when many changes are being made in the list of attractions. Along Broadway old plays were moving out toward the road and new plays were being brought in to replace them at the rate of six and seven and oftentimes as many as ten and twelve a week. Under these conditions "In Abraham's Bosom" was reviewed more or less casually and dismissed.

Some weeks later, as it was about to be withdrawn, there were rumors that the play was being considered seriously for the Pulitzer prize. Under the stimulus of this added interest the

Provincetowners moved their production uptown to the Garrick. Here it continued for several weeks more, and here it was seen for the first time by many of the leading drama critics. Their reports were favorable and in some instances highly enthusiastic.

Again, following a discouraging lack of interest on the part of the general public, "In Abraham's Bosom" was withdrawn. And then, in May, came the Pulitzer award.

Immediately a new interest was inspired in Prof. Green's work, the Provincetown Players revived "Abraham" in their Village Theatre and there it continued for six weeks to excellent returns.

"In Abraham's Bosom" is divided into seven long and short scenes, and covers a passage of twenty-one years in time. Though it goes no farther back than 1885 for its beginnings, it is in effect primitive drama in type and content. The impression is of an episodic study of problems and people belonging to a day far more distant than actually is the case.

The opening scene is in the turpentine woods of Eastern North Carolina, near a spring at the foot of a hill.

"The immediate foreground is open and clear save for a spongy growth of grass and sickly ground creepers. In the rear a wide-spreading tangle of reeds, briars and alder bushes. At the right the great body of a pine, gashed and barked by the turpentine farmer's ax, lifts straight from the earth. To the left a log lies rotting in the embrace of wild ivy. . . . The newly scraped blazes on the pines show through the brush like the downward spreading beards of old men, suggestive of the ancient gnomes of the woods, mysterious and silently watchful."

From the woods comes the sound of axes against the trees, accompanied by the rhythmic chant of the cutters. Occasionally a cutter breaks into a highly mournful song,

> "Oh, my feets wuh wet—wid de sunrise dew,
> De mawning stah—wuh a witness, too.
> 'Way, 'way up in de Rock of Ages,
> In God's bosom gwine be my pillah." . . .

Now it is dinner time and the call to "Git yo' peas, ev'body!" brings three perspiring negroes into the foreground. Here they quench their thirst by throwing themselves flat before the spring. Now they recover the dinner pails they have left hanging to the limb of a bush. One is young, one is older, one is little. They are all dressed in nondescript clothes, ragged and covered with the glaze of raw turpentine.

The negroes are playful and quarrelsome by turns. Bud, who

is young, would tease Puny, who is little and dumb, and Lije, who is older, would keep them apart and hold their attention to their food and their hour of rest.

The ax of a third cutter is still heard in the wood. That would be Abe, who never knows when to quit, according to the others. Getting worse an' worse, too, Abe is. Used to be the champeen hacker of the woods and the swamps until that time the white folks hanged Charlie Sampson on a telegram pole and shot his body full o' holes! Since then Abe just ain't been any good at workin'; just thinkin', thinkin', all the time. Both Colonel Mack and his son, Lonnie, have been noticing it. Been speakin' about it, too, talking rough to Abe about it. But it don't do no good.

Abe ain't safe, Lije allows. Abe talks too much. Talks too much to white folks. "Sump'n on he mind," Lije thinks; "some'n deep worry 'im, trouble—"

"Trouble about de nigger, wanter rise him up wid eddication—fact!" reports Bud.

"Hunh," ejaculates Puny; "rise him up to git a rope roun' his neck. Nigger's place down de bottom. Git buried in he own graveyard, don't mind out."

But Abe, "he gwine climb," it seems. Lije has heard him tell the Colonel that. And Lije feels that Abe is all mixed up, "bad mixed up all down inside," because he is half black and half white.

"De white blood in him comin' to de top," ventures Puny. "Dat make him want-a climb up and be sump'n. Nigger gwine hol' him down dough. Part of him take adder de Colonel, part adder his muh, 'vision and misery inside."

It ain't the white blood or the black, according to Bud, that is causing all Abe's trouble. It's the damned books he is always reading. There's one of them now, on Abe's dinner bucket. A 'rithmatic!

"Give a nigger a book and des' well shoot him," says Bud. "All de white folks tell you dat."

And what does it matter if Abe does learn to cipher right up to the Colonel? And the Colonel makes him a woods boss? Ain't no nigger goin' to work fo' no nigger! Leastways not Bud.

They call Abe again, giving him his full title this time: "Aberham McCranie!"

"Yeh, yuh, Aberham Lincoln, whut drapped he freedom from de balloon; you better git yo' grub!"

Abe comes now. "He is a young negro with a touch of the

mulatto in him, of 25 or 26, tall and powerfully built, dressed much like the others in cap and turpentine-glazed clothes. He puts his ax by the pine at the right, pulls off his cap and fans himself, while he pinches his sweaty shirt loose from his skin. His shaggy head, forehead and jaw are marked with will and intelligence. But his wide nostril and a slumbrous flash in his eye that now and then shows itself suggest a passionate and dangerous person when aroused. From the change in the actions of the others when he enters it is evident that they respect and even fear him."

Abe isn't interested in Bud or Puny or Lije. Nor in his dinner. He's just interested in his book. He's goin' to eat later— Yeh, charges Bud, when that Goldie woman comes bringing him pies an' things. Bud would be threateningly jealous if he were not afraid of Abe, and if Abe were not warning him to keep his head shut. Abe'll eat when he wants to and do problems when he wants to, and this particular problem has been worrying him two or three days. He just can't make it come out according to the white man's answer in the book.

Suddenly Abe gets the answer, and is overjoyed with his victory. He had been carrying two 'stid o' one, that's where he made his mistake. He would tell Puny and Bud and Lije, but all three are comfortably dozing by now and not interested. Abe's face "sinks into a sort of hopeless brooding."

"Yeh, sleep, sleep, sleep yo' life away," he mutters, scorning them. "I figger foh you, foh me, foh all de black in de world to lead 'em up out'n ignorance. Dey don't listen, dey don't heah me, dey in de wilderness, don't wanta be led. Dey sleep, sleep in bondage. (*He bows his head between his knees.*) Sleep in sin. (*Presently.*) Time me to eat."

The men have not gone back to their work when Colonel Mc-Cranie and his son Lonnie appear. They don't often come in the middle of the day, and Abe is hopeful this visit is being made so Colonel Mack can tell him about the school.

"The Colonel carries a riding whip. He is a stout, run-down old Southerner with all the signs of moral and intellectual decadence upon him. Lechery, whiskey, and levity of living have taken their toll of him, and yet he has retained a kind of native good-naturedness. His shirt front and once pointed beard are stained with the drippings of tobacco juice. There is something in his bearing and in the contour of his face that resembles Abe. His son, a heavyish florid young man of twenty-three or four, walks behind him."

It is not school news the Colonel brings to his workers. He only wants to see how they are doing and to transfer them to another job later. As for Lonnie, he has come, apparently, in the hope of having trouble with Abe. Lonnie has warned Abe before to let books alone and pay more attention to his job, and now, when Abe audibly regrets the Colonel's news that the white folks don't care much about the school idea, believin' it might be better to wait a while, Lonnie warns him about bein' sassy.

LONNIE—He's done told you two or three times, can't you hear?

ABE (*his eyes flashing and his voice shaking with sudden uncontrollable anger*)—Yeh, yeh, I hear 'im. Dem white folks don't keer—dey—

LONNIE (*stepping before him*)—Look out! none of your sass. Pa's already done more for you than you deserve. He even stood up for you and they laughing at him there in town.

ABE (*trembling*)—Yeh, yeh, I knows. But dem white folks don't think— I going to show 'em, I—

LONNIE (*pushing himself before him*)—Dry up. Not another word.

ABE (*his voice breaking almost into a sob*)—Don't talk to me lak dat, Mr. Lonnie. Stop him, Colonel Mack, 'fore I hurt him. (*The other negroes draw off into a knot by the pine tree, mumbling in excitement and fear.*)

COLONEL—Stop, Lonnie! Abe, don't you talk to my son like that.

LONNIE—By God, I'm going to take some of the airs off'n him right now. You've gone around here getting sorrier and more worthless every day for the last year. What you need is a good beating, and I'm gonna give it to you. (*He steps backwards and snatches the whip from his father's hand.*)

COLONEL—Stop that, Lonnie!

LONNIE—Keep out of this yourself. (*He comes towards* ABE.) I'll beat his black hide off'n him.

ABE—Keep 'im back dere, Colonel Mack. I mought kill him! Keep 'im off.

LONNIE—Kill him! All right, do it. There, damn you! (*He strikes* ABE *across the face with his whip. With a snarl* ABE *springs upon him, tears the whip from his hands and hurls him headlong into the thicket of briars and bushes. Then he stands with his hands and head hanging down, his body shaking like one with the palsy.*)

PUNY (*screaming*)—You done kilt Mr. Lonnie! Oh, Lawdy, Lawdy!

COLONEL (*running to* LONNIE, *who is crawling up out of the mud with his clothes and skin torn. He is sobbing and cursing*)— Are you hurt? How bad are you hurt?

LONNIE—Let me get at that son of a bitch and I'll kill him dead. (*Moaning.*) Oh, I'll beat his brains out with one o' them axes.

COLONEL—If you ain't dead, you'd better keep your hands off'n him. I'll fix him. (*He reaches down and picks up the whip. Thundering.*) Git down on your knees, Abe! Git down, you slave! I'm gonna beat you. (ABE *jerks his head up in defiance, but before the stern face of the* COLONEL *his strength goes out of him. He puts his hands up in supplication.*)

ABE—Don't beat me, Colonel Mack, don't beat me wid dat whip!

COLONEL—Git down on your knees! I've beat many a slave, and I'll show you how it feels. (*He strikes him several blows.*)

ABE (*falling on his knees*)—Oh, Lawd, have muhcy upon me! (*The* COLONEL *begins to beat him, blow upon blow.* PUNY, BUD *and* LIJE *stand near the pine in breathless anxiety.*)

PUNY—De Colonel'll kill 'im!

BUD (*seizing his arm*)—Shet dat mouf, nigger!

COLONEL (*as he brings the whip down*)—Let this be a lesson to you to the end of your life!

ABE (*his back twitching under the whip, his voice broken*)— Muhcy, Colonel Mack, muhcy!

COLONEL—You struck a white man, you struck my son.

ABE (*raising his tear-stained face*)—I yo' son too, you my daddy. (*He throws himself down before him, embracing his feet. The* COLONEL *lowers the whip, then drops it behind him.*)

LONNIE (*his voice husky with rage*)—You hear what he say? Hear what he called you? (*He seizes the whip and in a blind rage strikes the prostrate* ABE *again and again.*)

COLONEL (*stepping between them*)—Stop it! Give me that whip. (LONNIE *nervelessly hesitates and then reluctantly hands him the whip.*) Go on back out to the road and wait for me. Trot! (LONNIE *in disgust and rage finally goes off at the left nursing his face and his arms.*) Get up, Abe. Get up, I say. (ABE *sits up, hugging his face between his knees. The* COLONEL *wets his handkerchief in the spring, and with his hands on* ABE'S *head bathes the bruises on his neck and shoulders.*)

ABE (*in a voice grown strangely dignified and quiet*)—Thank 'ee, thank 'ee, Colonel Mack.

COLONEL (*breathing heavily*)—Thanky nothing. I had to beat you, Abe, had to. Think no more about it. Dangerous thing, hitting a white man. But this is the end of it. Won't be no law, nothing but this. Put some tar and honey on yourself to-night and you'll be all right to-morrow.

Goldie, coming through the bushes at the back of the spring, rushes forward when she sees them. Goldie "is a tall, sinuous young mulatto. She carries a bucket in her hand." Tenderly Goldie takes over the soothing of Abe's bruised neck and body, cooing over him as a mother would over an unhappy child. The Colonel leaves Abe in her charge.

At first Abe denies that any one has hurt him and then, stung to anger, he threatens the annihilation of his enemies. He would start after them, dragging Goldie with him as she tries to hold him back, if Lije and Bud did not stop him. Why should he go fix it to git himself hung up on a telegram pole? Bud wants to know that.

Now Abe is calm again and resigned. He's just a fool, a crazy fool. He knows that.

Goldie is comforting, though she sobs a little at sight of his poor back. Gradually her comforting appeals to Abe and, as in a dream, he is ready to follow where she leads.

GOLDIE (*her face alight, a sort of reckless and unreal abandonment upon her*)—I knows where dere's a cool place under a big tree. And dey's cool green moss dere and soft leaves. Le's go dere, boy. I gwine tend to you and feed you. (*She moves across towards the Right, leading* ABE *like a child.*) We make us a bed dere, honey. (LIJE *sits up watching them.*) Us forgit de 'membrance o' all dis trouble. (*A kind of ecstasy breaking in her voice.*) Dere de birds sing and we hear de little branch running over de rocks. Cool dere, sweet dere, you kin sleep, honey, rest dere, baby. Yo' mammy, yo' chile, gwine love you, make you fohgit.

ABE (*moved out of himself*)—Yeh, yeh, I come wid you. I don't keer foh nothing, not nothing no mo'. You, des' you'n' me.

GOLDIE—Ain't no worl', ain't no Lije and Bud, nobody. Us gwine make us a 'biding place and a pillah under dat green tree. (*In sweet oblivion.*) Feel yo' arms around me, my lips on yo'n.

We go singing up to heaben, honey, togedder—togedder. (*They go off, her voice gradually dying away like a nun's chant.*)

BUD (*breaking a sapling in his grasp*)—Gwine off, gwine off in de woods togedder dere lak hawgs.

PUNY (*bounding up, his body shaking in lascivious delight*)— I gwine watch 'em—hee-hee—I gwine watch 'em.

LIJE (*knocking him back*)—Bedder stay out'n dat woods. Abe kill you.

PUNY (*standing up by the pine tree*)—Kin see 'em, her still aleading 'im.

LIJE (*standing up and peering off to the Right*)—Dere on de cool moss and de sof' green leaves.

BUD (*stripping the limbs from the top of the broken sapling*)— Ain't gwine look. Dey fools, bofe fools. (*Raging out.*) Dere she go playing de hawg. Didn't know she lak dat. (*He sucks in his breath with the sound of eating something.*) Wisht to Gohd I knowed she lak dat. I de man foh her. Bud Gaskins. I tame her, Gohd damn her, I tame her down and take dat speerit out'n her. (*He crowds out his chest and walks up and down.*)

PUNY (*grasping* LIJE's *arm*)—Cain't hardly see 'em no mo', kin you?

LIJE—Kin hardly.

BUD (*his anger and jealousy disappearing in physical emotion and vulgar curiosity*)—Whah dey now?

LIJE (*pointing*)—Dere, dere, dey crossing de branch now.

PUNY (*breathlessly*)—I see 'em. I see 'em. He arm 'round her now, her head on he shoulder. (*He capers in his excitement.*) Lawd! Lawd!

BUD (*with a loud brutal laugh as he slaps* LIJE *on the back*)— On de sof' green moss.

LIJE (*laughing back and dragging his harp across his mouth*)— Whah de leaves is cool.

PUNY—Cain't see 'em no mo'. (*He whirls about and turns a handspring.*) Whoopee, folkses! Gwine run away wid myse'f!

BUD (*his eyes shining*)—Down whah de branch water run. (*He shuffles a jig among the leaves.*)

LIJE (*blowing upon his harp*)—Singing raght up to heaben! (*He plays more wildly as they all drop into a barbaric dance that gradually mounts into a Dionysiac frenzy.*)

PUNY—Heaben!

BUD—Jesus, Lawd, Fadder and Son!

LIJE (*singing loudly as they dance, the music running into a quick thumping rhythm*)—

My feets wuh wet wid de sunrise dew,
De mawning stah wuh a witness too.
'Way, 'way up in de Rock of Ages,
In God's bosom gwine be my pillah.

(*They gambol, turn and twist, run on all fours, rear themselves up on their haunches, cavort like goats.*)

PUNY—In God's bosom—hanh!

BUD—In who bosom?

LIJE—In who bosom, bubber! (*A loud halloo comes down from the hill in the rear, unnoticed by them.*)

PUNY—In Goldie's bosom. Hee-hee-hee!

BUD AND LIJE—Haw-haw-haw! Hee-hee-hee! In God's bosom gwine be my pillah. (*The halloo is repeated.*)

LIJE—Hyuh, dere dat Gabe calling us. Better git, or de Colonel have dat stick on our back. (*They gather up their buckets and axes,* PUNY *clambers up the pine a few feet and drops to the ground.*)

BUD—Kin see?

PUNY—See nothing. Hee-hee!

LIJE—Gut to leave 'em now. Abe ketch it 'gin don't mind out. He not coming wid us.

BUD—He done foh now. Dat gal gut him hard and fast. (*Snorting scornfully.*) Books, books! Rise 'em up, lak hell!

LIJE—I done told you. Heart say dis, head say dat. Bad mixtry. Bad. Crazy!

PUNY (*shouting*)—Heigh, you, Gabe! Coming! (*They move out at the rear up the hill, singing, laughing and jostling each other.*)

'Way, 'way down by de sweet branch water
In her bosom gwine be he pillah!

Hee-hee—haw—haw—!

(*Their loud, brutally mocking laughter floats back behind them.*)

### SCENE 2

It is a spring day, three years later. In Abraham McCranie's two-room cabin, barely furnished, a bed juts out into the room. On the bed, weakly shooing the flies away, lies Goldie. Sitting by the fire, holding an infant in her arms and rocking back and forth is Goldie's mother, Muh Mack—"a chocolate-colored negress near sixty, dressed in a long, dirty wrapper, and bare-footed. Her graying hair is wrapped in pigtails and stands around her head Medusa-like. A long snuff-stick protrudes from her mouth, and now and then the fire sputters with a frying noise as she spits into it."

Goldie is worried. Two children before this one have died. One when it was three days old. The other at four days. Now this baby has reached its fourth day, and he may go too.

Not according to the beliefs and prophecies of Muh Mack. This here is a strong and muscled infant, fit to live to be a hundred. "Dem udder po' little 'uns puny, bawn to die."

Still, Goldie can't forget them, how little they were and hungry. Nor how Mr. Lonnie done cut down the plum bushes and plowed up the hedge row where they were buried! And Abe didn't stop him!

"Cain't blame Abe," Muh Mack insists. "He stiff neck. God break his spirit. Gi' 'im two dead 'uns to fetch 'im down. He bedder humble now. (*Talking half to herself.*) He talk proud lak, gwine raise up big son, leader 'mong men. Fust 'un come thin, liddle lak rat. He hate 'im. He die. God call 'im. Second come, Ol' Moster keep him liddle, thin. He die too. Abe gitting down to sackcloff and ashes. God see him down crying foh muhcy, He send dis 'un, strong. Israel man. He gwine flourish, he gwine wax."

Abe's lost faith, too, Goldie laments. He doesn't take any interest in his new son. Probably be dead in a week, he says. Abe's still messin' around with his ol' books. Everything going wrong. Crops. Everything.

Now Abe is in from the fields, bringin' his hoe with him. Goldie gasps her horror! Hoes in a house bring bad luck! Awful bad luck! Might bring something on the baby! Muh Mack also explodes with wrath at sight of the hoe. Let Abe throw it out! Goldie's too weak to be worried!

They're a set of fools, Abe says. All niggers is ign'ant and bline. Believin' everything has a sign 'tached to it!

Abe is low. Very low. Nothing that Goldie can say has any cheering effect upon him. Nothing has gone right with Abe for a long, long time. He can't raise chillun, can't raise crap, can't raise nothin'! He hasn't any money, not even any shoes, and he won't ask the Colonel. He at least has pride, and he can't forget that beating at the spring! Everything's mortgaged! Everything's spent! What good's it goin' to do if Goldie does get up in a week and go back to working in the fields with him?

ABE—Make no difference. Wuk our guts out do no good. I tell you, gal, de nigger is down, down. De white man up dere high, setting up wid God, up dere in his favor. He git eve'ything, nigger git de scraps, leavings. (*Flaring out.*) Ain't no God foh de nigger, dat's white man's God. Dat come to me down in de new ground. (*He sits down again, tapping his feet on the floor.*)

GOLDIE (*wiping her eyes*)—Honey, you gut to stop talking lak dat. Cain't be bad luck allus. I'se 'feared when you talk dat wild talk. God heah it he do. (MUH MACK *comes and stands in the door.*) He mought be doing all dis to make us good, make us humble down befo' him.

ABE—Humble down, hell! Look at de udder niggers den. Dey shout and carry on in de church, pray and pay de preachers in deir blindness. Dey humble. What do God do? Starve 'em to deaf. Kill 'em off lak flies wid consumption. Dey dying 'long de river same as de chillun in de wilderness.

MUH MACK—You blaspheaming, da's whut you doing. No wonder Gohd take yo' babies 'way, no wonder he make yo' mule die, blast down yo' plan's an' send de crows and cold weather and root lice to destroy yo' craps. (*Her eyes flashing.*) You gut to change yo' ways. Some day he gwine re'ch down from de clouds and grab you by de scruff o' de neck and break you cross he knee. He gi'n you fine baby chile, you don't thank him. You gut to fall down, pray, git low, git humble. (*Her voice rises into a semi-chant.*) You dere, Jesus, heah my prayer. Dis heah sinner, he weeked, he blaspheam. Save him and save dis po' liddle baby.

GOLDIE (*weeping over the child*)—Do, Lawd, heah our prayer.

Muh Mack is praying eloquently, mostly that the Lord will destroy all Abe's old books, when a call from Colonel McCranie interrupts her. The Colonel has changed in three years. "He is stouter, his face mottled, and he walks with difficulty, propped on a stick."

He has come now to see the baby. Now he takes the infant from Goldie and holds him up to find him heavy, and strong. Which brings memories crowding back on Muh Mack.

"Lawd, it all comes to me ag'in," says she. "Jest such a day as dis thirty yeah ago you come down heah and hold Abe up dat-a-way."

And the Colonel, looking long through the window, answers

her. "Time hurries on, it goes by in a hurry. . . . Yes, Callie, we're getting old."

"For an instant all differences are passed away and they are four human beings aware of the strangeness of their lives, conscious of what queer relationships have fastened them together."

Then the baby cries and the spell is broken.

Now the Colonel recalls the real object of his visit. He has come to bring Abe a deed of gift to the cottage and twenty-five acres of land surrounding it.

They are all greatly excited by the Colonel's generosity, and embarrass him a little saying so. But it is what he wants to do and he is glad to do it. Abe's had a pretty hard time of it the last three years. But he's the only nigger in the whole country that's worth a durn. The Colonel is glad Abe's keeping up his books, too. Doesn't want him to give up, like Lonnie did. Lonnie ain't worth a damn. That's the Colonel's opinion of Lonnie.

Then there is another surprise for Abe. The Colonel has made arrangements for him to try school teaching in the fall and see what he can do with it.

"I'm going to have that old Quillie house fixed up and put some benches in it and a blackboard," says the Colonel. "I'll get two Negroes to serve with me on the school board and we'll try you out. I been reading your books, too, Abe."

Abe takes a great breath as he cries exultantly:

"I gwine teach school—at last!"

There is rejoicing now. Abe's going to take care of his son now, and raise him up right, like the Colonel said. His eyes are shining and his heart is light and he is ready to forgive everything. Even the beating by the spring.

Now Abe is offering up in prayer his thanks for all the great good that has come to him and his. Praying to the black man's God, the white man's God, the one and only God that he be heard!

As he prays Goldie and Muh Mack add their pleadings and their soulful endorsements.

ABE (*raising his head up, his eyes closed*)—Heah us, heah us, heah me dis day, heah my po' prayer. Fohgive me my sins, my blaspheamy. Wipe out de evil o' my weeked days. Purify, make clean, fohgit de 'membrance o' my transgression. Now heah I do humble down, I do cohnfess. Lift me, raise me, up, up!

MUH MACK—Hallelujah!

GOLDIE—Amen.

ABE (*bowing his head in a storm of grief*)—Re'ch down yo' hand and gimme stren'th. Now I draw nigh, I feel yo' sperit. Save me, save me now! (MUH MACK *and* GOLDIE *pray and moan aloud. Presently* ABE *stands up and cries out exultantly.*) He save me, he done save me! He done fohgive me!

MUH MACK (*clapping her hands wildly*)—Bless de Lawd, bless um!

GOLDIE (*faintly*)—Thank Jesus, save my baby and my husban'. (ABE *is silent a moment, his face working with emotion. He turns and bends down over the bed.*)

ABE—Po' little fellow, he sleep and rest. (*He puts his arms around* GOLDIE *and she clings to him.*) Honey chile, I changed. I gwine take new holt. From dis day I begins. I sorry foh all de past. (*He loosens her arms from around his neck and stands up, a strange set look on his face.*) I gwine keep heart now, look up, rise. I gwine lead. (*Looking down at the baby.*) I gwine raise him up a light unto peoples. He be a new Moses, he bring de chillun out of bondage, out'n sin and ign'ance. (*He turns suddenly and goes to the bucket at the left, pours some water out in a pan and sets it on the bed. Then he bends down and lifts the baby in his hand.* MUH MACK *looks up, drying her eyes.*)

GOLDIE—Whut dat, Abe? Whut dat you doing?

ABE (*dipping his hand in the water and holding the child aloft, his face lighted up in a beatific smile*)—On dis day I names you Douglass. You gwine be same lak him. Yeh, better. You gwine be a light in darkness, a mighty man. (*He dips his hand into the water and sprinkles the child.*) I baptize you and consecrate you to de salvation ob my people dis day! Amen! (*The women stare at him transfixed, caught out of themselves. He bends his head and stands with the child stretched before him as if making an offering to some god.*)

## SCENE 3

That same winter Abe's school was started in the old Quillie house, "a negro cabin of one bare room, now fitted up as a schoolhouse." It is furnished with "a squat, rusty, cast-iron stove, the pipe of which reels up a few feet and then topples over into an elbow to run through the wall." There is a rickety table for teacher, four or five rough pine benches "worn slick by restless students," and a small blackboard nailed to the wall.

Abe is the first to arrive this particular school day morning. He comes in carrying his lunch bucket and two or three books. "He is wearing an old overcoat and a derby hat, both making some claims to a threadbare decency." He starts a fire in the stove and is ready for his pupils.

But the pupils do not come. He shouts the call to books and rings the bell without result. Plainly disturbed, but determined to go on, he laboriously writes the day's motto on the blackboard: "January 21. An idle brain is the devil's workshop."

Three students straggle in—"a lazy, slumbrous girl of eighteen or twenty, a stout, thick-lipped youth about the same age, and a little, serious-faced, ragged boy of ten."

Abe is encouraged by the sight of them and would hurry with the order of the day to make up the time they have lost. But they are not interested. The two older children, Neilly and Lanie, find it difficult to suppress their amusement at the proceedings. They exchange fleeting smiles as though conscious of a secret they are sharing.

Abe is too interested to notice them. He is irritably disappointed at the tardiness of the other pupils, angered when Neilly and Lanie report that none are coming. Abe will go on with the school just the same. He orders them to their seats and sternly rebukes Lanie for her giggling.

It is Eddie, the little fellow, who finally breaks the news to Abe. "Mr. Mack," Eddie calls, in a high, frightened quaver, "dey all say de school ain't gwine run no mo' an' dey ain't coming."

Abe won't believe it. He won't give up. They got to show him! Again he orders the children to their seats. He calls the roll. The three answer "Presunt," and Lanie giggles.

Now the spelling lesson. But only little Eddie knows that. Lanie and Neilly don't even try. What's the use, if there ain't goin' to be no mo' school?

Abe stands Lanie in the corner for giggling. She is there, her face to the wall, when Puny arrives. Puny is in to warm his hands and, incidentally, as a member of the school board, to confirm the news that there ain't goin' to be no mo' school.

PUNY—You des' well quit de school business raght heah and now. Dey ain't gwine send to you no mo'.

ABE—What's the trouble?

PUNY—Trouble! You gone and done it, you has, when you beat Will Ragland's boy yistidy. Will so mad he kin kill you.

ABE (*anger rising in his voice*)—Needn't think I'm skeahed of him.

PUNY—I knows you ain't. But you wants to keep on teaching, don't you?

ABE—Yeh, and I'm going to.

PUNY—Nunh-unh, you ain't neiver. Will went 'round last night and gut everybody to say dey won't gwine send to you no mo'. Dey ain't gwine stand foh no nigger beating deir young 'uns.

ABE (*angrily*)—I had a right to beat him. I couldn't make him work no other way, and 'sides he told a lie to me. Said he didn't eat up po' little Sis Maffis' dinner. Several of 'em seen him do it.

PUNY—Can't he'p it. You beat 'im so dey had to have a doctor foh him, and Will done gone to de sher'ff to git out papers foh you.

ABE (*starting out of his chair*)—Gwine have me 'rested?

PUNY—He is dat. And mo', I reckon. And my advice to you is to git f'om heah. As a member of de school boa'd I say, bedder leave.

ABE—He think he kin run me 'way?

PUNY—Don't know what he think. Know I wouldn't lak to lie in no white man's jail-house, dat's me.

ABE—De otheh members of the boa'd know 'bout it?

PUNY—Us had a meeting last night.

ABE—What dey say?

PUNY (*fumbling in his pockets*)—Dey all side wid Will, 'count o' de beating and 'count o' dat speech you made in chu'ch last Sunday.

ABE—Wuh Mr. Lonnie dere?

PUNY—He dere and he send dis heah writing to you. (*He pulls a note from his pocket and hands it to* ABE, *who opens it excitedly.*)

ABE (*clenching his fist*)—Dat man say heah—God— He say de boa'd done all 'cided de school got to stop. (*He tears the note to pieces and throws it in the stove.*) He say dere he know a good job in Raleigh at public wuk he kin git me. (*Bitterly.*) Say I do better at dat dan farming or school. (*Pacing the floor, he throws his hand above his head.*) Nanh, anh—suh, I sets a oaf on high, I ain't going let 'em run me off. Dey cain't skeah me. Dey cain't run me off lak I stole sump'n'. (*He turns on* PUNY *with blazing eyes and* EDDIE *watches him, terrified.*) Why you all vote dat way? Whyn't you stand up and vote foh me? You know I trying do right. You weak, coward, no backbone.

PUNY (*backing towards the door*)—I ain't gut nothing 'gin you, Abe. Why you 'buse me?

ABE—Git out o' heah. All o' you down on me. Dat speech was so. It was right. Dat beating was right. (*Crying out.*) I ain't gwine give in. Dey cain't run me. You cain't run me. I fight 'em. I stay heah. Let 'em putt me in de jail, I last till de jail rot down. (*He moves menacingly towards* PUNY, *who flees through the door and slams it after him.*) I come through deir bars, deir iron won't hold me. I'll git dere, I'll come. My flesh will be as tough as deir iron! (*He goes to the table and picks up his books. He opens the Bible and stands thinking. Dropping into his chair, he sits with his elbow on the table and his chin in his hand, gazing into the distance. The anger and bitterness gradually pass from his face.*) Dat man's talk, proud. Cain't push through 'thout help—(*putting his hand on the Bible*)—'thout help from up there. (*He bows his head on the table.* EDDIE *begins to sob and, leaving his seat timidly, approaches* ABE's *bent form, gulping and wiping his nose and eyes with his sleeve.* ABE *looks up and puts his arm around him.*) Son, this heah's the last of this school. But we cain't stop, we got to keep on. (*EDDIE leans his head against him, his sobs increasing.*) Got to keep studying, got to keep climbing. (*After a moment he stands up and writes across the board, "This School is stopped for a while."* LANIE *and* NEILLY *come inquiringly in.*) Chillun, ain't goin' to be no mo' school till mebbe next yeah. You kin go home. (*LANIE giggles and* NEILLY *looks at him with familiar condescension.*) But I wants to dismiss with a word of prayer. (*At a sign from him* EDDIE *falls on his knees by the table. He gets down at his chair.*) Our Father, where two or three is gathered— (*NEILLY and* LANIE *look at him, pick up their buckets and scurry out giggling and laughing loudly.* ABE *springs to his feet, his face blank with astonishment. He calls after them furiously.*) Heigh, heigh, you! (*They are heard going off, their sharp laughter softening in the distance.*)

NEILLY—'Fo' Gohd, he down on his knees!

LANIE (*her voice growing faint*)—Yeh, and he 'bout kilt Arth yistiddy.

NEILLY—Haw—haw—haw.

LANIE—Hee—hee—hee.

Their voices die away. The curtain falls.

## SCENE 4

It is fifteen years later, the scene a room in the poverty-stricken Negro section of Durham, North Carolina. Goldie is washing at a tub resting on a goods box. Muh Mack, "bent under a slat bonnet," is dozing at the fireplace. A bed at the back of the room is piled with rough washing.

"For several minutes neither of the women says anything. Goldie washes heavily at the tub, her body bent and disfigured with the years of toil and poverty and the violence of childbirth. She wrings out a garment and takes it to the fireplace." Muh Mack resents being disturbed, but Goldie refuses to favor her. The years have taken toll of Goldie. "Her movements are slow, ox-like, and in her eyes now and then comes a sort of vacant look, as if some deadening disease had had its way within her brain, or as if trouble and worry have hardened her beyond the possibility of enthusiasm or grief anymore."

It is supper time and there is no supper, or money to buy supper with. "Ain't mo'n 'nough to fill my old hollow toof," according to Muh Mack. And what there is is far from appealing. "I et dat old meat and cawn bread till it makes me heave to look at it."

Somethin's got to be done about food, protests Muh Mack. Goldie can't go on washin' without anything to eat. Abe can't go on working on coffee and bread forever. "No wonder he look lak a shadow and cain't ha'f do his work. . . . How you gwine keep washing foh folks an' you don't eat?"

"Oh, Lawd Gohd in heaven, I don't know!" wails Goldie.

There is one fifty-cent piece left. That will buy some liver for Abe. But when Goldie looks for the money that's gone, too. Some one done stole it, and it is Goldie's fixed conviction that Muh Mack took it and gave it to Douglass to spend "foh ice cream and mess."

"Don't keer 'f I did," sulks Muh Mack. "Po' boy do widout all de time."

The situation is desperate. No more money. No more credit. Abe's pay day still twenty-four hours away. They all ought to go back home. That's where they ought to go, according to Muh Mack. Everything's been goin' wrong for fifteen years. And all because of Abe! That ol' fool, Abe!

Stick by him? Why should Goldie stick by him, when he'd drug her from pillar to post for fifteen years. He's sick, says Goldie. Was he sick when he got into co't over beatin' that

Raglands boy and lost all his land? Muh Mack wants to know. Was he sick when he got "cutting up a rust in Raleigh" an' de niggers an' white folks run him out of there? Same ol' story in Greensboro—got in a row wid somebody and had to leave!

"Things'll be crosswise wid 'im till dey straighten 'em out in de grave," that's Muh Mack's opinion. "If all dat shooting and killing in Wilmington wouldn't make 'im do better, nothing in de Gohd's world kin."

Still Goldie is determined to stick by Abe. Let Muh Mack know that and stop her talking.

"C'ose you gwine stay by 'im—and starve, too. Foh dat's what you'll do. Whut he don't spend on medicine he do on dem old lodges and sich and books and newspapers. And gits turned out'n eve'y one of 'em foh his speeches and wild talk, he do. (*With grim satisfaction.*) Shoveling dat coal down at de power house reckon'll hold him down foh a while. (*With an afterthought.*) Hold 'im down till somebody crack his haid wid a shovel and tu'n 'im off. (*Stirring the fire and then folding up her hands.*) I done said my say-so now. Do no good, 'caze you so wropped up in de fool."

"No, it won't do no good," flares Goldie. "I gwine stick by him. Dey ain't never done 'im right. Dey all been down on 'im f'om de fust. He gwine be a big man yit. Dem udder niggers do de dirty work and take whut dey kin git. Dey de lowdown trash. He gwine git him a big school some dese days."

"He-hee—hee," Muh Mack laughs scornfully. "Listen at him. He cain't teach nothing. De niggeh school teachers round hyuh know mo'n a minute dan Abe do in a week. Dey been to college at Raleigh and Greensboro and no telling whah. And dey gut some sense 'sides deir learning. Dat li'l Eddie Williams has. He done gone th'ough dat Shaw school in Raleigh and is off doing big wuk. Why couldn't Abe do sump'n lak dat!"

"Shet up, I tell you."

The power house whistle has blown. They know Abe is on his way home. Goldie is off to the grocer's, hoping for one more extension of credit. Muh Mack is laying the table when Douglass comes.

"He is a young Negro in short trousers, fifteen or sixteen years old, black as Muh Mack, and with something of a wild and worthless spirit already beginning to show in his face."

Muh Mack is happy Douglass has come, but a little mad at him. He done fergit to bring her anything wid dat fifty cents he spent. Douglass had got into a matching game at the hot-dawg stand and had to treat some of the fellows. That's where the fifty cents went. And if Muh Mack tells on him he—he—well, he won't play nary piece for her for mebbe two weeks.

He has fetched his guitar now, his good old "box," and is strumming it with amazing dexterity. The rhythms and the songs Douglass fits them to bring great content to Muh Mack. She skips heavily but happily to the music. Then Abe interrupts them.

Abe comes from work dragging a heavy box after him and carrying his dinner pail. He is begrimed with coal dust and the sight of Douglass and the "box" puts him in an ugly mood. "Put down dat damn guitah, you good-foh-nothing!" he shouts at the boy.

Nor can he be mollified by the chatter of Muh Mack. He breaks up the box, stirs up the fire and decides to lie down for a minute, till his head clears up. Then he will attend to Douglass!

Abe's manner terrifies Muh Mack and Douglass. The boy wails and whimpers before the wrath to come. Now Goldie is back from the grocer's with trouble piled on trouble. The grocer laughed at her—and Muh Mack knows why. Muh Mack and Douglass. But Abe mustn't know. He'd kill—

They have a time getting Abe to sit down to what there is to eat. Goldie is in tears, and the sight of these distresses Abe. He knows how hard it has been for her, and now there's this other—

But worse than all to Abe is Douglass' failure. Spendin' his mammy's good money on wuthless niggers! But that ain't what he is goin' to be beat for.

"De teacher stop me on de street and tell me you doing wuss'n ever in yo' books and she done had to putt you back in third reader. (*Swallowing his third cup of coffee down with a hunk of bread, he stands up and stares into the distance.*) Heah we done labor and sweat foh you, fix foh you to rise up and be sump'n'. Eight yeah you been going to school and you won't work, you won't learn. (*He strikes the table with his fist, and the lamp flickers and almost goes out.*) You ain't no good. Onct I thought you gwine go on, climb, rise high and lead. . . . I teach you to fool wid dem low niggers! I git you out'n dem trifling ways or I'll break yo' back in two. (*He sits down and jerks the boy across his knee and begins beating him blindly.*) I name you foh a great man, a man what stand high lak de sun, and you turn out to be de lowest of de low! Change yo' name, dat's what you better do. (*With a cuff on the cheek he hurls him across the room, where he falls, sobbing and wailing, on the floor.*) Shet dat fuss up! (DOUGLASS' *sobs gradually cease.* GOLDIE *starts toward him, but* ABE *jerks her back.*) Let 'im lie dere, de skunk and coward."

Muh Mack's protests are hysterical. She's going to find her another place to stay. As for that, they will all have to find another place to stay, Abe warns them. He's lost his job at the power house. Just by standing up for his rights. A white man sassed him and Abe sassed back, and a crowd of them run him off the place, God damn 'em—

GOLDIE (*coming over to* ABE's *chair and dropping on her knees beside him*)—Abe, Abe, le's go back. Please do. Le's go back whah we growed up. Ain't no home foh us in no town. We gut to git back to de country. Dat's whah we belong. (*She lays her head in his lap.*)

ABE (*looking down at her tenderly*)—Yeh, yeh, honey. We is gwine back. Adder all dese yeahs I knows now de town ain't no place foh us. Fifteen yeah we been trying to make it and couldn't. Dat's what I was going to tell you. All de signs been ag'in us. I orter knowed it after three or fo' yeahs. Back home de place foh us. Back in our own country. (*Staring before him and a smile suddenly sweetening the hardness of his face.*) We go back dere and take a new start. We going to build up on a new foundation. Took all dese yeahs to show me. (*His voice rising exultantly.*) Dere's whah my work is cut out to be. It come to me dis evening while I walked on de street. (*Standing up.*) Seem lak sump'n' spoke to me and said go back down on de Cape Fair River. I heard it plain lak a voice talking. "Dese streets and dese peoples ain't yo' peoples. Yo'n is de kind what works and labors wid de earf and de sun. Dem who knows de earf and the fullness thereof. Dere's whah yo' harvest is to be." And den when I come face to face wid de ruining of my boy, in my anger I see de way clear. We going back, we going back. And dere at last I knows I'm going to build up and lead! And my boy going to be a man. (*Looking at* DOUGLASS *with a hint of pleadingness.*) Ain't it so? (*But* DOUGLASS *only stares at him coldly.*)

GOLDIE (*looking up at him*)—I knows you will. I feel it des' de way you do. I keep telling Muh Mack some day you gwine git dere.

ABE (*gazing down at her*)—Dese heahs all been sent foh our trial, ain't dey, honey?

GOLDIE—Yeh, yeh, we been tried all foh a purpose.

ABE—And now we ready, ain't we, honey?

GOLDIE—We ready to go back and start all over.

MUH MACK (*repeating uncertainly*)—To start all over.

ABE—To build us a monument from generation unto generation.

GOLDIE (*softly, the tears pouring from her eyes*)—Yeh, yeh.

ABE—And all dis sin and tribulation and sorrow will be forgot, passed away, wiped out till de judgment, won't it, chile?

GOLDIE—It will, oh, I knows it will. We done suffered our share and Old Moster gwine be good to us now.

ABE—Good! Yeh, good! (*He sits with bowed head.*)

The curtain falls.

## SCENE 5

Near the close of a November day, back in the McCranie cabin three years later, Abe is at work on a speech and Muh Mack is, as usual, dozing before the fire under the same slat bonnet. A dirty pink fascinator is thrown across her shoulders, grown bony now.

"The room shows some sign of improvement," and "Abe is better dressed and more alert than formerly." He is greatly interested in his work, but also conscious that it is supper time and Goldie is not home to fix the food. Muh Mack is of no help. The rheumatiz and the misery have about done for her. Furthermore Muh Mack is not at all sure Abe deserves any supper, or anything else. Still messin' around with his books and speeches, again in trouble with Mr. Lonnie because the crops aren't what they should be and, worst of all, still hard against his own son, that po' boy Douglass, keepin' him "driv off lak a homeless dawg!"

None of the old lady's protesting reaches Abe. He has made his decision about Douglass and it stands. To-night he is sure he is to receive the support he needs for the establishment of his school. His speech is the best he has done yet. So good is it that he insists on reading parts of it to Muh Mack, who doesn't want to hear it, nor understands what she is forced to hear. Just disgusted, that's what Muh Mack is.

"Ladies and gentlemen," begins Abe, rising with dignity from his chair, his speech noticeably more gentle and more cultivated than formerly, "Ladies and gentlemen, this night is going to mean much in the lives of each and every one of us, big and little. . . . It marks the founding of the Cape Fair Training school, an institution that will one day be a light to other institutions round about. It is our aim here, with the few teachers and facilities we can provide, to offer education to the colored children amongst us and offer it cheap. . . ."

"Ignorance means sin, and sin means destruction, destruction before the law and destruction in a man's own heart. The Negro will rise when his chareckter is of the nature to cause him to rise—for on that the future of the race depends, and that chareckter is mostly to be built by education, for it cannot exist in ignorance. . . ."

He is striding up and down in front of Muh Mack, but she has dozed off again under his eloquence.

"A little over forty years ago the white man's power covered us like the night. Through war and destruction we was freed. But it was freedom of the body and not freedom of the mind. It means nothing. It don't exist. What we need is thinking people, people who will not let the body rule the head. And again I cry out, education . . .

"I don't say the colored ought to be made equal to the white in society, now. We are not ready for it yet. But I do say we have equal rights to education and free thought and living our lives. With that all the rest will come. . . .

"And what will stop us in the end from growing into a great Negro college, a university, a light on a hill, a place the pride of both black and white? . . ."

"Ain't that the truth, Muh Mack?" he asks anxiously. "Ain't that a speech equal to the best of the white, ain't it?"

"Lawd Jesus, you's enough to wake de daid," answers Muh Mack. "And you brung on yo' cough ag'in."

Further than that she cannot go. All his life Abe's hollered Lawd and followed Devil, as Muh Mack sees it. Now he's putting so much time on his school mess Mr. Lonnie's down on him again. Nor can she see any excuse in his explanation that he is not really a farmer, that his business is with schools, with learnin', in bringing the truth to the ignorant and the blind.

Now he is ready for the meeting in the Quillie house. He has his speech in his pocket and his plug hat on his head. As he goes he issues one last warning about Douglass. Let him never put foot in that house again.

"They ain't no man, flesh of my flesh or not, going to lie, rotten with liquor and crooks, around me. That's what I been talking against for twenty years."

Muh Mack—He mought a changed and want to do bedder.

Abe (*coming back into the room*)—Changed enough so he like to got arrested yesterday and it his first day back.

Muh Mack (*pleading in a high quavering voice*)—But I gut to see him. He's been gone two yeah.

Abe—Let him come if he dares. You ruint him with your tales and wuthless guitar playing and I don't want nothing more to do with him.

Muh Mack (*mumbling to herself*)—I's gwine see him 'fo' he goes 'way back yander ef I has to crawl slam over de river.

Abe (*with brightening eye*)—You heard me. He ain't no longer mine, and that's the end of it.

Muh Mack (*bursting into a rage*)—And yo' ain't none o' mine. You's gut all de high notions of old Colonel Mack and de white folks and don't keer nothing foh yo' own. Git on. (*He stands looking at the floor, hesitating over something.*) Whut you skeered of, de dark?

Abe (*shuddering and going across the room and getting an old overcoat from a nail*)—Yes, I'm afraid of it. You're right, I'm none of yours, nor my own mother either. You know what I am—no, I dunno whut I am. Sometime I think that's de trouble. (*Sharply.*) No, no, de trouble out there, around me, everywhere around me. (*The despondent look comes back to his face and he speaks more calmly.*) I'll cut across the fields the near way. And tell Goldie not to worry. I'll be back by ten with the school good as started. (*At the door he turns back again and calls to the old woman earnestly.*) Muh Mack, don't let her worry, don't. (*But the old woman is asleep.*) Let her sleep, let us all sleep. (*He goes out softly, closing the door behind him.*)

## SCENE 6

An hour later, at a spot where "a sandy country road twists out of the gloom of scrubby oaks and bushes," Abe staggers out of the darkness and falls panting at the road's edge. His hat is gone and his clothes torn. "His learning and pitiful efforts at cultural speech have dropped away like a worn-out garment and left him a criminal."

He is mumbling, holding his sides with his hands and rocking his head in pain." From his mumbling it is learned that he has been attacked and has defended himself. "Oh, my breast feel lak it'll bust." "Yeh, I outrun you, you po' white trash!

. . . God damn 'em to hell! Dey don't give me no chance.
Dey stop every crack, nail up every do' and shet me in. Dey
stomp on me, squash me, mash me in de ground lak a worm.
Dey ain't no place foh me. I lost, ain't no home, no 'biding
place. . . ."

In the distance a light twinkles in a barn. Soon Lonnie Mc-
Cranie appears, stout and middle-aged now. Lonnie recognizes
Abe, and in the dark listens to his story of the speech that was
to be delivered at the Quillie house and of what happened.

"When I got there they done run them lazy niggers off and
told me I had to go. (*Grimly.*) Dey couldn't skeer me though.
I went on in de house and started my speech. And den—
(*Throwing out his arms wildly.*) Mr. Lonnie, help me git back
at 'em. Help me git de law on 'em."

Lonnie is not sympathetic. Far from it. Serves Abe right.
Lonnie always said that. Truer now than it ever was before.
Lonnie has been looking over Abe's crop and has found it rotting in the fields. He has levied on it and is going to take it
over and Abe's through.

"Call it taking away from you if you want to," shouts Lonnie.
"I'm done of you. Next year you can hunt another place."

"Den you's a damn thief, white man."

His face working in uncontrollable rage, Abe rushes at Lonnie,
crushing him to the ground as Lonnie swings his lantern and
brings it with a crash down on Abe's head. "In the darkness
the two rocking forms are seen gripping each other's throats
under the moon."

Now Abe has choked the life out of Lonnie's body and beaten
his head against the stones. There is blood on his hands that
he can't wipe off on his trousers. And there are ha'nts and
visions stealing through his crazed brain.

"The trees seem to change their characteristics and become a
wild seething of mocking, menacing hands stretched forth from
all sides at him."

He views again the scenes at Charlie Sampson's hanging. And
now he sees the figures of a good looking Negress of twenty and
a dandified white man about thirty dressed in the fashions of
the fifties. He recognizes them as Colonel Mack and the lady
who was his Mammy and sees them disappearing in the under-
brush "lak hawgs," and yells pitifully after them.

Abe, stumbling over the body of the dead Lonnie, is rushing
madly down the road as the curtain falls.

## SCENE 7

A half hour later Douglass has arrived at the McCranie cottage and is giving Muh Mack an account of his travels. Douglass "is now about nineteen years old, and has developed into a reckless, dissipated youth, dressed in the cheap, flashy clothes of a sport."

Douglass is disgusted and defiant. "Let them dere Norveners put Pap in print foh what he's trying to do foh de niggers. Ef dey could see him now down a po' dirt fahmer dey'd not think he's such a sma't man. Let him read his books and git new idees. Dey won't change de nigger in him, not by a damn sight."

Muh Mack is of a mind to endorse Douglass' attitude, but she is more interested in those tales of adventure he has been telling. Douglass is feeling his gin a little now, and is a little ugly and defiant. He can remember days in jail and days on rock piles cause he had tried to do some of those things he had heard his pap preach about, those things 'bout there being no difference 'twixt de cullud and de white.

Things have gone badly with Douglass, but he has learned one lesson his old man will never learn—"dat we belongs down wid de pick and de sludge hammer and de tee-arn and de steam shovel, and de heavy things—at de bottom doing de dirty work foh de white man, dat's it. And he ain't gwine stand foh us to be educated out'n it nuther."

Now Douglass gets out his old guitar and is reminding Muh Mack of the good old days they used to have a-singin' and a-dancin'. Muh Mack has risen from her chair, pulled her skirt up over her scrawny shanks and is cutting several of the old steps when Goldie stands, astonished, at the door. "Her face is worn and haggard, and the strained, vacant look in her eyes has deepened." She clings to Douglass convulsively and cries a little as he holds her awkwardly. She warns him against agging his pap on. They mustn't have trouble. Abe ain't well.

There isn't much time for a visit, not enough for Douglass to find out just what is wrong with his mother that she should look so strange. A noise on the porch signals Abe's coming. Douglass escapes to the kitchen with his guitar.

Abe's face is bruised, his clothes are torn, he staggers as he walks. Muh Mack knows the signs. "Dey's been adder him!"

Abe shuts their yowling and warns them to get away. Everything's finished and at the end. But when he tries to tell Goldie what happened at the school house he can't quite remember.

"They was a crowd of white men at de door with dough-faces over their faces. Said wa'n't going to be no meeting. Dey beat me, run me off. And dey give me till to-morrow to git outen de country. You got to git away, foh it's worse'n dat— oh, it is! (*Calmly and without bitterness.*) Who you reckon set 'em on me? Who you think it was told 'em about de trouble I been in before? Yeh, and he made it out terribler'n it was. Douglass told 'em. . . . He done it. My own flesh and blood. No! No! he was but ain't no more! (*Gloomily.*) But I don't blame him—dey ain't no blaming nobody no longer."

He tells them of his running from the school house, of his meeting Mr. Lonnie, and of the murder that followed when they fought in the dark. Briefly he is calm again and resigned.

"This is the way it was meant to be and I'm glad it's ended," he says. The next moment "he stands with his fists to his temples and then flings out his arms in a wide gesture.

"Oh, damn 'em," he shouts. "Don't dey know I want to do all for de best. (*Shaking his fists at the shadows.*) I tell you, I tell you I wanted—I've tried to make it come right. (*Lowering his head.*) And now it's come to dis."

Douglass is in from the kitchen. He can't stand the charge that he had betrayed his pap. He didn't mean—he never thought—

"Who you?" coldly demands Abe. "A leader, a king among men! Here's Douglass," he tells the women, "and you can go wid him."

Douglass and Muh Mack take to the fields, but Goldie will not go. Outside the approach of the pursuers becomes insistently louder. Abe has taken Goldie's arms from around his neck and has placed her back in the chair. Now he stands looking strangely at her. Even as he shakes her by the shoulders she is no more than dumbly aroused.

ABE—Tell me, what is it, Goldie! What ails you, gal? (*She sits looking dumbly at him and he draws away from her. Presently there is a sound of stamping feet outside, and voices slip in like the whispering of leaves. A stone is thrown against the house, then another, and another. One crashes through the window and strikes the lamp. The room is left in semi-darkness. ABE with a sob of overwhelming terror falls upon his knees. Twisting his great hands together, he casts up his eyes and cries in a loud voice.*) God, God, where is you now! Where is you, God! (*He begins half sobbing and chanting.*) You has helped befo', help me now. Is you up dere? Heah my voice! (*Fear takes possession of him.*) Blast me, Lawd, in yo' thunder and lightning, if it is yo' will! Ketch me away in de whirlwind, foh I'm a sinner. Yo' will, yo' will, not mine. Let fiah and brimstone burn me to ashes and scatter me on de earf. (*Gasping.*) I've tried, I've tried to walk de path, but I'm po' and sinful. . . . Give me peace, rest—rest in yo' bosom—if it is dy will. Save me, Jesus, save me! (*He falls sobbing to the floor.*)

VOICE (*outside*)—Come out of there, you dirty nigger! (*A shudder runs through him, and his sobs grow less violent.*) Come out! Come out! (*Another stone crashes through the room. As if ashamed of his weakness,* ABE *rises from the floor. He speaks firmly to the shadows.*)

ABE—In the end it was so intended. (*Looking around him.*) And I end here where I begun. (*He bursts out in a loud voice.*) Yet they're asleep, asleep, and I can't wake 'em!

VOICES—He's in there! . . . I hear him talking! . . . He's done talking now, goddam him! . . . We'll show him the law all right! . . . He's got a gun! . . . Shoot him like a dog! . . .

ABE (*wiping his brow and again speaking in the rôle of the educator trying to convince his everlastingly silent hearers*)— But they'll wake up, they'll wake—a crack of thunder and deep divided from deep—a light! A light, and it will be! (GOLDIE *still sits hunched over in her chair. As he speaks he goes to the door at the left.*) We got to be free, freedom of the soul and of the mind. Ignorance means sin and sin means destruction. (*Shouting.*) Freedom! Freedom! (*Lifting up his voice.*) Yea, yea, it was writ, "Man that is born of woman is of few days and full of trouble. . . ." Lak de wind wid no home. Ayh, ayh, nigger man, nigger man— (*He opens the door.*) I go talk to 'em, I go meet 'em—

VOICE—Hell! Look out! There he is!

ABE—Yea, guns and killings is in vain. (*He steps out on the porch.*) What we need is to—to—(*his words are cut short by a roar from several guns. He staggers and falls with his head in the doorway*)—and we must have—have— (*At the sound of the guns,* GOLDIE *springs to her feet. For an instant everything is still. Then several shots are fired into* ABE'S *body.*)

VOICE—Quit the shooting. He's dead as a damned door! Now everybody get away from here—no talking, no talking. Keep quiet—quiet. (*There is the sound of shuffling footsteps and men leaping the fence. Voices come back into the room.*)

VOICES—Yeh, mum's it. . . . He won't raise no more disturbances! . . . (*The voices grow more faint.*) What a bloody murder he done! . . . He's still now, by God! . . . It's the only way to have peace, peace. . . . Peace, by God! . . .

(GOLDIE *moves towards the door where* ABE *lies. Halfway across the room she stops and screams and then drops down beside his body. The wind blows through the house setting the sparks flying.*)

# THE PLAYS AND THEIR AUTHORS

"Broadway." Drama in three acts by Philip Dunning and George Abbott. Copyright, 1926, by the authors. Published and copyrighted, 1926, by George H. Doran & Co., New York.

Philip Dunning, still in his thirties, has been an actor and a stage manager most of his life in the theatre, which dates back fifteen years. He was, in the estimation of every one except Philip Dunning, a mere child when he decided to quit Meriden, Connecticut, where he was born, and study life excitingly in the show business rather than dully in school. For one summer he served time as a magician's assistant in a medicine show, being the boy who escaped miraculously four times a day after having been carefully locked in a mail sack and lowered into a tank of water where he might reasonably be expected to drown. After that experience, which lasted through one vacation, he refused to go back to school. For years he did whatever came to his hand to do. He danced and sang in vaudeville, did skits and bits, played in stock and wrote plays. He peddled "Broadway" in script form under various titles—"A White Little Guy," "The Bright Lights" and "The Roaring Forties" among them. He sold it finally to Jed Harris, who called in George Abbott to point up the script and serve as stage director. He has been working the last year on another play, "The Kid Brother," which he is writing with Jack Donahue, the dancer.

Mr. Abbott, as co-author of "The Fall Guy," has appeared in these volumes before (1924-25). He also is an actor, though of late seasons he has been so much in demand as collaborator and director he has had little time for anything else. He was born in Hamburg, New York, educated at the University of Rochester, and studied playwriting with Prof. Geo. Pierce Baker, then at Harvard. He wrote several plays that he did not sell, acted many parts in stock, became a play reader for John Golden, met James Gleason when both were touring with "Dulcy," agreed to edit and rewrite "The Fall Guy," and was thus started upon the interesting and profitable career that it is safe to predict is still approaching its peak.

"Saturday's Children." Comedy in three acts by Maxwell Anderson. Copyright, 1926, by the author. Copyright and published, 1927, by Longmans Green & Co., New York.

Maxwell Anderson's first appearance in this current history of the drama was in the issue of 1924-25, which was the season he and Laurence Stallings wrote "What Price Glory?" He is a Pennsylvanian, born in the town of Atlantic, and his father was the Rev. William Lincoln Anderson, leader of the Baptist flock. During his school years the family moved West and the son graduated from the University of North Dakota. Following the profession of instructor Mr. Anderson was associated first with the faculty of his home university and later with those of Leland Stanford and Whittier colleges in California. He later gave up his professorships to become an editorial writer, which brought him eventually to the New York *World*. His first play was "The White Desert."

"Chicago." Drama in three acts by Maurine Watkins. Copyright, 1926, by the author. Published and copyrighted, 1927, by Alfred A. Knopf, New York.

Maurine Watkins has enjoyed one of those exciting adventures in the theatre that keep novice playwrights burning father's midnight oil. And yet her years, or at least her months, of preparation were more numerous than is generally known. She was born in Kentucky, reared in Indianapolis, graduated from Butler College and went to Radcliffe. She began writing plays at school and collected $500 advance on one she sold to Leo Ditrichstein. So hopeful of her future was that actor that he asked her to collaborate with him on a second play, which she did while he was playing "The Business Widow" in Chicago during the season of 1924. The Ditrichsteins were going back to New York, Miss Watkins had her trunks packed and was headed for her home in Indianapolis, when she suddenly decided to try newspaper work. She applied for a job on the Chicago *Tribune,* worked as a reporter for several months, saved her money and went to New York to write a play. She studied with Professor Baker at Yale while she wrote "Chicago," sold it and achieved success overnight.

"The Constant Wife." Comedy in three acts by William Somerset Maugham. Copyright, 1926, by the author. Published and copyrighted, 1927, by George H. Doran & Co., New York.

W. Somerset Maugham is a physician turned author. He is an Englishman born in Paris in 1874, educated at King's College, Canterbury and Heidelberg, served as interne at St. Thomas's Hospital and took to writing novels in 1897. One called "Mrs. Craddock" was the most successful of his earlier output, and "Moon and Sixpence" one of the greatest of his later successes. He turned to plays with "A Man of Honor," and during the later years of Charles Frohman's life furnished that manager with a series of light comedies, including "Lady Frederick," "Jack Staw," "Mrs. Dot," etc. He served as a medic at the front during the war, and wrote a war-time comedy called "Too Many Husbands." "The Circle," included in the 1921-22 volume of "The Best Plays" series, was one of his American successes. It was from his short story, "Miss Thompson," that the four-year sensation, "Rain," was fashioned.

"The Play's the Thing." Comedy in three acts by Ferenc Molnar, adapted by P. G. Wodehouse. Copyright, 1926, by the authors. Published and copyrighted, 1927, by Brentano's, New York.

Ferenc Molnar has made one previous appearance in these books—as the author of "Liliom," which was a success of the season of 1920-21. He is probably the best known of the Hungarian authors, was born in Budapest in 1878, graduated from the universities of Budapest and Geneva, and has been writing plays since 1902, when a piece of his called "The Doctor" was produced. Previous to that he had tried his hand at journalism. By American playgoers he is known as the author of "The Devil," "The Phantom Rival," "Where Ignorance is Bliss" and "Liliom," but none of these attained the success of "The Play's the Thing."

Pelham Granville Wodehouse, who made the adaptation of "The Play's the Thing," born in Guildford, England, in 1881, and educated at Dulwich College, joined the staff of the London *Globe* when he left college and succeeded to the editorship of the "By the Way" column in that periodical. He came to America and was dramatic critic of *Vanity Fair* when he took to writing for the theatre. His first play, written in collaboration with John Stapleton, was "A Gentleman of Leisure." His output was rather steady from then on and he gained fame when he collaborated with Guy Bolton on a series of musical comedies including "Have a Heart," "Leave It to Jane," "Oh, Boy" and "Oh, Lady, Lady." He has written many short stories for *The Saturday Evening Post* and the magazines. "The Play's the Thing" was his first adaptation, and was followed by "Her Cardboard Lover."

"The Road to Rome." Comedy in three acts by Robert Emmet Sherwood. Copyright, 1926, by the author. Copyrighted and published, 1927, by Charles Scribners' Sons, New York.

Robert Emmet Sherwood is one of a small group of distinguished playwrights who can point with pardonable pride to the fact that his first play was a success. His first play to be produced, at least. He may have practiced on several others, but if so he has not publicly confessed. Mr. Sherwood having been born, 1896, in New Rochelle, which is no more than forty-five minutes from Broadway on the better trains, got his A.B. from Harvard in 1918 and took naturally to writing. He was dramatic editor and special contributor to *Vanity Fair* in 1919-20, and since 1920 has been associate editor and editor of *Life*. He also looks after the moving picture reviews for that weekly and writes a syndicated weekly article on the latest moving pictures. In 1922-23 he edited a companion volume to "The Best Plays" called "The Best Moving Pictures of 1922-23." He is married and lives in Manhattan.

"The Silver Cord." Drama in three acts by Sidney Howard. Copyright, 1926, by the author. Published and copyrighted, 1927, by Charles Scribners' Sons, New York.

Sidney Howard, a Californian in his early thirties, established himself as a playwright by winning the Pulitzer prize offered for the best American play produced during the year 1924. This was "They Knew What They Wanted," produced by the Theatre Guild, and included in the 1924-25 issue of "The Best Plays." This year he further distinguished himself by selling the Guild two plays, "The Silver Cord" and "Ned McCobb's Daughter." These were added to the repertory of that organization within a few weeks of each other and both were popularly acclaimed. Mr.

Howard is another of the successful playwrights who studied with Professor Baker at Harvard, and he has done his bit of newspaper reporting. He is the author of many magazine stories and a novel, "The Labor Spy."

"The Cradle Song." Drama in two acts by Gregorio Martinez Sierra. Adapted by John Garrett Underhill. Copyrighted, 1915-17-19-21, by the adapter. Published and copyrighted, 1922, by E. P. Dutton & Co.

G. Martinez Sierra is the most prominent of present-day writers for the Spanish theatre. He was born in Madrid in 1881, and educated at the University of Madrid. Out of school he turned first to story writing, publishing, under the chaperonage of Jacinto Benevente, a book entitled "El Poema del Trabajo" ("The Song of Labor"). He followed this with several volumes of prose poems, and in 1904 the first of his novels, "The Humble Truth," was published. In 1899 Benevente had organized the Spanish Art Theatre and young Sierra joined with him, playing many parts in the semi-professional productions. It was not until nearly ten years later that he turned to playwriting, and not until 1911 that he achieved a definite success with "The Cradle Song." This play, which has been freely translated, was given a few matinée performances in English by Augustin Duncan some years ago, but not until Eva Le Gallienne included it in her Civic Theatre repertory this season did it attract attention. The program acknowledges Señora Maria Martinez Sierra as part author of the play. During the season of 1926-27 Señor Sierra, who has succeeded to the direction of the Spanish Art Theatre, brought his company to New York for a fortnight's repertory. They were on their way home to Spain, following a tour of South American cities.

"Daisy Mayme." Comedy in three acts by George Kelly. Copyright, 1926, by the author. Copyrighted and published, 1927, by Little, Brown & Co., Boston.

George Kelly is also a frequent and valued contributor to "The Best Plays" collection. His "Show-off" was included in the 1923-24 volume and his "Craig's Wife," the Pulitzer prize winner in 1925-26, was a feature of last year's book. He is, as therein stated, a Philadelphian approaching his middle thirties. He was for years a successful actor on, and a successful writer of sketches for, the vaudeville stage. Since turning to the writing of long plays he has produced "The Torchbearers," "The Show-off," "Craig's Wife" and "Daisy Mayme."

"In Abraham's Bosom." Drama in seven scenes by Paul Green. Copyright, 1926, by the author. Copyrighted and published, 1927, by Robert M. McBride & Co., New York.

Paul Green, winner of the Pulitzer prize for having written what the committee of awards decided was the best American drama of 1926, is a true son of the South. He was born on a farm near Lillington, N. C., March 17, 1894, grew up a farmer's son, working during the summer and getting a little schooling in the winter. He was graduated from the Buie Creek academy in 1914, and taught a country school for two years. He was admitted to the University of North Carolina in 1916, and enlisted in the army in 1917. He served as a private, corporal, sergeant and sergeant-major with the 105th Engineers, 30th division, and was later made a second lieutenant. He went back to the University in 1919 and was graduated in 1921. He later did graduate work at Cornell and became a member of the faculty of his alma mater. Two volumes of his plays, "Lonesome Road" and "The Lord's Will," were published in 1925.

# PLAYS PRODUCED IN NEW YORK

## June 15, 1926—June 15, 1927

## THE MAN FROM TORONTO

### (28 performances)

Comedy in three acts by Douglas Murray. Produced by Bannister and Powell, in association with Miller and Goldreyer, at the Selwyn Theatre, New York, June 17th, 1926.

Cast of characters—

| | |
|---|---|
| Martha | Peg Entwistle |
| Robert | Gavin Muir |
| Mrs. Calthorpe | Beatrice Hendricks |
| Mrs. Hubbard | Marion Stephenson |
| Minnie | Mona Hungerford |
| Mr. Priestly | George Graham |
| Fergis Wimbush | Curtis Cooksey |
| Ada | Lota Sanders |
| Ruth Wimbush | Ethel Martin |

Acts I, II and III.—Mrs. Calthorpe's Summer Cottage, Teignmouth, Devonshire, England.

Staged by Albert Bannister.

Mrs. Calthorpe, still young and attractive, is, by the terms of a rich man's will, given in marriage to Fergis Wimbush, a large he-person of Canada. When Fergis comes to call Mrs. Calthorpe pretends she is her own parlor maid. She wants to have a look at him. He falls in love with her and is ready to give up his share of the fortune to marry her. Which he doesn't have to do.

## ZIEGFELD'S REVUE

### ("No Foolin'")

### (108 performances)

Revue in two acts. Music by Rudolf Friml; lyrics by Gene Buck, Irving Cæsar and James Hanley; tableaux by Ben Ali

Haggin. Produced by Florenz Ziegfeld at the Globe Theatre, New York, June 24th, 1926.

Principals engaged—

| | |
|---|---|
| James Barton | Rae Dooley |
| Andrew Tombes | Louise Brown |
| Charles King | Edna Leedom |
| Irving Fisher | Beth Berri |
| Lew Christy | Polly Walker |
| Arthur (Bugs) Baer | Peggy Fears |
| Moran and Mack | Claire Luce |
| Genesko | Mary Jane |
| Yacht Club Entertainers | Greta Nissen |
| George Moeser | Helen O'Shea |
| Victor Munro | Barbara Newberry |
| Owen Harvey | Yvonne Occent |
| | Kay English |

Staged by Florenz Ziegfeld and John Boyle.


## MY MAGNOLIA

### (4 performances)

All-colored revue in two acts. Book by Alex C. Rogers and Eddie Hunter; music by C. Luckey Roberts; lyrics by Alex C. Rogers. Produced by Walter Campbell at the Mansfield Theatre, New York, July 8th, 1926.

Cast of characters—

| | |
|---|---|
| Peggy Switch | Hilda Rogers |
| Harvey | Paul Bass |
| Jodey | Percy Colston |
| Mr. Workem | Lionel Monagas |
| Henry Upson (Oof Dah) | Dink Stewart |
| Jasper Downson | Barrington Carter |
| Johnny Page | George Randol |
| Chef | Claude Lawson |
| Dusty Snow | Alberta Perkins |
| Sherman (Head Porter) | Eddie Hunter |
| Jenny | Estelle Floyd |
| Widow Love | Lena Sanford Roberts |
| Grenadine | Mabel Gant |
| Magnolia | Catherine Parker |

Acts I and II.—In and Around Harlem's "Black Belt," New York, and New Orleans.

Staged by the Authors.

A series of colored sketches and specialties strung on a thin thread of story.

## THE BLONDE SINNER

(173 performances)

Farce with music in three acts by Leon DeCosta. Produced by Musicomedies, Inc., at the Cort Theatre, New York, July 14th, 1926.

Cast of characters—

George Hemmingworth..............................Ralph Bunker
Betty Hemmingworth...............................Enid Markey
Flash Pinkney.....................................Ruth Stevens
Adonis Mulberry..................................Clif Heckinger
Jack Conelly....................................Harold De Becker
Alfred Bird.....................................Russell Morrison
Ida.............................................Marjorie Gateson
Mike Reilly.........................................Matt Hanley
Alexander Homer.................................Frank Kingdon
James Manton....................................Howard St. John
Charleston Maid....................................Margy Lane

Acts I, II and III.—Hemmingworths' Living Room in an Exclusive Manor in Long Island, N. Y.

Staged by Edwin Vail.

The Hemmingworths, renting a cottage at the seashore, take in a lot of comic boarders to help reduce the overhead. Search for a certain blonde co-respondent, with suspicion landing on Mrs. Hemmingworth, provides the complications.

## HONEST LIARS

(96 performances)

Farce in three acts by Robert Weenolsen and Sherrill Webb. Produced by George MacFarlane at the Sam H. Harris Theatre, New York, July 19th, 1926.

Cast of characters—

Minnie.......................................Margaret Walker
Dr. Harold Stoddard..........................Alfred Kappeler
Mrs. Patty Stoddard...........................Kathleen Lowry
Dr. Sherwood................................Ainsworth Arnold
Helen Sherwood..............................Adelaide Rondelle
Miss Smee.....................................Harriet Harbaugh
Mr. Bunne..........................................Neil Pratt
Dickie Chambers.............................Robert Woolsey
Red Mike...........................................Jay Wilson
Tom.........................................Ralph Whittleweed
Aloyus..........................................Vincent Strain

Acts I, II and III.—In the Sherwood Sanitarium, a privately owned hospital in the Suburbs of Philadelphia.

Staged by Frank Smithson.

Fun in a sanitarium which includes among its patients a slightly demented comedian. A patented anesthetic machine permits the disposal of troublesome characters at any time. An eloping pair, escaping from a raided roadhouse, are considerably embarrassed to discover a pair of abandoned twins on the rear seat.

## BARE FACTS OF 1926

### (107 performances)

Revue in two acts. Sketches by Stuart Hamill; lyrics by Henry Myers; music by Charles M. Schwab. Produced by Kathleen Kirkwood, in association with Murray Phillips, at the Triangle Theatre, New York, July 16, 1926.

Principals engaged—

Rupert Lucas
Micjael Burroy
Joseph Battle
Stephen Draper
Courtenay Travers
Mel Tyler
Frank Marshall
    Staged by Kathleen Kirkwood.

Mary Doerr
Roberta Pierre
Nina Navarre
Lorette Hurley
Amey Steere
Lucy Parker
Sydney Haygooni

## PYRAMIDS

### (32 performances)

Drama in a prologue and three acts by Samuel Ruskin Golding. Produced by Ramsey Wallace and Frank Martins at the George M. Cohan Theatre, New York, July 19th, 1926.

Cast of characters—

Martin Van Cott................................Charles Waldron
Joan Amory....................................Carroll McComas
Muriel Rankin....................................Madeline Grey
Cooper Rankin.................................Donald Campbell
Robert Amory........................................Roy Gordon
Neil Gilroy...........................................Guy Milham
Ushikibo.....................................Harry D. Southard
Nolan.......................................Robert W. Lawrence
Ferguson .........................................James Barrett
Inspector Farrell.................................Carlton Brickert
    Prologue—Fifth Avenue. Act I.—Amsterdam Avenue. Acts II and III.—Madison Avenue.
    Staged by Priestly Morrison.

Robert Amory, a young corporation lawyer, having an expensive wife, gambles with his employer's money, hoping to buy her jewels. Caught, the employer, Martin Van Cott, offers to let Amory off in trade for Mrs. Amory's affections. Mrs. Amory indignantly spurns the offer, but later agrees to live with Van Cott if he will get her husband a pardon. Van Cott works rather to keep Amory in jail. Amory escapes, there is a shot, Van Cott is dead and everybody suspects the Jap butler, who also liked Mrs. Amory.

## AMERICANA

### (224 performances)

Musical revue by J. P. McEvoy. Music by Con Conrad and Henry Souvaine; special numbers by George Gershwin, Philip Charig, Ira Gershwin and Morrie Ryskind. Produced by Richard Herndon at the Belmont Theatre, New York, July 26, 1926.

Principals engaged—

| | |
|---|---|
| Roy Atwell | Maryon Dale |
| Lew Brice | Roberta Bellinger |
| Tom Button | Betty Compton |
| Charles Butterworth | Harriette Burke |
| Edgar Gardner | Georgia Ingram |
| | Arline Gardner |

Staged by Allen Dinehart and Larry Ceballos.

## NO MORE WOMEN

### (6 performances)

Comedy in three acts by Samuel Shipman and Neil Twomey. Produced by Schwab and Mandel at the Ambassador Theatre, New York, August 3, 1926.

Cast of characters—

| | |
|---|---|
| Mel Hardy | John Marston |
| Dick Rogers | Charles Ritchie |
| Wah-No-Tee | James La Curto |
| Nee-a-Tah | Mildred Brown |
| Lorna Morton | Nana Bryant |
| Nancy | Mildred McLeod |
| Rufus R. Ralston | O. J. Vanasse |
| Bill Slade | Charles Bickford |

Acts I, II and III.—Living Room of Mel Hardy's Lodge, Cody, Wyoming.

Staged by Edgar MacGregor.

Mel Hardy, hating women after having been jilted by Lorna Morton, establishes a misogynist's camp in the woods. In drifts Nancy, a bar'foot waif, whose father beats her. Following Nancy is Bill Slade, a rough Western Petruchio, who has bought the

girl for $500.   Hardy protects the girl by diverting Bill's atten-
tion to Lorna Morton, the vamp, who captures his fancy.


## NIC NAX OF 1926

### (13 performances)

Musical revue in two acts.  Words by Paul W. Porter, Matt
Kennedy and Roger Gray; music by Gitz Rice and Werner
Janssen.  Produced by George Mooser at the Cort Theatre, New
York, August 2, 1926.

Principals engaged—

| | |
|---|---|
| Nancy Gibbs | Gitz Rice |
| Irene Olsen | Frederick Santley |
| Katherine Witchie | Roger Gray |
| Estelle Hunt | Ralph Riggs |
| Suzanne Bennett | Harry Short |
| Lorraine Sherwood | Sam Summers |
| Helen Wehrle | Nat Nazarro, Jr. |

Staged by Paul W. Porter and Jack Conners.


## MY COUNTRY

### (48 performances)

Comedy in three acts by William J. Perlman.  Produced by
Independent Producing Company at the Chanin's 46th Street
Theatre, New York, August 9, 1926.

Cast of characters—

Robert Van Dorn ...............................Frederick Burton
Julia..........................................Louise Randolph
Alice..........................................Marguerite Mosier
Bob ...........................................Earl House
Nathan Blumberg................................Lee Kohlmar
Mollie ........................................Pola Carter
Lester ........................................Roy R. Bucklee
Frank Palmieri.................................Joseph B. Verdi
Marianna......................................Erin O'Brien-Moore
Patrick Mulcahy...............................Eddie O'Connor
    Acts I, II and III.—Living Room at Van Dorn's, Suburb of New
York.
    Staged by Charles Judels.

Robert Van Dorn, seven-generation American from old Dutch
stock, refuses to accept his country as the melting-pot of the
world.  When, with her mother's consent, his daughter Alice wants
to marry her next-door chum, Lester Blumberg, Van Dorn rebels
and quits home.  They get him back for his own silver wedding

anniversary, however, and he is made to see that America is America, whatever he may think of his neighbors.


## LOOSE ANKLES

### (168 performances)

Comedy in three acts by Sam Janney. Produced by Brock Pemberton at the Biltmore Theatre, New York, August 16, 1926.

Cast of characters—

| | |
|---|---|
| Betty Brent | Carlotta Irwin |
| Ann Harper | Kathleen Comegys |
| Frances Drayton | Leonore Sorsby |
| Agnes | Jeanne De Me |
| Jasper | Kenneth Lawton |
| Harvey | Fred House |
| Aunt Sarah | Ethel Martin |
| Jessica | Barbara Gray |
| Ethel | Moon Carroll |
| Aunt Katherine | Lavinia Shannon |
| Major Ainsworth Elling | George W. Barbier |
| Andy Barton | Osgood Perkins |
| Terry Francis | Charles D. Brown |
| Linton Hawkins | Frank Lyon |
| Gil Barry | Harold Vermilyea |
| J. Esmelton Stotes | Robert Lucius Cook |

Acts I, II and III.—Ann Harper's Home in Gramercy Park and a Furnished Room in the Fifties, New York.
Staged by Brock Pemberton.

Ann Harper, forced to marry if she is to get the money, according to the terms of another of those wills, determines to stage a scandal by way of reprisal. She advertises for a willing eloper and draws Gil Barry, a nice boy but in the clutch of circumstances and a trio of grafting dancing sheiks with whom he lives. Loving Ann, Gil refuses to be a party to any scheme that would cloud her name. Which, as it turns out, he doesn't have to do, seeing Ann loves him, too.


## THE LITTLE SPITFIRE

### (200 performances)

Comedy in three acts by Myron C. Fagan. Produced by B. F. Witbeck at the Cort Theatre, New York, August 16, 1926.

Cast of characters—

| | |
|---|---|
| Marty Gorman | Russell Mack |
| Gertrude Gorman | Eileen Wilson |
| "Gypsy" | Sylvia Field |

Frank Gorman.................................Andrew Lawlor, Jr.
James Ralston................................Raymond Van Sickle
Peter Ralston.................................A. H. Van Buren
Mrs. Ralston............................Theresa Maxwell Conover
Patricia Longworth...............................Peggy Allenby
Stanley Markham................................Dudley Hawley
Brooks..........................................Frank Thomas
A Bell Boy........................................Walter Glass
    Act I.—A Suite in a New York Hotel. Act II.—Home of the
Ralstons and Canoe Place Inn. Act III.—The Gorman Apartment
in the Bronx.
    Staged by A. H. Van Buren.

Gypsy is a chorus girl who marries James Ralston, a son of
wealth whose Southampton family is of the stage society type
suffering from tilted noses and receding chins. James is pretty
square, even after his relatives make it appear that Gypsy has
returned to her old admirer, Stanley Markham. He lets Gypsy
go back to the chorus, but he goes after her long before she is
able to land a job.


# SUNSHINE

## (15 performances)

Comedy in three acts by Henry C. White. Produced by Paul
M. Trebitsch at the Lyric Theatre, New York, August 17, 1926.

Cast of characters—

Laffy Putnam.................................Hobart Cavanaugh
Hettie Perkins..................................Georgia Harvey
Charlie Wood.....................................Robert Craig
Emily Whitaker................................Eleanor Griffith
David Whitaker....................................O. P. Heggie
John B. Florham................................Byron Beasley
Patience Dusenberry...................................Ruth Lee
    Acts I and III.—Dave Whitaker's Law Office, Abbeyville, Con-
necticut. Act II.—Dave Whitaker's Home.
    Staged by Victor Morley.

They call David Whitaker, country town lawyer, "Sunshine"
because he is so darned kindly. Which makes it hard for him the
day John B. Florham, the big perfumery man, walks into his
office and tells him the story of how he betrayed David's wife as
a girl and how David's daughter, Emily, is really the child of
that meeting out there on the Kansas prairies. David knows he
ought to kill Florham, but he just can't bring scandal on Emily.
They compromise and tell the girl the story as a bit of interesting
fiction. Thus she is forced to choose between them, without
really knowing for sure that she is the girl. She sticks with
David.

## THE HOME TOWNERS

(64 performances)

Farce comedy in three acts by George M. Cohan. Produced at the Hudson Theatre, New York, August 23, 1926.

Cast of characters—

| | |
|---|---|
| "Vic" Arnold | William Elliott |
| P. H. Bancroft | Robert McWade |
| Casey | William Walcott |
| "Waly" Calhoon | Chester Morris |
| Joe Roberts | Walter Plimmer, Jr. |
| Lottie Bancroft | Georgia Caine |
| Bell Boy | Spencer Bentley |
| Maid | Doris Freeman |
| Beth Calhoon | Peg Entwistle |
| Mort Calhoon | Ben Johnson |
| Nellie Calhoon | Florence Earle |
| Stone | Walter Calligan |

Acts I and III.—Arnold's New York Apartment. Act II.—A Suite at the Waldorf.

Staged by John Meehan; supervised by George Cohan.

Vic Arnold, having left South Bend as a boy and made a couple of million dollars in New York, decides to marry Beth Calhoon, young daughter of Park Avenue, and sends for his old pal, P. H. Bancroft, to act as best man. Bancroft, cynical, suspicious and mean-spirited in the Main street fashion, suspects Vic of being the victim of the usual New York grafters and insists on exposing the Calhoons. As it happens he is all wrong, but before Arnold can prove it to him the romance stands in serious danger of being wrecked. Then Bancroft sneaks ashamedly back to South Bend, convinced that not all the 6,000,000 New Yorkers are crooks.

## HENRY—BEHAVE

(96 performances)

Farce comedy by Lawrence Langner. Produced by Gustav Blum at the Bayes Theatre, New York, August 23, 1926.

Cast of characters—

| | |
|---|---|
| Susan | Violet Hill |
| Henry Wilton | John Cumberland |
| Kate Wilton | Justina Wayne |
| Dick Wilton | Elisha Cook, Jr. |
| Blanche Wilton | Gail De Hart |
| Mrs. Huxley | Carrie Weller |
| Alton B. Stevens | Beresford Lovett |

```
Westcott P. Bennett..........................Edward G. Robinson
Evelyn Hollis.......................................Gladys Lloyd
Arthur Courtney..............................Waldo Edwards
Archibald Musgrove.........................Charles De Bevoise
Adelaide Musgrove................................Irene Young
Beatrice Beamish..................................Lorraine Lally
Anthony Alexander................................Pat O'Brien
George..........................................Jacob Zollinger
Frank Adair.....................................James Newcombe
Geraldine Tussant.................................Mary Walsh
Clement Courtney............................Walton Butterfield
Lavinia Courtney...........................Charlyne Courtland
Policeman.........................................Darrell Starnes
```
    Acts I and III.—The Dining-room in the Wilton Home, Melton-on-
the-Sound, L. I.  Act II.—The Melton Yacht Club.
    Staged by Gustav Blum.

Henry Wilton, a Long Island realtor, is fearfully strict. Won't let his grown children stay out late. Won't have any liquor at the golf club. Frowns upon intimate dancing. Then he is hit by a taxi and loses all memory of the last twenty years. Acting as he did as a boy, he cuts up scandalously with the girls and drinks himself tight with the boys. Bumped back to normality he decides to be a more liberal citizen and run for congress.

## EARL CARROLL VANITIES

### (303 performances)

Revue in two acts; lyrics and music by Grace Henry and Morris Hamilton; sketches by Stanley Rauh and Wm. A. Grew. Produced by Earl Carroll at the Earl Carroll Theatre, New York, August 24, 1926.

### Principals engaged—

| | |
|---|---|
| Julius Tannen | Yvette Rugel |
| Harry Delf | Dorothy Knapp |
| Robert Rhodes | Florence Brady |
| Mack and Moran | Thelma White |
| Charles Dale | Magda de Bries |
| Joe Smith | Bernice Speer |
| Bernard Dudley | Hazel Bowman |
| M. De Jari | Bebe Stanton |
| Norman Frescott | Isabel Mohr |
| Gilbert Wells | Patterson Twins |

    Staged by Earl Carroll.  Dances by David Bennett.

## THE GHOST TRAIN

(61 performances)

Mystery drama in three acts by Arnold Ridley. Produced by A. H. Woods and Arch Selwyn at the Eltinge Theatre, New York, August 25, 1926.

Cast of characters—

| | |
|---|---|
| Richard Winthrop | Robert Rendel |
| Elsie Winthrop | Gypsy O'Brien |
| Saul Hodgkin | Walter Wilson |
| Charles Murdock | John Williams |
| Peggy Murdock | Claudette Colbert |
| Miss Bourne | Gladys Ffolliott |
| Teddie Deakin | Eric Blore |
| Julia Price | Isobel Elsom |
| Herbert Price | Arthur Barry |
| John Sterling | Henry Mowbray |
| Jackson | Arthur J. Wood |

Acts I, II and III.—Waiting-room of the Station at Clear Vale Junction, Near Rockland, Maine.

Staged by Norman Houston.

A party of travelers, held up by a wreck, miss their train connections and are forced to spend a night in a haunted railway station up near Rockland, Me. The station agent tells them the story of the ghost train that periodically comes out of nowhere, rushes past the station with all lights blazing, and disappears. To look on it means certain death. Many eerie things happen in the dark, the train makes its scheduled trip and everybody is properly scared. Then the exposé. It is a device of crooks to keep the law hounds away.

## THE DONOVAN AFFAIR

(128 performances)

Drama in three acts by Owen Davis. Produced by Albert Lewis, in association with Donald Davis, at the Fulton Theatre, New York, August 30, 1926.

Cast of characters—

| | |
|---|---|
| Carney | Joseph Robison |
| John Killain | Paul Harvey |
| Jean Rankin | Miriam Doyle |
| David Cornish | Niles Welch |
| Lydia Rankin | Eleanor Woodruff |
| Peter Rankin | Robert T. Haines |
| Ben Holt | Chas. C. Wilson |
| Anne Holt | Renita Randolph |
| Ruth Linsey | Phœbe Foster |

Neil Linsey........................................Robert Hudson
Horace Carter.....................................Edwin Stanley
Nelson..............................................Ray Collins
Mary.............................................Georgie Lee Hall
Professor Donovan...............................Edwin Maxwell
Mrs. Dowd........................................Merle Stanton
Dr. Morris..........................................Frank Taylor
Roberts...........................................Jefferson Hall
　　Acts I, II and III.—In the Library of Peter Rankin in West-
chester.
　　Staged by Albert Lewis.

The night the Donovans gave a dinner Jack Donovan was
boasting of the luminosity of his turquoise ring. They turned
out the lights to see the ring shine and when they turned them on
Donovan was sprawled over the table dead. Some one had
slipped the game knife between his ribs. Then it transpires that
the ring was supposed to wield a wicked influence over women
and several in the cast who had suffered wanted to be rid of
the ring and its owner. One of them did the murder. But not
any of those you most suspect.


## SERVICE FOR TWO

### (24 performances)

Comedy in three acts by Martin Flavin. Produced by A. L.
Erlanger at the Gaiety Theatre, New York, August 30, 1926.

Cast of characters—

Edith..............................................Florence Fair
Sam ..............................................Hugh Wakefield
Peggy ........................................... Marion Coakley
Aunt Augusta....................................Grace Griswold
Katie..................................................Lida Kane
A Page .............................................. Ross Hertz
A Waiter........................................Edward Jephson
A Guest...........................................Harry Neville
　　Acts I, II and III.—In the Hotel Alabaster, New York.
　　Staged by B. Iden Payne.

Sam and Edith, married in England, where Sam is the Earl of
Bagshote, are on their way to western America. They stop at
the Hotel Alabaster, New York. Peggy from the cinemas discovers Sam's name on the register and that his room is next to
hers. Having flirted desperately with him in the old days, Peg
hopes to renew the relations, gets Sam into her room, feeds him
Scotch, and finally turns him over to his startled bride for what
he is, a silly old thing.

## THE ADORABLE LIAR

(32 performances)

Comedy in three acts by Roy Briant and Harry Durant. Produced by Edgar Selwyn at the 49th Street Theatre, New York, August 30, 1926.

Cast of characters—

| | |
|---|---|
| Rupert Barry | Henry Stephenson |
| Josephine Barry | Mary Horne Morrison |
| Elton Moors | Tom Wise |
| Joyce Barry | Beatrice Blinn |
| Mark Roque | William B. Mack |
| Karith Barry | Dorothy Burgess |
| Alan Davis | Eric Dressler |
| Tansy Roque | Nelly Neil |

Acts I and III.—Living Room of Rupert Barry's Bungalow in a Little Florida Village. Act II.—The Girls' Bedroom.

Staged by Edgar Selwyn.

Karith Barry is 17 and incurably imaginative. Romance is her life, and she awaits the coming of her Sir Galahad on a white steed. As it happens he comes in a white auto and is a Florida realtor named Alan Davis. And he is more or less seriously pursued by an eager young vamp named Tansy Roque, who swears he has made her promises. Karith, determined to save Alan, and glowing with the thought that she may compromise herself, inveigles him into her room at midnight, is caught and suffers several minor humiliations. But she gets her realtor.

## POTASH AND PERLMUTTER, DETECTIVES

(47 performances)

Comedy in three acts by Montague Glass and Jules Eckert Goodman. Produced by A. H. Woods at the Ritz Theatre, New York, August 31, 1926.

Cast of characters—

| | |
|---|---|
| Babette Imerglick | Annette Hoffman |
| Henry D. Feldman | Max Waizman |
| Kent J. Goldstein | Hartley Power |
| Rosie Potash | Mathilde Cottrelly |
| Abe Potash | Ludwig Satz |
| Mawruss Perlmutter | Robert Leonard |
| Tegner | Edwin Walter |
| George McAdam | Charles Gotthold |
| Jean McAdam | Hope Sutherland |
| Hedges | Robert Vivian |
| Hal Mason | Brandon Peters |
| Henry Dubois | Harry Hanlon |

```
Letty..........................................Patricia O'Connor
Mrs. McAdam...................................Isabel O'Madigan
Cunningham.......................................Allen Jenkins
Sigmund Fried......................................Arthur Dunn
      Act I.—The Coplin Detective Agency.  Act II.—Home of George
McAdam, Nohampton, L. I.  Act III.—The Jail at Nohampton.
      Staged by Bertram Harrison.
```

Abe and Mawruss are named as executors of the Coplin Detective Agency and induced to carry on the business. But the first jewelry robbery they investigate gets them into jail, charged with the possession of the gems. They talk and laugh themselves out of this predicament by 11 P.M. evenings and 5 P.M. matinées.


## SHE COULDN'T SAY NO

### (71 performances)

Farce in three acts by B. M. Kaye. Produced by A. E. and R. R. Riskin at the Booth Theatre, New York, August 31, 1926.

Cast of characters—

```
Walter Turnbull..................................Ralph Kellard
Christopher Morton...............................Chester Clute
Alice Hinsdale..................................Florence Moore
Eddie Page........................................Frank Beaston
Eliphalet Potter..................................Joseph Dailey
Mary Hudson........................................Helen Spring
Hank Smith........................................Louis Haines
Ely Sweezey.......................................John A. Regan
Ezra Pine...........................................Paul Porter
Pansy Hooper.....................................Fay Courteney
Judge Jenkins......................................Walter Jones
Clerk of Court.......................................Ollor Doyll
      Act I.—Law Office of Turnbull and Johnson, New York.  Act
II.—Palace Hotel, Kerricksville, N. Y.  Act III.—The Court Room,
Kerricksville, N. Y.
      Staged by Rollo Lloyd.
```

Alice Hinsdale, a stenographer in the office of Walter Turnbull, secretly loves Walter and wants to help him. While he is away from the office she conspires with his other friends to accept a breach of promise case the winning of which will mean much to him. She goes upstate to try the case and discovers Walter on the opposite side. She goes through with the burlesque trial and wins. Explanations fix everything.

## IF I WAS RICH

(92 performances)

Play in three acts by William Anthony McGuire. Produced by William Anthony McGuire at the Mansfield Theatre, New York, September 2, 1926.

Cast of characters—

| | |
|---|---|
| Jimmy Sterling | Joe Laurie, Jr. |
| Henry King | Al Ochs |
| R. Murray Pembrook | Joseph Kilgour |
| William Dunroy | Ray Walburn |
| Elizabeth McCue | Ruth Donnelly |
| John Splevin | Charles Dow Clark |
| Ruth Sterling | Mildred McLeod |
| Muriel Martin | Lu McGuire |
| Harold Rogers | G. D. Byron |
| Beatrice Van Ness | Mildred Lillard |
| Mildred Dellham | Vola Price |
| Tillie | Dorothy Fenron |
| Mrs. Pembrook | Isabelle Randolph |
| Peggy Burton | May McCabe |
| George Hildreth | Fred Irving Lewis |
| Lieutenant Spaulding | John T. Doyle |
| Richard McDermott | Joseph Baird |
| Burke | Howard Hull Gibson |

Acts I and III.—James Sterling's Apartment. Act II.—The Pembrook Home on Long Island.

Staged by William Anthony McGuire.

Jimmy Sterling is what his friends describe as a great little guy, a hard-working shipping clerk at $40 a week. Ruth Sterling is a well-meaning wife, but extravagant. Success, she thinks, consists in tricking people into thinking you are something you are not. Finally she forces Jimmy to try it and he lies himself into a comic contact with a rich man and his society friends. When exposure comes Jimmy is whipped for half an act and Mrs. Sterling is revealed as the would-be mistress of a man she works for. Then they agree to play the game of life on the level.

## SOUR GRAPES

(40 performances)

Comedy in three acts by Vincent Lawrence. Produced by William Harris, Jr., at the Longacre Theatre, New York, September 6, 1926.

Cast of characters—

| | |
|---|---|
| James Milburn | Frank Conroy |
| Phillips | James Kearney |

Alice Overton ........................................ Alice Brady
John Overton ........................................ John Halliday
Marjorie Lawson ................................... Flora Sheffield
    Acts I, II and III.—A Room in the Overtons' House.

John and Alice Overton, much in love when they married, have grown restless and subconsciously indifferent to each other. James Milburn, engaged to Marjorie Lawson, both mutual friends of the Overtons, suddenly declares his passion for Alice Overton and she admits her liking for him.   They agree to face Overton and Marjorie, confess their love, ask a release from all obligations and get married.   The arrangement is all right with Overton, but Marjorie, who has given herself to Milburn, is facing motherhood. Learning this Milburn promptly accepts his fate and marries Marjorie.   Which leaves the Overtons, their indifference confessed, facing an unhappy future.   It is John's suggestion that they try the game of pretending a love neither feels in the hope that the old love may be revived.   Which they do.


## CASTLES IN THE AIR

### (160 performances)

Musical comedy in three acts.   Book and lyrics by Raymond W. Peck; musical score by Percy Wenrich; dances by John Boyle. Produced by James W. Elliott at the Selwyn Theatre, New York, September 6, 1926.

Cast of characters—

Amos ........................................ Robert Williamson
Annie Moore ...................................... Joyce White
George Sedgwick ................................. Allen Waterous
Philip Rodman .................................... Stanley Forde
Mme. Joujou Durant ............................. Claire Madjette
Evelyn Devine ................................... Vivienne Segal
Count Draga ..................................... Richard Farrell
Monty Blair .................................... Bernard Granville
John Brown .................................... J. Harold Murray
General Slodak ................................... Walter Edwin
Kemlar ......................................... William Hasson
The Chancellor .................................. Gregory Ratoff
Lieutenant ...................................... Edward Gorman
The Queen Regent ................................ Thais Lawton
Ballet Dancer ................................. Mary Hutchinson
    Act I.—Evelyn's 21 Club, Westchester.   Act II.—The Castle.   Act III.—The Rodman Garden, Westchester.   August.
    Staged by James W. Elliott.

Monty Blair and John Brown, out of college and on adventure bent, are touring Westchester County in a battered flivver.   Inquiring for a roadhouse they are directed by a joker to a private society club, where Monty, being a cutup, introduces John as the exiled prince of Latavia. The boys don't fool Philip Rodman any, but when his rich ward, Evelyn Devine, evinces an interest in John, after she has indicated a fancy for title hunting, Rodman decides to rent a Latavian castle and speed the false romance to cure her. In Latavia, with everything ready for the exposure and arrest of John, he turns out to be a real prince after all, and later there is much joy and merrymaking.

## WHAT'S THE USE

### (9 performances)

Comedy in four acts by Pauline Fain. Produced by Fain Pro-ductions, Inc., at the Princess Theatre, New York, September 6, 1926.

Cast of characters—

| | |
|---|---|
| Mrs. Ginsberg | Dora Kashinsky |
| Mrs. Brown | Eleanor Warren |
| Rita Ginsberg | Yvonne Manon |
| Mr. Salen | Herman Hershberg |
| Mrs. Salen | Helen Gropper |
| William Salen | Harry R. Irving |
| Elsie Salen | Lillian Shrewsbury |
| Dr. Leonard Salen | Santos Orteaga |
| Mary Field | Edna Mink |

Acts I, III and IV.—Mrs. Ginsberg's Flat on Washington Heights.
Act II.—Dr. Salen's Apartment.
Staged by Argyle Campbell.

William Salen marries Rita Ginsberg and treats her something fierce until the play's end, when he brings her a thousand dollars and announces that not only has he invented a new dance that is a riot, but that he also owns a night club.

## NO TRESPASSING

### (23 performances)

Comedy in three acts by John Hunter Booth. Produced by Hassard Short at the Sam H. Harris Theatre, New York, September 7, 1926.

Cast of characters—

| | |
|---|---|
| Edythe Warren | Josephine Drake |
| Tom Widdemer | W. E. Lawrence |
| Grace Hewitt | Diantha Pattison |
| Guy Warren | Edwin Nicander |
| Carol Widdemer | Juliette Day |

Zoe Galt..........................................Kay Johnson
Jack Truesdale...................................Charles Ritchie
Bassett.............................................Basil Smith
Bob Hewitt........................................Nicholas Joy
David Druce......................................Russell Hicks
    Acts I, II and III.—In the Long Island Home of the Hewitts.
    Staged by Hassard Short.

Bob Hewitt, meeting his old college mate, David Druce, on Broadway, invites him to spend the week-end at the Hewitt place down Long Island. David is a minister specializing in saving the souls of savages. The week-enders, full of cocktails, politely bait David, and Zoe Galt, most attractive of the unattached vamps, wagers she can bring about his fall by Monday. Her summer house campaign failing, Zoe invades David's sleeping rooms, and fails again. Then she denounces him as a churchly cheat, only to sue for his pardon next afternoon and ask him to marry and reform her. Which he, being in love, agrees to do.


## QUEEN HIGH

### (332 performances)

Musical comedy in three acts. Book by Laurence Schwab and B. G. De Sylva; music by Lewis E. Gensler; lyrics by B. G. De Sylva. Produced by Laurence Schwab at the Ambassador Theatre, New York, September 8, 1926.

Cast of characters—

T. Boggs Johns...................................Charles Ruggles
George Nettleton.................................Frank McIntyre
Richard Johns...................................Clarence Nordstrom
Jimmy.............................................Edwin Michaels
Jerry Vanderholt.................................John Rutherford
Polly Nettleton..................................Mary Lawlor
Mrs. Nellie Nettleton............................Helen Carrington
Florence Cole.....................................Luella Gear
Coddles.............................................Gaile Beverly
Patricia............................................June Odea
Kitty...............................................Barbara Grace
    Act I.—The Showroom of the Eureka Novelty Co. Acts II and
    III.—The Westchester Home of the Nettletons.
    Staged by Edgar McGregor and Sammy Lee.

T. Boggs Johns and George Nettleton, being associated in the garter and novelty business, quarrel and agree to leave the decision as to which shall run the business for a year to poker hands dealt cold. The loser, during the same period, must serve the winner as butler. Nettleton wins and Boggs is the comic butler for the next two acts.

## NUMBER 7

### (37 performances)

Drama in three acts by J. Jefferson Farjeon. Produced by Earl Carroll at the Times Square Theatre, New York, September 8, 1926.

Cast of characters—

| | |
|---|---|
| Eddie Scott | William Gregory |
| Gilbert Fordyce | J. W. Austin |
| Ben | Harry McNaughton |
| Rose Ackroyd | Lois Meredith |
| Nora | Eden Gray |
| Henry | Austin Fairman |
| Brant | Reginald Barlow |
| Ackroyd | Marshall Vincent |
| Smith | Fred Eric |

Acts I, II and III.—In an Untenanted House During a Thick Fog, in London.

Staged by Earl Carroll and Henry Stillman.

Gilbert Fordyce, investigating the mysterious goings on at the house known as No. 7, finds Ben, a comic sailor, loitering in the street and forces him into the house as a suspect. On the second floor they find a corpse, and before they are able to round up the band of crooks using the place as a get-away rendezvous, they have many wild experiences beloved of those auditors who squeal easily.

## TWO GIRLS WANTED

### (324 performances)

Comedy in three acts by Gladys B. Unger. Produced by John Golden at the Little Theatre, New York, September 9, 1926.

Cast of characters—

| | |
|---|---|
| Marianna Miller | Nydia Westman |
| Sarah Miller | Charlotte Denniston |
| Mrs. Gock | May Duryea |
| Miss Timoney | Mary Philips |
| Mrs. Delafield | Beverly Sitgreaves |
| Edna Delafield | Grace Menken |
| Dexter Wright | William Hanley |
| William Moody | Herbert Saunders |
| Philip Hancock | Frank Monroe |
| Jack Terry | Charles Laite |
| Michael | James C. Lane |
| Johnny | John Humphrey |

Act I.—Bedroom of Marianna and Sarah Miller at Mrs. Gock's Rooming House and the President's Room in the Office of the Hancock Equipment Company. Act II.—Mrs. Delafield's Country Home, Ardsley, N. Y.

Staged by Winchell Smith.

Marianna and Sarah Miller are in New York, living in a cheap rooming house and cooking their breakfasts in their trunk. Marianna is a stenographer and Sarah a clerk. Marianna meets and loves Dexter Wright, a broker, and when she learns that he is engaged to Edna Delafield is so hurt she agrees to go with Sarah and accept a job in a Westchester home, she to be second girl and Sarah the cook. It happens to be the home of Dexter Wright's fiancée, and Marianna has an unhappy time of it until she is able to help Dexter through a business crisis and learns that he never loved Edna anyhow.

## NAUGHTY RIQUETTE

### (88 performances)

Musical comedy in two acts. Book and lyrics by Harry B. Smith; adapted from the German of R. Schanzer and E. Welisch. Produced by the Messrs. Shubert at the Cosmopolitan Theatre, New York, September 13, 1926.

Cast of characters—

| | |
|---|---|
| Faverolle | Walter Armin |
| Alphonse La Fleur | George A. Schiller |
| Clarisse | Audrey Maple |
| Gaston Riviere | Alexander Gray |
| Simone | Connie Emerald |
| Yvette | Lenoria Spiro |
| Theophile Michu | Stanley Lupino |
| Bardou | Joseph Spree |
| Riquette Duval | Mitzi |
| Liane De Soucy | Mary Marlowe |
| Dupont | Oliver Hagan |
| Maurel | Peter Hawley |
| Abri-Dabri | Edward Basse |
| Lord Dillington | Oliver Hagan |
| Maitre d'Hotel | Joseph Spree |
| Prof. DuBose | Walter Armin |
| Dean | Sylvan Lee |
| Julie | Jane Moore |
| Colonel Latour | Oliver Hagan |
| Captain Duroc | Peter Hawley |

Act I.—Central Telephone Exchange, Paris. Acts II and III.—Lounge of the Hotel Sunbeam, Near Monte Carlo.
Staged by J. J. Shubert.

Riquette Duval, telephone operator, needs money quickly to send her sick brother to the seashore. To get it she agrees to act as the "fire screen" for Gaston Riviere, who wants to carry on with Clarisse La Fleur, a married woman. Riquette will pretend to be Gaston's travelling companion to divert suspicion from Clarisse. At Monte Carlo, however, Gaston discovers that it is Riquette he loves, and finally gets the thought over to her in a couple of songs.

## HENRY'S HAREM

(8 performances)

Farce comedy in three acts by Fred Ballard and Arthur Stern. Produced by The Playshop, Inc., at the Greenwich Village Theatre, New York, September 13, 1926.

The Haremers—

| | |
|---|---|
| Katherine | Joan Storm |
| Dolly | Belle Green |
| Polly | Ruth MacMullen |
| Edith | Beatrice Loring |
| Henry | Al Roberts |
| Ann | Olive Reeves-Smith |
| Jake | Earl Mayne |
| Jimmie | John Lewis |
| Danny | Burt Payne |
| Billy | Albert Ward |
| Casey | Edwin Vickery |
| Rainey | Robert McCarthy |

Acts I, II and III.—Henry's Harem, Atlantic City.

Henry has promised father that he will not marry until his three sisters are provided with mates. Falling in love with Ann, Henry wants to get married, and to hurry off the sisters gives a sort of engagement party, stimulates the interest of the visiting prospects by serving punch and finally tricks everybody into being engaged to somebody.

## JUST LIFE

(79 performances)

Drama in three acts by John Bowie. Produced by Jacob Oppenheimer at the Henry Miller Theatre, New York, Sept. 14, 1926.

Cast of characters—

| | |
|---|---|
| Meg Chase | Vivian Tobin |
| Dick Fellows | Norman Foster |
| Robert Henning | Boyd Marshall |
| Drusinda | Jane Burby |
| Gordon Chase | Clyde Fillmore |
| Grace Norton | Ethel Wilson |
| Florence Silsby | Elaine Ivans |
| Philip Post | Franklin Parker |
| Madame Bernice Chase | Marjorie Rambeau |
| Forbes | James A. Boshell |
| Eileen Hier | Lea Penman |
| Miss Austen | Mary Wall |

Acts I, II and III.—Drawing Room in the Park Avenue Apartment, New York, of Mr. and Mrs. Gordon Chase.

Staged by Oscar Eagle.

Mme. Bernice was once "the mocking bird of the century," but her voice went back on her and she settled down to Park Avenue domesticity with her husband, her daughter and her pearls. Husband cheated and Mme. Bernice sold the pearls to keep him out of jail. Then she went back to singing in the cheaper London concert halls. Returning home unexpectedly, she discovers her husband wrapped in the arms of his secretary and her daughter more or less on the loose. She divorces husband, sees daughter married and goes back to her operatic career.

## COUNTESS MARITZA

### (318 performances)

Musical play in three acts. Book and lyrics from the original of Julius Brammer and Alfred Grunwald by Harry B. Smith; music by Emmerich Kalman. Produced by the Messrs. Lee and J. J. Shubert at the Shubert Theatre, New York, September 18, 1926.

Cast of characters—

```
Nepomuk................................................Arthur Rogers
Count Tassilo Endrody............................Walter Woolf
Bela Torek......................................Louis E. Miller
Tscheko.........................................Hugh Chilvers
Lazlo............................................Arthur Geary
Manja............................................Odette Myrtil
Stefan...........................................Nat Wagner
Servant.........................................Frank Sinnott
Zingo..........................................Harry K. Morton
Countess Maritza................................Yvonne D'Arle
Lisa.............................................Vivian Hart
Prince Populescu................................George Hassell
First Officer....................................C. H. Tolman
Baron Koloman Szupan...........................Carl Randall
Freda........................................Marjorie Peterson
Princess Bozena Klopensheim.....................Florence Edney
     Prologue—Grand Salon in the Château of Count Tassilo Endrody.
Act I.—Garden of Countess Maritza's Château in a Balkan State.
Acts II and III.—Drawing Room of Countess Maritza's Château.
     Staged by J. J. Shubert.
```

Count Tassilo loves the Countess Maritza, but hesitates to tell her so for fear she will think him a fortune hunter. He stoops to conquer her by seeking a job as her overseer. Together they revel in duets and stolen love confessions until the countess grows suspicious as well as jealous and sends Tassilo away. When she discovers the truth about him she calls him back.

## BROADWAY

### (332 performances)

Drama in three acts by Philip Dunning and George Abbott. Produced by Jed Harris at the Broadhurst Theatre, New York, September 16, 1926.

Cast of characters—

| | |
|---|---|
| Nick Verdis | Paul Porcasi |
| Roy Lane | Lee Tracy |
| Lil Rice | Clare Woodbury |
| Katie | Ann Preston |
| Joe | Joseph Spurin-Calleia |
| Mazie Smith | Mildred Wall |
| Ruby | Edith Van Cleve |
| Pearl | Eloise Stream |
| Grace | Molly Ricardel |
| Ann | Constance Brown |
| "Billie" Moore | Sylvia Field |
| Steve Crandall | Robert Gleckler |
| Dolph | Henry Sherwood |
| "Porky" Thompson | William Foran |
| "Scar" Edwards | John Wray |
| Dan McCorn | Thomas Jackson |
| Benny | Frank Verigun |
| Larry | Millard Mitchell |
| Mike | Roy R. Lloyd |

Acts I, II and III.—In the Private Party Room of the Paradise Night Club, New York City.

Staged by Philip Dunning and George Abbott.

See page 32.

## KEPT

### (11 performances)

Comedy in three acts by Pierre Gendron. Produced by Chamberlain Brown at the Comedy Theatre, New York, September 17, 1926.

Cast of characters—

| | |
|---|---|
| Ruby | Emma Wise |
| Dr. Wilkins | Jack Bennett |
| Harold Russell | Edgar Henning |
| Lucille Manion | Valerie Valaire |
| Mary Dawn | Marie Curtis |
| Netty Estel | Minnie Dupree |
| Marjorie Norton | Lenita Lane |
| Norman Henderson | Robert Williams |
| Frank Fagin | Philip Heege |
| Vera Robins | Zola Talma |
| Frederic J. Norton | Edmund Elton |
| Wanda | Dorothy Estabrook |

Act I.—Old Colonial Inn, Danbury Corners. Acts II and III.—Norman's Apartment, New York City.

Staged by Ira Hards.

Netty Estel, come upon trying days in her middle years, is living in an old ladies' home when she finds Norman Henderson drunk and badly injured in an automobile smash-up. She nurses him back to sobriety and consciousness and when he proposes that she let him adopt her as a mother she agrees and goes happily to live with him in New York. All goes well until Norman gets drunk again and throws Netty out of his apartment at the suggestion of his mistress, Vera Robins. They are two kept women, insists this sweetheart, but only one of them is earning her keep. Sober again, Norman begs his way to Netty's forgiveness.

## SCOTCH MIST

(16 performances)

Comedy in three acts by Patrick Hastings. Produced by The Dramatists' Theatre, Inc., at the Klaw Theatre, New York, September 20, 1916.

Cast of characters—

```
Freddie Lansing...................................David Tearle
Mary Denvers..................................Rosalinde Fuller
Betty...........................................Lorna Lawrence
Alice...........................................Audrey Ridgwell
Claude Montague................................Harold Webster
Jonathan Waterhouse...............................Percy Moore
Sir Lawson Denvers.................................Fred Tiden
Merton..............................................Billy Hedges
David Campbell................................Philip Merivale
Elizabeth...........................................Carrie Glenn
        Act I.—In Sir Lawson Denvers' House, London.  Acts II and
III.—The Castle at Kinlochie, Scotland.
        Staged by Edward Childs Carpenter.
```

Mary, loved by Sir Lawson Denvers and David Campbell, chooses Sir Lawson and some time later, growing restless at home, regrets she had not taken David. Teasing David into paying some attention to her, he attacks her in his Scotch castle, turning over the lamp and bringing the matter to an issue. Which in the end leaves Mary without either a husband or a lover.

## THE RAMBLERS

(289 performances)

Musical comedy in two acts. Book by Guy Bolton, Bert Kalmar and Harry Ruby; lyrics and music by Bert Kalmar and

Harry Ruby. Produced by Philip Goodman at the Lyric Theatre, New York, September 20, 1926.

Cast of characters—

| | |
|---|---|
| Nettie Field | Norma Gallo |
| Black Pedro | William E. Browning |
| Pancho | Horton Spurr |
| Joe Small | Lloyd Pedrick |
| Anita | Eleanor Dawn |
| Neil Farnham | William Sully |
| Carter | Alfred Watson |
| Dapper Dan | Richy Craig, Jr. |
| Jenny Wren | Ruth Tester |
| Hazel Knott | Winefride Verina |
| Lotta Moore | Nita Jacques |
| Prof. Cunningham | Bobby Clark |
| Sparrow | Paul McCullough |
| Ronald Roche | Blaine Cordner |
| Billy Shannon | Jack Whiting |
| Ruth Chester | Marie Saxon |
| Fanny Furst | Georgia O'Ramsey |
| The Father | Henry Permane |
| Lida Belmont | Marguerite Murray |
| Bootlegger | John Klendon |
| Cissie O'Hearn | Bonnie Murray |

Act I.—At Tia Juana and Beverley Hills, California. Act II.—"On the Lot" at Fanny Furst's Movie Studio at Hollywood.
Staged by Philip Goodman.

Cunningham and Sparrow outwit both the authorities and their librettists along the Mexican border at Tia Juana.

## HONEYMOON LANE

### (317 performances)

Musical comedy in a prologue and two acts. Book, lyrics and music by Eddie Dowling and James Hanley. Produced by A. L. Erlanger at the Knickerbocker Theatre, New York, September 20, 1926.

Cast of characters—

| | |
|---|---|
| Mary Brown | Pauline Mason |
| Ruth Adams | Martha Morton |
| Honey Duke | Johnny Marvin |
| Tim Murphy | Eddie Dowling |
| John Brown | George Pauncefort |
| Ted Kleinz | Al Sexton |
| Ethel Jackson | Florentine Gosnova |
| Matty Pathe | Gordon Dooley |
| Florence O'Denishawn | Florence O'Denishawn |
| Dream Man | Worthe Faulkner |
| Station Master | Jerre McAuliffe |
| Conductor | John McAvoy |
| Tiny Little | Kate Smith |
| Porter | Dick Wheaton |
| A Passenger | Alyce Johnstone |
| Mrs. Nelligan | Josie Intropodi |

```
Addie..........................................Adelaide Seaman
Mazie Buck.....................................Helyn Eby-Rock
Jessie..............................................Ivy Palmer
Leo Scamp...........................................Leo Beers
The Boss.......................................Bernard Randall
Patrick Kelly......................................D. J. Sullivan
Elsie.............................................Ethel Allys
Edith............................................Edith Sheldon
```
Prologue—Exterior of Mary Brown's Home, Canningville, Pa. Act I.—The W. H. Kleinze Pickle Factory, Canningville, Pa. Act II.—Back Stage and Round About a Theatre.

Staged by Edgar MacGregor.

Tim Murphy hoped to marry Mary Brown back in their old home town, but Mary was dead set on going on the stage. In New York she makes her way through the chorus of a musical comedy and Tim comes on just in time to save her from a flesh hound or two.

## FANNY

### (63 performances)

Melodramatic comedy in three acts by Willard Mack and David Belasco. Produced by David Belasco at the Lyceum Theatre, New York, September 21, 1926.

Cast of characters—

```
"Doggie" Davis.................................Francis Pierlot
"Humpty" Riggs...............................Spencer Charters
"Slim" Hawkins...................................Louis Mason
Joe White.......................................Warren William
"Gyp" Gradyear.................................John Cromwell
High Low........................................Samuel S. Lee
"Hollywood" Haswell..........................George Sherwood
Nora Cassell.......................................Ruth Dayton
Miss Leah Mendoza................................Jane Ellison
Fanny Fiebaum...................................Fannie Brice
```
Acts I, II and III.—The Living-room of David Mendoza, Late Proprietor of the XY Ranch, Near Horse Blanket, Arizona.

Staged by David Belasco.

Fanny Fiebaum, serving the philanthropic Miss Leah Mendoza as companion and friend, foils a would-be robber band in Arizona. Miss Leah's brother has hidden $60,000 on his ranch and then died. The chief robber finds the money, but before he can get away with it Fanny has introduced him to herself as a Yiddish vamp who takes it right away from him, money, belt and everything.

## YELLOW

### (135 performances)

Melodrama in three acts by Margaret Vernon. Produced by George M. Cohan at the National Theatre, New York, September 21, 1926.

Cast of characters—

| | |
|---|---|
| Hotel Porter, at N. Y. Hotel | Joseph Guthrie |
| "Val" Parker | Chester Morris |
| Hotel Waiter, at N. Y. Hotel | Jose Rivas |
| "Polly" | Selena Royle |
| Jack Crompton | Hale Hamilton |
| Jen Wilkes | Marjorie Wood |
| Daisy Lingard | Shirley Warde |
| Jimmy Wilkes | Spencer Tracy |
| Thomas W. Sayre | Frank Kingdon |
| Mrs. Sayre | Jane Wheatley |
| Paul | Richard Freeman |
| Donaldson | Daniel Pennell |
| Carrie Williams | Eva Cassanova |
| Welles | Martin Malloy |
| Inspector Graney | Harry Bannister |
| Louis | H. Paul Ducet |
| Cigarette Girl | Mary Meehan |
| Page Boy | Walter Hale |
| Check Girl | Helen Macks |
| An Old Roue | Frank Burbeck |
| Policeman | Paul Hanson |

Act I.—The Wilkes Downtown Apartment. Act II.—The Sayre Estate, Orange County. Act III.—Jack Crompton's Apartment and a Fashionable Restaurant.

Staged by John Meehan.

Val Parker deserts Daisy Lingard, with whom he has been living for six months, to marry Polly Sayre of his own social set. On the eve of his departure for Europe on his honeymoon he hands $5,000 to his best friend, Jack Crompton, tells him of Daisy, confesses she is going to become a mother and asks him to square it. Daisy refuses the money and goes on the street to support the child. Parker, back from Europe, and out of love with his wife, tries to resume relations with Daisy. She finally shoots him, but he does not die. In the end Daisy is sinking lower and lower and Parker, divorced, has been ordered by the police to leave town.

## SANDALWOOD

### (39 performances)

Drama in three acts by Owen Davis and Fulton Oursler. Produced by Robert Milton at the Gaiety Theatre, New York, September 22, 1926.

Cast of characters—

```
Eddie Carpenter ............................... William Harrigan
Lucy.............................................. Pauline Lord
Dr. Carpenter.................................... Joseph Brennan
Mrs. Carpenter.................................... Marion Ballou
Rev. Harold Carpenter............................ Douglas Wood
Minnie...................................... Mabel Montgomery
George ........................................... Robert Strange
Belle............................................... Eva Condon
Faith Waring....................................... Gilda Leary
Joe Spindell....................................... Stanley Jessop
Dr. Clarke......................................... James Seeley
```
    Acts I, II and III.—At the Home of the Carpenters.
    Staged by Robert Milton.

Eddie Carpenter is sick and determined to die. He finds life piffling and the world thickly inhabited with pifflers. Nobody can do anything with Eddie until Faith Waring, a beautiful pagan with whom he has been in love for some time, walks into his sick room and promises to get him well if Lucy Carpenter, his wife, will step aside. The doctor advises Lucy to agree, Faith moves in, and Eddie gets well. Then Faith wants him to leave Lucy, who can never understand or appreciate him. But Eddie, growing strong physically, loses his pagan courage and in the end Faith gives him back to Lucy.

## THE SHELF

### (32 performances)

Comedy drama by Dorrance Davis. Produced by William B. Friedlander at the Morosco Theatre, New York, September 27, 1926.

Cast of characters—

```
Stanley Risdale .................................... Louis Kimball
Emma Smith ......................................... Jessie Ralph
Mrs. Chetswold.................................... Leah Winslow
Mrs. Plummer .................................... Lotta Linthicum
Miss Batterson..................................... Thelma Ritter
John Wendham .............................. Frederick Truesdell
Caroline Wendham .................................. Lee Patrick
Stella Amaranth..................................... Frances Starr
```

Baldwin Custard ................................. Lawrence Leslie
U. S. Senator Risdale.............................. Arthur Byron
The Rev. Herbert Chetswold........................ Donald Meek
  Acts I, II and III.—The Sun Parlor of John Wendham's Home,
Kiwanisport.
  Staged by William B. Friedlander.

Stella Amaranth, entering her forties, hears one of the country
cats where she is visiting declare that she (Stella) is old enough
to be laid on the shelf. To prove the lady wrong Stella starts
a more or less sensational campaign of vamping. She sells kisses
at a bazar, fascinates a senator's young son, lures a governor into
granting her many favors and finally stirs the senator himself
to amorous action.

## THE JUDGE'S HUSBAND

### (120 performances)

Comedy in three acts by William Hodge. Produced by Lee
Shubert at the 49th Street Theatre, New York, September 27,
1926.

Cast of characters—

Marg........................................... Jessie Crommette
Stella......................................... Dorothy Walters
John Findley.................................. Chas. F. McCarthy
Alice Kirby...................................... Ruth Lyons
Mrs. Judge Kirby ............................... Gladys Hanson
Joe Kirby ....................................... William Hodge
Harry Fitch.................................. Alexander Clark, Jr.
Dan Reynolds.................................... Richard Gordon
Sophie.......................................... Marie Haynes
Clerk of the Court............................... Francesca Hill
Court Stenographer................................. Irene Blare
  Acts I and III.—The Kirby Home, Wave Crest, Connecticut. Act
II.—Superior Court, Court House, Fairfield County.
  Staged by Thomas Coffin Cook.

Joe Kirby has taught his wife so much law that she has gone
into politics and been elected a judge. Joe takes over the house
management in her place and when he disappears for two days
and two nights the judge assumes that he spent them with one of
the maids. She sues Joe for divorce and hears her own case. One
of her suitors is her attorney, but after Joe gets through cross-
examining him he is not so popular. Then it is shown that Joe
was out saving his daughter from a scrape those nights he didn't
get home and the judge is glad to forgive all.

## GENTLEMEN PREFER BLONDES
(199 performances)

Comedy in three acts by Anita Loos and John Emerson. Produced by Edgar Selwyn at the Times Square Theatre, New York, September 28, 1926.

Cast of characters—

| | |
|---|---|
| Dorothy Shaw | Edna Hibbard |
| Harry | Harold Thomas |
| Gloria Atwell | Ruth Raymonde |
| Lorelei Lee | June Walker |
| Henry Spoffard | Frank Morgan |
| Lady Beekman | Grace Hampton |
| Sir Francis Beekman | G. P. Huntley |
| Mrs. Spoffard | Mrs. Jacques Martin |
| Miss Chapman | Katherine Brook |
| Leon | Daniel Wolf |
| Connie | Vivian Purcell |
| Robert Broussard | Georges Romain |
| Louis Broussard | Adrian Rosley |
| Gus Eisman | Arthur S. Ross |
| H. Gilbertson Montrose | Bruce Huntley |
| Dickie | Edwina Prue |
| William Gwynn | Roy Gorham |
| Lulu | Grace Burgess |
| Herb | Richard Brandlon |
| Ann Spoffard | Grace Cornell |
| Old Spoffard | Will T. Hays |

Act I.—Royal Suite of an Ocean Liner.    Act II.—A Sitting Room in the Ritz Hotel, Paris.    Act III.—Lorelei's Apartment, New York. Staged by Edgar Selwyn.

Lorelei Lee, a wise little blonde from Little Rock, is being educated in New York by Gus Eisman of the button profession. With her pal, Dorothy, Mr. Eisman sends Lorelei to Paris to broaden her mind and wait for him. On the boat over Lorelei meets and is greatly attracted to Henry Spoffard, a literary person. In London she extracts a diamond tiara from Sir Francis Beekman, and in Paris she becomes more or less involved with the Broussard brothers, who are Lady Beekman's lawyers. By the time Mr. Eisman gets to Paris, there are several problems to be adjusted, so Dorothy decides to marry Mr. Spoffard.

## THE WOMAN DISPUTED

(87 performances)

Melodrama of the Great War by Denison Clift. Produced by A. H. Woods at the Forrest Theatre, New York, September 28, 1926.

Cast of characters—

| | |
|---|---|
| A Passerby | John Anthony |
| A Blind Man | J. K. Newman |
| Two Soldiers | { Robert Cummings<br>{ Henry Von Rhau |
| Marriette | Andrew Corday |
| A Waif | Jackie Grattan |
| A Thief | W. Bradley Ward |
| Two Men | { B. J. McOwen<br>{ Hall Symonds |
| A Woman | Louise Quinn |
| Marie-Ange | Ann Harding |
| First Policeman | Charles Hammond |
| Second Policeman | Richard Bradshaw |
| Capt. Friedrich Von Hartmann | Lowell Sherman |
| Lieut. "Yank" Trinkard, of the Foreign Legion | Louis Calhern |
| Sergeant Bauer | Robert Cummings |
| Sergeant Franz | Henry Von Rhau |
| An Orderly | Hall Symonds |
| Lieut. Bittner | W. Bradley Ward |
| A Father | J. K. Newman |
| A Grandfather | Royal Thayer |
| A Boy | Jackie Grattan |
| Comte Hubert Debreville | Charles Hammond |
| Comtesse Debreville | Viola Roache |
| M. Henri Dardignac | B. J. McOwen |
| Mlle. Jacqueline Dardignac | Vera Tompkins |
| Father Rochambeau | Crane Wilbur |
| Lieut. Gregory | John Anthony |
| Sergeant Drake | Richard Bradshaw |
| An American Soldier | Joseph Burton |

Act I.—Street in a City in Alsace, 1914. Marie-Ange's Room. Act II.—The Cathedral of La Harpe, 1918. Act III.—The Cathedral. Staged by Crane Wilbur.

Marie-Ange, out of luck on the farm, goes to a city in Alsace and, being unjustly jailed by the police, takes to the streets when she is free. A man shoots himself in her room; his brother, Captain Von Hartmann, calls to investigate and takes a fancy to Marie-Ange. So does his friend, Yank Trinkard of the Foreign Legion. Comes the war. Marie-Ange flies to the arms of Yank, which makes Von Hartmann bitter. In a shell-wrecked cathedral in France, Von Hartmann, meeting Marie-Ange again seeks to force her to his will. She agrees to go with him if he will release a party of civilian prisoners. She knows one of these is a French spy. The spy gets through, brings on Yank and the Americans, Von Hartmann is arrested and Marie-Ange is forgiven.

## THE CAPTIVE

(160 performances)

Drama in three acts adapted by Arthur Hornblow, Jr., from "La Prisonnière" by Edouard Bourdet. Produced by the Charles Frohman Company at the Empire Theatre, New York, September 29, 1926.

Cast of characters—

| | |
|---|---|
| Gisele De Montcel | Ann Trevor |
| Mlle. Marchand | Winifred Fraser |
| Josephine | Minna Phillips |
| De Montcel | Norman Trevor |
| Irene De Montcel | Helen Menken |
| Jacques Virieu | Basil Rathbone |
| Georges | Arthur Lewis |
| Françoise Meillant | Ann Andrews |
| D'Aiguines | Arthur Wontner |

Act I.—Irene De Montcel's Room. Acts II and III.—The Study in Jacques Virieu's Apartment.
Staged by Gilbert Miller.

Irene de Montcel, ordered by her diplomatist father to be prepared to move from Paris to Brussels, refuses to go. De Montcel, suspecting Irene is held by the fascination a degenerate woman companion exerts for her, insists upon her going. To escape submission Irene begs a girlhood sweetheart, Jacques Virieu, to marry her. Jacques, though warned by the husband of the degenerate that such a marriage cannot be successful, agrees to Irene's proposal. A year later they are returned from their honeymoon. Their marriage has been a failure and Irene, still under the influence of her friend, deserts her husband.

## RED BLINDS

(20 performances)

Play in three acts, by Lord Lathom, produced by Lord Lathom at the Maxime Elliot Theatre. New York, September 30, 1926.

Cast of characters—

| | |
|---|---|
| Lady Kerandel | Gertrude Kingston |
| Florence | Iris Hoey |
| Shout | Alec Harford |
| Maurice Benn | Mackenzie Ward |
| Amy | Cicely Oates |
| Arthur Grimm | Campbell Gullan |
| Ned Burton | Cyril Raymond |

Act I.—A Drawing Room in Mayfair, London. Acts II and III.—Florence's Boudoir.
Staged by Wallett Waller.

Florence, caught cheating by her suspicious husband, frankly confesses her early adoption of the oldest profession. Deserted by both husband and lover she defiantly goes to Deauville in search of another man.

## HAPPY GO LUCKY

### (52 performances)

Musical comedy in three acts; book and lyrics by **Helena Phillips Evans**; music by Lucien Denni. Produced by **A. L. Erlanger** at the Liberty Theatre, New York, September 30, 1926.

Cast of characters—

```
Chester Chapin.....................................Taylor Holmes
Mildred Chapin .....................................Nydia D'Arnell
Robert Chapin ..........................................John Kane
Lucy Manning........................................Edith Shayne
Courtney Thompson................................Jack Squires
Mabel Holly.....................................Betty Gallagher
Roy Hayden .................................... Ralph Whitehead
Dawson ...........................................Herbert Belmore
Laura La Guerre..............................Madeline Cameron
Elsie Dayly .......................................Lina Abarbanell
Kate..............................................Ethel Mulholland
Clara.............................................Mary Bothwell
       Acts I, II and III.—The Home of Chester Chapin.
       Staged by Fred G. Latham.
```

Chester Chapin, growing crabbed and impossible as a family man, is the despair of his children and his housekeeper sister until the day one of them reads that repeated doses of flattery, subtly administered, will make a lamb of any man. They try it and it works. Then Chester discovers the plot and threatens reprisals. All happy at the finish.

## THE IMMORTAL THIEF

### (25 performances)

Spectacle drama by Tom Barry. Produced by Walter Hampden at Hampden's Theatre, New York, October 2, 1926.

Cast of characters—

```
Silenus Geta ........................................Ernest Rowan
Poetar ................................................. Cecil Yapp
Three Thieves..........J. P. Wilson, Marcel Dill, F. Thomas Gomez
Old Thief of Bagdad...................................P. J. Kelly
Ben Sarken........................................Dallas Anderson
Naomi ............................................. Marie Adels
```

Marius Rufinus.................................Walter Hampden
His Mother........................................Mabel Moore
His Old Nurse...........................Adelaide Fitz Allen
Septimus Celsus......................................C. Norman Hammond
An Old Official of the Law.....................William H. Sams
A Young Official.................................Howard Claney
Asper.............................................Hart Jenks
An Egyptian King...................................Howard Galt
An Ethiopian Prince...............................F. R. Colton
A Syrian...........................................Stuart Miller
A Phœnician......................................Gordon Hart
A False Prophet....................................J. P. Wilson
Merzah............................................Suzanne Jackson
Her Daughter.....................................Edith Barrett
Pharaoh's Daughter...........................Grania O'Malley
Greek Maidens................................... { Hope Cary
                                                 { Ruth Seward
Keeper of the Bordello.......................Robert Paton Gibbs
A Hasheesh Eater....................................P. J. Kelly
A Camel Driver.....................................Marcel Dill
A Sailor Spy......................................Louis Polan
A Peddler Spy.....................................Basil Grant
An Old Boatman..................................Anthony Andre
A Beggar..............................................F. Thomas Gomez
Bordello Girls.......Eudora Hunner, Grace Morton, Caroline Meade
A Wine Girl.......................................Dorothy Scott
James the Less....................................Stanley Howlett
Son of a Widow....................................Gordon Hart
    Staged by Mr. Hampden.

Marius Rufinus, cruel leader of a band of thieves in Jerusalem during the closing days of Christ's ministry on earth, seeking escape to Damascus, is apprehended by the authorities. Touched with the faith of salvation held out by his mother as a follower of the Nazarene, Marius takes the sin of murder on himself to save a girl he has wronged. He is crucified at the right hand of the Savior and the promise of absolution is held out to him.


## DEEP RIVER

### (32 performances)

Native opera in three acts; book and lyrics by Laurence Stallings; music by Frank Harling. Produced by Arthur Hopkins at the Imperial Theatre, New York, October 4, 1926.

Cast of characters—

Tizan...............................................Julius Bledsoe
Octavie.........................................Rose McClendon
Sara..............................................Bessie Allison
Julie..............................................Gladys White
Henri.............................................Rollo Dix
Paul.............................................Andre Dumont
Jules.............................................David Sager
Garcon........................................Frederick McGurk
M. Brusard.......................................Luis Aberni
Hutchins.......................................Arthur Campbell
Mugette..........................................Lottice Howell

```
Colonel Streatfield.............................Frederick Burton
Hazzard Streatfield.............................Roberto Ardelli
Hercule.........................................Antonio Salerno
The Announcer...................................Frank Harrison
Mother of Mugette...............................Louisa Ronstadt
The Queen.......................................Charlotte Murray
Waiting Women—Katherine Parker, Carrie Giles, Cora Gary, Alberta
                      Dougal.
```
    Act I.—Café of the Theatre Orleans.  Act II.—The Place Congo.
Showing a voodoo meeting.  Act III.—Patio at Mr. Hercule's Quadroon Ball.
    Staged by Arthur Hopkins.

In the New Orleans of 1835 it was the custom for the rich
Creole gentlemen to select their favorites from among the débu-
tantes at the quadroon ball, and thereafter maintain them under
their protection.  On the occasion of one such ball three Ken-
tuckians, the two Messrs. Streatfield and Hutchins, propose to
join the revelry.  Hazzard Streatfield, meeting Muguette, the
loveliest of that season's quadroons, falls in love with her, but is
violently opposed by M. Brusard, the leader of Creole society.
Brusard, resenting the insults of Streatfield, kills him in a duel.
Later, after Muguette has sought a voodoo charm to help her
win Hazzard Streatfield, Hazzard and Brusard kill each other,
leaving the girl to one of the less attractive of her suitors.


## TREAT 'EM ROUGH

### (24 performances)

Comedy in three acts by Frederick and Fanny Hatton.  Produced by Richard Herndon at the Klaw Theatre, New York,
October 4, 1926.

Cast of characters—

```
Dan Carson.....................................George Torrence
Marco..........................................Walter Connolly
Joe............................................M. Charles Palazzi
Beppo .........................................Himself
Rosie Moore....................................May Hopkins
Lisa Toselli...................................Nedda Harrigan
Trixie Colette.................................Helen Landis
Gus............................................Robert Dye
Mimi La Verne..................................Marguerite Forrest
Pansy La Motte.................................Myrtle Miller
Tony Barudi....................................Allan Dinehart
Tomasso Salvatore..............................William Ricciardi
Buff...........................................John Shanks
Sergeant Burns.................................James Manning
Nora O'Hare....................................Genevieve Tobin
Father Flynn...................................Thomas Mac Larnie
Demetrius......................................Jack Rigo
Lola Carson....................................Helene Sinnott
Susi...........................................Lois Shore
```
    Acts I, II and III.—A Room in the Apartment of Tomasso Salva-
tore, Above the Café Salvatore, New York City.
    Staged by Allan Dinehart.

Tony Barudi is the little boss of a low cabaret of which his adopted father, Tomasso Salvatore, is big boss and proprietor. Tony is rough with the girls of the place, taking his pick of them and demanding the obedient service of the discarded. He catches a bit of a Tartar, however, when he tries his rough tricks on Nora O'Hare, not long enough from County Roscommon to have lost either her accent or her fighting spirit. He has to love and marry Nora before he can even start taming her.

## THE GOOD FELLOW

(7 performances)

Comedy in three acts by George S. Kaufman and Herman J. Mankiewicz. Produced by Crosby Gaige at the Playhouse Theatre, New York, October 5, 1926.

Cast of characters—

Mrs. Kent ........................................ Clara Blandick
Mrs. Helton ...................................... Jennet Adair
Ethel Helton ..................................... Ethel Taylor
Dan Ripley ....................................... Walter Baldwin, Jr.
Jim Helton ....................................... John E. Hazzard
Tom Drayton ...................................... Lester Vail
Charlie Arbuckle ................................. Robert Burlen
Harry Barker ..................................... Earle Craddock
Fred Busby ....................................... W. W. Shuttleworth
Harry Branders ................................... Forest Zimmer
Frank Reynolds ................................... Morris Ankrum
Willie Curtis .................................... Lester Neilson
Bill Cutler ...................................... Victor Kilian
Louis Fender ..................................... Stanley Andrews
Ed Mullins ....................................... Stewart Masten
Saul Rabinowitz .................................. Jacob Kingsberry
   Acts I, II and III.—An Evening in September, the Home of the
Heltons in Wilkes-Barre, Pennsylvania.
   Staged by Howard Lindsay and George S. Kaufman.

Jim Helton is one of the most successful of the back-slappers of Wilkes-Barre, Pa. Good old scout and champion joiner, being the Grand Napoleon of the ancient Order of Corsicans is his proudest lodge honor. To bring the Corsican convention to Wilkes-Barre, Jim agrees to raise $10,000. The citizens and the brothers fail him and he has to pawn his life insurance and hold up his daughter's fiancé to get the money. Exposure does for Jim, but he gets a good job out of it and wins the forgiveness of his folks.

## BLACK BOY

### (37 performances)

Comedy drama in three acts by Jim Tully and Frank Dazey. Produced by Horace Liveright at the Comedy Theatre, New York, October 6, 1926.

Cast of characters—

```
Black Boy...............................................Paul Robeson
Irene...................................................Edith  Warren
"Shrimp"...............................................Fuller Mellish, Jr.
"Square Deal"..................................Edward Redding
"Mauler"....................................Charles Henderson
"Whitey".......................................Edward  Gargan
"Eddie".................................................James Ford
"Yellow"......................................Percy  Verwayen
"Squint"...........................................Robert Collyer
Langhorne Dubree.................................Henry Troy
Chauffeur...........................................G. O. Taylor
Radio Announcer.....................Major J. Andrew White
    Acts I and III.—Interior of the Training Camp.  Act II.—Black
Boy's Apartment in Harlem.
    Staged by David Burton.
```

Black Boy is just a roustabout colored boy until the day he wanders into the training camp of "The Mauler." They offer him $10 to work as a sparring partner, and what he does to "The Mauler" is sufficient to convince the latter's manager that Black Boy can become a champion. In two years he is sitting on the top of the world, surrounded by cheap luxuries and cheaper parasites, including the girl he lives with, Irene. Dissipation does for him his next fight, the bums desert him and he discovers that Irene is black in place of white. Defeated, he goes back to his old life.

## THE JEWELED TREE

### (37 performances)

Egyptian dramatic fantasy, period 1350 B.C., by Garrett Chatfield Pier. Produced by the Pierce Tollman Corporation at the 48th Street Theatre, New York, October 7, 1926.

Cast of characters—

```
Senebes...............................................Carol Chase
Tua...................................................Anna Alexander
Abee....................................................Rita  Morarity
Ankhamon........................................Frank Jamison
Deddi..............................................Arthur  Bowyer
Thuya...........................................Frederica  Going
Anteff........................................Richard  Nicholls
```

```
Queen Ankhesen...................................Olive Valerie
Hotep ...........................................Pat Walsh
Tuee.............................................George Thornton
Mena.............................................Ward McAllister
Rames............................................Walter Petrie
Khnum............................................Leslie King
Nutaree .........................................Thomas Holding
First Mermaid ...................................Mignon Ranseer
Second Mermaid ..................................Raina Darling
Third Mermaid....................................Louise Mainland
Fourth Mermaid...................................Nellie Leach
First Shade......................................Pat Walsh
Second Shade.....................................George Thornton
Face-Turned-Backward ............................Ivan Triesault
Hathor ..........................................Fraun Koski
Ata..............................................Reva Greenwood
First Chamberlain................................Milton Thomann
Second Chamberlain ..............................Raymond O'Brien
First Guard .....................................William Yeatry
Second Guard.....................................Bert Lannon
Third Guard......................................Stuart Lee Kann
Fourth Guard.....................................Jack Clifford
Meryt............................................Magda Bennett
Nofret ..........................................Alice Wynne
Tiya ............................................Peggy Cornell
Nana ............................................Nellie Savage
Taya ............................................Karen Taft
Miya ............................................Celeste Dubois
Atotha ..........................................Doris Bryant
Ahmes ...........................................Ivan Triesault
```
The Period of the Play Is the 18th Egyptian Dynasty, Shortly After the Death of King Tut-ank-hamen.

Staged by Lawrence Marston.

The Queen Ankhesen, widow of Tut-ank-hamen, desiring to live forever and be forever beautiful, sends her young fiancé, Rames, in search of the fabled jeweled tree, the fruit of which guarantees eternal youth. Rames, braving many dangers, finds the tree and also Ata, the soul of the tree, who is very beautiful herself. Returning to the Queen he gives her the golden apple, which turns her hair gray and her face ugly and he is thereafter free to wed Ata, whom the gods make mortal as a favor to him.

## THE LION TAMER

(29 performances)

Satirical fable by Alfred Savoir, translated from the French by Winifred Katzin. Produced at the Neighborhood Theatre, New York, October 7, 1926.

Cast of characters—

```
Bartender........................................Charles Romano
The Clown .......................................Blanche Talmud
The Snake Charmer................................Lily Lubell
Lord John Lonsdale...............................Ian Maclaren
Gregoire ........................................Marc Loebell
Arabella ........................................Dorothy Sands
```

Angelo...........................................Otto Hulicius
Vicomte des Adrets..............................Albert Carroll
A Servant......................................Richard Randolph
Program Boy......................................George Heller
 Act I.—The Bar Outside the Circus. Act II.—Lord Lonsdale's Château Near Paris. Act III.—Back at the Circus.
 Staged by Agnes Morgan.

Lord John Lonsdale, representing idealism and intellectual justice, seeks to satisfy his longing to see àn oppressor beaten by following a circus in the hope of being present for the day the lions turn and rend the lion tamer, who stands for brute force and vulgarity. But the lions love their tamer. Then Lord John seeks to crush the oppressor another way. He engages a professional lover to deceive him. The lover pleases the lion tamer's wife very much, but merely separates her temporarily from her husband. After which Lord John seeks to replace the professional lover and, failing in his desires, feeds himself to the lions.


## BUY, BUY, BABY

### (12 performances)

Farce in three acts by Russell Medcraft and Norma Mitchell based on a play by Francis R. Bellamy and Lawton Mackall. Produced by Bertram Harrison at the Princess Theatre, New York, October 7, 1926.

Cast of characters—

Betty Hamilton.....................................Shirley Booth
Norah............................................. Mabel Colcord
Harold Boland.................................... Maurice Burke
Pauline Lunt...................................... Veree Teasdale
Janice Marvin................................Laura Hope Crews
Ronald Bradford................................Edwin Nicander
Carteret Flotten ................................ Malcolm Duncan
Esmeralda Pottle................................Alison Skipworth
A Burglar........................................Charles Mather
Henry Marvin....................................Thurston Hall
 Acts I, II and III.—The Marvin Living Room, Bronxville.

Esmeralda Pottle, excited by the declining birthrate, as applied to her own kin, promises a million dollars to the first of her near relatives to become a parent. As at the time of the offer some of the younger kin are married and some are not, some are at home and some are in foreign parts, the scramble to bring all parties within reach of the prize is at least hectic. Nephew Harold, sometime secretly married to Betty Hamilton, finally qualifies by producing a 3-months-old heir.

## TRAGIC 18

### (9 performances)

A play in three acts by Maurice Clark; produced by Fuguet, Inc. (in association with Murray Phillips) at the Charles Hopkins Theatre, New York, October 9, 1926.

Cast of characters—

| | |
|---|---|
| Bill Bowman | Frank Roberts |
| Teddy Bowman | Neil Martin |
| Sam Joseph | Homer Barton |
| Sue Le Staire | Beatrice Maude |
| Dot Dixon | Maude Hanaford |
| Mrs. Bowman | Jennie Eustace |
| Frankie Givney | Dixie Loftin |

Acts I and II.—New York Apartment of Bill Bowman and Sam Joseph. Act III.—A Vestibule in an Old Apartment House and the Apartment of Dot Dixon.

Staged by Murray Phillips.

Teddy Bowman, in New York getting a start, falls desperately in love with Dot Dixon of the chorus. His younger brother, Bill, tries to break up the match and sends for Mrs. Bowman. Dot finally confesses a previous marriage and a 5-months-old baby, and gives Teddy back to his mother.

## JUAREZ AND MAXIMILIAN

### (48 performances)

Dramatic history in three phases and thirteen pictures, by Franz Werfel; produced by the Theatre Guild at the Guild Theatre, New York, October 11, 1926.

Cast of characters—

| | |
|---|---|
| Clarke | Stanley DeWolfe |
| Elizea | Philip Loeb |
| City Deputy of Chihuahua | Philip Leigh |
| Mariano Escobedo | Harold Clurman |
| Porfirio Diaz | Edward G. Robinson |
| Riva-Palacio | Morris Carnovsky |
| Maximilian | Alfred Lunt |
| Captain Miguel Lopez | Edward Van Sloan |
| Doctor Basch | Albert Bruning |
| Grill | John Rynne |
| Madame Barrio | Cheryl Crawford |
| State Councillor Stephen Herzfield | Earle Larimore |
| Carlotta | Clare Eames |
| Archbishop Labastida of Mexico and Puebla | Dudley Digges |
| Theodosio Lares | Perry Ivins |
| Lawyer Siliceo | Erskine Sanford |
| General Tomas Mejia | Philip Loeb |
| François Achille Bazaine | Arnold Daly |
| Edouard Pierron | Maurice McRae |

```
Iturbide..........................................Alfred  Lewis
Blasio ..........................................Sanford  Meisner
General  Marquez...................................Dan  Walker
General  Miramon...............................Charles  Allais
Corporal  Winberger............................Stanley  DeWolfe
Yapitan..........................................Philip  Leigh
Polyphemie.......................................Harold  Clurman
Princess  Agnes  Salm..........................Margalo  Gillmore
José  Rincon  Gallardo............................Erskine  Sanford
Official..........................................Roland  Twombley
Canon  Soria.....................................Morris  Carnovsky
     Staged by Philip Moeller.
```

The thirteen pictures are taken from scenes in and about the imperial palace in Mexico City, the pleasure palace at Chapultepec, and the headquarters of both armies in the field.

Covering that period of Maximilian's occupancy of the throne of Mexico from the autumn of 1865 to the summer of 1867.


## AN AMERICAN TRAGEDY

### (216 performances)

Drama by Patrick Kearney from the novel by Theodore Dreiser. Produced by Horace Liveright at the Longacre Theatre, New York, October 11, 1926.

Cast of characters—

In Prologue
```
Clyde  Griffiths...................................Morgan  Farley
Elvira  Griffiths...............................Caroline  Newcombe
Asa  Griffiths.......................................Frank  Moran
Hester  Griffiths....................................Olive  Mercer
A  Girl...........................................Marian  Florance
A  Young  Man ....................................Sydney  Coburn
Another  Girl........................................Joan  Brown
Another  Young  Man.............................Harry  Arnold
```

In the Play
```
Mrs. Samuel  Griffiths.............................Grace  Griswold
Bella  Griffiths.....................................Janet  McLeay
Gilbert  Griffiths............................House  Baker  Jameson
Samuel  Griffiths..................................Walter  Walker
Clyde  Griffiths...................................Morgan  Farley
Sondra  Finchley..................................Miriam  Hopkins
Jill  Trumbull........................................Sally  Bates
Whiggam .........................................Bert  Wilcox
Roberta  Alden.................................Katherine  Wilson
Stuart  Finchley....................................Philip  Jones
Bertine  Cranston...........................Martha  Lee  Manners
Harley  Baggott....................................Jack  Quigley
Dr.  Glenn........................................Arthur  Hughes
Mrs.  Peyton.......................................Violet  Andrews
An  Innkeeper.......................................John  Wheeler
A  Deputy  Sheriff................................Sydney  Coburn
Orville  Mason ...................................Albert  Phillips
Alvin  Belknap...................................Willard  Dashiell
Ruben  Jephson...................................Anthony  Brown
Burton  Burleigh ..................................Bert  Wilcox
Bailiff..........................................Harold  McCreery
```

```
Clerk of the Court...........................Frank Rutherford
Judge Oberwaltzer..................................Philip Wood
Second Guard.....................................Frank Horan
Third Guard...................................Frank Rutherford
    Staged by Edward Goodman.
```

Clyde Griffiths, son of small town evangelists, feels the thrill of the freer physical life when he goes to Lycurgus, New York, and begins his career in a factory. Meeting Roberta Alden, a pretty factory girl, he loves and seduces her. Later he meets Sondra Finchley of the society Finchleys and would be rid of Roberta, who is expectant. Taking Roberta for a row on the lake, Griffiths either knocks or permits her to fall into the water and drown. He denies the act of murder, but a jury refuses to believe him and he is sent to the chair.


## CRISS CROSS

### (206 performances)

Musical comedy in two acts and a prologue. Music by Jerome Kern; libretto by Otto Harbach and Anne Caldwell. Produced by Charles Dillingham at the Globe Theatre, New York, October 12, 1926.

Cast of characters—

```
Countess de Pavazac..............................Allene Stone
Yasmini.........................................Dorothy Francis
Renee...........................................Primrose Caryll
Khadra.........................................Kathryn Burnside
Lucie.............................................Lydia Scott
Fifi..............................................Beth Meakins
Badoura.........................................Phyllis Pearce
Marie..............................................Lucie Monroe
Arlette.............................................Pearl Eaton
Babette...........................................Alice Donahue
Suzette.........................................Virginia Franck
Paulette.........................................Marjorie Leet
Miquette.........................................Danzi Goodell
Jeanne...........................................Bobby Breslau
Goldie Digger ...................................Dorothy Bate
Selima..............................................Lydia Scott
Captain Carleton ..................................Roy Hoyer
Ilphrahim Benani.................................Oscar Ragland
Professor Mazeroux...............................John Lambert
Maestro Viaggiatore.............................Auguste Aramini
The Marabout of Oran...........................Ralph Thomson
An Argentine; a Soldier; a Juggler.................Charles Baum
The Cure.........................................George Herman
Cassim............................................Mark Truscott
Iadid.............................................Jack Shannon
Nissim...........................................Frank Lambert
"Susie"............................Joseph Schrode, Thomas Bell
Dolly Day.........................................Dorothy Stone
Christopher Cross...................................Fred Stone
```

Prologue—Town Hollow in Fable-land.  Act I.—Outside a School in Southern France.  Act II.—Benani's Home in Algiers.  The Bazaar of Jadid.  The Jar of Ali Baba.  Terrace in the Palace Garden. The Diamond Palace.
Staged by R. H. Burnside.

Christopher Cross, being a resourceful aviator, manages to help Captain Carleton save Dolly Day from the designing schemes of Benani, who would rob her of her birthright and a considerable fortune.

## WE AMERICANS

### (118 performances)

Drama in three acts by Milton Herbert Gropper and Max Siegel.  Produced by Sam H. Harris at the Sam H. Harris Theatre, New York, October 12, 1926.

Cast of characters—

| | |
|---|---|
| Mrs. Levine | Clara Langsner |
| Morris Levine | Muni Wisenfrend |
| Beth Levine | Ailsa Lawson |
| Phil Levine | Luther Adler |
| Samuel Korn | Charles Ellis |
| Mr. Albertini | Jules Bennett |
| Mrs. Albertini | Josephine Wehn |
| Mr. Goldberg | Sam Mann |
| Mrs. Goldberg | Ethel Henin |
| O'Dougall | Jerome Kennedy |
| Mr. Horowitz | Morris Strassberg |
| Mrs. Horowitz | Ann Lowenworth |
| Chaim Horowitz | Herbert Polesie |
| Jacob Marcus | William E. Morris |
| Clarence Williams | Lackaye Grant |
| Helen Dale | Ruth Lee |
| Leo Lanheim | George Baxter |
| Anna Philipescu | Sylvia Hoffman |
| Song Lee | Mann Wada |
| Mrs. Peterson | Nancy Allan |
| Mr. Finkel | Milton C. Herman |

Acts I and III.—Home of the Levines.  Act II.—Night School.
Staged by Sam Forrest.

Beth Levine, graduated from high school and eager to go higher socially, finds life at home with her well-meaning but ignorant Jewish parents intolerable.  She tells them frankly they have made no attempt to keep pace with life in America, or even to become good American citizens.  Stung and hurt by Beth's criticism, the parents, after she leaves them, go to night school to improve themselves.  Beth does not find everything as rosy as she had hoped, and in time is happy to return to her home and her girlhood's sweetheart.

## THEY ALL WANT SOMETHING

(62 performances)

Comedy in three acts by Courtenay Savage from the novel, "The Dark Chapter," by E. J. Rath. Produced by Herman Gantvoort at Wallack's Theatre, New York, October 12, 1926.

Cast of characters—

| | |
|---|---|
| Kane Kilbourne | Kenneth Richards |
| Hilda Kilbourne | Katherine Revner |
| Mr. Kilbourne | Charles S. Abbe |
| Mrs. Kilbourne | Camilla Crume |
| Grosvenor | Joseph Greene |
| Billy Kilbourne | Billy Quinn |
| Wade Rawlins | William T. Tilden, 2nd |
| Herb Wheeler | Wills Claire |
| Valerie | Valerie Dade |
| Virginia | Virginia Morris |
| Minnie Harlan | Irene Shirley |
| Jack Merrill | Edward Downes |
| Chauncey Smith | Donald MacMillan |
| Annabelle | Helene Ambrose |

Acts I, II and III.—On the Living Porch of the Summer Residence of Mr. Kilbourne, Near Ridgefield, Connecticut.
Staged by Alonzo Price.

Wade Rawlins, rich and a trifle eccentric, assumes the disguise of a comic strip tramp and goes in search of adventure and story material. At the Kilbournes' he finds Mrs. Kilbourne interested in the reclamation of tramps and is able to save Hilda, the daughter, and the other Kilbournes several kinds of embarrassment. After which he comes out of hiding and is happily engaged to Hilda.

## THE HUMBLE

(21 performances)

Drama in three acts by Laurence Irving, based on Dostoevsky's novel, "Crime and Punishment." Produced by Carl Reed at the Greenwich Village Theatre, New York, October 13, 1926.

Cast of characters—

| | |
|---|---|
| Kashkin | Thomas Chalmers |
| Dr. Zozimoff | Junius Matthews |
| Nastasia | Mae Noble |
| Rodion Raskolnikoff | Basil Sydney |
| Sonia Martinova | Mary Ellis |
| Gromoff | David Landau |
| Doonia Romanova | Florence Mason |
| Pulcheria | Kate DeBecker |
| Katinka | Verna Dean |

```
Keller ................................................ Franklyn Fox
Solski ................................................ Maurice Fein
Koltzoff ............................................. Curtis Karpe
Mikolka ............................................. George Bratt
Dmitri ............................................... Wallace House
Bezak ............................................. Sydney Greenstreet
Sergeant of Police ................................. V. P. Newmark
A Policeman ......................................... T. H. Bunch
Another Policeman ................................... Arthur Gray
Cossacks ...................... Michel Barroy and Barington White
```

Act I.—Rodion's Room in the Yamskaya. Act II.—An Island in the Neva Near St. Petersburg. Act III.—Gromoff's Room in the Yamskaya. Sonia's Room in the Same House. In and About the City of St. Petersburg, Russia, in the year 1866.

Staged by Bertram Forsyth.

Rodion Raskolnikoff, an atheistic student in pre-revolutionary Russia, is smarting under the burdens of the poor and the alleged persecutions of the church. If the law permits laborers' lives to be sacrificed in progressive building enterprises, should it not justify the taking of life in society to rid the world of oppressors? Living up to his theories, he murders Gromoff, who would harm Sonia, a sad child but pure. The police trail Rodion until he is forced to confess and goes to jail.

## THE STRAW HAT

### (57 performances)

A comedy in three acts, adapted from the French of Labiche, by Paul Tulane and Agnes Hamilton Jones. Produced by The American Laboratory Theatre, New York, October 14, 1926.

Cast of characters—

```
Gillette Rapide ..................................... Arthur Sircom
Helene .............................................. Anne Schmidt
Papa Rontonton ..................................... Donald Keyes
Mme. Rontonton ..................................... Dora Schwartz
Uncle Absinthe ..................................... Richard Skinner
Bobbin .............................................. Morton Brown
Felix ............................................... Harold Hecht
M. Feroce Detour ................................... George Auerbach
Anisette Detour .................................... Martha Johnson
Virginia ............................................ Roberta Renys
Emile Gunsonover .................................... Louis Quince
Baroness Creme de la Creme .......................... Stella Adler
Yvette .............................................. Adelaide George
Vicomte Achilles de Pseudobarde ..................... Sam Hartman
Clara ............................................... Florence House
M. Slocome Fussbudgette ............................ Robert H. Gordon
Rosalie Brouhaha .................................... Frances Wilson
```

Act I.—A Room in Gillette's House. Clara's Millinery Shop. Act II.—At the Baroness Creme de la Creme's. Act III.—A Street in Paris.

Staged by Richard Boleslavsky.

## WHITE WINGS

(27 performances)

Fantastic comedy in four acts by Philip Barry. Produced by Winthrop Ames at the Booth Theatre, New York, October 15, 1926.

Cast of characters—

Joseph (a Horse)......................................George Ali
Mary Todd.....................................Winifred Lenihan
Archie Inch.........................................Tom Powers
Herbert...........................................J. M. Kerrigan
Mr. Ernest Inch.................................William Norris
Paul Pillsbury....................................Donald McKee
Ralph Otis.......................................Earl McDonald
Clyde Sims.........................................Ben Lackland
Kit Canari....................................Donald MacDonald
Mrs. Fanny K. Inch..............................Jessie Graham
Major Philip E. Inch...........................Albert Tavernier
Charlie Todd...................................Arthur B. Allen
Dr. Derby.........................................Earl McDonald
Dr. Bowles.......................................Donald McKee
A Taxi-driver......................................Ben Lackland
A City Employee..............................Phil M. Sheridan
     Act I.—The Boulevard. Acts II, III and IV.—The Parkway, an
American City Between 1895 and 1915.
     Staged by Winthrop Ames.

In 1895 the Inches have for three generations been the most successful and the proudest of street cleaning white wings. Archie Inch is so impressed with the honor and glory attaching to his humble but necessary calling that he forbids himself the joy of a budding romance in which Mary Todd, daughter of Janitor Todd, figures. A horseless carriage invention of Mary's father finally puts the horse out of business and the Inches' occupation is gone. Not until then is Archie willing to acknowledge defeat and love Mary.

## ON APPROVAL

(96 performances)

Comedy in three acts by Frederick Lonsdale. Produced by Charles Dillingham at the Gaiety Theatre, New York, October 18, 1926.

Cast of characters—

Helen Hayle.................................Kathlene MacDonell
Mrs. Wislack................................Violet Kemble Cooper

```
Richard Halton.................................Wallace Eddinger
The Duke of Bristol............................Hugh Wakefield
    Act I.—Helen's House in Mayfair, London.  Acts II and III.—
Mrs. Wislack's House in Scotland.
    Staged by Athole Stewart.
```

Mrs. Wislack, having been once bitten, is twice shy of matrimony. She has taken some sort of fancy to Richard Halton, however, and proposes that they spend a month in her house in Scotland, observing each other as closely as possible without the customary marital intimacies. At the end of the month they will decide. They are followed to Scotland by Helen Hayle, daughter of a pickle millionaire, and the impecunious Duke of Bristol, considering the sale of his title to Miss Hayle. Life becomes more or less unbearable for the four. Halton and Miss Hayle sneak away in a snowstorm, leaving the irascible Duke and the catty Mrs. Wislack to hate each other and discover just how disagreeable each really is.

## GOD LOVES US

### (30 performances)

Drama in three acts by J. P. McEvoy. Produced by The Actors' Theatre (Kenneth Macgowan, director), at the Maxine Elliott Theatre, October 18, 1926.

Cast of characters—

```
Lucille..........................................Dorothy Peterson
Myrtle............................................Evelyn Keller
George............................................Elmer Cornell
Hector MacInerny Midge............................J. C. Nugent
Tommy......................................Douglass Montgomery
Mrs. Midge........................................Helen Lowell
Officer..........................................Ellsworth Jones
Radio Announcer....................................Seth Kendall
Prof. Ambrose Glutz...............................Harold Evans
Inspector ......................................Joseph McInerny
Rev. Harold Klump.................................John Carmody
Hadley...........................................Charles Gibney
George W. Dawson, Pres. of Dawson & Co. "Greeting Cards for All
    Occasions"...................................Malcolm Williams
Dawson, Jr. .......................................Cebra Graves
Cashier............................................Seth Kendall
President of "Go-Getters".........................Sherling Oliver
Song Leader.....................................Frederic A. Bryan
Harry Schmotz....................................Cliffman Jewell
Gentleman Known as "Al".........................Henry Gurvey
Butcher Boy......................................Willard Tobias
    Acts I, II and III.—The Home of Midge and the Officers of Daw-
son and Co.
    Staged by Kenneth Macgowan.
```

Hector Midge for twenty-five years has written greeting cards and served as assistant sales manager for Dawson & Co., hoping one day to be made sales manager. When the job is open Dawson gives it to his upstart son, who promptly fires Midge. After three months' search for another job Midge, beaten in spirit, takes back his old job at his old salary and goes toiling on with the rest of the slaves. A later change made in the play when it was re-titled "The Go-Getters" sends Midge into the West as a book salesman.

## KATJA

### (112 performances)

Operetta in three acts by Frederick Lonsdale; lyrics by Harry Graham; music by Jean Gilbert; additional scenes written and arranged by Isabel Leighton; additional lyrics by Clifford Grey. Produced by the Messrs. Shubert at the 44th Street Theatre, New York, October 18, 1926.

Cast of characters—

| | |
|---|---|
| Maud Sumerdal | Dorothy Whitmore |
| Leander Billdorff | Jack Sheehan |
| Count Orpitch | Bruce Winston |
| Patricia | Doris Patston |
| Ivo, Prince of Ogladin | Dennis Hoey |
| Katja Karina, Princess Ilanoff | Lilian Davies |
| Edouard | John Adair |
| Carl, Prince of Karuja | Allan Prior |
| Simon | Oscar Figman |
| Andre | Frank Hemmingway |
| Amilie | Mary Buckley |
| Hortense | Betty Allen |
| Louise | Julia Strong |
| Henri | Tom Green |
| Sergeant of Police | Jack Walsh |
| Boscart | Oscar Figman |
| Inspector of Police | Frank Walters |
| Vladimir | Valodia Vestoff |
| Natasha | Martha Mason |
| Annette | Kitty Coleman |

Act I.—Reception Room, Villa of Count Orpitch. Act II.—Room in Prince Carl's Villa. Act III.—Office of the Chief of Police at Monte Carlo.

Staged by J. C. Huffman, Lewis Morton and Max Scheck. Supervised by J. J. Shubert.

Katja Karina, the Princess Ilanoff, having been deposed, partly through the intrigues of Carl, Prince Karuja, becomes Katja, the dancer. As such she charms Carl, who never has seen her, into a love affair, from which they are melodiously extricated by 11:15 P.M.

## THE NOOSE

### (197 performances)

Drama by Willard Mack from a story by H. H. Van Loan. Produced by Mrs. Henry B. Harris by arrangement with Martin Sampter, at the Hudson Theatre, New York, October 20, 1926.

Cast of characters—

| | |
|---|---|
| Craig.............................................. | Hans Robert |
| John Bancroft................................. | Lester Lonergan |
| Bill Chase...................................... | Ralph Locke |
| Stella Bancroft................................ | Anne Shoemaker |
| Nickie Elkins.................................. | Rex Cherryman |
| Hughes......................................... | George Thompson |
| A Waiter....................................... | Ralph Adams |
| Dave Stern..................................... | Harry Bulger, Jr. |
| Jack Grattan................................... | Jack Daley |
| Tommy Jordan................................. | Charles Brown |
| Georgie......................................... | Mae Clark |
| Frances......................................... | Dorothy Sheppard |
| Patsy........................................... | Erenay Weaver |
| Gladys.......................................... | Maryland Jarbeau |
| Dot............................................. | Barbara Stanwyck |
| "Come On" Conly............................. | Wilfred Lucas |
| Buck Gordon................................... | George Nash |
| Seth McMillan................................. | George Barnum |
| Miss Devoy..................................... | Carolyn Clarke |
| Phyllis.......................................... | Helen Flint |

Acts I and III.—Governor Bancroft's Home. Act II.—Conly's Office, in the Box Stall Night Club.

Staged by Willard Mack.

Nickie Elkins, in his early twenties, is about to be hanged for a murder he refuses not only to explain but even to discuss. The governor has refused the appeal of Nickie's attorney for a reprieve and his own wife's sympathetic interest in the boy's case does not alter his determination. The action flashes back eight weeks to the commission of the crime. Nickie, having been brought up with crooks, has killed the leader of his gang, Buck Gordon, when the latter threatened to use his knowledge that the boy is the son of the governor's wife, born out of wedlock, to save the gang from going to prison. Nickie is ready to hang rather than bring scandal into his mother's life. Neither the governor or his wife ever learns the real truth, but Nickie's life is saved and a pardon probable.

## SURE FIRE

### (37 performances)

Comedy in three acts by Rolph Murphy. Produced by Boothe, Gleason and Truex at the Waldorf Theatre, New York, October 20, 1926.

Cast of characters—

| | |
|---|---|
| Alice | Donnee Waldron |
| John Kenderton | William Jeffrey |
| Louise Schuyler | Ann Winston |
| Robert Ford | Robert Armstrong |
| Alfred Lowell | Hugh O'Connell |
| Walt Henderson | Stephen Maley |
| Herby Brewster | Gene Lockhart |
| Jane Cole | Nancy Sheridan |
| George Reynolds | Paul Huber |
| Sarah Cole | Mina C. Gleason |
| Philip Cole | Norman Foster |
| Peggy Vere | Lee Smith |
| Congressman Blaine | James Seeley |

Prologue—Office of John Kenderton, Times Square, New York.
Acts I, II and III.—The Post Office, Clayville.
    Staged by Rollo Lloyd.

Robert Ford, a highbrow playwright living and working in Greenwich Village, refuses to write the sure-fire type of hokum drama, refuses to believe, in fact, that it even remotely reflects life. On a wager he goes to Clayville, Indiana, and runs plump into the plot concerned with the gray-haired postmistress with a pretty daughter who is about to be sold out by the village skinflint because she has used the mortgage money to pay her son's gambling debts. Convinced, Ford becomes his own hero, pays off the mortgage and writes that kind of play.

## THE WILD ROSE

### (61 performances)

Musical comedy in two acts. Book and lyrics by Otto Harbach and Oscar Hammerstein, 2nd; music by Rudolf Friml. Produced by Arthur Hammerstein at the Martin Beck Theatre, New York, October 20, 1926.

Cast of characters—

| | |
|---|---|
| Baron Frederick | Joseph Macaulay |
| General Hodenberg | Len Mence |
| "Monty" Travers | Joseph Santley |
| "Buddy" Haines | Gus Shy |
| Luella Holtz | Inez Courtney |

Gideon Holtz ........................................William Collier
Countess Nita........................................Nana Bryant
King Augustus III................................Fuller Mellish
Princess Elise......................................Desiree Ellinger
Carl ...................................................Jerome Daley
Peter ..................................................Neil Stone
Zeppo .................................................Dink Trout
The Flower Vender.................................George Djimos
    Act I.—Outside of the Casino at Monte Carlo.  Act II.—In and
Around the Palace at Borovina.
    Staged by William J. Wilson.

"Monty" Travers, an adventuresome young American, meets and wildly loves the Princess Elise of Borovina at Monte Carlo. Later he learns who she is and that her father, King Augustus, is in danger of being gypped by American oil speculators and deposed by native bolshevists. Breaking the bank "Monty" stuffs a satchel full of francs and flies to his lady's protection. It looks at the finish as though they might marry and raise duets.

## THE LADDER

### (264 performances)

Drama in three acts by J. Frank Davis. Produced by Brock Pemberton at the Mansfield Theatre, New York, October 22, 1926.

Cast of characters—

    Act I.—The Present Time.  The Home of Stephen Pennock, New
                   York City

Margaret Newell.............................Antoinette Perry
Stephen Pennock..................................Hugh Buckler
Betty Pennock......................................Irene Purcell
William Matteson................................Ross Alexander
Bellwood ............................................Edgar Stehli
Roger Crane .......................................Vernon Steele

    Scene 2—The Year 1300 A. D.  The Great Hall of the Earl of
                Orleton's Castle, England

Wat of Hampshire.........................Edward J. McNamara
Master William Warren.........................Ross Alexander
Betty Hackett......................................Irene Purcell
Sir Roger Clifford.................................Vernon Steele
Lady Mortimer.....................................Minnie Milne
Sir John Mortimer..............................Julius McVicker
Sir Henry Maule..................................Carl Anthony
Mistress Ellen....................................Anita Damrosch
Mistress Judith....................................Sallie Sanford
Stephen, Earl of Orleton...........................Hugh Buckler
The Abbot of Winfield.......................Montague Rutherfurd
Lady Margaret Percy............................Antoinette Perry
Master Peter Marsh.................................Edgar Stehli

    Act II.—The Year 1670 A. D.  The House of Mistress Sanderson
                on Pall Mall, London

Lady Colepepper....................................Minnie Milne
Mistress Margaret Sanderson.....................Antoinette Perry
Mistress Betty Holden..............................Irene Purcell
Mistress Berinthia Davenport......... ...........Anita Damrosch
Lucy..................................................Sallie Sanford

Stephen, Earl of Arlington..........................Hugh Buckler
Sir George Etheredge.......................Montague Rutherfurd
Sir Anthony Finch.................................Edgar Stehli
Ensign Marshall.................................Leonard Carey
Brooks.......................................George Carmichael
Lord William Sedley.............................Ross Alexander
Johnson .........................................Julius McVicker
Captain Roger Harcourt..........................Vernon Steele

Act III.—Scene 1—The Year 1844 A. D. The Home of John
Covill, New York City.

Welcome Jones...................................Sallie Sanford
Mrs. Porter........................................Minnie Milne
Mrs. Bowles.....................................Anita Damrosch
John Covill......................................Julius McVicker
Margaret Wright...............................Antoinette Perry
Roger Covill......................................Vernon Steele
Ranney ...........................................Edgar Stehli
Senator Henry.....................................Carl Anthony
Stephen Quinn....................................Hugh Buckler
William Covill...................................Ross Alexander
Betty Lee ........................................Irene Purcell

Scene 2—The Present Time. The Home of Stephen Pennock, New
York City.

Margaret Newell...............................Antoinette Perry
Roger Crane.......................................Vernon Steele
Peter Bellwood...................................Edgar Stehli
Staged by Brock Pemberton.

Margaret Newell is pestered prettily but seriously by two
lovers, Stephen Pennock, her widowed brother-in-law, and Roger
Crane, more attractive but rather vacillating. One night when
they had been talking of the eastern religions and the theory of
reincarnation, Margaret dozes off to dream of the time she was
Lady Margaret Percy in the old England of 1830; again when
she was Mistress Margaret Sanderson, actress, in 1670; and
finally when she was plain Margaret Wright in colonial New
York, 1844. She wakes up to know Roger is the boy.

## DAISY MAYME

### (112 performances)

Comedy in three acts by George Kelly. Produced by Rosalie
Stewart at The Playhouse, New York, October 25, 1926.

Cast of characters—

Ruth Fenner.........................................Nadea Hall
Mrs. Laura Fenner.................................Alma Kruger
Mrs. Olly Kipax.................................Josephine Hull
Cliff Mettinger.................................Carlton Brickert
May Phillips.......................................Madge Evans
Daisy Mayme Plunkett.............................Jessie Busley
Charlie Snyder.....................................Frank Rowan
Mr. Filoon...........................................Roy Fant
Acts I, II and III.—A Room in the Home of Cliff Mettinger.
Staged by George Kelly.

See page 281.

## SATURDAY NIGHT

(13 performances)

A play by Jacinto Benevente. Produced by the Civic Repertory Theatre, New York, October 25, 1926.

Cast of characters—

| | |
|---|---|
| Princess Etelvina | Hilda Plowright |
| Prince Michael | Sayre Crawley |
| The Duke of Suavia | Eugene Wellesley |
| Edith | Martha Leavitt |
| Prince Florencio | Paul Leyssac |
| Lady Seymour | Ruth Lavington |
| The Countess Rinaldi | Beatrice Terry |
| Leonardo | Alan Birmingham |
| Harry Lucenti | Marlyn Brown |
| Servant | Conway Washburne |
| Lord Seymour | Barlowe Borland |
| The Signore | David Belbridge |
| Imperia | Eva Le Gallienne |
| Cashier | Diana Rust |
| Ruhu-Sahib | Harold Moulton |
| Esther | Mimi Lehman |
| Juliette | Georgiana Brown |
| Waiter | Arthur Jacobson |
| Mr. Jacob | Egon Brecher |
| An Artist | Ian Emery |
| Tobacco | Sydney Machat |
| Mme. Jenny | Mary Ward |
| Cornac | Prince Singh |
| Rosina | Winthrop Wayne |
| Pepita | Isabel Jones |
| Mme. Lelia | Beatrice de Neergaard |
| Nunu | Hardie Albright |
| Tommy | Allan Campbell |
| Lelia's Husband | Wesley John |
| Donina | Rose Hobart |
| Zaida | Ruth Wilton |
| Flower Woman | Agnes McCarthy |
| Bareback Rider | Grace Carlisle |
| Male Dancer | Robert F. Ross |
| 3rd Sailor | Wesley John |
| Gaetano | Arthur Jacobson |
| 2nd Sailor | John F. Miller |
| 1st Sailor | Don Vere |
| Cecco | Sydney Machat |
| Commissary of Police | Gordon Pascal |
| An Unknown | Barlowe Borland |
| Majesta | Leona Roberts |
| Pietro | Edwin Cooper |
| Celeste | Françoise Du Moulin |
| Teresina | Georgiana Brown |
| Nelly | Martha Leavitt |
| Fanny | Margaret C. Love |
| Accordion Player | Alexander Ivanoff |
| Servant | Russell Hopkins |
| English Girl | Nancy Bevill |

Staged by Eva Le Gallienne.

The rise of Imperia from sculptor's model to prince's consort, and a story of debauchery among the royal idlers of early Italy.

## RAQUEL MELLER

### (13 performances)

A recital by Mlle. Meller, assisted by an orchestra under the direction of Victor Baravelle. Presented by E. Ray Goetz at the Henry Miller Theatre, New York, October 25, 1926.

"La Farandula Pasa" (Poor Pierrot)
"Nena"
"Tus Ojus" (Your Eyes)
"Mariana"
"El Peligro de las Rosas" (Beware of the Rose!)
"La Mujer d'en Manelic" (The Wife of Manelic)
"Noi de la Mare" (Joy and Pangs of Motherhood)
"El Relicario" (The Charm)
"Flor de Te" (Tea Blossom)
"Ay! Cipriano" (Naughty Cipriano!)
"Diguili que Vengui" (Tell Him to Come!)
"La Virgen Roja" (The Red Virgin)
"La Tarde del Corpus" (The Procession)

"La Monteria" (Grandmother's Dress)
"Manola"
"La Hija del Carcelero" (The Jailer's Daughter)
"La Reina del Cortijo" (The Peasant Queen)
"Mimosa"
"La Violetera" (The Violet Girl)
"Flor del Mal" (Flower of Sin)
"Siempre Flor" (The Eternal Flower)
"Gitanillo" (Gypsy Sweetheart)
"Mis Amores" (My Loves)
"El Pescadero" (The Fishmonger)
"La Mujer del Torero" (The Wife of the Bullfighter)
"Como la Flor" (Like the Flower)

The return of the Spanish diseuse was not as sensational as her first engagement, the previous season, but she enjoyed a profitable season of special matinées at the Henry Miller Theatre preceding a road tour.


## AUTUMN FIRE

### (71 performances)

Comedy drama in three acts by T. C. Murray. Produced by John L. Shine at the Klaw Theatre, New York, October 26, 1926.

Cast of characters—

Ellen Keegan...................... ......................Una O'Connor
Nance Desmond............................Julie Hartley-Milburn
Owen Keegan......................................John L. Shine
Michael Keegan ...................................... Felix Irwin
Mrs. Desmond.................................Caroline Morrison
Tom Furlong.................................Clement O'Loghlen
Molly Hurley.............................Mary Hartley-Milburn
Morgan Keegan.......................................Lloyd Neal
Acts I and III.—Owen Keegan's Farmhouse. Act II.—Mrs. Desmond's Cottage.
Staged by George Vivian.

Owen Keegan, sixty if he's a day, gets an idea that he is almost as young as he used to be and that he should marry Nance

Desmond and enjoy life. Nance, really in love with Owen's son Michael, agrees to marry Owen because of the property and the social advantages involved and goes through with her promise, even after Owen has been thrown from a horse he was trying to tame, and seriously injured. A year later Owen sees Michael kissing Nance, realizes that youth calls to youth, and cleans out his house. Michael goes away, but probably not for long.


## CAPONSACCHI

### (269 performances)

Drama in prologue and three acts by Arthur Goodrich and Rose A. Palmer based upon Robert Browning's "The Ring and the Book." Produced by Walter Hampden at Hampden's Theatre, New York, October 26, 1926.

Cast of characters—

| | |
|---|---|
| Giotti | Anthony Andre |
| Melchior | Marcel Dill |
| Andrea | Gordon Hart |
| Montini | Louis Polan |
| Pope Innocent XII | Stanley Howlett |
| Guido Franceschini | Ernest Rowan |
| Caponsacchi | Walter Hampden |
| Tommati | Hart Jenks |
| Venturini | P. J. Kelly |
| Scalchi | Robert Paton Gibbs |
| Gherardi | Dallas Anderson |
| Pietro Comparini | J. P. Wilson |
| Violante Comparini | Suzanne Jackson |
| Pompilia | Edith Barrett |
| Canon Conti | Cecil Yapp |
| Governor of Arezzo | C. Norman Hammond |
| Archbishop of Arezzo | Edwin Cushman |
| Margherita | Marie Adels |
| Salvatore | Howard Claney |
| Peppina | Grania O'Malley |
| Innkeeper at Castelnuovo | William H. Sams |
| His Servant | Albert West |
| Marinetta | Eudora Hunner |
| Guard at Castelnuovo | G. Tom Gomez |

Prologue and Epilogue—A Court of Justice at the Vatican. Act I.—The Carnival. Act II.—Caponsacchi's Cell, Arezzo. Street Outside Guido's Palace, Arezzo. The Inn at Castelnuovo. Act III.—A Court of Justice at the Vatican. Pietro's Villa, Rome.
Staged by Walter Hampden.

Caponsacchi, the noble priest of "The Ring and the Book," is on trial before the ecclesiastic court, charged with the murder of Pompilia and her parents. As he begins his testimony in defense the lights fade and the action goes back to the story of Guido Franceschini's plot to marry Pompilia, kill her and her parents and inherit the estates, and Caponsacchi's noble effort to save her and remain true to his vows despite his consuming love for the girl. Back to the trial and a dramatic decision by Pope Innocent XII in defense of truth, honor and Caponsacchi.


## THREE SISTERS

### (39 performances)

Drama by Anton Tchekov. Produced by the Civic Repertory Theatre at the Civic Repertory, New York, November 8, 1926.

Cast of characters—

```
Olga...............................................Beatrice  Terry
Irina..................................................Rose  Hobart
Baron Nikolay Lvovitch Tusenbach.................Harold  Moulton
Vassily Vassilyevitch Solyony......................Sydney  Machat
Ivan Romanitch Tchebutykin........................Sayre  Crawley
Masha.........................................Eva Le Gallienne
Anfisa..........................................Leona  Roberts
Ferapont........................................Marlyn  Brown
Orderly.........................................Gordon  Pascal
Lt.-Gov. Alexander Ignatyevitch Vershinin............Egon  Brecher
Andrey Sergeyevitch Prozorov................... Alan  Birmingham
Fyodor Illyitch Kuligin.............................Paul  Leyssac
Natalya Ivanovna...........................Beatrice de Neergaard
Alexey Petrovitch Fedotik........................Hardie  Albright
Vladimir Karkovitch Roddey..........................Ian  Emery
Maid... ...........................................Ruth  Wilton
Musician..........................................Nancy  Bevill
      Acts I, II and III.—The House and Gardens of the Prozorovs in
   a Provincial Town in Russia.
      Staged by Eva Le Gallienne.
```

In a Russian garrison town, Olga, Irina and Masha Prozorov find life dull and without promise. A regiment moves in, Masha indulges a sort of spinster love romance with the Lieutenant-Governor, and there is a flair of life for a time, during which Olga and Irina marry unhappily. Then the regiment moves away and things settle to their old level of hopeless boredom.


## GENTLE GRAFTERS

### (13 performances)

A play in three acts by Owen Davis. Produced by Sam H. Harris at the Music Box, New York, October 27, 1926.

Cast of characters—

```
Cora Blake...................................Charlotte  Granville
Mary Doyle.......................................Lucille  Sears
Ellen...............................................Liane  Carrera
```

Delivery Man......................................Walter Brown
Sally..........................................Katharine Alexander
Jim Merrick.......................................Morgan Wallace
Dick Cameron.......................................Robert Keith
Kitty Doyle.......................................Helene Lackaye
Jerry Doyle......................................Charles Kennedy
Dan McClung........................................Guy Nichols
Tom Morton........................................Charles Ritchie
Billy Dexter.......................................William David
Roberts...........................................Fred E. Strong
    Acts I, II and III.—Late Afternoon in December. New York City.
    Staged by Sam Forrest.

When Sally was seventeen her mother died, leaving her daughter without funds, expensive tastes and a determination to be even with men because of the love trick one of them had played her mother. Adopting Cora Blake as a sort of chaperon, Sally proceeds to support the two of them by gold digging. She lets her generous and expectant men friends donate what they will and gives nothing in return but her smiles and her thanks. Then she falls in love with Dick Cameron, poor but clean, who loves her. She wants to marry Dick, but Cora, the chaperon, wants her to become the mistress of Jim Merrick instead and lies to her about Dick. When it is too late Sally discovers the trick. She feels like killing herself, but goes out on a party instead.


## THE PEARL OF GREAT PRICE

### (32 performances)

Drama-spectacle in prologue, seven scenes and an epilogue. Book by Robert McLaughlin. Produced by the Messrs. Shubert at the Century Theatre, New York, November 1, 1926.

Cast of characters—

Adventure........................................John Nicholson
Any Man's Sister..................................Margot Kelly
Bailiff..............................................Peter Doyle
Beauty..........................................Dagmar Oakland
Beggar..........................................Booth Franklin
Blasé...........................................Booth Franklin
Bore..............................................Albert Froom
Cringe..............................................H. Kurasaki
Death...........................................Booth Franklin
Despair........................................Florence Pendleton
Drink.............................................John Nicholson
Envy......................................Mrs. William Faversham
Fame............................................Richard Temple
Folly.............................................Myrtle Adams
Foreman of the Jury...............................John Nicholson
Greed.............................................Edward Favor
Humanity.........................................Richard Temple
Hunger..............................................Peter Doyle
Idle Rich..........................................Frank Green
Indolence..........................................Helen Tucker

```
Law .................................................Albert Froom
Lesbia .............................................. Marie Desyls
Loneliness ......................................... Millie James
Love ..........................................Reginald Sheffield
Lure.............................................Bernice Gardner
Lust..............................................Eugene Ordway
Luxury .............................................Julia Hoyt
Luxury's Attendants
    Flip .............................................Sydna Black
    Flounce .......................................Adele Ranson
    Flirt...........................................Irma Bertrand
    Pert ..........................................Hazel Goodwin
    Primp..........................................Adele LeRoy
    Swish ............................................Mae Welch
    Swirl..........................................Francis Kelly
    Smirk............................................Betty Webb
Mother of Pilgrim..................................Effie Shannon
Orgy ..................................................Valdeo
Pander ..........................................Marion Kerby
Pilgrim.......................................Claudette Colbert
Preen ......................................Kathleen Cambridge
Prejudice .......................................Elmer Grandin
Pride..............................................Marie Pettes
Prudence ......................................Lalive Brownell
Queer..............................................Ross Neal
Quill..........................................William Du Pont
Slander........................................Millie Butterfield
Shame ..........................................Amelia Bingham
Smug ...........................................Herbert Ashton
Truth ..........................................Malcolm Fassett
Vanity.......................................Marcella Swanson
Vulgarity..........................................Lee Beggs
Want ...........................................William Du Pont
Wanton ..........................................Irene Whipple
```

Prologue—"The Little House Among the Hollyhocks." The Play—"The Abode of Luxury." "The Morn of Promise." "The Threshold of Fame." "The Street of Indecision." "Where Souls Are Put in Pawn." "The Auction Room of Shame." "The Court of Humanity." Epilogue—"The Trysting Place of Happiness."
Staged by J. C. Huffman.

When the mother of Pilgrim died all she had to leave her daughter was the Little House Among the Hollyhocks, which was mortgaged, and her (Pilgrim's) chastity, which she advised the girl to wear as a pearl of great price around her neck. Thereafter many evil men tried to possess themselves of Pilgrim's pearl, starting with Idle Rich. She is invited to Fame's studio to pose in nothing at all, but refuses to take off the pearl. Thrown into the street, Want and Despair escort her finally to the old House of Shame, where Pander and the rest of the girls and boys try to cheat and rob her of her heritage. But finally her chubby-faced True Love, who has been away with Adventure, comes for her and everything is probably for the best.

## LOOSE ENDS

(40 performances)

Drama in three acts by Dion Titheradge. Produced by Sam H. Harris at the Ritz Theatre, New York, November 1, 1926.

Cast of characters—

| | |
|---|---|
| Deborah Bryce | Alison Bradshaw |
| Cyril Gayling | Michael Braddell |
| Sarah Britt | Ethel Griffies |
| Nina Grant | Violet Heming |
| Hester | Bernice Beldon |
| Brenda Fallon | Molly Kerr |
| Ralph Carteret | Stanley Logan |
| Malcolm Forres | Dion Titheradge |
| Winton Penner | Charles Quartermaine |
| Reid | Vera Nielson |

Acts I and II.—Drawing Room in Nina Grant's Flat. Act III.—Brenda Fallon's Sitting Room.
Staged by Dion Titheradge.

Nina Grant, West End actress of standing in London, ran down Malcolm Forres while she was motoring in the park. Picking him up and carrying him to her apartment to be assured that he had suffered no serious injury, she ended by falling in love with him and marrying him. He was at least a much cleaner and finer type than any of her gin-and-scandal set. A year or so later Nina discovers that Malcolm, who is quite disgusted with her friends, is himself a released convict sentenced to serve a life term for murder. And yet he dare criticize her life and that of her set! She thinks she wants a divorce and he is willing she should have it. But she changes her mind finally and also her attitude toward life as it is lived nowadays.


## SEED OF THE BRUTE

(80 performances)

Drama in three acts by Knowles Entrikin. Produced by the Messrs. Wm. A. Brady, Jr., and Dwight Deere Wiman at the Little Theatre, New York, November 1, 1926.

Cast of characters—

| | |
|---|---|
| Lizzie Saunders | Hilda Vaughn |
| Calvin Roberts | Robert Ames |
| Lafe Bratton | Claude Cooper |
| Molly Warner Carr | Adele Carples |
| John Roberts | Donn Cook |
| Anne Emerson Roberts | Doris Rankin |
| Barbara Davis | Jane Seymour |

Judge Hannibal Emerson..........................David Glassford
David Carr.......................................Harold Elliott
Matthew Carr....................................Sydney Booth
    Prologue—Calvin Roberts' Barn.   Acts I and II.——The Living
Room of the Emerson Mansion.   Act III.—Molly Carr's Cottage, a
small Illinois County Seat.
    Staged by the Author.

Calvin Roberts is a strong, uneducated man and a political power in a small mid-western town.  He marries Anne Emerson of the cultured Emersons, but lives an increasingly lonely life because of the little they have in common.  His son, John, takes after his mother's side of the family and comes home from college practically a stranger to his father.  Calvin finds himself opposed to David Carr, a chum of John's, whose father has bought him the local newspaper.

Carr is determined to drive the Roberts' political ring out of existence.  Drawn to Carr despite this opposition, Roberts discovers that he is his illegitimate son.  But, seed of the brute though he may be, Carr repudiates the relationship and Roberts is left to fight out his life's problems alone.

## THE MASTER BUILDER

### (29 performances)

Drama by Henrik Ibsen.  Produced by the Civic Repertory at the Civic Repertory, New York, November 1, 1926.

Cast of characters—

Knut Brovik.....................................Sydney Machat
Kaia Folsi......................................Ruth Wilton
Ragnar Brovik...................................Harold Moulton
Halvard Solness.................................Egon Brecher
Aline Solness...................................Beatrice Terry
Doctor Herdal...................................Sayre Crawley
Miss Hilda Wangel..............................Eva Le Gallienne
    Act I.—Solness' Workroom.   Act II.—Drawing Room in Solness'
House.   Act III.—Verandah of Solness' House.
    Staged by Eva Le Gallienne.

See "Best Plays of 1925-26."

## THE PLAY'S THE THING

### (260 performances)

Comedy in three acts by Ferenc Molnar. Adapted by P. G. Wodehouse. Produced by the Charles Frohman Company at the Henry Miller Theatre, New York, November 3, 1926.

Cast of characters—

| | |
|---|---|
| Mansky | Hubert Druce |
| Sandor Turai | Holbrook Blinn |
| Albert Adam | Edward Crandall |
| Johann Dwornitschek | Ralph Nairn |
| Almady | Reginald Owen |
| Ilona Szabo | Catherine Dale Owen |
| Mell | Claud Allister |
| Lackeys | { Stephen Kendal<br>{ John Gerard |

Acts I, II and III.—A Room in a Castle on the Italian Riviera, a Saturday in Spring.

Staged by Holbrook Blinn.

See page 193.

## THE LITTLE CLAY CART

### (39 performances)

A Hindu drama, translated from the original Sanskrit by Arthur William Ryder. Revived at Neighborhood Playhouse, New York, November 8, 1926.

Cast of characters—

| | |
|---|---|
| The Singer with the Sitar | Prosulla Kumar Shoshal |
| The Musician with the Esrai | Sarat Lahiri |
| The Stage Manager | George Stillwell |
| Charudatta | Ian Maclaren |
| Maitreya | Edgar Kent |
| Rohasena | Lois Shore |
| Vardhamanaka | Walter Geer |
| Radanika | Dorothy Sands |
| Charudatta's Wife | Lily Lubell |
| Vasantasena | Betty Linley |
| Madanika | Paula Trueman |
| A Maid | Irene Lewisohn |
| Vasantasena's Mother | Dorothy Sands |
| Santhanaka | Marc Loebell |
| Sthavaraka | Otto Hulicius |
| A Courtier | John F. Roche |
| A Shampooer Who Turns Monk | Albert Carroll |
| Mathura | Joseph N. Thayer |
| Darduraka | Otto Hulicius |
| A Gambler | George Hoag |
| Sharvilaka | Theodore Hecht |
| Aryaka | Anton Bundsman |
| Chandanaka | George Stillwell |
| Viraka | George Hoag |
| The Beadle | Ralph Geddes |

```
The Judge.......................................George Stillwell
The Clerk........................................Anton Bundsman
The Gild Warden.................................Joseph N. Thayer
Courtroom Guards...............William Challee, John D. Haggart
Goha.................................................John Roche
Ahinta..............................................Walter Geer
Executioner's Guards................Horace Michael, David Lewis
    The City of Ujjayini (Called Also Avanti) and Its Environs.
    Staged by Agnes Morgan and Irene Lewisohn.
```

See "Best Plays of 1924-25."

## FIRST LOVE

### (50 performances)

Comedy in three acts, adapted by Zoe Akins from the French play "Pile ou Face," by Louis Verneuil. Produced by the Messrs. Shubert at the Booth Theatre, New York, November 8, 1926.

Cast of characters—

```
Delabudelière.......................................Orlando Daly
Count de Varigny..................................Bruce McRae
Julien.............................................Robert Davis
M. Courteil.....................................Leonard Booker
Prince Silaf-Erzerioun.......................Mortimer H. Weldon
Jean..............................................Geoffrey Kerr
Maica................................................Fay Bainter
Dominique........................................George Marion
    Act I.—47 Avenue du Parc Monceau, Paris. Act II.—An Attic
in the Quartier Latin. Act III.—21 Rue d'Aumale.
    Staged by George Marion.
```

Maica, having nursed Jean, a fellow lodger, through pneumonia, stays on as his mistress for three years. Jean is the son of the Count de Varigny and has left home because his father objected to his ambition to be a composer. Now the count is eager that Jean shall marry a rich girl and acquire financial independence. Maica, thinking to sell herself rather than permit Jean to do practically the same thing, offers herself to a rich man who has been writing her and who, it transpires, is Jean's father. Learning the truth of the situation the Count de Varigny forgives the lovers.

## OH, KAY

### (256 performances)

Musical comedy in two acts. Book by Guy Bolton and P. G. Wodehouse; music by George Gershwin; lyrics by Ira Gershwin.

Produced by Messrs. Alex A. Aarons and Vinton Freedley at the Imperial Theatre, New York, November 8, 1926.

Cast of characters—

| | |
|---|---|
| Molly Morse | Betty Compton |
| Peggy | Janette Gilmore |
| The Duke | Gerald Oliver Smith |
| Larry Potter | Harland Dixon |
| Phil Ruxton | Marion Fairbanks |
| Dolly Ruxton | Madeleine Fairbanks |
| "Shorty" McGee | Victor Moore |
| Constance Appleton | Sascha Beaumont |
| Jimmy Winter | Oscar Shaw |
| Kay | Gertrude Lawrence |
| Revenue Officer Jansen | Harry T. Shannon |
| Mae | Constance Carpenter |
| Daisy | Paulette Winston |
| Judge Appleton | Frank Gardiner |

Victor Arden and Phil Ohman at the Pianos.

Acts I, II and III.—In and Around Jimmy's House, Beachampton, Long Island.

Staged by John Harwood and Sammy Lee.

The Duke is a titled Englishman who turns his yacht, which is all he has left after the war, into a rum runner. His sister, Kay, accompanies him to America, comes ashore when the crew is landing the liquor, takes refuge from a storm in the home of Jimmy Winter, falls in love with Jimmy and marries him after he is successfully rid of a couple of previous marital entanglements.

## NAKED

### (32 performances)

A play in three acts by Luigi Pirandello. English translation by Arthur Livingston. Produced by Augustin Duncan at the Princess Theatre, New York, November 8, 1926.

Cast of characters—

| | |
|---|---|
| Ersilia Drei | Marguerite Risser |
| Ludovico Nota | Augustin Duncan |
| Signoria Onoria | Mattie Keene |
| Alfredo Cantavalle | Porter Hall |
| Franco Laspiga | Carlin Crandall |
| Emma | Georgiana Von Tornow |
| Grotti | Carroll Ashburn |

Acts I, II and III.—In Ludovica Nota's Study on a Busy Street in Rome.

Staged by Augustin Duncan.

Ersilia Drei, out of harmony with living, decides to kill herself, is restrained by Ludovico Nota, a novelist, and Franco Laspiga, a reporter. Undecided whether to marry the reporter, run

away with a lover, or live with the novelist, Ersilia concludes
again that life is a cheat and concludes a second time that death
is the true solution of her muddled existence.


## GAY PAREE

### (175 performances)

Revue in two acts. Dialogue by Harold Atteridge. Music and
lyrics by Alberta Nichols and Mann Holiner. Produced by the
Messrs. Shubert at the Winter Garden, New York, November 9,
1926.

Principals engaged—

| | |
|---|---|
| Chic Sale | Winnie Lightner |
| Max Hoffman, Jr. | Mary Milburn |
| Richard Bold | Helen Wehrle |
| Frank Gaby | Jane Aubert |
| Douglass Leavitt | Alice Boulden |
| Newton Alexander | Margie Finley |
| Chester Fredericks | Azeada Charkouie |
| Jack Haley | Lorraine Weimer |
| Ben Holmes | Gay Paree Girls |
| Al Wohlman | |

Staged by J. J. Shubert, Felix Seymour and J. C. Huffman.


## HEAD OR TAIL

### (7 performances)

A comedy in three acts by Laszlo Lakatos, adapted from the
Hungarian by Garrick Truman. Produced by Henry Baron at
the Waldorf Theatre, New York, November 9, 1926.

Cast of characters—

| | |
|---|---|
| Andor Tamas | Philip Merivale |
| Kitty Tamas | Estelle Winwood |
| Dr. Gunther | Charles Halton |
| Mr. Upmann | William J. Barwald |
| Ilona | Doris Underwood |
| Mama | Grace Filkins |
| Edwin Paris | Allyn Joslyn |
| Marie | Angela Jacob |

In Act II.

| | |
|---|---|
| Bubus | Allyn Joslyn |
| Madame | Grace Filkins |
| Baby | Doris Underwood |
| Katie | Estelle Winwood |
| The Director | William J. Barwald |
| The Editor | Charles Halton |
| Martha | Angela Jacob |

A Man.................................................Carl Reed
A Woman.........................................Mary Holmes
    Acts I and III.—Drawing Room in Andor Tamas' Home in Buda-
pest.   Intermezzo.  Entrance to the Opera Bar.  Act II.—Interior
of Opera Bar.
    Staged by Clarke Silvernail.

## JOHN GABRIEL BORKMAN

### (15 performances)

A play in four acts by Henrik Ibsen.  Produced by the Civic
Repertory Theatre, November 9, 1926.

Cast of characters—

Gunhild Borkman................................Beatrice Terry
Malena....................................Beatrice de Neergaard
Ella Rentheim.................................Eva Le Gallienne
Mrs. Fanny Wilton................................Ellida Pierra
Erhardt Borkman................................Hardie Albright
John Gabriel Borkman ............................. Egon Brecher
Frida Foldal........................................ Ruth Wilton
Vilhelm Foldal.................................. Sayre Crawley
    Acts I and III.—Mrs. Borkman's Drawing Room.  Act II.—The
Great Gallery.  Act IV.—An Open Space Outside the Main Building.
The Action Takes Place During the Course of One Evening.
    Staged by G. E. Calthrop.

See "Best Plays of 1925-26."

## OLD BILL, M. P.

### (23 performances)

Comedy in three acts by Bruce Bairnsfather; music by Abel
Baer.  Produced by Charles Coburn at the Biltmore Theatre,
New York, November 10, 1926.

Cast of characters—

Maggie .............................................Helen Hanlon
Kate..........................................Helen Tilden
Bert................. ⎰           ⎰ Charles McNaughton
Alf................. ⎬ Three Pals ⎬   Charles E. Jordan
Old Bill............ ⎱           ⎱   Charles Coburn
Lady Barbara .....................................Audrey Ridgwell
Lord Hadenham............................Lawrence D'Orsay
A Constable.................................N. St. Clair Hales
Wells...............................................Leonard Ide
Lord Bledlow.........................................C. T. Davis
Mr. Clayton........................................James Jolley
Molly Parsons................................... Evelyn Clayton
Bessie Martin....................................Lillian Spencer
Suzanne Constance Saunderson...................Josephine Willis
Raleigh...........................................Thomas P. Tracy
Fenelli.......................................N. St. Clair Hales
Maxwell .........................................Herbert Ranson

Mrs. Bradley..................................Susanna Lawrance
Bob Martin........................................Roy Cochrane
Jim Bailey.....................................George Fitzgerald
Tom Lloyd.....................................Lawrence Sterner
Ed Brown..........................................Henry Carvill
Steve Graddon..................................Guido Alexander
Frank Lewis...........................................F. H. Day
Ned Denton...................................Leighton Converse
Jim Neil..........................................Allan Cromer
Mr. Montague..............................Wallace Widdecombe
Baxter.........................................Herbert Belmore
A Footman.....................................Guido Alexander
Dave Long..........................................Colin Hunter
Joe Darvil...........................................Paul Dane
Pete Saunders............................George V. Denny, Jr.
Jack Grey..........................................George Lamb
A Woman.........................................Nancy De Silva
Clerk of Court..................................Thomas P. Tracy
Mr. Ingram........................................Roy Cochrane
Inspector Ferguson...............................Henry Carvill
Mr. Morton, M.P. .............................George Fitzgerald
Mr. Chisel.........................................George Lamb
A Postman.........................................Colin Hunter
  Staged by Henry Herbert.

The hero of "The Better Ole" in politics standing for parliament and working in the coal mines. With Bert and Alf, Old Bill is imprisoned in a mine following an explosion but finally rescued.


## THE EMPEROR JONES

### (61 performances)

A play by Eugene O'Neill. Produced by Mayfair Productions at the Mayfair Theatre, New York, November 10, 1926.

Cast of characters—

An Old Native Woman.............................Hazel Mason
Harry Smithers......................................Moss Hart
Brutus Jones, Emperor..........................Charles S. Gilpin
Lem............................................Arthur Ames
Soldiers, Adherents of Lem, the Little Formless Fears
Jeff..............................................John Blue
The Negro Convicts..George Blue, John Ray, Harry Crow, James Lee
The Prison Guard..................................John Reid
The Planters........................George Frey, Harold Mays
The Spectators............................Mary Pine, Mae Ford
The Auctioneer......................................Hugh Rice
The Slaves........George Blue, John Ray, Harry Crow, James Lee
The Congo Witch Doctor........................Kenneth Harris
The Crocodile God ................................
  The action takes place on a West Indian Island not yet self-determined by white marines. The form of government is, for the moment, an empire.

See "Best Plays of 1920-21."

## THE SQUALL

(262 performances)

Drama in three acts by Jean Bart. Produced by A. L. Jones and Morris Green at the 48th Street Theatre, New York, November 11, 1926.

Cast of characters—

| | |
|---|---|
| Manuela | Mary Fowler |
| Pedro | Hugh Kidder |
| Dona Paca | Ida Mulle |
| Finito | Romney Brent |
| Anita | Dorothy Stickney |
| Juan Mendez | Horace Braham |
| Padre Molina | Charles R. Burrows |
| Don Diego | Henry O'Neill |
| Dolores Mendez | Blanche Yurka |
| Jose Mendez | Lee Baker |
| Nubi | Suzanne Caubet |
| El Moro | Ali Yousuff |

Acts I, II and III.—The Living Room of the Mendez Household Located in Quejano, Near Granada.

Staged by Lionel Atwill.

Nubi, a wild gypsy girl, blows into the home of the Mendez' on the wings of a squall, pursued by El Moro, her chief. Pleading for protection, the Mendez hide and keep Nubi when the gypsies move on. She rewards their kindness by seducing José, the father, and Juan, the son, not to mention Pedro, the hired man. Then El Moro comes back and takes her home.

## PRINCESS TURANDOT

(26 performances)

A fantasy adapted from the Russian version by Harry G. Alsberg and Isaac Don Levine. Intermezzo by Lewis Waller. Produced by Carlo Gozzi at Provincetown, November 12, 1926.

Cast of characters—

| | |
|---|---|
| Tartaglia }<br>Ishmael } | J. Edward Bromberg |
| Pantalone | Victor Sharoff |
| Brigella | Harold McGee |
| Princess Turandot | Barbara Bulgakov |
| Kalaf | Kirby Hawkes |
| Adelma | Leni Stengel |
| Altoum | Jasper Deeter |
| Skirina | Sada Gordon |
| Timur | George Frame Brown |
| Zelima | Muriel Campbell |
| Barak | Moss Fleisig |

Slave Girl..........................................Sheba Strunsky
The Sages.........Edward Robbin, Boris Marshmallow, Ferd Nofer
    Acts I, II and III.—In and Around Pekin, China, in the 13th
Century.
    Staged by Leo Bulgakov.

The Princess Turandot is a male-hating lady who swears she will marry no man who cannot guess the three hardest riddles she can think up. Many try and suffer death as a penalty of failure. Then Prince Kalaf guesses the riddles, but forswears marriage when he discovers how the Princess feels about men. Finally the Princess comes down from her high throne and there is joy at the court.


## PYGMALION

### (143 performances)

Comedy in five acts by Bernard Shaw. Produced by the Theatre Guild at the Guild Theatre, New York, November 15, 1926.

Cast of characters—

Clara Hill..........................................Phyllis Connard
Mrs. Eynsford Hill.............................Winifred Hanley
A Bystander.......................................Charles Cardon
Freddy Hill......................................Charles Courtneidge
Eliza Doolittle....................................Lynn Fontanne
Colonel Pickering..................................J. W. Austin
Another Bystander..............................Bernard Savage
The Sarcastic Bystander............................Leigh Lovel
An Elderly Gentleman..........................Thomas Meegan
An Elderly Lady....................................Kitty Wilson
Henry Higgins..................................Reginald Mason
Taxi Driver.....................................Edward Hartford
Mrs. Pearce........................................Beryl Mercer
Alfred Doolittle..................................Henry Travers
Mrs. Higgins.....................................Helen Westley
The Maid..........................................Dorothy Fletcher
    Act I.—Covent Garden at 11.15 P.M. Acts II and IV.—Higgins'
Laboratory in Wimpole Street. Act III and V.—Drawing Room.
    Staged by Dudley Digges.

Professor Higgins, specializing in phonetics, wagers his friend, Colonel Pickering, that by teaching Liza, a flower girl, the speech and manners of a lady he can introduce her at a royal garden party as a duchess and have her so accepted by society. The experiment is a success, but what to do with the remade Eliza after that is a problem. There is a hint that she stays on and looks after the Professor, who has grown more or less dependent upon her.

## GERTIE

### (248 performances)

Comedy-drama in three acts by Tadema Bussière. Produced by Gustav Blum at the Bayes Theatre, New York, November 15, 1926.

Cast of characters—

| | |
|---|---|
| Mrs. Flynn | Carrie Lowe |
| Jimmie | Elisha Cook, Jr. |
| Jones | Allen Nagle |
| Amy | Marienne Francks |
| Joe | Jimmie Scott |
| Steve | Pat O'Brien |
| Gertie | Constance McKay |
| Sylvester Cunningham | Edward Reese |
| Jarvis | Waldo Edwards |
| A Policeman | Edward Goff |

Acts I, II and III.—In Gertie's Room, Mrs. Flynn's Rooming House on West 66th Street, New York.
Directed by Gustav Blum.

Gertie, an attractive working girl, can sell herself to an aristocrat, Sylvester Cunningham, but the night he comes to her drunk and she knows his intentions are altogether dishonorable, she throws him out and decides to stick to Steve, the honest garage man, who has loyally loved her through it all.

## A PROUD WOMAN

### (7 performances)

A comedy in three acts by Arthur Richman. Produced by Edgar Selwyn at the Maxine Elliott Theatre, New York, November 15, 1926.

Cast of characters—

| | |
|---|---|
| Mrs. Merritt | Margaret Wycherley |
| Frank Baldwin | Percy Ames |
| Selma | Madeleine King |
| Senator Norton | Brandon Evans |
| Marion Taylor | Florence Eldridge |
| Edgar Merritt | John Marston |
| Julia Cates | Elizabeth Risdon |
| Wilbur Cates | Herbert Yost |
| Edith Norton | Anne Morrison |

Acts I, II and III.—At the Merritts', New York City.
Staged by John Hayden.

Marion Taylor, come to New York from the West to earn her living, meets and loves Edgar Merritt, an upstanding young lawyer of family. They are quickly engaged and about to be married, when Marion's sister, Julia Cates, a proud and selfish woman, comes on for the ceremony, instills the suspicion in Marion's mind that she is being made cheap by the Merritts because she is, to them, just a working girl and finally induces Marion to break off the match. Marion realizes her mistake in the end, but is so disgusted with herself for having listened to her sister that she goes away to think things over, leaving her erstwhile fiancé waiting hopefully.

## LILY SUE

### (47 performances)

Melodrama in three acts by Willard Mack. Produced by David Belasco at the Lyceum Theatre, New York, November 16, 1926.

Cast of characters—

| | |
|---|---|
| Harve Pedley | Huron L. Blyden |
| Phronia | Florence Gerald |
| Lily Sue | Beth Merrill |
| Asa | Leslie M. Hunt |
| "Duke" Adams | Curtis Cooksey |
| Louis Lingard } Lance Lingard } | Joseph Sweeney |
| Joe Holly | Willard Mack |
| "Stonewall" Billings | James Grady |
| Charlie Highhorse | William Courtleigh |
| Mina Keason | Beatrice Banyard Mack |
| Uncle Johnny Hines | Robert Wayne |
| Jerry | Arnold Davidson |
| Luke | John Wheeler |
| Jake | Earl Craddock |
| Jack | Edmond Norris |
| Buck | Jose Yovin |
| Tom | John Clemence |
| Pete | Franklin Klein |
| Bill | F. Raymond |
| Jim | Edward Kelly |

Act I.—The Pedley Ranch Near Sweet Grass, Montana. Act II.—The Ranch Dooryard. Act III.—Interior of the Ranch House. The Jail Near Sweet Grass.

Staged by David Belasco.

Lily Sue Pedley is the eighteen-year-old daughter of a family of nomadic homesteaders in the West. Much admired by many men she is most desired by Joe Holly, the sheriff, Duke Adams, a handsome cowhand, and Louis Lingard, a no-good rancher. Lingard, caught peeping at Lily as she disrobes in a tent with a light in it, is shot and killed. Duke is suspected and arrested by the sheriff. The Lingard gang, bent on lynching Duke, surround the jail and are about to hang Duke when Lily Sue rides furiously to his rescue. It was her brother Asa who did the killing for defensible reasons of his own.

## TWINKLE, TWINKLE

### (167 performances)

Musical comedy in two acts. Books and lyrics by Harlan Thompson; music by Harry Archer; additional scenes and numbers by Kalmar and Ruby. Produced by Louis F. Werba at the Liberty Theatre, New York, November 16, 1926.

Cast of characters—

```
Jack Wyndham....................................Joseph Lertora
Florence Devereaux...........................Perqueta Courtney
Louise................................................Elise Bonwit
Dolores....  ......................................Dorothy Martin
Suzette.............................................Anita Firman
June..................................................Diana Day
Gloria................................................Ann Kelly
Sam Gibson.................................William J. McCarthy
A Cutie...........................................Therese Kelly
Alice James.........................................Ona Munson
Jennie.............................................Patty Hastings
Richard Grey.....................................Alan Edwards
Harry..............................................John Sheehan
Telegraph Operator..................................John Gray
P. G. (Peachy) Robinson..........................Joe E. Brown
Bessie Smith........................................Flo Lewis
Jane Robinson.....................................Frances Upton
```
Act I.—Private Car of Alice James. A Railroad Crossing. Railroad Eating House, Pleasantville, Kansas. Outside Mrs. Green's Boarding House. Act II.—Garden of Mrs. Green's Boarding House. Staged by Frank Craven, Julian Alfred and Harry Puck.

Alice James, a famous movie star, fed up with the Hollywood crew, drops off the train at a small town in Kansas and becomes a waitress in the station eating house. Pursued by rival film directors and also by a hick detective, P. G. Robinson, Alice is finally exposed, but not before she has met, loved and promised to marry Richard Grey.

## THE WITCH

### (28 performances)

Drama in four acts by John Mansfield (from the Norwegian by H. Wiers-Jensen). Produced by Carl Reed at the Greenwich Village Theatre, New York, November 18, 1926.

Cast of characters—

```
Merete Beyer...............................Adelaide Fitz Allan
Bente.........................................Genevieve Dolaro
Anne Pedersdotter..................................Alice Brady
Jorund..........................................Louise Lorimer
David............................................Wallace House
Herlofs-Marte...............................Maria Ouspenskaya
Martin............................................Hugh Huntley
```

```
Absolon..........................................David  Landau
Leader of Town Guards.........................George Blackwood
Jost................................................. Arthur  Gray
Hendrik............................................ V. P. Newmark
Master Klaus....................................James C. Malaidy
Master Laurentius.............................. Erskine  Sanford
Master Johannes.............................. Harold DeBecker
Jens Schelotrup.............................. Henry  Buckler
```
      Act I.—Dooryard of Absolon's House.  Acts II and III.—A Room
in Absolon's House.  Act IV.—The Choir of Bergen Cathedral in
the Year 1574.
      Directed by Hubert Osborne.

Anne Pedersdotter, daughter of a woman suspected of witchcraft in sixteenth-century Norway, is married at an early age to
Absolon, the palace chaplain who is many years her senior.
Martin, Absolon's son, by a former marriage, on a visit home is
greatly desired by Anne, who, hearing the story of her mother's
power over men, tries it successfully on the boy.  It works so
well she next wishes her husband dead, and he succumbs to a
stroke.  Anne is arrested by the church authorities, held for
witchcraft and goes mad when put to the test of touching the
corpse of Absolon.

## MOZART

### (32 performances)

Comedy in three acts by Sacha Guitry; music by Reynaldo
Hahn; English version by Ashley Dukes; prologue by Brian
Hooker.  Produced by E. Ray Goetz at the Music Box Theatre,
New York, November 22, 1926.

### Cast of characters—

```
Madame d'Epinay..................................Lucile Watson
Mlle. Marie-Anne de Saint-Pons...................Frieda Inescort
Grimaud..........................................Harold Heaton
Louise..............................................Jeanne Greene
Marquis de Chambreuil............................Stewart Baird
Baron von Grimm..................................Frank Cellier
La Guimard......................................Martha Lorber
Mozart...........................................Irene Bordoni
Mon. Vestris......................................J. Blake Scott
```
      The Action Passes in the Home of Madame d'Epinay in Paris in
the Year 1778.
      Staged by William H. Gilmore and Norman Loring.

Mozart, in his early twenties, is in Paris visiting the Baron
von Grimm, his friend and patron.  In search of love and inspiration the youthful composer attracts the attentions of many
ladies, and is so interested in love that his muse practically de-

serts him. Finally Von Grimm, disappointed and a little jealous, sends him home.

## UP THE LINE

### (24 performances)

Drama in three acts by Henry Fisk Carlton. Produced by Richard Herndon at the Morosco Theatre, New York, November 22, 1926.

Cast of characters—

| | |
|---|---|
| Ma | Lydia Willmore |
| Effie | Florence Johns |
| Jenny | Dorothy Estabrook |
| Slug | Louis Calhern |
| Rat | Barry Macollum |
| Big Bill | Carleton Macy |
| Happy | Daniel Kelly |
| Jarnigan | Pat S. Barrett |
| Nels | J. Malcom Dunn |
| John | Lynne Berry |
| Blackie | Harlan Briggs |
| Ruth | Elizabeth Wragge |

Acts I, II and III.—In the Mess Shack of a Ranch House in North Dakota.

Staged by Allan Dinehart.

Effie, hired girl on one of the Jarnigan ranches in North Dakota, longs passionately for the romance of life and travel in the great outside world. Slug, one of the peregrinating wobblies, hired for the harvest, fills her mind with stories of his adventures. Effie falls in love with Slug, and when she cannot leave her invalid mother to follow him he stays with her. They are married. Slug grows restless and would move on. Effie knows that she is to have a child, and when Slug wants to move on lets him go. Eight years later, nothing having been heard of Slug, she marries Nels, an honest Swede. Then Slug comes back and would stay with Effie and their child. But she sends him away again.

## THIS WAS A MAN

### (31 performances)

Comedy in three acts by Noel Coward. Produced by Basil Dean, Inc., at the Klaw Theatre, New York, November 23, 1926.

Cast of characters—

| | |
|---|---|
| Carol Churt | Francine Larrimore |
| Harry Challoner | Terence Neill |

```
Edward Churt...................................A. E. Matthews
Lady Margot Butler.............................Violet Campbell
Berry...........................................Leonard Loan
Lord Romford.................................Mackenzie Ward
Zoe St. Mervyn......................................Auriol Lee
Major Evelyn Bathurst............................Nigel Bruce
Blackwell........................................Horace Pollock
```
    Acts I and III.—Edward Churt's Studio in Knightsbridge, London. Act II.—Evelyn Bathurst's Flat in Half-Moon Street, London. Staged by Basil Dean.

Edward Churt, knowing that his wife Carol is quite frequently and rather boldly unfaithful to him, follows the easier course of shutting his eyes to the situation rather than create a scandal and suffer the humiliations of court action. His good friend, Major Bathurst, thinking to expose Carol and serve his friend, invites her to his rooms, where she entraps him, and he also stays the night. The Major honorably confesses his sins next morning, which stirs Churt to a promise of action against Carol.

## LA LOCANDIERA

### (*The Mistress of the Inn*)

### (31 performances)

Comedy in three acts. Translated and adapted from the Italian of Carlo Goldoni by Helen Lohmann. Produced by the Civic Repertory Theatre at the Civic Repertory Theatre, New York, December 6, 1926.

Cast of characters—

```
The Marquis of Forlipopoli.......................Sayre Crawley
The Count of Albafiorita..........................Paul Leyssac
Fabrizio......................................Alan Birmingham
The Cavalier of Ripafratta.......................Egon Brecher
Mirandolina...................................Eva Le Gallienne
Servant to the Cavalier.........................Barlowe Borland
Ortensia........................................Beatrice Terry
Djaneira...............................Beatrice de Neergaard
```
    Acts I, II and III.—In an Inn, 18th-century Italy. Staged by Eva Le Gallienne.

Mirandolina, the attractive mistress of an inn, is sought by many of her lodgers, but has little use for men until the Cavalier of Ripafratta defies her. He has no more use for women than she has for men. Mirandolina successfully brings him to his knees with a proposal and then marries Fabrizio, her younger and more attractive helper

## THE CONSTANT WIFE

(233 performances)

Comedy in three acts by W. Somerset Maugham. Produced by the Charles Frohman Company at the Elliott Theatre, New York, November 29, 1926.

Cast of characters—

| | |
|---|---|
| Mrs. Culver | Mabel Terry-Lewis |
| Bentley | Thomas A. Braidon |
| Martha Culver | Cora Witherspoon |
| Barbara Fawcett | Jeanette Sherwin |
| Constance Middleton | Ethel Barrymore |
| Marie-Louise Durham | Veree Teasdale |
| John Middleton, F.R. C.S. | C. Aubrey Smith |
| Bernard Kersal | Frank Conroy |
| Mortimer Durham | Walter Kingsford |

The Action of the Play Takes Place in John's House in Harley Street, London.

Staged by Gilbert Miller.

See page 118.

## NED McCOBB'S DAUGHTER

(132 performances)

A play in three acts by Sidney Howard. Produced by the Theatre Guild at the John Golden Theatre, New York, November 29, 1926.

Cast of characters—

| | |
|---|---|
| Carrie Callahan | Clare Eames |
| First Federal Man | Maurice McRae |
| Nat Glidden | Philip Loeb |
| Second Federal Man | Morris Carnovsky |
| Jenny | Margalo Gillmore |
| Babe Callahan | Alfred Lunt |
| Captain Ned McCobb | Albert Perry |
| George Callahan | Earle Larimore |
| Lawyer Grover | Edward G. Robinson |
| Ben McCobb | Philip Leigh |

Act I.—Inside "Carrie's Spa" at the Merrybay Terminus of the Kennebec Ferry. Acts II and III.—The Parlor of the Old McCobb Homestead.

Staged by Philip Moeller.

Carrie Callahan, running a spa in Merrybay, Maine, is married to George Callahan, a worthless Irishman from Boston. George's brother, Babe, who has taken to bootlegging, stops at the spa, and when George is arrested for stealing $2,000 from the ferry company, offers to pay the money and keep him out of jail if Carrie will let him use her barn as a storage place for his liquor. Carrie, forced by circumstances to accept the offer, ends by tricking Babe out of his money.

## MAITRESSE DE ROI

### (48 performances)

An historical play in four acts and one tableau by M. M. Adolphe Aderer and Armand Ephraim; music by M. Arthur Honegger. Produced by the Messrs. Shubert at the Cosmopolitan Theatre, New York, November 30, 1926.

Cast of characters—

| | |
|---|---|
| Comtesse Du Barry | Mme. Cécile Sorel |
| Comtesse De Montauran | Mlle. Marie-Louise Berger |
| Zamore | Mlle. Inger de Friis |
| Louise | Mlle. Paulette Noizeux |
| Marie Deliant | Mme. Farnel |
| La Femme de la Halle | Mlle. Gabrielle Calvi |
| 1er Mannequin | Mme. Olga Livinoff |
| Mme. Bertin | Mme. Jeanne Despa |
| 2eme. Mannequin | Mme. Jeanne Frison |
| 3eme Mannequin | Mme. Frappier |
| Une Suivante | Mme. Marthe Réal |
| Une Femme du Peuple | Mme. Helen Vox |
| S. M. Louis XV | M. Louis Ravet |
| De Lambry | M. Rolla Norman |
| Marquis de Lubersac | M. Charles Gerval |
| Le Maier | M. Guy Favières |
| L'Abbe Delille | M. Marc Darnault |
| Maitre Lepot | M. Selmar |
| Drouias | M. Jacques Dapoigny |
| Roettier | M. Harout |
| Zamore | M. Moros |
| Deliant | M. Pierre Sentés |
| Roger | M. Eddy Fastré |
| Le Nonce | M. Jean Martini |
| Denizot | M. Pierre Vérat |
| Samson | M. André Marcel |
| L'Executeur | M. André Gilbert |
| Le Maire | M. Paul George |

Staged by M. Komisarjevski.

The drama of du Barry, picking the famous mistress up when she was spending a part of Louis XV's money to lessen the wants of her favorite poets and painters, carrying her through a rescue of and flirtation with the handsome guardsman, De-Laubry and ending with her incarceration and death upon the guillotine in the Revolution. The Sorel repertoire also included "Le Misanthrope," "L'Aventurière," "La Dame Aux Camelias," and "Le Demi Monde."

## BEYOND THE HORIZON

(79 performances)

Drama in three acts by Eugene O'Neill. Revived by The Actors Theatre at the Mansfield Theatre, New York, November 30, 1926.

Cast of characters—

| | |
|---|---|
| James Mayo | Malcolm Williams |
| Kate Mayo | Judith Lowry |
| Captain Dick Scott | Albert Tavernier |
| Andrew Mayo | Thomas Chalmers |
| Robert Mayo | Robert Keith |
| Ruth Atkins | Aline MacMahon |
| Mrs. Atkins | Eleanor Wesselhoeft |
| Mary | Elaine Koch |
| Ben | Victor Kilian |
| Doctor Fawcett | Joseph McInerney |

Acts I, II and III.—The Mayo Farm Overlooking the Sea.

See "Best Plays of 1919-20."

## THE DESERT SONG

(228 performances)

Operetta in two acts; music by Sigmund Romberg; book by Otto Harbach, Oscar Hammerstein, 2nd, and Frank Mandel. Produced by Messrs. Laurence Schwab and Frank Mandel at the Casino Theatre, New York, November 30, 1926.

Cast of characters—

| | |
|---|---|
| Sid El Kar | William O'Neal |
| Mindar | O. J. Vanasse |
| Hassi | Earle Mitchell |
| Benjamin Kidd | Eddie Buzzell |
| Captain Paul Fontaine | Glen Dale |
| Azuri | Pearl Regay |
| Sergeant La Vergne | Albert Baron |
| Sergeant DuBassac | Charles Davis |
| Margot Bonvalet | Vivienne Segal |
| General Birabeau | Edmund Elton |
| Pierre Birabeau | Robert Halliday |
| Susan | Nellie Breen |
| Ethel | Elmira Lane |
| Ali Ben Ali | Lyle Evans |
| Clementina | Margaret Irving |
| Neri | Rachel May Clark |
| Hadji | Chas. Morgan |

Acts I and II.—In the Riff Mountains and General Birabeau's Home, Northern Africa.

Staged by Arthur Hurley and Robert Connelly.

Pierre Birabeau, having espoused the cause of the Riffs to protect them from the cruelties of his own commanding officer, finds himself opposed in the campaign by his own father. Disguised as the Red Shadow he leads the Riffians in many successful campaigns, escaping detection by pretending to be half-witted at home. Assisting in the abduction of the girl he loves, Margot Bonvalet, he makes passionate love to her in the desert as his rebel self and wins her hand when exposure follows.

## SAY IT WITH FLOWERS

### (2 performances)

A farce comedy in three acts by Luigi Pirandello, translated by Alice Rohe. Produced by Brock Pemberton at the Garrick Theatre, December 3, 1926.

Cast of characters—

| | |
|---|---|
| Rosario | Mary Tupper |
| Toto Pulejo | Maxwell Sholes |
| Prof. Paolino | Osgood Perkins |
| Mrs. Petella | Carlotta Irwin |
| Nono | Willard Tobias |
| Giglio | Paul Jones |
| Belli | Teddy Jones |
| Dr. Nino Pulejo | Charles D. Brown |
| Grazia | Ethel Martin |
| A Sailor | John Saunders |
| Captain Petella | Hugh Buckler |

Act I.—Prof. Paolino's Study. Acts II and III.—The Home of the Petellas. In an Italian Seaside City.

Staged by Brock Pemberton.

Professor Paolino, carrying on an affair with Mrs. Petella during her sailor husband's absence, is keen to be relieved of threatened responsibilities by effecting a reconciliation between the Petellas, who have long been estranged. While Captain Petella is home briefly, the professor manages a dinner for him that is highly seasoned and very wet. If reconciliation follows Mrs. Petella is to put a potted plant on the balcony. Next day the balcony is a mass of flowers and the Petella home a wreck.

## THE PIRATES OF PENZANCE

### (128 performances)

A comic opera in two acts. Produced by the Gilbert and Sullivan Opera Company at the Plymouth Theatre, New York, December 6, 1926.

Cast of characters—

| | |
|---|---|
| Richard | John Barclay |
| Samuel | J. Humbird Duffey |

Frederic...........................................William Williams
Major-General Stanley.............................Ernest Lawford
His Orderly.........................................Bert Prival
Edward............................................William C. Gordon
A Doctor of Divinity................................Bert Prival
Mabel.............................................Ruth Thomas
Kate..............................................Sybil Sterling
Edith.............................................Eleanor Edson
Isabel............................................Adele Sanderson
Maud.............................................Paula Langlen
Ruth.............................................Vera Ross
    Act I.—A Rocky Seashore on the Coast of Cornwall, England.
Act II.—A Ruined Chapel on General Stanley's Estate.
    Staged by Winthrop Ames.

The second of the Winthrop Ames revivals of the Gilbert-Sullivan repertoire, following his successful reintroduction of "Iolanthe" the previous season.


## SLAVES ALL

### (8 performances)


A play in three acts by Edward Percy. Produced by William A. Brady at the Bijou Theatre, December 6, 1926.

Cast of characters—

Squitch............................................Stanley Drewitt
George Squitch...................................Reginald Sheffield
Jenny Venn....................................Marguerite Mosier
Ann Rigordan......................................Vera Allen
Julia Rigordan....................................Marian Abbott
Charlotte Holdsworth....................Nancie Halliwell Hobbes
Dr. Felix Burn...............................T. Wigney Percyval
Rev. Matthew Holdsworth........................Halliwell Hobbes
John Rigordan......................................Lionel Atwill
Captain Sheamus Blagdon.........................Herbert Ashton
    Acts I, II and III.—Dining-room of the Rigordans' Home at Tunbridge Wells.
    Staged by Lumsden Hare.

John Rigordan, a writer who suffers periodical cravings for alcoholic stimulation, is cut off by his older sister, Julia, from participation in his father's estate. He has some thought of putting poison in his sister's soup and marrying the housemaid. But sister takes an overdose of laudanum and saves him the trouble. He discovers after Julia's death that the housemaid is his own niece.

## THIS WOMAN BUSINESS
(47 performances)

A comedy in three acts by Benn W. Levy. Produced by Dr. Louis Sunshine at the Ritz Theatre, December 7, 1926.

Cast of characters—

| | |
|---|---|
| Hodges | George Thorpe |
| Honey | Henry Kendall |
| Nettlebank | Elena Aldcroft |
| Crofts | George Graham |
| Brown | Edward Rigby |
| Bingham | O. P. Heggie |
| Trent | J. Augustus Keogh |
| Crawford | Genevieve Tobin |
| Addleshaw | John Heath Goldsworthy |

Acts I, II and III.—The Living-room of Hodges' Country House in Cornwall.

Staged by Edward Rigby.

Hodges, being a woman hater, invites five or six other men of similar views to spend a peaceful and Eveless holiday at his country place. In pops Crawford, a London typist disgusted with life and about to become a thief. The misogynists take her in, set her straight and she ends by marrying Hodges.

## THE CONSTANT NYMPH
(148 performances)

A play in three acts by Margaret Kennedy and Basil Dean, Produced at the Selwyn Theatre, New York, December 9, 1926, by George C. Tyler and Basil Dean.

Cast of characters—

| | |
|---|---|
| Lewis Dodd | Glenn Anders |
| Linda Cowlard | Marion Warring-Manley |
| Kate Sanger | Olive Reeves-Smith |
| Katerina | Loretta Higgins |
| Kiril Trigorin | Paul Ker |
| Paulina Sanger | Louise Huntington |
| Teresa Sanger | Beatrix Thomson |
| Jacob Birnbaum | Louis Sorin |
| Antonia Sanger | Ruth Nugent |
| Roberto | Harry Sothern |
| Susan | Gloria May Kelly |
| Florence Churchill | Lotus Robb |
| Charles Churchill | Edward Emery |
| Millicent Gregory | Jane Savile |
| Sir Bartlemy Pugh | Sidney Paxton |
| Peveril Leyburn | Leo Carroll |
| Erda Leyburn | Olive Reeves-Smith |
| Dr. Dawson | J. H. Brewer |
| Lydia Mainwaring | Loretta Higgins |

```
Robert Mainwaring..............................Percy Baverstock
An Usher........................................William Evans
A Fireman..................................Thomas Coffin Cooke
A Clerk..................................... Harry M. Cooke
Madame Marxse...............................Katherine Stewart
```
Act I.—"Sanger's Circus." The Living-room at the Karindehutte, Austrian Tyrol. Act II.—"The Silver Sty." Act III.—The Artists' Room in Queen's Hall, London, and the Pension Marxse in Brussels.
Staged by Basil Dean.

The Sangers, Lewis Dodd, Trigorin and Birnbaum are living more or less unconventionally in the Tyrol. Sanger dies, his cousins, the Churchills, come on to straighten matters out and take Teresa and Paulina back to England to school. Florence Churchill fascinates and marries Dodd, who later repents the match and knows, at last, that it is Teresa he really loves, as she worships him. Teresa elopes with Dodd to Brussels and dies in a pension.

## THE TRUMPET SHALL SOUND

### (30 performances)

A play in three acts by Thornton N. Wilder. Produced by the American Laboratory Theatre, December 10, 1927.

Cast of characters—

```
Peter Magnus.....................Robert H. Gordon
Sarah Budie.............................Jane Barry
Flora................................Helen Coburn
Nestor.............................. Sam Hartman
Keeter..............................Arthur Sircom
Dabney............................ Louis V. Quince
Sodestrom.......................Erna Obermeyer
Flecker..........................Blanch Tancock
Charles............................Walter Duggan
Gaylord.........................George Auerbach
DelVale............................Anne Schmidt
Miller...........................Frances Titsworth
Dexter........................Herbert V. Gellendre
Goss............................George Macready
```
Act I.—The Great Drawing-room of Peter Magnus' New York Mansion, Washington Square North, in the Fall of 1871. Act II.—The Same. Six Weeks Later. Act III.—The Same. Five Days Later.
Staged by Richard Boleslavsky.

Peter Magnus, returning to his Washington Square mansion after a considerable absence, discovers that his servants have turned it into a rooming house and collected therein a motley crew of roomers. In place of turning them out, Peter, ruled by his inner Christian conscience, seeks to improve their spiritual natures and finally departs in peace leaving the mansion to the unfortunates.

## THE DYBBUK

### (111 performances of repertory)

A dramatic legend in three acts by S. Ansky. Music by I. Engel. Produced by the Habima Players of Moscow at the Mansfield Theatre, December 13, 1926.

Cast of characters—

| | |
|---|---|
| First Batlan | Raikin Ben-Ari |
| Second Batlan | Benno Schneider |
| Third Batlan | Ben-Chaim |
| Meier | B. Tschemeritsky |
| Chonon | L. Warshawer |
| Hennoch | Benjamin Zemach |
| Messenger | A. Prudkin |
| Ascher | E. Winiar |
| Gnesia | Ch. Grober |
| Sender | D. Itkin |
| Lea | Anna Rovina |
| Friede | Tmima Yudelwitch |
| Gitel | Tamar Robins |
| Basia | F. Lubitsch |
| Sender's Relatives | Miriam Goldin / L. Pudalower / Bath-Ami / Zwi Friedlander |

Beggars—

| | |
|---|---|
| Zundel | I. Winiar |
| Schulem | Ben-Chaim |
| Delphen | Raikin Ben-Ari |
| Refual | Aron Meskin |
| Berchik | S. Brook |
| Dvosia | Winiar-Katchur |
| Dreisel | Ch. Grober |
| Yachna | Chava Adelman |
| Nechuma | Anna Paduit |
| An Old Woman | Chana Hendler |
| Rivke | Elisheva Factorowitch |
| Elka | Ina Govinskaya |
| Menashe | Benjamin Zemach |
| Nacman | J. Bertonow |
| Mendel | Benno Schneider |
| Asrial, the Tzadik of Miropol | Naum L. Zemach |
| Michuel | Zwi Friedlander |
| Shameshon, Rabbi of Miropol | B. Tschemerinsky |
| Chassidim | S. Brook / Efroti-Chechik / Aron Meskin / A. Baratz / E. Golland / Ch. Hendler / J. Bertonow / L. Warshawer |
| Voice Off Stage in Third Act | E. Golland |

Staged by E. Vachtangov.

The original Hebrew version of "The Dybbuk," which was followed by the adapters of that version of the Ansky drama printed in "The Best Plays of 1925-26." During the engagement, the Habima also presented: "The Eternal Jew," and "The Deluge."

## HOWDY, KING

### (40 performances)

A comedy in three acts by Mark Swan. Produced by Anne Nichols at the Morosco Theatre, New York, December 13, 1926.

Cast of characters—

| | |
|---|---|
| Ruiz | David Leonard |
| Guest of Hotel | Eleanor Z. Audley |
| Tourist | Hamilton Philips |
| His Wife | Marion Bushee |
| Waiter | Frank Reyman |
| Guest of Hotel | Hazel Cooper |
| Ortega | Alfred Kappeler |
| Prince Sargossa | Byron Beasley |
| Marcia Bond | Lorna Elliott |
| Helen Bond | Harriet MacGibbon |
| Jefferson Bond | Louis Frohoff |
| Baron Felipe La Varra | Douglas Mac Pherson |
| Johnny North | Minor Watson |
| Larry O'Moore | Frank Otto |
| Duke D'Alvar | G. Davison Clark |
| Countess Isabella D'Alvar | Anna Kostant |
| Baroness Carlotta Varcia | Leneta Lane |
| An Attendant | Dorothy Beresford |

Duke D'Alvar's Mountain Guard
{ Ruppert May
Walter Stewart
Franklin Wait
John Triggs

Palace Guard
{ William Beer
Neil Bridges
George Toll
Frank Mayne

Act I.—An Afternoon in Nice. Act II.—The Saracen Tower in Eldorado and the Throne Room. Act III.—Private Apartment of the King.

Staged by Clifford Brooke.

Johnny North, from Texas, in Europe selling horses, meets up with an American rodeo along the Riviera. Taking a cowboy's place he attracts the attention of and is attracted by a traveling American, Helen Bond, and proceeds to follow her thereafter. About the time Helen's parents are taking her to Eldorado, Johnny learns that he really is a descendant of Juan Northe, king of that mythical kingdom, and really in line for the throne. Mixing with the Eldoradan politicians who would crown him, he is properly enthroned as king when the Bonds arrive. Thereafter he carries on his love campaign and conquers a revolution from that advantage.

## HANGMAN'S HOUSE

### (8 performances)

A drama in four acts by Willard Mack. Dramatized from a novel of Donn Byrne. Produced by William A. Brady, Jr., and

Dwight Deere Wiman, at the Forrest Theatre, December 16, 1926.

Cast of characters—

| | |
|---|---|
| Neddy Joe | Charles Kennedy |
| A Gardener | Emmet O'Reilly |
| A Boy | William Pearce |
| Dermot McDermot | Walter Abel |
| Anne McDermot | Katherine Emmet |
| Lord Chief Justice O'Brien | Joseph Kilgour |
| John D'Arcy | Frank Shannon |
| Connaught O'Brien | Katherine Alexander |
| "Citizen" Hogan | Percy Waram |
| Murphy | Felix Haney |
| Larry Mason | Clement O'Loghlen |
| Paddy Talbot | Walter Kenney |
| Mr. Doyle | R. Henry Handon |
| Mr. McSweeney | Emmet O'Reilly |
| Mickey Regan | Jack McGraw |
| Robinson | Ralph Cullinan |

Acts I, II and III.—In and Around Dermotstown, Ireland.
Staged by William A. Brady, Jr.

Dermot McDermot is in love with and hopes to marry Connaught O'Brien, but Lord Chief Justice O'Brien, her father, known as "the hangman," is dead set on her taking the flashier John D'Arcy. Connaught is obedient but unhappy, and after a year of misery, and more particularly after proving D'Arcy was betting against her derby entry, the Bard of Amagh, which Dermot McDermot rides to victory, Conny gives the villain the gate and knows Dermot for the true love he is.


## THE DYBBUK

### (41 performances)

Play in three acts by S. Ansky. Revived by the Neighborhood Theatre, New York, December 16, 1926.

Cast of characters—

| | |
|---|---|
| First Batlan (Professional Prayer Man) | Edgar Kent |
| Second Batlan | Cecil Clovelly |
| Third Batlan | George Bratt |
| Meyer, Shamos (Sexton) | Walter Geer |
| Meshulach (the Messenger) | Ian Maclaren |
| Channon | Albert Carroll |
| Hennoch | Otto Hulicius |
| An Old Woman | Mary George |
| Leah | Betty Linley |
| Frade | Dorothy Sands |
| Gitl | Paula Trueman |
| Asher | David Lewis |
| Reb Sender | Marc Loebell |

Beggars of Brianits:

| | |
|---|---|
| Fishke | George Hoag |
| Leyser | George Heller |

Moysheh ........................................William Challee
Zeydl ..........................................David Lewis
Shlemiel .......................................Joseph H. Thayer
Tsippe .........................................Grace Stickley
Neche ..........................................Sadie Sussman
Rivke ..........................................Blanche Talmud
Draesl .........................................Irene Lewisohn
Elke ...........................................Hannah Herman
Klippe .........................................Sophie Bernsohn
Nechame ........................................Frances Cowles
The Bratt ......................................Lois Shore
Musician .......................................Sidney Shapiro
Basye ..........................................Lily Lubell
Reb Nachman ....................................George Bratt
Menashe ........................................Theodore Hecht
Reb Mendl ......................................Cecil Clovelly
Rabbi Aesrael (the Tsadik) .....................Edgar Kent
Rabbi Michoel ..................................Theodore Hecht
Rabbi Shamshon .................................Otto Hulicius
Dayanim ....................Walter Geer and George Hoag
    Act I.—Synagogue in Brianits.  Act II.—A Courtyard of Sender's
House in Brianits.  Act III.—The Tsadik's Prayer Room.

See "Best Plays of 1925-26."


# OH, PLEASE

## (75 performances)

Farce revue in two acts founded on a story by Maurice Hennequin and Pierre Veber.  Produced by Charles Dillingham at the Fulton Theatre, New York, December 17, 1926.

Cast of characters—

Emma Bliss .....................................Helen Broderick
Miss Fall River ................................Pearl Hight
Miss South Bend ................................Blanche Latell
Miss Topeka ....................................Gertrude Clemens
Miss Walla Walla ...............................Josephine Sabel
Jane Jones .....................................Irma Irving
Peter Perkins ..................................Nelson Snow
Buddy Trescott .................................Charles Columbus
Jack Gates .....................................Nick Long, Jr.
Nicodemus Bliss ................................Charles Winninger
Fay Follette ...................................Kitty Kelly
Thelma Tiffany .................................Gertrude McDonald
Ruth King ......................................Dolores Farris
Clarice Cartier ................................Cynthia MacVae
Lily Valli .....................................Beatrice Lillie
Robert Vandeleur ...............................Charles Purcell
Peter Perkins ..................................Robert Baldwin
Dick Mason .....................................Lloyd Carder
Ted Foster .....................................James Garrett
Sammy Sands ....................................Richard Bennett
Billy Lan ......................................Charles Angle
Joe Dillard ....................................Jack Wilson
Chester Case ...................................Leon Canova
Marjorie Kenyon ................................Dorothie Bigelow
    Act I.—Bungalow of Nicodemus Bliss in Flower City, California.
Act II.—Display Room of Vandeleur Perfume Company in New
York.  The Bliss House, New Rochelle and a Lawn Fête at Vandeleur's Estate, Westchester.
    Staged by Hassard Short.

Something from the French about a perfume factory run by Nicodemus Bliss who gets into trouble when his wife thinks he is carrying on with Lily Valli, the actress.


## TWELFTH NIGHT

### (26 performances)

Comedy by William Shakespeare. Revived by Civic Repertory Company at the Civic Repertory Theatre, New York, December 20, 1926.

Cast of characters—

| | |
|---|---|
| Orsino | Harold Moulton |
| Sebastian | Hardie Albright |
| Antonio | Barlowe Borland |
| Sea Captain | Robert F. Ross |
| Valentine | Ian Emery |
| Curio | Edwin Cooper |
| Sir Toby Belch | Egon Brecher |
| Sir Andrew Aguecheek | Wesley John |
| Malvolio | Sayre Crawley |
| Fabian | Marlyn Brown |
| Feste | Alan Birmingham |
| Olivia | Beatrice Terry |
| Viola | Eva Le Gallienne |
| Maria | Josephine Hutchinson |
| 1st Officer | Gordan Pascal |
| 2nd Officer | Arthur Jacobson |
| Priest | Robert F. Ross |
| Ladies, Attendant on Olivia | Margaret C. Love, Agnes McCarthy, Hilda Plowright |
| Pages at the Court of Orsino | Ruth Wilton, Martha Leavitt |

Staged by Eva Le Gallienne.


## THE SILVER CORD

### (112 performances)

Play in three acts by Sidney Howard; produced by the Theatre Guild at the John Golden Theatre, New York, December 20, 1926.

Cast of characters—

| | |
|---|---|
| Hester | Margalo Gillmore |
| David | Elliot Cabot |
| Christina | Elisabeth Risdon |
| Robert | Earle Larimore |
| Mrs. Phelps | Laura Hope Crews |
| Maid | Barbara Bruce |

Acts I, II and III.—In Mrs. Phelps' House Which Is Situated in One of the More Mature Residential Developments of an Eastern American City.

Staged by John Cromwell.

See page 220.

## THE GREAT ADVENTURE

(45 performances)

Comedy in three acts by Arnold Bennett. Revived by Reginald Pole at the Princess Theatre, New York, December 22, 1926.

Cast of characters—

| | |
|---|---|
| Albert Shawn | George Thompson |
| Ilam Carve | Reginald Pole |
| Dr. Pascoe | Wheeler Dryden |
| Edward Horning | Wayne Whitten |
| Janet Cannot | Spring Byington |
| Cyrus Carve | C. T. Van Voorhis |
| Father Looe | Charles Lowden |
| Honoria Looe | Miriam Cutler |
| Peter Horning | Harry Green |
| Ebag | Henry Mowbray |
| James Shawn | Wheeler Dryden |
| John Shawn | Harry Green |
| Mrs. Albert Shawn | Ruth Vivian |
| Lord Leonard Alcar | George Fitzgerald |
| Texel | Lowden Adams |

Staged by Reginald Pole.

Ilam Carve, a timid artist grown sick to death of fawning idolaters, disappears and permits the body of his dead valet, Albert Shawn, to be buried as that of himself. Carve is thus forced not only to read his most laudatory obituaries, but to be witness to his own funeral when Shawn's body is buried in state in Westminster Abbey.

## THE HONOR OF THE FAMILY

(33 performances)

Play in four acts adapted by Paul M. Potter from the play "La Rabouilleuse" by Emile Fabre. Produced by Charles Frohman, Inc., at the Booth Theatre, New York, December 25, 1926.

Cast of characters—

| | |
|---|---|
| La Vedie | Julia Shaw |
| Orsanto | D. V. Deering |
| Borniche | William Clark |
| Commandant Max Gilet | Courtney White |
| Flora Brazier | Jessie Royce Landis |
| Captain Renard | Edward Butler |
| Joseph Bridau | Harry Burkhardt |
| Madame Bridau | Eugenie Woodward |
| Jean-Jacques Rouget | Robert Harrison |
| Colonel Philippe Bridau | Otis Skinner |
| Kouski | Harry Burkhardt |
| General Carpentier | Wilson Reynolds |

Commandant Mignonnet......................William F. Granger
Captain Potel........................................Albert Berg
    Acts I, II, III and IV.—At the Home of the Bridaus in Issoudun,
Near Bourges, 1824.

A revival of the familiar story of Col. Philippe Bridau's vigorous house cleaning when he descends upon his miserly uncle's home and clears it of the cheats and conspirators who would do him and his wrong.

## NIGHT HAWK

### (144 performances)

Drama in three acts by Roland Oliver. Revived by Lepane Amusement Company at the Frolic Theatre, New York, December 25, 1926.

Cast of characters—

Agnes Merrill....................................Pam Browning
Dr. Perry Colt....................................Frank Thomas
Walter Colt.......................................Martin Burton
Maisie Buck....................................Carroll McComas
Mrs. Hayes.................................. Marguerite Tebeau
    Acts I, II and III.—In the Consultation Room of Dr. Colt, New
York City.

See "The Best Plays of 1924-25."

## MOZART

### (40 performances)

Comedy in three acts by Sacha Guitry. Music by Reynaldo Hahn. Produced by A. H. Woods at the 46th Street Theatre, December 27, 1926.

Cast of characters—

Mozart......................................Yvonne Printemps
Baron von Grimm................................Sacha Guitry
Madame d'Epinay.........................Mme. Germaine Gallois
Marie-Anne de Saint-Pons.........................Mlle. J. Leclerc
La Guimard........................Mlle. A. Ritchy (de l'Opera)
The Marquis de Chambreuil........................M. de Garcin
Vestris................................M. Marionno (de l'Opera)
A Lackey.........................................M. A. Chanot
A Servant........................................Mlle. R. Senac
    The Action of the Play Passes in the Home of Madame d'Epinay
in Paris, in the Year 1778.
    Staged by Sacha Guitry.

The French original of the play given in an English translation and included previously in this record.

## THE PADRE

(32 performances)

Play in four acts adapted by Stanley Logan from the French. Produced by Wm. A. Brady at the Ritz Theatre, New York, December 27, 1926.

Cast of characters—

| | |
|---|---|
| Alexandre Grandin | Arthur Bowyer |
| Georges Lebedin | John M. Troughton |
| Maurice Tremoulet | Albert Froom |
| Alice | Marcella Swanson |
| Alphonse Dupuis | Richard Temple |
| Charles Gaussat | Henry Major |
| Josephe Marius | A. C. Frothingham Lysons |
| Father Pellegrin | Leo Carrillo |
| Count Pierre De Sableuse | Stanley Logan |
| Florent | George Schiller |
| Poilu | By Himself |
| Genevieve Cousinet | Vivian Tobin |
| Madame Cousinet | Nana Bryant |
| Monsieur Cousinet | Robert Lee Allan |
| Monseigneur Sibue | John M. Kline |
| Monsieur Plumoiseau | Richard Temple |
| Senator Berthier | Caryll Gillen |
| Madame Berthier | May Anderson |
| Joseph | Albert Froom |
| The Chausseur | Harold Grau |
| Victorine | May Anderson |
| Paulette | Elaine Ivans |
| Georges | A. C. Frothingham Lysons |
| Policeman | James Brook |
| Lauthier | John M. Troughton |
| The Cardinal | Elwyn Eaton |

Acts I and II.—The Hotel de la Poste Sableuse and the Salon of the Château de Sableuse. Act III.—Restaurant of the Abbaye Thelme. Act IV.—The Palace of the Cardinal.

Staged by Stanley Logan.

Father Pellegrin, having been through the war and acquired the speech and much of the viewpoint of his soldier pals, finds himself returned to church work and quite unpopular with the politically conspiring monseigneurs of his diocese. Father Pellegrin, as a "good scout," refuses to be humbled, gets himself into difficulties by questioning the motives of his richest parishioners and is about to be set down when an understanding cardinal interferes in his behalf. The original play, "Mon Curé Chez Les Riche," was written by André de Lorde and Pierre Chaine.

## PEGGY-ANN

(197 performances)

Musical comedy in two acts. Book by Herbert Fields; music by Richard Rodgers; lyrics by Lorenz Hart. Produced by Lew

Fields and Lyle D. Andrews at the Vanderbilt Theatre, New York, December 27, 1926.

Cast of characters—

| | |
|---|---|
| Mrs. Frost | Lulu McConnell |
| Mr. Frost | Grant Simpson |
| Dolores Barnes | Edith Meiser |
| Alice Frost | Betty Starbuck |
| Guy Pendleton | Lester Cole |
| Sally Day | Dorothy Roy |
| Peggy-Ann | Helen Ford |
| Arnold Small | Fuller Mellish, Jr. |
| Patricia Seymour | Margaret Breen |
| Freddie Shawn | Jack Thompson |
| A Policeman | Patrick Rafferty |
| Miss Flint | Marion Trabue |
| A Sailor | Howard Eames |
| Mr. Fish | Harold Mellish |
| Steward | G. Douglas Evans |

Act I.—In the Boarding-house of Mrs. Barnes, Glens Falls, N. Y., and in New York as Peggy Dreams it May Be.
Book staged by Robert Milton.

Peggy-Ann, helping Ma with the work of a boarding house in Glens Falls, N. Y., has no chance to go anywhere, or see anything. Her greatest ambition is to be married to Guy Pendleton, to whom she has been engaged for three years, and to go to New York, and she is fearfully unhappy when her catty older sister makes fun of her. With everybody out of the house Peggy-Ann dreams herself married and rich in New York, enjoying many fantastic and amusing adventures. She awakes to find herself still at home, but Guy with a job and prospects.

## WOODEN KIMONO

### (197 performances)

Melodramatic mystery comedy in three acts by John Floyd. Produced by Frederick Stanhope and Jacques Froehlich at the Martin Beck Theatre, New York, December 27, 1926.

Cast of characters—

| | |
|---|---|
| Clara Malcom | Leonore Harris |
| Sandock | Bennett Southard |
| Sheriff Jott | Worthington Romaine |
| Roger Malcom | William Norton |
| Ethan Malcom | Sam Coit |
| Dr. Graham | Hermann Lieb |
| Peter Mullen | Robert Bentley |
| Richard Halstead, 1st | Alden Chase |
| Richard Halstead, 2nd | Leslie Austen |
| Mary Madders | Jean Dixon |

Agatha Bloom.....................................Helen Carew
John Dryden...................................Dudley Clements
   Acts I and II.—Interior of Red Owl Tavern.  Act III.—Cellar
of Mullen's House.
   Staged by Frederick Stanhope.

A story of dope peddlers and their pursuers.  The title from
a coffin-like box in which a demented old gentleman insists upon
spending most of the evening.


## WHAT NEVER DIES

### (39 performances)

Comedy in three acts by Alexander Engel.  Translated by
Ernest Boyd.  Produced by David Belasco at the Lyceum
Theatre, New York, December 28, 1926.

Cast of characters—

Rosina Von Dollereder...........................Haidee Wright
Tiburtius...........................................E. H. Sothern
Pius.............................................Moffat Johnston
Benedict.........................................Ernest Cossart
Dorothea..............................................Hilda Spong
Aggie...................................... Katherine B. Standing
Edith.........................................Carolyn Ferriday
Annie.................................................Rose Farrell
Hugo Odersky...................................France Bendtsen
Fiammetta.......................................Rosalinde Fuller
Elena............................................. Eleanor Shaw
Luigi Bartoli.......................................Guido Nadzo
Cesare Tomaselli...............................Campbell Gullan
Peter............................................Albert G. Andrews
Annie's Governess........................Margaret Knapp Waller
Nina.................................................Betty Brenska
Pietro...........................................Santos Ortega
Elena's Governess.............................Myrrha Alhambra
Bertha................................................Clara Cubitt
   Acts I, II and III.—The Dollereder Estate, Near Vienna and the
Villa of Tiburtius, Near Rome.
   Staged by David Belasco.

Tiburtius Von Dollereder, still hot-blooded at 65, craftily
deserts his settled sons of 40 and 42 and marries a young Italian.
The family, thinking Tiburtius is living in sin with the lady, call
in the Von Dollereder grandmother to use her influence to curb
Tiburtius and conserve the Von Dollereder fortune he is spending.
Grandmother, mildly protesting at first, visits Tiburtius's ménage,
meets his wife and their six-year-old child, is charmed with the
whole achievement and proudly bids Tiburtius continue his strike
for freedom.

## BETSY

### (39 performances)

Musical comedy in two acts, words by Irving Cæsar and David Freedman, lyrics by Lorenz Hart and music by Richard Rodgers. Produced by Florenz Ziegfeld at the New Amsterdam Theatre, New York, December 28, 1926.

Cast of characters—

| | |
|---|---|
| Stonewall Moskowitz | Al Shean |
| Mama Kitzel | Pauline Hoffman |
| Louie | Jimmy Hussey |
| Joseph | Ralph Whitehead |
| Moe | Dan Healy |
| Betsy | Belle Baker |
| Ruth | Bobby Perkins |
| Archie | Allen Kearns |
| Winnie Hill | Madeline Cameron |
| Flora Dale | Evelyn Law |
| May Meadow | Barbara Newberry |
| Tom Maguire | Ed Hickey |
| Dan Kelly | Jack White |
| Tex Brown | Phil Ryley |
| Mrs. Brown | Vanita La Nier |

Acts I and II.—On the East Side of New York and at Coney Island.

Staged by William Anthony McGuire and Sammy Lee.

Louie, Joseph and Moe Kitzel want to get married, but Mama Kitzel won't let them until they have found a husband for their older sister Betsy. They try to sell Bet to a youthful pigeon fancier, Archie, but he loves her younger sister Ruth. And so it goes until 11 o'clock when things just naturally right themselves.

## DEVIL IN THE CHEESE

### (157 performances)

Fantastic comedy in three acts by Tom Cushing. Produced by the Charles Hopkins Company at the Charles Hopkins Theatre, New York, December 29, 1926.

Cast of characters—

| | |
|---|---|
| Jimmie Chard | Fredric March |
| Dr. Pointell Jones | Dwight Frye |
| Mr. Quigley | Robert McWade |
| Mrs. Quigley | Catherine Calhoun Doucet |
| Goldina Quigley | Linda Watkins |
| Chubbock | George Riddell |
| Father Petros | Bela Lugosi |
| Constantinos | Earl MacDonald |
| Min | Frank Norman Hearn |
| An Idea of Mr. Quigley | Earl MacDonald |

A Gorilla..........................................Hooper Bunch
The Cannibal Chief...............................Joseph Hazel
     Acts I and III.—The Monastery of Meteora.   Act II.—Inside
Goldina's Head.
     Staged by Charles Hopkins.

Mr. Quigley, an archæologist, accepts the invitation of Father Petros to do a little digging around the monastery of Meteora. He takes his family with him, hoping thus to lose Jimmie Chard, who has been pursuing Goldina Quigley. Goldina rebels and not being able to understand, Mr. Quigley wishes he could see just what is in her mind. When he eats a piece of cheese dug up with an ancient vase he gets his wish. The spirit of the cheese takes him inside Goldina's head and he discovers how much in love and how incurably romantic she really is. When he wakes, and Jimmie is the only one with wit enough to save the party from bandits, Mr. Quigley is glad to welcome him into the family.

## NEW YORK EXCHANGE

### (82 performances)

Play in two acts by Peter Glenny. Produced by Ivan L. Wright Productions, Inc., at the Klaw Theatre, New York, December 30, 1926.

Cast of characters—

Dallas Dinon......................................Lelya LeNoir
Sally Parks.......................................Sydney Shields
Leonard Baxter....................................Roy Gordon
Bobbie............................................Doris Underwood
Lester............................................Read Wight
Mrs. Fullerton-Joyce..........................Mabel Montgomery
Mrs. Ella May Morton..........................Alison Skipworth
Sammie............................................Harold Minjir
Dr. Scratch.......................................Charles Moore
Sylvia Class......................................Mona Bundoon
Ernest............................................Donn Cook
Stefano DeAngelo..................................James LaCurto
Sunshine..........................................Gladys Thompson
Shadow............................................George Cartier
Waiter............................................Samuel Baron
Chauffeur.........................................Charles Wilton
Landlady.......................................Celeste St. Gaudens
Rosie.............................................Agnes Klem
Chef d'Orchestre..................................George LeSoir
Ruby..............................................Jane Olive Ward
Robert............................................Herbert M. Kollman
     Act I.—At Dallas Dinon's Night Club.  A Night in January.  Act
II.—Ernest's Room, Fronting West End Avenue.  A Night in May.
Act III.—Ernest's Suite in Paris.  Three Years Later.
     Staged by Clarke Silvernail.

Ernest, who has the makings of a first-class tenor, is loved by Sally Parks, a musical comedy star, but stolen by Ella May Morton, an aging lady with a passion for youthful companionship. After being supported for some time by Ella May, Ernie breaks his bonds, referring to his patroness finally as a "philanthropic louse," and returns presumably to normality and Sally.

## CHICAGO

### (172 performances)

Satirical comedy in three acts by Maurine Watkins. Produced by Sam H. Harris at the Music Box Theatre, New York, December 30, 1926.

Cast of characters—

| | |
|---|---|
| Roxie Hart | Francine Larrimore |
| Fred Casely | Doan Borup |
| Jake | Charles A. Bickford |
| Amos Hart | Charles Halton |
| Sergeant Murdock | Charles Slattery |
| Martin S. Harrison | Robert Barrat |
| Babe | Arthur R. Vinton |
| Slats | G. Albert Smith |
| Mrs. Morton | Isabelle Winlocke |
| Velma | Juliette Crosby |
| Liz | Dorothy Stickney |
| Billy Flynn | Edward Ellis |
| Mary Sunshine | Eda Heineman |
| Moonshine Maggie | Ferike Boros |
| Go-To-Hell Kitty | Edith Fitzgerald |
| Bailiffs | Carl De Mal, George Lanning |
| Judge Canton | Milano Tilden |
| Woman Reporter | Wilma Thompson |
| First Man Reporter | George Cowell |
| Clerk of the Court | Charles Kuhn |
| First Photographer | James C. Pall |
| Stenographer | Vincent York |
| Foreman of the Jury | G. W. Anspake |
| Cameramen | Thomas Poland, Al Milliken |

Act I.—Roxie's Bedroom. South Side, Chicago. Act II.— Women's Ward, Cook County Jail. Act III.—Prisoners' Room in Criminal Court Building and Judge Canton's Court.

Staged by George Abbott.

See page 94.

## BLACK COCKATOO

### (4 performances)

A melodrama in three acts, by Samuel Ruskin Golding. Produced by Frank Martins at the Comedy Theatre, December 30, 1926.

Cast of characters—

| | |
|---|---|
| Quincy Ting | James R. Fulton |
| Duke | George Le Guere |

Barry Flynn ................................. Harry D. Southard
Lily Chang ..................................... Anne Forrest
Henry Moy ..................................... Edward Forbes
Roy Beekman ..................................... James Crane
Noel Lawford ................................. Charles Hampden
Frances Bradley ................................. Bee Morosco
Manny Pitkin ............................... William R. Randall
Detective ......................................... Carl Reed
Detective .............................. Robert C. Cunningham
Olsen's Orchestra
Acts I and III.—Lily Chang's Apartment in the Upper Forties.
Act II.—"The Black Cockatoo."
Staged by Edgar MacGregor.

Lily Chang, a half-caste from the Straits Settlement, runs a night club in New York, is padlocked, gets Roy Beekman, the district attorney, tight, makes him believe he has married her, releases him when she discovers she loves him, becomes involved in dope smuggling and is saved in the end when the district attorney makes their marriage real.

## IN ABRAHAM'S BOSOM

### (116 performances)

A folk tragedy in seven scenes by Paul Green. Produced by the Provincetown Players at the Provincetown Theatre, New York, December 30, 1926.

Cast of characters—

Bud Gaskins ..................................... Frank Wilson
Lije Hunneycutt ................................. Thomas Mosley
Puny Avery ..................................... James Dunmore
Abraham McCranie ............................... Julius Bledsoe
Colonel McCranie ............................... L. Rufus Hill
Lonnie McCranie ................................. H. Ben Smith
Goldie McAllister ............................. Rose McClendon
Muh Mack ..................................... Abbie Mitchell
Douglass McCranie ............................... R. J. Huey
Eddie Williams ................................. Melvin Greene
Lanie Horton ............................... Armithine Lattimer
Neilly McNeill ............................... Stanley Greene
Seven Scenes in and Near the Turpentine Woods of Eastern North Carolina. the Summer of 1885.
Staged by Jasper Deeter.

See page 325.

## THE BROTHERS KARAMAZOV

### (56 performances)

Play in five acts, based on the Dostoevsky novel, by Jacques Copeau and Jean Croue, translated by Rosalind Ivan. Produced by the Theatre Guild at the Guild Theatre, New York, January 3, 1927.

Cast of characters—

| | |
|---|---|
| Feodor Pavlovitch Karamazov | Dudley Digges |
| Dmitri Feodorovitch Karamazov | Alfred Lunt |
| Ivan Feodorovitch Karamazov | George Gaul |
| Aliocha Feodorovitch Karamazov | Morris Carnovsky |
| Smerdiakow | Edward G. Robinson |
| Father Zossima | Philip Leigh |
| Grigori Vassiliev | Henry Travers |
| Lieutenant Moussialovitch | Herbert Ashton |
| Vroubleski | Philip Loeb |
| Trifon Boriston | Charles Carden |
| Andrey | Charles Courtniedge |
| Gregory Illitch | Thomas Meegan |
| Chief of Police | Bernard Savage |
| Katerina Ivanovna Verhovovtseva | Clare Eames |
| Agrafena Alexandrovna Svetlov | Lynn Fontanne |
| A Maid | Dorothy Fletcher |
| Arina | Phyllis Connard |
| Stepanide | Dorothy Fletcher |

Act I.—Courtyard in the Monastery. Act II.—Katerina's Room. Act III.—The Living-room at Feodor Pavlovitch's. Acts IV and V.—The Inn at Mokroe.

Time—1865. Place—Russia, Near Moscow.

Staged by Philip Moeller.

In this telescoped version of the Dostoevsky novel the decline and fall of the Karamazov family include the failure of Aliocha to find happiness in religion, the emotional resentment of Dmitri at his father, Feodor's, attempt to cheat him of his mother's inheritance; the tragic love of Ivan for Katerina, and of Katerina's equally futile passion for Dmitri, and the latter's unhappy infatuation for the harlot, Agrafena, whom the father seeks to buy and is killed by his bastard son, Smerdiakow. Everybody is a little mad in the end.

## THE NIGHTINGALE

### (96 performances)

A musical romance based on the life of Jenny Lind. Book and lyrics by Guy Bolton and P. G. Wodehouse. Music by Armand Vecsey. Produced by the Messrs. Shubert at the Jolson Theatre, January 3, 1927.

Cast of characters—

| | |
|---|---|
| Major-General Gurnee | Lucius Henderson |
| Mrs. Gurnee | Sophie Everett |
| Mr. Carp | Stanley Lupino |
| Colonel Wainwright | John Gaines |
| Mrs. Vischer Van Loo | Clara Palmer |
| Alice Wainwright | Eileen Van Biene |

```
Captain Joe Archer.................................Robert Hobbs
Piper.............................................Thomas Whiteley
Josephine.........................................Violet Carlson
Cadet Officer.....................................Donald Black
Jenny Lind........................................Eleanor Painter
Whistler..........................................Harold Woodward
Stephen Rutherford................................Nicholas Joy
Captain Rex Gurnee................................Glen Dale
P. T. Barnum......................................Tom Wise
Colonel Robert E. Lee.............................Victor Bozardt
Dolly.............................................Eileen Carmody
Susan.............................................Arline Melburn
Otto Goldschmidt..................................Wm. Tucker
Signor Belletti...................................Ivan Dneproff
Butler............................................John Gaines
Footman...........................................Neal Frank
Usher.............................................Robert Harper
Cornelius Vanderbilt..............................Victor Bozardt
```
Act I.—The Terrace of the Old Hotel at West Point.   Act II.—
Jenny Lind's Bedroom in a New York Hotel.  2—Outside the Hotel.
3—Steve Rutherford's House.   Act III.—1—The Lobby of Castle
Garden.  2—The Stage of Castle Garden.
Staged by Lewis Morton.

A dovetailing of certain biographical incidents and a free use
of a justifiable imagination by which Jenny Lind is the heroine
of a lyrical flirtation with a dashing West Pointer, Captain
Gurnee. For a day or two her manager, P. T. Barnum, is all at
sea as to what to do if he loses Jenny to romance, but the singer
decides finally that she would be doing Captain Gurnee a wrong
if she were to marry him and bravely bids him farewell.

## BALLYHOO

### (7 performances)

Play in three acts by Kate Horton. Produced by Russell
Janney at the 49th Street Theatre, January 4, 1927.

### Cast of characters—

```
Uncle Jeff........................................W. H. Post
Belden............................................William Sellery
Mrs. Belden.......................................Adelaide Hibbard
Doris.............................................Arline Blackburn
Texas Dan.........................................Hugh O'Connell
Slow Joe..........................................Earle H. Mayne
Cameron MacDonald.................................Eric Dressler
The Hardy Brothers................................{ Smith E. Frazier
                                                  { James Green
Starlight Lil.....................................Minna Gombell
The Judge of the Races............................Morgan Wallace
Judy MacDonald....................................Kathryn Givney
Muriel Benedict...................................Louise Carter
A Barker..........................................Kent Thurber
```
Act I.—Dressing-room Back of the Stage of a Tent Vaudeville
Show Playing a Middle Western Fair.   Act II.—Ballyhoo Stand
and Grounds Before the Tent.   Act III.—Same as Act I.
Staged by Richard Boleslavsky.

Starlight Lil, champion rider for a wagon show out west, fascinates and encourages Cameron MacDonald, a society youth, to love her. But she loves him too much to let him marry her and so pretends to give herself to another man to disgust Cameron. She only succeeds in driving him to other and worse women, and then they are both nearly killed by Starlight's favorite mount, Mesquite.

## LACE PETTICOAT

### (15 performances)

Musical comedy of Old New Orleans, in two acts, by Stewart St. Clair, lyrics by Howard Johnson; music by Emil Gerstenberger and Carl Carlton. Produced by Carl Carlton at the Forrest Theatre, January 4, 1927.

Cast of characters—

| | |
|---|---|
| Marie | Erma Chase |
| Lisette | Ruth Matlock |
| Raymond de la Lange | Luis Alberni |
| Jules | Gerald Moore |
| Louis | Cullen Clewis |
| Mammy Dinah | Mercedes Gilbert |
| Professor Bonalli | James C. Morton |
| Bozo | Joseph Spree |
| Leontine Pantard | Stella Mayhew |
| Clarice | Elcie Peck |
| Dominic Deni DeLaBouregard de Grand Pre | Richard Powell |
| Renita | Vivian Hart |
| Paul Joscelyn | Tom Burke |
| Pere Modeste | A. S. Byron |

Act I.—The Flower Market in Old Orleans. Act II.—The Old Cathedral and the Mardi Gras.
Staged by Carl Carlton.

Paul Joscelyn of the army loves Renita and wants to marry her. Raymond de la Lange, a Creole of prominence, also loves her but isn't eager for marriage. To separate Renita and Paul, Raymond tells the girl she is a quadroon. But Raymond lies, as is proved after Renita has been made fearfully unhappy for an hour or so.

## JUNK

### (9 performances)

Play in three acts by Edwin B. Self. Produced by Messrs. Shesgreen and Vroom at the Garrick Theatre, January 5, 1927.

Cast of characters—

| | |
|---|---|
| Grandmother | Alice May Tuck |
| Nancy | Marguerite Mosier |

```
Ernest John.....................................Sydney Greenstreet
"Chick" Prall.........................................Calvin Thomas
Jim, the Gunman.......................................Doan Borup
Gobknuckle...........................................Jay Fassett
First Prison Guard..............................George V. Denny
Second Prison Guard.............................Hamilton Swift
Dr. Schelling......................................Herbert Ranson
Old Sal..............................................Emma Dunn
David...............................................John Maroney
Jean Prall.......................................Marguerite Mosier
```
     Act I.—An American Farm House.  Acts II and III.—Home of
Ernest John and a Corner of Governor Prall's Study.
     Staged by Charles Coburn.

Ernest John, a love-inspired hobo, seeks to help all unhappy
folk with whom he comes in contact.  He even agrees to take
part in a bank robbery in order that there may be money enough
for an operation to help grandmother, and Nancy, whom Ernest
John loves more than any of the others.  Then he gives up
Nancy to her true love and returns to the road.  Twenty-five
years later Ernest John is a junk man, but still kindly.  He helps
Nancy's husband, who is now governor, by killing the man who
seeks to blackmail the governor about the old bank robbery.  And
then Ernest John dies from a bullet the blackmailer put in
him.


## TOMMY

### (192 performances)

Comedy in three acts by Howard Lindsay and Bertrand Robinson.  Produced at the Gaiety Theatre, New York, January 10,
1927.

Cast of characters—
```
Mrs. Wilson .....................................Florence Walcott
Marie Thurber....................................Peg Entwistle
Bernard..............................................Alan Bunce
Mrs. Thurber.....................................Maidel Turner
Mr. Thurber........................................Lloyd Neal
David Tuttle........................................Sidney Toler
Tommy Mills....................................William Janney
Judge Wilson ......................................Ben Johnson
```
     Acts I, II and III.—Living-room in the Thurber Home.
     Staged by the Authors.

Marie Thurber really loves Tommy Mills, but because her
family is so determined she will marry him she turns for relief
to Bernard, the snappy salesman.  To save the situation, Uncle
Dave, the town's political boss, wisely decides to oppose Tommy.
This he does with such fervor the Thurbers finally throw the boy
out.  Then Marie flies to Tommy's defense and all is as it was
planned.

## ARABIAN NIGHTMARE

("The Galloping Sheik")

(24 performances)

Fantastic comedy in three acts by David Tearle and Dominick Colaizzi. Produced by Clarke Painter at the Cort Theatre, January 10, 1927.

Cast of characters—

| | |
|---|---|
| Sarah Frisbee | Ethel Strickland |
| Caroline Twiggam | Helen Lowell |
| Mamie Marshall | Marion Coakley |
| Bobbie Mudge | Lorin Raker |
| Burglar | Percy Moore |
| Mr. Horatio Bumble | Seth Arnold |
| Midar | Stephen Wright |
| Jameel | Charles Millward |
| Rasheeda | Catherine Willard |
| Arabian Minstrel | Charles Quigley |
| Mamoon | William Miles |
| Lady of the Harem | Emilie Corson |

Act I.—Living-room in Caroline Twiggam's House, Amesbury, Mass. Act II.—Room in a Castle on the Edge of the Arabian Desert. Act III.—Harem in the Palace.

Mamie Marshall, tired of the routine of life in a small town and hungering wildly for a sheik-adventure or two as they are lived in the movies, inherits enough money to take her and her aunt to the desert, sheik-hunting. There she is captured, dragged to a harem, discreetly manhandled and finally rescued by her little old small-town boy.

## GHOSTS

(24 performances)

Drama in three acts by Henrik Ibsen. Translated by William Archer, revised by Harrison Grey Fiske. Revived by Charles D. Coburn and Patterson McNutt at the Mansfield Theatre, January 10, 1927.

Cast of characters—

| | |
|---|---|
| Mrs. Helen Alving | Mrs. Fiske |
| Oswald Alving | Theodore St. John |
| Pastor Manders | Walter Ringham |
| Regina Engstrand | Jarvis Kerr |
| Jacob Engstrand | William C. Masson |

The Action Takes Place in the Living-room of Mrs. Alving's Country Home at Rosenvold, Overlooking One of the Large Fjords of Western Norway.

Staged by Harrison Grey Fiske.

A slightly modernized version of the Archer translation which makes no particular change except to put the cast in modern clothes.

## PIGGY

### (83 performances)

Musical comedy in two acts adapted by Daniel Kusell and Alfred Jackson from "The Rich Mr. Hoggenheimer" by Harry B. Smith and Ludwig Englander. Produced by William B. Friedlander, Inc., at the Royale Theatre, New York, January 11, 1927.

Cast of characters—

| | |
|---|---|
| Butler | James Jolley |
| Mrs. Hoggenheimer | Lotta Linthicum |
| Hon. Cecil Puffington | Harry McNaughton |
| Bobby Hunter | Brooke Johns |
| Signor Charli-Oppin | Rodolpho Badaloni |
| Monsieur Hohuho | Eddie Conrad |
| Suzanne Fair | Wanda Lyon |
| Piggy Hoggenheimer | Sam Bernard |
| Lord Tyrone | Beresford Lovett |
| Second Man | Paul Winkopp |
| Valet | Dan Corbett |
| Deck Steward | John Crone |
| Hotsie | Goodee Montgomery |
| Totsie | George Clifford |
| Guy Hoggenheimer | Paul Frawley |
| Betty Marshall | Marion Marschante |
| Lady Mildred Vane | Gladys Baxter |
| Maid | Rosalind Bernard |
| Mr. Shapiro | John Cronin |
| Edna | Joan Carter-Waddell |
| Inspector | James Jolley |

Act I.—In Hoggenheimer's London Home and on an Ocean Liner.
Act II.—Garden of an Estate at Great Neck, L. I.
Staged by William B. Friedlander.

A revised and musicalized version of "The Rich Mr. Hoggenheimer" of twenty years ago, relating the adventures of a wealthy vulgarian who tries to marry his son to the daughter of a lord and is forced to come to America finally to try to reclaim him from a pretty shop girl. The boy clings to the shop girl.

## THE CLAW

(60 performances of repertory)

A fantasy in one act by Lewis Waller and Dermot Darby. Produced by the American Grand Guignol at the Grove Street Theatre, New York, January 12, 1927.

Cast of characters—

| | |
|---|---|
| Jim | Marshall Vincent |
| Phyllis | Gladys Renavent |
| The Waiter | Michel Ferrolle |
| Lila | Feroll Moore |
| Mark | Denis Gurney |
| Eric | Baron Hepburn |

Two thrillers and two shockers taken from the repertoire of the original Grand Guignol, including "The Claw," a drama in one act by Jean Sartene, adapted by Dermot Darby; "The Last Torture," a melodrama in one act by Jean Bideau, adapted by Georges Renavent; and "Maid of All Work," a farce in one act by Dermot Darby, from the farce "Petite Bonne Serieuse," by MM. Eminory and J. Manoussi.

## BYE BYE, BONNIE

(125 performances)

Musical comedy in two acts by Louis Simon and Bide Dudley. Produced by L. Lawrence Weber at the Ritz Theatre, New York, January 13, 1927.

Cast of characters—

| | |
|---|---|
| Flossie | Laine Blaire |
| Charles Phillips | Georgie Hale |
| Mrs. Noah Z. Shrivell | Mabel Acker |
| Ted Williams | Rudolph Cameron |
| Dottie | Dorothy Van Alst |
| Margie | Margie Royce |
| Babs | Blanche Krebs |
| Flo | Florence Parker |
| Bonnie Quinlin | Dorothy Burgess |
| Noah Z. Shrivell | Louis Simon |
| Bill Briggins | Charles Henderson |
| Alice | Sue Saunders |
| Jefferson Sparks | Charles Wheeler |
| Sanford Alden | Cecil Owen |
| "Butch" Hogan | William Frawley |
| Warden | Cecil Owen |
| Keeper | Charles Henderson |
| "Mugsie" | Bernard Cavanaugh |
| Ruby | Ruby Keeler |
| Simpson | John Clemson |
| Alan Moran and Walter Feldkamp at the Pianos | |

Act I.—Office of The Shrivell Soft Soap Company, Shrivelton,
N. J.  Act II.—Warden's Office, Welfare Island and at Shrivell's
Home.
Staged by Edgar McGregor.

Bonnie, a stenographer, goes with her employer, Noah Shrivell,
to a night club to help him entertain certain buyers.  She also
helps Mr. Shrivell buy liquor for his friends.  Then Mr. Shrivell,
hitherto an ardent dry, goes to jail for thirty days.  During his
absence, his friends elect him to Congress on the wet ticket, after
which Bonnie marries Ted Williams.


## WHERE'S YOUR HUSBAND?

### (19 performances)

A new farce in three acts by Ben S. Gross; produced by George
Bamman at the Greenwich Village Theatre, New York, January
14, 1927.

Cast of characters—

| | |
|---|---|
| Mary Weston | Zola Talma |
| Billy Weston | Sam Hines |
| Steve Benson | Myron Paulson |
| Tony Blanchard | Eugene Donovan |
| Elsie Benson | Betty Laurence |
| Eliza Scroggins | Alice Fischer |
| Daniel Scroggins | Harry Lewellyn |
| Mazie Macumber | Kate-Pier Roemer |
| Bobbie Ellsworth | Mark Haight |

Acts I, II and III.—The Benson Home in the Westchester Suburbs.
Staged by George Bamman.

Elsie Benson's Uncle Daniel is likely to leave her $50,000 if
he likes her husband.  The day uncle is calling Elsie and her husband quarrel and husband runs away.  Rather than lose a chance
at the inheritance Elsie borrows a husband.  And her friend
borrows another for her.  So she has two and many complications.  The same day Aunt Eliza takes a drink or two too much
out of her stocking flask and becomes enamored of a professional
sheik who is supposed to be one of the husbands.

## THE BARKER

(172 performances)

Play in three acts by Kenyon Nicholson.  Produced by Charles
L. Wagner, in association with Edgar Selwyn, at the Biltmore
Theatre, New York, January 18, 1927.

Cast of characters—

| | |
|---|---|
| Nifty Miller | Walter Huston |
| Hap Spissell | Al Roberts |
| T-Bone | Philip Heege |
| Pop Morgan | Albert Hyde |
| A Hick | Ross Hertz |
| Carrie | Eleanor W. Williams |
| Colonel Gowdy | George W. Barbier |
| Lou | Claudette Colbert |
| Sailor West | John Irwin |
| Chris Miller | Norman Foster |
| Maw Benson | Florence Gerald |
| Doc Rice | Raymond Bramley |
| Cleo | Mae Hopkins |
| Hawaiian Trio | { Nakoloilani  Pakuakini  Pakalaka |

Acts I, II and III.—In and Around the Tents of Colonel Gowdy's
Big City Shows.
Staged by Priestly Morrison.

Nifty Miller has grown up in the tent show business and is at
the moment ballyhoo man for the Gowdy Shows.  He is determined his son Chris shall not follow in his footsteps.  Chris is
being educated and is going to be a lawyer.  But Chris joins the
show for his vacation and pleads for a chance to stay only a few
weeks.  During that time he is vamped by Lou, the snake
charmer, at the behest of Carrie, Nifty's jealous girl.  Then Lou
and Chris discover their love is on the level and defy Nifty to
separate them.  Nifty thinks he will quit the show at the last,
but is drawn back.

## THE VIRGIN MAN

(63 performances)

Comedy of youth and love in three acts by William Francis
Dugan.  Produced by the Times Square Productions at the Princess Theatre, New York, January 18, 1927.

Cast of characters—

| | |
|---|---|
| Peggy | Virginia Smith |
| Hughie | Don Dillaway |
| Nellie | Betty Alden |

```
Elsa ................................................ Dorothy Hall
Conway .............................................. Joseph Baird
Elevator Boy ..........................................Paul Clare
Tom .................................................Charles Horn
     Acts I, II and III.—Living-room in Conway's Riverside Drive
Apartment.
     Staged by William Francis Dugan.
```

Hughie from Yale, an innocent who has never been really kissed, visits his guardian in New York and immediately attracts three wild women. All three try their Broadway tricks on him, but he successfully defends himself. He goes back to Yale as pure as when he left there, which is pretty pure.

## SAM ABRAMOVITCH

### (15 performances)

A play of life in three acts by François Porche; adapted by Charlton Andrews. Produced by Anne Nichols at the National Theatre, New York, January 18, 1927.

Cast of characters—

```
Sara Abramovitch................................Mary Fowler
Aunt Miriam...............................Ruth Chorpenning
Lazarus..........................................Richard Abbott
Sam Abramovitch........................Pedro de Cordoba
Landlord .............................................Will Marsh
Moses Rosenfeld ...................................Arthur Hohl
Wolf Joseph .......................................Lee Kohlmar
Housekeeper.......................................Kate Morgan
Maid ..............................................Maud Brooks
Professor Ranke ...............................Ainsworth Arnold
An Irish Immigrant Woman.........................Kate Morgan
A German Immigrant Woman.......................Leah Hanna
Inspector...........................................Gerald Cornell
First Excluded Man..................................John Davis
Second Excluded Man...........................Ernest Howard
Deported Man.....................................Charles Adams
A Fat Immigrant..................................Vyvyan Dobbie
A Jewish Immgirant..............................Mark Adams
An Italian Immigrant...........................Edward Chodorov
An Italian Immigrant Woman.......................Lillian Okun
A Small Boy...............................George Offerman, Jr.
Commissioner....................................Fred Fairbanks
Well Dressed Woman............................Edna Washburn
Matron .........................................Marie Offerman
An Orphan Boy.................................Charles Walters
Second Jewish Immigrant.........................Harry Barker
Beryl Aaron.....................................Richard Abbott
Eli Frankel...................................C. Maclean Savage
Ber Zussman...................................Edward Chodorov
Ruth .............................................Adele Ronson
Zmira.......................................Ruth Chorpenning
Fradil............................................Mark Adams
First Policeman..............................William Frederic
First Broker...................................Ernest Howard
Second Broker.....................................John Davis
First Clerk.....................................Gerald Cornell
Second Clerk......................................Kirk Ames
```

Attendant.........................................Harry Barker
Secretary.........................................Charles Adams
Dixon.............................................William Frederic
Sloog.............................................Edward Chodorov
A Friend of Sam's.................................Richard Freeman
Rebecca...........................................Maud Brooks
Esther............................................Julia Cohn
A Mover...........................................Harry Barker
    Acts I, II and III.—A Pilgrimage That Carries from a Garret in
Dresden to a Rich Apartment in New York.
    Staged by Clifford Brooke.

In Dresden Sam Abramovitch, a visionary young Jew from Astrakan, seeks the inspiration of the great scientific economist, Professor Ranke, with whom he would like to fight for the redemption of the souls of all men, Jew and Gentile. The professor is cold to the proposition and Abramovitch, realizing he must have money, even to be an idealist, goes to America and becomes a tailor. In a few years he is an employer, then an owner of co-operative shops, then a great broker. Rich beyond his dreams, he continues to pour his gold, as he thinks, into great philanthropies, only to learn that his radical friends have used the money to foment strife. At the peak of his miseries his 15-year-old son dies, he is beaten in Wall Street and life looks dark. But with a new faith and his loyal wife he fights on.

## LADY ALONE

### (44 performances)

Play in three acts by Laetitia McDonald. Produced by L. Lawrence Weber, in association with David Wallace, at the Forrest Theatre, New York, January 20, 1927.

Cast of characters—

Clarisse Carter......................................Lee Smith
Kathryn Peters.................................Dorothy Overend
Paul Forsythe.................................Edward H. Wever
Craig Neilson..................................Austin Fairman
Mrs. Virginia Lane.............................Louise Galloway
Rev. Dr. Boomer...................................Kirk Brown
Nina Hopkins......................................Alice Brady
Stephen Brett..................................Joseph Kilgour
Regan...........................................William Leith
U. S. Marshal.............................William W. Crimans
Messenger.......................................Spencer Bentley
    Acts I, II and III.—Nina's Apartment in a Remodeled Brown-
stone House, New York.
    Staged by David Wallace.

Nina Hopkins, young and attractive, has made rather a bust of her life financially. Born of a flighty mother, hers has been a pillar-to-post existence, until she has practically made up her mind to marry Stephen Brett, 20 years older than she, for the protection his name and money will give her. Then she meets again a married man with whom she had once fallen desperately in love, the old charm is still potent and on his agreement to get a long-delayed divorce and marry her, Nina takes on the marital relation without benefit of clergy. The divorce granted, the lover, Craig Neilson, weakens. He will lose his mother's money if he marries again. So he decides to go to Africa on a hunt. And Nina pours herself an overdose of sleeping medicine and peacefully dies.

## DAMN THE TEARS

### (11 performances)

An ironic play in two acts by William Gaston. Produced by Alexander McKaig at the Garrick Theatre, New York, January 21, 1927.

Cast of characters—

| | |
|---|---|
| Buckland Steele | Ralph Morgan |
| Odile | Eleanor Griffith |
| Hon. Timothy Mulvahey | John Washburn |
| Johnny O'Shay | Elmer Cornell |
| Bill Vincent | Harry Winston |
| Manager | Frederick Bryan |
| Mr. Steele | Reginald Barlow |
| Mrs. Steele | Florence Rylander |
| Lilian | Joan Storm |
| May | Jean Bourdelle |
| Pete | William Rainey |
| Secretary | Seth Kendall |
| Stenographer | Joyce Benner |
| Attendant | Hugh Kidder |
| Officer | James Martin |
| Clerk | Halliam Bosworth |
| Judge | Frederick Bryan |
| Landlady | Joan Storm |
| Mr. Street | Reginald Barlow |
| Buck as a Boy | Edwin Phillips |
| Palmira | Virginia Farmer |

Acts I and II.—A Pilgrimage from a Baseball Field Through the World and Back.

Staged by Sigourney Thayer.

Buckland Steele, a popular athlete and promising student at college, suffers a brainstorm the day he fails his ball team when a hit is needed. In a huff he breaks training and is fired from the squad. Thereafter his decline is rapid and fantastic. He tries to study law and fails, he tries to write and fails. He takes to dissipation to relieve his mental torture and winds up back in the ball park, a harmless, witless, mumbling old vagabond, with an officer waiting to jail him as a vagrant.

## THE CRADLE SONG

(57 performances)

Comedy in two acts with an interlude in verse by Gregorio and Maria Martinez Sierra. Translated into English by John Garrett Underhill. Produced by the Civic Repertory Theatre, New York, January 24, 1927.

Cast of characters—

Sister Sagrario .......................................Ruth Wilton
Sister Marcella ...........................Beatrice de Neergaard
The Prioress ......................................... Beatrice Terry
Sister Joanna of the Cross......................Eva Le Gallienne
The Mistress of Novices.............................Mary Ward
The Vicaress .......................................Leona Roberts
Sister Tornera.................................Margaret G. Love
Sister Inez........................................Hilda Plowright
A Countryman ...................................Barlowe Borland
Sister Maria Jesus...............................Chalee Hubbard
The Doctor ......................................... Egon Brecher
Teresa ....................................Josephine Hutchinson
Antonio............................................Hardie Albright
     Acts I and II.—Convent of Enclosed Dominican Monks, Spain.

See page 256.

## THE LOVE THIEF

("Praying Curve")

(32 performances)

Drama in three acts by Martin Brown. Produced by Phil Werner and Michael Goldreyer at the Eltinge Theatre, New York, January 24, 1927.

Cast of characters—

Ferdie...............................................Jay Hanna
Minnie...............................................Grace Huff
Pup Bridges.....................................Walter Connolly
Jake ............................................William B. Mack
Daisy Bell........................................ Mona Bruns
Ham Purdy ...................................John W. Ransone
The Angel...................................Frank M. Thomas
The Earl........................................W. W. Shuttleworth
     Act I.—Jake's Place.   Act II.—At Praying Curve.   Act III.—
Daisy's Room in Joe Bayle's Grand Switch Hotel.
     Staged by Frank Keenan.

First called "Praying Curve." Daisy Bell, a tough lady of a tougher speakeasy, has been corresponding for two years with a dope fiend who had gone west for his health and, as she believed, got religion. The urge to join him is so strong that she finally breaks the bonds of evil that hold her and goes out. Then she discovers that her own dope fiend is dead and this eloquent letter writer is a pal who has taken his name and has really reformed. She will have nothing to do with the deceiver, who also goes back to the drink in his disappointment. Facing an act of heroism and a big emotional crisis, the two redeemed children try a fresh start.

## ROSE-MARIE

### (48 performances)

Musical play in two acts, book and lyrics by Otto Harbach and Oscar Hammerstein 2d; music by Rudolph Friml and Herbert Stothart. Revived by Arthur Hammerstein at the Century Theatre, New York, January 24, 1927.

Cast of characters—

```
Sergeant Malone................................Charles Meakins
Lady Jane.............................................Peggy Pates
Black Eagle...........................................Neil Moore
Edward Hawley.....................................James Moore
Emile La Flamme.............................Frank Harrington
Wanda...............................................Grace Wells
Hardboiled Herman...........................Houston Richards
Jim Kenyon......................................Paul Donah
Rose-Marie La Flamme.....................Ethel Louise Wright
Ethel Brander.....................................Karyl Kunkel
     Act I.—In the Canadian Rockies. Act II.—In Quebec and at the
Château Frontenac.
     Staged by Paul Dickey, Supervised by Arthur Hammerstein.
```

See "Best Plays of 1924-25."

## YOURS TRULY

### (129 performances)

Musical play in two acts, book and lyrics by Clyde North and Anne Caldwell, music by Raymond Hubbell. Produced by Gene Buck at the Shubert Theatre, New York, January 25, 1927.

Cast of characters—

```
Shuffling Bill.........................................Jack Squires
Joey Ling.............................................Jack Stanley
Mac..................................................John Kearney
Phil.................................................David Herblin
Mike.................................................Edgar Nelson
```

```
Diana............................................Irene Dunne
J. P. Stillwell..................................Theodore Babcock
Helen...........................................Eleanor Terry
Truly...........................................Leon Errol
Bonzolino.......................................Vic Casmore
Ruth............................................Audrey Berry
Scats...........................................Ina Williams
Mary Stillwell..................................Marion Harris
Bandit..........................................David Herblin
Dinty Moore.....................................Harry Kelly
Chang...........................................Greek Evans
Who's This......................................Geneva Mitchell
What's Her Name.................................Anastasia Reilly
A Bowery Rose...................................Hilda Ferguson
Tillie Dupont...................................Lotta Fanning
Minnie Fletcher.................................Joy Sutphen
Old "Pop".......................................Earl Van Horn
Cynthia Jones...................................Inez Van Horn
Tom.............................................Harry Long
Abe Levy........................................Ronald Wyse
Wing Sing.......................................Charles Wheeler
Paquita.........................................Aida DeMaris
Jimmie..........................................Jimmie McCallion
Herbert.........................................Herbert Schwartz
Chinese Girls...........Peggy Frawley, Eleanor Sweet, Dolly Pross
```
    Act I.—Mission Square, New York City.  Act II.—Estate of J. P.
Stillwell, a Street Back of Dinty Moore's.  The "Mission."  Under-
neath Dinty Moore's and Chang's "Open Door Night Club."
    Staged by Paul Dickey and Ralph Reader, Under the Supervision
of Gene Buck.

Mary Stillwell, anxious to do good in the world, takes to the
social settlements and the singing of night-club classics.   Followed into Chinatown by her millionaire father, who hopes to
bring her back home, she eludes father, who is shanghaied by
certain parties and everybody is invited to a party at the Stillwell home in the name of father, who is in no position to object.


## SATURDAY'S CHILDREN

### (167 performances)

Comedy in three acts by Maxwell Anderson.  Produced by the
Actor's Theatre, Inc., at the Booth Theatre, New York, January
26, 1927.

Cast of characters—

```
Florrie Sands...................................Ruth Hammond
Willie Sands....................................Richard Barbee
Mrs. Halevy.....................................Lucia Moore
Bobby...........................................Ruth Gordon
Mr. Halevy......................................Frederick Perry
Rims O'Neil.....................................Roger Pryor
Mrs. Gorlik.....................................Beulah Bondi
```
    Acts I and II.—At the Halevy's.  Act III.—Small Room in Mrs.
Gorlik's Boarding House.
    Staged by Guthrie McClintic.

See page 63.

## HONOR BE DAMNED!

### (45 performances)

A story of to-day in three acts. Produced by Willard Mack by arrangement with David Belasco at the Morosco Theatre, New York, January 26, 1927.

Cast of characters—

| | |
|---|---|
| John Connell | Willard Mack |
| Mrs. Connell | Lizzie McCall |
| Mary Connell | Ruth King |
| Beebe Dawley | Beatrice Banyard |
| Agnes Delrae | Ethel Gray Terry |
| "Big" Tom Reynolds | William Courtleigh |
| Lou Buckley | Carl Gerard |
| Sammie Stern | George Cleveland |
| Ted McBride | Harry English |
| Phil McGoveny | Thomas F. Tracey |
| Andrew Roby | Huron L. Blyden |

Acts I, II and III.—The Home of the Connells in West 57th Street, New York.

Staged by Willard Mack.

John Connell, product of the east side, self-educated and famous as a criminal lawyer, admits his loyalty to his crowd and tries to remain true to it. He "springs" his pals with the aid of political influence, but he keeps his mother and sister away from contact with them. Or thinks he does. Then he discovers that the man he has agreed to defend for a defenseless murder is also the man who has seduced his sister. His reaction is highly emotional, but he decides to go through with it.

## THE SCARLET LILY

### ("The Red Lily")

### (57 performances)

A new play of the day after the Big Parade by David Arnold Balch. Produced by Sanford E. Stanton at the Comedy Theatre, New York, January 29, 1927.

Cast of characters—

| | |
|---|---|
| Mrs. Strong | Jennie A. Eustace |
| Debbie | Isabel Dawn |
| Ira Strong | Carleton Macy |
| Hattie Watkins | Kathleen Lowry |
| Calvin Gallup | John Paul Lewis |
| Elmer Strong of the A. E. F. | Malcolm Fassett |
| Marcelle | Marguerite Risser |

```
Sam Strong........................................Bert Gorman
Rev. Mr. Simpson..............................Duncan Penwarden
Earl Watkins...................................Edwin Ledding
```
    Acts I, II and III.—Sitting-room in the Strong Farmhouse, Vermont.
    Staged by E. J. Blunkall.

Touched up a bit after the opening, when it was known as "The Red Lily." Elmer Strong, A. E. F. hero, brings home the wife he married in Bordeaux, Marcelle of the Coq d'Or. The New England Strongs are a little suspicious, and trouble follows when Earl Watkins recognizes Marcelle as the young woman who took his fifty francs and failed to make good a promise. Marcelle, exposed, asks to be sent back to the Coq d'Or, though her old life is a thing of the past forever, and Elmer stands by for a happy ending.


# THE BOTTOM OF THE CUP

## (6 performances)

Play in three acts by John Tucker Battle and William J. Perlman. Produced by the Mayfair Productions at the Mayfair Theatre, New York, January 31, 1927.

Cast of characters—

```
Mammy Lou.......................................Eva Benton
Rosalie Fitzhugh..............................Adelaide Rondelle
Colonel Fitzhugh.............................William Thompson
Doctor Jeffrey.....................................Cass Burt
Charles Thompson............................Daniel L. Haynes
Sheriff Bolton...............................Harlan E. Knight
Robert Kinney.................................Roderick Maybee
Willis Thompson.............................George W. Nixon
A Detective......................................Warren K. Hill
```
    Acts I, II and III.—Mammy Lou's Cabin, Mississippi Delta.
    Staged by Henry Stillman.

Charles Thompson, negro, has been sent north and educated by Col. Fitzhugh, on whose plantation the Thompsons have lived for generations. He returns south imbued with a desire to found a college for his people but runs into tragedies that stop him. His beloved missy, Rosalie Fitzhugh, has been betrayed by Robert Kinney. His brother Willie has helped Kinney with a bank robbery and Kinney kills him. Charles, seeking to set things straight, sacrifices himself, sends Kinney, reformed, to marry Rosalie, and gives himself up to a mob of lynchers as the real bank robber.

## TRELAWNEY OF THE WELLS

(56 performances)

Comedy in four acts by Arthur Wing Pinero. Revived by George C. Tyler at the New Amsterdam Theatre, New York, January 31, 1927.

Cast of characters—

James Telfer ........................................ Wilton Lackay
Mrs. Telfer (Miss Violet Sylvester) ............ Henrietta Crosman
Augustus Colpoys .................................... Otto Kruger
Ferdinand Gadd ................................... John E. Kellard
Tom Wrench ........................................ Rollo Peters
Avonia Bunn ...................................... Estelle Winwood
Rose Trelawney ................................... Helen Gahagan
Imogen Parrott ................................... Pauline Lord
O'Dwyer .......................................... J. M. Kerrigan
Mr. Denzil ....................................... Gerald Rogers
Mr. Mortimer ............................... Matthew Smith, Jr.
Mr. Hunston ...................................... J. F. Foster
Miss Brewster .................................... Peggy Whiffen
Hallkeeper at the Pantheon ....................... Robert Lansing
Vice Chancellor Sir William Gower, Kt. ............ John Drew
Miss Trafalgar Gower ............................. Effie Shannon
Arthur Gower ..................................... Eric Dressler
Clara De Foenix .................................. Frieda Inescort
Captain De Foenix ........................... Lawrence D'Orsay
Mrs. Mossop ................................. Mrs. Thos. Whiffen
Mr. Ablett ....................................... O. P. Heggie
Charles .......................................... Gerald Rogers
Sarah ............................................ Peggy Whiffen
   Acts I and III.—Mr. and Mrs. Telfer's Lodgings. Act II.—At Sir William Gower's in Cavendish Square. Act IV.—On the Stage of the Pantheon Theatre.
   Staged by George C. Tyler.

"Best Plays of 1924-25."

## THE ROAD TO ROME

(159 performances)

Play in three acts by Robert Emmet Sherwood. Produced by William A. Brady, Jr., and Dwight Deere Wiman at the Playhouse Theatre, New York, January 31, 1927.

Cast of characters—

Varius ........................................... Fairfax Burgher
Meta ............................................. Joyce Carey
Fabia ............................................ Jessie Ralph
Fabius ........................................... Richie Ling
Amytis ........................................... Jane Cowl
Tanus ............................................ Peter Meade
Scipio ........................................... Charles Brokaw
Cato ............................................. William Pearce
Drusus ......................................... William R. Randall

```
Sertorius.........................................Lionel  Hogarth
Tibullus...........................................Alfred  Webster
Sergeant..........................................Jock  McGraw
Corporal...........................................Lewis  Martin
First Guard.................................Clement O'Loghlen
Second Guard...................................Ben  Lackland
Third Guard................................ Walter A. Kinsella
Fourth Guard......................................John McNulty
Fifth Guard.......................................Peter  Meade
Thotmes.........................................Lionel  Hogarth
Hasdrubal..........................................Louis Hector
Maherbal...........................................Alfred  Webster
Carthalo...........................................Harold  Moffet
Mago...........................................Barry  Jones
Hannibal.........................................Philip  Merivale
Bala................................................Gert  Pouncy
```
Act I.—A Courtyard in the House of Fabius Maximus at Rome.
Acts II and III.—Hannibal's Headquarters in a Temple About Three
Miles East of Rome.
Staged by Lester Lonergan.

See page 153.


# FOR BETTER OR WORSE

## (16 performances)

Comedy drama in three acts by Allen de Lano.  Produced at
the Mansfield Theatre, New York, January 31, 1927.

Cast of characters—

```
Mary........................................... Gladys  Hurlbut
Mrs. Parsons......................................Edith  Spencer
Henry.............................................Joseph  Prosser
George Parsons....................................Tom  Powers
Mr. Parsons.......................................Wilmer  Walter
Doctor Graves.......................................Tom  Irwin
Fanny..............................................Edna  Leslie
```
Acts I, II and III.—Parsons' Home in a Small American Town.
Staged by Tom Powers.

George Parsons, having seduced Mary, an orphan-slavey in his
home, makes her an honest woman by marrying her for better
or worse.  Being collegiate and particular, Parsons can't stand
the more or less illiterate Mary, even as the mother of his child,
and in a moment's passion threatens to kill his offspring.  The
child is saved when Mary swears it isn't George's.

## TRIAL MARRIAGE

### (24 performances)

Drama in three acts by Michael Kallesser. Produced by Michael Kallesser at Wallacks Theatre, New York, January 31, 1927.

Cast of characters—

| | |
|---|---|
| Peggy Hall | Grace Valentine |
| Dick Saunders | Howard St. John |
| Mrs. Mills | Lou Ripley |
| Jack Wales | G. Pat Collins |
| Tony Spalls | Rodolpho Badaloni |

Acts I, II and III.—Home of Dick Saunders, New York City.
Staged by George Smithfield.

Peggy Hall is living with Dick Saunders on a trial marriage basis. Saunders tires of the arrangement and quits. Jack Wales takes his place and tries to make a harlot of Peggy. Saunders, back from South America and rich, refuses to take Peggy back when he learns about Wales and Peggy dies in his arms when Wales, a dope fiend by this time, shoots her.

## THE DARK

### (15 performances)

Drama in three acts by Martin Brown. Produced by William A. Brady, Jr., and Dwight Deere Wiman at the Lyceum Theatre, New York, February 1, 1927.

Cast of characters—

| | |
|---|---|
| Chris Landers | Louis Calhern |
| Flora Cort | Juliette Day |
| Sue Maddox | Julia Hoyt |
| Nicholas Trask | Stanley Logan |
| Vonnie Wallace | Saxon Kling |
| Rita Landers | Ann Andrews |
| Peanuts | Warren McCollum |
| Hopkins | Walter Colligan |

Acts I and II.—The Landers' Country House. Act III.—Rita's Sitting-room.
Staged by George Cukor.

Chris and Rita Landers are more or less happily married when Chris, trying to invent a new electric tube, suffers the loss of both eyes. The next year he spends in growing increasingly suspicious of his wife, whom he suspects of ceasing to love him since his face is scarred and he is obliged to wear a mask. Finally, unable to stand the strain longer, he forces a confession of her growing abhorrence of him and her attachment for another man and then pulls the mask from his face that she may gaze upon his ugliness. The sight moves her to deep pity and her love is restored.

## THE WANDERING JEW
### (15 performances)

A play in four phases by E. Temple Thurston, based on the ancient legend of the Wandering Jew. Produced at the Cosmopolitan Theatre, New York, February 1, 1927.

Cast of characters—

Phase 1—Jerusalem on the Day of the Crucifixion
Scene—A Room in the House of Matathias, the Jew

| | |
|---|---|
| Judith | Hutin Britton |
| Rachel | Vera Hurst |
| Matathias | Matheson Lang |
| Du Guesclin | Roland Arthur |

Phase 2—Syria in the Time of the First Crusade
Scene 1—A Tourney Outside the Walls of Antioch

| | |
|---|---|
| Du Guesclin | Roland Arthur |
| Boemond, Prince of Tarentum | Shayle Gardner |
| Godfrey, Duke of Normandy | Philip Cunningham, Jr. |
| Raymond of Toulouse | George Butler |
| Issachar | Ernest Bodkin |
| Joanne de Beaudricourt | Winifred Izard |
| The Unknown Knight | Matheson Lang |

Scene 2—The Knight's Tent

| | |
|---|---|
| Phireus | Denham Lewis |

Phase 3—Sicily in the Thirteenth Century
Scene—The House of Matteo Bottadio, the Jew, in Palermo

| | |
|---|---|
| Mario | Arnold Rooke |
| Andrea Michelotti | Ernest Bodkin |
| Matteo Bottadio, the Jew | Matheson Lang |
| Gianella Bottadio | Hutin Britton |
| Pietro Morelli | Shayle Gardner |

Phase 4—Spain in the Middle Ages
Scene 1—A Room in the House of Matteos Battadios,
a Doctor in Seville

| | |
|---|---|
| Al Kazar | Philip Cunningham, Jr. |
| Lazzaro Zapportas | Arnold Rooke |
| Maria Zapportas | Helen Simon |
| Arnaldo Zapportas | Elsie Judge |
| Matteos Battadios, the Jew | Matheson Lang |
| Olalla Quintana | Winifred Izard |
| Gonzalez Ferara | Shayle Gardner |
| Alonzo Castro | Alfred Dean |

Scene 2—The Tribunal Chamber of the Inquisition

| | |
|---|---|
| Juan de Texada | George Butler |
| Councillor | Geo. Smith |
| Councillor | William Walker |
| Officer of the Inquisition | Thomas Long |
| Officer of the Inquisition | Fred Hall |
| Men-at-Arms | Walter Plinge and Roland Arthur |

Scene 3—A Public Place
Staged by Matheson Lang.

See "Best Plays of 1921-22."

## RIO RITA

### (157 performances)

Musical Comedy in two acts by Guy Bolton and Fred Thompson. Produced by Florenz Ziegfeld at the Ziegfeld Theatre, New York, February 2, 1927.

Cast of characters—

| | |
|---|---|
| Padrone | Juan Villasana |
| Reporter | Al Clair |
| Roberto Ferguson | George Baxter |
| Carmen | Helen C. Clive |
| Ed Lovett | Robert Woolsey |
| Grim Gomez | Fred Dalton |
| General Enrique Joselito Esteban | Vincent Serrano |
| Raquel | Gladys Glad |
| Conchita | Marion Benda |
| Juanita | Dorothy Wegman |
| Lolita | Peggy Blake |
| Beppo | Kay English |
| Rio Rita | Ethelind Terry |
| Chick Bean | Bert Wheeler |
| Dolly | Ada-May |
| Jim | J. Harold Murray |
| Sergeant McGinn | Harry Ratcliffe |
| Sergeant Wilkins | Donald Douglas |
| Davalos | Alf P. James |
| Escamillo | Pedro Rubin |
| Capt. Gonzales | Alberto Carillo |
| Herminia | Collette |
| Katie Bean | Noel Francis |
| Montezuma's Daughter | Katherine Burke |

Acts I and II.—On the Shores of the Rio Grande.
Staged by John Harwood.

Jim, the captain of a company of Texas Rangers, is over the border looking for a bandit. Rio Rita's brother is suspected, which makes it tough for Jim and Rita to love each other, especially as Jim has a conscience and Gen. Esteban, the Mexican authority, loves her too. Fortunately the right bandit is discovered at curtain time.

## PINWHEEL

### (4 performances)

A play of New York by Francis Edwards Faragoh. Produced at the Neighborhood Playhouse, February 7, 1927.

Cast of characters—

| | |
|---|---|
| The Jane | Dorothy Sands |
| The Guy | Marc Loebell |
| The Lady Friend | Paula Trueman |
| The Bookkeeper | Albert Carroll |

```
The Fast Woman .................................... Lily Lubell
Her Companion .................................... George Heller
Radio Voice....................................... Theodore Hecht
Manager........................................... George Bratt
Worker ........................................... Theodore Hecht
1st Mrs. ......................................... Grace Stickley
2nd Mrs. ......................................... Mary George
Sugar Daddy ...................................... Otto Hulicius
     Staged by Alice Lewishon.
```

An allegorical drama in which a Jane and a Guy wander through the adventure with life that is New York, suffering defeat when the Jane, tied to Guy, prefers the Bookkeeper and kills him when she knows that she is losing him.


## THE ADVENTUROUS AGE

### (16 performances)

Comedy in three acts by Frederick Witney. Produced at the Mansfield Theatre, New York, February 7, 1927.

Cast of characters—

```
Hodder ........................................... Gordon Richards
Barbara Rivers.................................... Cecile Dixon
Nicholas Rivers................................... Terence Neill
Leonard Rivers.................................... Halliwell Hobbes
Adela Rivers...................................... Mrs. Patrick Campbell
Dr. Hamish Meluish ............................... David Clyde
Mavis Gore ....................................... Joan Vivian-Reis
     Acts I, II and III.—Mrs. Rivers' House in Surrey.
     Staged by George C. Tyler.
```

Adela Rivers, 45, but not ready to give up a last try for romance, is thinking of a Cook's Tour in search of amorous adventure when her mind is diverted by the appearance of her daughter's Scotch suitor, Hamish Meluish. Adela embarrasses Hamish with her attentions, but is finally put in her place by her children.


## SINNER

### (128 performances)

Comedy in three acts by Thompson Buchanan. Produced by Richard Herndon, by arrangement with W. Herbert Adams, at the Klaw Theatre, New York, February 7, 1927.

Cast of characters—

```
Ebenezer Standish ................................ Daniel Kelly
Cynthia Pemberton................................. Claiborne Foster
```

Tom Page...........................................Allan Dinehart
Jimmy La Farge.....................................Hugh Huntley
Mrs. John Pemberton, Sr. ........................Merle Maddern
John Pemberton, Sr. ..............................Richard Temple
Estelle Pemberton....................................Vera Allen
Billy Lawrence.................................Geoffrey Harwood
Watkins..........................................William Stone
John Pemberton, Jr. ................................Ray Walburn
 Act I.—Ebenezer's Roadhouse, Westport, Conn.  Acts II and III.
—Home of Tom Page.
 Staged by Allan Dinehart.

Cynthia Pemberton, sought by Tom Page while his divorce is pending, indulges in a pre-marital honeymoon and then, when Page is free, decides she is afraid of marriage.  However, they are married, and Page becomes engrossed in money-making. Cynthia turns to Jimmy La Farge for comfort and the expected happens.  Then Cynthia insists marriage is all she expected it would be and declares herself forever through with both men. She is again whipped when her husband, reverting to the old-fashioned ways, slaps her into a state of adoration and obedience.

## FOG

### (96 performances)

Play in three acts by John Willard.  Produced by Lorton Productions, Inc., at the National Theatre, New York, February 7, 1927.

Cast of characters—

Olaf................................................Ben Hendricks
Charlie.............................................Robert Keith
Eunice.........................................Vivienne Osborne
Elmer Dixon............................Alexander Clarke, Jr.
Lord Jim..................................  ............Wilfred Jessup
Scraggs........................................ Frank McHugh
Eph Kelly......................................Charles Dow Clark
Jeelo.........................................Edward Colebrook
Darcy........................................ Hugh O'Connell
 Act I.—A Private Wharf.  Acts II and III.—Cabin of the "Night Bird."
 Staged by Arthur Hurley.

Charlie and Eunice, among others, are lured at night to a deserted dock sticking out into the Great South Bay, Long Island.  There they hear a shot and a commotion aboard a mystery yacht, tied up alongside, and foolishly rush aboard.  First thing they know they are drifting towards the sea with a crazy captain.  Many things happen to awe, disturb, distress, startle and amaze them, but Charlie and Eunice are safe in each other's arms at the finish.

## JUDY

### (96 performances)

Musical comedy in two acts by Mark Swan. Produced by John Henry Mears at the Royale Theatre, New York, February 7, 1927.

Cast of characters—

| | |
|---|---|
| Tom Stanton | George Meeker |
| Dick Wetherbee | Edward Allen |
| Harry Danforth | Frank Beaston |
| Anita | Magda Bennett |
| Babette | Elizabeth Mears |
| Jack Lethbridge | Charles Purcell |
| Mrs. Maguire | Lida Kane |
| Lucy Lethbridge | Alice Mackenzie |
| Judy Drummond | Queenie Smith |
| Nathan Gridley | James Seeley |
| Mathew Lethbridge | John T. Dwyer |

Acts I and II.—The Rookery in Greenwich Village.

Staged by Bobby Connolly.

Judy, as a farce, was called "Judy Drops In." Judy is the stepdaughter of a bad man who locks her out one night when she is late. She is picked up by a Greenwich Village bachelor, who is much surprised to find her a good girl, and thereafter she lives on and keeps house for him and his chums, chaperoned by the janitress. Finally she marries the best of the boys.

## THE STRAWBERRY BLONDE

### (24 performances)

Comedy in three acts by Martin Brown. Produced at the Bijou Theatre, New York, February 7, 1927.

Cast of characters—

| | |
|---|---|
| Bessie Salute | Helen Joy |
| Fern Linkworthy | Maida Reade |
| Manon Linkworthy | Frances Victory |
| Peer Lepreen | William Pike |
| Pearl Lepreen | Julie Ring |
| Herbie Salute | George Anderson |
| Irma Trand | Mary Frey |
| Sammie Hermahammer | Bert Chapman |
| Adolf Linkworthy | Frank Howson |
| Old Mrs. Linkworthy | Enid Gray |

Acts I, II and III.—Salute's Flat in Wilpod Court, Astoria, New York.

Staged by George Anderson.

Herbie Salute, being red-headed and attractive to women, is fearfully embarrassed when three red-headed babies are born in the apartment house in which he and his wife, Bessie, are residents. Bessie is also embarrassed, and suspicious. Scandal threatens. Then it is proved that there are other red-headed men still at liberty.

## OFF-KEY

### (16 performances)

Drama in three acts by Arthur Cæsar. Produced by Robert V. Newman at the Belmont Theatre, New York, February 8, 1927.

Cast of characters—

| | |
|---|---|
| Ann | Margaret Douglass |
| Helen Clark | Katherine Revner |
| Tommy Neville | Albert Hackett |
| Kenneth Reynolds | McKay Morris |
| Alice Reynolds | Florence Eldridge |
| Cora Stevenson | Lucile Watson |
| Charles Ames | Kenneth Hunter |

Alice Reynolds had lived for some months with Charles Ames before she married the novelist, Kenneth Reynolds. Later the men meet, and because her husband is one of the liberal novelists, Alice makes a clean breast of everything. Kenneth pretends not to mind, but later his thoughts strike in and he is fit for any crime. There is a compromise at the end.

## LALLY

### (63 performances)

Play in three acts by Henry Stillman. Produced by Carl Reed, in association with Norman C. Stoneham, at the Greenwich Village Theatre, New York, February 8, 1927.

Cast of characters—

| | |
|---|---|
| Isolde Lally | Patricia Barclay |
| Brunhilde Lally | Helen Kingstead |
| Elsa Lally | Erin O'Brien-Moore |
| Stravinski Lally | Robert Collyer |
| Lally | Claude Rains |
| Izzyitch | Benedict MacQuarrie |
| Felicia de Mendoza | Zola Talma |
| Matilda | Kate McComb |
| Elizabeth Lally | Augusta Durgeon |
| Angelique | Genevieve Dolaro |
| Malvinski | France Bendtsen |

```
Cranston Thompson....................................F. H. Day
Archibald Higgins................................Gerald Hamer
Judith Montifiori................................Anne Morrison
Giovanni........................................Owen Meech
Ronald Byrde.................................Reginald Malcolm
    Acts I, II and III.—The Living-room, Lally's House, Somewhere
on the Hudson.
    Staged by John D. Williams.
```

Lally is a genius, an orchestra leader and a composer. In his suburban home he lives with his four irresponsible children and an excitable mistress, Mrs. Lally having been dead some years. Feeling the need of a soul-lifting inspiration if he is to finish his latest work, Lally prevails upon Judith Montfiori to stay near him and fires his mistress. In three weeks the composition is finished and Lally is in love with Judith. She will neither marry nor live with him, however. She leaves him, knowing that out of his imagined misery and longing he will do his best work.

## GRANITE

### (70 performances)

Play in three acts by Clemence Dane. Produced by the American Laboratory Theatre, New York, February 11, 1927.

Cast of characters—

```
Penny Holt.....................................Frances Wilson
Jordan Morris............................Herbert V. Gellendre
Judith............................................Blanch Tancock
Prosper........................................George Macready
A Nameless Man.............................Robert H. Gordon
A Clergyman...................................Roland Coombs
    Acts I, II and III.—Living-room of a Farm on Lundy's Island, in
the Second Decade of the Last Century.
    Staged by Richard Boleslavsky.
```

Judith, who yearns for life, is doomed to live on a granite island in the sea, with a granite-willed husband. The husband being murdered, Judith acquires another, but he turns out as bad. Then a handsome stranger does for the second, by pushing him into the sea. Judith, claimed as reward, is more miserable than before.

## SPELLBOUND

(3 performances)

Drama in three acts by Walter Elwood. Produced by Mary Forrest at the Klaw Theatre, New York, February 15, 1927.

Cast of characters—

Martin Tingue ........................................Bert West
Calvin Tingue... ...............................James G. Morton
Ella Van Valzeh..................................Esther Stockton
Nick Tingue...........................................Arthur Gray
Abbie Van Valzeh..............................Lottie Salisbury
Harvey Tingue..................................Richard Bowler
Ada Tingue...............................Adelaide Fitz Allen
    Acts I, II and III.—In the Tingue Cottage.

Ada Tingue, reading as a young woman that certain pellets dropped in a drinker's coffee would cure him of the pernicious craving for alcohol, seeks to anticipate the temptations of their manhood by feeding the pellets to her sons. As a result one is paralyzed below the waist, the other rendered dumb, while the mother goes away as a missionary devoting herself to saving souls. Eighteen years later she returns, slightly demented, and is duly exposed. Her sons fortunately recover.

## A LADY IN LOVE

(16 performances)

Comedy in three acts by Dorrance Davis. Produced by A. E. and R. R. Riskin at the Lyceum Theatre, New York, February 21, 1927.

Cast of characters—

Snivel................................................Alf Helton
Betty.............................................Jane Salisbury
Sophia..........................................Liane Carrera
Sir Barnaby........................................Rollo Lloyd
Clarissa............................................Peggy Wood
Sir Jeremy..................................Sydney Greenstreet
Constant...........................................Allyn Joslyn
Bragdon.........................................Gavin Gordon
La Roche............................................Julian Noa
Tapgood.........................................Lester Paul
Bloodshot..........................................Walter Jones
Moll..............................................Dennie Moore
Sadie..........................................Natalie Moorhead
Jenny.........................................Dorothy Estabrook
Constable...........................................Paul Lester
    Act I.—Living-room at Sir Barnaby's and Stag's Head Inn.  Act II.—Garden between homes of Sir Barnaby and Sir Jeremy.  Act III.—The Living-room and the Garden.  Mayfair, England, 1680. Staged by Rollo Lloyd.

Clarissa has been married seven years to Sir Barnaby, whom she took to save her father from the debtors' prison. Then Bragdon, her girlhood's lover, returns to town. Determined to see Bragdon, Clarissa schemes to have Sir Barnaby invite him to the house. Later, when the jealous Sir Barnaby has Bragdon set upon, the lover pretends to be dead and Clarissa induces Sir Barnaby to have the body removed to her rooms to see if she cannot bring the poor young man back to life. Which she does. And also gets a divorce.

## WINDOW PANES

### (32 performances)

Drama in three acts by Olga Printzlau. Produced by Charles L. Wagner at the Mansfield Theatre, New York, February 21, 1927.

Cast of characters—

| | |
|---|---|
| Artem Tiapkin | Charles Dalton |
| Marya | Eileen Huban |
| Misha | Cathryn Randolph |
| Peter | Craig Williams |
| Louiskoff | John Brewster |
| Efim | Frederick Knight |
| Ivan | Olive Behrens |
| Adevitch | Theresa Kilburn |
| Balidor | Brandon Peters |
| Ritka | Ruth Findlay |
| A Wanderer | Henry Herbert |
| Dvine | Catherine Haydon |
| Thora | Millie Aston |
| An Officer | Roy Cochran |
| Leo | Charles Allais |
| Sonia | Grace Lynn |
| Alexief | Benjamin Osipow |
| Stephan | Stephen Zebrock |

Acts I, II and III.—Artem Tiapkin's Hut in a Hamlet Near the Black Sea.

Staged by Henry Herbert.

A local soothsayer of a Russian village has foretold the second coming of Christ. The peasants, led by Artem Tiapkin, go to the village chapel to wait. Marya, wife of Artem, remains at her cottage with her dumb son, hoping the Master may pass her door and hear her prayers. A Wanderer begs a glass of water. Hearing the legend, he bids Marya be of good faith. The Savior will come to those whose hearts and minds are open for his reception. Let her see that the window panes of her soul are cleared of the gathered dust of ignorance and the light will shine in. In demonstration he clears the dust from the windows of the hut and the sunlight chases away the shadows. In a talk with the boy the Wanderer clears the misunderstanding from his mind and the child is mute no longer. The returning villagers marvel at the miracle, but Artem, the doubter, follows after the Wanderer and slays him as a political refugee on whose head a price has been set. Crazed by remorse, Artem hangs himself in atonement.

## SET A THIEF—

### (80 performances)

Mystery melodrama in three acts by Edward E. Paramore. Produced at the Empire Theatre, New York, February 21, 1927.

Cast of characters—

| | |
|---|---|
| Florence | Gladys Feldman |
| Payson | Earl House |
| Walter Marston | Calvin Thomas |
| Mrs. Dowling | Margaret Wycherly |
| Anne Dowling | Natacha Rambova |
| Tom Bennett | James Spottswood |
| Hannah | Nellie Fillmore |
| J. Frothingham Melville | Richard Coolidge |
| Rosie Ray | Martha Madison |
| Dayton | Carlton Rivers |
| Jack Harrington | Brandon Evans |
| Inspector Crowder | Frederic Burt |
| Nolan | Artie Kaufman |

Acts I, II and III.—In the Library of Walter Marston's Home in New York City.

Staged by Alexander Leftwich.

Walter Marston, banker, needs a couple of millions and conspires to rob himself. He might have fooled the detectives and the lawyers, but he could not fool his old Auntie Dowling, who is a sort of watchful Mrs. Grumpy. He is duly exposed at 11 P.M.

## POLLY OF HOLLYWOOD

### (24 performances)

Musical comedy in two acts by Will Morrissey. Produced by Harry L. Cort at the George M. Cohan Theatre, New York, February 21, 1927.

Cast of characters—

| | |
|---|---|
| Polly | Midgie Miller |
| Roderick | William Friend |

```
Gambler ........................................ Edward Gargan
Sheriff ................................................ Jerome Daly
Pablo .............................................. Hugh Kidder
Valencia ........................................ Bertee Beaumont
Tom Dix ........................................ Dave Ferguson
Chick ............................................ Franker Woods
Nelse ............................................ Earle S. Dewey
Driver ................................................ John Agee
Roberta ........................................ Marguerite Zender
Assistant Director ................................. Willard Hall
Camera Man ......................................... Matty Fain
Property Man ...................................... R. Luketas
Greener .......................................... Robert G. Pitkin
Julie ................................................ Alice Wood
Irene .............................................. Lillian Jordan
Abe Stein .......................................... Barney Ward
Moe Stein ......................................... Hugh Herbert
Hymie Cohen ...................................... Jacob Prank
Typist .............................................. Anna Mycue
Deenora and Berinoff ................................... Dancers
        Staged by William Morrissey.
```

The one about the little country girl who met a great director
and went into the movies—but not very far in.


## WHAT ANN BROUGHT HOME

### (96 performances)

Comedy in three acts by Larry E. Johnson. Produced by
Earl Carroll at Wallack's Theatre, New York, February 21, 1927.

Cast of characters—

```
Sam Bennet ........................................ Erman Seavy
Hattie Bennet ................................. Marion Stephenson
Alma ............................................... Peggy Shannon
Bert Hardcastle .................................. Cecil W. Secrest
Uncle Henry ...................................... Edward Poland
Ann ................................................. Mayo Methot
Dudley Purdy .................................... William Hanley
Nina ............................................... Lenore Sorsby
J. T. Raymond ...................................... George Earle
    Acts I, II and III.—Front Room in Sam Bennet's Home, Bennet's
Mills, Ind.
        Staged by Earl Carroll.
```

Ann, having married Dudley one day when she was in town
shopping, brings him home and suffers great chagrin when her
smart relatives accept him as a day-dreaming dumbbell without
brains or ideas. But Dudley fools them by turning the greatest
realty deal in the town's history and Ann proudly takes him
away on a second honeymoon.

## CRIME

(133 performances)

Melodrama of New York's underworld in four acts by Samuel Shipman and John B. Hymer. Produced by A. H. Woods at the Eltinge Theatre, New York, February 22, 1927.

Cast of characters—

| | |
|---|---|
| Annabelle Porter | Sylvia Sidney |
| Tommy Brown | Douglass Montgomery |
| Woman | Mary Smith |
| Man | Charles P. Mather |
| Officer | Clifton Self |
| Rocky Morse | Chester Morris |
| Spat | Earle Mayne |
| Dorothy Palmer | Kay Johnson |
| Frank Smiley | Gustav Yorke |
| Marjorie Grey | Katherine Francis |
| Stella Smiley | Josephine Deffry |
| William A. Emory | Walter D. Greene |
| Eugene Fenmore | James Rennie |
| Mouse Turner | Claude Cooper |
| Billy | Marvin Oreck |
| Spud | Jack LaRue |
| Dinkey | Michael Markham |
| Jimmy | Walter Power |
| Ken | Philip M. Sheridan |
| Hortense | Barbara Barondess |
| Henry | Clifton Self |
| Pedestrian No. 1 | Spurr K. Gould |
| Pedestrian No. 2 | Cleve Delland |
| Clerk | Irving H. Rapper |
| Spectator | Neill Bridges |
| Waiter No. 1 | Eddie Kelly |
| Waiter No. 2 | Jess Romer |
| Fluffy Girl | Marie Cole |
| Old Gentleman | Jack Thomson |
| Manager of Club | William Boulias |
| Milly | Carol Baldwin |
| Capt. Gargan | John O'Meara |
| Lieut. Tierney | Charles P. Mather |
| Inspector McGuinness | E. F. Bostwick |
| Tony | John Ward |
| Stenographer | De Lancey Cleveland |
| Voice on Radio | R. H. Irving |

Staged by A. H. Van Buren.

Act I.—1—A Secluded Spot in Central Park. 2—The Living-room of Frank Smiley's Apartment on Riverside Drive. Act II.—1—The Living-room at Eugene Fenmore's. Act III.—1—Exterior of Goldberg's Jewelry Shop on Broadway. 2—Eugene Fenmore's. Act IV.—1—The "Hellsden Club." 2—Office of Inspector of Police.

Tommy and Annabelle are held up in the park and Tommy is robbed of his $130 wedding money. Tommy decides to be even and holds up the hold-ups. The hold-ups, members of the famous Gene Fenmore gang, overcome Tommy and Annabelle and force them to join the gang. Fenmore plans a big jewelry store robbery, using Tommy and Annabelle as decoys. The kids are arrested, a gang girl squeals on Fenmore and all three are headed for the chair when Fenmore confesses to save Tommy and Annabelle.

## RIGHT YOU ARE IF YOU THINK YOU ARE

### (48 performances)

Parable in three acts by Luigi Pirandello. Produced by the Theatre Guild, Inc., at the Guild Theatre, New York, March 2, 1927.

Cast of characters—

| | |
|---|---|
| Lamberto Laudisi | Reginald Mason |
| Signora Frola | Beryl Mercer |
| Ponza | Edward G. Robinson |
| Signora Ponza | Armina Marshall |
| Commendatore Aggazi | Morris Carnovsky |
| Amalia | Laura Hope Crews |
| Dina | Phyllis Connard |
| Sirelli | Henry Travers |
| Signora Sirelli | Elisabeth Risdon |
| The Prefect | J. W. Austin |
| Centuri | Philip Loeb |
| Signora Cini | Helen Westley |
| Signora Nenni | Dorothy Fletcher |
| The Butler | Maurice McRae |
| A Gentleman | Philip Leigh |

Acts I, II and III.—Parlor in Commendatore Aggazi's House in a Small Italian Town.

Staged by Philip Moeller.

The Ponzas have recently moved to an Italian village, bringing Mrs. Ponza's mother with them. They occupy separate apartments, and the two women never see each other save at a distance. Gossip forces an explanation. Ponza insists his mother-in-law, Signora Frola, is a little crazy. She thinks, he says, that her daughter is still his wife, though her daughter has been dead for four years. Signora Frola, being questioned, insists that it is her son-in-law who is a little crazy. He thinks his first wife died and that he married again, when as a matter of fact he has never been married but once. Then the young Mrs. Ponza is called and calmly insists that she is both the first and second wife of Ponza. Tragic circumstances that, they insist, need not be explained compel the three of them to live as they do.

## PUPPETS OF PASSION

(12 performances)

Play in three acts by Rosso di San Secondo, adapted by Ernst Boyd and Eduardo Ciannelli. Produced at the Masque Theatre, New York, February 24, 1927.

Cast of characters—

| | |
|---|---|
| The Gentleman in Grey | Frank Morgan |
| Attendant | Erskine Sanford |
| Messenger Boy | Joseph Bascetta |
| The Gentleman in Mourning | Manart Kippen |
| First Workingman | Chauncey Causland |
| Second Workingman | George Sinclair |
| The Lady in the Blue Fox Fur | Rose Hobart |
| The Opera Singer | Gilda Leary |
| A Lady | Elaine Davies |
| A Gentleman | Edward Fetbroth |
| Telegraph Boy | Chester Erskin |
| A Bride | Edith Leitner |
| A Bridegroom | Paul E. Martin |
| First Dancer | Caddie Carr |
| Maid | Mrs. Charles Willard |
| Second Dancer | Anne Tarshis |
| Maitre D'Hotel | Eduardo Ciannelli |
| Waiters | Antonio Salerno / Giorgio Romano / Ernesto Valente |
| A Man About Town | Santos Ortega |
| A Solo Dancer | Evelyn Sabin |
| The Unexpected Guest | Craig Ward |

Staged by David Burton.

A Gentleman in Grey, a Gentleman in Mourning and a Lady in Blue Fox Furs meet in a telegraph office. Each has suffered a love tragedy and each is a little mad. They seek to console each other, but the love madness will not release them. The Gentleman in Grey kills himself. The Lady of the Furs returns to the lover who beats her. The Gentleman in Mourning is left to wonder what this sorry scheme of things is all about.


## BABBLING BROOKES

(3 performances)

Progressive comedy by E. D. Thomas. Produced by Russell Fanning, Inc., at the Edyth Totten Theatre, New York, February 25, 1927.

Cast of characters—

1927

| | |
|---|---|
| Aunt Babby | Clara Thropp |
| Uncle Bihl | George Neville |

```
Twin A............................................Viola Munroe
B. B. Brooke, Attorney............................Helen Weston
Bobby Arnold....................................Parker Fennelly
```

#### 1847

```
Michael Brooke..................................Charles Gibney
Zeke Tuttle....................................Charles Bunnell
Hank Arnold.................. ....................B. M. Conning
Chief of the Shinnecocks.......................William Frederic
Belle Brooke.......................................Edyth Totten
```

#### 1867

```
Michael Brooke, Junior...........................B. M. Conning
The Bride......................................Phyllis Frederick
Zeke Tuttle....................................Charles Bunnell
Mrs. Ada Horton......................................Edna May
Una............................................Frances Kennan
```

#### 1890

```
Miketta Brooke.................................Eleanor Laning
Belle Brooke.......................................Edyth Totten
```

#### 1923

```
Belle Brooke.......................................Edyth Totten
Granny Una.....................................Frances Kennan
Bub................................................Viola Munro
```

#### 1927

```
Aunt Babby........................................Clara Thropp
B. B., Now Mrs. Arnold............................Helen Weston
Uncle Bihl.......................................George Neville
```

#### Album

```
Michael Brooke..................................Charles Gibney
Michael Brooke, Junior...........................B. M. Conning
Miketta Brooke..................................Eleanor Laning
Chief of the Shinnecock's......................William Frederic
Belle Brooke.......................................Edyth Totten
     Staged by Edyth Totten.
```

The early Brookes helped to build up a section of Long Island and got to running with the Shinnecock Indians. One seduced a princess. She cursed his family and prayed that all the Brookes' children be girls. And they were. Which made it difficult to settle up the estate of old Somebody Brooke, who died in 1927. Belle Brooke, lady attorney, turned the trick, however.


### MONEY FROM HOME

(32 performances)

Comedy in three acts by Frank Craven. Produced by A. L. Erlanger at the Fulton Theatre, New York, February 28, 1927.

Cast of characters—

```
Jennie Patrick....................................Shirley Warde
Nannie Bauer...................................Camilla Dalberg
Hermann Bauer......................................John Ravold
Newton Chester................................Frederick Graham
```

```
Mrs. Chester....................................Adora Andrews
Dr. James Durham...............................Frank Craven
"Jakey" Getz.........................................John Diggs
George Peters...................................Leo Donnelly
Bell Boy.........................................Beacher Zebbs
    Acts I and III.—Home of Jennie Patrick, Falls Creek, Pa.  Act
II.—Chancellor Arms Hotel, New York.
    Staged by Frank Craven.
```

Jennie Patrick, waitress, inherits $5,000 in Pennsylvania and is willing to spend it all on one good time in New York. There she meets Doc Durham, a smart medic who has given up practice for confidence work. The Doc is after Jennie's money, which he assumes to be limitless, and marries her to get it. When he discovers she was telling the truth he is ready to run. An explosion in a factory holds him over, reinspires him with a love of his profession and causes him to know that he really loves Jen.

## WE ALL DO

### (8 performances)

Comedy in three acts by Knud Wiberg and Marcel Strauss. Produced by George MacFarlane at the Bijou Theatre, New York, February 28, 1927.

Cast of characters—

```
Winnifred Chester...........................Virginia Williams
Charles Chester...............................Carleton Hildreth
Pauline Chester...............................Anne Shoemaker
Geoffrey Chester...............................Charles Richman
Reverend Dr. Chester.............................Orlando Daly
Countess D'Albini............................Kathryn Givney
Count Antonio D'Albini.........................Herbert Clark
Allan Conover................................H. Reeves-Smith
Williams.......................................Raymond O'Brien
    Acts I, II and III.—Early Evening in the Living-room of the
Chester Home, New York City.
    Staged by Marcel Strauss.
```

Pauline Chester knows that her lawyer husband, Geoffrey, is living with the Countess D'Albini, but so long as it keeps him away from home she does not much care. When her daughter Winnifred wants to marry the Countess's son, Antonio, however, there is trouble. Geoffrey and the Countess both object. Pauline sees no reason why the young people should not be happy, and threatens to uncover the whole scandal if they are interfered with. Then she runs away with an old flame of her own.

## LOUD SPEAKER

### (42 performances)

Farce in three acts by John Howard Lawson. Produced by the New Playwrights Theatre at the 52nd Street Theatre, New York, March 7, 1927.

Cast of characters—

| | |
|---|---|
| Harry U. Collins | Seth Kendall |
| Peterson | Porter Hall |
| Emma Collins | Margaret Douglass |
| Maid | Isobel Stahl |
| Clare Collins | Agnes Lumbard |
| Josephus | Leonard Sillman |
| Johnnie Dunne | Romney Brent |
| Floradora Finnigan | Hilda Manners |
| A Stranger with a Beard | Benjamin Osipow |
| Dorothy Dunne | Reba Garden |
| Armenian Iky | Maurice Fein |
| 1st Reporter | Benjamin Kamsler |
| 2nd Reporter | Bernard L. Gottlieb |
| 3rd Reporter | Miriam Gumble |
| 1st Photographer | Russell Wright |
| 2nd Photographer | Boyd Clarke |

Staged by Harry Wagstaff Gribble.

A fantastic and futuristic farce detailing ironically the campaign of a man who runs for the governorship of New York. He is the usual political weathercock until he gets full of synthetic gin and tells the voters to go to hell by radio. This guarantees his election.

## INHERITORS

### (17 performances)

Play in three acts by Susan Glaspell. Revived by the Civic Repertory Theatre at the Civic Repertory Theatre, New York, March 15, 1927.

Cast of characters—

| | |
|---|---|
| Smith | Gordon Pascal |
| Grandmother | Leona Roberts |
| Silas Morton | Robert F. Ross |
| Felix Fejevary, 1st | Egon Brecher |
| Felix | Alan Birmingham |
| Senator Lewis | J. Edward Bromberg |
| Horace | John Eldridge |
| Doris | Ruth Wilton |
| Fussie | Oahlee Hubbard |
| Madeline Fejevary Morton | Josephine Hutchinson |
| Aunt Isabel | Eva Le Gallienne |
| Harry | Harold Moulton |
| Professor Holden | Sayre Crawley |
| Ira Morton | Robert F. Ross |
| Emil Johnson | Wesley John |

Acts I and III.—Sitting-room of the Mortons' Farmhouse in the Middle West.   Act II.—A Corridor in the Library of Morton College. Staged by Eva Le Gallienne.

Silas Morton, in 1879, gave his best land to a mid-west college that thought might be made free in America.   In 1920 certain of the Morton College disciples are jailed as slackers and there is no freedom.   Madeline Morton, however, carries on.   Her mother died for the Swedes, her brother for the French, her sweetheart goes to jail as a conscientious objector in 1917 and she smashes a policeman with a tennis racket in defense of some Hindu Reds.

## THE HEAVEN TAPPERS

(9 performances)

Play in three acts by George Scarborough and Annette Westbay.   Produced by Lee Shubert in association with Edwin Carewe at the Forrest Theatre, New York, March 8, 1927.

Cast of characters—

David Calvin, alias "The Parson"................Charles Waldron
Bud Ketcham....................................Thomas Chalmers
Kent Hardy..................................... Reginald Barlow
Warden........................................... Thomas Gunn
Chaplain Francis................................John M. Kline
Kid Short......................................Frank Marlowe
Pop Peters........................................Joseph Allen
Red Belwyn....................................Margaret Lawrence
Devil Ace Gilson................................Louis Bennison
Cap Mayhorn......................................John Benson
Dock Tolliver....................................Harry Clarens
Mrs. Gilson....................................Florence Gerald
Mrs. Ketcham..................................Lule Warrenton
Old Jud..........................................Frank Williams
Lafe Ketcham.....................................Charles Abbe

Act I.—Cell-room in a Federal Penitentiary and in the Blue Ridge Mountains Six Months Later.   Acts II and III.—Home of Devil Ace Gilson.
Staged by Edwin Carewe.

"Parson" Calvin, out of jail, calls his gang together in the south where the moonshiners are reported rolling in wealth. Disguising himself and two others as traveling prophets, he preaches religion to the mountaineers and sets his woman, "Red" Belwyn, on Devil Ace Gilson, leader of the moonshiners.   Devil Ace has a way of poisoning those who interfere with his business, but he falls for "Red" and through her really does get religion.   She is herself converted by the faith she has inspired, which puts the "Parson" out of business and makes nearly everybody good.

## EARTH

### (24 performances)

An expressionistic play in seven scenes by Em Jo Basshe. Produced by the New Playwrights at the 52nd Street Theatre, New York, March 9, 1927.

Cast of characters—

| | |
|---|---|
| Deborah | Inez Clough |
| Brother Elijah | Daniel L. Haynes |
| Abner | Hayes Pryor |
| Senon | William Townsend |
| Mary | Marie Young |
| Sera | Ruth Carr |
| Dinah | Dannie Morgan |
| Naomi | Elsie Winslow |
| Suzanna | Geraldine Evans |
| Barnabas | Hemsley Winfield |
| Moses | H. Webster Elkins |
| Mathias | Jerome N. Addison |
| Ebenezer | McKinley Reeves |
| Peter | Harold Des Verney |

In and Around a Clearing in the Early Eighties.
Staged by Russell Wright and Hemsley Winfield.

Deborah, colored, mother of six children, all dead, protests to the Lord and begs the return of Walter, her best beloved. At a religious shrine in the hills, where the flock meets to be led in prayer and worship by Brother Elijah, who is blind, Deborah is adjudged a sinner and stricken down.

## THE NEW YORKERS

### (52 performances)

Musical revue in two acts; book and lyrics by Jo Swerling and Henry Myers; music by Arthur Schwartz, Edgar Fairchild and Charles M. Schwab. Produced by Milton Bender at the Edyth Totten Theatre, New York, March 10, 1927.

Principals engaged—

| | |
|---|---|
| Chester Clute | Tamara Drasin |
| Rima Swan | Mona Sorel |
| Florence Faun | Elaine Lauren |
| Lilyan Lauren | Dorothy Hoffman |
| Isabel Zehner | Milton Laurence |
| Sue Baxter | Dorothy Daye |
| Milt Collins | Harry Benson |
| Benn Trivers | Roberta Gale |
| Gay LaSalle | Wes. L. Robertson |
| Genevieve Ames | Charles Bender |
| Elaine Gerard | |

## MENACE

(24 performances)

Drama in three acts by Arthur M. Brilant. Produced by James E. Kenney at the 49th Street Theatre, New York, March 14, 1927.

Cast of characters—

| | |
|---|---|
| Kama | Maud Durand |
| Lattimer | Jack Roseleigh |
| Setsu | Eve Casanova |
| Michi | Wyrley Birch |
| Okuma | Richard Bowler |
| Lorna Patterson | Pauline MacLean |
| Arnold Ross | Joseph Granby |
| Seth Jackson | Tom Reynolds |
| Warden | Alan Ramsay |

Acts I, II and III.—In the Living-room of Lattimer's Hut on an Island in Japan.

Staged by Arthur Hurley.

Setsu, a daughter of the Samaurai who was educated at Smith, is back on an island off Tokio and is harboring Lattimer, a white man, wanted in the states. Setsu is in love with Lattimer, but his interest in her is merely casual. Detectives from the states, including the daughter of the prison warden who helped Lattimer escape, take the fugitive back home and Setsu thinks seriously of committing hara-kiri.

## THE MYSTERY SHIP

(109 performances)

Mystery melodrama in three acts, by Edgar M. Schoenberg and Milton Silver. Produced by Gustav Blum at the Garrick Theatre, New York, March 14, 1927.

Cast of characters—

| | |
|---|---|
| Burke | Leighton Meehan |
| Conway | Arthur C. Morris |
| Mrs. Chickering | Elizabeth Irving |
| Anthony Langdon | Wallace Erskine |
| Capt. O'Donnell | Joseph R. Garry |
| Albert Gardner | Sherling Oliver |
| Mildred Langdon | Marion Swayne |
| Thomas Chickering | Ellis McClellan |
| Pete | Bob Spear |
| Dr. Emory | George D. Winn |
| Stowe | Robert J. Lance |

Acts I, II and III.—On Board a Ship at Sea.

Staged by Gustav Blum.

A man is found dead in his cabin bunk on a ship at sea, following a revolver shot. A three-act search for his murderers, also for the corpse, which later disappears, reveals a plot to rob an insurance company of many thousands of dollars. The man was only playing dead.

## THAT FRENCH LADY

### (47 performances)

Comedy-drama in three acts by Samuel Shipman and Neil Twomey. Produced by A. L. Jones and Morris Green at the Ritz Theatre, New York, March 15, 1927.

Cast of characters—

Martha ................................................Marie Reichardt
Gertrude Kraft ...................................... Mary Loane
Fred Kraft .......................................... Robert Williams
Karl Kraft .......................................... Louis Mann
Michael Maloney.....................................Brandon Tynan
Madame Nina de Poulet...........................Clara Lipman
Stella Kraft ........................................ Marian Stokes
Toinette ........................................... Jeanne La Motte

Acts I, II and III.—Living-room in Karl Kraft's Home, Lexington Avenue, New York.
Staged by Louis Mann.

Karl Kraft, pro-German banker, is fearfully excited when his A.E.F. son returns from France with Nina de Poulet. Kraft believes there is an affair between them. Later he discovers Mme. de Poulet is his son's mother-in-law, investigating his American home to see whether or not it is fit for her daughter.

## HER CARDBOARD LOVER

### (100 performances)

Play in three acts by Jacques Deval; adapted by Valerie Wyngate and P. G. Wodehouse. Produced by Gilbert Miller and A. H. Woods at the Empire Theatre, New York, March 21, 1927.

Cast of characters—

Monsieur Bonnavant..............................Ernest Stallard
Charly..............................................Arthur Lewis
Paul Guisard........................................Terence Neil
Andre Sallicel .....................................Leslie Howard
A Croupier..........................................Charles Esdale
Simone .............................................Jeanne Eagels
Cloak Room Attendant............................Henry Vincent
Tony Lagorce.......................................Stanley Logan
Albine .............................................Valerie Wyngate

Act I.—Bar of the Baccarat Room, Hendaye. Act II and III.—Simone's Bedroom in Her Paris Apartment.
Staged by Gilbert Miller.

Simone, having divorced a husband with whom she still is in love, thinks she may avoid a temptation to return to him by hiring another man to make love to her. She thus accepts the ardent attentions of Andre Sallicel. Andre is persistent and very much in earnest. So much so that he finally routs Tony Lagorce, the former husband, and is accepted as Simone's true mate.

## LUCKY

### (71 performances)

Musical comedy in two acts by Otto Harbach, Bert Kalmar, Harry Ruby and Jerome Kern. Produced by Charles Dillingham at the New Amsterdam Theatre, New York, March 22, 1927.

Cast of characters—

| | |
|---|---|
| Cyngie | Kumara Singha |
| Chuck Dugan | Henry Mowbray |
| A Pearl Thief | Bert Gould |
| Finch | Martin Berkeley |
| Barlow | Paul Everton |
| Jack Mansfield | Joseph Santley |
| Notoya | Kathryn Hamill |
| Teddy Travers | Richard (Skeet) Gallagher |
| First Tourist | Joan Clement |
| Second Tourist | Jeanne Fonda |
| Long Ling | Al Ochs |
| Charlie Simpson | Walter Catlett |
| Strawberry | Princess White Deer |
| Grace Mansfield | Ivy Sawyer |
| Mazie Maxwell | Ruby Keeler |
| Lucky | Mary Eaton |
| Officer | Hugh Francis Murphy |
| The High Priest | Charles Gibney |
| Mendicant Monks | Fred Wilson, Stanley McClelland, Hal Clovis Emile Cote. |
| First Waiter | Fred Lenox |
| Second Waiter | George Ferguson |
| Third Waiter | Al Wyart |
| Page | Charles Eaton |
| Wilton | Richard Farrell |
| Shellbach | Charles Mitchell |

Paul Whiteman and His Orchestra

Act I.—Scene 1—Pearl Village, Ceylon. 2—A Sacred Bo Tree. 3—Music Room of the S. S. Washington. 4—A Street in Columbo, Ceylon. 5—Exterior Buddhist Temple. Act II.—Scene 1—Green Room of Cabaret. 2—A Doorway on East Twelfth Street. 3—Paul Whiteman and His Orchestra. 4—Dance Floor of Cabaret.
Staged by Hassard Short.

Lucky is a Ceylonese pearl fisher who gives all the pearls she finds to her supposed father, Barlow, who is really a crook. Jack Mansfield, touring Ceylon, falls in love with Lucky, thus complicating his own love affairs but creating a romance that is happily consummated at 11 P.M.

## THE SPIDER

(100 performances)

Mystery melodrama in three acts by Fulton Oursler and Lowell Brentano. Produced by Albert Lewis and Sam H. Harris at the 46th Street Theatre, New York, March 22, 1927.

Cast of characters—

ACT I.—The Show

| | |
|---|---|
| A—Overture | Tivoli Theatre Orchestra |
| B—News Reel | International News Service |
| C—Mack & La Rue | The Skating Marvels of the Century |
| D—Lytell & Fant | The Chocolate Cake-Eaters |
| E—Chatrand, the Great | The Master Magician |

Assisted by Alexander, the Boy with the Radio Eyes

| | |
|---|---|
| The Manager | Wm. E. Morris |
| The Man | Donald Mackenzie |
| The Girl | Eleanor Griffith |
| The Sergeant | John O. Hewitt |
| The Doctor | Arthur Stuart Hull |
| Bill | John Burkell |
| Dick | Anton Ascher |
| Mrs. Wimbleton | Priscilla Knowles |
| Harry | Edw. Mann |
| The Reporter | Murray Alper |
| The House Leader | Walter Travers |
| The Inspector | Thomas Findlay |
| Officer Simpson | John Rogers |
| Officer Burke | Harry Phillippi |
| Officer Shayne | John Kelly |
| Officer Casey | Alfred Goldie |
| Officer Dougherty | D. J. Flanagan |
| Officer Jones | Charles Hamlin |
| Officer Thornton | Clifford Stone |
| Alexander | Roy Hargrave |
| Tommy | H. Yano |
| Estelle | Germaine Giroux |
| Chartrand, The Great | John Halliday |

Act II.—Scene 1—Chatrand's Dressing-room. 2—Before the Curtain. 3—The Stage. Act III.—Scene 1—The Manager's Office. 2—Before the Curtain. 3—The Stage.

The Action of the Play Takes Place During a Performance at the Tivoli Vaudeville Theatre, New York.

Staged by Albert Lewis.

Chatrand, the magician, has picked up in Washington a boy suffering an attack of amnesia who is psychically gifted. He calls him Alexander, the boy with the radio eyes, and makes him a feature of his act, asking any one in the audience who recognizes him to tell who he is. At the performance with which the play starts Alexander makes startling statements regarding a spider locket submitted to him in a mind-reading test by a young woman in the audience. The young woman's escort objects, the lights go out mysteriously, there is a shot and when the lights are turned up the objecting patron is found murdered in the aisle. The police take charge, an investigation follows and the young woman of the locket is proved to be Alexander's sister, her escort the leader of a dope ring who held the young folks in his power.

## THE CROWN PRINCE

### (45 performances)

Royal romance in three acts, by Zoe Akin; from the Hungarian by Ernest Vajda. Produced by L. Lawrence Weber at the Forrest Theatre, New York, March 23, 1927.

Cast of characters—

| | |
|---|---|
| Vercel | Jerome Lawler |
| Personal Lackey | Dennis Cleugh |
| Herr Schmitt | Ferdinand Gottschalk |
| The Equerry | C. W. Van Voorhis |
| The Crown Prince | Basil Sydney |
| First Lackey | Samuel Rosen |
| Adjutant Von Stucken | Harold Heaton |
| Charlotte | Kay Strozzi |
| Anna | Mary Ellis |
| The Emperor | Henry Stephenson |
| Meyer | Arthur Bowyer |

Act I.—Palace of the Crown Prince. Acts II and III.—Kleyerdorf.

Staged by Lawrence Marston.

The author here gives his version of the unsolved tragedy that occurred in the royal house of Austria in 1889. At that time the Crown Prince was found dead in his castle at Meyerling. In the play his death is explained in his love for the Baroness Anna, whom he brought to the court in defiance of his father's wishes and his cold and ambitious wife's protest. Nor would he give Anna up. The Emperor thereupon sought to turn Anna's mind against the Crown Prince and finally induced her to put poison drops in her lover's coffee on promise that she should become the mistress of the Emperor and possibly queen. In the end Anna prefers to drink the rest of the poison and die with her lover.

## SAVAGES UNDER THE SKIN

### (28 performances)

Play in three acts by Harry L. Foster and Wynn Proctor. Produced by Carl Reed at the Greenwich Village Theatre, New York, March 24, 1927.

Cast of characters—

| | |
|---|---|
| Wong | Harold De Becker |
| Rev. Brown | William B. Mack |

```
Chumley Satterthwaite Bannerman...............J. Malcolm Dunn
Datu Babu.......................................Najid Assif
Francis Xavier O'Rourke..........................Louis Calhern
Old Native.....................................Frank De Silva
Tanya............................................. Marie Elek
Maya.........................................Princess Almica
Prince Hadi......................................Clay Clement
Edith Brown....................................Flora Sheffield
Shorty...........................................Jack Veitch
A Native Dancer............................Valentina Rasehouba
    Staged by John D. Williams.
```

Francis O'Rourke, son of a missionary who once ruled the
Island of Saba Saba, in the South Seas, and was murdered by
the natives, returns to avenge his parent's death and becomes the
Mussolini of Saba Saba. He is opposed by Reverend Brown,
a new missionary, who helps to educate Prince Hadi, the hereditary ruler of the island. Hadi returns from Oxford, starts a
rebellion and rules briefly. Then the natives are whipped again
and O'Rourke resumes his reign.


## MARINERS

### (16 performances)

Drama in three acts by Clemence Dane. Produced by The
Actors' Theatre, Inc. (Guthrie McClintic, director), at the
Plymouth Theatre, New York, March 28, 1927.

Cast of characters—

```
Rev. Benjamin Cobb............................Arthur Wontner
Miss Ann Shepperley.............................Haidee Wright
Mrs. Bewley......................................Ethel Griffies
Miss Pym.........................................Beulah Bondi
Joan Shepperley.................................Mary Kennedy
Violet Bewley.................................. Emily Hammond
Lady Sara Shepperley........................Evelyn Walsh Hall
George Shepperley.............................George Fitzgerald
Sir James Fowler................................Gilbert Douglas
Dr. Ludlow Bell..............................T. Wigney Percyval
A Maid......................................... Madeline Barr
Gerry Despard...................................Hugh Sinclair
Lily Cobb........................................Pauline Lord
Flo Sanders...................................Geraldine Koerpel
    Acts I, II and III.—Living-room at the Rectory and the Drawing-
room at the Shepperleys'.
    Staged by Guthrie McClintic.
```

The Rev. Benjamin Cobb, honor student at college, marries
Lily, the daughter of an inn keeper, hoping to mold her to his
heart's desire. Lily, through the years, grows increasingly suspicious and neurotic, becomes jealous of her husband and finally
hopelessly messes up his life and his work. In the end the
Reverend Cobb dies of the flu and Lily, overcome by remorse, is
found dead on the fresh turned earth of his grave.

## RUFUS LeMAIRE'S AFFAIRS

### (56 performances)

Revue in two acts; music by Martin Broones; book and lyrics by Ballard Macdonald; additional skits by Andy Rice. Produced by Rufus LeMaire at the Majestic Theatre, New York, March 28, 1927.

Principals engaged—

| | |
|---|---|
| Ted Lewis | Charlotte Greenwood |
| Lester Allen | Beth Berri |
| John Price Jones | Line Basquette |
| William Halligan | Peggy Fears |
| Lon Hascall | Mary Lewis |
| John Hamilton | Sally Starr |
| Lester Dorr | Bobbe Arnst |
| Sunny Dale | Albertina Rasch Girls |

Staged by William Halligan, Jack Hascall and Albertina Rasch.

## CHERRY BLOSSOMS

### (56 performances)

Musical play in three acts, adapted from "The Willow Tree," by Benrimo and Harrison Rhodes; book and lyrics by Harry B. Smith; music by Sigmund Romberg. Produced by the Messrs. Shubert at the 44th Street Theatre, New York, March 28, 1927.

Cast of characters—

| | |
|---|---|
| Stella Maywood | Ann Milburn |
| Jefferey Fuller | James Marshall |
| George Washington Goto | Bernard Gorcey |
| Imaru | Frederick Kaufman |
| Kamura | Fred Harper |
| O-San Dam | Goodie Galloway |
| Yo-San | Desiree Ellinger |
| Ned Hamilton | Howard Marsh |
| First Shop Girl | Marie Laval |
| Second Shop Girl | Ronnie Madison |
| Tomotado | William Pringle |
| Shimamura | Frank Greene |
| The Bonze | Harold Kravitt |
| Nogo | Frank Davenport |
| Street Singer | Sylvia Peterson |
| Mary Temple | Gladys Baxter |
| First Officer | El Thompson |
| Second Officer | Dan Douglas |
| Larry Fuller | Walter Tenney |
| O-Yuki-San | Desiree Ellinger |
| Kiku San | Marion Keeler |
| A Geisha Dancer | Verona |

Act I.—Japanese Bazaar and Curio Shop. Act II.—The Willow Garden of Hamilton's Home. Act III.—Tea House of the Yoshiura. Staged by Lew Morton.

Ned Hamilton, a touring American, out of love with an English sweetheart, buys a statue of the princess of the willow tree of a Japanese merchant. Hearing the legend that the princess, carved from the heart of a willow tree, may come to life if he puts a mirror, the soul of woman, in her bodice, Ned tries it. The princess, pretty Yo-Susa-San, who has been substituted by the merchant for the statue, does come to life and lives happily with Hamilton until his English princess comes in search of him and he goes back to England with her.

## LOST

### (8 performances)

Drama in three acts by A. E. Thomas and George Agnew Chamberlain. Produced by Ramsey Wallace at the Mansfield Theatre, New York, March 28, 1927.

Cast of characters—

| | |
|---|---|
| Glen Lansing | Barbara Ramsey |
| J. Y. Wayne | George Henry Trader |
| Ada | Florence Archibald |
| Mrs. Lansing | Louise Mackintosh |
| Gerald Lansing | Ramsey Wallace |
| Alice Lansing | Mona Kingsley |
| Alan Wayne | James Crane |
| Macguire | R. Webb Lawrence |
| Honoria | Mercedes Gilbert |
| Bonifacio | Leon C. Timberlake |
| Jones | Harry Davenport |
| Margarita | Rosalinde Fuller |
| Lieber | Edward Van Sloan |

Act I.—Country Home of the Lansings. Acts II and III.—Alan Wayne's Camp, Brazil.
Staged by Rollo Lloyd.

Gerald Lansing and his wife, Alice, being unhappy, Alice turns to Alan Wayne for comfort. Alan and Alice decide to elope to South America, but Alice turns back at the railway station. Gerald, hearing of the elopement, misses Alice's return and goes to South America to kill Wayne. In Brazil the two men meet and agree to fight it out as soon as Wayne, who is in a fever, is well. Meantime Wayne, suffering remorse, sends for Alice. She arrives only to find that her husband has gone native and is living with Margarita, a half caste. Gerald feels bound to stick to his native wife, but Margarita, realizing she is in the way, throws herself over a cliff.

## THE LEGEND OF LEONORA

### (16 performances)

Comedy in three acts by Sir James M. Barrie. Revived by arrangement with Charles Frohman, Inc., at the Ritz Theatre, New York, March 29, 1927.

Cast of characters—

```
Mr. Justice Grim Dyke...........................Moffat Johnston
Sir Roderick Peripety..............................Leonard Willey
Captain Rottray, R. N. ............................Bruce McRae
Mr. Tovey.........................................George Thorpe
Mr. Lebetter.....................................Edward Cooper
Railway Guard...................................Richard Simpson
Foreman of Jury................................J. F. Robertson
Juryman......................................George H. Wiseman
Juryman........................................William Newman
Clerk...........................................Kenneth Lawton
Usher...........................................Harry Holliday
Policeman.......................................Richard Rawson
Leonora...........................................Grace George
Lady Peripety.....................................Adele Ronson
Mrs. Tovey.......................................Nelly Malcolm
Maid..............................................Jane Maurice
        Act I.—Living-room in the Tovey's Home.  Act II.—The Court
Room.  Act III.—Living-room in Leonora's Home.
        Staged by Edward Elsner.
```

Leonora, being an old-fashioned mother, requests a fellow traveler to close the window of their compartment because her daughter Milly has a sniffy cold. The traveler refuses and Leonora pushes him off the train, closing the window herself. She is arrested, charged with murder and brought to trial, but she so charms the judge and jury that she easily convinces them of the justice of her act and is triumphantly acquitted.

## SCALAWAG

### (7 performances)

Play in three acts by David Higgins and Bennett Musson. Produced by Cast Productions, Inc. (direction Sanford E. Stanton), at the 49th Street Theatre, New York, March 29, 1927.

Cast of characters—

```
Jonas Beebe.......................................Carleton Macy
Ab Whiffen.......................................Charles Lewis
Lem Simkins......................................Joseph Burton
"Aunt Lib".......................................Camilla Crume
Sam Appleby........................................David Higgins
Malvinia..........................................Daphne Kendall
Myra Appleby.......................................Isabel Dawn
```

```
Tom Rinnell.....................................Edwin Redding
Judge Westcott..............................Duncan Penwarden
Jim Allison........................................Robert Toms
Larry Maddern...................................Max Waizman
    Acts I and III.—"The General Grant Garage."  Act II.—"Living-
room in Jonas' Home," Clear Water Springs, Vermont.
    Staged by E. J. Blunkall.
```

"Uncle Sam" Appleby, a lovable ne'er-do-well living in a prohibition district, undertakes to help his partner's grandson,
Jonas Beebe, who returns from the war a little shattered but
still in love with his boyhood sweetheart, Myra Appleby. Jonas,
aiding a war buddy turned bootlegger, gets into trouble with the
law, needs $2,000 to pay his fine. "Uncle Sam" and Myra raise
the money and the judge overlooks the evidence.


## FOG-BOUND

### (27 performances)

Drama in three acts by Hugh Stanislaus Stange. Produced
by Richard Herndon at the Belmont Theatre, New York, April 1,
1927.

Cast of characters—

```
Mrs. Penny.......................................Clara Blandick
Annabel Jones........................................Lois Ross
Hester Penny.......................................Nance O'Neil
Doctor Bill..................................W. W. Shuttleworth
Lem Ross........................................Curtis Cooksey
Cap'n Joshua Penny.............................Porter Fennelly
Cap'n Ezra Tuttle..............................Alfred Hickman
Nell Tuttle.......................................Betty Linley
Mary Howell......................................Dorothy Ellin
Frank Smith.....................................William Johnstone
Gersham Smith..................................Porter Fennelly
    Acts I, II and III.—In Front of the Penny Home on the Sand
Dunes Near Montauk Point, Long Island.
    Staged by Alfred Hickman.
```

In 1882 Hester Penny, in love with a sailor, Lem Ross, is
forced by her parents to marry the village parson, Ezra Tuttle.
Eighteen years later Lem returns and wants Hester. She, living
unhappily with Tuttle, a cruel fanatic, agrees to run away with
Lem but is dissuaded by fear her daughter, Nell, will suffer the
stings of a bitter community which has already ostracised one
such girl whose mother had similarly sought freedom with the
man she loved.

## SPREAD EAGLE

(80 performances)

Drama in three acts by George S. Brooks and Walter B. Lister. Produced by Jed Harris at the Martin Beck Theatre, New York, April 4, 1927.

Cast of characters—

| | |
|---|---|
| Grace | Virginia Farmer |
| Peter | Lester Nielson |
| Joe Cobb | Osgood Perkins |
| Bill Davis | Charles D. Brown |
| Lois Henderson | Brenda Bond |
| General Ramon Angel de Castro | Felix Krembs |
| Martin Henderson | Fritz Williams |
| Charles Parkman | Allen Vincent |
| Mike Riordan | Donald Meek |
| Rosalie Kent | Aline MacMahon |
| Manuel | Eduardo Sanchez |
| Father Estrella | Malcolm Duncan |
| Captain | Herbert Courtney |
| Colonel Rojas | Jose Rivas |
| Theatre Manager | Frank E. Dae |
| Radio Announcer | Vincent Yorke |
| Brigadier General Wagner, U. S. A. | Fred House |
| Sentry | Harry M. Cooke |

Act I.—Martin Henderson's Office. Act II.—Scene 1—Office Shack of Spread Eagle Mining Company at Mercedes, Mexico. 2—The Stage of a New York Theatre. 3—Broadcasting Station WPIX. 4—A Broadway Motion Picture Theatre. Act III.—Henderson's Private Car at Matamoras, Mexico.

Staged by George Abbott.

Martin Henderson, big business billionaire who hopes for intervention in Mexico to make his mining interests secure, hires young Parkman, son of an ex-president of the United States, and sends him to Mexico, knowing that he is likely to be shot by General De Castro, whose revolution Henderson has secretly financed. Parkman is shot and the United States goes to war with Mexico. Then Parkman returns, having only been wounded, and weakly agrees to remain silent, partly because of his love for Henderson's daughter and partly because he may be falsely shown up as a coward through Henderson's influence.

## LYRIC DRAMA

(31 performances)

Produced by the Neighborhood Playhouse, New York, April 5, 1927, under the direction of Irene Lewisohn, with incidental music by Howard Barlow.

I—"Tone Pictures" and "The White Peacock," by Charles T. Griffes. Dancers: Sophie Bernsohn, Christine Burton, Eppie Epstein, Lillian Schweitzer, Bertha Slutzker and Gita Ruker.

II—Commedia Dell' Arte, translated from the Italian by Amelia Defries.

Cast of characters—

| | |
|---|---|
| Isabella | Dorothy Sands |
| Columbina | Paula Trueman |
| Arlecchino | Albert Carroll |
| Pantalone | Marc Loebell |
| Mezzetino | Ian Maclaren |
| Pedrolino | Otto Hulicius |
| Giove | J. Blake Scott |
| Joy | Christine Burton |
| Sorrow | Sophie Bernsohn |
| Singers | Selma Leigh, Sol Friedman |
| Louis XIV | George Hoag |
| Lady in Waiting | Eppie Epstein |
| Madame de M. | Gita Zucker |

III—Ritornell, dance romance by Irene Lewisohn and Francis Edward Faragoh, arranged to Bela Bartok's dance suite. The dancers: George Heller, George Hoag, John D. Haggart, Joseph H. Thayer, Jack Seulutrinic, Lily Lubell, Sadie Sussman, Sophie Bernsohn, Lillian Schweitzer, Eppie Epstein, J. Blake Scott, George Bratt, Albert Carroll, Blanche Talmud, Sol Friedman, Margaret Bickel, Bertha Slutzer, L. F. Ellsworth, Marion Friedsburg.

## HEARTS ARE TRUMPS

### (21 performances)

Comedy in three acts by Felix Gandera. Produced by Henry Baron at the Morosco Theatre, New York, April 7, 1927.

Cast of characters—

| | |
|---|---|
| Raoul de Trembly-Matour | Frank Morgan |
| Madame Millois | Alice Fischer |
| Arlette Millois | Vivian Martin |
| Guingleau | Edward Douglas |
| Le Huchard | C. H. Croker-King |
| Marc | William Phelps |
| Lefol | Ignatio Martinetti |
| Sylvine | Betty McLean |
| Gilbert | Percy Winter |
| Upholsterer | Albert J. Aubrey |
| Dominique | Cecil Clovelly |
| M. Palette | George Spelvin |
| Madame Palette | Grace Ade |
| Madame Silvain | Katherine Lorimer |
| Madame Rotchirs | Venie Atherton |

Miss Murray.....................................Lois Wales Winter
Berthe..........................................Betty Warwick
    Act I.—Near Saint-Jean-de-Luz.  Act II.—Village Near Puy-de-
Dome.  Act III.—In Paris.
    Staged by J. Clifford Brooke.

Arlette, led by her ambitious mother into a marriage with one who pretends to be the Comte de Trembley-Matour, discovers her groom to be an imposter. Going in search of the real count, in the hope of having her marriage annulled, Arlette discovers her husband in name only to be charming and decides to stay on and not marry her young cousin, with whom she thought she was in love.

## RAPID TRANSIT

### (20 performances)

Satiric comedy in seven scenes by Lajos N. Egri; translated by Gustav Davidson; adapted by Charles Recht. Produced by the Provincetown Players, in association with Horace Liveright, at the Provincetown Theatre, New York, April 7, 1927.

Cast of characters—

Imre Szabo....................................Joseph Macaulay
A Voice.......................................Harold McGee
First Merchant................................John Alcorn
Second Merchant...............................John Beistel
First Sales Inspector.........................William Challee
Second Sales Inspector........................Richard Skinner
Policeman.....................................Guy Fuguet
Walking Tax Inspector.........................Rolland Twombley
Breathing Tax Inspector.......................Donald Marye
Pedestrian....................................Edward Franz
Thief.........................................Donald MacGinnis
A Woman.......................................Rachel Sewall
Her Child.....................................Victor Kilian
First Newsboy.................................Christine Diemer
A Husband.....................................Geoffry Warnick
A Wife........................................Louise Lorimer
Ilona.........................................Mary Fowler
Velver........................................Goldwin Patten
Otto..........................................David Belbridge
Sandor........................................Moss Flesig
Captain Gavoy.................................Clarence Derwent
A Maid........................................Blanche Collins
A Gossip......................................Louise Bradley
Gossip........................................Lusy Shrieve
Gossip........................................Dorothee Nolan
Gossip........................................Barbara Benedict
A Maid........................................Juliet Brenon
Mrs. Kotlack..................................Rebekah Kennett
A Cripple.....................................Emile Carboneri
2nd Newsboy...................................Louis Barretta
Sergeant Fonyoi...............................James Martin
    Scenes 1, 4 and 6—Hakuba-Hekuba Land.  2—Velver's Office.
3—Szabo's Home.  5—Court Room.
    Staged by James Light.

Imre Szabo, living in Hakuba, escapes to the adjoining world of Hekuba, where the whole span of life is achieved in twenty-four hours.   How to make the most of so brief a life, and on what particular virtues to concentrate, worries him considerably, particularly when wives present their husbands with babies in a few minutes that are full grown a quarter hour later.   It gives him a chance to rail against most of the foolish injustices of life as we live it.


## BIG LAKE

### (11 performances)

Drama in two parts by Lynn Riggs.   Produced by the American Laboratory Theatre, New York, April 11, 1927.

Cast of characters—

| | |
|---|---|
| Betty | Helen Coburn |
| Lloyd | Frank Burk |
| Elly | Stella Adler |
| Butch | Grover Burgess |
| Sheriff | Louis V. Quince |
| Plank | John S. Clarke, Jr. |
| Joe | Francis Fergusson |
| Miss Meredith | Frances Williams |
| Bud Bickel | Sam Hartman |
| The Davis Boy | Harold Hecht |

Part I.—The Woods.   Part II.—The Lake and the Cabin in Indian Territory.

Staged by George Auerbach.

Out in Oklahoma Betty and Lloyd, tremulous in the grip of a first love, precede other picnickers to the shores of Big Lake, which spells freedom and release and misty romance to them. They borrow a boat from Butch Adams, a bootlegger who has that morning murdered a man, and are in the middle of the lake when the sheriff comes for Butch.   Butch makes the sheriff believe that Lloyd committed the murder and yells to him to row in.   Lloyd exultantly refuses, the sheriff shoots him dead and Betty throws herself out of the boat and is drowned.

## THE SECOND MAN

(44 performances)

Comedy in three acts by S. N. Behrman. Produced by the Theatre Guild under the direction of Philip Moeller at the Guild Theatre, New York, April 11, 1927.

Cast of Characters—

Mrs. Kendall Frayne...........................Lynn Fontanne
Clark Storey.... .....................................Alfred Lunt
Alistin Lowe......................................Earle Larimore
Monica Grey...................................Margalo Gillmore
Albert......................................Edward Hartford
    Acts I, II and III.—Storey's Studio in West Fifty-sixth Street.
Staged by Philip Moeller.

Clark Storey, an irresponsible novelist, loving life and luxury and determined to enjoy both, is loved by two women, the rich Mrs. Frayne and the younger and eager Monica Grey. Determined to marry Mrs. Frayne, though he is more strongly attracted physically to Monica, he throws the latter over. Monica thereupon swears falsely that she is to become the mother of his child. Storey accepts his fate, but his attitude convinces Monica that he does not love her. She turns to Alistin Lowe, a less colorful but more sincere suitor, and Storey is left to make up with Mrs. Frayne, if he can.


## RUTHERFORD & SON

(23 performances)

Drama by Githa Sowerby. Produced in revival by the Lenox Hill Players at the Grove Street Theatre, New York, April 12, 1927.

Cast of characters—

John Rutherford...............................Louis John Latzer
Richard, son................................David V. Schenker
John, son...............................Mitchell Padraic Marcus
Janet, daughter............................Mary Wolston-Hallet
Ann, sister...........................................Eve Saxen
Mary.........................................Florence Mann
Martin.........................................Jerome Seplow
Mrs. Henderson...........................Yetta Samuels Ellis
    Staged by Charles Friedman.

John Rutherford, a hard man and strong, has devoted thirty years to the building up of the business of Rutherford & Son. Now he meets the opposition of his daughter and his sons, but will not give way.  He is dominant and strong to the end, and finally compromises when he is forced to bargain with his daughter for the right to train her child to carry on the business.  He can have him, she says, after the boy is ten years old.  But in ten years she knows her father will no longer be able to make any one afraid of him.

## ONE GLORIOUS HOUR

### (20 performances)

Romantic comedy in three acts, translated by Ella Barnett from the German.  Produced by Murray Phillips at the Selwyn Theatre, New York, April 14, 1927.

Cast of characters—

```
Roland......................................Effiingham  Pinto
Wiczek.........................................Herbert  Yost
Armin..............................................Jay  Fassett
Eric.............................................Ullrich  Haupt
Maria......................................Vivienne  Osborne
Stranger...........................................Carl  Reed
Lancken.......................................Joseph  Kilgour
Stein.............................................Karl  Huebl
Thea..........................................Gladys  Wilson
Hildegarde.....................................Gail  De Hart
     Acts I, II and III.—At a Lodge in the Wilderness Somewhere
in Central Europe.
     Staged by Ullrich Haupt.
```

The Baroness Maria, restless at home, escapes in a rowboat and is cast by the winds on the opposite shore of a lake.  She is rescued by Eric, a sonneteer living with Roland, a pianist, and Armin, a painter, in a castle.  For eight days Maria stays on. They all love her and all respect her, even in a bathing suit. Then she lures Eric into the moonlight for an hour of freedom, after which her father comes and takes her home.

## THE TIGHTWAD

### (9 performances)

Play in three acts by Robert Keith.  Produced by the Messrs. Shubert at the 49th Street Theatre, New York, April 16, 1927.

Cast of characters—

```
John Taylor.....................................Alexander  Clark
Mrs. Taylor........................................Leah  Winslow
```

Edna Taylor...................................Lucile Nikolas
Mamie Harris.................................. Marie Carroll
Elmer Taylor..................................Allen Moore
Orval Stone...................................Cebra Graves
Tommy Jordan................................. King Calder
    Acts I, II and III.—Living-room of Taylor Home in Quincey, Ill.
    Staged by A. H. Van Buren.

Tommy Jordan is a spender. Rather take a chance at getting rich quick than budget his accounts and save his money. Edna Taylor is a saver. She won't marry Tommy until he reforms, which turns Tommy into a sealed-pocket tightwad. Within a year he has humiliated Edna and disgusted Edna's folks. Also invested all the Taylor family savings in a business that looks like a bust. But when the business turns prosperous Tommy is again the white-haired boy and promises to loosen up his pocket clasps just a little.


## LOVE IS LIKE THAT

### (24 performances)

Romantic comedy in three acts by S. N. Behrman and Kenyon Nicholson. Produced by A. L. Jones and Morris Green by arrangement with Stuart Walker at the Cort Theatre, New York, April 18, 1927.

Cast of characters—

Maid..............................................Della Vanna
Kay Gurlitz.....................................Catharine Willard
Graham Delano...............................Edward H. Wever
Mrs. James Gordon Parmenter......................Lucile Watson
Jesse Hopper....................................John T. Doyle
Kate Mumford...................................Minna Phillips
Cassandra Hopper..................................Ann Davis
Vladimir Dubriski.............................. Basil Rathbone
Michael Irshov.................................Charles Richman
Natasha.......................................Barbara Bulgakov
Grigori..........................................Percy Shostac
    Act I.—Living-room of Mrs. Parmenter's House in New York.
    Acts II and III.—Mrs. Parmenter's Studio Apartment.
    Staged by Dudley Digges.

Cassandra Hopper, returning from Europe, stops a stowaway from throwing himself overboard. Stowaway turns out to be Prince Vladimir Dubriski, exiled Russian. Cassandra brings him home, to the consternation of her new-rich family and the joy of her friends. The Prince falls in love with her, but her heart is true to Graham Delano, her western sweetheart. Then the prince, to rid himself of an entangling widow, Kay Gurlitz, insists his assumed title is false and that he is only a valet. Kay drops him and he retires heart-shocked but with dignity.

## LADY DO

### (56 performances)

Revue in prologue and two acts; book by Jack McClellan and Albert Cowles; lyrics by Sam M. Lewis and Joe Young; music by Abel Baer. Produced by Frank L. Teller at the Liberty Theatre, New York, April 18, 1927.

Cast of characters—

### THE PROLOGUE

| | |
|---|---|
| Dorothy | Nancy Welford |
| A Bricklayer | James A. Waites |
| Buddy | Karyl Norman |

### THE PLAY

| | |
|---|---|
| "Pop" Poulet | Luis Alberni |
| First Gendarme | James A. Waites |
| Second Gendarme | Philip Duey |
| Louis | Paul Darnelle |
| Fifi | Ninon Natalie |
| Mimi | Marguerite Duane |
| Henri | Glenn McComas |
| Marcel | Henry Shope |
| Georgette | Ada Winston |
| Marie | Jean Watson |
| Henriette | Jane Swanson |
| Georges | Leonard Saxon |
| Duke De Corsona | Joseph Lertora |
| William Walthal | A. S. Byron |
| Mrs. Walthal | Maude Odell |
| Marion Hobart | Frances Upton |
| Powers | Ralph Whitehead |
| Dorothy Walthal | Nancy Welford |
| Valda De Corsona | Harriett Lorraine |
| Fleurette | Rita Dunne |
| The Paris Rose | Karyl Norman |
| Jacques | Billy Skinner |
| Buddy Rose | Karyl Norman |
| Pat Perkins | Lew Hearn |
| Jack | Slyvan Lee |
| Jill | Jane Moore |
| Rita | Rita Howard |
| Helen | Helen Fables |
| Rose Walthal | Karyl Norman |
| A Flunkey | Julio Alvarez |
| Another Flunkey | Philip Duey |
| The Nurse | Juanita Zerbe |

Act I.—Scene 1—"Pop" Poulet's Café, Paris! 2—Somewhere on the Atlantic. 3—Lawn of the Walthal Estate, Roslyn, L. I. Act II.—Interior of the Walthal Home.

Staged by Edgar J. Macgregor.

One in which Buddy, learning to impersonate females as a soldier, turns his falsetto talent to account in winning Dorothy after the war.

## MR. PIM PASSES BY

### (36 performances)

A comedy in three acts by A. A. Milne. Revived by the Theatre Guild, Inc., at the Garrick Theatre, New York, April 18, 1927.

Cast of characters—

```
Anne...........................................Armina Marshall
Carraway Pim...................................Erskine Sanford
Dinah............................................Helen Chandler
Brian Strange.......................................Gavin Muir
Olivia Marden.................................Laura Hope Crews
George Marden, J. P.............................Dudley Digges
Lady Marden.......................................Helen Westley
```
Acts I, II and III.—The Morning-room at the Marden House, Buckinghamshire.

Staged by Philip Moeller.

Mr. Pim, passing by the Mardens', stops in to reveal, inadvertently, that he has met the man who was Mrs. Marden's first husband and supposed to have been seven years dead. The news is greatly exciting to the intensively British George Marden, who fears he has been living in sin, and dire things threaten until Mr. Pim passes by again and is extremely helpful in straightening matters out.

## THE JAZZ SINGER

### (16 performances)

Comedy drama in three acts by Samson Raphaelson. Produced by Albert Lewis in association with Sam H. Harris, at the Century Theatre, New York, April 18, 1927.

Cast of characters—

#### ACT I AND III

The Home of Cantor Rabinowitz, Lower East Side, New York.
```
Moey..............................................George Shafer
Cantor Rabinowitz...............................Jacob Shoengold
Sara Rabinowitz...............................Dorothy Raymond
Udelson.................................................Sam Jaffe
Clarence Kahn...................................Robert Milford
Jack Robin........................................George Jessel
```

#### ACT II

"Back Stage" of the Music Box Theatre, New York.
```
Harry Lee.........................................Edward Arnold
Eddie Carter...........................................Aborn Adler
Mary Dale.............................................Lillian Taiz
Gene.....................................................Ted Athey
Randolph Dillings................................Maxwell Selser
Miss Glynn.....................................Betty De Pascue
```

Franklyn Forbes.................................Robert Fradola
Stage Doorman...................................Tom Johnstone
Sam Post.........................................Arthur Lane
Avery Jordan....................................Joseph Hopkins
Ima Bagg.......................................Imogene Bethune
Levy..........................................Samuel Silverbrush
Dr. O'Shaughnessy................................Tony Kennedy
    Staged by Albert Lewis.

Jakie Rabinowitz, runaway son of Cantor Rabinowitz, is on the point of making his début as a jazz singer in a big revue on Broadway when he hears his father is dying and calling upon him to take up the work of the cantor which has been a Rabinowitz honor for generations. Jake struggles, but heeds the race call.

## THE THIEF

### (64 performances)

Play in three acts by Henri Bernstein; adapted by C. Haddon Chambers. Revived by William A. Brady in association with Lee Shubert at the Ritz Theatre, New York, April 22, 1927.

Cast of characters—

Richard Voysin....................................Lionel Atwill
Raymond Lagardes................................Gilbert Emery
M. Zambault.....................................Orlando Daly
Fernand Lagardes........................Anthony Kemble Cooper
Butler...........................................William Leith
Marie Louise Voysin................................Alice Brady
Isabelle Lagardes................................Mona Kingsley
    Acts I and III.—Drawing-room of M. Lagardes. Act II.—A Bedroom.
    Staged by Lionel Atwill.

Money missed from the home of the Lagardes is traced to the son, Fernand. Fernand, accused, is willing to take the blame because of his love for Mme. Voysin, a guest and old friend of the family, but M. Voysin accidentally traps his wife into a confession of guilt and the truth is dramatically exposed.

## THE GOSSIPY SEX

### (23 performances)

Farce in three acts by Lawrence Grattan. Produced by John Golden at the Mansfield Theatre, New York, April 19, 1927.

Cast of characters—

John Bowen....................................Thomas W. Ross
Alice Bowen....................................Florence Mason

```
Milton Norris.......................................John Cherry
Hilda Norris.......................................Eva Condon
Gerald Kenyon..................................Norval Keedwell
Anna Sterling......................................Una Merkle
Philip Baxter....................................Philip Barrison
Flossie Baxter.......................................Helen Weir
Chief Mason.....................................Ralph Theadore
Mazie Mason.....................................Grace Menken
Richard Foster..................................George Spelvin
Briggs...........................................Harry Forsman
Martha..............................................Joan Carvel
Danny Grundy...................................Lynne Overman
    Acts I, II and III.—At the Home of Mr. and Mrs. Bowen One
Summer Evening.
    Staged by Sam Forrest.
```

Danny Grundy is a salesman and a gossip. Wanting to interest people he naturally acquires the habit of talking about the things that interest them, which usually is concerned with the questionable activities of their friends. A casual guest at the John Bowen's party, he all but breaks up the Baxter marriage, sets the Norrises against the Bowens and leads Mr. Mason to think Mrs. Mason has colored blood.

## THE COMIC

### (15 performances)

Play in three acts by Lajos Luria; English version by James L. A. Burrell and Lawrence R. Brown. Produced by John Jay Scholl and William J. Perlman at the Masque Theatre, New York, April 19, 1927.

Cast of characters—

```
The Comedian.....................................J. C. Nugent
The Actress...................................Patricia Collinge
The Author......................................Cyril Keightley
The Pupil........................................Rex O'Malley
The Manager...................................Malcolm Williams
    Acts I, II and III.—Garden Room of a summer Villa on Lake
Balaton, Hungary.
    Staged by J. C. Nugent.
```

A play within a play in which the Comedian suspects the Actress is going too far with the Author and sets them acting out prepared scenes as a test. Being warned in time by the Pupil, they fool the Comedian, and in the end the Actress turns from both Author and Comedian to take up with the Manager.

## GOAT ALLEY

### (13 performances)

Drama in three acts by Ernest Howard Culbertson. Revised by the Toussaint Players at the Princess Theatre, New York, April 20, 1927.

Cast of characters—

| | |
|---|---|
| Lucy Belle Dorsey | Evelyn Ellis |
| Slim Dorsey | Edward Thompson |
| Sam Reed | A. B. Comathière |
| Aunt Rebecca | Elizabeth Williams |
| Lizzie Gibbs | Dorothy Paul |
| Jeff Bisbee | J. Louis Johnson |
| Chick Avery | Baron Bryan |
| Jeremiah Pocher | Hayes Prior |
| Fanny Dorsey | Margaret Petty |
| Israel Dorsey | George Watson |
| Policeman | Jack Carter |

Acts I, II and III.—Sitting-room in Lucy Belle's Home, Goat Alley, Washington, D. C.

Staged by Egon Brecher of Civic Repertory Theatre.

See "Best Plays of 1921-22."

## THE FIELD GOD

### (45 performances)

Play in four acts by Paul Green. Produced by Edwin R. Wolfe, Inc., at the Greenwich Village Theatre, New York, April 21, 1927.

Cast of characters—

| | |
|---|---|
| Neill Sykes | Ben Smith |
| Hardy Gilchrist | Fritz Leiber |
| Etta Gilchrist | Adelaide Fitz-Allen |
| Mag | Clara Thropp |
| Lonie | Lillie Brayton |
| Rhoda Campbell | Ruth Mason |
| Sion Alford | Claudine Mintz |
| Jacob Alford | Arthur Ellen |
| Aunt Margaret | Bessie Mar English |
| Mrs. Jones | Marion Fredreic |
| Mrs. Jernigan | Lillian Ardell |
| A Preacher | James G. Morton |

Acts I, II and III.—Yard and Rear Part of the Gilchrist House. A Farm in Eastern North Carolina.

Staged by Edwin R. Wolfe.

Hardy Gilchrist, denying the God of his neighbors, attributes his success to hard work and honorable dealing with all men. His invalid wife seeks to bring him into the church, but he stands defiantly outside. When Hardy is brought low by his love for

Rhoda Campbell, a niece, and his wife dies of a stroke, the church folk accept it as a visitation of divine wrath. Hardy marries Rhoda, is ostracised and prayed for and finally, after many tor ments, is given to see the light.


## WALL STREET

### (21 performances)

Romantic melodrama in three acts by James N. Rosenberg. Produced by The Stagers, Inc. (Edward Goodman, director), at the Hudson Theatre, New York, April 20, 1927.

Cast of characters—

| | |
|---|---|
| Anne Perry | Margaret Douglass |
| John H. Perry | Arthur Hohl |
| A Board Boy | Frank Russo |
| Another | Walter Ferrell |
| A Customer | Edwin Macdonald |
| Another Customer | James Symington |
| Another Customer, Later a Banker | B. H. MacMahon |
| Another Customer | Albert Henry |
| Cyrus B. Tomlinson | Robert Robson |
| A Customers' Man | Lewis McMichael |
| Another | Frederic A. Bryan |
| Mitchell Marfield | Alfred Swenson |
| William Patterson | Ernest Howard |
| Macdonald | Arthur Hughes |
| A Newsboy | Mountford Adams |
| Margaret Patterson | Mary Law |
| John Hewlett | John Warner |
| Mrs. Templeton | Dorothy Rudd |
| Mrs. de Coudret | Rita Vale |
| Schuyler Bruce | Robert Robson |
| Peter Breckenridge | Powell York |
| Violet Smithers | Kathryn Kohler |
| O'Reilly | John Grey |
| Bishop Lincoln | Seth Kendall |
| Senator Folsom | Frederick Burton |
| A Banker | John McGovern |
| Serge Borosky | David Lewis |
| A Trained Nurse | Dorothy Libaire |
| Burton | Jack Quigley |
| A Woman Customer | Dorothy Libaire |
| William Thompson, Asst. District Attorney | Samuel Levine |
| A Visitor to the Stock Exchange | Marie Hobson |
| President of the Stock Exchange | Henry Brown |

Prologue—Perry's Home in Nelsonville. Act I.—Scene 1—Customers' Room of Patterson and Marfield, Stock Brokers. 2 and 4— Private Office of William Patterson. 3 and 5—A Street. 6—Perry's Flat on Third Avenue. Act II.—John H. Perry's Home on Fifth Avenue. Act III.—Private Office, Perry & Son, No. 2 Wall Street. Staged by Edward Goodman.

John H. Perry, small-town reared and ambitious, has a chance to go to the big city. Promises Anne, his wife, that if he goes and is successful he will quit. In New York Perry, become a broker's clerk, maneuvers himself into a position in which he can take a crooked fortune away from his crooked employers and force himself into the firm. His wife goes back to the small town, taking their infant son. Perry marries his employer's daughter, who deserts him for an Italian singer. Twenty years later, the first wife having died, Perry takes his son in with him and son turns out a typical Perry, predatory and unscrupulous. Son finally smashes things, kills himself and leaves father, in an invalid's chair, trying to square things with the world.

## HOUSE OF SHADOWS

### (29 performances)

Play in four acts by Leigh Hutty. Produced by William A. Brady, Jr., and Dwight Deere Wiman in association with J. H. Del Bondio at the Longacre Theatre, New York, April 21, 1927.

Cast of characters—

| | |
|---|---|
| Real Estate Agent | James W. Wallace |
| Professor | Tom Powers |
| Darkey's Wife | Abbie Mitchell |
| Darkey | Tom Moseley |
| Girl | Marguerite Churchill |
| Crook | James S. Barrett |
| Phantom Husband | Frank Peters |
| Phantom Wife | Alden Gay |
| Pirate Lover | John See |
| Policeman | Leslie Cooley |
| Old Man | Frank Peters |

Act I.—Gate of an Old Mansion on the Hudson. Acts II and IV.—Living-room in the Old Mansion. Act III.—Scene 1—A Subterranean Passageway in the Mansion. 2—A Walled Room at the End of the Passageway.

College professor, exposing great American ghost stories, rents haunted house on Hudson, meets strange girl who has dashed into house out of storm to escape pursuing villain. Professor, girl and villain find themselves in walled passage leading to room filled with pirate treasure. Villain dies of shock, professor and girl finally get out and uncover crazy miser as guardian of gold and creator of thrills.

## HIT THE DECK

### (60 performances)

Musical comedy in two acts; adapted from the play "Shore Leave." Book by Herbert Fields; lyrics by Leo Robin and Clifford Grey; music by Vincent Youmans. Produced by Lew Fields and Vincent Youmans at the Belasco Theatre, New York, April 25, 1927.

Cast of characters—

| | |
|---|---|
| Donkey | Brian Donlevy |
| Dinty | Arnold Brown |
| Marine | Jack Bruns |
| "Battling" Smith | Franker Woods |
| Chick | Ben Carswell |
| Gus | Cliff Whitcomb |
| Bob | Robert Duenwihe |
| Lavinia | Stella Hayhew |
| Loulou | Louise Groody |
| Lieut. Alan Clark | John McCauley |
| Toddy Gaie | Bobbie Perkins |
| Charlotte Payne | Madeline Cameron |
| Mat | Roger Gray |
| Bilge | Charles King |
| Bunny | Edward Allen |
| Capt. Roberts | Jerome Dailey |
| Ah Lung | Anthony Knilling |
| Mun Fang | Billy Sobel |
| Rita | Peggy Conway |
| Coolie | Ah Chong |
| Four Missionaries | Locust Sisters |

Act I.—Loulou's Coffee House and the Deck of the U. S. S. "Nebraska." Act II.—A Seaport Town in Ch.na. 2, A Mandarin's home. 3, Loulou's Coffee House.

Staged by Lew Fields, Seymour Felix and Alexander Leftwich.

Loulou, keeper of coffee house on a Newport dock, falls in love with "Bilge" Smith, gob. Bill, being shy, Loulou is forced to follow him around the world to ask him to marry her. "Bilge" is willing until he discovers she has come into money. She finally has to sign that away before he will listen to reason. So she assigns the inheritance to her first born.

## THE CIRCUS PRINCESS

### (61 performances)

Revue in prologue and three acts. Book and lyrics from the original of Julius Brammer and Alfred Grunwald by Harry B. Smith; music by Emmerich Kalman. Produced by the Messrs. Lee and J. J. Shubert at the Winter Garden, New York, April 25, 1927.

Cast of characters—

| | |
|---|---|
| Loris | Roy Vitalis |
| Nicholas | Starr Jones |
| Paul | Herbert Lyle |
| Constantine | Harry Shackelford |
| Ivan Panin | Joseph Toner |

```
Prince Alexis Orloff..............................Guy Robertson
Prince Palinska....................................Arthur Barry
Stanislavsky.....................................Robert O'Connor
Pinelli...........................................James C. Morton
Baron Sakuskine.................................Stanley Harrison
Lieutenant Petrovitch..............................Frank Horn
Princess Fedora Palinska.........................Desiree Tabor
Commissionaire..................................Edmund Ruffner
Grand Duke Serjius...............................George Hassell
His Adjutant.........................................Starr Jones
Toni Schumberger....................................Ted Doner
Fritzi Burgstaller, alias Mabel Gibson..................Gloria Foy
Barmaid..........................................Virginia Hassell
Mr. X. ............................................Guy Robertson
Poodles Hanneford and Family.......................Themselves
An Old Clown......................................Fred Derrick
A Clown.........................................Oscar Lowande
Footman.........................................Edouard Grobe
1st Cossack...................................Poodles Hanneford
2nd Cossack...................................James C. Morton
Majordomo......................................Edmund Ruffner
An Officer........................................Henry Lyle
Archbishop..........................................John Henry
Pelican........................................George Bickel
1st Waiter.......................................James C. Morton
Bus Boy......................................Poodles Hanneford
Porter.............................................Billy Culloo
Frau Schumberger.............................Florence Morrison
```
     Prologue—Cardroom in the Officers' Club in St. Petersburg.  Act
I.—Circus Stanislavsky in St. Petersburg.  Act II.—Ballroom in the
Palace of the Grand Duke Serjius.  Act III.—Lobby of the Arch-
duke Charles Hotel in Vienna.
     Staged by J. C. Huffman.

Prince Orloff, cut off by his uncle, joins the circus as a masked
marvel.  Later meets and loves his uncle's widow, Princess Pa-
linska, and marries her under one of his hereditary titles.  Exposed as a circus performer, the princess leaves him.  Asserting
his princely rights, Orloff also leaves the princess.  Third act and
all's well.

## MIXED DOUBLES

### (15 performances)

Farcical comedy in three acts by Frank Stayton.  Produced by
the Messrs. Shubert at the Bijou Theatre, New York, April 26,
1927.

## Cast of characters—

```
Barrett............................................Roy Cochrane
Rev. Arthur Escott................................William Eville
Sir John Dorle...................................Thurston Hall
Betty..........................................Margaret Lawrence
Rose...........................................Marcella Swanson
Reggie Ervine.......................................Eric Blore
Lady Audrey Irvine.............................Marion Coakley
Howell Jamess.....................................John Williams
Ian McConochie.................................Russell Morrison
```
     Acts I, II and III.—Hall of Sir John's House in Sussex.

Sir John marries Betty believing her to be a sod widow. Betty's first, Reggie, turns up married to Lady Audrey. To make matters worse Betty has grabbed the name of the maid's intended and told Sir John she really was married to him. The maid's intended also turns up. Which goes on until 10:30 P.M.

## ENCHANTMENT

### (13 performances)

Comedy in three acts by Joseph Jefferson Farjeon. Produced by Enchantment, Inc. (under the auspices of the American Theatre Association), at the Edyth Totten Theatre, New York, April 27, 1927.

Cast of characters—

Elsie Garden ..................................... Alison Bradshaw
Arthur Bowen ...................................... Leslie Barrie
Bill ............................................. Edward Rigby
Robert Benger ...................................... A. P. Kaye
Lady Constance Bowater ......................... Pamela Simpson
The Duke of Porthurst .............................. Alan Hollis
        Acts I, II and III.—In a Snowbound English Country Cottage.
    Staged by Robert Rendel.

Elsie Garden and Arthur Bowen, leaving a snowbound train, break into a snowbound cottage seeking warmth and shelter. Under the spell of the adventure they pretend they are Lord This and Lady That. Two other passengers similarly gathered, Robert Benger and Bill, a tramp, pretend they are Blood, a great detective, and Peace, a notorious criminal. Then come Lady Constance and the Duke of Porthurst. Sensing what is going on, they in turn pretend to be quite common, the butler and the maid in fact, and serve dinner to the others. Then the storm breaks, the "guests" go back to the station and her ladyship and the Duke are revealed as the real owners of the cottage.

## THE ROAD TO HAPPINESS

### (16 performances of repertory)

Drama in three acts by Martinez Sierra and Eduardo Marquina. Produced by Crosby Gaige at the Forrest Theatre, New York, May 2, 1927.

Cast of characters—

The Blind Man ...................................... A. Tudela
Blanca Rosa ................................... Catalina Barcena

```
A Farmer..........................................V. Plasencia
Lorenzo.......................................L. Perez de Leon
Justina...........................................R. Satorres
Casilda.........................................M. Larrabeiti
Martina.........................................T. Fernandez
Leandra........................................M. del C. Gil
The Aviator.......................................M. Collado
The Mechanic.......................................R. Mazo
Melchoro........................................F. Fernandez
Faquirre......................................L. Garcia Ortega
Catita...........................................R. Satorres
Justamante......................................M. Larrabeiti
Sibila...............................................M. Leal
Pericanta.........................................A. G. Alonso
First Gypsy.....................................M. del C. Gil
Second Gypsy.....................................T. Fernandez
A Wagon Driver...............................J. Alburquerque
Cayetana.........................................C. Fernandez
Damian...........................................L. Manrique
Ignacia...........................................L. Alvarez
A Wanderer..........................................A. Tudela
```

**Blanca Rosa,** an orphan, is counseled by a wandering blind man to beware the city, never to beg, to be gay and to accept sorrows as they come. After he dies Blanca seeks to follow his precepts and suffers much, being loved too passionately by the husband of a woman who befriends her, fought over by two young gypsies into whose camp she is taken and finally promised in marriage to a cripple. Her only true love is an aviator, and he flies away, leaving her mostly her memories.

During this engagement of the Spanish Art Theatre the Sierra players also presented "The Romantic Young Lady," "The Girl and the Cat," "The Blind Heart," "The Cradle Song," "Angela Maria," "The Royal Peacock" and "Pygmalion."

## THE LADY SCREAMS

### (8 performances)

**Play** in three acts by Everett Chantler. Produced by Charles J. Mulligan at the Selwyn Theatre, New York, May 2, 1927.

Cast of characters—

```
Michael..........................................Ralph Cullinan
Maid............................................Millicent Grayson
Lucy West.........................................Betty Weston
Mrs. West........................................Eleanor Daniels
Richard Gordon................................W. D. Heppenstal
Ruth Harrison...................................Dana Desboro
Walter Henson...................................Anthony Hughes
Robert Irwin.......................................Grant Mills
Helen Taylor...................................Frances Halliday
Doctor Brown...................................Edward Broadley
Captain Kenney...................................John Campbell
Officer Holmes...................................Allan Tower
     Acts I, II and III.—Home of Ruth Harrison.
     Staged by Edward Broadley.
```

Lucy West, having shot a man, is paroled in the care of a rich woman. She falls in love with the woman's son, is pursued by the crook she shot, and screams rather than take part in the robbery of the house.

## THE SEVENTH HEART

### (8 performances)

Musical comedy in three acts by Sarah Ellis Hyman. Produced by Lionel Productions, Inc., at the Mayfair Theatre, New York, May 2, 1927.

Cast of characters—

| | |
|---|---|
| Maybelle Wright | Sylvia Beecher |
| Clara Stewart | Aileen Poe |
| Mrs. Thorne | Mary Moore |
| Mazie Kennedy | Mildred Kent |
| Gloria Higgins | Barbara Weeks |
| Jane | Helen Gray |
| Harold Kennedy (passing under the name of Colonel Barrie) | Arthur Brander |
| Jack Stewart | Ralph Dunn |
| Charlie Stewart | Charles Garland |
| Robert Kennedy | A. Trevor Bland |
| Captain Dix | Robert Farrell |
| Tommy Watkins | Armand Lauret |
| James Marshall | Francis Felton |
| Miranda Jones | A Young Widow |
| Julia, the Romantic Lady | A Dancer |
| Martha | The Little School Teacher |
| Pansy | A Toe Dancer |
| Daisy Cerina Brown | An Old Maid |
| Violet | The Oriental Girl |
| The Spanish Lily | The Phantom Love |

Acts I, II and III.—The Stewart Villa, Palm Beach, Florida.
Staged by Edward Elsner.

## LITTLE THEATRE TOURNAMENT

### (7 performances)

Conducted by Walter Hartwig, in coöperation with the Manhattan Little Theatre Club, Inc., for the David Belasco Trophy, at Frolic Theatre, New York, the week of May 2, 1927.

### MONDAY EVENING, MAY 2

The Union Players of Bay Ridge, Brooklyn, in "The Drums of Oude," by Austin Strong.
The Cast—

| | |
|---|---|
| Captain Hector McGregor | David W. Taylor |
| Lieutenant Alan Hartley | Donald Helm |

Sergeant McDougal...............................Robert L. Neill
Stewart, the Sentry...........................Alexander Ballantyne
Two Hindustani Servants.......H. Arthur Eade and Charles Fields
Mrs. Jack Clayton, Hartley's Sister..................Elsie H. Neill
Scene—The Interior of a Palace in Northern India, Occupied by
British Troops.

The Krigwa Players Little Negro Theatre of Harlem in "The Fool's
Errand," by Eulalie Spence.
The Cast—
Cassie, a Busybody..................................Ethel Bennett
Sister Williams, the Minister's Wife.................Marian King
Doug, Father of Maza...........................William Jackson
Parson Williams.......................................Ira Reid
Maza, Daughter of Doug.........................Doralyne Spence
Jud, a Suitor of Maza...........................Malcolm Dodson
Freddie, Another Suitor ...........................William Holly
Mom, Mother of Maza ...........................Ardelle Dabney
Brethren and Sisters of the Church Council—Minnie Brown, Inez
Bennett, Louise Robinson, George Lee, Samuel Carthan, Levi Alex-
ander.
Scene: Living-room of Doug's Home.

The Association Players of the 92nd Street Y.M.H.A. in "Confes-
sion," by Kenyon Nicholson.
The Cast—
Germaine .....................................Ethel Leventhal
Mme. Bertharde....................................Ruth Zakrow
Skeet ..............................................Henry Chuck
Walt .................................................I. Fell
Scene—"Buvette du Bon Temps," a Café, near an American Rest
Camp on the Outskirts of Bar-la-Duc, France.
Directed by Myron E. Sattler.

## TUESDAY EVENING, MAY 3

The Unity Players of Montclair, New Jersey, in "The Giant's Stair,"
by Wilbur Daniel Steele.
The Cast—
Til Jessup.....................................Percita West Gardner
Mrs. Weatherburn, Her Sister..............Florence Wolff Klaber
Edwin Dane, the Sheriff........................Fortescue Metcalf
Cantpole.........................................Lewis Kimball
Scene—Kitchen of the Weatherburn Farm Situated at the Upper
End of a Mountain Valley.
Directed by Percita West Gardner.

The Lighthouse Players of the New York Association for the Blind
of Manhattan in "Manikin and Minikin," by Alfred Kreymborg.
The Cast—
Manikin..........................................Rose Resnick
Minikin..........................................Ruth Askenas
The Scene Represents Two Basque Figures on a Mantel Shelf.

The Thalian Players of the Bronx Y.M.H.A. in the Third Act of
"Disraeli," by Louise N. Parker.
The Cast—
Potter, Disraeli's Gardener........................Samuel Roland
Bascot, Disraeli's Butler...........................Charles D'Yuro
Flooks, a Postman................................Julius Sobelmann
The Rt. Hon. Benjamin Disraeli, M.P. ............John H. Brown
Clarissa, Lady Pevensey........................Mollie Buchsbaum
Lady Beaconsfield ...............................Ida Tannenbaum
Mr. Hugh Meyers...............................Emanuel Berliner
Mrs. Noel Travers...............................Natalie Krellman
Sir Michael Probert, Bart. ..........................Oscar Donner
Scene—At Hughenden, Disraeli's Country Home.

## WEDNESDAY EVENING, MAY 4

The Brookside Open-air Theatre of Mount Kisco, New York, in "The Immortal Beloved," by Martia Leonard.
The Cast—
Anton Felix Schinler, Friend and Biographer of Beethoven........
.............................................Charles Haubiel
A Lady.................................................Jane King
Scene—In Carlsbad, July, 1862.

The Indianapolis Theatre Guild of Indianapolis, Indiana, in "The Second Act," by Maurice C. Tull.
The Cast—
Phylis Wray........................................Eleanor Tull
Mary MacDowell.....................................Betti Black
Bridget...........................................Georgia Fricker
Walls............................................Joseph Henninger
Lady of Beautiful Dreams........................Elizabeth Wetzel
Demon of Dreadful Dreams............................M. C. Tuil
Helen Gibbs...................................Ruth McInnis Todd
Scene—An Impressionistic Furnished Room.
Staged by Maurice C. Tull.

The Gardens Players of Forest Hills, Long Island, in "History as Was," by Maurice Marks.
The Cast—
### I.
Ramese I.........................................Morton Savell
Secretary........................................Cameron Shipp
A Dancer.........................................Lucile Fulton
Starret............................................Homer Croy
Slaves.......................Calvert Cole and William Hampton
### II.
Cohen............................................Harold Dobrer
Stenographer.....................................Blanche Lopez
Sir Walter Raleigh..............................Walter Claypoole
First Tailor....................................Anthony Leonard
Second Tailor....................................Maurice Mayer
### III.
Napoleon........................................Lawson Paynter
Sergeant.........................................Clarence Perry
Soldier............................................Frank Heinz
Josephine.........................................Arlene Kiliani
Directed by Bertha E. Mandel.

League of American Pen Women, Inc. (New York Branch), Manhattan, in "Values," by Aïda Rodman DeMilt.
The Cast—
Leander Bliss, an Oysterman...................Gerald MacDonald
Jed, His Son...................................Richardson Brown
Debby Ann, Jed's Wife............................Anna Barnouw
Scene—A Fisherman's Cottage, Long Island.

## THURSDAY EVENING, MAY 5

The Charlotte High School Players of Charlotte, North Carolina, in "Jazz and Minuet," by Ruth Giorloff.
The Cast—
Mrs. Van Hayden.................................Martha Dulin
Eleanor Prudence Van Hayden.............Alice Houston Quarles
Prudence Van Hayden, the Great-Great-Aunt.........Nancy Watts
Richard Townsend, Eleanor's Lover...............Lawrence Miller
Robert Trowbridge............................Marshall Pritchett
Nettie, the Modern Maid........................Jane McLaughlin
Lucy, Maid of Colonial Days.....................Frances Martin
Milord Devereaux..................................John Everett
Scene—Living-room of Mrs. Van Hayden's Apartment.
Directed by Ethel Rea and Luisa Duis.

The Memphis Little Theatre of Memphis, Tennessee, in "The Delta Wife," by Walter McClellan.
The Cast—
Hamer Mathes....................................Clifford Penland
Cora Mathes.......................................Allison Davant
Scene—A Room in Mathes' Cabin, Just Behind the Levee in the Delta of the Great River.
Directed by Colin Clements.

The Welwyn Garden City Theatre Society of Welwyn Garden City, England, in "Mr. Sampson," by Charles Lee.
The Cast—
Caroline Stevens......⎱ Two Maiden Sisters ⎰.........Elsie Colson
Catherine Stevens.....⎰                    ⎱.......Lilian Hinton
Mr. Sampson, Their Tenant Next Door.............Ernest Selley
Scene—The Kitchen of a Cottage on a Moorland in the West Country of England.
Directed by C. B. Purdom.

The Mansfield Players of Manhattan in "Off Col'uh," by Amy L. Weber.
The Cast—
Miles Johnson, Proprietor of the Cotton Wood Club...............
.......................................... George H. Snowden
Priscilla Williams, Cabaret Artist and Cashier.......Juanita Stewart
John Jackson, Tap Dancer and Doorman..............Leon Drake
Scene—The Cotton Wood Club, Harlem, New York City.

FRIDAY EVENING, MAY 6

The Derita Players of Derita, North Carolina, in "The Last of the Lowries," by Paul Green.
The Cast—
Cumba Lowrie, the Aged Mother of the Lowries.................
....................................Margaret Ellen Alexander
Jane, Her Daughter..................................Ruth Ellis
Mayno, Cumba's Daughter-in-Law..................Barbara Garris
Henry Berry Lowrie, Last of the Outlaw Gang......Marvin Hunter
Scene—The Rough Home of the Lowrie Gang in Scuffletown, a Swampy Region of Robeson County, North Carolina.

The Barnswallows Association of Wellesley College, Wellesley, Massachusetts, in "The Stronger," by August Strindberg.
The Cast—
Madame X ...................................Norma Holzman
Mademoiselle Y...............................Margaret McCarty
Scene—A Corner in a Ladies' Café.
The Play Produced by Ellen Bartlett.

The Little Theatre of Tulsa, Oklahoma, in "Waitin'," by Elizabeth Copmann.
The Cast—
Hazel, Keeper of an Oil Country Lease-house......Neyneen Farrell
Ed, Her Husband, a Driller..................Edward M. Gallaher
John Trowbridge, an Oil Producer..............Harold E. Stewart
Julia, His Wife .................................. Kathryn Gavin
Scene—Combination Kitchen, Dining-room and Office of an Oil Country Lease-house.
Prizes were awarded the Welwyn Garden City Theatre Society of Welwyn Garden City, England; the Krigwa Players Little Negro Theatre of Harlem, New York City; the Brookside Open-air Theatre of Mount Kisco, New York; the Memphis Little Theatre of Memphis, Tennessee. The Association Players of the 92nd Street Y.M.H.A., New York City, received honorable mention. The Belasco trophy went to the Welwyn Garden City Theatre Society for their production, "Mr. Sampson."

## A NIGHT IN SPAIN

(50 performances)

Revue in two acts; book by Harold Atteridge; music by Jean Schwartz; lyrics by Al Byram. Produced by the Messrs. Shubert at the 44th Street Theatre, New York, May 3, 1927.

Principals engaged—

| | |
|---|---|
| Phil Baker | Grace Bowman |
| Sid Silver | Helen Kane |
| Ted Healy | Grace Hayes |
| George Anderson | Betty Healy |
| Stanley Rogers | Barbera |
| Jay Brennan | Rhea Mason |
| Bert Gardener | Bernice Gardener |
| J. Colvil Dunn | Helba Huara |
| Shemp Howard | Lola Raine |
| Tito Coral | Andreini orchestra |
| Trainor Brothers | |

Staged by Gertrude Hoffman and Charles Judels.

## TRIPLE CROSSED

(48 performances)

Mystery melodrama in three acts by F. S. Merlin. Produced by Robert Rockmore at the Morosco Theatre, New York, May 5, 1927.

Cast of characters—

| | |
|---|---|
| Henry | Frank Horton |
| Phillipa Callender | Patricia Barron |
| Ridgely | Robert Toms |
| Taber Van Buren | Frederick Smith |
| Hastings | Victor Killian |

Acts I, II and III.—Living-room of the Callender's Apartment.
Staged by F. S. Merlin.

During the performance of a triangle play a switch is made in the property pistols used and the hero accidentally kills the villain. Search being made for the man who substituted the real for the phony revolver many persons in the audience are suspected and the police take charge. It is decided to play the scene a second time, and this time the villain really is killed. Not by a bullet but by poisoned liquor supplied by the property man.

## OH, ERNEST!

### (44 performances)

Musical comedy in two acts; book and lyrics by Francis De-Will; music by Robert Hood Bowers. Produced by P. T. Rossiter at the Royale Theatre, New York, May 9, 1927.

Cast of characters—

```
Sir Percy Middowshire..........................William Jordan
James Lane.........................................Ralph Riggs
Algernon Moncrieff............................Harry McNaughton
Jessica Esmond....................................Phyllis Austin
Hon. John Worthing, J. P. ...........................Hal Forde
Lady Bracknell....................................Flavia Arcaro
Hon. Gwendolen Fairfax........................Marjorie Gateson
Martha........................................Katharine Witchie
Jane.............................................Vivian Marlowe
Cecily Cardew....................................Dorothy Dilley
Miss Prism........................................Sonia Winfield
Rev. Canon Chasuble, D.D. ........................Jethro Warner
Pollyanna Montague...........................Barbara Newberry
Peggy Vernon....................................Patricia Wynne
Anne Aubrey....................................Edith Mae Wright
Clarice Chitworth.................................Dimples Riede
Evelyn Stuart...................................Dorothea Mabie
     Act I.—Algernon Moncrieff's Rooms, London.  Act II.—The Gar-
den Manor House, Woolton.
     Staged by William J. Wilson.
```

A musicalized version of Wilde's "The Importance of Being Earnest."

## JULIE

### (8 performances)

Play in three acts by Corning White. Produced by Homeric Productions, Inc., at the Lyceum Theatre, New York, May 9, 1927.

Cast of characters—

```
Ezra...........................................John Daly Murphy
Mrs. Stone....................................Blanche Friderici
Lee Stone...................................Alexander Clark, Jr.
Pierre...........................................Edward Arnold
Maman........................................Alison Skipworth
Julie.............................................Betty Pierce
Phœbe.........................................Mildred Southwick
     Acts I and III.—Kitchen of the Farm House of the Stones.  Act
II.—The Shack of Maman.
     Staged by Arthur Hurley.
```

Julie was a good girl and remained good right up to the last act, despite the efforts of her wicked foster mother, old Maman, to sell her to Pierre, the rich bootlegger. And the baby wasn't Julie's either. Old Maman was keeping it for the rich blonde, Phœbe, but the truth found her out.


## KATY DID

### (8 performances)

Comedy in three acts by Willis Maxwell Goodhue. Produced by Edward Whiteside and J. J. Levinson at Daly's Theatre, New York, May 9, 1927.

Cast of characters—

| | |
|---|---|
| Eddie Carson | Edgar Nelson |
| Pansy McGuirk | Genevieve Williams |
| Katie O'Donovan | Juliette Day |
| Carlo Emarri | Romney Brent |
| Ferenczy | Karl Stall |
| Prolix | Charles E. Bird |
| Amalia | Carolyne McLean |
| Virginia Hampton | Adelaide Rondelle |
| Anthony Noland | Stanley De Wolfe |

Act I.—First Episode—Corner in Childs'. 2, In Front of Childs'. 3, Small Furnished Room. Act II.—Furnished Apartment on the Lower West Side. Act III.—Private Parlor at the Waldorf Astoria, and Again in the Furnished Apartment.

Staged by Oscar Eagle.


## KEMPY

### (45 performances)

Comedy in three acts by J. C. Nugent and Elliott Nugent. Revived by Murray Phillips at the Hudson Theatre, New York, May 11, 1927.

Cast of characters—

| | |
|---|---|
| Ruth Bence | Ruth Nugent |
| "Dad" Bence | J. C. Nugent |
| "Ma" Bence | Clara Blandick |
| Jane Wade | Frederica Going |
| Katherine Bence | Norma Lee |
| Ben Wade | Edd Russell |
| "Kempy" James | Elliott Nugent |
| "Duke" Merrill | William J. Kelly |

Acts I, II and III.—Living-room in the Bence Home in a Small New Jersey Town.

Staged by J. C. Nugent.

See "Best Plays of 1921-22."

## HE LOVED THE LADIES

(6 performances)

Comedy in three acts by Herbert Hall Winslow. Produced by the Lepane Amusement Company at the Frolic Theatre, New York, May 10, 1927.

Cast of characters—

| | |
|---|---|
| Col. Sam Buckland | John Carmody |
| Mrs. Stoddard | Ada Lytton Barber |
| Andrew May | Lyons Wickland |
| Mrs. Buckland | Gertrude Fowler |
| Judge Burton Stoddard | Herbert Fortier |
| Phillipa Lee | Isabel Dawn |
| Bess Welcome | Helen Tucker |
| Jack Welcome | Tom Morgan |
| Margaret Jellicoe | Louise Carter |
| Audrey Le Salle | Lillian Ross |
| Wallin | Thomas V. Morrison |
| Lily Lou | Chona Paula |
| Bobolink | Ernie Mack |
| Syncopated Bully Girls | Cora Youngblood Corson's Band |

Acts I, II and III.—Living-room of the Late Hamilton Wayne's Home, Waynesburg, New York.

Staged by Jack Roseleigh.

Hamilton Wayne, founder of Waynesburg, is dead. Andrew May, nephew, is thought to be his heir. Second and later will names Audrey Le Salle, an illegitimate daughter previously unknown, as heir. Audrey comes to Waynesburg, collects the millions, and begins spending them wildly. Snippy society ladies would run her out of town. She finds letters in Wayne's effects indicating that he had had affairs with most all the ladies, and her tormentors agree to drop the scandal. Audrey marries Andrew and all is well.

## ONE FOR ALL

(3 performances)

Play in three acts by Ernest and Louise Cortis. Produced by The Whitehouse Productions, Inc., at the Greenwich Village Theatre, New York, May 13, 1927.

Cast of characters—

| | |
|---|---|
| Claude Severns | Walton Butterfield |
| Leonora Varillo | Ethel Jackson |
| Cora Gansevoort | Jennie A. Eustace |
| Bertram Chattox | Beresford Lovett |
| Dempsey | N. R. Cregan |
| Molly Gansevoort | Madeline Delmar |

```
Eric Brent.........................................Allyn Joslyn
Alicia Pomeroy.....................................Lelya Le Noir
   Prologue—Conservatory in the Gansevoort Mansion. Acts I and
III.—Living-room in the Brent's Home. Act II.—Alicia Pomeroy's
Apartment, Riverside Drive, New York City.
   Staged by Jasper Deeter.
```

Molly Gansevoort, in love with Eric Brent, insists on marrying him even though he tells her he must forego the rewards of matrimony until he has discovered a serum that will cure tuberculosis. A year later Molly and Eric are broke and Eric must have $9,000 to bring his experiments to a successful issue. To get the money Molly sells herself to Bertram. Eric wins fame and success, but some months later Molly must account for a child of which he is not the father. Realizing what his wife has done Eric forgives her.

## THE WHITE SISTER

Opera by Clement Giglio based on Marion Crawford's novel. Produced at Wallack's Theatre, New York, May 17, 1927.

Cast of characters—

```
Sister Giovanna..................................Josie Jones
Countess Chiaramonte............................Maria Spinelli
Captain Giovanni................................Eugene Scudder
Lieutenant Basile................................Enzo Sarafini
Monsignor Seracinesca............................George Puliti
Bresca........................................Alexander Giglio
Inspector..........................................S. Gridelli
Doctor.............................................G. Magni
```

Sister Giovanna, taking to a convent when she hears of her fiancé's death in the wars, later learns of his escape and is seriously and persistently tempted to forswear her vows but manages to remain loyal and pure.

## GRAND STREET FOLLIES

### (30 performances)

Musical revue. Book and lyrics by Agnes Morgan; music by Max Ewing. Produced at the Neighborhood Theatre, New York, May 19, 1927.

Principals engaged—

| | |
|---|---|
| Albert Carroll | Dorothy Sands |
| Marc Loebell | Agnes Morgan |
| Otto Hulicius | Aline Bernstein |
| John F. Roche | Lois Shore |

Junius Matthews
Geo. Bratt
Ralph Geddis
J. Blake Scott
Geo. Hoag
Bert Farjeon
Edmond Rickett
Geo. Heller
   Staged by Agnes Morgan.

Lily Lubell
Blanche Talmud
Sadie Sussman
Mae Noble
Polaire Weissman
Edla Frankau
Ethel Frankau
Odna Brandeis

## RUDDIGORE

### (19 performances)

Operetta in two acts by W. S. Gilbert and Arthur Sullivan. Produced by Lawrence J. Anhalt at the Cosmopolitan Theatre, New York, May 20, 1927.

Cast of characters—

MORTALS

Robin Oakapple ................................... Alexander Clark
Richard Dauntless................................. Craig Campbell
Sir Despard Murgatroyd.......................... William Danforth
Old Adam Goodheart............................. Harvey Howard
Rose Maybud..................................... Violet Carlson
Mad Margaret................................... Sarah M. Edwards
Dame Hannah.................................... Dorothy Pilzer
Zorah ............................................. Ruth Ramsey
Ruth ............................................... Juliet Buell

GHOSTS

Sir Rupert Murgatroyd ........................... Robert Willard
Sir Jasper Murgatroyd ............................. John Russell
Sir Lionel Murgatroyd........................... Henry Riebeselle
Sir Conrad Murgatroyd........................... Hugh Sorenson
Sir Desmond Murgatroyd.......................... Noel Harland
Sir Gilbert Murgatroyd........................... Donald Black
Sir Mervyn Murgatroyd ........................... Paul Shorran

—AND—

Sir Roderic Murgatroyd......................... Herbert Waterous
   Act I.—The Fishing Village of Rederring in Cornwall. Act II.—Picture Gallery in Ruddigore Castle.
   Staged by Charles Jones.

## PATIENCE

### (16 performances)

Operetta in two acts by W. S. Gilbert and Arthur Sullivan. Produced by Perke Hamberg Productions, Inc., at the Masque Theatre, New York, May 23, 1927.

Cast of characters—

Reginald Bunthorne................................. James Watts
Archibald Grosvenor ............................. Joseph Macaulay
Mr. Bunthorne's Solicitor........................ Hartley Gregson

Col. Calverley....................................William Langan
Maj. Murgatroyd................................Dudley Marwick
Lieut. the Duke of Dunstable......................Harold Hansen
The Lady Angela................................Beatrice Kneale
The Lady Saphir...................................Elinor Edeson
The Lady Ella................................Margaret Schilling
The Lady Jane..................................Bernice Mershon
Patience............................................Vivian Hart
    Act I.—Exterior of Castle Bunthorne.  Act II.—A Glade.
    Staged by Robert Milton.


## TALES OF RIGO

### (20 performances)

Music drama in three acts.  Drama by Maurice V. Samuels, based on a story by Hyman Adler; music and lyrics by Ben Schwartz.  Produced by J. Oppenheimer at the Lyric Theater, New York, May 30, 1927.

Cast of characters—

Maria...........................................Mildred Holland
Roberts.........................................Maurice M. Fein
Bones..................................................Jay Fassett
Jose.................................................Hugh Kidder
Rigo...............................................Hyman Adler
Zita.................................................Mira Nirska
Seton..............................................David Leonard
Vivien Ranger.............................Marguerite Borough
Ralph Clark....................................Warren Sterling
Mrs. Ranger.....................................Madeline Grey
Henry Clark...................................George Stillwell
C. Marsden..........................................Carl Reed
Mrs. Marsden..................................Gladys Wilson
Pablo.............................................Samuel Nusbam
Kashi..............................................Walter Deloff
Buzi..............................................Andrew Salama
    Acts I and III.—Rigo's Camp of Gypsy Vagrants.  Act II.—
Scene 1—Interior of Gypsy Tent. 2—Drawing-room of Mrs. Ranger's Home.
    Staged by Clarence Derwent.

Zita, brought up in the gypsy camp of Rigo, the violinist, falls in love with Ralph Clark, who is in society.  Then she learns from her foster father that Ralph is her half-brother.  Foster father was mistaken, however, and love conquers all.


## MERRY-GO-ROUND

### (19 performances)

Musical comedy in two parts; book and lyrics by Morrie Ryskind and Howard Dietz; music by Henry Souvaine and Jay

Gorney.   Produced by Richard Herndon at the Klaw Theatre, New York, May 31, 1927.

Principals engaged—

William Collier
Philip Loeb
Don Barclay
Leonard Sillman
Clifford Walker
William Liebling
Etienne Girardot
James Jolly
Daniel Higgins
    Staged by Allan Dinehart.

Marie Cahill
Evelyn Bennett
Libby Holman
Blanche Fleming
Louise Richardson
Joyce Booth
Mary Stills
Maryon Dale
Pan-American Quartet

## A VERY WISE VIRGIN

### (16 performances)

Comedy in three acts by Sam Janney.   Produced by the author at the Bijou Theatre, New York, June 2, 1927.

Cast of characters—

Betty Brent....................................Joan Bourdelle
Emma...........................................Doris Bryant
Elise Foster...................................Gail DeHart
Herbert Ferris.................................Dennis Cleugh
Dan Steel......................................John Buckler
Aunt Caroline..................................Ethel Martin
Narka Dianina..................................Joan Gordon
    Act I.—Elise Foster's Home.   Before Dinner.   Act II.—The Same. After Dinner.   Act III.—The Same.   The Next Morning.

Betty Brent believes in the freedom of the flapper and vamps her men friends with impunity.   "It's a wise virgin who knows her own boiling point," declares Betty and she knows.   Winning Dan Steel away from her best friend, Elise Foster, Betty loses him promptly to Narka Dianina, a Russian charmer with the moral standards of a Bolshevist.   Then Betty marries the family doctor and Dan goes back to Elise.

## JULIUS CÆSAR

### (8 performances)

Drama by William Shakespeare.   Revived by the Players' Club at the New Amsterdam Theatre, New York, June 6, 1927.

Cast of characters—

Julius Cæsar...................................William Courtleigh
Octavius Cæsar.................................Frederick Worlock

```
Marcus Antonius................................James Rennie
Flavius.........................................Harry Davenport
Marrullus........................................Lawrence Cecil
Marcus Brutus....................................Tyrone Power
Cassius........................................Basil Rathbone
Casca..........................................Herbert Ranson
Trebonius........................................Joseph Kilgour
Cinna.........................................David Glassford
Decius Brutus...................................Pedro De Cordoba
Metellus Cimber....·...........................Roland Bottomley
Popilius Lena.....................................Frazer Coulter
Titinius........................................Kenneth Hunter
Pindarus..........................................Doan Borup
A Soothsayer......................................Ivan Simpson
A Cobbler........................................James T. Powers
Servius............................................Edgar Kent
Cæsar's Servant...................................Harry Forsman
1st Citizen......................................Thomas Chalmers
2nd Citizen.......................................Edwin T. Emery
3rd Citizen.........................................Laura Burt
Lucius........................................... Mary Eaton
Calpurnia........................................ Marion Coakley
Portia.......................................... Mary Young
      Staged by John Craig.
```

# LOMBARDI, LTD.

## (12 performances)

Comedy in three acts by Frederic and Fanny Hatton. Revived by Murray Phillips' Repertory Theatre at the George M. Cohan Theatre, New York, June 6, 1927.

## Cast of characters—

```
Yvette...........................................Marion Martin
Daisy............................................ Eunice Hunt
Muriel..........................................Adele Leroy
James Hodgkins...................................John Saunders
An Expressman....................................Edward Shaw
Tito Lombardi....................................Leo Carrillo
Norah Blake......................................Helen Deddens
Phyllis Manning....................................Rita Vale
Millie McNeal.....................................Marion Abbott
Robert Tarrant...................................Beresford Lovett
Lida Moore......................................Audrey Ridgewell
Riccardo Tosello.................................Philip Tonge
Max Strohm.........................................Arthur Ross
Mrs. Warrington Brown.................Evelyn Carter Carrington
Eloise........................................Barbara Weeks
      Acts I, II and III.—Lombardi's Studio at the Shop.
      Staged by Cecil Owen.
```

Tito Lombardi, dressmaker, is desperately in love with a favorite mannikin, Phyllis Manning. Phyllis ditches Tito for a broker, but he is consoled by the true love of Norah Blake, his "right-hand man."

## TALK ABOUT GIRLS

### (3 performances)

Musical comedy in two acts; book by William Carey Duncan, based on a play by John Hunter Booth; lyrics by Irving Caesar; music by Harold Orlob and Stephen Jones. Produced by Harry H. Oshrin and Sam H. Grisman at the Waldorf Theatre, New York, June 14, 1927.

Cast of characters—

| | |
|---|---|
| Jane Riker | Frances Upton |
| Andrew Lowe | William Cook |
| Henry Quill | Robert Jarvis |
| General Weston | Edwin Forsberg |
| Elsie | Lillian Michel |
| Calvin Lowe | Spencer Charters |
| Abigail | Madelyn Killeen |
| Sue Weston | Jane Taylor |
| Charles Parsons | Floyd Marion |
| Mrs. Alden | Florence Earle |
| Philip Alden | Russell Mack |
| Dan Mason | Andrew Tombes |
| J. W. Savage | Bernard McOwen |
| Simmons | John Meehan, Jr. |
| George V. Grubble | Joseph Smiley |

Act I.—Outside Mrs. Alden's Home, Lower Falls, Mass. Act II.—Living-room at Mrs. Alden's.
Staged by John Harwood.

Philip Alden, broke and a failure in New York, accepts a ride back to his old home town of Lower Falls in a Rolls-Royce driven by a chance acquaintance, Dan Mason. Lower Falls, in the midst of a boost-the-home-town week, accepts Philip as the owner of the Rolls and a New York success. He teeters at the edge of exposure for two acts and then puts through a power-plant deal and makes good, especially with Sue Weston.

## BABY MINE

### (12 performances)

Comedy in three acts by Margaret Mayo. Revived by John Tuerk at the 46th Street Theatre, New York, June 9, 1927.

Cast of characters—

| | |
|---|---|
| Zoie | Lee Patrick |
| Jimmy Jenks | Roscoe Arbuckle |
| Alfred Hardy | Humphrey Bogart |
| His Secretary | W. J. Paul |
| Aggie | Floy La Pointe |
| Maggie O'Flarety | Zelma Tiden |
| Rosa Gatti | Anna Kostant |

```
Finnigan..........................................M. Tello Webb
Michael O'Flarety................................W. J. Brady
Donaghey.........................................Jerome Jordan
      Act I.—Zoie's Sitting-room.   Act II and III.—Zoie's Bedroom.
```

Zoie Hardy, having quarreled with her much loved but very exacting husband, Alfred, is accused of refusing deliberately to accept the obligations of motherhood. To win Alfred back she announces her expectations and is thereafter obliged to borrow an infant against the return of her husband. Jimmy Jenks, willing but dumb, arranges to borrow a baby and finally produces three, thus creating two hours of confusion and many complications.

## THE WOMAN OF BRONZE

### (1 performance)

Drama in three acts by Henry Kistemaeckers and Eugene Delard. Adapted from the French by Paul Kester. Revived by Murray Phillips at the Lyric Theatre, New York, June 15, 1927.

Cast of characters—

```
Strelsky..........................................Walter Tietjens
Maude Randall.................................. Lucille Morrison
Billy Byrd ...........................................Hall Taggart
Tom Randall...................................... Carl Young
Leonard Hunt....................................Pedro De Cordoba
Mary Courtney...................................Marion Barney
Mrs. Graham....................................Harriet Sterling
Sylvia Morton..................................... Mary Fowler
Paddy Griggs.....................................Ralph Morgan
Mrs. Randall...................................Virginia Chauvenet
Douglas Graham.................................Richard Temple
Dorothy Barker...................................Elma Roiton
James..         .....................................Harry Barfoot
Vivian Hunt....................................Margaret Anglin
Reginald Morton...............................Clarence Derwent
Papa Bonnelli................................M. Charles Palazzi
George............................................John Brewster
Ellen...........................................Catherine Haydon
      Acts I, II and III.—Loggia of Leonard Hunt's Studio.
      Staged by Cecil Owen.
```

See "Best Plays of 1920-21."

# STATISTICAL SUMMARY

## (Plays Which Ended Runs After June 15, 1926)

| Plays | Number Performances | Plays | Number Performances |
|---|---|---|---|
| Alias the Deacon | 277 | Laff That Off | 390 |
| At Mrs. Beam's | 222 | Last of Mrs. Cheyney, The | 385 |
| | | Love in a Mist | 118 |
| Bride of the Lamb | 109 | Lulu Belle | 461 |
| Cocoanuts, The | 377 | Merry World, The | 85 |
| Cradle Snatchers, The | 478 | | |
| Craig's Wife | 360 | Night in Paris, A | 335 |
| Earl Carroll's Vanities | 440 | One Man's Woman | 158 |
| | | One of the Family | 238 |
| Garrick Gaieties | 174 | | |
| Geo. White's Scandals | 424 | Patsy, The | 245 |
| Girl Friend, The | 409 | Pomeroy's Past | 94 |
| Grand St. Follies, 1926 | 53 | | |
| Great God Brown | 271 | Sex | 375 |
| Great Temptations | 197 | Shanghai Gesture, The | 206 |
| | | Song of the Flame | 219 |
| Half-naked Truth, The | 38 | Square Crooks | 150 |
| House of Usher | 198 | Sunny | 517 |
| Importance of Being | | Tip Toes | 192 |
| Earnest, The | 70 | | |
| Iolanthe | 255 | Vagabond King, The | 511 |
| Kitty's Kisses | 170 | What Every Woman Knows | 268 |
| Kongo | 135 | Wisdom Tooth, The | 160 |

Note—The number of performances played by each attraction during the season of 1926-27 will be found added to the following record of productions.

# PLAYS THAT HAVE RUN OVER 500 PERFORMANCES ON BROADWAY

## To June 15, 1927

| Plays | Number Performances | Plays | Number Performances |
|-------|---------------------|-------|---------------------|
| Abie's Irish Rose | 2,179 | Student Prince | 608 |
| Lightnin' | 1,291 | Adonis | 603 |
| The Bat | 867 | Kiki | 600 |
| The First Year | 760 | Blossom Time | 592 |
| Seventh Heaven | 704 | The Show-off | 571 |
| White Cargo | 702 | Sally | 570 |
| Peg o' My Heart | 692 | The Music Master | 540 |
| East Is West | 680 | The Boomerang | 522 |
| Irene | 670 | Sunny | 517 |
| A Trip to Chinatown | 657 | The Vagabond King | 511 |
| Rain | 648 | Shuffle Along | 504 |
| Is Zat So? | 618 | | |

# WHERE AND WHEN THEY WERE BORN

Abarbanell, Lina .............Berlin ...................1880
Abbott, George .............Hamburg, N. Y. .........1895
Adams, Maude .............Salt Lake City, Utah .....1872
Adelaide, La Petite .........Cohoes, N. Y. ...........1890
Allen, Viola ................Huntsville, Ala. .........1869
Ames, Robert .............Hartford, Conn. .........1893
Ames, Winthrop .............North Easton, Mass. .....1871
Anglin, Margaret ...........Ottawa, Canada ........1876
Anson, A. E. ...............England .............1879
Arbuckle, Maclyn ...........San Antonio, Texas .....1866
Arliss, George .............London, England .......1868
Arthur, Julia ...............Hamilton, Ont. .........1869
Atwell, Roy ...............Syracuse, N. Y. .........1880
Atwill, Lionel .............London, England .......1885

Bacon, Frank ........... ....California .............1864
Bainter, Fay ...............Los Angeles, Cal. ........1892
Barbee, Richard ............Lafayette, Ind. .........1887
Barrie, James Matthew .......Kirriemuir, N. B. ........1860
Barrymore, Ethel ...........Philadelphia, Pa. ........1879
Barrymore, John ............Philadelphia, Pa., ........1882
Barrymore, Lionel ..........London, England .......1878
Bates, Blanche .............Portland, Ore. ...........1873
Bayes, Nora ...............Milwaukee, Wis. .........1880
Beban, George .............San Francisco, Cal. ......1873
Beckley, Beatrice ..........Roedean, England .......1885
Best, Edna ................England .............1901
Beecher, Janet .............Chicago, Ill. ...........1884
Belasco, David .............San Francisco, Cal. ......1862
Ben-Ami, Jacob ............Minsk, Russia ...........1890
Bennett, Richard ...........Cass County, Ind. .......1873
Bennett, Wilda .............Asbury Park, N. J. .......1894
Benrimo, J. Harry ..........San Francisco, Cal. ......1874
Berlin, Irving .............Russia ...............1888
Bernard, Barney ...........Rochester, N. Y. ........1877
Bernard, Sam ..............Birmingham, England ....1863

Bernhardt, Sarah ............Paris, France ............1844
Bingham, Amelia ............Hickville, Ohio ..........1869
Binney, Constance ..........Philadelphia, Pa. ........1900
Blackmer, Sidney ............Salisbury, N. C. ..........1896
Blinn, Holbrook ............San Francisco, Cal. ......1872
Boland, Mary ..............Detroit, Mich. ..........1880
Bordoni, Irene ..............Paris, France ..........1895
Brady, Alice ..............New York ..............1892
Brady, William A. ..........San Francisco, Cal ......1863
Breese, Edmund ............Brooklyn, N. Y. ..........1871
Brian, Donald ..............St. John's, N. F. ..........1871
Broadhurst, George H. ........England ..............1866
Bruns, Julia ..............St. Louis ..............1895
Bryant, Charles ............England ..............1879
Brooks, Virginia Fox ........New York ..............1893
Buchanan, Jack ............England ..............1892
Buchanan, Thompson ........Louisville, Ky. ..........1877
Burke, Billie ..............Washington, D. C. .......1885
Burton, Frederick ..........Indiana ..............1871
Byron, Arthur ..............Brooklyn, N. Y. ..........1872

Cadell, Jean ..............Edinburgh ..............1884
Cahill, Marie ..............Brooklyn, N. Y. ..........1871
Cantor, Eddie ..............New York ..............1894
Campbell, Mrs. Patrick ......England ..............1865
Carle, Richard ............Somerville, Mass. ........1871
Carlisle, Alexandra ..........Yorkshire, England ......1886
Carr, Alexander ............Russia ..............1878
Carter, Mrs. Leslie ..........Lexington, Ky. ..........1862
Catlett, Walter ............San Francisco, Cal. ......1889
Cawthorne, Joseph ..........New York ..............1868
Chaplin, Charles Spencer ....London ..............1889
Chatterton, Ruth ..........New York ..............1893
Cherry, Charles ............England ..............1872
Claire, Ina ................Washington, D. C. .......1892
Clarke, Marguerite ..........Cincinnati, Ohio ........1887
Cliffe, H. Cooper ..........England ..............1862
Clifford, Kathleen ..........Charlottesville, Va. .......1887
Coburn, Charles ............Macon, Ga. ..............1877
Coghlan, Gertrude ..........England ..............1879
Coghlan, Rose ............Petersborough, England ...1850
Cohan, George M. ..........Providence, R. I. ........1878
Cohan, Georgette ..........Los Angeles, Cal. ........1900

Colbert, Claudette ..........Paris .................1905
Collier, Constance ...........Windsor, England ........1882
Collier, William .............New York ..............1866
Collinge, Patricia ...........Dublin, Ireland ..........1894
Collins, José ................London, England ........1896
Conroy, Frank ...............London, England ........1885
Cooper, Violet Kemble .......London, England ........1890
Cornell, Katherine ..........Buffalo, N. Y. ...........1900
Corrigan, Emmett ............Amsterdam, Holland .....1871
Corthell, Herbert ............Boston, Mass. ...........1875
Courtenay, William ..........Worcester, Mass. ........1875
Courtleigh, William ..........Guelph, Ont. ............1869
Coward, Noel ...............England ................1899
Cowl, Jane .................Boston, Mass. ...........1887
Crane, William H. ...........Leicester, Mass. .........1845
Craven, Frank ..............Boston, Mass. ...........1875
Crews, Laura Hope ..........San Francisco, Cal. ......1880
Crosman, Henrietta ..........Wheeling, W. Va. ........1865
Crothers, Rachel ............Bloomington, Ill. ........1878
Cumberland, John ...........St. John, N. B. ..........1880

Dale, Alan .................Birmingham, England ....1861
Dale, Margaret .............Philadelphia, Pa. ........1880
Dalton, Charles .............England ................1864
Daly, Arnold ................New York ..............1875
Daniels, Frank ..............Dayton, Ohio ...........1860
Dawn, Hazel ................Ogden, Utah ............1891
Day, Edith .................Minneapolis, Minn. ......1896
De Angelis, Jefferson ........San Francisco, Cal. ......1859
Dean, Julia .................St. Paul, Minn. ..........1880
De Belleville, Frederic .......Belgium ................1857
De Cordoba, Pedro ..........New York ..............1881
Dickson, Dorothy ............Kansas City ............1898
Dillingham, Charles B. ........Hartford, Conn. .........1868
Dinehart, Allan ..............Missoula, Mont. .........1889
Ditrichstein, Leo ............Temesbar, Hungary ......1865
Dixey, Henry E. ............Boston, Mass. ...........1859
Dodson, John E. ............London, England ........1857
Dolly, Rosy ................Hungary ...............1892
Dolly, Jennie ...............Hungary ...............1892
Donnelly, Dorothy Agnes .....New York..............1880
Doro, Marie ................Duncannon, Pa. .........1882
D'Orsay, Lawrence ..........England ................1860

Dressler, Marie ..............Cobourg, Canada.........1869
Drew, John ................Philadelphia, Pa. ........1853
Drew, Louise ..............New York ..............1884
Druce, Herbert ..............England ................1870
Duncan, Isadora ...........San Francisco, Cal. ......1880
Duncan, Augustin ..........San Francisco, Cal. ......1873
Dunn, Emma ..............England ................1875
Dupree, Minnie ............San Francisco, Cal. ......1875
Duse, Eleanora ............Vigerano, Italy .........1859

Eagels, Jeanne .............Kansas City, Mo. ........1894
Eames, Clare ...............Hartford, Conn. .........1896
Eddinger, Wallace ..........New York .............1881
Edeson, Robert ............Baltimore, Md. ..........1868
Eldridge, Florence ..........Brooklyn, N. Y.........1901
Ellis, Mary ................New York .............1900
Elliston, Grace .............Wheeling, W. Va. ........1881
Ellinger, Desirée ............Manchester .............1895
Elliott, Gertrude ...........Rockland, Me. ..........1874
Elliott, Maxine .............Rockland, Me. ..........1871
Elliott, William ............Boston, Mass. ..........1885
Ellsler, Effie ...............Philadelphia, Pa. ........1898
Eltinge, Julian .............Boston, Mass. ..........1883
Emerson, John .............Sandusky, Ohio .........1874
Errol, Leon ................Sydney, Australia ........1881
Ewell, Lois ................Memphis, Tenn. .........1885

Fairbanks, Douglas .........Denver, Colo. ..........1883
Farnum, Dustin ............Hampton Beach, N. H. ...1874
Farnum, William ...........Boston, Mass. ..........1876
Farrar, Geraldine ...........Melrose, Mass. .........1883
Faversham, William .........Warwickshire, England ...1868
Fealy, Maude ..............Memphis, Tenn. .........1883
Fenwick, Irene .............Chicago, Ill. ...........1887
Ferguson, Elsie .............New York .............1883
Fields, Lewis ..............New York .............1867
Findlay, Ruth ..............New York .............1897
Fischer, Alice .............Indiana ...............1869
Fisher, Lola ...............Chicago, Ill. ...........1892
Fiske, Minnie Maddern .......New Orleans, La. ........1867
Fontanne, Lynn ............London, England ........1882
Forbes-Robertson, Sir J. ......London, England ........1853
Foy, Edward Fitzgerald ......New York .............1854

Huston, Walter ............Toronto ...............1884
Hussey, James ............Chicago ..............1891

Illington, Margaret .........Bloomington, Ill. ........1881
Irving, Isabel ..............Bridgeport, Conn. ........1871
Irwin, May ...............Whitby, Ont. ...........1862

Janis, Elsie ..............Delaware, Ohio .........1889
Joel, Clara ................Jersey City, N. J. ........1890
Jolson, Al ................Washington, D. C. .......1883

Keane, Doris ..............Michigan ..............1885
Keenan, Frank ............Dubuque, Ia. ..........1858
Keightley, Cyril ............New South Wales, Aus. ...1875
Kennedy, Madge ...........Chicago, Ill. ...........1890
Kerrigan, J. M. ............Dublin, Ireland .........1885
Kerr, Geoffrey ............London, England .......1895
Kershaw, Willette ..........Clifton Heights, Mo. .....1890
Kosta, Tessa ..............Chicago, Ill. ...........1893
Kruger, Otto ..............Toledo, Ohio ..........1895

Lackaye, Wilton ...........Virginia ..............1862
Larrimore, Francine ........Russia ...............1888
La Rue, Grace ............Kansas City, Mo. ........1882
Lauder, Harry ............Portobello, England .....1870
Lawton, Thais .............Louisville, Ky. ..........1881
Lawrence, Gertrude .........London ..............1898
Lawrence, Margaret .........Trenton, N. J. ..........1890
Lean, Cecil ...............Illinois ...............1878
Le Gallienne, Eva ..........London, England ........1900
Levey, Ethel ..............San Francisco, Cal. ......1881
Lewis, Ada ................New York .............1871
Logan, Stanley ............Earlsfield, England ......1885
Lewis, Mabel Terry .........London, England ........1872
Loraine, Robert ...........England ..............1876
Lord, Pauline ............Hanford, Cal. ..........1890
Lorraine, Lillian ..........San Francisco, Cal. ......1892
Lou-Tellegen ............Holland ..............1881
Lunt, Alfred ..............Milwaukee, Wis. ........1893

Mack, Andrew ............Boston, Mass. ..........1863
Mack, Willard ............Ontario, Canada .........1873
Mackay, Elsie ............London, England ........1894

MacKellar, Helen ..........Canada ...............1896
Mann, Louis ...............New York .............1865
Mantell, Robert B. .........Ayrshire, Scotland .......1854
Marinoff, Fania ............Russia ................1892
Merivale, Philip ............India .................1886
Marlowe, Julia .............Caldbeck, England ......1870
Matthews, A. E. ...........Bridlington, England .....1869
Matthison, Edith Wynne .....England ...............1875
Maude, Cyril ..............London, England ........1862
McIntyre, Frank ...........Ann Arbor, Mich. .......1879
McRae, Bruce .............India .................1867
Meighan, Thomas ..........Pittsburgh .............1879
Melba, Nellie .............Melbourne, Australia .....1866
Mellish, Fuller ............England ...............1865
Mercer, Beryl .............Seville, Spain ..........1882
Miller, Henry .............London, England ........1859
Miller, Marylin ...........Findlay, Ohio ..........1898
Mitchell, Grant ...........Columbus, Ohio ........1874
Mitzi (Hajos) .............Budapest ..............1891
Moores, Clara .............Omaha, Neb. ..........1897
Morris, Clara .............Toronto, Canada ........1846
Murphy, Tim ..............Rupert, Vt. ............1860

Nash, Florence ............Troy, N. Y. ...........1888
Nash, Mary ...............Troy, N. Y. ...........1885
Nazimova, Mme. ...........Crimea, Russia .........1879
Nielsen, Alice .............Nashville, Tenn. ........1876

Olcott, Chauncey ...........Providence, R. I. .......1862
O'Neill, Eugene Gladstone ....New York .............1888
O'Neil, Nance .............Oakland, Cal. ..........1875
O'Ramey, Georgia ..........Mansfield, Ohio ........1886

Painter, Eleanor ...........Iowa ...............1890
Pawle, Lenox ..............London, England ........1872
Pennington, Ann ...........Philadelphia, Pa. ........1898
Pickford, Mary ............Toronto ..............1893
Post, Guy Bates ...........Seattle, Wash. ..........1875
Powers, James T. ..........New York .............1862
Power, Tyrone .............London, England ........1869

Rambeau, Marjorie .........San Francisco, Cal. ......1889
Rathbone, Basil ............Johannesburg ..........1892

Tell, Alma ................New York .............1892
Tell, Olive ................New York .............1894
Terry, Ellen ...............Coventry, England ......1848
Thomas, Augustus ..........St. Louis, Mo. .........1859
Thomas, John Charles .......Baltimore, Md. .........1887
Tinney, Frank .............Philadelphia, Pa. ........1878
Tobin, Genevieve ..........New York .............1901
Tobin, Vivian ..............New York .............1903
Toler, Sidney .............Warrensburg, Mo. ........1874
Trevor, Norman ............Calcutta ..............1877
Truex, Ernest .............Denver, Colo. ...........1890
Tynan, Brandon ............Dublin, Ireland .........1879

Ulric, Lenore .............New Ulm, Minn. ........1897

Valentine, Grace ...........Indianapolis, Ind. .......1892
Varesi, Gilda ..............Milan, Italy ...........1887
Victor, Josephine ..........Hungary ..............1891

Wainwright, Marie .........Philadelphia, Pa. ........1853
Walker, June ..............New York .............1904
Walker, Charlotte ..........Galveston, Texas ........1878
Warfield, David ............San Francisco, Cal. ......1866
Warwick, Robert ...........Sacramento, Cal. ........1878
Ware, Helen ...............San Francisco, Cal. ......1877
Weber, Jos. ...............New York .............1867
Welford, Dallas ............Liverpool, England ......1874
Westley, Helen ............Brooklyn, N. Y. .........1879
Westman, Nydia ............White Plains, N. Y. ......1906
Whiffen, Mrs. Thomas .......London, England ........1845
Whiteside, Walker ..........Logansport, Ind. .........1869
Wilson, Francis ............Philadelphia, Pa. ........1854
Winant, Forrest ............New York .............1888
Winwood, Estelle ..........England ..............1883
Wise, Thomas A. ...........England ..............1865
Wood, Peggy ..............Philadelphia, Pa. ........1886
Wycherly, Margaret ........England ..............1883
Wyndham, Olive ...........Chicago, Ill. ...........1886
Wynn, Ed. ................Philadelphia, Pa. .........1886

Zabelle, Flora .............Constantinople .........1885
Ziegfeld, Florenz, Jr. ........Chicago, Ill. ...........1867

# NECROLOGY

## June 15, 1926—June 15, 1927

Alfred Hollingsworth, actor, 52. Prominent in Shakespearean revivals on the Pacific coast. Died Glendale, Cal., June 20, 1926.

Julian Mitchell, stage director, 72. Originally a dancer at Niblo's Gardens. Began directing productions when he was 20; staged thirteen of the nineteen "Ziegfeld Follies" produced during his lifetime. Married to Bessie Clayton, dancer, for thirty years. Died Long Branch, N. J., June 24, 1926.

Lincoln J. Carter, playwright, 61. Twenty-five years ago prominent writer of sensational melodramas, including "The Fast Mail," "The Tornado," "The Heart of Chicago," "Remember the Maine," etc. Born the day of Lincoln's assassination, named for martyred president. Died at summer home near Goshen, Ind., July 13, 1926.

Roshanara, dancer. Family name Olive Craddock. For many years specialized in Eastern dances, organizing her own troupe in 1913 and touring America. Died Asheville, N. C., July 14, 1926.

Edouard Durand, actor, 55. For thirty years prominent in French-American characterizations. Born France, died Porchester, N. Y., July 31, 1926.

Harry Harwood, actor, 78. Member of the Daniel Frohman and Augustin Daly stock companies and played in support of many stars. Born New York City; died Portland, Me., August 1, 1926.

Izrael Zangwill, playwright, 62. Wrote "Children of the Ghetto," "Merely Mary Ann," "The Serio-comic Governess," "Nurse Marjorie," "The Melting Pot," and other plays. Born, London, 1864; died Midhurst, Sussex, England, August 1, 1926.

William Owens, actor, 63. Played in support of many stars, including Julia Marlowe, Ada Rehan and Lewis Morrison. Finished in pictures. Died Chicago, August 20, 1926.

Ben Welch, comedian. For many years prominent in vaudeville

Lost his eyesight in 1921, but continued his monologue for five years. Died Smithtown, L. I., September 2, 1926.

George Appleton, manager, 82. For many years manager, first for Nat C. Goodwin, later for Maxine Elliott (then Mrs. Goodwin). Manager of Maxine Elliott Theatre, New York, since its erection. Died New York, September 5, 1926.

Will H. Deming, actor, 55. Popular light comedian for many years, after starting as an usher in Hooley's theatre, Chicago, and getting his early training with the Harry O. Stubbs' stock company in Columbus, Ohio. Also an early associate of Lincoln J. Carter's. Died London, England, September 13, 1926.

Frank Norcross, actor, 70. Supported many of the old stars, being at one time Fanny Davenport's leading man. Finished in pictures. Died Glendale, Cal., September 13, 1926.

Joseph Holland, actor, 67. Prominent years ago in Charles Frohman's companies; afterward starred jointly with his brother, E. M. Holland. It was the death of George Holland, father of Joseph and E. M., that brought about the naming of "The Little Church Around the Corner." Died New York, September 25, 1926.

Tom Thumb, midget comedian, 84. Famed attraction of circuses and museums for sixty years. Family name was Darius Adner Alden. Died Los Angeles, Cal., September 24, 1926.

Charles B. Hanford, actor, 67. Shakespearean star for many years, a contemporary of Frederick Warde, Louis James, Helena Modjeska and others. Prominent as Washington, D. C., amateur before adopting profession. Died Washington, October 16, 1926.

Lola Fisher, actress, 34. Popular comédienne during last years of her career, which started in 1914. Played in "Good Gracious, Annabelle" and "Be Calm, Camilla," and was with all-star company playing "The Rivals," her last engagement. Born Chicago, 1892. Died Yonkers, N. Y., October 15, 1926.

Harry Houdini, magician, 54. The successor of Herrmann, Kellar, etc., and an independent worker for many years, specializing in escapes from handcuffs and packing cases. Late years devoted much study to the exposure of fake spiritualists. Born Atkinson, Wis. Family name Weiss. Died Detroit, Mich., October 31, 1926.

James K. Hackett, actor, 57. Prominent figure as star and

manager in American theatres for forty years. His first big success, "The Prisoner of Zenda." His last years devoted to Shakespearean revivals, notably "Macbeth," which he played in Paris at the invitation of the French government. Son of James A. Hackett, born Wolf Island, Ontario, 1869. Died Paris, November 8, 1926.

George Hanlon, acrobat and comedian, 82. A member of the Hanlon family, entertainers of a past generation. Died New York, November 6, 1926.

Walter M. Wilson, actor and stage director, 52. Prominent in theatre activities and the designer of the Jefferson window for "The Little Church Around the Corner." Died New Haven, Conn., November 13, 1926.

Helena Frederick, prima donna, 44. A member at one time of the Bostonian's organization, later prima donna for many musical comedies. Died Beacon, N. Y., November 19, 1926.

William Beach, actor, 52. An actor from boyhood, and prominent both in the support of the older stars, and in western stock companies. Died Philadelphia, December 1, 1926.

Charles Ringling, circus man, 64. Sixth of the seven Ringling brothers and for years in charge of the firm's finances. Born McGregor, Ia.; died Sarasota, Fla., December 3, 1926.

Charles Belmont Davis, critic, 60. A writer and brother of Richard Harding Davis. Last years devoted to play reviewing for the New York *Herald-Tribune*. Born Philadelphia, Pa.; died Asheville, N. C., December 10, 1926.

Arnold Daly, actor, 52. Began as an office boy for Charles Frohman, drifted into acting and established himself when he produced Bernard Shaw's "Candida" and later other Shaw dramas. Born Brooklyn, N. Y.; died New York, January 13, 1927.

Bruce Edwards, manager, 54. For thirty years general manager for Charles Dillingham enterprises. Born Scotland; died New York, January 16, 1927.

Grace Van Studdiford, singer, 54. Sang at the Metropolitan in "Martha," later turned to light opera and was notably successful as the prima donna of DeKoven and Smith's "The Red Feather." Born Lafayette, Ind.; died Fort Wayne, Ind., January 29, 1927.

Byron Beasley, actor, 55. For many years prominent as a leading man. Was playing in "Howdy, King" in Detroit, when he died, January 28, 1927.

Roi Cooper Megrue, playwright, 43. Author of "Tea for Three,"

"It Pays to Advertise" (with Walter Hackett); "Under Cover," "Under Fire," "Her Own Way" and "Among the Girls." Died New York, February 27, 1927.

Frank C. Egan, producer, 55. Well known for many years on the Pacific coast as a teacher and dramatic coach. Produced many plays in the Little Theatres, notably "White Collars." Born Chicago, died Los Angeles, March 5, 1927.

Harry Montague, author and actor, 83. Old-time composer of "Pull Down the Blinds" and other songs. Manager of theatres in San Francisco and Denver. Died Amityville, L. I., March 20, 1927.

James A. Byrne, acrobatic comedian, 59. One of the Byrne brothers who achieved fame in "Eight Bells," which they played for twenty years. Was later in "Superba." Born Norwich, Conn.; died Camden, N. J., March 19, 1927.

Thomas Conkey, baritone, 45. Last engagement with the Municipal Opera Company of St. Louis. Died New York, April 3, 1927.

Gilda Leary, actress, 31. Prominent in leading rôles after her American début in "Daddy Long Legs." Played in "A Prince There Was," "Sandalwood" and "Puppets of Passion." Born England, died New York, April 17, 1927.

Kitty Morton, actress, 65. Second of the Four Mortons, and mother of Clara and Paul Morton. Appeared with one or more of the Mortons in vaudeville for forty-six years. Born Detroit, Mich.; died New York, April 25, 1927.

Earl Williams, actor, 44. Prominent in support of many stars and in western stock companies. Last fifteen years devoted to pictures. Born Sacramento, Cal.; died Hollywood, Cal., April 25, 1927.

George W. Sammis, manager, 72. For years associated with the productions of the Shuberts and later with those of A. L. Erlanger. Died Sound Beach, Conn., April, 1927.

Ernest Ball, song writer, 49. Composer of approximately 300 songs, many of which proved popular. Among them "Mother Machree," "Love Me and the World Is Mine," "Till the Sands of the Desert Grow Cold" and "Let the World Go By." Born Cleveland, Ohio; died Santa Ana, Cal., while on tour.

Bruce McRae, actor, 60. Prominent as leading man for many years, playing in support of prominent stars, notably Ethel Barrymore. Last engagement with Grace George in "The

Legend of Leonora." Born India, died New York, May 7, 1927.

Anna Eva Fay, mind reader and mystic, 64. For years the most famous entertainer devoting her psychic powers to vaudeville. Became internationally known and had many imitators. Retired in 1924. Born Southington, Ohio, died Melrose Highlands, Mass., May 12, 1927.

Sam Bernard, comedian, 64. For fifty years a popular entertainer playing dialect parts. One of the old Weber and Fields stars and later a star in "The Rich Mr. Hoggenheimer," rewritten finally as "Piggy." His greatest hits were scored in "Friendly Enemies," with Louis Mann; "The Girl from Kay's," "The Casino Girl," etc. Born Birmingham, England; died on shipboard May 16, 1927.

Maurice Mouvet, dancer, 40. The first of the cabaret ballroom dancers to attract international attention. Frequently appeared in stage productions, dancing at different times with Florence Walton, Joan Sawyer, Barbara Bennett, Lenore Hughes and Eleanora Ambrose. Born Switzerland, died Lausanne, Switzerland, May 18, 1927.

James S. Metcalfe, dramatic critic, 68. For many years prominent in theatre world as critic and essayist. Dramatic editor for *Life* for thirty-one years, latterly with Wall Street *Journal*. Married Elizabeth Tyree, Frohman actress, in 1904. Born Buffalo, N. Y.; died New York, May 26, 1927.

Denman Maley, comedian, 50. Played in the Hoyt comedies years ago, starting with "A Black Sheep." Last engagement in "The Butter-and-Egg Man." Born Holyoke, Mass.; died Collingswood, N. J., May 22, 1927.

Robert C. Hilliard, actor, 70. Known for years as the handsomest, as well as one of the best leading men on the native stage. Succeeded Maurice Barrymore as leading man for Lily Langtry, played under the direction of David Belasco, and later starred in "A Fool There Was" and "The Argyle Case." Played "The Littlest Girl" in vaudeville for years. Born New York, died New York, June 6, 1927.

James Doyle, dancer, 38. Gained prominence in musical comedies as the Doyle half of the Dixon and Doyle team of dancers. Several seasons with Fred Stone. Born Lowell, Mass.; died New York, June 13, 1927.

# INDEX OF AUTHORS

553

# INDEX OF PLAYS AND CASTS